D1557896

Praise for *Political Assassinations and Attempts in US History*

"J. Michael Martinez's new book about political assassins is a must read and is a book which I heartedly recommend. His book adds a crucial historical dimension to our understanding of the motives which have driven assassins and would-be assassins in US history."

—Mel Ayton, author of *Hunting The President: Threats, Plots and Assassination Attempts - From FDR to Obama*

"In J. Michael Martinez's new book *Political Assassinations and Attempts in US History,* he does a brilliant job of putting US presidential assassinations and attempts under a microscope for an insightful and sobering view of US history."

—Greg Stebben, author of *White House Confidential*

"In this study of American political assassinations, J. Michael Martinez not only takes us through what happened in the past, but also delves into the minds and motivations of the assassins to help as we look into the future. Can we learn from the patterns and predict the next assassination? Maybe, maybe not, but this fascinating book provides a deeper understanding into the warning signs which, unfortunately, may be all too plentiful in today's political climate."

—Mike Farris, author of *A Death in the Islands: The Unwritten Law and the Last Trial of Clarence Darrow*

"Original and evocative, this book examines within the historical context the nature of assassinations perpetrated against twenty-five American political figures. Grappling with this perplexing issue, Martinez probes the jagged edge of human psychology. He offers a provocative explanation of the underlying motives behind political assassinations, assigning them to five categories. This theoretical construct combines the complexity and the contingence of violence in America."

—Orville Vernon Burton, professor, Clemson University and author *The Age of Lincoln*

"In *Political Assassinations and Attempts in US History*, Martinez thoughtfully examines political assassinations in America to understand not just the historically important question of *what* happened, but, perhaps more importantly, the intriguing one of *why* individuals resorted to violence against prominent political figures. In quest of their motivations, Martinez distributes the twenty-five assassins he has identified into five categories that range from rational beings to crazy ones to "others." Why political assassinations seem to be increasing since the nineteenth century is an obvious matter of great concern to lovers of liberty in a republic solidly based on the rule of law— and most especially so in times when partisan political discourse is coarser, participants more passionate, and self-governed individuals seemingly rarer."

—William D. Richardson, distinguished professor emeritus,
University of South Dakota, and author of *Democracy,
Bureaucracy, and Character: Founding Thought*

"In *Political Assassinations and Attempts in US History*, J. Michael Martinez provides an incisive description and analysis of a problem that has plagued nations and communities. Based on twenty-five instances of violence against elected officials and public figures in the United States, the book contributes new insight to long-standing issue."

—Jeffrey L. Brudney, PhD, Betty and Dan Cameron family
distinguished professor of innovation in the nonprofit sector,
University of North Carolina Wilmington

"The USA is a uniquely and hugely violent place as this book demonstrates. This is so because it was birthed in genocide against Native Americans and in the enslavement of black Africans. Assassination, which is a political murder, has been used against government figures and by the government itself. The killing of President John Fitzgerald Kennedy altered world history in as much as he set his course against the Cold War. Likewise, the murder of Malcolm X set back the struggle for black freedom. The USA has been at war almost continually since I was born in 1942. As the leader of the student nonviolent coordinating committee, H. Rap Brown, famously observed: 'violence is as American as apple pie.'"

—Attorney Michael Steven Smith, co-host,
Law and Disorder Radio and author of *The Assassination of Che Guevara*

POLITICAL ASSASSINATIONS AND ATTEMPTS IN US HISTORY

POLITICAL ASSASSINATIONS AND ATTEMPTS IN US HISTORY

The Lasting Effects of Gun Violence Against American Political Leaders

J. Michael Martinez

Carrel Books may be purchased in bulk at special discounts for sales promotion, corporate gifts, fund-raising, or educational purposes. Special editions can also be created to specifications. For details, contact the Special Sales Department, Carrel Book, 307 West 36th Street, 11th Floor, New York, NY 10018 or carrelbooks@skyhorsepublishing.com.

Carrel Books® is a registered trademark of Skyhorse Publishing, Inc.®, a Delaware corporation.

Visit our website at www.carrelbooks.com

10 9 8 7 6 5 4 3 2 1

Library of Congress Cataloging-in-Publication Data is available on file.

Cover design by Rain Saukas
Cover photos courtesy of the Library of Congress

Print ISBN: 978-1-63144-070-0
Ebook ISBN: 978-1-63144-071-7

Printed in the United States of America

This book is for Arya Rayne Carter, a beautiful grandchild,
from papa

Dream on, dream on, of bloody deeds and death.

—William Shakespeare, *King Richard III*, Act V, Scene 3

TABLE OF CONTENTS

LIST OF PHOTOGRAPHS

PREFACE AND ACKNOWLEDGMENTS

"Oh, my God, they've shot Bobby Kennedy!"

My mother literally gasped, dropping the cigarette from her lips as she drove me to day care early one morning in June 1968. I remember giggling from the back seat as I watched her hastily pull the car to the shoulder of the road. Safely parked, she bent and swept ashes from her lap before the embers could burn her thighs. I could not stop laughing at her predicament. When she turned and glanced at me, however, I saw a look of anguish and horror plastered on her face. Although she did not utter a reproachful word, I fell silent. That look told me she was in no mood to trifle with a silly child.

This long-ago incident occurred before 24/7 news programs existed. Senator Robert F. Kennedy had been shot in the early morning hours of June 5, just after midnight on the West Coast (around 3:00 a.m. in South Carolina, where we lived at the time), and so word of the assault had not yet filtered into the hinterlands. Unaware of the tumultuous events in California hours earlier, Mom followed our usual routine that day. She turned on the car radio as we drove along the highway. Within minutes, the announcer interrupted the music to report on the latest tragedy. It was the first we had heard of it.

At five years of age, I wasn't altogether sure who Bobby Kennedy was, but the news of his shooting impressed me mightily. My mother appeared unflappable to me in those days. It must have been a major event to trigger such a dramatic reaction from her. I recall walking around the day-care center on that June 5, and whenever I encountered an adult, I would loudly exclaim, mimicking my mother's reaction, "Oh, my God, they've shot Bobby Kennedy!" I could not understand why the adults laughed as I announced the terrible news. With the passing years, I came to understand that the message did not elicit laughter; it was the earnestness of a little wide-eyed messenger blurting out such big news. To this day, news of the Bobby Kennedy shooting remains my first vivid memory of an event that occurred outside my immediate family.

It would be too melodramatic, not to mention factually inaccurate, to say that my fascination with the subject of political assassinations was born on the day that Bobby Kennedy was shot down. Instead, the impetus for this book, as for all of my books, began with a simple question: *Why?* Why would someone resort to violence aimed at a public figure? What is to be gained, especially since the assassin more often than not is caught and punished with prolonged imprisonment and sometimes execution? It is tempting to say, "Well, all these assassins and would-be assassins are crazy, and there is no telling what a lunatic will do." Yes, it is tempting to reach such a knee-jerk conclusion but, as these pages hopefully make clear, the story is not quite so conceptually or factually simple.

In researching this book, I chose to focus on twenty-five assassinations and attempted assassinations of American political figures with that simple question in mind: Why? Why did these men and women act on their violent impulses? As I worked on this book, I wondered whether I should focus primarily on the political figures who were assaulted or the persons who assaulted them. In the end, I focused on both, but the organizing principle—assessing the motives of killers and would-be killers according to a five-tiered typology—required judgments about the probable motives of the men and women who believed that violent acts were necessary.

As I have learned repeatedly throughout my writing career, no one produces a book alone. I was assisted along the way by many helpful souls. First and foremost, I thank Niels Aaboe, formerly executive editor at Skyhorse Publishing, who worked with me on two books at Skyhorse and one at Rowman & Littlefield. Niels was patient and encouraging through every step of the laborious publication process. To my great sorrow, he left Skyhorse shortly before I completed the manuscript. I was fortunate that Veronica (Ronnie) Alvarado stepped in to see the project through to its culmination.

A good friend, the very talented Gabriel Botet, assisted me in locating many of the photographs included in the book. When the images were unavailable in a suitable resolution, Gabriel was instrumental in manipulating the pixels and performing some sort of magic that enhanced their quality. I can never repay his many kindnesses.

I was fortunate to receive assistance from exceptional librarians and archivists, including (in alphabetical order): Michal Gorlin Becker, director of Operations, the Shapell Manuscript Foundation; Germain J. Bienvenu, PhD,

Special Collections, Public Services, Louisiana State University Libraries; Charlene Bonnette, MLIS, CA, head preservation librarian, Louisiana Collection, State Library of Louisiana; Tyler Bouyér, customer service associate, Getty Images; William M. Cross, JD, MSLS, director, Copyright & Digital Scholarship Center, North Carolina State University Libraries; Danielle Grundel, archivist technician, Idaho State Archives, Division of the Idaho State Historical Society; and Erica Varela of the *Los Angeles Times*. I also relied on assistance form the staff of the Horace W. Sturgis Library at Kennesaw State University (KSU). These kind folks provided guidance about the interlibrary loan process. KSU has been my academic home since 1998, and Sturgis library personnel have assisted me on many previous books.

I cannot, of course, forget family and friends who helped me along the journey. I now have nine grandchildren—Brianna Marie Carter; Aswad Elisha "Ellie" Woodson; Christopher Kainan Carter; Skylar Renee Kula; Emma Kay Lynne Woodson; Nero Blake Carter; Arya Rayne Carter; Rory Daulton; and Dawson Daulton—and they are always a delight and an inspiration. Ellie and Emma live with me, and their nonstop antics frequently amuse (and occasionally annoy) me when I step away from my research and writing.

Thanks also to loved ones who helped ease the load, including Keith W. Smith, a valued friend of more than thirty years; Chuck Redmon, another treasured friend of many years; Shirley Hardrick, housekeeper and babysitter extraordinaire; and Dr. William D. Richardson, my mentor and dissertation director at Georgia State University, who recently retired as the Odeen-Swanson Distinguished Professor of Political Science, chair of the Department of Political Science, and director of the W. O. Farber Center for Civic Leadership at the University of South Dakota. Dr. Richardson also was kind enough to review the manuscript and provide a jacket blurb.

I also must extend heartfelt appreciation to family members who are fellow writers: Chris Mead (cousin), Loren B. Mead (uncle), Walter Russell Mead (cousin), Robert Sidney Mellette (cousin), William W. Mellette (uncle), and Jim Wise (cousin). They have inspired me in myriad ways throughout the years.

Needless to say (but I will say it, anyway) any errors or omissions in fact or interpretation are my fault, and mine alone.

Monroe, Georgia
March 2017

INTRODUCTION

On August 9, 2016, when Republican presidential nominee (and later 45th president of the United States) Donald J. Trump spoke at a political rally in Wilmington, North Carolina, he alluded to the darker side of American politics, namely political assassinations. Speaking of former secretary of state Hillary Clinton, his Democratic rival, Trump said, "Hillary wants to abolish—essentially abolish the Second Amendment. By the way, if she gets to pick, if she gets to pick her judges, nothing you can do, folks. Although the Second Amendment people, maybe there is, I don't know." Trump later claimed that his off-the-cuff remark was not serious. His campaign surrogates offered a slightly different interpretation, arguing that he was serious, but not about assassination. He was asking Second Amendment supporters to mobilize their political resources in favor of a Republican candidate so that Clinton could not appoint Supreme Court justices who would approve gun control measures limiting the right to bear arms.[1]

Skeptics believe, however, that Trump was suggesting, albeit elliptically, that his supporters assassinate either Secretary Clinton or her Supreme Court nominees. Trump's offhand musing was reminiscent of English King Henry II's reputed comment about Thomas Becket, "Who will rid me of this troublesome priest," or words to that effect. Not long after the king posed his question aloud, four knights hacked Becket to death inside Canterbury Cathedral. Trump could claim, just as Henry II did, that his comments were not intended as a call to action, but merely a reflection of his exasperation at disagreements with a bitter rival. Apologists suggest that a speaker bears no responsibility for how listeners construe rhetorical questions. The only person responsible for assassinating, or attempting to assassinate, another person is the perpetrator who acts violently with the intent to cause harm.

Whether he meant to or not, Trump was tapping into a potent tradition in American politics. Throughout its storied history, the United States has earned a reputation as a violent society. Denizens of other nations sometimes look upon Americans as reckless cowboys, owing to a "Wild West," cavalier attitude about violence, especially episodes involving guns. As part of this less-than-hallowed tradition, public figures have fallen prey to many an assassin's bullet. In an effort to understand the ramifications of these incidents, this book examines the history of violence perpetrated against American political figures (as opposed to pogroms and deliberate acts of violence undertaken by political figures against the masses).

Before 1835, when house painter Richard Lawrence fired two pistols at President Andrew Jackson, political assassination was not a part of the American experience. Violence occurred frequently during the early history of the republic—and dueling was still practiced in some states—but deliberate attempts to snuff out the life of a political leader were virtually unknown. With the death of the founding generation and the tremendous growth of the US population during the 1830s, times and sensibilities changed. It was a turbulent era. The Jackson administration democratized the electorate, empowering the lower classes to participate in political affairs as never before. Immigration exploded as numerous peoples from far-off lands flooded into the New World. The rise of the abolitionist movement called attention to the divisive slavery issue, thereby exposing a rift between North and South that would grow in coming decades. The prevalence of violence as a potential solution to a political problem in American history dates from this time.

Of course, violence has been employed to achieve political objectives throughout human history; assassinations and assassination attempts are not unique to the United States. Antiquity is filled with examples of political murders. When Julius Caesar was felled by assassins in 44 BCE, political murders were already a longstanding tradition. This book, however, focuses on assassinations (and attempts) in the American republic.

Nine American presidents—Andrew Jackson in 1835, Abraham Lincoln in 1865, James A. Garfield in 1881, William McKinley in 1901, Harry S. Truman in 1950, John F. Kennedy in 1963, Richard Nixon in 1974, Gerald Ford twice in 1975, and Ronald Reagan in 1981—have been the targets of assassins. (Even this statement is a bit inaccurate because most, if not all, presidents and presidential candidates have received messages containing threats. The focus here is on serious threats where the person acted on the impulse to kill or maim.) President-elect Franklin D. Roosevelt was also a target shortly before he was sworn into office in 1933. Moreover, three presidential candidates—Theodore Roosevelt in 1912, Robert F. Kennedy in 1968, and George Wallace in 1972—were shot by assailants. Roosevelt and Wallace survived, but

Robert Kennedy did not. In addition to presidents and candidates for the presidency, as of this writing, eight governors, seven US senators, nine US House members, eleven mayors, seventeen state legislators, and eleven judges have been victims of political violence. No other nation with a population of over fifty million people has witnessed as many political assassinations or attempts.

The etymology of the word "assassination" also antedates the American experience. Its origin is uncertain, but some historians believe that it derives from the word *hashshāshīyīn*, which shares the same route as "hashish." The assassins were a group of Persian killers working in Iran from the eighth to the fourteenth centuries. Whether these killers acted under the influence of hashish remains a point of contention among scholars. In any case, by the time William Shakespeare wrote *Macbeth* early in the seventeenth century, "assassination" referred to political murder. In Act I, Scene 7, of the famous play, Macbeth remarks, "If it were done when 'tis done, then 'twere well/ It were done quickly. If the assassination/ Could trammel up the consequence, and catch/ With his surcease success; that but this blow/ Might be the be-all and the end-all here, But here, upon this bank and shoal of time,/ We'd jump the life to come."

In the twenty-first century, an "assassin" is anyone who kills a prominent political figure. By extension, a would-be assassin is anyone who attempts to kill a prominent political figure and fails. The term "political figure" need not refer to an elected official, although often that is the case. A political figure can be someone who influences public policy even if he or she does not hold elective office. Joseph Smith, founder of the Mormon Church, never held office, but he influenced the course of the nineteenth-century politics. Malcolm X and Martin Luther King, Jr., never stood for election, but they were enormously influential civil rights leaders during the twentieth century. These men are included because of their connection to, and influence on, the political process. Such personages can be distinguished from the attempted murder of artist Andy Warhol and the shooting of rock musician John Lennon. Although both Warhol and Lennon occupied a public space on the margins of the political process, they were primarily creative artists and were not famous and influential owing to their politics. Therefore, they are not included in the book.

Naturally, these violent episodes trigger a series of important questions. First, why has the United States—a country constructed on a bedrock of the rule of law and firmly committed to due process—been so susceptible to political violence? Attacks on public figures were rare in colonial America. When violence occurred, it usually resulted from riots by mobs or from duels, such as the infamous contest between Alexander Hamilton and Aaron Burr in 1804.

The rarity of political violence early in the history of the republic raises several additional questions. Why did violence against political figures increase during the nineteenth century? Did the nation's culture or politics change and, if so, how? Did political violence increase during the twentieth century and, if so, why? What, if anything, can be done to reduce or eliminate such attacks? This book addresses these questions by examining twenty-five instances of violence against elected officials and public figures in American history.

A book on political assassinations can be organized in several ways. The most obvious method is to discuss the violent episodes chronologically. The chronological approach has the advantage of simplicity, and it can be useful in understanding how violence aimed at public figures changes over time. By examining assaults in historical context, the author can illustrate the evolving sensibilities of assailants, their targets, and the American people. Unfortunately, while such an approach can provide a broad overview of the social, cultural, historical, political, and religious conditions of the era—a macroscopic view—it generally does not provide a glimpse into the specific reasons that the assailants felt compelled to act—a microscopic view. The chronological approach can answer what happened, but not necessarily *why* it happened. To understand the "why," something else is required.

Accordingly, *Political Assassinations and Attempts in US History* moves beyond the chronological approach and relies on a typology of assassins designed to explicate motives. This classification system is a modification of the structure James W. Clarke employed in his 1982 book *American Assassins: The Darker Side of Politics*.[2] Assassins are divided into five categories according to their intentions. The individuals and groups within each category possess common characteristics that explain, to some extent, why they acted as they did. Clarke argued that although discussing historical context is helpful, delving into motives is crucial to understanding why assailants act against political figures. His theoretical construct is especially insightful in exploring what the individual assailants hoped to accomplish.

Philosophers sometimes refer to an exploration of motives as the quest to understand "intentionality." Many thinkers working within the Western intellectual tradition have contended that the central feature of "personhood" is the idea that individuals possess free will and make choices based on their will. The French philosopher and mathematician René Descartes placed intentionality at the heart of his philosophy when he famously stated that "I think therefore I am." The only reality I know for certain is my own existence and intentions.

Intentionality is the key feature in the Anglo-American system of jurisprudence. Criminal law is predicated on the concept that persons who violate the laws of the nation-state must be punished for their transgressions. Yet a prohibited act can only be deemed a "transgression" if the person who acted knew or should have known that the act was a violation of the law. Children, persons acting on a mistake of fact, and the mentally ill are not punished if they are unable to form or possess the requisite bad intent.

Anyone familiar with the concept of *mens rea* (a guilty mind) in criminal law will caution that understanding intentions is at best an uncertain enterprise. Criminologists examine indicia of intent, but no one claims to understand human motivations with any reasonable degree of certainty. The point is well taken. Moreover, discriminating readers may disagree with the classification of a particular person in one category versus another. Nonetheless, despite the potential hazards inherent in delving into the psychology of the human mind, attempting to discern motives can be useful in understanding would-be assassins.

Of the five categories of intentionality employed in this book, Type 1 is a category reserved for rational actors who understand the political purpose of killing a public figure. These types of actors are zealots who seek to advance a political cause by eliminating a prominent individual who stands in their way. Cause and effect are important for a Type 1 assassin. Perhaps the public figure is the architect, or perceived architect, of a policy that negatively affects the actor. In other cases, the assassin's target is a symbol of a distasteful regime and, therefore, removing the symbol is tantamount to a symbolic victory. While these types of actors may be neurotic or emotionally disturbed, they first and foremost are driven by a rational desire to remove a troublesome public figure. Mentally healthy individuals may question whether any would-be assassin is genuinely "rational," but the desire to kill an offender is rational in the sense that the actor understands the nature of the act—that is, distinguishes between right and wrong as well as fact and fantasy—and works to achieve a political goal.

A Type 2 assassin, by contrast with a Type 1 actor, is motivated by an egocentric need for recognition. Although this type of actor is not necessarily cognitively impaired or delusional, he or she is less interested in achieving a political goal than a Type 1 assassin is. As a person with low self-esteem, a Type 2 actor seeks to compensate for a lack of social status, and the most efficient way to garner attention is by killing a high-status person. A nobody becomes a somebody when the nobody kills a somebody. From that point on, whenever historians speak of Person X, they invariably must speak of Person Y. The assassin has then affected public policy, but the political repercussions are secondary considerations. So while changing public policy is crucial for a Type 1 actor, it is but an ancillary outcome for a Type 2 personality.

The Type 3 actor is far more isolated and emotionally disturbed than a Type 1 or Type 2 actor. In modern parlance, a Type 3 individual is a sociopath, feeling no compunction about taking the life of another human being. A Type 1 or Type 2 actor understands that assassination will cause pain to the person who is killed and his or her family, but believes that the benefits outweigh the costs. A Type 3 actor is incapable of empathizing with the target. This kind of killer believes that life is so meaningless and devoid of purpose that the death of another human being carries no moral consequences. An example of this type is a killer for hire who accepts payment to assassinate a public official. He or she is driven only by the desire to earn a fee. Another example is a person who believes that a public official personifies a hated segment of society and therefore seeks to remove the official. In short, a Type 3 actor perceives reality accurately, but he or she has no capacity to respond emotionally.

A Type 4 actor is essentially what a layperson would call "crazy." This type of would-be assassin suffers from extreme emotional or cognitive distortion. In some cases, the individual suffers from hallucinations and has only a tenuous hold on reality. When questioned, a Type 4 actor often explains that he or she heard voices inside his or her head telling him or her to act. He or she acts against a prominent public figure because he or she believes that the figure is somehow responsible for all manner of real or imagined maladies. Like a Type 3 assailant, a Type 4 personality is isolated from friends or family, or at best enjoys strained social relationships. The difficulty with anticipating the actions of a Type 4 offender is that this person acts based on an irrational motive, which means that it is almost impossible to predict his or her actions beforehand. Although neighbors and coworkers may sense that the person is maladjusted and ideally should receive mental health treatment, the lack xxii • POLITICAL ASSASSINATIONS AND ATTEMPTS IN US HISTORY

of an effective psychological or psychiatric intervention does not necessarily mean that the person will harm himself or others.

Finally, Type 5 is reserved for "miscellaneous" or "other" motives. In other words, the person or persons acted for a variety of motives, some of which are unknown or unknowable. When a lynch mob killed Joseph Smith in 1844, most members of the mob were incensed at the beliefs and behaviors of the Mormon leadership. Given the psychology of mob behavior, however, it is impossible to identify the motives of the individuals who participated in the murder. Some assassins, such as Carl Weiss, the man who shot Louisiana politician Huey P. Long, act on inscrutable motives. Long was a charismatic, larger-than-life political figure. It would be easy and convenient to assume that Weiss opposed Long's policies and therefore, in keeping with a Type 1 actor, sought to eliminate the object of his wrath to accomplish a political purpose. Yet the historical record suggests that Weiss was not an outspoken critic of the Long administration. Prior to the time that he shot Long in 1935, Weiss appeared to be happily married with a well-adjusted family life. He was a physician and apparently well respected. Because he did not evince the attributes typically associated with assassins, his motives are difficult to fathom. Perhaps Weiss was a Type 1 killer, harboring enormous animosity against Huey Long's political agenda. Perhaps Weiss was sliding into the type of madness associated with a Type 4 personality. The available evidence does not provide a definitive conclusion. In these types of cases, the best that can be said is that the would-be assassin acted for reasons that may never be understood.

In the pages that follow, readers will discover a variety of individuals and motives. The common link among all of them is that they believed violence was the answer to a perplexing problem. To make sense of the complex individuals and their crimes, the book is organized chronologically according to the type of assassin. Thus, Type 1 assassins are discussed from the earliest in time to the latest. Similarly, Type 2, Type 3, Type 4, and Type 5 assassins are discussed using the same format. The earliest case covered here dates from 1835, when Richard Lawrence (Type 4) attacked Andrew Jackson, while the latest episode occurred when Jared Lee Loughner (Type 4) shot Arizona Congresswoman Gabrielle Giffords in 2011. Regrettably, given the long tradition of political violence in the United States, other cases may occur in the years to come.

PART I

TYPE 1 ACTORS

Chapter 1

"SIC SEMPER TYRANNIS":
ABRAHAM LINCOLN (1865)

One of the most infamous assassinations in American history occurred on April 14, 1865, when the acclaimed stage actor John Wilkes Booth shot President Abraham Lincoln with a .44-caliber Deringer pistol while the president watched a play at Ford's Theatre in Washington, DC. Booth escaped through a back door moments after horrified theatregoers witnessed the assassin leap from a balcony and land on the stage. Unconscious and mortally wounded, Lincoln slumped in his chair, never to look on the world again. When it was clear that the wounded president would not survive a journey to the White House, doctors directed that his body be carried out of the theatre so the great man would not expire on the floor of the presidential box. The following morning at 7:22, the president died. Already popular for guiding the nation through its darkest hours, the martyred Lincoln ascended into the pantheon of American heroes, forever after memorialized as a man of granite, an icon for the ages.[3]

Nothing in Lincoln's early life or career suggested that one day he would be regarded as a giant figure in American history. In a campaign biography, he characterized his humble origins as the "short and simple annals of the poor." When he first considered a run for the presidency, the coarse, homely, under-educated prairie lawyer from Illinois was a dark horse candidate in a field of stellar thoroughbreds, including New York Senator William H. Seward and former Ohio Governor Salmon P. Chase. Having served but a single term in the US House of Representatives and eight years in the state legislature, Lincoln appeared ill-suited for high office.[4]

Yet appearances can be deceiving. Despite his lack of formal education and his slim resume, Lincoln had developed a remarkably nuanced view of slavery, the most important, and contentious, issue of the day. Navigating between the abolitionists who sought to emancipate slaves immediately and apologists for the peculiar institution who wished to preserve the status quo,

Lincoln argued that the Constitution protected slavery where it already existed, but the federal government could prevent its spread into the territories. He was on record expressing his private distaste for the institution, but he recognized that an elected official must follow constitutional requirements and statutory dictates despite his personal predilections.

Lincoln came to national attention when he unsuccessfully ran for a US Senate seat against the prominent Illinois politician Stephen A. Douglas, the incumbent senator, in 1858. In a series of well-publicized debates, the two men grappled over slavery and its effect on the nation. Douglas was by far the better known of the two candidates, but Lincoln held his own in the debates and emerged as a promising national political figure. Although Lincoln lost the battle for the Senate, he arguably won the war for public attention. He used his new-found prominence to position himself as a viable alternative to Republican presidential hopefuls who had amassed too many political opponents to capture the party's nomination in 1860. It was a brilliant strategy. Lincoln became a compromise candidate for the Republican presidential nomination when the bigger names failed to secure the requisite votes at the party convention.[5]

He was elected to the nation's highest office in 1860, at precisely the moment when the Union was fracturing. Southern state leaders had spent decades, they believed, ground under the boot heels of an oppressive federal government. Time and again Southerners had threatened to secede from the Union rather than submit to federal limitations on the institution of slavery. As early as the 1830s, when President Andrew Jackson threatened to use force against South Carolina during the Nullification Crisis, the precarious state of the Union had caused no small amount of consternation among leaders on both sides of the Mason-Dixon line.[6]

The incoming president initially underestimated the nature and extent of secession threats. National lawmakers—notably Lincoln's political hero, Henry Clay—had cobbled together compromises to forestall disunion for decades, and Lincoln hoped that another accommodation could be reached. Despite last-minute wrangling among several influential political leaders, a compromise was not in the offing. Lincoln nonetheless was an optimist; he believed that Southern men would come to their senses if he could assuage their fears about an obdurate federal government interfering with state rights. In his inaugural address, the president assured hostile factions that "In *your* hands, my dissatisfied fellow-countrymen, and not in *mine*, is the momentous issue of civil war. The Government will not assail *you*. You can have no conflict without being yourselves the aggressors"[7]

Alas, despite Lincoln's eloquent plea for sectional rapprochement, the better angels of our nature could not be found. Thirty-nine days into the Lincoln administration, the rebels in Charleston, South Carolina, fired on Fort Sumter, a federal military installation. War had descended on the nation. No one knew that it would become a bloody, internecine affair that would claim the lives of more than 2 percent of the population, but it was clear that history had changed forever. Lincoln reluctantly issued a call for volunteers to put down the rebellion by force. Long-threatened civil war had become a reality.[8]

And so Abraham Lincoln became a wartime president, overseeing four arduous years of bloodshed, deprivation, and discord. As with so much in his life and career, he grew into his job. He had almost no military experience save for a few months in 1832 when he served in the Illinois state militia during the Black Hawk War, and yet Lincoln educated himself on strategy and tactics. When he could not find a suitable commander to claim consistent battlefield victories, he stepped into the breach as much as he could before he tapped Ulysses S. Grant to serve as general in chief late in the war. Lincoln was not a commander in the field, but he knew the kind of general officer that he needed. He used his new-found knowledge to help him find the right man at the right time.[9]

Essentially a moderate, cautious politician when the war began, Lincoln evolved over time. He resisted pressure from abolitionists as well as some Radical Republicans in Congress to emancipate the slaves, fearing that he would alienate Border State representatives if he moved too quickly or outpaced Northern public opinion on slavery. When he recognized the advantages of issuing an emancipation proclamation as a wartime measure, Lincoln decreed that slaves in the rebellious states were free as of January 1, 1863. It was not the wholesale assault on the peculiar institution that the Radicals had desired, but Lincoln went beyond his predecessors in issuing his proclamation. Later, he lobbied to enact a constitutional amendment to outlaw slavery throughout the nation. The states ratified the amendment in December 1865, eight months after Lincoln's assassination.[10]

When he learned that Confederate General Robert E. Lee had surrendered his army near Appomattox Courthouse, Virginia, on April 9, 1865, Lincoln was elated. Rebel armies still marched in the field, but the president

1.1 By 1865, Abraham Lincoln had aged markedly after four years of civil war. Courtesy of the Library of Congress.

believed that the rebellion would soon end. Despite the hardships he and the nation had endured, in April 1865 Lincoln believed that better days were ahead.[11]

As the war wound to a conclusion and the prospects for national unity improved, a group of conspirators plotted to kidnap or kill the president. John Wilkes Booth, a celebrated actor from a prominent family of actors, served as the leader of the cabal. Booth was the ninth of ten children born to Junius Brutus Booth, an English actor known for his vivid portrayals of Shakespearean characters.

John Wilkes grew to adulthood with little structure or discipline in his life. He was fourteen years old when his father died in 1852. Three years later, he followed in his father's footsteps by becoming an actor. His elder brother,

Edwin, was a prominent actor in his own right, which led to a not-so-good-natured sibling rivalry. Another brother, Junius Brutus Booth, Jr., was also a well-known thespian, but he was seventeen years older than John Wilkes and therefore not a serious competitor.[12]

By all accounts, the handsome, charismatic Booth was a talented if somewhat undisciplined actor. His physical attractiveness and hail-fellow-well-met bonhomie made him a popular public figure as well as "a star of the first magnitude." President Lincoln saw John Wilkes Booth perform in a play, *The Marble Heart*, on November 9, 1863. Booth's kindness and generosity to friends and strangers alike became well-known, presenting a stark contrast to the portrait of a crazed radical that became the standard narrative following the Lincoln assassination.[13]

If John Wilkes Booth was such a fun-loving, kind, gregarious friend to all, his actions in the eighteen months leading up to the assassination appear inexplicable—until they are placed in the context of the times. Washington, DC, was for all intents and purposes a Southern city. Loose talk circulated throughout the capital. Shady characters engaged in talk of conspiracies, but most dastardly deeds only consisted of the empty threats and broken promises uttered by disgruntled Southern sympathizers who developed bold plans but almost never followed through. It was clear, however, that Southerners loathed Abraham Lincoln, referring to him as a tyrant who desired nothing so much as the subjugation of the South and the destruction of her cherished traditions. Booth revered the Southern Confederacy and worried that the Union might prevail, destroying the Southern way of life. Exposed to the vitriol espoused by his colleagues as well as in numerous pro-Southern newspaper editorials, Booth came to hate the man in the White House who was pushing for the rebels' capitulation.[14]

As Southern fortunes deteriorated throughout 1864, Booth resolved to act in defense of his beloved Confederacy. He had never served in the Confederate Army, but he was anxious to serve the cause. With the hour growing late, Booth recognized that desperate times call for desperate measures. In October 1864, he traveled to Montréal, a haven for Confederate spies and agents provocateurs, perhaps to meet with representatives of the Confederate government, although no conclusive link has ever been demonstrated. Whether he acted in concert with Confederate agents or on his own initiative, Booth hatched a plan to kidnap the president of the United States and hold him for ransom.

1.2 The dashing John Wilkes Booth, a Southern sympathizer and prominent actor, loathed Abraham Lincoln, and resolved to see the president kidnapped or killed. Courtesy of the Library of Congress.

The original plan was to abduct the president while Lincoln visited the Soldiers' Home near Washington, DC. After traveling on back roads into southern Maryland with his captive in tow, Booth would hold Lincoln hostage far away from the protection of Union soldiers. It was a bold plan requiring multiple parties to assist in the abduction and getaway.

Booth reached out to four pro-Southern men, all of whom brought a different skill to the table: John Surratt, Jr., was a Confederate spy who knew the back roads of southern Maryland and could prove invaluable in eluding capture; George Atzerodt was a boatman who knew the waters they would likely encounter as they fled with the captured president in tow; Lewis Powell (also known as Lewis Payne or Lewis Paine) was an ex-Confederate soldier with a powerful physique and a fierce disposition who could be counted on to employ violence, as necessary; and Booth apparently selected the last man, David Herold, a simpleton, because Herold was loyal to a fault. Other persons may have been involved in the initial planning as well, but their participation in the conspiracy was never clear.[15]

Booth soon recognized that kidnapping the president was unrealistic and unnecessarily complicated. Abducting Lincoln with only a handful of men and fleeing along back roads patrolled by Union troops probably would lead to the conspirators' arrest, trial, conviction, and execution. Moreover, Booth was not sure how long the Southern Confederacy would remain viable. By late 1864, Southern armies had suffered a series of crushing military defeats. Confederate General Robert E. Lee was stuck in Petersburg, Virginia, as General Ulysses S. Grant besieged the city. Grant's trusted lieutenant, General William T. Sherman, was cutting a swath of destruction through Georgia. Confederate General John Bell Hood had suffered a disastrous defeat in fierce fighting during the Franklin-Nashville campaign in Tennessee. If Booth and his band were resolved to act, they must act boldly—and soon.[16]

If he could not seize the president for strategic advantage, Booth could cut off the head of the snake. He believed that he could create chaos—and thus benefit the Southern cause—in Washington by assassinating President Lincoln, Vice President Andrew Johnson, Secretary of State William Seward, and General Grant.

In the modern era, approaching a president of the United States is difficult owing to the extraordinary security precautions in place to ensure his safety. During much of the nineteenth century, however, presidents were readily accessible to the public. Booth bragged that he might have assassinated Lincoln as the newly reelected president delivered his inaugural address on March 4, 1865. As an important person about town, the charismatic young actor enjoyed access to places where he could get at Lincoln at his discretion. Yet as winter turned to spring, Booth hesitated to implement his plan.[17]

His indecision ended as the Confederacy collapsed. On April 11, two days after Lee's surrender, Lincoln appeared on a White House balcony to address a crowd of well-wishers standing below. Booth was among the onlookers as the president spoke. "Let us all join in doing the acts necessary to restoring the proper relations between these states and the Union," Lincoln called to the crowd. He outlined his Reconstruction plan in Louisiana and suggested that he might support universal manhood suffrage, allowing "very intelligent" blacks to vote.[18]

Booth was disgusted by what he heard. This coarse buffoon who had destroyed the Southern Confederacy would now allow black men to vote in federal elections. The angry young man turned to a friend and exclaimed, "That means nigger citizenship. Now, by God, I'll put him through. That is the last speech he will ever make."[19]

Booth made good on his promise. His plans solidified on April 14 when he learned that Lincoln and Grant would attend a performance at Ford's Theatre that evening. It would be a convenient opportunity to snuff out the lives of two loathsome tyrants while Booth's confederates acted against other high-ranking government officials. As Booth shot the president and his chief butcher, the plan was for Atzerodt to assassinate Vice President Johnson while Lewis Powell killed Seward—with Herold's assistance, if necessary.[20]

Booth arranged for a horse to be waiting at the rear door of the theatre that evening. Sneaking up behind Lincoln and Grant, he would fire a pistol at the unsuspecting prey, dash from the building, jump on his horse, and ride away into the night. Booth entertained delusions of grandeur, believing that he would be hailed as a hero, at least in the South, for disposing of two villains. As he expressed it in a letter that he handed to a fellow actor, John Matthews, "The world may censure me for what I am about to do, but I am sure posterity will justify me."[21]

Shortly after ten that evening, as the play *Our American Cousin* was showing, Booth made his way to Ford's Theatre. His presence in the theatre was not alarming. He was a well-known actor and had performed many times at the venue. He even had his mailed delivered there. As he ambled through the theatre, Booth approached Lincoln's valet, Charles Forbes, and handed him a card, presumably the actor's calling card. It was not unusual for a prominent actor such as Booth to request a brief audience with the president to offer his regards. Forbes spoke to Booth for a moment before the actor approached the door to the presidential box.[22]

The presidential box contained two barriers—an exterior door that opened from the hallway into a small vestibule, and an interior door that led to the enclosure where the president and his entourage would sit in chairs to view the performance. Booth entered the exterior door without being challenged or asked to state his business. The man who was supposed to guard the door, John Frederick Parker of the District of Columbia Metropolitan Police Department, had departed, reputedly to lounge in a nearby tavern.

Inside the vestibule, to Booth's surprise, no one watched over the president. Booth had come equipped with a knife to slash his way through one or more presidential bodyguards, but he realized that a blitz attack was unnecessary.

Wedging a wooden stick between the wall and the door leading to the presidential box, Booth prepared for the assault. He had thought ahead. By barring the exterior door, he was confident that he could carry out his work without interference. Someone, perhaps Booth himself, had drilled a peephole in the interior door leading from the vestibule to the box. The assassin-in-waiting could look through the hole and see the president sitting in a rocking chair with the left side of his face exposed to the audience of 1,700 people, most of whom sat in seats configured along the floor. The president's wife, Mary Todd Lincoln, sat to his immediate right. A young couple, Clara Harris, the daughter of New York Senator Ira Harris, and her fiancé, Major Henry Rathbone, had joined the presidential party for the evening after General Grant had cancelled plans to attend.[23]

Although he had never appeared in the play, Booth was familiar with the script for *Our American Cousin*. In one scene, a character walks onstage and utters a line that usually provokes widespread laughter in the audience. Booth intended to step through the interior door leading from the vestibule to the presidential box at that moment, aim his .44-caliber Deringer pistol, and fire into the president's brain. He hoped that the noise of the laughter would buy him precious seconds. During the inevitable confusion, he would flee to safety before armed guards could impede his escape.

This part of the plot worked perfectly. At precisely the appointed time, Booth stepped through the door, lifted his arm, and fired his pistol point-blank into the back of Lincoln's head. The bullet entered the president's skull behind his left ear and lodged above his right eye. Lincoln, instantly rendered unconscious by the bullet, slumped in his chair.[24]

The crowd initially believed the noise was part of the play. Within seconds of the blast, Major Rathbone, an experienced army officer who recognized the sound of gunfire, sprang from his chair and lunged, apparently intent on preventing the assassin's escape. Booth was prepared for exactly such a contingency. Dropping the Deringer, he pulled a dagger from his pocket and slashed the major from elbow to shoulder. Rathbone staggered backward.

Always attuned to drama, Booth leapt from the box onto the stage below. He may have snagged his foot on a prop and broken his leg when he landed. Some scholars question this version of the story, suggesting that Booth fled out

1.3 This famous Currier & Ives drawing imagines the moment when Booth shot the president in Ford's Theatre on April 14, 1865. Courtesy of the Library of Congress.

the back of the theatre far too quickly to have broken his leg during the jump. Perhaps he broke it later, during his mad dash from the scene of the crime.

In any case, Booth understood that he must scurry from the theatre as quickly as possible to elude the authorities, but he would not be denied his greatest moment on the stage. Rising to his full height, he exclaimed "Sic semper tyrannis" ("thus ever to tyrants"), the state motto of Virginia. Some eyewitnesses heard him shout, "I have done it; the South is avenged!" Accounts varied as to the exact wording, but everyone agreed that a man had leapt from the presidential box to the stage below and uttered a few words before he rushed backstage.[25]

As for the other conspirators, they were supposed to act in concert with Booth, murdering their targets at the same time that the actor assassinated the president. Here the plot unraveled. Atzerodt lost his nerve and did not attack Vice President Johnson. Instead, he spent the evening drowning his sorrows in alcohol. Lewis Powell showed up at Secretary Seward's house and stabbed the bedridden man, but he, too, failed in his assignment. Seward had been grievously injured in a recent carriage accident and was recuperating in his bed. He suffered serious stab wounds, but survived the attack.[26]

In the meantime, the scene at Ford's Theatre dissolved into chaos. Mary Todd Lincoln wailed incessantly as two doctors from the audience, Charles Leale and Charles Sabin Taft, removed the president from his chair and laid him on the floor so they could examine the wound. Feeling with his hand, Leale discovered the hole in Lincoln's head. He attempted to dig the bullet from the hole, but he could not find the object. He and Dr. Taft realized that the damage was massive. "His wound is mortal," Dr. Leale announced. "It is impossible for him to recover." Sometime during these minutes, the lead actress from the play, Laura Keene, entered the presidential box and cradled the dying man's head in her lap.[27]

If he could not save his patient's life, Dr. Leale could stabilize Lincoln's condition by removing blood clots from the head wound with his hand. He understood that Lincoln would not survive a journey back to the White House, but Leale did not want the president to die on the theatre floor. He and Dr. Taft agreed that the mortally wounded man must be moved to a bed where he could rest comfortably.

A group of onlookers carried the president's enormous frame from the theatre. They did not have a destination in mind until they heard a man, Henry Safford, shouting, "Bring him in here! Bring him in here!" Safford was a lodger in a boarding house across from Ford's Theatre owned by William Petersen, a German tailor. At Safford's invitation, the crowd of men carried the prostrate Abraham Lincoln into a back bedroom of the Petersen house. They had to lay his six-foot, four-inch body diagonally on the bed because Lincoln was too tall to rest fully prone on the small mattress.[28]

By this time, word spread that Lincoln had been shot. A procession of important persons congregated at the Petersen house to check on the president's condition. Secretary of War Edwin Stanton took charge, issuing orders and even directing that Mary Todd Lincoln be taken from the room after she could not control her hysteria. Throughout the night, Stanton dispatched orders to government personnel and military officers to search for Booth. No one knew where the assailant had fled, but Stanton was determined to track him down.

Apart from Stanton and Secretary of the Navy Gideon Welles, no one milling about the Petersen house quite knew what to do. The president's wife was inconsolable, occasionally falling quiet, but often crying aloud in her grief. The doctors felt impotent; they had done all they could do, but it was a matter of time before the patient expired. Nineteenth-century medicine could not save his life.[29]

Lincoln survived longer than his doctors had anticipated. He died in the early morning hours of April 15, at 7:22 a.m., nine hours after the shooting, having never regained consciousness. It was Easter Sunday—a day known by many Americans forever after as "Black Easter." Present at Lincoln's death-bed, Secretary Stanton uttered a phrase that soon became famous: "Now, he belongs to the ages."[30]

The news electrified the nation. On the eve of the Union triumph in the Civil War, the man who had guided his nation through its worst days was struck dead by the forces of darkness and evil. Many Americans believed that the Confederate leadership must have been behind the conspiracy. It was inconceivable that Booth and his small band of ruffians could have engineered the plot without Southern support.[31]

During his life, Lincoln engendered a wide range of opinion. Some citizens viewed him as an uneducated country bumpkin ill-suited for the presidency. Others considered him a wise, benevolent father figure who had grown into his role as the commander in chief of a war-torn nation. Confederates believed he was a fiend hell-bent on emancipating their slaves and destroying the South. Soldiers and former slaves called him "Father Abraham." He was vacillating, decisive, tyrannical, bumbling, cruel, gentle, peace-loving, war-crazy, and anything else his detractors and supporters cared to project onto him.[32]

With his death, Lincoln was transformed into an iconic figure. Gone was the vacillating flesh-and-blood politician struggling to find his way through a monstrous civil war. In his place, a new figure emerged, a "man of granite," a giant among men, an untouchable legend. Observing the myths that sprang up as soon as Lincoln died, a journalist shrewdly remarked that the assassination "has made it impossible to speak the truth of Abraham Lincoln hereafter."[33]

The nation grieved as never before. Even George Washington's death almost sixty-six years earlier had not been met with such an outpouring of heartfelt agony. The nation's first president had died of natural causes while in retirement, but Lincoln had been the victim of an assassin's bullet, his life snuffed out at the beginning of what promised to be a momentous second term. By all rights, his service to the nation should not have ended so soon.

Schools and businesses shut down. Flags flew at half-mast for weeks. Lincoln's body lay on display in the East Room of the White House on April 17, where 25,000 people—some waiting up to six hours to gain entry—filed past to catch one last glimpse at the martyr. Ten days after Lincoln died, his remains were transferred to a private rail car for a 1,700-mile journey to his hometown of Springfield, Illinois, for interment. Americans still in mourning lined the track for much of the journey.[34]

Even as the nation grieved for its fallen hero, the search was on for the president's assassin. His identity was never in doubt. A large number of eye-witnesses had identified John Wilkes Booth, a prominent actor, as the man who leapt from the presidential box onto the stage at Ford's Theatre. With the assault on Secretary of State Seward that same evening, everyone under-stood that Booth probably was part of a conspiracy to topple the leaders of the executive branch of the federal government. The extent of the conspiracy was not yet known.[35]

Booth escaped from the capital city as quickly as possible. Within thirty minutes of the shooting, he approached a sentinel, Sergeant Silas T. Cobb of the 3rd Massachusetts Heavy Artillery, at the Navy Yard Bridge leading from Washington, DC, into Maryland. The gunman hoped that he had reached the bridge before news of the assassination spread throughout the city.

Sgt. Cobb was not supposed to allow anyone to cross the bridge after dark. Always the master thespian, Booth appeared calm and collected. He said that he did not know the bridge closed at nightfall. He had hoped to traverse the dark road by the light of the moon; therefore, he had waited to begin his journey until he was sure the moon filled the night sky. Unaware that Booth would soon be the most sought-after man in the country, the sergeant waved him through. Booth's co-conspirator, David Herold, crossed the same bridge an hour later and met up with Booth in Maryland. The two men collected weapons they had hidden previously at a tavern in Surrattsville, Maryland.[36]

Booth's injured leg presented a complication, but not an insurmount-able obstacle. He and Herold rode their horses to the home of Dr. Samuel A. Mudd in southern Maryland. A physician, Mudd examined the leg and deter-mined that it was broken. He set the leg in a splint and arranged for Booth to procure a set of crutches. Mudd's role in the assassination has remained a point of contention since that evening. He later claimed that he knew noth-ing of the assassination and only treated Booth because the man required medical attention. Yet even after he learned of the assassination and Booth's probable guilt, Mudd hesitated to contact the authorities. Whether he was an accomplice after the fact or an innocent man caught in Booth's web of deceit, Mudd paid a price for his efforts that night. Arrested and put on trial, he served a prison sentence until 1869. Most historians remain skeptical that the doctor was as innocent as he claimed.[37]

After leaving Mudd's house, Booth and Herold made their way to Rich Hill, an estate owned by Samuel Cox, Sr., a loyal Southern man, near Bel Alton, Maryland. Cox enlisted the assistance of another trusted fellow, Thomas Jones, who hid the fugitives in a swamp for five days until they could cross the Potomac River into Virginia. By April 24, Booth and Herold had left Maryland and found refuge at Richard H. Garrett's farm, Locust Hill, near Port Royal, Virginia. Assuming an alias, Booth lied to Garrett, telling the man nothing about the assassination. He said that he was a Confederate soldier returning home from the war.[38]

Garrett suspected that his two visitors had lied, but before he acted on his suspicions, Union soldiers from the 16th New York Cavalry arrived. Booth had been the subject of an intense manhunt in the eleven days since Lincoln had died. Initially, his pursuers had searched the Maryland countryside, following his trail from the Navy Yard Bridge. Eventually, Union troops realized that Booth and Herold had crossed the river into Virginia. Two strangers traveling on horseback, with one of the men sporting a broken leg, attracted attention. By April 26, the soldiers found the conspirators hiding in the Garrett family barn.[39]

Ordered to surrender or the soldiers would burn the barn within fifteen minutes, Booth vowed never to be taken alive. Davey Herold was less willing to die. He chose to surrender, and Booth agreed to let him go. After Herold was alone inside the barn, Booth negotiated with his captors. The soldiers wanted to take him alive so they could question him about the assassination plot. Booth simply refused to lay down his weapons or leave the barn. Fearful that the armed fugitive would never surrender and might cause further damage, the soldiers set fire to the barn, confident that Booth would have no choice but to rush outside to escape the flames.[40]

As fire engulfed the building, one soldier, Sergeant Thomas P. "Boston" Corbett, eyed the assassin through a slit in the wall. Told that Booth was pointing a carbine rifle at a fellow soldier, Corbett aimed his pistol and fired. The bullet struck Booth in the back of the head, severing his spinal cord. Soldiers scurried into the burning barn and carried the wounded assassin outside, placing his body beside a grove of locust trees. When the heat from the fire grew too intense, they carried Booth onto the porch of the Garrett home.

He was in agony. Able to speak only in a hoarse whisper, Booth said, "Tell my mother I die for my country." After he asked a soldier to lift his hands so that he could gaze on them, Booth muttered, "useless, useless." He died on the porch of the Garrett House two hours after he was shot on April 26, 1865.[41]

Lincoln's assassin was dead, but some of his confederates remained at large. Secretary Stanton and the army wasted little time in pursuing leads. Anyone who might have participated in the scheme was rounded up for questioning and possible prosecution. Investigators gradually narrowed the list to nine suspects. One man, Edman (sometimes spelled "Edmund") "Ned" Spangler, a thirty-nine-year-old stagehand at Ford's Theatre who unwittingly held the reins of John Wilkes Booth's horse briefly during the night of the assassination, was not part of the conspiracy, but he was in the wrong place at the wrong time. Spangler was arrested, released, and arrested again. Later, he was convicted on dubious evidence for his role in the conspiracy and sentenced to serve six years in prison. Spangler served slightly less than four years until President Andrew Johnson pardoned him before Johnson left office in March 1869.[42]

Michael O'Laughlen and Samuel Arnold were early recruits in the original plot to kidnap Lincoln, but they dropped out before Booth orchestrated the assassination. Both men were sentenced to life in prison. O'Laughlen died of yellow fever in 1867, but Arnold was among the men President Johnson pardoned in 1869. Dr. Samuel Mudd, convicted and sentenced to life imprisonment, also won a pardon in 1869.[43]

John H. Surratt, Jr., had met with John Wilkes Booth on several occasions in late 1864 and early 1865. He was a Confederate courier and spy as well as a willing participant in the kidnapping scheme. When Booth shot the president on April 14, Surratt was in Elmira, New York. Recognizing that he probably would be arrested, he fled to Montréal. Later, he served under the alias John Watson in the Ninth Company of the Pontifical Zouaves in the Papal States before he was recognized and arrested. Surratt escaped to Italy and traveled on to Alexandria, Egypt. Arrested by US officials in Egypt, he was shipped back to the United States for trial. Unlike the other conspirators, who were tried by a military commission, Surratt was tried by a civilian court. He won his release following a mistrial in 1867.[44]

The four major defendants—Lewis Powell, George Atzerodt, David Herold, and Mary Surratt—were tried by a nine-member military tribunal, convicted, and sentenced to death. Critics, notably former Lincoln Attorney

General Edward Bates and Secretary of the Navy Gideon Welles, argued that the conspirators should have been tried by a civilian court. Military tribunals are only appropriate when civilian courts cannot operate owing to an insurrection, but the war had ended by the time the Lincoln conspirators were captured and bound over for trial. (An 1866 United States Supreme Court case, *Ex Parte Milligan*, eventually reached this same conclusion.) In response to the criticism, Lincoln's second attorney general, James Speed, contended that the military nature of the conspiracy and the existence of martial law in the District of Columbia necessitated trial by a military tribunal. President Johnson agreed.[45]

Powell, Atzerodt, and Herold had been active participants in the Lincoln assassination plan, but Mary Surratt's culpability was a matter of dispute. She owned the boarding house where the conspirators met to discuss the plans to abduct or kill President Lincoln. Her son, John, was a Confederate spy and an integral member of the cabal. By all accounts, Mary Surratt was a Confederate sympathizer, but whether she actively plotted to assassinate Lincoln is not known. Questionable evidence convicted her. She delivered a package of "shooting irons" to the tavern in Surrattsville on the day of the assassination. The tavern keeper's testimony that she told him "there will be parties here tonight who will call for them" was the most damning evidence against her. Whether she understood why Booth and his co-conspirators needed the package was never clear.[46]

Being tried outside of the civilian courts placed the defendants at a significant disadvantage. In a civil court of law, a guilty verdict against a criminal defendant must be unanimous. If the defendant is convicted, he or she can appeal the decision to a higher court. Defendants enjoy constitutional protections such as due process of law. By contrast, a military commission can convict a defendant by a simple majority vote. A death penalty can be imposed with a two-thirds majority. A defendant can only appeal a conviction to the president of the United States. In light of the passions surrounding the assassination of the now almost universally revered Abraham Lincoln, the four defendants knew they faced formidable odds against an acquittal.[47]

In a seven-week trial that featured 366 witnesses and produced a 4,900-page transcript, members of the military commission sifted through evidence against the three men and one woman accused of planning the president's murder. After meeting in secret from June 29 until July 5, 1865, the tribunal convicted the four major defendants and sentenced them to be executed. The

1.4 Members of the military commission that tried the Lincoln conspirators are shown, standing left to right: Brigadier General Thomas M. Harris; Major General Lew Wallace; Major General August V. Kautz; and Brevet Brigadier General Henry L. Burnett, assistant judge advocate general. Seated left to right: Lieutenant Colonel David R. Clendenin; Colonel C. H. Tompkins; Brigadier General Albion P. Howe; Brigadier General James Ekin; Major General David Hunter; Brigadier General Robert S. Foster; Ohio Congressman John A. Bingham, assistant judge advocate general; and Brigadier General Joseph Holt, judge advocate general. Courtesy of the Library of Congress.

prisoners learned the following day that they would be hanged on July 7. President Johnson declined to commute their sentences.

Mary Surratt's supporters attempted to see the president to beg for leniency, but he refused to meet with them. When her attorneys secured a writ of habeas corpus from a judge ordering that Mary Surratt be released into civilian custody, Johnson suspended the writ. He ordered that the defendants be hanged on July 7 between 10:00 a.m. and 2:00 p.m. The prisoners were housed in the old prison on the grounds of the Washington Arsenal, and there they would be executed.[48]

It was an excruciatingly hot day when the four condemned felons shuffled to the gallows accompanied by clergymen and four soldiers from Company F of the Fourteenth Veteran Reserves. Around 1:15 p.m. on July 7, the group emerged from the prison into the courtyard where a gallows platform had been erected. Brevet Major General John F. Hartranft, commander of the prison, led the way. The crowd, estimated at between 1,000 and 3,000 people, mostly soldiers, watched from the courtyard as well as from adjacent windows and rooftops.[49]

Wearing a black veil that obscured her face, Mary Surratt followed General Hartranft. She was so weak and feeble that she required assistance from two army officers, one on each arm. The veil also made it difficult to see. When she told a soldier that her wrists hurt because they were bound too tightly, he assured her, "Well, it won't hurt long."

George Atzerodt came next. He, too, appeared unable to walk without assistance from two army officers. He was heard to cry, "God help me now! Oh! Oh! Oh!" Next was Davey Herold, who also walked with assistance from two well-placed soldiers.

The most remarkable prisoner of all, noticed by many observers, came last. Lewis Powell, defiant to the end, strutted "like a king to be crowned," in the words of a journalist who watched the scene unfold. After a gust of wind blew the hat from Powell's head, Reverend Abram Dunn Gillette retrieved it and placed it on the condemned man's head. "Thank you, doctor," Powell said, smiling. "I won't be needing it much longer."[50]

After they climbed the thirteen steps of the scaffold, the prisoners sat in chairs while their guards knelt to bind their legs with white cloth. Two ministers whispered in Mary Surratt's ear while she waited. Soldiers standing on the platform held parasols over her head to shield her from the sun. With the preliminaries concluded, General Hartranft read the verdict. Afterward, Reverend Gillette addressed the crowd and offered a prayer. Speeches and prayers from the other ministers followed.

After all the words were spoken, the prisoners were pulled from their chairs and positioned next to the four nooses. Soldiers pinioned their arms behind their bodies. Mary Surratt said, "Please don't let me fall." George Atzerodt trembled as he spoke. "Gentlemen, take warn . . ." Overcome with emotion, he could not finish the sentence. "Goodbye gentlemen who are before me now," he finally managed to say. "May we all meet in the next world." The hangman, Captain Christian Rath, and his four assistants placed white hoods on the prisoners' heads. Atzerodt muttered something unintelligible before calling out, "Don't choke me." Herold and Powell remained silent.[51]

When Rath was satisfied that everything was in place, he clapped his hands three times. On the third clap, the four soldiers standing beneath the platform kicked the supports holding the trap doors in place. The doors sprang open and the prisoners fell through. Their bodies jerked violently. Mary Surratt appeared to die instantly, but the others danced for several minutes. (She

1.5 The Lincoln conspirators were quickly dispatched to the gallows. This photograph, snapped by the legendary photographer Alexander Gardner, shows the bodies immediately after the hanging. Courtesy of the Library of Congress.

became the first woman ever executed by the United States federal government.) Herold wet himself. Atzerodt convulsed before falling still. Lewis Powell writhed and swung for five minutes. Twenty minutes after the hanging, all four were pronounced dead. Their bodies were cut down and placed in simple pine coffins to be buried in shallow graves against the prison wall.[52]

And so one of the most infamous assassinations in American history ended with the deaths of the conspirators in what some critics deemed a rush to judgment. The architect of the crime, John Wilkes Booth, had already paid for his deeds with his life, but the need for revenge remained strong among members of the Johnson administration as well as the Northern public. If agents of the federal government could not punish the trigger man, they could exact vengeance against his accomplices.[53]

Booth's motives remain controversial. Some observers have characterized him as a Type 2 killer. According to this view, Booth was primarily a vain, egocentric actor with little control over his emotions. Because he could not compete with his more famous father and brothers, the young actor initiated a bold crime that would eclipse their fame forever. Killing Abraham Lincoln would ensure that the name "John Wilkes Booth" lived on in the pages of history.

The problem with this theory is that it presupposes that John Wilkes Booth was a non-entity seeking to transform himself into a well-known public figure. Killing the president of the United States presumably would complete such a transformation. Yet Booth was a young, handsome, charismatic public figure in his own right. If he had not yet attained the same level of fame as his family members, he had many years left to prove himself. Type 2 killers frequently act owing to feelings of rejection and worthlessness in their lives. Taking the life of a public figure enhances their stature. John Wilkes Booth already enjoyed a level of prominence unknown to all but a handful of Americans.

Although Booth undoubtedly understood that assassinating the president would make him even more famous than he already was, he appeared to act primarily for political motives. If this is the case, he was a classic Type 1 assassin. After the Confederate States of America suffered a series of battlefield defeats and President Lincoln was reelected in 1864, Booth became increasingly despondent. The Southland that he loved so much was imperiled. He held Abraham Lincoln personally responsible for the wretched state of affairs in the South. Killing the tyrannical president might alleviate the suffering of Southerners and improve the prospects for a negotiated settlement to resolve differences between the North and the South. Even if it was too late to affect the outcome of the war, shooting Lincoln was the most effective way of punishing the loathsome creature.

Booth believed that history would judge him kindly. He was sadly mistaken. Generations of Americans have come to revere the historical memory of Abraham Lincoln. They entertain a far different opinion of John Wilkes Booth. For the overwhelming majority of Americans as well as citizens throughout the world, Booth remains one of the most reviled miscreants in the nation's history.[54]

Chapter 2

"I KILLED THE PRESIDENT FOR THE GOOD OF THE LABORING PEOPLE, THE GOOD PEOPLE. I AM NOT SORRY FOR MY CRIME": WILLIAM MCKINLEY (1901)

President William McKinley has come down through history as a remote, old-fashioned, stodgy historical figure. When he is remembered, if at all, it is because he was assassinated in 1901, an event that propelled the legendary man of action Theodore Roosevelt into the presidency. Unlike the giants of American politics such as George Washington, Abraham Lincoln, and Franklin D. Roosevelt, President McKinley is little known, and his accomplishments are seldom appreciated by generations of Americans. He stares out of old photographs with his dark, piercing eyes, thinning, slicked-back hair, and a vaguely menacing expression that appears to reveal a humorless, colorless placeholder who temporarily occupied the executive chair until a better man could be found.[55]

Yet the McKinley who walked the earth for fifty-eight years was not quite as sterile and unappealing as facile historical memory would suggest. He left behind a mixed legacy, but he could cite notable achievements. Under his leadership, the United States won a "splendid little war" with Spain to establish a presence in Cuba and the Far East. The national economy rebounded following a disastrous downturn in 1893. The country appeared on the international stage as a global power for the first time, and Americans felt proud of their ascendancy. The challenges of suppressing a nasty insurrection in the Philippines and combating charges of American imperialism tarnished McKinley's reputation, but he gradually earned the respect and even admiration of many Americans during his time in office.

Far from being cold and aloof, William McKinley loved people. One of his favorite activities in public life was to mingle with his constituents—a conviviality that may have contributed to his death because McKinley's insistence on greeting the public allowed his assassin to venture close enough to shoot the man. By all accounts, McKinley always had a kind word for his assistants and associates. As a young congressman, he enjoyed a well-deserved reputation as one of the most congenial fellows in Washington, DC. More than that, he eschewed extreme partisanship in favor of compromise through consensus-building. One colleague, Tom Reed, wryly observed that "My opponents in Congress go at me tooth and nail, but they always apologize to William when they are going to call him names."[56]

Although he had served with distinction in the Union army during the Civil War and steadily paid his political dues as a congressman and later governor of Ohio, McKinley was not one of those men who had burned with presidential ambition since his youth. It is difficult to say exactly when he began to harbor ambitions to live in the White House. His name surfaced as a possible Republican candidate was early as 1892. By 1895, he was scouting

2.1 William McKinley, twenty-fifth president of the United States from 1897 until 1901, is perhaps best remembered for his assassination in September 1901. Courtesy of the Library of Congress.

the terrain. Mark Hanna, a fellow Ohioan known as a kingmaker for his masterful ability to manipulate the political system, became a key supporter.[57]

McKinley had the right resume for the job during the 1890s. His affiliation with Ohio, an important Midwestern bellwether state, made his candidacy strategically beneficial. Three of Ohio's native sons—Ulysses S. Grant, Rutherford B. Hayes, and James A. Garfield—had already been elevated to the presidency, attesting to the importance of the Buckeye State in national politics. (The number is five if William Henry Harrison and his grandson, Benjamin, are counted, although they made their names outside of Ohio.) McKinley knew President Hayes from their mutual wartime service. One story told of Hayes as a senior officer in McKinley's regiment witnessing the younger man's bravery under fire during the Battle of Antietam in 1862. According to the popular recounting of the event, Hayes turned to a fellow officer and remarked, "Keep your eye on that young man. There is something in him." Both men made their names in 1876, when Hayes won a disputed presidential election and McKinley secured a seat in the US House of Representatives.[58]

Never flashy or charismatic, McKinley presented himself as steady and rock solid, a sober man well-suited to lead the nation through sober times. He had compiled a solid record as a pro-business Republican who also understood the problems of the middle class. As a member of Congress in 1890, he championed high protective tariffs through legislation that bore his name. It was an issue near and dear to many Republican hearts and wallets. After losing his congressional reelection bid in 1890, McKinley went home and won the Ohio gubernatorial post. From there, with Hanna's help, he was positioned to seek the presidency.[59]

This affable, rotund fellow was a creature of his time and place. McKinley was not a wealthy robber baron, but neither did he understand the plight of the lower classes. He had never known hunger, homelessness, or the hopeless despair of the working man. Instead, he was the epitome of the small town, marginally affluent, Protestant, church-going white citizen of good faith who could not fathom the wretched conditions of Negroes, immigrants, or the working poor. He was a devoted family man who doted on his frail wife, Ida, and thought himself a good Christian man. Oblivious to others outside of his station, he most likely would have been incredulous to learn that for some poor souls, he had become a symbol of American greed and imperialism.

He did not intentionally oppress anyone. In fact, he was flexible on the issues dividing rich and poor. McKinley initially waffled on the currency question, one of the most pressing matters of the 1890s. Farmers and the working poor preferred currency backed by silver, which would ensure that more money could be circulated even as it promoted inflation. Businessmen preferred the gold standard, which they believed would stabilize the currency and ensure economic prosperity in the long run. The issue was crucial for elected officials at all levels of government because the Panic of 1893 had led to a deep recession that spread mass suffering and economic hardship. Falling in line with his class, McKinley eventually supported the gold standard, thereby assuring party elders that he was a man who could be trusted to carry out core Republican policies if he won the presidency.[60]

The presidential contest of 1896 became a transformative election. The United States underwent enormous changes at the end of the nineteenth century as the country moved from a largely rural, agricultural economy to an urban, industrialized one. Immigrants streamed onto American shores in record numbers in search of better lives. Business associations that seemed more acquisitive and less congenial than many Americans believed desirable gradually replaced kinship relations that had been so important to white Anglo-Saxon Protestants of an earlier age. The election reflected the changes and the tumult that ordinary citizens felt.

If William McKinley became the standard-bearer for a party of big business interests and the gold standard, his Democratic opponent was a worthy counterweight. William Jennings Bryan, a former Nebraska congressman, emerged as the nominee of both the People's Party and the Democratic Party. An old-style stump orator, he had built a career as a populist who argued in favor of low tariffs to assist farmers, but he was not a leader in the agrarian revolt of the 1890s. He came late to the silver currency platform but, like many a politician who spies a political opening, he arrived with a vengeance. Confessing that he did not fully grasp the nuances of his new agenda, Bryan bluntly told the press that "the people of Nebraska are for free silver and I am for free silver. I will look up the arguments later."[61]

In the early stages of the general election race, Bryan appeared to be a genuine threat. His campaign rallies generated huge crowds of enthusiastic farmers and laborers who hung on his every word. During the Democratic National Convention in Chicago on July 9, 1896, Bryan's "Cross of Gold" speech became one of the most memorable addresses in American political history.[62]

Despite his powerful oratory, Bryan could not overcome McKinley's advantages. Conservatives feared Bryan's radicalism and populists thought that he was the wrong messenger to carry a populist banner. When the polls closed in November, McKinley captured the presidency with 271 electoral votes to Bryan's 176 votes, an Electoral College landslide of more than 61 percent. The popular vote told a different tale: McKinley prevailed by about 600,000 votes out of 13.5 million ballots cast, hardly a resounding victory. Republicans carried twenty-three states compared with twenty-two states for the Democrats. Bryan performed well in the South and in the western states, but he lost the heavily populated northeastern states.[63]

The incoming president appeared to be a solid Republican who vowed in his inaugural address not to pursue "wars of conquest" and to "avoid the temptation of territorial aggression." His supporters believed that he would engage in the same type of genial consensus-building efforts he had pursued throughout his political career. At the outset, he seemed to be in track to be a caretaker president, keeping the tariff in place, promoting the gold standard, and protecting the interests of the investor class. Mark Hanna, now a US senator, could not have been more pleased.[64]

And then events intervened to change the trajectory of American history, as so often happens. When the Cuban exile José Julián Martí Pérez led a revolt in Cuba in 1895, US public opinion supported his efforts. After he came into office in 1897, McKinley faced enormous pressure to assist the rebels in their struggle against Spanish control of Cuba. By that time, Martí was dead and the Cuban independence movement appeared to be foundering. American business-men feared that their island investments were imperiled while newspapers such as William Randolph Hearst's *New York Journal* and Joseph Pulitzer's *New York World* competed to see who could sling the most effective propaganda in favor of American intervention.

Bowing to the pressure, McKinley dispatched an American ship, the USS *Maine*, to protect American interests. When the ship exploded in Havana Harbor on the evening of February 15, 1898, American outrage reached new heights, propelled by the press. McKinley could no longer resist the drumbeat for intervention. On April 25, Congress declared war and American soldiers and sailors landed on the island toward the end of June. After a short series of battles, the United States emerged triumphant, pushing the Spanish out of Cuba and establishing an American presence in Puerto Rico, Guam, and the Philippines. Thus, America became a major player on the world stage, and McKinley, the reluctant imperialist, became the leader of a new empire.[65]

The president eventually won a second term with the slogan "Prosperity at Home and Prestige Abroad." He also made a decision that would hold enormous consequences for the presidency. Theodore Roosevelt joined his ticket as his vice president. Garret Hobart, vice president during McKinley's first term, had been a valued friend and confidant, but Hobart died in 1899 owing to a bad heart. McKinley finished the term without a second in command. In the meantime, Roosevelt had been rising steadily through the ranks, holding a series of state and national offices, including the governorship of New York. He appeared to be an inspired vice-presidential pick.[66]

Aside from his energy as a public official, Roosevelt was a man of action who won battlefield glory. His name became instantly recognizable when he led the First US Volunteer Cavalry Regiment, nicknamed the Rough Riders, on a mad charge along a grassy slope on the San Juan Heights of Cuba during the Spanish American War. Although the episode was hardly a noteworthy battle in the annals of American history, Roosevelt demonstrated physical bravery and, with able assistance from newspapers, parlayed his exploits into a public relations bonanza. When McKinley included the colorful, energetic Roosevelt on the ticket in 1900, the addition strengthened an already strong candidacy. Although Hanna expressed misgivings about including the "cowboy" in the administration, he could take comfort in the likelihood that the new vice president, having relinquished the governorship of New York, was politically neutered.[67]

With his reelection, McKinley solidified his image as a symbol of the might and majesty of the United States. It was an image that the president and many Americans relished, but a small faction, the anarchists, were repulsed by the nation's capitalist zeal and its growing imperialist impulses. For turn-of-the-century anarchists, the newly emergent empire of the United States represented much of what was wrong with the world.

While anarchism dates back to the Greeks of the third century BCE, English thinker William Godwin developed the modern theory at the end of the eighteenth century. He had seen the dehumanizing effects of industrialization in England as well as the rise of totalitarian states throughout much of Europe. Godwin came to believe that all governments are inherently corrosive and corrupt. Human beings can only thrive if they face life free from encumbrances and oppressive institutions that stifle freedom. If individuals are left alone and not forced to act against their will, invariably they will fall back on reason and live in harmony with each other. When human beings misbehave, the underlying cause is a lack of education. The central task of life is to acquire enough education to understand how to live as a rational, autonomous human being. It was an orderly view of a chaotic world.[68]

Although many anarchists remained committed to peaceful resistance to government action, extremists argued that governments would oppress the citizenry unless they were stopped by acts of violence. Johann Most, a German American anarchist, popularized the concept of the "propaganda of the deed," which involved an organized campaign of terror against political institutions as a means of advancing the anarchist cause. Practitioners of this form of anarchism prided themselves on their ability to strike at governments by attacking their citizens through public acts of violence.[69]

Anarchism never attracted large numbers of adherents in the United States, but the fear of government-hating terrorists spread dramatically in the early years of the twentieth century. To hear fear-mongers tell the tale, anarchists lurked around every corner. The terror that Americans felt only emboldened the extremists. Johann Most's heir apparent, the Italian immigrant Luigi Galleani, led an effort to terrorize the citizenry during the 1910s. His devoted followers, the Galleanists, favored bomb attacks in crowded cities as a means of calling attention to the failures of Western, highly industrialized governments. Any self-professed anarchist, even if he or she emphatically rejected the propaganda of the deed, risked being characterized as a dangerous radical who was merely biding his time before erupting into violence.[70]

Arguably the most famous (or infamous) American anarchist was a Russian Jew, Emma Goldman, who came to the United States in 1885 as an adolescent. She embraced the anarchist cause while reading about the Haymarket riot, a dramatic clash between Chicago police and striking workers. Some unknown soul hurled dynamite at the police during the demonstration. In response, officers fired on the crowd. When the smoke cleared, eight policeman and numerous civilians died. As a result of the intense media coverage, the stereotype of the "bomb-throwing anarchist" was born and gained credence in the court of public opinion. Goldman, once denounced as a "rebel woman," empathized with the workers killed in the melee. She decided that all governments were corrupt and destroyed human freedom. To share her passion with her fellow man, she took to writing fierce editorials and speaking

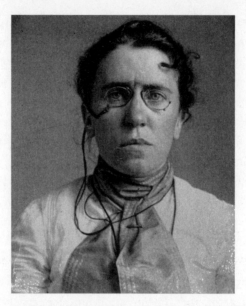

2.2 Leon Czolgosz claimed that he was inspired to kill President McKinley by the well-known anarchist Emma Goldman, pictured here. Courtesy of the Library of Congress.

out at anarchist rallies, discovering that she was a gifted rabble-rouser. Many Americans saw "Red Emma" as a genuine threat to law and order in the republic, but disenfranchised peoples, especially recent immigrants, hailed her as a brave champion of individualism and free speech.[71]

One young man drawn to the anti-government message was Leon Czolgosz, a twenty-eight-year-old son of Polish Catholic immigrants. He spent much of his early life working in factories and came to view the anarchist perspective on oppressive governments as inspired. Czolgosz approached Goldman as she prepared to speak at a rally in Cleveland, Ohio, on May 5, 1901, and asked for recommendations on readings. Without thinking much about it, she uttered a few suggestions and returned to her preparations. She encountered him again on July 12, 1901, as she was leaving the Chicago home of Abraham Isaak, publisher of the anarchist newspaper *Free Society*. She remembered this odd character, who introduced himself as Nieman (German for "no man"), as the fellow she had spoken with in Cleveland. Nieman accompanied her on a Chicago elevated train to the home of several friends. She left him there and departed, never to see him again. Later, after Czolgosz became known as McKinley's assassin, she recalled him as "very young, a mere youth, of medium height, well built and carrying himself very erect. But it was his face that held me, a most sensitive face, with delicate pink complexion. . . ."[72]

The pink-cheeked youth was a loner. At the age of twenty-five, he apparently suffered a nervous breakdown. For a time, he moved back to his family's farm in Warrensville, Ohio, but he grew listless, refused to help out, and quarreled frequently with family members, especially his stepmother.[73]

Czolgosz was fascinated by the assassination of King Umberto I of Italy on July 29, 1900. The anarchist triggerman, Gaetano Bresci, claimed that he acted on behalf of the people. This noble motive resonated with the strange young man. Inspired by Bresci's courageous deed, Emma Goldman's impassioned rhetoric, and his readings in anarchist literature, Czolgosz resolved to make something of his aimless life. He would strike out at the symbol of American oppression: President William McKinley. (He apparently failed to notice that Goldman's speeches did not call for violence.)[74]

Using his favorite alias, Fred C. Nieman, he traveled to Buffalo, New York, site of the Pan-American Exposition of 1901. The exposition was a world's fair situated on 350 acres of land in Buffalo and scheduled to last from May 1 until November 2, 1901. President McKinley had promised to attend earlier in the year, but he had been delayed. Now he was scheduled to appear at the Temple of Music at 4:00 p.m. on September 6. He delivered a well-received speech to an estimated crowd of 116,000 people the day before. Always happy to greet his constituents, the president looked forward to shaking hands with as many common citizens as he could meet in the allotted time.[75]

In the meantime, Fred Nieman entered a Buffalo hardware store and purchased a new .32-caliber Iver Johnson revolver, paying $4.50 for the weapon. It was the same model that Bresci had used to kill Umberto I. Safely ensconced in a hotel room, he practiced wrapping the revolver in a white handkerchief to disguise his intent until the last possible moment.[76]

Unaware of his date with Czolgosz, McKinley awoke on September 6 as a guest in the posh home of Exposition president John G. Milburn. After setting off on an invigorating early morning walk, he boarded a train for a sightseeing excursion to nearby Niagara Falls. He returned in time to enter the stately Temple of Music to greet the public. Unbeknownst to McKinley, Czolgosz had followed the presidential entourage to Niagara in hopes of getting a shot at his target. When he realized that he would never get close enough to shoot the president, the would-be assassin returned to Buffalo. His only hope was to mingle with the crowd waiting to see McKinley inside the Temple of Music. He knew that he might be searched or called out before he could complete his task, but the slow-moving reception line was Czolgosz's last and best opportunity to strike a blow for anarchism.[77]

Shortly before 4:00 p.m., McKinley took his place on the dais in the Temple of Music with his personal secretary, George B. Cortelyou, on his right and John Milburn on his left. Satisfied with the accommodations, he turned to his security detail and gave the order. "Let them come," he said. Someone threw open the doors and the assembled masses swarmed inside.

The first man to speak to the president, Dr. Clinton Colegrove of Holland, New York, cryptically said, "George Washington, Abraham Lincoln, and President McKinley." Presumably the remark was meant as a compliment, categorizing the incumbent with two of the nation's great presidents from the past. McKinley smiled and graciously moved the gentleman along so he could greet the rest of the well-wishers in line.[78]

As the crowd shuffled through the room, Secret Service agents focused on a swarthy-looking man who fit the stereotype of an Italian anarchist. Their inattention allowed Leon Czolgosz to remain what he had been throughout most of his life—the invisible fellow that never stood out in a crowd. No one noticed that he had his right hand stuffed inside his pocket.

A large African American, James Parker, a six-foot-four-inch waiter from Atlanta, grew irritated at the man standing in front of him. The fellow simply would not keep up with the rest of the line. "If you can't go faster, at least let me by," he finally exclaimed in exasperation. The man, Nieman, ignored him and focused on the president standing on the dais, all the while continuing his slow shuffle forward.[79]

The moment of reckoning arrived. Nieman/Czolgosz stood face-to-face with the object of his hatred. President McKinley extended his right hand while the odd young man lifted his left. In a swift motion that appeared out of character for a man who had been so sluggish in his movements, Czolgosz whipped his right hand from his pocket. He held his .32 caliber revolver concealed beneath a white handkerchief. Before anyone had time to react, the sound of two firecrackers erupted in the room. A small cloud of smoke wafted up from the scene.

The president clutched his midriff and staggered, surprised at the assault. He remained on his feet, but clearly he had been injured. After a few seconds

2.3 Self-professed anarchist Leon Czolgosz is depicted in this drawing at the moment when he shot President McKinley on September 6, 1901. Courtesy of the Library of Congress.

when everyone was too stunned to move, bystanders sprang into action. James Parker was the first to strike Czolgosz, punching him in the neck while he reached for the revolver. Several officers in the security detail jumped into action, smashing their fists into the assailant and driving him to the ground. Czolgosz cried out, "I done my duty."[80]

Incredibly, McKinley himself stopped the beating. Detective John Geary reached out and caught the president, who appeared on the verge of collapse. As Geary, Cortelyou, and Milburn escorted the stricken man over torn bunting and into a nearby chair, McKinley looked at the scene unfolding behind him. He supposedly said, "Don't let them hurt him" or "Be easy with him, boys." The words had their intended effect, and the officers stopped pummeling the now-subdued Czolgosz, who was bleeding from his eyes and nose. The group hustled him away to a nearby room for questioning.

McKinley initially insisted that his injuries were not severe, but within minutes it was clear that he was mistaken. As the color drained from his face and he grew weak, the president turned to his secretary to utter a simple message. His wife, Ida, was a fragile woman under the best of circumstances, and McKinley worried that she would not take the news well. "My wife—be careful, Cortelyou, how you tell her—oh, be careful!"[81]

Initially, the police feared that the gunman had been a part of a conspiracy. Under questioning, the suspect gave his name as Fred Nieman and said that he had acted alone. He claimed to be a blacksmith born in Detroit. As the interrogation continued, he professed his allegiance to anarchism and told his inquisitors that he was a disciple of Emma Goldman. The next day, he elaborated on his motives, telling the detectives that "I know what will happen to me—if the President dies I will be hung. I want to say to be published—'I killed President McKinley because I done my duty. I don't believe in one man having so much service, and another man should have none.'"[82]

Investigators immediately followed up on the assassin's claims to be an anarchist. As police rounded up the usual suspects, Emma Goldman was in St. Louis. When she first heard that the shooter claimed to have been inspired by her words, she was stunned. She opened a newspaper and recognized the man in the photograph. "Why, that's Nieman!" Realizing that she would have to cooperate with police, she bought a train ticket to Chicago. After hiding out briefly, she surrendered to the authorities. The investigation later verified that Czolgosz acted alone.[83]

While the authorities spoke with the assailant, the president's condition was dire. Eighteen minutes after the shooting, an electric ambulance transported him to the Exposition hospital. It was not a state-of-the-art facility, having been designed as a temporary area to treat minor ailments such as heat exhaustion, upset stomachs, and minor aches, pains, and scrapes. The equipment and personnel necessary to treat a major gunshot wound to the abdomen were unavailable. Dr. Herman Mynter, a physician who had met McKinley the preceding day, was called in to treat the wounded man. Mynter was not the Exposition doctor, but he was the only medical professional on hand at the time of the shooting. McKinley recognized the man. "Doctor, when I met you yesterday, I did not imagine that today I should have to ask you for a favor," the president joked. Another physician, a gynecologist named Dr. Matthew D. Mann, arrived to offer assistance as well.[84]

The doctors attempted to remove the bullets from McKinley's abdomen. The president's obesity, the poor lighting in the operating theater, the doctors' inexperience in treating gunshot wounds, their lack of basic equipment such as retractors, and the doctors' willingness to explore the patient's wound without proper sterilization made the procedure especially dangerous. Dr. Mann inserted his hands into the bleeding abdomen and fished around for bullets. The first bullet easily fell from the president's stomach, but the second one proved to be elusive. The doctors left it inside and stitched up the wounded man.[85]

Transported back to John Milburn's home to recuperate, McKinley initially appeared to be on the mend. Medical reports were so optimistic that Vice President Roosevelt departed on a family camping trip in the Adirondack Mountains, a dozen miles from the nearest telephone or telegraph. The president was conscious and alert, asking for copies of the latest newspapers so he could keep abreast of the news.[86]

By September 12, six days after the shooting, the president's health began to decline. It was an alarming development. He had been doing so well. Unfortunately, gangrene infected the walls of his stomach, and the primitive medicine of the time could not stop the patient's blood from being poisoned as a result. By the early morning hours of September 14, McKinley was not long for the world. "God's will be done, not ours," he told his wife. Ida leaned in close and sang the words to one of the president's favorite hymns, "Nearer, My God, to Thee." He drifted in and out of consciousness until he died, quietly, at 2:15 a.m. on Saturday, September 14, 1901.[87]

Leon Czolgosz was arraigned on murder charges nine days after the president's death. The defendant initially entered a guilty plea, but the judge refused to accept it. A trial would be held. Despite press accounts of the defiant anarchist, Czolgosz retreated into his usual shyness, seldom speaking or showing emotion. A photograph purportedly showing the assassin behind bars circulated in national publications, contributing to the public image of a lunatic anarchist—a caged beast—as the killer of a beloved, martyred president. The image did not resemble the Leon Czolgosz with cherubic features known to his family and acquaintances, but it became fixed in the public imagination, nonetheless.[88]

The trial proceeded rapidly. Czolgosz did not cooperate with his attorneys, which meant that his defense was perfunctory at best. One possible defense was insanity, but the prisoner would not speak to the psychologists assigned to his case. They eventually declared him sane. In the few pretrial statements he made, Czolgosz clearly set forth a rational position, even if most Americans found it distasteful. "I don't believe in the Republican form

2.4 This photograph is purported to be an image of Leon Czolgosz behind bars after he shot President McKinley. Courtesy of the Library of Congress.

of government and I don't believe we should have any rulers," he said. "It is right to kill them."[89]

To no one's surprise, the jury rendered a guilty verdict in thirty-three minutes, and the judge sentenced the defendant to die in the electric chair at the prison in Auburn, New York. On October 29, 1901, jailers led Leon Czolgosz to the electric chair and strapped him down for his execution. "I killed the president for the good of the laboring people, the good people," he said. "I am not sorry for my crime but I am sorry I can't see my father." A few minutes after 7:00 a.m., a searing jolt of 1,700 volts of electricity killed him.[90]

A subsequent autopsy revealed no organic abnormalities. He was a normal "good-looking, youthful" body. According to one account, the assassin's brother allowed the prison to dispose of the body. Another account suggested that when his family asked for the corpse so that he could be buried, prison officials refused. Instead, they disposed of Leon Czolgosz's body in a prison grave without a casket, submerging his remains in "six barrels of quicklime and a carboy of sulphuric acid."[91]

By contrast, William McKinley's body was shipped by train from Buffalo, New York, to Washington, DC, arriving on the evening of Monday, September 16, 1901. The dead president's coffin spent the night in the East Room of the White House surrounded by an honor guard. His widow, Ida, visited once that evening. The following day, White House officials had the coffin moved to the Capitol for a state funeral. After the service concluded, the widow followed the flag-draped coffin down the long east steps of the Capitol to join a funeral procession to the train depot. William McKinley's body traveled back to Canton, Ohio, his hometown, for interment.[92]

In the aftermath of the third assassination of an American president, physicians, psychologists, historians, and political scientists debated Czolgosz's state of mind. Whenever someone takes it upon himself to kill a public figure, the reaction is almost always that the person must be mentally unhinged. Well-adjusted individuals do not physically lash out at strangers, no matter how much they dislike a public figure's policies or statements. Yet all the available evidence suggests that Czolgosz was sane. He embraced a political ideology at odds with mainstream American political thought, but his decision to embrace anarchy was hardly the act of a lunatic. His words and actions leading up to the crime and after the crime suggest an orderly, calm, and rational actor who should be taken at his word. Leon Czolgosz insisted that he had done his duty and did not regret his actions. He was a typical Type 1 assassin—a person who knows what he is doing and acts freely and rationally.

Chapter 3

"I SAW MURDER—NO, NOT MURDER, A THOUSAND TIMES WORSE THAN MURDER—I SAW ANARCHY WAVE ITS FIRST BLOODY TRIUMPH IN IDAHO": FRANK STEUNENBERG (1905)

The landscape was reminiscent of a Currier & Ives print. Blanketed in snow, a cozy hamlet situated west of Boise, Idaho, presented an idyllic scene of early-twentieth-century American serenity. A solitary figure, bundled up to escape the cold, ambled along a snowy street in Caldwell, a small burg but a steadily growing commercial hub, on one of the last days of the year. The governor, as he was still called by his fellow citizens despite having left office years earlier, was a prominent personality in town. Life was good, and the governor basked in the glow of his prosperity.

On the evening of December 30, 1905, he was still in a festive mood following the Christmas holiday. In a spirit of conviviality, he made the rounds to chat with friends and associates. He visited his doctor. He stopped at the bank he co-owned with his brother. He briefly read a newspaper in the Saratoga Hotel. He then returned home with plans to spend a quiet evening with his family. As he closed the gate to the white picket fence separating his house from the sidewalk, the governor ignited a bomb that knocked him from his feet and blew a hole in the right side of his body, ravaging his limbs.

Alarmed by the deafening noise and a gigantic flash of light, his wife and thirteen-year-old daughter raced from inside the house and knelt over their beloved paterfamilias, who lay prostrate on the cold ground, bleeding profusely from grievous wounds. It was a grisly scene, a vivid contrast from the idyll that had existed minutes earlier. The right side of Frank Steunenberg's body had absorbed the brunt of a ferocious blast. His right arm was almost completely ripped from his body and his right leg was mangled. Both legs were broken near the ankles. Local doctors rushed to his side after neighbors had lifted the governor and carried him inside his house, but they could tell he was not long for the world. Frank Steunenberg, the fourth governor of Idaho, died a few hours after the explosion at the ripe old age of forty-four.[93]

No one knew what had happened or how to respond to the unprecedented act of violence. In the minutes after the explosion, the governor's stunned wife, Belle, remarked to her brother-in-law that "Frank has shot himself somehow." Steunenberg also thought he had been gunned down. "Who shot me?" he asked as his mangled body lay in the street.[94]

It was not a gunshot. Investigators soon recognized that the contraption was a bomb rigged to explode when the governor closed the gate to his fence and stepped into his yard. Suspicion immediately fell on local mine workers. If anyone harbored a grudge toward the mostly beloved local politician, miners were the logical suspects.

No one could forget the terrible events from five years earlier. In 1900, a dispute erupted between mine owners and their workers in the silver mines of Coeur d'Alene, which resulted in bombs exploding in the offices of the mining company. Fearful of civil unrest, Governor Steunenberg declared martial law and dispatched troops to keep the peace. Keeping the peace meant herding 1,000 miners into a series of empty railroad boxcars. They remained locked up for months without the benefit of due process of law. The governor had been elected with labor support, but many miners viewed Steunenberg's actions as nothing less than a betrayal. He was no longer in office by 1905, but laborers were not quick to forget—or forgive.[95]

Caldwell was still a small place when the bomb exploded in 1905, and few unfamiliar people could slip in and out of town without inviting scrutiny. Investigators almost immediately focused on a strange character who called himself Thomas Hogan. The suspicious man, often immaculately adorned in a dark three-piece suit, a dapper bowler hat, and clean-shaven, had been spotted in Caldwell on and off again since September. On December 13, he registered at the Saratoga Hotel, one of the sites that Governor Steunenberg had visited in the minutes before the bombing. Hogan said he hailed from Denver, and he impressed his acquaintances throughout the town as a fellow who was "well supplied with money." When pressed, he uttered vague reasons for being in town, none of which made much sense. Caldwell was not

3.1 Former Idaho Governor Frank Steunenberg, pictured here in 1900, died from a bomb blast on December 30, 1905. Courtesy of the Idaho State Archives.

a renowned tourist destination. Despite its growing commercial interests, it was hardly a place where businessmen congregated.

Hogan bragged at various times about being a gambler, an itinerant sheep dealer, and a real-estate speculator. He slept late—a rarity in a town where most blue-collar workers rose before the sun—and he spent most of his waking time lounging in the hotel bar. Yet for all of his odd behavior, he did not appear to be a sinister character, just a bit strange.

Still, he was an outsider, and he struck the locals as a little too cavalier about the dramatic death of the beloved ex-governor. When everyone else was reeling with shock and dismay over the explosion that had extinguished one of the leading lights of the community, Hogan was offering up business deals and inquiring about real property for sale. It appeared unseemly and more than a little suspicious for this interloper to be living it up at such a deeply emotional time. George Froman, an ex-marshal and one of the dozen or so self-appointed members of a citizens committee looking into the matter, did not hesitate to share his opinion of Hogan. "There's the man we should be watching," he told a friend as he pointed to the suspect. "I'm convinced that he either did the job or knows who did." Froman succinctly summarized the prevailing sentiment. "He's been hanging around here for months doing nothing. He has plenty of money, but he doesn't have any business here. And a coupla times he asked about Frank."[96]

The citizens needed to get to the bottom of the matter. While Hogan was out one day, the group arranged to have his hotel room searched. (This was an era before Fourth Amendment search-and-seizure rules were firmly established.) What they found was disturbing. Towels draped over the door-knobs prevented anyone from peeking through the keyholes. The chamber pots contained Plaster of Paris, which may have held the bomb components together. Traces of powder on the carpet suggested that dynamite had been placed inside the room recently.[97]

Early in the New Year, a local judge agreed to issue a warrant for Hogan's arrest. Called to account for the murder, the defendant initially acted bemused. He understood why the locals were suspicious, but appeared unruffled as he repeatedly proclaimed his innocence. Yes, he was a strange man temporarily living in town without a visible means of support and yes, he appeared unfazed by the dramatic events of late, but those facts alone did not mean that he was the offender.[98]

Even as this Hogan character came under scrutiny, state and local officials wondered whether the governor's assassination had been part of an elaborate conspiracy. Steunenberg's troubled relationship with the miners was well known. Hogan, if he turned out to be the culprit, might have acted at the behest of a cabal that looked to create ongoing strife for government leaders and mine owners. To get to the bottom of the crime, the locals hired a detective firm, the Thiel Agency. Later, they brought in perhaps the premier firm, the Pinkerton National Detective Agency, to replace Thiel in identifying and apprehending the guilty person or persons.[99]

The use of a private detective agency to investigate a public crime was not as unusual as it might seem. The methods employed in criminal investigations early in the twentieth century were markedly different from what they would become in later years. In the eighteenth century, citizens feared a government with too much power because it might oppress individuals.

In many communities, inhabitants resisted the effort to organize a police force. If crimes occurred, citizens would cobble together a temporary investigatory body that set out to protect the public from reprobates who would disturb the peace. By the mid-nineteenth century, police forces had arisen in metropolitan areas, but their professionalism and integrity varied widely. Some states and localities preferred to retain private agencies to pursue criminals. Aside from not having to fund permanent police forces, community leaders could limit the corruption and abuses that ran rampant among police officers in big cities, where the distinction between a law-enforcement official and a criminal was not always clear.[100]

The Pinkerton Agency began in 1850, when a Scottish-born security man and spy, Allan Pinkerton, founded his eponymous firm, and quickly rose to fame by uncovering a plot to assassinate President-elect Lincoln in 1861.[101] By the early 1900s, Pinkerton agents had established a reputation as champions of the capitalist class, ruthless investigators determined to break laborers in favor of management. In hiring the agency to follow leads in the Steunenberg murder, the townspeople sent an unmistakable message: they believed that revenge-minded miners had ordered the former governor's assassination. The most famous of all the Pinkerton men at the time, James McParland, took the lead in the case, ensuring that the matter would generate national headlines.

McParland was a living legend. He had been a detective for three decades, and had captured the public imagination as few law enforcement personnel had. Early in his career, he had worked undercover in the coal region of Pennsylvania investigating a series of murders perpetrated by Irish labor activists. He later served as a crucial witness in trials that transformed him into a symbol of the heroic law-and-order officer. So great was his fame that Sir Arthur Conan Doyle wrote of a meeting between the fictional beau idéal of a detective, Sherlock Holmes, and McParland in *The Valley of Fear*.[102]

As he took over from the Thiel Agency, McParland got right to work. He was certain that the suspect was their man, and McParland knew how to extract useful information. He persuaded the state's present governor, Frank Robert Gooding, to have Hogan transferred to the state penitentiary in Boise. Afterward, the great detective had the prisoner placed into solitary confinement. Visiting the suspect several times, McParland relied on alternate forms of rhetoric. He told the man that the evidence against him was overwhelming and more than enough to have him executed. Next, McParland expressed sympathy for Hogan's plight and acknowledged that the inmate was merely a tool of larger interests. The men he was protecting would not assist him should Hogan be judged guilty. His benefactors would not hesitate to disavow any relationship with him, and the poor man would die alone. Hogan did not recognize the famous detective during their first encounter, but later he realized who McParland was, and he was flattered. The world's foremost sleuth was spending time on Hogan's case, and it appealed to the suspect's ego.[103]

After being questioned repeatedly about the Steunenberg affair, the suspect broke down, exactly as McParland had anticipated. Hogan had experienced enough. He would not serve as the fall guy for his masters. It turned out that the strange man in custody was not named Thomas Hogan. He confessed that he was Harry Orchard, which also was an alias. He was born Albert Edward Horsley in Canada in 1866. He spent most of his life flittering from one dead-end job to another before he fell into mining as an occupation. A man apparently willing to do anything to advance his own ends, Orchard said that he had planted bombs and engaged in all manner of mischief on numerous occasions.

He was a shadowy figure, a man of many names and talents. Orchard, as he was generally called during the Steunenberg trial, had been seen in and around Coeur d'Alene, Idaho, during a period of labor unrest back in 1899. He may or may not have taken part in violent acts aimed at mine owners. Orchard's participation was murky, but he was seen in the company of officials from the Western Federation of Miners (WFM), a powerful union, which suggested that he probably was in cahoots with union bosses.[104]

The extraordinary tale unraveled quickly. Orchard said that he had killed the former governor on orders from two union leaders—WFM president Charles Moyer as well as general secretary William "Big Bill" Haywood. He signed a sixty-four-page confession outlining his long history of working as terrorist-in-chief for the WFM. In light of Orchard's propensity to lie, the accusations were not as damning as they might have been, but they were enough to allow prosecutors to prepare a case against the union leaders.[105]

The explosive story confirmed citizens' worst fears. The out-of-control miners had murdered Steunenberg in a cowardly act that threatened to undermine the established social order. Moyer and Haywood must be extradited from Colorado and brought to Idaho for trial. Unfortunately for prosecutors, the uncorroborated word of a confessed liar like Harry Orchard was insufficient to obtain an extradition order for Moyer and Haywood to be brought to Idaho.

McParland and the Pinkertons were unperturbed. They arranged for Moyer, Haywood, and a third man implicated in the plot, George Pettibone, to be apprehended and forcibly dragged to Idaho for trial in February 1906. Whether the act of detaining the men and rushing them by train across the border to stand trial on criminal charges amounted to kidnapping became a matter of no small dispute. On learning of the unorthodox and possibly illegal extradition, a WFM attorney, Edmund Richardson, traveled to Idaho to file a writ of habeas corpus seeking the defendants' immediate release. When

3.2 In 1908, Harry Orchard (born Albert Edward Horsley) pleaded guilty to the crime of assassinating Steunenberg. This photograph dates from January 1906, around the time of Orchard's arrest. Reprinted from *The Confessions and Autobiography of Harry Orchard* (1907).

he lost in the Idaho courts, he filed an appeal with the United States Supreme Court.[106]

The Supreme Court of that era was generally conservative and respectful of state rights as well as hallowed federalism principles—perhaps too respectful, according to detractors. Presented with a petition to intervene into the affairs of a state criminal trial, the justices expressed their skepticism at the propriety of such a course of action. Writing for the court majority in *Pettibone v. Nichols*, Associate Justice John Marshall Harlan affirmed the lower courts' rulings. In the majority's view, the court should not delve into the methods by which the defendants came into the jurisdiction. Otherwise, criminal defendants might be freed from custody only to flee without standing trial for their alleged crimes. The court held that "neither the Constitution nor laws of the United States entitled the person so held to be discharged from custody and allowed to depart from the state. If, as suggested, the application of these principles may be attended by mischievous consequences involving the personal safety of individuals within the limits of the respective states, the remedy is with the lawmaking department of the government."[107]

Having lost their habeas corpus challenges, the three defendants were bound over to stand trial. Prosecutors pursued other defendants as well, attempting to cut a deal with several suspects in exchange for testimony against the others. During this phase of the case, McParland remained actively involved, searching for witnesses, suppressing evidence, and leaving no stone unturned in his efforts to convict Messrs. Moyer, Haywood, and Pettibone. When a Pinkerton man pursued suspects to be brought to justice, he would employ whatever tactics were necessary and expedient.[108]

As they prepared for trial, the prosecution added William Borah to the team. A gifted trial lawyer and orator who had just been elected to the US Senate, Borah accepted the case as a means of raising his profile on the eve of his congressional career. James H. Hawley, arguably Idaho's preeminent trial attorney and Borah's occasional antagonist, agreed to prosecute the case as well. It was a stellar lineup, indicating that the mine owners would leave nothing to chance in avenging the ex-governor's murder.[109]

Not to be outdone, the defense secured the services of famed Chicago-based attorney Clarence Darrow. When he joined the defense team in March 1906, Darrow was already a prominent lawyer with several well-known cases under his belt, and he was on his way to a storied career that would resonate long after his death. Recognizing that he was facing a formidable prosecution team, Darrow got right to work, using his legendary powers of persuasion to good effect. He apparently convinced James Lillard, the uncle of a defendant and crucial prosecution witness named Steve Adams, to speak with his nephew. After their meeting, Adams recanted a damaging confession that would have bolstered the prosecution's case.[110]

The presence of all-star attorneys, along with the labor dispute as a backdrop, ensured that the Steunenberg murder case would become one of the most sensational trials of the era. Everyone knew that the issue was not confined to determining who murdered Frank Steunenberg, the former Idaho governor, as important as that question was to his friends and supporters. In many respects, the contest served as a proxy fight between mine owners and miners. In engaging James McParland and the Pinkerton Agency along with Borah and Hawley, the prosecutors were declaring war on the miners in general and the WFM in particular. With Darrow at the helm, the defense served notice that the trial would become a platform for championing the little man over elite interests.[111]

As everyone expected, the matter became a *cause célèbre*. Despite (or perhaps because of) McParland's participation and the political nature of the proceedings, millions of Americans, especially those of modest means, empathized with the miners. They knew what it was like to suffer at the hands of affluent capitalists who cared more for profits than for the suffering of their fellow man. Working people believed that the mine owners must not be allowed to subvert the union, or the rich and privileged would once again take advantage of the poor and weak.

Faced with the emotional appeal of the unions, McParland and his team desperately wanted to win through whatever means were necessary. The great detective tried to influence press accounts by planting stories and reporting on favorable developments. He also planted a spy known as "Operative 21" on the defense team to provide surreptitious reports on the case. In the meantime, Governor Gooding constantly intervened, offering his assistance to the prosecution. Even President Theodore Roosevelt, whose antipathy for labor radicals was well known, repeatedly offered unsolicited advice on bringing the defendants to justice. The president's *ex parte* communications with Supreme Court justices in the *Pettibone v. Nichols* case left even his admirers irked at his callous disregard for constitutional safeguards.[112]

3.3 The three principal defendants in the Steunenberg assassination trial are pictured here in 1907 (left to right): Western Federation of Miners (WFM) President Charles Moyer; WFM General Secretary William "Big Bill" Haywood; and miner George Pettibone. Unknown origin, circa 1907.

Harry Orchard was the central prosecution witness when the trial commenced in Boise in mid-1907. During his twenty-six hours on the stand, Orchard reiterated his written confession, painstakingly spelling out the bombings and violence he had employed on behalf of the WFM over the years. Prosecutors introduced eighty additional witnesses as the trial dragged on for months. For their part, Darrow and the defense lawyers presented over one hundred witnesses. Closing arguments consumed two weeks of the trial.[113]

As expected, Darrow's summation attracted the largest share of media attention. He was at his best, alternately using humor, anger, and pathos to move the jurors during the eleven-hour and fifteen-minute oration. One onlooker marveled at the lawyer's physical prowess, remarking that Darrow "brings into action every muscle of his body in emphasizing his sentences. He waves his hands. He shrugs his shoulders; he wags and nods and tosses his head about. He bends his knees and he twists his body. And his contortions, if he were not so serious about them, would be almost as interesting as what he says."[114]

What he said was interesting enough. Predictably, Darrow lit into Harry Orchard, questioning everything about the notorious liar's credibility. "I don't believe that this man was ever really in the employ of anybody. I don't believe he ever had any allegiance to the Mine Owners Association, to the Pinkertons, to the Western Federation of Miners, to his family, to his kindred, to his God, or to anything human or divine," he thundered. In Darrow's estimation, Orchard "was a soldier of fortune, ready to pick up a penny or a dollar or any other sum in any way that was easy . . . to serve the mine owners, to serve the Western Federation, to serve the devil if he got his price, and his price was cheap."[115]

Darrow understood that the WFM was associated with violence and to argue that the miners were innocent victims of a witch hunt would strain credulity. With few attractive options, he chose to confront the issue head-on. "I don't mean to tell this jury that labor organizations do no wrong," he said. "I know them too well for that. They do wrong often, and sometimes brutally; they are sometimes cruel; they are often unjust; they are frequently corrupt. . . ." Having acknowledged the weakness in his case, Darrow cast the trial in broader terms, arguing that unions are defenders of the poor and downtrodden.

It was a masterful performance capped by one of Darrow's most eloquent perorations. He extolled Haywood's virtues as a great labor leader unafraid to die if convicted and sentenced to be executed:

> Other men have died before. Other men have died in the same cause in which Bill Haywood has risked his life, men strong with devotion, men who love liberty, men who love their fellow men, patriots who have raised their voices in defense of the poor, in defense of justice, have made their good fight and have met death on the scaffold, on the rack, in the flame and they will meet it again until the world grows old and gray. Bill Haywood is no better than the rest. He can die if die he needs, he can die if this jury decrees it; but, oh, gentlemen, don't think for a moment that if you hang him you will crucify the labor movement of the world.[116]

In Darrow's view, the jury possessed an awesome responsibility. The jurors' "guilty" verdict against Bill Haywood would not destroy the labor movement while a "not guilty" verdict would embolden the weak and oppressed to take heart at American justice. Darrow's words dripped with hyperbole:

> Out on the broad prairies where men toil with their hands, out on the wide ocean where men are tossed and buffeted on the waves, through our mills and factories, and down deep under the earth, thousands of men and women and children, men who labor, men who suffer, women and children weary with care and toil, these men and these women and these children will kneel tonight and ask their God to guide your judgment. These men and these women and these little children, the poor, the weak, and the suffering of the world will stretch out their hands to this jury, and implore you to save Haywood's life.[117]

Rising to the occasion, Bill Borah joined co-counsel Hawley in summing up the prosecution's case. Borah reminded the jury that organized labor was not on trial. "It is simply a trial for murder," he said. Whereas Darrow attempted to put elite miner owners on trial, Borah argued for deciding the case on narrower grounds. Much of his summation focused on the evidence assembled against the defendants. He also reminded the jury that although Darrow and Hawley were eloquent public speakers—"They have been brought here because of their power to sway the minds of men"—the central task was to determine who killed Frank Steunenberg and punish the culprits appropriately.[118]

"I remembered again the awful thing of December 30, 1905, a night which has taken ten years to the life of some who are in this courtroom now," he said, matching Darrow's emotional appeal. "I felt again its cold and icy chill, faced the drifting snow and peered at last into the darkness for the sacred spot where last lay the body of my dead friend, and saw true, only too true, the stain of his life's blood upon the whitened earth." In a brief departure from his strategy of focusing on Frank Steunenberg, the man at the core of the case, Borah suggested that the killing was part of darker forces at work in the United States. "I saw Idaho dishonored and disgraced. I saw murder—no, not murder, a thousand times worse than murder—I saw anarchy wave its first bloody triumph in Idaho."[119]

3.4 The legendary trial lawyer Clarence Darrow, pictured here, worked with the defense team on behalf of Bill Haywood during the Steunenberg murder trial. Courtesy of the Library of Congress.

Clarence Darrow had lectured the jury on its duty, and William Borah would do the same:

> If the defendant is entitled to his liberty, let him have it. But, on the other hand, if the evidence in this case discloses the author of this crime, then there is no higher duty to be imposed upon citizens than the faithful discharge of that particular duty. Some of you men have stood the test and trial in the protection of the American flag. But you never had a duty imposed upon you which required more intelligence, more manhood, more courage than that which the people of Idaho assign to you this night in the final discharge of your duty.[120]

Borah's appeal lasted five hours and fifty-one minutes, about half of Darrow's closing argument. Observers rated it highly. At the conclusion, Bill

Haywood reputedly turned to one of his defense attorneys and muttered, "Well, I have heard the best of them in the country, but Borah beats them all."[121]

Despite the prosecution's legal talent and the plethora of evidence, the jury acquitted Haywood of the charges. In a second trial, George Pettibone also won an acquittal. Recognizing that the case against Moyer could not stand in the wake of his co-conspirators' acquittals, prosecutors dropped the charges. As for Harry Orchard, he entered a guilty plea for his role as the bomber in the Steunenberg murder. Initially sentenced the death, he won a reprieve when the penalty was commuted to life in prison. He died at the state penitentiary in Boise in 1954.[122]

The Steunenberg assassination, largely forgotten today by the general public, was one of the most infamous episodes of violence in American history at the turn of the twentieth century. Aside from the trial verdicts, the question of whether Moyer, Haywood, and Pettibone, or any of their associates, were behind the murder was never answered satisfactorily. It was certainly possible that these men, and perhaps others, planned the killing. With the passage of more than a century, it is likely that no one will ever know with certainty what happened on that cold winter's evening in Caldwell, Idaho. What is indisputable is that labor and management conflicts, sometimes vicious, frequently bloody, and occasionally murderous, plagued the American landscape for decades to come.[123]

One fact appears reasonably clear: Harry Orchard, also known as Thomas Hogan and Albert Edward Horsley, was a Type 1 actor. Whether acting on orders from the miners' union or on his own initiative, he killed Frank Steunenberg for political purposes. The former governor had betrayed the labor movement, and he had to be punished. Bombing was a frequent tactic used by the WFM, and it was the method of choice in Steunenberg's assassination. In his zeal to avenge a wrong, Orchard acted on the clearest of motives. He believed that if he killed the man who had hurt the miners, he would send a message that labor would not kowtow to the elite, moneyed interests. One might question his timing—why kill a former governor who had been out of office for years?—but his reasoning was comprehensible. He was fully aware of what he was doing, and he was willing to do what was required to suit his political ends.[124]

Chapter 4

"IT ALL HAPPENED SO RAPIDLY. I DIDN'T REALLY KNOW WHAT THE HELL WAS GOING ON": HARRY S. TRUMAN (1950)

Harry S. Truman was not one of those fellows who believed he was destined for great things. As a young man, he never expressed a burning desire to become president of the United States. Some figures experience a fire in the belly so intense that they will stop at nothing to capture high political office. A self-effacing man by disposition, Truman did not envision himself ensconced in the White House even after he became a well-regarded senator with a prestigious national reputation. His unlikely political career was not forged from the fiery furnace of personal ambition, but through the calm, cool calculus of opportunity. After his clothing business failed, Truman associated with the Pendergast machine of Kansas City, which helped him secure a series of minor political positions that amounted to little more than sinecures. Truman eventually won a seat in the United States Senate as a Democrat representing Missouri, and that should have been the apex of his political career. Yet he avoided making too many enemies and carved out a niche investigating waste and fraud in military expenditures as the head of a Senate committee that brought him national acclaim. Tapped to join the ticket with an ailing Franklin D. Roosevelt when the incumbent ran for an unprecedented fourth term, Truman had served as vice president for only eighty-two days when FDR died of a cerebral hemorrhage.

Suddenly thrust into the presidency, the man from Missouri was widely regarded as ill-fitted for his position, especially when compared with his predecessor. The patrician Roosevelt had been groomed for great things throughout his life, and he possessed a shrewd, nuanced view of political power that became legendary. By contrast, Harry Truman appeared utterly guileless. It was difficult to imagine this son of Missouri engaging in political machinations of any sort, despite his ties to Pendergast. Truman's public persona suggested that he was an accidental chief executive who would serve out his term as unobtrusively as possible until someone of a higher stature could assume control. After all, the new chief did not fit the mold of what a president should be. He spoke in the plain, sincere cadences of the Midwestern haberdasher he had once been. He famously refused to indulge in the political gamesmanship that had so delighted Franklin Roosevelt. FDR could be equally charming, generous, eloquent, crafty, duplicitous, opportunistic, and ruthless, but with Harry Truman, what you saw was what you got—or at least that was the popular view.

The new president possessed greater political acumen than was appreciated when he assumed office in 1945. Glimmers of things to come could be seen by the discerning few who examined his work as a Senate investigator during his days as head of the Truman committee. It was not clear if such competence would transfer from the legislative to the executive branch. He seemed bereft of political instinct at the outset, a man hopelessly in over his head. As he grew into his new role, Truman came to appreciate and master the intricacies of wielding political power in a compound republic. Americans began to see evidence of the steel in Truman's spine, and many observers liked what they saw. Eventually, he garnered respect even from detractors who realized that the president was not as callow as he initially appeared.

Truman fashioned a career from defying expectations and beating odds. Despite the likelihood of electoral defeat among voters weary of Democratic executive control, Truman wrangled a second term as the nation's chief magistrate. In so doing, he influenced the course of post–World War II public policy for the next half century.[125]

He faced numerous international problems during his second term. Concern over the "red menace" spreading across Asia and Europe heightened tensions in the Cold War. The Soviet Union exploded a nuclear device in August 1949. Communists under Mao Zedong expelled the nationalist Chiang Kai-shek from China that same year. When a simmering dispute on the Korean peninsula erupted into violence in June 1950, Truman believed that he must contain communist advances or face a mounting threat on America's shores in the not-too-distant future. To that end, he dispatched troops. Suddenly, the Cold War turned hot, and the United States was engulfed in a violent police action half a world away. Previously, the Truman administration had supported the formation of the North Atlantic Treaty Organization (NATO) in Europe, approved an airlift to assist free citizens of West Berlin, and supported peoples resisting aggression in places such as Greece and Turkey.[126]

Of all the issues confronting Truman as he entered his sixth year in office, the question of Puerto Rican independence consumed little of his time and energy. This lack of attention was precisely the problem in the eyes of some critics. The Caribbean island, an unincorporated US territory, was home to a growing nationalist movement. The more zealous proponents of Puerto Rican nationalism plotted to make a strong statement against American imperialism, and the strongest statement possible was to confront US political leaders through violence.

The nationalists were not personally angry at Harry Truman. His record toward Puerto Rico was fairly progressive, especially when measured against previous presidents. He had named the first native Puerto Rican as governor of the island and he even spoke of extending Social Security benefits to Puerto Rican citizens. Truman's offense was that he was president of the United States, and therefore a symbol of the might and majesty of the American government. The most effective way to publicize the plight of the island's nationalists and push for Puerto Rican independence was to strike out at the symbol.[127]

Two committed nationalists, Griselio Torresola and Oscar Collazo, took it upon themselves to act. Torresola came to the cause through family ties, but Collazo joined after careful deliberation. Both men were poorly educated, impoverished, and yearning to engage in a dramatic action that would highlight the injustices perpetrated against Puerto Rico by the imperialist United States. Yet their temperaments were different. Collazo was known as the more stable family man while his younger counterpart was impetuous and insolent.

The two men met in New York City in October 1950. They had known each other in passing in Puerto Rico, but they were hardly close friends. Collazo was more than a decade older than Torresola, and they traveled in different social circles. They were reunited by a common purpose. The younger man was determined to do his part for Puerto Rican independence; he sought out Collazo to discuss whether they should return to the island to fight in an uprising initiated by nationalist leader Pedro Albizu Campos on October 30. Rather than fight on the home front, the pair resolved to travel to Washington and assault President Truman. Collazo subsequently recalled that "by coming to Washington and making some kind of demonstration in the capital of this nation, we would be in a better situation to make the

4.1 Puerto Rican nationalists targeted President Harry S. Truman, pictured here, for assassination because he was a symbol of American imperialism. Courtesy of the Library of Congress.

American people understand the real situation in Puerto Rico; that Puerto Rico has no government; there is no Government of Puerto Rico."[128]

Torresola was familiar with weapons, but Collazo was a neophyte. Evidence suggests that the men spent a day loading and unloading guns so that Collazo could master weapons in advance of the assault. They also familiarized themselves with the layout of the Blair House, the presidential guest residence across from the White House on Pennsylvania Avenue. The United States government purchased the property in 1942 to accommodate official visitors, but it served a variety of purposes. The White House was undergoing a major renovation in the fall of 1950, and the president and his wife temporarily resided at Blair House while the work was performed. The move proved to be fortuitous for Collazo and Torresola. The guest residence was closer to the road than the White House and therefore more vulnerable to a blitz attack.[129]

On the morning of Wednesday, November 1, 1950, the duo visited Blair House to scout out the location. After expressing brief misgivings, they reiterated their determination to carry out the plan. They left to eat lunch and return to their hotel. Torresola continued the weapons tutorial before they departed for their rendezvous with history. Just after 2:00 p.m., they returned to Blair House in a taxicab.[130]

Three White House policemen were visible outside the residence, but they did not notice anything especially unusual or alarming about two gentlemen dressed in dark business suits. According to the plan, Collazo would approach the front of Blair House while Torresola sought to gain entry through a rear door. They did not know if the president was home, but they "just took a chance," in Collazo's words, that he would be there and accessible. As fate would have it, Truman was there. He was upstairs napping in a second-floor bedroom that faced the road.[131]

Around 2:19 p.m., Collazo brazenly walked up to a Capitol police officer, Donald T. Birdzell, and pointed a Walther P-38 semiautomatic nine millimeter pistol at the man, firing at point blank range. Collazo's lack of training proved to be a handicap. He had not released the safety; consequently, the gun did not discharge. Fumbling to correct the problem, Collazo squeezed the trigger at precisely the moment when Birdzell took notice of the gunman. The bullet struck the officer in the knee, sending Birdzell to the pavement and alerting nearby security personnel that something was amiss. The assassin had lost the crucial element of surprise.[132]

In the guard booth at the east end of Blair House, not far from the scene of the shooting, US Secret Service agent Floyd Boring and White House police officer Joseph Davidson stood on patrol. "I'd come out more or less to chat," Boring recalled. "It all happened so rapidly. I didn't really know what the hell was going on."[133]

Wounded and experiencing excruciating pain, Birdzell crawled from the scene, drawing the shooter's attention away from the entrance to Blair House. Collazo hesitated, uncertain of what to do. The hesitation allowed Boring and Davidson time to scamper over to the front of Blair House. Had Collazo charged through the front door immediately, he might have shot Truman before reinforcements could arrive to impede his efforts.

Boring and Davidson realized that Blair House was under attack. They drew their weapons and fired repeatedly at the assailant. Collazo was pinned down, unable to enter the residence. He returned fire as best he could, but he was outnumbered and outgunned. Finally, he was struck in the head and arm by two .38 bullets. He collapsed, badly hurt and incapacitated, in front of the building.[134]

4.2 Would-be assassin Oscar Collazo lies wounded near the steps of the Blair House on November 1, 1950. Courtesy of Acme, Harry S. Truman Library & Museum, National Archives & Records Administration.

As the Collazo drama unfolded in front of Blair House, Griselio Torresola approached a guard station on the west side of Pennsylvania Avenue. He spoke in a loud voice, presumably to divert attention from the noise of the gunfire echoing from the front entrance. Inside the guard booth, Officer Leslie Coffelt was talking with White House policeman Joseph Downs, a plainclothes officer on duty that afternoon. Coffelt heard the commotion and turned his head as Torresola approached. The officer had no time to react. Torresola raised his nine millimeter German Luger semiautomatic pistol and fired four times inside the small guard shack. Three shots slammed into Coffelt's chest and abdomen, and a fourth bullet penetrated his policeman's tunic. He slumped in his chair, mortally wounded.[135]

Joseph Downs, startled by the shooting, was reaching for his weapon as Torresola pointed the Luger in his direction and fired. Injured in the hip, back, and neck, the policeman staggered away and entered a basement door, denying the gunman an immediate entrance into Blair House. It was an inspired move, allowing Downs to scream for help before Torresola could react.[136]

The assassin faced a choice: he could try and force his way inside the rear entrance to Blair House or he could come to Collazo's assistance. The intensity of the shootout no doubt caused the young man to choose the latter course. He rounded the corner of the residence to see Officer Birdzell pointing his service revolver at Collazo. Torresola fired and hit Birdzell in the knee. Now wounded in both knees, the officer collapsed.[137]

With his partner out of the fight and his gun empty of bullets, Torresola stopped to reload. At that moment, a disoriented President Truman, waking from his nap, stuck his head out the window to see what was causing so much commotion. Earlier in the day, he had enjoyed a modest lunch with his wife and mother-in-law before retiring for a nap. He was scheduled to attend a ceremony unveiling a statue of British Field Marshal Sir John Gill at Arlington National Cemetery in less than an hour. When he looked out the window, Truman was thirty feet away from his would-be assassin. Fortunately, Torresola did not spy the object of his assault.[138]

While Torresola reloaded, Officer Coffelt, dying, somehow got to his feet and staggered from the guard booth. He squeezed off one final round before he fell to the ground. The bullet ripped into Torresola's head two inches above his ear on a slight upward angle, instantly killing him. Officer Coffelt survived for four hours before he died at a local hospital. The gun battle with Collazo and Torresola had lasted less than one minute.[139]

Suddenly, everyone was in motion. As the Secret Service and police officers converged on Blair House, no one knew whether additional assassins were lurking somewhere nearby or if a conspiracy existed to attack Truman at a later time. Investigators fanned out to find answers. The press soon learned of the affair and arrived in droves. A rumor spread that Truman had been assassinated after ambulances were spotted departing the scene.[140]

Truman bounded down the stairs within minutes of the shooting and prepared to depart for his appointment at Arlington National Cemetery. He arrived as police officers examined Collazo's badly wounded body in front of Blair House. If he was upset by the episode, the president never showed it. When someone asked whether he intended to honor his afternoon commitment, he appeared surprised by the question. "Why, of course," he said.[141]

As he delivered his remarks during the visit to Arlington that afternoon, Truman did not mention the shooting. He appeared unconcerned until he learned that Officer Coffelt had died. The president participated in a subsequent ceremony honoring the slain policeman, expressing his appreciation for Coffelt's sacrifice and characterizing the slain man as one of the best officers on the White House security detail.[142]

4.3 Griselio Torresola's dead body lies near the Blair House following an assassination attempt against President Truman on November 1, 1950. Courtesy of Acme, Harry S. Truman Library & Museum, National Archives & Records Administration.

Truman was philosophical about the attack. "A president has to expect these things," he said with no display of emotion. Even though he recognized the danger, he was determined not to allow the incident to alter his routine completely. He enjoyed a morning walk around the city and often traveled with only a small security detail.[143]

Despite his desire to return to his regular activities, Truman understood that the world was a dangerous place and a leader could ill afford to ignore the realities of the modern presidency. Collazo and Torresola served notice that a president could not blithely ignore lurking threats, however much he might lament the loss of his freedom of movement. Accordingly, Truman's security detail eventually grew to at least a dozen Secret Service agents.[144]

In the meantime, Oscar Collazo survived his wounds and was called to answer for his crimes. His attorney counseled the defendant to enter an insanity plea, but Collazo adamantly refused. The two nationalists acted for political reasons, as classic Type 1 killers always do. The paramount motivation was to highlight the inequities inherent in the relationship between the United States and Puerto Rico. Seeking refuge in an insanity plea would negate everything Collazo and Torresola had accomplished. If a price was to be paid, Collazo was willing to pay it. Thus, to no one's surprise, he was charged with homicide in the death of Officer Coffelt. He also faced several counts of assault with intent to kill the president and members of his security force. Convicted of all charges on March 7, 1951, Oscar Collazo was sentenced to be executed. Far from being despondent, he looked forward to martyrdom as a means of publicizing the gross injustices perpetrated by the United States against Puerto Ricans.[145]

In June 1952, President Truman surprised and enraged Collazo when the president commuted the sentence to life imprisonment, robbing the convicted man of the martyrdom he desperately craved. As Truman explained, Puerto Rico did not impose capital punishment on criminal defendants; therefore, the United States would not do so in this case. Instead of becoming a hero to all independence-minded Puerto Ricans by dying in the electric chair, defiant until the end, Collazo faced the unappealing prospect of wasting away behind bars for decades, forgotten by all but a handful of his compatriots. It was an ignominious fate for a man who sought political superstardom.[146]

In 1979, President Jimmy Carter commuted Collazo's sentence, allowing the defendant to secure an immediate release. The world had changed markedly in those three decades. Most notably, the Puerto Rican independence movement had more or less collapsed, and few islanders cared much about an old man spouting out a tirade on US injustices. Collazo found pockets of support, though. The Puerto Rican Cultural Center of Chicago, Illinois, featured a pro-independence mural depicting Collazo and Torresola as heroes of the Puerto Rican nationalist movement. Cuban President Fidel Castro toasted Collazo as a hero for striking against the imperialistic United States. The old man returned to Puerto Rico, living out his years as a quaint relic of a long-gone age. He died on February 21, 1994, at the age of eighty.[147]

The Puerto Rican nationalists reinforce the understanding of Type 1 assassins as rational actors. These men did not hear voices urging them to commit their crimes, nor were they sociopaths projecting their own feelings of inadequacy onto their victims. Type 1 attackers seek to advance a political purpose, and they believe that violently striking out at a prominent target is the most effective means of achieving the goal. Sadly, these actors seek a short cut for establishing political legitimacy. Rather than going through the normal channels of political lobbying by building coalitions and persuading decision-makers of the rightness of their cause, they rely on violence as the ultimate expression of their discontent.[148]

Chapter 5

"RFK MUST DIE": ROBERT F. KENNEDY (1968)

Robert Francis Kennedy (RFK) was the seventh child of Joseph P. Kennedy, Sr., and Rose Fitzgerald Kennedy, founders of a dynasty that dominated the US political landscape during the second half of the twentieth century. Young Bobby came of age as a child of privilege. His father amassed a fortune as a financier (and a bootlegger during Prohibition), and enjoyed a modest political career of his own. Joseph, Sr., a feisty, proud Irish Catholic from Boston, was determined that his family would reach the top of the social and political hierarchy. No amount of money was too much to ensure the success of his progeny—elite private educations, the right connections, and the best jobs. After his eldest son, Joseph, Jr., died in World War II, the paterfamilias pushed his surviving sons to excel in the rough-and-tumble world of politics. Armed with formidable intellects and a taste for political blood sport, they succeeded beyond all expectations save their father's. The second son, John, served as the thirty-fifth president of the United States from January 1961 until his assassination in November 1963. The youngest son, Edward M. "Ted" Kennedy, became a prominent senator from Massachusetts, serving in office from 1962 until his death in 2009. The middle son, Bobby, served as attorney general in John's presidential administration and later won a seat in the US Senate representing the state of New York.[149]

After the murder of President Kennedy, Bobby was adrift. He was still a young man—he turned thirty-eight years old two days before his brother's assassination—and yet he stood at a crossroads. Bobby had spent most of his professional life working at his brother's side, serving as John's closest confidant. His identity was intertwined with protecting and advancing his elder brother's political career. Without that close familial bond, the path forward seemed to disintegrate. Bobby stayed on as Lyndon Johnson's attorney general well into 1964, but it was clear that his status as a trusted adviser had ended. President Johnson was all too aware that the Kennedys looked on him as a rube—and, worse, a rube standing in the way of a second Kennedy's rise to the presidency. Confirming Johnson's suspicions, RFK could barely control his temper when he was forced to meet with the new president. He loathed the man who had stepped into his brother's shoes. Bobby eventually bowed out of the administration and spent the next several years as a senator criticizing LBJ's Vietnam War policies.[150]

Like many public figures, Bobby Kennedy was a complicated man who appeared to embrace innumerable political inconsistencies. He started his career as a conservative congressional staffer for a committee chaired by Wisconsin Senator Joseph McCarthy, the demagogue who eventually came to epitomize the xenophobic anti-communists. Early in his career, RFK was a veritable law-and-order man, a zealous government prosecutor who chased after mobsters and racketeers with undisguised glee. Later, as part of his brother's administration, he turned his attention to deposing Cuban dictator Fidel Castro, that irritating symbol of communist ascendancy. RFK, like

5.1 Robert F. Kennedy made a name for himself as his brother John's aggressive enforcer and political strategist. He later served as the attorney general in the JFK administration. Courtesy of the Library of Congress.

many of his contemporaries, accepted the domino theory, which posited the now-discredited notion that if representatives of the free world did not actively oppose the specter of global communism, soon the red menace figuratively would spread to the United States as a cancer that, if unchecked, metastasizes throughout the human body. The young government lawyer of the late 1950s and early 1960s was a Cold Warrior who focused more on happenings in the rice paddies of far-off Asian dictatorships than on the haunting inequities of the ghettoes of Watts or the cotton fields of rural Mississippi.[151]

The Bobby Kennedy of his brother's era became a different man as the 1960s progressed. His life was a work in progress. Following his election to the US Senate in November 1964, he secured a front-row seat to the enormous changes occurring in the country and around the world. The young conservative brawler who so often had been described as "ruthless" and "relentless" evolved into a liberal icon with a soft spot for the poor, children, the elderly, and people of color. As attorney general, he had been slow to support the civil rights movement, but the times they were a-changin'. The New York senator was far more supportive and empathetic than the administration official had been less than half a decade earlier.[152]

Because he was a Kennedy and the next male in line after John's death, many assumed he would run for the presidency in due course. When RFK appeared at the 1964 Democratic convention, the ovation extended beyond the normal applause afforded party leaders. Bobby was visibly moved. Of course, he understood that the applause was not just for him, but also an expression of nostalgia for the hopes and ideals that were dashed when his brother was assassinated.[153]

Although Bobby considered announcing his candidacy for the presidency in 1968, the time was not ripe. If he waited until 1972, he would still be a young man and perhaps he would not face an incumbent president seeking reelection. The political calculus soon changed. After Senator Eugene McCarthy demonstrated President Johnson's vulnerability by coming within a hair's breadth of winning the New Hampshire Democratic presidential primary, RFK entered the race. Despite lingering animosity among some liberals who believed that Bobby had been too timid to challenge Johnson just yet, the senator was confident that he could capture the nomination and eventually the presidency. His odds improved enormously on March 31, 1968, when President Johnson unexpectedly announced that he would not seek reelection.[154]

5.2 Robert F. Kennedy, heir apparent to his slain brother, John, campaigned to win the Democratic presidential nomination in 1968. In this photograph, a worried-looking security official, Bill Barry, holds Kennedy so that well-wishers will not pull the candidate into the crowd. Courtesy of the Evan Freed personal collection.

Now a full-fledged presidential candidate, Bobby Kennedy hit the road with as much vigor as he could muster. It was a dangerous enterprise, and his friends and family expressed concern for his safety. RFK frequently held political rallies before thousands of screaming attendees. To some observers, he resembled a rock star reaching out to adoring fans who wanted to touch or grope him, but the hysteria could be worrisome. Everyone knew that charisma attracts dangerous people. For his part, Bobby accepted the possibility of violence with a bemused fatalism. After a bomb threat was phoned in to a rally in Salt Lake City at the end of March, RFK joked, "That's what I call opening my campaign with a bang."[155]

The year 1968 was one of the most tumultuous in recent decades as violence erupted in ghettoes, on college campuses, and in hundreds of venues, small and large, across America. On April 4, a gunman shot and killed the civil rights activist Martin Luther King, Jr., in Memphis, Tennessee. Bobby announced the news to a stunned crowd in Indianapolis. With yet another iconic '60s public figure lying dead from an assassin's bullet, Kennedy loyalists feared that a deranged gunman seeking instant notoriety might set his sights on Bobby.[156]

The fear became reality. During the spring of 1968, a young Palestinian with Jordanian citizenship, Sirhan Bishara Sirhan, turned his attention to the popular presidential candidate with the famous name. Sirhan seethed with anger and resentment over RFK's apparent support for Israel at the expense of the Arab cause. Violence became the preferred means of expressing that anger.[157]

Sirhan was born in Jerusalem on March 19, 1944, and moved to Pasadena, California, shortly before his thirteenth birthday. He later recalled his reluctance to immigrate to the United States. "I didn't want to leave; I wanted to stay in my own country with my own people," he explained."[158]

By all accounts, Sirhan's father, Bishara, ruled the family with an iron fist. He never liked his new country, believing that American culture was too permissive and led to immorality. Despite the father's beliefs that the family was becoming too Americanized, the Sirhans maintained most of their religious and ethnic identities. They spoke Arabic at home, read Arab newspapers, listened to Arab music, and honored Arab customs. They took pride in their ability to encounter American popular culture without succumbing to temptation.

Young Sirhan was an indifferent student. He finished high school and briefly attended Pasadena City College, but poor performance led to his dismissal. Afterward, he held a series of menial, poorly paid jobs. He was described as taciturn, but hardly obsequious. When provoked, he responded in a fury. His hair-trigger temper resulted in many heated arguments. Sirhan also suffered a head injury when he fell from a horse in 1966, which may have contributed to his aggressiveness. It was clear to anyone who deigned to notice that something was odd about this young man.[159]

His worried mother helped her strange son secure a job at an organic health food store. He worked there from September 1967 until March 1968. To Sirhan's boss and co-workers, he appeared fanatical about his Arab roots and heritage. He was also irascible and refused to take orders. Thin-skinned and quick to take offense, Sirhan constantly blamed others for his mistakes and shortcomings. His boss fired him when Sirhan became too difficult to handle.[160]

For the next three months, Sirhan was at loose ends. It is difficult to know exactly when he resolved to stalk Bobby Kennedy, but it may have been in May 1968, when he read a news article about the senator's support for selling fifty jet bombers to Israel. That same month, Sirhan watched a CBS Television documentary titled *The Story of Robert Kennedy*, part of which discussed Kennedy's visit to Palestine in 1948. Although the documentary did not specifically state that the senator supported Israel, the program showed an Israeli flag flapping in the breeze, and Sirhan became convinced that RFK was an enemy to all Arabs.

Well before he showed an interest in Senator Kennedy, Sirhan had been fascinated with the subject of assassinations. Even as a child, he had read books and stories about infamous political murders. When Martin Luther King, Jr., was assassinated on April 4, Sirhan followed news reports with great interest. The stories about Bobby Kennedy's support for Israel may have pushed him to act, but Sirhan had long been convinced that violence was a legitimate form of problem resolution.[161]

Beginning in late May 1968, Sirhan methodically plotted to shoot RFK. He left many clues that allowed subsequent investigators to track his movements. He appeared at a Kennedy political rally in Los Angeles on May 24, perhaps to scout it out. On June 1, he purchased two boxes of .22-caliber hollow-point bullets from the Lock, Stock, and Barrel Gun Shop in San Gabriel. In his journals, he pledged that he would shoot Robert Kennedy no later than June 5.[162]

Sirhan traveled to San Diego on June 3 when he learned that the candidate would speak at the El Cortez Hotel. Unable to get close enough to Kennedy, the would-be assassin returned to Pasadena. The following day, Sirhan visited the San Gabriel Valley Gun Club and practiced his rapid-fire shooting techniques. After the gun club closed at 5:00 pm, he ate a hamburger at a Bob's Big Boy restaurant before heading over to the Ambassador Hotel on Wilshire Boulevard in Los Angeles. The senator was scheduled to await the results of the California Democratic Primary in the hotel that evening. With luck, Sirhan could get close enough to shoot Kennedy when the candidate addressed his supporters.[163]

Sirhan was seen lurking about the hotel several hours before the senator was expected to enter the Embassy Ballroom. Eyewitnesses later reported that the odd young man spoke about Kennedy with great disdain to several members of the crowd. Of course, no one knew he had come equipped with a .22-caliber Iver-Johnson Cadet revolver.

As the hours passed and the election returns were tabulated, the crowd grew in size. Kennedy was poised to win a major victory, an important milestone in his quest to win the presidency. Shortly before the senator appeared to speak with his followers, Sirhan was spotted moving around the kitchen pantry. Several onlookers initially thought he was a kitchen worker until they realized that he was not wearing an employee uniform. He was asked to leave the area, but somehow he reappeared a short time later.[164]

In the meantime, Kennedy, flush with victory after winning the California primary, appeared in the main ballroom around midnight and briefly spoke to the crowd. Immediately afterward, the senator and his entourage moved away from the stage. Unable to navigate through the throngs of people, RFK suggested that he and his staff exit through a back door. Someone pointed to the kitchen. It was around 12:15 in the morning when they moved into the pantry. Seventy-seven people crowded into the tight space, although only eighteen became what police later called "key witnesses."[165]

Sirhan was elated. After all the mistakes and missed opportunities of recent days, he had planned his attack perfectly. He had mulled over the likely routes that Kennedy would use to leave the ballroom, and the kitchen had seemed a logical choice. It was inspired guesswork. Because he had been unable to approach Senator Kennedy, Sirhan had waited until Senator Kennedy approached him. Now, in the wee morning hours of June 5, here came his prey. The pantry was a long narrow space crammed with people, but the security staff was standing too far away from RFK to stop a determined assassin from completing his task.

Sirhan had but a brief moment to act. Stepping away from an ice machine from a distance of a few feet, he raised his revolver and aimed at point blank range. One nearby witness claimed he heard the gunman exclaim, "Kennedy, you son of a bitch!" Leaning against a steam table, Sirhan fired off two shots, paused, and pressed the trigger repeatedly, unleashing a series of staccato blasts that struck five people in addition to Robert Kennedy. Paul Schrade, a United Automobile Workers union official; Ira Goldstein, a 19-year-old radio reporter; William Weisel of ABC TV; Elizabeth Evans, a friend of a Kennedy campaign aide; and Irwin Stroll, an adolescent campaign volunteer, were victims of Sirhan's fusillade that night. Despite their injuries, all five survived.[166]

Robert Kennedy was not as fortunate as the other persons crowded into the pantry. He took two bullets in the back and one in the head, with a fourth bullet passing through his jacket. The head wound was grave, entering his skull and destroying the mastoid bone just behind his right ear. Grabbing part-time security guard Thane Cesar's clip-on tie, the senator fell to the floor while several bystanders—including former football-player-turned-Kennedy-bodyguard Rosey Grier; journalist and literary critic George Plimpton; Karl Uecker, the hotel's assistant maître d'; and Rafer Johnson, a Gold-medal decathlete—wrestled with Sirhan to remove his gun and subdue him before he could escape.[167]

Witnesses heard a *pop-pop-pop* noise before they recognized the source. Warren Rogers, a journalist and Kennedy admirer, later wrote, "I remember thinking at the time that whenever I heard gunshots, they always sounded like firecrackers, and I wondered why they always sounded like firecrackers." Rogers soon found himself part of the melee. Pressed against Sirhan in the struggle to disarm the gunman, Rogers noted his "swarthy complexion and black curly hair."[168]

When they realized that someone had discharged a gun, spectators screamed and fled in the ensuing chaos. Hotel busboy Juan Romero knelt and spoke gently to the fatally wounded man sprawled on the floor. "Come on, Mr. Kennedy," he said. "You can make it." RFK muttered a reply: "Is everybody all right?" *Los Angeles Times* photographer Boris Yaro captured the moment in a series of photographs that soon became famous around the world. Another Kennedy had been shot down in his prime.[169]

Bill Barry, RFK's security man, had lost sight of the senator in the crowd. When he finally caught up, he joined in the struggle with Sirhan. Satisfied that the shooter no longer posed a threat, he turned his attention to Robert Kennedy. He slipped off his suit jacket and slid it under the wounded man's head. "I knew immediately it was a .22, a small caliber, so I hoped it wouldn't be so bad," Barry recalled, "but then I saw the hole in the senator's head, and I knew."[170]

5.3 *Los Angeles Times* photographer Boris Yaro snapped this photograph of a mortally wounded Robert F. Kennedy lying on the floor of the Ambassador Hotel kitchen moments after Sirhan Sirhan shot the senator. Busboy Juan Romero kneels at Kennedy's side. Courtesy of Boris Yaro and the *Los Angeles Times*.

Two doctors, Stanley R. Abo and Martin Esther, treated RFK at the scene. Finding the head wound, Dr. Abo tried to keep a clot from forming. Ethel, Bobby's wife, knelt and spoke to him in soothing tones despite her own feelings of horror. Warren Rogers later described the dramatic scene: "There, on his back, his shirt torn wide, his mouth open, his eyes rolling back in his head, his bloodied right hand clutching a rosary, his right ear a red smear, a blood-soaked handkerchief on his bare stomach, lay Bob Kennedy." RFK recognized his wife and whispered her name.[171]

As someone called for an ambulance and onlookers tried to make the stricken man as comfortable as possible, members of the Kennedy entourage restrained the assailant. George Plimpton later remembered how calm Sirhan appeared. While everyone else was shouting and panicky, moving in a whirlwind of activity, the assassin was composed, almost serene. Plimpton shuddered when he recalled "those utterly cold, utterly expressionless eyes of his." Someone else thought he heard Sirhan say, "I did it for my country," or words to that effect.[172]

An ambulance arrived around 12:23 a.m. As the attendants lifted her husband to place him onto a stretcher, Ethel called out, "gently, gently." Robert Kennedy had been awake until this time, but he closed his eyes and lost consciousness. The attendants loaded him into the ambulance for the short trip to Central Receiving Hospital. Billy Barry and Warren Rogers rode in the front seat while Ethel Kennedy, campaign aide Fred Dutton, and RFK's sister Jean rode in the back of the ambulance with the attendant.[173]

RFK was still alive, but comatose. He had lost a prodigious amount of blood while lying on the kitchen floor. Bullet fragments were lodged in his head.

Satisfied that they had done all they could to stabilize the patient, doctors agreed to transmit Kennedy to Good Samaritan Hospital a few blocks away to undergo brain surgery. A team of neurosurgeons was on hand when the ambulance arrived. The surgeons spent more than three hours attempting to repair the damage, but the injury was too severe. Robert Kennedy died twenty-hours and twenty-nine minutes after he was shot.[174]

The senator's press secretary, Frank Mankiewicz, had issued periodic briefings since the news broke. At 1:59 a.m. on June 6, he faced the press corps to provide one last bulletin. Visibly shaken and choking back tears, Mankiewicz struggled to speak. "I have a short announcement to read which I will read at this time," he said. "Senator Robert Francis Kennedy died at 1:44 a.m. today, June 6,

1968. With Senator Kennedy at the time of his death was his wife Ethel, his sisters, Mrs. Patricia Lawford, and Mrs. Stephen Smith, his brother in law, Stephen Smith, and his sister-in-law, Mrs. John F. Kennedy. He was 42 years old."[175]

As for the man who had slain "The Once and Future King," as someone scrawled on the wall in crayon five feet from where RFK had fallen inside the hotel kitchen, he was handed over to police officers within minutes of the shooting. Transported to the Rampart Division of the Los Angeles Police Department, Sirhan appeared lucid and rational, in one officer's opinion, but under the influence of drugs or alcohol, according to another. A suspect's state of mind is always crucial for understanding the crime, although sometimes it can be difficult to discern the assailant's motives. California State Assembly Speaker Jesse Unruh accompanied Sirhan to the police station that morning. When Unruh asked why Sirhan had committed the crime, the suspect snapped, "Do you think I'm crazy, so you can use it in evidence against me?" Later, after he was transferred to police department headquarters in the Parker Center, Sirhan was interrogated. The interrogating officer saw no evidence of irrationality, declaring Sirhan "one of the most intelligent people I have ever attempted to interrogate."[176]

The officer said "attempted to interrogate" because Sirhan refused to cooperate. He would not reveal his name, stating that "I think I shall remain incognito." He was incarcerated in the medical ward so he could be treated for a broken finger, a sprained ankle, and severe bruises he sustained as he tussled with the crowd inside the Ambassador Hotel. The following morning, his brothers Adel and Munir appeared in the police station after having seen Sirhan on television. In this way, the authorities learned the identity of the man who had shot Robert F. Kennedy.[177]

His guilt was never in doubt. During an interrogation on June 9, Sirhan admitted that he had killed RFK. He agreed to plead guilty in court provided he received a "guarantee of life having a chance to tell my story on the witness stand, plus another guarantee of parole after seven years. I absolutely want a guarantee of that." The court would not agree to such conditions, ensuring that a trial ensued.[178]

Sirhan's defense attorneys pushed for a diminished-capacity plea despite his family's opposition. In the Arab world, admitting to diminished capacity brings shame to the killer's relatives. Sirhan also resisted such a plea. He told his attorneys that he was sane when he shot Senator Kennedy. Eventually, for reasons that are unclear, Sirhan acquiesced and accepted his attorneys'

5.4 Sirhan Sirhan, shown here in his mug shot, assassinated Senator Robert F. Kennedy in Los Angeles in June 1968. Courtesy of the California Department of Corrections.

advice. They were anxious to avoid a death penalty, but Sirhan later told Judge Herbert V. Walker, "I will ask to be executed."[179]

His trial began in January 1969. From the outset, the defendant presented constant problems. He seemed to change his mind about his plea at various stages. He also expressed his desire to discharge defense counsel. Judge Walker continued the trial and refused to dismiss Sirhan's attorneys. To no one's surprise, on April 17, 1969, the jury returned a guilty verdict.[180]

During the penalty phase, the jury sentenced Sirhan to die in the gas chamber. Judge Walker upheld the jury verdict despite a letter from the Kennedy family requesting clemency. "My brother was a man of love and sentiment and compassion," Senator Edward M. Kennedy wrote on his family's behalf. "He would not have wanted his death to be the cause for the taking of another life." Judge Walker listened to the evidence, but ultimately chose to uphold the death penalty because the sentence for first degree murder in California was execution.[181]

Although Judge Walker was correct that state law provided for the death penalty, the likelihood of Sirhan's execution was remote. The state had unofficially banned executions in 1967. On February 18, 1972, the California Supreme Court officially extended the ban when it held in *The People of the State of California v. Robert Page Anderson* that the death penalty as applied in

California violated the Eighth Amendment of the United States Constitution. Sirhan Sirhan's sentence thus became life in prison.[182]

Sirhan's punishment was not quite the end of the story. In the years following the trial and sentencing, a series of conspiracy theories arose. Some commentators argued that a second shooter must have been present owing to the physical evidence. The nature of RFK's injuries, the angle of the bullet holes in the kitchen pantry, and missing photographs and physical evidence suggested to persons with a penchant for believing in conspiracies that a hidden cabal had engineered the senator's assassination. Still other theorists mused that Sirhan may have been programmed to kill RFK because the gunman appeared to be in a "dissociative state" when he pulled the trigger. A popular 1962 film, *The Manchurian Candidate*, based on a book of the same name, portrayed an assassin who was hypnotized to kill a senator, and Sirhan was supposedly working in this vein. Despite the alleged plots concerning multiple shooters and the powers-that-be behind the killing, no credible evidence has ever surfaced to indicate that anyone other than Sirhan Sirhan assassinated Robert F. Kennedy.[183]

Conspiracies notwithstanding, Sirhan sometimes has been characterized as a lone-wolf assassin who sought to gain notoriety for killing a famous person. In light of his social awkwardness and loner persona, such an interpretation is appealing. If he were a lone gunman seeking a higher status for killing a well-known public figure, Sirhan would be characterized as a classic Type 2 killer, especially if he sought to impress a loved one by carrying out the act. While a desire for recognition might have been a motivating factor, the weight of the evidence suggests that he was driven to kill by his political disagreements with Senator Kennedy's policy on Israel.

If Sirhan's diminished-capacity plea and the presence of conspirators lurking behind the assassination are discounted, the assassin appears to be a Type 1 killer. Sirhan was rational: He meticulously planned the murder after he learned of the senator's pro-Israeli policies. On several occasions, and in notebooks that he kept, Sirhan expressed his disgust with RFK's politics. "RFK must die," he proclaimed. Moreover, except on rare occasions when he has granted interviews or sought parole, he has avoided publicity. If he were a Type 2 killer in search of media fame, he would shout from the rooftops at every opportunity about how he performed this deed and why he should be associated in the public mind with Robert Kennedy. For the most part, he has not sought out the limelight. He has become, in the words of one historian of the RFK assassination, the "forgotten terrorist."[184]

PART II

TYPE 2 ACTORS

Chapter 6

"IT'S JUST THAT WE WILL NEVER BE YOUNG AGAIN": JOHN F. KENNEDY (1963)

Friday, November 22, 1963, became a date forever enshrined in the hearts and minds of Americans old enough to recall what they were doing when they heard the news. Their bright young president, just forty-six years old, was shot and killed by an assassin while riding in a motorcade through the streets of Dallas, Texas. His death and the death of his assassin just two days later changed the nation. The newspaper columnist Mary McGrory, a Kennedy confidante and admirer, lamented that "we'll never laugh again." Daniel Patrick Moynihan, later a US senator, was serving as a Kennedy aide at the time. "Heavens, Mary, we'll laugh again," he assured her. "It's just that we will never be young again."[185]

Kennedy, often affectionately known by his initials, was the rare public figure whose death transformed him into something he had never been in life: A cultural hero. During his life, he had been an icon to young people, but he also had been an elected official, which meant that he amassed his share of political enemies. William Manchester, an early historian of the assassination, wrote that "Martyrdom had transformed John Kennedy so swiftly that even those closest to him found adjustment difficult. Friday morning he had been a popular but controversial young President." Within days, his status changed. "Death had swept away both affection and enmity; they had been replaced by idolatry."[186]

The living, breathing president had faced a host of seemingly intractable problems during the fall of 1963. After many delays and false starts, he had announced his support for a civil rights bill only three months earlier, but his legislative agenda was stalled in Congress. He fretted over the increasing number of military advisers ensconced in Southeast Asia, debating whether he should continue to escalate the conflict or pursue some other course of action. After his death, an endless debate raged over whether JFK would have committed ground troops or withdrawn from Vietnam. He faced Cold War confrontations across the globe, especially in Berlin and Cuba. Many old-line politicos and career military men, less than impressed with their commander in chief's celebrated vim and vigor, proved to be implacable foes to the New Frontier's progressive ideals. It had been a difficult presidency with a steep learning curve, but Kennedy believed that he at last understood the perils of his position and was ready to move forward into a brighter future.[187]

One daunting obstacle remained firmly fixed in his path. Facing a potentially hard-fought reelection campaign in 1964, the president agreed to visit Texas to patch up a growing rift in the state's Democratic Party ranks. His vice president, Lyndon B. Johnson, was supposed to be a tonic to what ailed the party in the Lone Star State, but even a shrewd political operative such as LBJ had not been able to make things right. JFK had been wary of the trip and worried about the divisiveness of Texas politics, but the visit appeared to have been going well aside from a bit of behind-the-scenes intraparty squabbling between Governor John Connally and Senator Ralph Yarborough. The governor's wife, Nellie Connally, riding in the open limousine with the president and the first lady moments before fatal shots were fired, turned to tell Kennedy, "You can't say that Dallas doesn't love you today, Mr. President." It was one of the last remarks that John Kennedy heard before an assassin ended his life. In an instant, everything changed.[188]

The JFK murder was shocking on multiple levels. Aside from the obvious horror of losing the nation's most visible and powerful elected official to a seemingly senseless act of violence, the event portended tumultuous changes in American life. Before the shooting, the nation had not lost a chief executive to a gunman since McKinley in 1901. Louisiana Senator Huey P. Long, a presidential aspirant, died by an assassin's hand in 1935 and President Harry Truman faced an attempt in 1950, but the Dallas slaying was a vividly successful reminder of the vulnerability of a national leader to a lone malcontent willing and able to step beyond the confines of an orderly society. Happening at a time when many Americans could watch live television coverage of the affair, including the subsequent funeral and the murder of the assassin, the Kennedy murder became a watershed moment.[189]

In retrospect, Moynihan's remark about the country losing its youth is eerily prescient. In the years that followed the Dallas slaying, the nation experienced multiple shootings and assassinations: Malcolm X in 1965, Martin

6.1 John F. Kennedy is seen here in 1961, during the first year of his presidency. Courtesy of the Library of Congress.

Luther King, Jr., and Robert F. Kennedy in 1968, Kent State and Jackson State in 1970, George C. Wallace in 1972, Gerald Ford (twice) in 1975, and Ronald Reagan in 1981. For millions of Americans, John Kennedy's death presaged a time of emotional turmoil and lost innocence in the nation.[190]

In the wake of the murder, conspiracy theories abounded. The president had been the target of a vicious cabal at various times thought to be directed by the US Central Intelligence Agency (CIA), communist agents, the mafia, Soviets, Cubans, white supremacists such as the Ku Klux Klan or the John Birch Society, and/or numerous other anti-Kennedy groups. Motion pictures such as Oliver Stone's 1991 thriller *JFK* set forth fanciful theories about unseen forces lurking in the shadows ready to launch a *coup d'état* at the first opportunity. The fictional account of such a plot, *Seven Days in May*, enjoyed success as a book and film during the 1960s.[191]

Even before his inauguration, Kennedy had been the target of assassination plots. On December 11, 1960, while the president-elect was vacationing at his family compound in Palm Beach, Florida, Richard Paul Pavlick, an anti-Catholic seventy-three-year-old former postal worker, planned to ram his car, filled with dynamite, into Kennedy's car, killing them both. Pavlick ultimately abandoned the plan, he later explained, when he spied Jacqueline Kennedy with her daughter, Caroline, and realized that she had recently given birth to a son. The Secret Service arrested the man before he could engineer a second attempt. Pavlick was found incompetent to stand trial and spent six years confined to a mental institution and a hospital.[192]

Other assassination plots surfaced. Perhaps the most chilling plan, thwarted by the Federal Bureau of Investigation (FBI) early in November 1963, called for shooters to take out President Kennedy during a ride in a motorcade in Chicago. Conspiracy theorists suggest that when that scheme failed, the unknown cabal switched its attention farther south. No credible evidence has ever surfaced to link the plots in Chicago and Dallas, but the lack of credibility has seldom dissuaded paranoids from insisting that a nexus exists between seemingly random events.[193]

Certainly the atmosphere in some areas of Texas was toxic. When JFK awoke in Fort Worth, Texas, on that fateful Friday morning, he learned of right-wing propaganda circulating throughout Dallas as well as a derogatory newspaper advertisement accusing him of treason and attacking his Catholic faith. Although initially irked, he eventually shrugged it off. Dallas enjoyed a reputation as "nut country," but he had a job to do. The president joked that any determined soul with a gun could take out a public figure. It was wise to undertake reasonable precautions, but the notion of absolute safety was an unattainable ideal.[194]

Kennedy's equanimity was not surprising. He knew that as a public figure, he was a possible target of assassins, but he was not overly concerned. The man had faced death many times during his life. As a naval officer in World War II, his PT boat had been sliced in two by a Japanese destroyer early one morning in 1943. Kennedy survived. Several times in his life his precarious health had led to scares where the possibility of his death was likely, but he had lived to tell the tale. If he had made it through those difficult situations intact, surely he faced nothing more lethal in the streets of Dallas during a routine political trip.[195]

The events on the morning of November 22 proceeded as planned. After delivering prepared remarks outside of his Fort Worth hotel, Kennedy and his entourage departed on Air Force One for a short ride to Love Field in nearby Dallas. The weather had been nasty of late, which meant the president might ride beneath a bullet-proof bubbletop fixed atop the presidential limousine when he traveled from the airport to the Dallas Trade Mart to deliver a speech. As luck would have it, the weather cleared shortly before the motorcade departed. The president decided he would ride in an open limousine so the crowds could get a look at him. The first lady would sit beside him while Governor Connally and his wife rode in the front seat near the driver. Vice President Johnson and his wife were also in the motorcade, but seated in a separate automobile.[196]

The enthusiastic crowd estimated at between 150,000 and 200,000 people surprised the officials riding in the cars. Although a few anti-Kennedy signs were sprinkled among the onlookers, the response was overwhelmingly positive. The parade route had been published in the newspaper, ensuring that spectators would know exactly where to position themselves to see the president whiz by that morning. The slow-moving motorcade was a politician's dream because it exposed the man of the hour to thousands of citizens—but it was also an assassin's delight for exactly the same reasons.[197]

One man who had learned of the president's visit with interest was a twenty-four-year-old ex-Marine named Lee Harvey Oswald. An odd, emotionally unstable young man, Oswald had immigrated to the Soviet Union after he left the Marines in 1959. He initially expressed his admiration for the Soviet style of government, but he soon became disillusioned. Returning to the United States with a wife and young daughter, he fell into a pattern of abusing his wife and drifting through a series of boring, dead-end jobs. He claimed to be an avowed Marxist, but his poor understanding of history and ideology and his anger toward the bureaucratization he witnessed in the Soviet Union left him a decidedly confused zealot. The only consistency in his life was his increasing frustration with his squalid circumstances.[198]

Oswald appeared to be searching for an idea he could believe in or an ideology that would meet his emotional needs. He came to believe that the answer to his restlessness could be found in Cuba. The island was under the rule of Fidel Castro, a fiery revolutionary who displaced the Batista regime in 1959. In Castro's Cuba, Marxist ideals could be realized without the large, bloated, unworkable bureaucracy that governed the USSR. Lee Oswald had found his Shangri-La.[199]

If he planned to leave the United States and reside in Cuba as an important member of the intelligentsia—for Oswald had no doubt that he possessed superior abilities that a visionary like Fidel Castro would appreciate—he must

6.2 President Kennedy is pictured riding in a motorcade in Dallas, Texas, on November 22, 1963, minutes before he was killed by an assassin's bullet. His wife, Jackie, sits next to him. Texas Governor John Connally and his wife, Nellie, are seated in the front. Courtesy of the Library of Congress.

establish his bona fides. The young marksman seized on what appeared to be the perfect plan. He would assassinate a right-wing partisan who publicly called for an invasion of Cuba. If Castro came to see that Oswald had forestalled further American intervention on the island, he would welcome the hero of the revolution into his lair with open arms.[200]

General Edwin A. Walker was the right-wing reactionary who had attracted the would-be assassin's attention. He had fashioned a career in the military, but Walker's extremist views eventually cost him his command. A fierce critic of the Kennedy administration, the general believed that JFK's much-vaunted performance during the Cuban missile crisis of 1962 had actually been disastrous. Instead of invading Cuba and driving the communists off the island when he had a prime opportunity, the president had sold out. Kennedy's nuanced approach to allowing Soviet Premier Nikita Khrushchev to remove the missiles in exchange for a no-invasion pledge was a sign of weakness. Walker also expressed his dissatisfaction with Kennedy's robust civil rights proposals. Oswald thought that if right-wing fanatics like Walker had their way, the United States—already a racist, imperialist nation—would only grow more vainglorious and militant in its quest to take over the world.

The would-be revolutionary resolved to shoot Walker, which would accomplish two goals. First, it would rid the world of a loud-mouth reactionary demagogue. Secondly, it would demonstrate to the Cubans that Oswald was a friend of the Revolution. Most convenient of all, Walker lived in Dallas and would be an easy target for a gunman.

On March 12, 1963, Oswald took a major step toward fulfilling his newly developed plan: he ordered a $29.95 6.5-millimeter Mannlicher-Carcano rifle from a Chicago mail-order firm. Shortly after it arrived, he posed for a series of photographs holding the rifle. Conspiracy theorists later dissected the photographs to explain why they were forgeries designed to implicate Oswald in the Kennedy assassination, transforming him into a patsy for unseen forces working behind the scenes. At the time that Oswald posed with his new rifle, however, he proudly told his wife, Marina, to give the photos to his daughter "to remember Papa by sometime."

Oswald began practicing with the rifle as well as reconnoitering General Walker's neighborhood. The timing of this is important, as Oswald tended to take extreme action when something went awry in his personal life. On Saturday, April 6, Oswald lost his job at a commercial photography firm. He claimed it was because FBI agents had added him to a watch list after he returned from the Soviet Union and they were harassing him. In reality, the employer fired him because Oswald was surly and difficult to deal with, especially when he read Russian-language newspapers during his breaks. Without a job to stabilize his mood swings, he felt ready to act.

Around 9:00 p.m. on April 10, General Walker sat a desk in his home when a bullet struck the wooden frame outside his window. The case remained unsolved at the time of the Kennedy assassination, but after Oswald was arrested, police investigators recognized that he was the likely culprit in the Walker incident. Having failed in his April shooting, Oswald buried the rifle near the general's house, walked to a nearby bus stop, and rode home.[201]

Anxious to find work and frustrated by his failing marriage, Oswald soon boarded a bus for New Orleans. He briefly worked in a coffee processing

6.3 Lee Harvey Oswald poses with his new rifle in the backyard of his apartment on West Neely Street in Dallas, Texas, in March 1963. Courtesy of the Warren Commission Report, Exhibit 133-A.

plant and began distributing literature on behalf of the Fair Play for Cuba Committee (FPCC). While in New Orleans, Oswald attracted attention. On August 9 and 16, he was arrested for brawling with anti-Castro activists incensed because he was passing out "Hands Off Cuba!" leaflets. He also appeared on two radio programs criticizing the administration's Cuban policies. Conspiracy theorists later suggested that Oswald met with nefarious forces to plan John Kennedy's assassination during this time, but the nature and scope of the meetings, if any, remains obscure. What is certain is that a pregnant Marina Oswald and her infant daughter came to live with Lee for a short time before returning to Dallas to live with her friend, Ruth Paine, in the nearby suburb of Irving, Texas.[202]

Oswald appeared in the Cuban Embassy in Mexico City on September 27, 1963, seeking a visa to travel to Cuba en route back to the Soviet Union. Embassy personnel alternated between bemusement and anger as Oswald demanded assistance owing to his efforts on behalf of the Castro regime. When he did not procure the visa, he supposedly made threats against President Kennedy, although accounts differed on what he said. In light of the young man's preposterous claims, it is doubtful whether anything he said that day impressed his interlocutors as credible. An angry, demoralized Oswald returned to Dallas empty-handed.[203]

Pregnant Marina Oswald and her infant daughter were now living with Ruth Paine in Irving. Lee, in the meantime, agreed to rent a cheap room in Dallas and search for employment. On October 1, Ruth Paine mentioned that the Texas School Book Depository had an opening. Lee applied, got the job, and started working on October 16. His second daughter, Audrey Rachel, was born four days later.[204]

Oswald was lonely. With his wife and children living in the suburbs, he had little to occupy his time apart from his mind-numbingly dull job of filling school-book orders. His pro-Cuban political activities provided an outlet for his restlessness, but Oswald nonetheless felt that his life was in a downward spiral. He occasionally hitched a ride to the suburbs on the weekends to spend time with his family, but the meetings were deeply unsatisfying. Lee belittled Marina and she in turn alternated between warmth and open hostility, sometimes questioning his manhood and challenging his ability to act as the breadwinner for his family. Later, after Marina discovered that her husband was living under an alias in Dallas, the couple fought bitterly. During the argument, Lee blamed his lack of financial stability on the FBI.[205]

In mid-November, as the announcement of Kennedy's motorcade route hit the newspapers, Lee Oswald apparently resolved to shoot the president. He did not harbor personal animosity toward JFK, although he was unhappy with the administration's policies on Cuba. The timing and the circumstances proved to be too convenient to ignore. Lee's personal life was unraveling. He wanted to prove his revolutionary zeal to the Cubans, he needed to demonstrate his manhood to his wife, and he desired a change in the emptiness of his day-to-day existence. Killing a famous man would recast Lee Harvey Oswald's pathetic life. He would be an important person for once.

The motorcade route passed by the Texas School Book Depository, and Lee possessed a rifle that would allow him to shoot at the target with ease. He had received training in marksmanship in the Marine Corps. With the motorcade slowing down to make the sharp turn at Dealey Plaza, it would not be difficult to take out the president.[206]

On Thursday, November 21, Oswald asked Wesley Frazier, a co-worker who lived near Ruth Paine, for a ride to Irving so Oswald could retrieve curtain rods for his apartment. Frazier agreed. In reality, the package of curtain rods was the Mannlicher-Carcano rifle that Oswald had hidden in Ruth Paine's garage.

When Oswald arrived at the Paine residence that Thursday evening, he broke his usual pattern. He did not visit Marina and the children on a fixed schedule, but when he did come, it was on the weekend. Marina was surprised by his early appearance. She was still upset about his use of an alias. When Lee asked to reconcile that night, Marina refused. Instead of spending a warm evening with his wife, he spent a sleepless night at the Paine house.[207]

Rising early the next morning, Lee did not kiss his wife goodbye. He left his wedding ring in a china cup along with $170—all the money he had. "Take it and buy everything you and Junie and Rachel need," he told Marina. His behavior struck her as odd, but she had no inkling of what Lee planned to do later that day. He walked over to the garage, picked up the supposed curtain rods, now wrapped in paper, and hitched a ride into the city with Wesley Frazier.[208]

Eyewitnesses later testified during the Warren Commission hearings that they saw Oswald in the Texas School Book Depository that day, although they were not always certain of the time. The last person who could place him in the building was a witness who believed Lee was standing on the first floor around noon. Another eyewitness remembered being on the sixth floor at 12:10 p.m., about twenty minutes before the assassination. He thought he was the only person there, but a pile of boxes obscured his view of what was later described as the sniper's nest. Oswald apparently stacked the boxes in the southeast corner of the sixth floor to hide from onlookers. There he waited next to an open window, rifle in hand.[209]

President Kennedy's motorcade appeared in front of the school-book depository at 12:30 p.m. Oswald fired three shots. One apparently missed completely. A second shot hit the president at the base of his neck, passing through his body and striking Governor Connally. The third bullet struck Kennedy in the head and proved to be fatal.[210]

Oswald hid the rifle under boxes and calmly walked away. Ninety seconds later, he encountered a police officer, Marrion L. Baker, and Oswald's supervisor, Roy Truly, in the second floor lunchroom. Because Truly identified Oswald as an employee, and the young man did not appear nervous or out of breath, the officer let him pass. The assassin walked out of the building seconds before authorities sealed the entrances. Truly later realized that Oswald was the only employee unaccounted for that day.[211]

Oswald caught a city bus, requesting a transfer pass. Only two blocks later he exited, presumably frustrated at the heavy traffic. Anxious to make good time, he hailed a taxicab to his rooming house at 1026 Beckley Avenue. He arrived about thirty minutes after the president had been shot. His housekeeper saw him scurrying to his room and she noticed him leaving a few minutes later wearing a jacket he had not worn earlier. The last time she spotted him, Oswald was standing at a nearby bus stop.[212]

Dallas police officer J. D. Tippit drove up next to Oswald at 1:15 p.m. The officer may have heard a broadcast about a suspect seen lurking in the window of the school book depository and decided that Oswald matched the description. In any case, Tippit asked Oswald a few questions from his car. Moments later, the officer opened the car door and stepped outside. As Tippit stood up from his patrol car, Oswald produced a .38-caliber revolver and shot the man four times. Nine eyewitnesses subsequently identified Oswald as the man who shot and killed Officer Tippit.[213]

Minutes later, a shoe store manager saw a man duck into the alcove of his store. Curious at this unusual behavior, he watched as the man crept up the street and entered the Texas Theatre without paying. The manager told the theatre clerk what he had seen, and the clerk called the police. When officers arrived, the theatre manager turned up the house lights so the shoe-store manager could point out the strange man. Unable to escape, that man, Lee Oswald, initially said, "Well, it is all over now," but he was not yet ready to surrender. Pulling his revolver from his pants, he pointed it at an officer before he was disarmed. A tussle ensued. Later, Oswald claimed that he had suffered a black eye because "a policeman hit me" and he was the victim of police brutality.[214]

He was arrested as a suspect in the shooting of Officer Tippit, but it did not take authorities long to realize that Oswald probably had killed President Kennedy, too. As the suspect was being questioned, an officer recognized Oswald's name. Lee Oswald was the sole employee missing from the school-book depository. He was arraigned for Tippit's murder that night but soon he would be charged with JFK's murder as well.[215]

Vice President Johnson had been riding in the motorcade when President Kennedy was slain. Part of the entourage diverted to Parkland Hospital after the shooting, Johnson soon learned that the president was dead. Anxious to secure the new president, the US Secret Service and Johnson's men hustled him out of the hospital and over to the presidential aircraft. Slightly more than two hours after the shooting, Johnson swore the oath of office as president. Federal judge Sarah T. Hughes swore him in as JFK's widow, Jackie, still wearing her blood-stained pink suit, looked on in numb horror. Cecil Stoughton's iconic photograph captured the historic scene for the world to see. Johnson had wanted Mrs. Kennedy in the photograph even though she

6.4 Lyndon B. Johnson takes the oath of office as the 36th president of the United States while the distraught former first lady Jackie Kennedy looks on. Courtesy of Cecil Stoughton, White House Photographs, John F. Kennedy Presidential Library and Museum, Boston.

was still suffering from the shock of watching her husband gunned down beside her, as her presence conveyed a sense of continuity and legitimacy to the new administration.[216]

From the first hours after the shooting, investigators wondered whether Oswald had been part of an elaborate conspiracy to murder the president. The assassin contributed to the controversy when he was paraded before reporters not long after his arrest and claimed that he had not killed anyone. He was a patsy, he said. The medical evidence clearly showed that the head wound had snuffed out the president's life, but the contamination of the body from efforts to resuscitate Kennedy and the subsequent autopsy at Bethesda Naval Hospital made it difficult to determine where the bullets originated. Footage from a homemade film shot by clothing manufacturer Abraham Zapruder showing the moment of impact further muddied the waters when it showed the president's head snapping backward even though Oswald fired his rifle from behind the motorcade.[217]

The *coup de grâce* occurred two days after JFK's death when Oswald died from an assassin's hand. Authorities were transferring him from the Dallas police headquarters to another facility when a local nightclub owner, Jack Ruby, stepped forward with a .38 revolver and fired. Oswald was hit in the abdomen and collapsed. The moment was broadcast live on NBC television and captured in a dramatic photograph by Bob Jackson of the *Dallas Times-Herald*. Transported to Parkland Hospital—the same facility where President Kennedy died—Lee Harvey Oswald died at 1:07 p.m., 107 minutes after he was shot.[218]

Jack Ruby's shady past and his apparent mob connections convinced many Americans that John F. Kennedy's murder was the result of a conspiracy. Oswald's strange comings and goings and his self-professed Marxist ties and pro-Cuba politics suggest that nefarious forces recruited him to take out the American head of state. Another scenario suggests that Oswald was an unwitting participant—either he did not pull the trigger and thus was framed, or he was brainwashed and forced to act against his will when he fired the rifle that day. In any case, according to most conspiracy theories, Jack Ruby was sent to kill Oswald (a "loose end") before the president's assassin could divulge the existence of the conspiracy. Legions of amateur sleuths came out of the woodwork to explain how one or more assassins also fired at the presidential motorcade from the grassy knoll outside of the school book

6.5 In this iconic photograph, cameraman Bob Jackson captured the moment when Jack Ruby shot and killed accused presidential assassin Lee Harvey Oswald. Courtesy of the Library of Congress, World-Telegram photo by Robert H. Jackson.

depository. The puppet-master of the entire performance was portrayed as everyone from Fidel Castro to Nikita Khrushchev to Lyndon Johnson.[219]

Johnson came into the presidency at a moment when many Americans, indeed much of the world population, knew little about him other than that he was a wheeler-dealer from Texas—the very state responsible for the murder of the beloved martyr—who had been a slimy political operative that ruthlessly used his position as Senate majority leader to advance his interests. He understood that he must solidify his position and claim his legitimacy as the nation's rightful president. One way to achieve his goal was to establish a commission to investigate the events leading up to the murders in Dallas and why they occurred. On November 29, 1963, he created the President's Commission on the Assassination of President Kennedy, commonly known as the Warren Commission after US Supreme Court Chief Justice Earl Warren, who chaired the group. Some potential members expressed reluctance to serve, fearing that the commission's investigation would raise as many questions as it answered. Nonetheless, the president insisted, and Lyndon Johnson could be a persuasive man. Aside from Chief Justice Warren, other members included two US senators (Richard B. Russell, Jr., of Georgia and John Sherman Cooper of Kentucky) and two US congressmen (Gerald R. Ford of Michigan, the House minority leader and later vice president and president, and Hale Boggs of Louisiana, the House majority whip). Allen W. Dulles, former director of the CIA, and John J. McCloy, former president of the World Bank, also served.[220]

The Warren Commission spent the better part of a year interviewing witnesses, collecting documents, and sifting through reports on Oswald, his associates, and the president's activities. The final report, numbering 888 pages, appeared in September 1964. Investigators concluded that Lee Harvey Oswald acted alone, as did Jack Ruby. Not surprisingly, the Warren Commission's findings, rather than ending the national obsession with the Kennedy assassination, as it was intended to do, was only the beginning. Three separate government investigations—a panel directed by US Attorney General Ramsey Clark in 1968, the United States President's Commission on CIA Activities within the United States (often called the Rockefeller Commission, after its chairman, Vice President Nelson Rockefeller), and the 1978–79 House Select Committee on Assassinations (HSCA)—reexamined the murder, sometimes agreeing with the Warren Commission report and sometimes taking issue with its conclusions. In the final analysis, as unsatisfying as it may be, no one can definitively say whether Lee Harvey Oswald acted alone in shooting President Kennedy on November 22, 1963, but the overwhelming weight of the evidence suggests that he did.[221]

Although the mystery of JFK's assassination will never be solved to everyone's satisfaction, evidence suggests that the president's killing was far more prosaic than conspiracy theorists believe. When his life is examined closely, Oswald appears to be a classic lone wolf gunman. He was a strange figure hovering around the fringes of organized groups. He may have met with anti-Kennedy figures when he was in New Orleans, Dallas, or Mexico City. His movements and associations were always a bit murky. He may even have resented the Kennedy administration's harsh policies toward Cuba and Fidel Castro. Nonetheless, no credible evidence exists to show his participation in an organized conspiracy.[222]

The overriding concern in Oswald's life—far outranking his Marxist ideology—was his family. He expressed genuine love for his wife and children even if he frequently acted abusive and moody. Counterfactual scenarios are always tricky, but a dispassionate observer can be forgiven for asking the "what if" question. What if Marina Oswald had reconciled with her husband on the evening of November 21, 1963? He probably would not have gathered up his curtain rods and headed into Dallas that day to alter the course of American history. If Lee Oswald somehow could have overcome his personality deficiencies and lived a typical middle class American life, as he sometimes told Marina he wanted, perhaps he would have been content to purchase a small house on a tiny tract of land, buy his wife the washing machine she desired, and revel in the growth and development of his young children.[223]

Lee's pattern of destructive behavior was tied to his personal circumstances. When he felt emasculated or powerless, he acted out his frustration by blaming others. The FBI was responsible for his inability to hold a steady job, not his own abysmal work habits. General Walker was responsible for the anti-Cuban feelings Lee had witnessed and read about. President Kennedy enjoyed the fame and popularity that Lee craved, but could never experience. With his personal life out of control and feeling unable to arrest its decline, Lee Oswald acted out by attacking a public figure in a desperate quest to gain acceptance, recognition, and status.

He was a Type 2 actor. He was not a fierce ideologue, as a Type 1 killer is, despite his insistence that he was a pro-Cuba Marxist. His political leanings were always a bit confused. His desire to kill Kennedy was not because he detested the president's politics. He simply needed to kill a famous man, and John Kennedy was one of the most famous men on the planet in 1963.

He was not a Type 3 nihilist that believes nothing matters. Lee Oswald's case was exactly the opposite. He lashed out violently not because he felt too little. He felt too much. Frustrated and angry that his sad, pathetic life was stuck in a rut, he resolved to change his circumstances by arming against a sea of troubles. He would show everyone that he was special. The way to accomplish this objective was to show them what he could do with a rifle. Gun violence was his prescription for demonstrating how much of an impact he could have on the world.

Oswald was not a Type 4 personality; he did not suffer from hallucinations or altered states of reality. Rational and balanced, but neurotic and emotionally needy, he used a gun to show others what he could do. He could not find the wherewithal to succeed in the normal avenues of human achievement, so he looked elsewhere. He was as far removed from John F. Kennedy as a man could be. Kennedy was handsome, charismatic, rich, famous, and powerful. Lee Harvey Oswald was none of those things. If he could take John Kennedy's life, however, he would earn his own measure of fame and prove to the world that he was somebody.[224]

An objection might be raised that Oswald fled the scene and subsequently denied his involvement in the shootings of Kennedy and Tippit. If he were so desperate for attention, why would he flatly deny his involvement when pressed to explain his actions? Oswald must have recognized that he could not evade capture for long. He had left virtually all of his money with his wife that morning. He had not established a safe house, a reliable means of transportation to effect escape, or a destination outside of Dallas where he could hide. Despite the supposed conspiracy supporting his efforts, Oswald was all alone in dealing with the aftermath of the assassination. Fleeing the building within minutes of the shooting, he surely understood that his absence would be noticed quickly. Running straight to his boarding house where eyewitnesses might see him would invite scrutiny. Riding a city bus away from the scene of the shooting was another odd activity. Entering a movie theatre without paying was yet another action that invited attention. Everything he did suggested that while Oswald sought a temporary reprieve from police custody, he had not planned to hide his identity indefinitely. "Everybody will know who I am now," he reputedly told a police officer when he was apprehended. Indeed, they did.[225]

The honors denied to Lee Harvey Oswald were bestowed on John Fitzgerald Kennedy. The president's body was flown back from Dallas to Washington, DC, and laid in the East Room of the White House for twenty-four hours. On Sunday, November 24, a horse-drawn caisson carried Kennedy to the US Capitol building to lie in state. In the course of eighteen hours, approximately 250,000 people viewed the coffin, some waiting in line for ten hours or longer. Dignitaries from over ninety countries arrived to pay their respects. Following a requiem mass at St. Matthew's Cathedral, JFK was laid to rest in a plot located in Arlington National Cemetery. His widow lit an eternal flame over the slain leader's grave.[226]

In the years since he was cut down at a relatively young age, John F. Kennedy has lived on in popular myth. Countless articles, books, films, songs, and other forms of media recall the president who seemed so full of hope and promise. He is one of the rare public servants to capture the public imagination. To have given so much for his country, even his life, has sustained the myth of the Kennedy presidency as a magical time, an American Camelot. It is likely that JFK is remembered fondly, at least in part, because he died so tragically with so much promise as yet unfulfilled.[227]

Chapter 7

"WHOEVER DIES IN PROJECT PANDORA'S BOX WILL BE DIRECTLY ATTRIBUTABLE TO THE WATERGATE SCANDAL": RICHARD M. NIXON (1974)

On February 22, 1974, bleary-eyed passengers lined up at Baltimore-Washington International Airport to shuffle onto a DC-9 airplane. It was a cold, overcast daybreak. Delta Flight 523 was scheduled to depart shortly after 7:00 a.m., bound for Atlanta, Georgia. For all intents and purposes, it was another routine Friday morning.

Suddenly, as the boarding process commenced, an agitated, heavy-set man appeared in the gate area. Walking up behind a Maryland Transportation Authority security guard, the man whipped open his raincoat, produced a .22-caliber pistol, and shot the guard twice at point blank range. One bullet tore through the officer's back, severing his aorta. The victim, twenty-four-year-old George Neal Ramsburg, never knew what hit him. He instantly fell dead as stunned onlookers recoiled in horror. The gunman did not speak.[228]

The rampage had only begun. In a swift, fluid motion surprising in such an overweight man, the assailant leapt over a security chain and scurried down the jetway, boarding the plane before anyone could react. As he entered the cockpit, the man fired a warning shot. "Fly this plane out of here," he ordered the startled pilots. Frightened flight attendants, recognizing that a crazed intruder was brandishing a gun, fled before they could be shot.

The pilot, Reese (Doug) Loftin, calmly explained that he could not take off until someone removed the wheel blocks from the plane's tires. The explanation drove the gunman into a rage. He pointed his gun at the co-pilot, Fred Jones, and fired a bullet into the man's stomach. "The next one will be in the head," he vowed.[229]

Still furious, the man reached out and grabbed a nearby passenger, a woman. "Help the man fly this plane," he screamed. When he heard an unidentified noise outside the plane, he pushed the woman away and fired two shots, striking Jones in the head and Loftin in the shoulder.

Loftin frantically called ground control, explaining that "this fellow, he shot us both" and declaring, "this is a state of emergency." He relayed the would-be hijacker's demands. "Get ahold of the ramp people and ask the people to come on out to unhook the tug."[230]

Loftin lost consciousness soon after he spoke to the tower officials. Now apoplectic, his face a red mask of fury, the gunman reloaded his .22 and turned his wrath on another passenger. Dragging a woman by her hair from her seat and thrusting her into the cockpit, he told her to fly the plane even though she was not a pilot. Frustrated as his plan unraveled, the man again shot Loftin and Jones. He ordered a flight attendant to close the airplane door or he would blow up the aircraft.

By this time, Anne Arundel County police officers arrived. They could not allow the plane to take off even if someone could be found to handle the controls. Despite their efforts to forge a peaceful resolution, the man would not listen to reason. When it became clear that the hijacker would not be placated, authorities resolved to act decisively to end the standoff.

Officer Charles Troyer, carrying the deceased George Ramsburg's .357 Magnum revolver, took charge, firing four rounds through the window of the aircraft door. One bullet struck the hostage in the thigh. In response to the hysterical woman's pleas, the assailant told her to return to her seat. Seconds later, two more shots flew through the window. Hit in the lower chest and stomach, the gunman fell to the floor. Writhing in pain, he turned the pistol on his right temple and pulled the trigger. As Officer Troyer and armed security personnel stormed through the door, they found a briefcase as well as a gasoline bomb strapped to the dead man's body.[231]

They soon identified the shooter as Samuel Joseph Byck, a forty-four-year-old, 5-foot, 11-inch, 250-pound former tire salesman. He had lived a troubled life. Born on January 30, 1930, to poor Jewish parents in south Philadelphia, Byck dropped out of high school in the ninth grade to help support his family. He floated from job to job before enlisting in the US Army in 1954, when he was twenty-four. He served for two years. Except for a minor AWOL offense, his record was undistinguished and gave no clue as to the turbulence of his later life. He earned an honorable discharge in 1956.[232]

His father died in 1957. In an unusual move, Samuel married a woman less than a month after his father's death, when a Jewish family is still in a period of mourning. By most accounts, his married life was traditional and happy, at least in the early years. He fathered four children—three daughters and a son—and appeared to be a middle-class, marginally prosperous breadwinner. Somewhere as the years passed, though, he lost his way. Samuel found that could not hold a job reliably, while his two brothers were gainfully employed. Their prosperity highlighted Samuel's failures to such an extent that he cut off all contact with his siblings. To a man whose life was spiraling downward, their success was too much to bear.

Arrested in November 1968 for receiving stolen goods, Samuel escaped prosecution when the case was dismissed in May 1969. Determined to get back on his feet financially, he applied for a loan from the Small Business Administration (SBA) so he could finance an operation where he would drive a refurbished school bus to various locations to show off brightly-colored tires. He was certain that his business plan would make him a wealthy entrepreneur.[233]

Yet all was not well. Recognizing that his mental health was deteriorating, Byck voluntarily checked into the Friends Psychiatric Hospital in Philadelphia for two months in 1972. He later described himself as "manic depressive, one of one million others." Despite this statement of apparent self-reflection, Byck did not genuinely believe he was mentally ill. He came to see that other people and forces beyond his control caused his problems.

During the early 1970s, his behavior became increasingly erratic as his chronic unemployment and failing marriage took their tolls on his life. In March 1972, Byck contacted a radical organization, the Black Liberation Army, contributing $500 and truck tires to the group. He sympathized with the plight of oppressed minorities because he, too, saw himself as oppressed. He reserved special vituperation for the Nixon administration, which he believed was corrupt and undermining the United States Constitution.[234]

For many Americans in the early 1970s, President Richard Milhous Nixon served as a symbol of much that was wrong with the country. He had built his early career on red-baiting elected officials and demonizing political enemies. Throughout his long career as a public figure, Nixon relied on demagoguery, capturing the presidency in 1968 by employing a southern strategy that obliquely

7.1 Richard Nixon, 37th president of the United States, inspired enormous animosity during his presidency (1969–1974). Courtesy of the Library of Congress.

appealed to latent racism. He also directed aides to spy on anti–Vietnam War protestors and compiled an enemies list to provide political payback to his opponents. Nothing, it seemed, was beyond the pale for Richard Nixon.[235]

As the rhetoric aimed at the president intensified during the 1972 election season, it did not take much for someone like Samuel Byck to recognize the appeal of a scapegoat. His wife had asked him to move out of the house in 1971. As a consequence, he had lost all semblance of normality in his life. If he could focus his anger and frustration on something or someone outside of himself, he did not have to accept responsibility for his failings or grapple with his own shortcomings. Richard Nixon became the target of his rage. Enthralled by the 1972 presidential campaign, he became an ardent enthusiast for Nixon's Democratic opponent, South Dakota Senator George McGovern.[236]

Unfortunately, Byck carried his support to extremes. The Secret Service first noticed this odd character in 1972 after Byck sent tape recordings to several public figures, including Connecticut Senator Abraham Ribicoff, medical scientist Jonas Salk, and musical composer Leonard Bernstein. He also uttered verbal threats against President Nixon when the SBA rejected Byck's loan request. In his mind, Nixon was directly responsible for the SBA's decision. When Secret Service agents interviewed him on October 16, 1972, however, Byck denied making anti-Nixon statements. An interviewer concluded that Byck was "quite intelligent and well read" and did not find any cause for concern. A psychiatrist who had treated Byck assured the agents that Byck is "a big talker who makes verbal threats and never acts on them."[237]

Although the psychiatrist believed that Byck would never act on his threats, clearly the man admired those who did. Byck was fascinated by news reports of Mark "Jimmy" Essex, who built a sniper's nest on the roof of a Howard Johnson's hotel in New Orleans and killed six people with a high-powered rifle before police gunned him down on January 12, 1973. Byck clipped newspaper articles about Essex and wrote on one clipping, "I'LL MEET YOU IN VALHALLA, MARK ESSEX—OK! SAMUEL BYCK."[238]

January 1973 became a pivotal month. Aside from his obsession with the Jimmy Essex case, Byck resolved to attend Nixon's second inauguration on January 20. On the 16th, he stopped at his estranged wife's house and borrowed her car. Arriving in Washington, DC, before the inaugural festivities commenced, he spoke with police officers about the preparations. For unknown reasons, he departed and drove to North Carolina before he turned and headed up to Long Island, New York, to visit relatives. He returned to Philadelphia sometime around January 22. Alerted that Byck had mysteriously disappeared and then just as mysteriously reappeared, authorities talked with him about his trip. He denied that he had planned to kill President Nixon. In fact, he vehemently assured his interlocutors that his mission in life was to ensure peace and harmony "between the races and peoples of the world." Even Byck recognized that his behavior was irrational and out of control. He checked into Philadelphia General Hospital for observation shortly after his talk with the authorities, but he was immediately released.[239]

Tracing Samuel Byck's activities for the rest of 1973 reveals a man whose mental illness was advancing. With his personal life deteriorating, he was convinced more than ever that he must raise a hue and cry about defects in the world. He wrote an impassioned, if ultimately incoherent, letter to Pennsylvania Senator Richard Schweiker about corruption within the Small Business Administration. Still incensed that the SBA had denied his loan request, Byck thought the senator should look into the obviously nefarious activities within the agency. Byck also penned a cryptic letter to the Israeli consulate containing a map of Egypt with the words "Israelis go home and let my brother alone" scrawled over the area of the Sinai Peninsula. The Secret Service showed up on his doorstep again. Byck explained that he wanted to show the Israelis that he, as a Jew, cared about peace in the Middle East.[240]

When his wife's petition for divorce was granted in September 1973, Byck spiraled downward at a rapid pace. That same month, he picketed outside of the White House displaying signs about Nixon's impeachment. Arrested for picketing without a permit, he inundated the National Park Service with requests for a permit. He appeared near the White House again on November 26 and November 30. Samuel Byck was becoming well-known to the Secret Service. Whether he was a harmless crank or a potential threat was never clear.[241]

In December, Byck's condition became markedly worse. He again wrote to Senator Schweiker. This time, Byck asked for the names of people who had received executive clemency from President Nixon. He also wrote to Senator McGovern objecting to McGovern's vote confirming Gerald Ford as Nixon's new vice president. Observing that the new vice president was Nixon's "echo," Byck wrote, "P.S. From the mind of Ford came Edsels." In the spirit of the Christmas season, he appeared in front of the White House dressed as Santa Claus. Byck occasionally stopped passersby with children to ask what the youngsters wanted for Christmas. He carried a placard reading, "Santa sez 'ALL I WANT FOR CHRISTMAS IS MY CONSTITUTIONAL RIGHT TO PEACEABLY PETITION MY GOVERNMENT FOR A REDRESS OF GRIEVANCE.'" Predictably, he carried another sign urging that Nixon be impeached.[242]

Early in 1974, Byck developed a concept he called "Pandora's Box." The plan reflected his intense antipathy toward the Nixon administration as well as his personal frustrations about his declining fortunes. He was determined to forge a meaning for his life, and he had finally found a way to move forward from his emotional cul-de-sac. In a series of tape recordings, he outlined a scheme to hijack a commercial airliner and crash it into the White House. "I will try to get the plane aloft and fly it towards the target area," he said. "By guise, threats or trickery, I hope to force the pilot to buzz the White House—I mean, sort of dive towards the White House." Byck probably was influenced by Army Private First Class Robert K. Preston, who stole a helicopter and "buzzed" the White House on February 17, 1974, before he was fired upon and forced to land. Unlike Preston, however, Byck did not intend to survive the episode. "When the plane is in this position, I will shoot the

7.2 Samuel Byck, pictured here expressing his outrage toward President Nixon, attempted to hijack an airplane and crash it into the White House in February 1974. Courtesy of Bettmann/Getty Images.

pilot and then in the last few minutes try to steer the plane into the target, which is the White House." Byck justified the operation as a necessary form of punishment for Nixon's crimes. "Whoever dies in Project Pandora's Box will be directly attributable to the Watergate scandals," he said.[243]

It all made sense in his skewed view of the world. If he gave his life in the service of a larger cause, he would be a martyred hero, an important person. He felt that his day-to-day life was a failure. He was chronically unemployed, estranged from his wife and children, and seldom noticed or appreciated unless he was picketing in front of the White House. When he crashed the jet and took out the dastardly Richard Nixon, he would live on in eternity.

Byck had stolen a gun from his only friend, an act which he regretted, but in his tape recordings he explained why it was necessary. He could no longer tolerate "seeing my country being raped and ravished almost before my very eyes. And I won't stand idly by and allow it to happen." The nation needed a hero, and Samuel Byck would be that hero. "They can call me misguided, if they like, but of course being misguided or being guided is only a matter of again, who is interpreting the action and what side of the fence you are sitting on."[244]

Classifying Samuel Byck in a typology of assassins is complicated, although the Type 2 category appears to be the best fit. A case might be made that he was a Type 1 assailant because he objected to the politics of the Nixon administration, and Type 1 actors typically are motivated by strong objections to the target's public policies. Alternatively, he might be seen as suffering from mental illness owing to his paranoia and frequent bouts of depression and psychiatric breakdowns, and thus a Type 4 actor. Those assassins experience cognitive distortion, hallucinations, delusions, and feelings of persecution.

The Type 1 classification assumes that the primary motivation is political. The shooter hopes to effect changes in public policy by engaging in a relatively straightforward political analysis: the target has developed and/or implemented a policy that I find to be highly objectionable. In Byck's case, however, he blamed Nixon for all manner of ills that the president did not cause. Byck was upset because the SBA had not approved his loan application, and he believed that Nixon had influenced the decision. This reasoning was fanciful. He transformed the president into a scapegoat for many social and political problems that Nixon could not control. This sort of muddled reasoning knocks Byck out of the Type 1 category. Whatever objections Byck had with respect to Nixon's policies were tangential to Byck's motives in attempting an assassination.

As for being a Type 4 actor, Byck certainly suffered from mental illness. Yet he was not out of touch with reality. Strange voices or visions did not direct his actions. He was lucid enough to understand that his actions would have consequences.[245]

Samuel Byck tried to assassinate Richard Nixon because he believed the act would give his life meaning. Byck's self-esteem was so low that he thought the only way he could prove his worth was to become an assassin. Like so many people who see themselves as nobodies, he came to see that an act of aggression aimed at a public figure would transform him into a somebody. He was a Type 2 assailant.[246]

Chapter 8

"THE SECURITY WAS SO STUPID. IT WAS LIKE AN INVITATION": GERALD R. FORD (1975)

Gerald Rudolph Ford, as of this writing, holds the dubious distinction of being the only man to serve as president of the United States who was never elected to that office or the vice president's office. He had fashioned a long career as a Michigan congressman when President Richard Nixon tapped him to serve as vice president in October 1973, following Spiro Agnew's resignation. Ten months later, Richard Nixon resigned as president to escape impeachment for his role in the Watergate scandal. As wildly improbable as it appeared, Gerald Ford had become the 38th president of the United States. He was sixty-one years old.[247]

The amiable Ford was neither inspiring nor charismatic, but he had earned a reputation as an open and honest politician in an era not noted for such qualities. At the time Nixon selected him to serve as vice president, Ford had been in public life for almost a quarter century, the last eight as House minority leader. He possessed the right mixture of experience and earnestness to restore public trust at a time of deep division within the nation. Although his decision to pardon Nixon for crimes that Nixon might have committed in September 1974 was controversial at the time, few observers ultimately doubted Gerald Ford's personal integrity.[248]

Yet Ford, despite his bland, wholesome public persona, was not universally beloved. In one incredible month—September 1975—he was the target of two assassination attempts only seventeen days apart. Aside from the proximity of the two attempts, another factor sparked curiosity. The assailants were women. American political assassins as a rule have been men, but the two people who came gunning for Ford were exceptions to the rule.[249]

The first would-be assassin, Lynette "Squeaky" Fromme, was a twenty-six-year-old devotee of notorious cult leader Charles Manson. Fromme was alienated from her family and adrift in the 1960s California counterculture when she stumbled upon Manson on the boardwalk at Venice Beach in 1967. She was immediately enthralled by the messianic Manson's philosophical musings, which mostly consisted of a New Age mysticism based supposedly on free love, doing what feels good, bucking societal expectations, and similar clichés of the era. Past his thin veneer of peace and love, Manson was a petty criminal who had been recognized as a violent, antisocial personality since childhood. By the late 1960s, he was a rock star wannabe who used his strange counterculture personality to entice vulnerable young men and women to join his "family." He briefly hung out with Dennis Wilson, a drummer in the Beach Boys rock group, and became obsessed with the lyrics from the Beatles' 1968 White Album. Manson believed that the lyrics from many songs on the album contained a secret code indicating that an apocalyptic race war would soon erupt.

The family grew violent during the summer of 1969 and initiated a series of gruesome murders, including two notorious home invasions that left seven victims dead—one of whom was the actress Sharon Tate, eight-and-a-half months pregnant—as a testament to the power of a murderous cult leader. Police initially failed to solve the killings, but they tied the Manson family to the crimes after they arrested the members at a desert ranch for other offenses. As investigators interrogated family members and searched for clues, they uncovered an elaborate cult of personality related to Manson. Even after he was convicted of conspiracy to commit murder and sentenced to death—the sentence was later changed to nine concurrent life sentences—Manson commanded allegiance from his devoted followers.[250]

Lynette Fromme was not directly implicated in the murders, so she remained free while Manson and other family members were incarcerated. Known as "Squeaky" because of her high-pitched voice, Fromme appeared innocent, even childlike, but her demeanor was deceiving. She possessed an iron will and ruthless determination. By all accounts, she was fully committed to her family and incensed that criminals such as Richard Nixon walked free and engaged in all manner of mischief while Manson, a Christ-like figure, languished behind bars. During Manson's trial, she and several other family members engaged in bizarre antics, disrupting courtroom proceedings and threatening witnesses. Their actions did not cease even after their leader was carted off to prison to serve out his life tucked away from society.[251]

In the years that followed, Squeaky Fromme never wavered in her devotion to the messiah. Whenever Manson was transferred to a new prison, she moved so she could be closer to him. She lived in San Francisco when he was sent to San Quentin Prison, and she relocated to Sacramento when he entered Folsom Prison in nearby Represa. Aside from physically moving, Fromme kept the faith, never voicing doubts about Manson's warped view of the world or expressing regret for the people hurt and killed by the family. She was investigated for new murders but somehow escaped long-term incarceration. Although she was suspected of having participated in some capacity, evidence was always lacking. In 1971, she served ninety days in jail for attempting to feed a hamburger laced with Lysergic acid diethylamide (LSD) to a witness in the Sharon Tate murder case, but prosecutors could never pin any killings on her.[252]

By 1975, as the nation entered a new era with a new president, interest in the Manson family subsided. To the extent that anyone thought about her, Fromme appeared to be just another relic of that crazy Age of Aquarius, a time that seemed quaint and unfathomable to a new generation on the rise. The Manson family and its escapades dropped from sight.

Yet Squeaky Fromme was determined to live out a second act in her American life. Still residing in Sacramento, she joined with Manson disciples Sandra Good and Susan Murphy to form an International People's Court of Retribution against environmental polluters. In the old days under Manson's tutelage, they had railed against the ill-defined Establishment, but now their focus sharpened. They aimed their rage at corporate executives and their families. The intent apparently was to develop a terrorist campaign forcing large companies to curb their destructive practices. When the plan fell through, Fromme decided that only Manson possessed the necessary grit and determination to carry out the family's schemes.

Focused once again on her mentor and savior, Fromme reached out to California Superior Court Judge Raymond Choate, the presiding officer at the original trial. She began by writing a letter asking that the judge reduce Charlie's sentence. She placed a follow-up telephone obliquely threatening the safety of Judge Choate's family. No one quite knew what to do about all of this. Fromme's appeals for attention fell on deaf ears.[253]

Around this same time, Fromme and Sandra Good sported red robes in a mystical attempt to call attention to Manson's plight. The women told the few in the press who would grant them an audience that they were praying for Manson's release or resurrection, for only he could offer salvation. To make the way for his inevitable return, we must "clean up the earth." The red robes, she explained, "are an example of the new morality. We must clean up the air, the water and the land. They're red with sacrifice, the blood of sacrifice." This sort of New Age mysticism played well in the late 1960s, especially in the aftermath of the Manson family murders when the news media sought to answer the question of why the cult turned to murder. In 1975, the specter of free-wheeling hippies traversing the countryside eager to satisfy their blood-lust by killing random folk in the dead of night seemed so remote as to be a virtual impossibility. Manson was locked up and counterculture types were a dying breed. All this free love gibberish was all so boring. The women failed to garner much press attention.[254]

The possibility of new acts of violence perpetrated by Manson's legion of followers may have appeared unlikely to most Americans, but no one informed the man behind the throne of the changing hour. In the summer of 1975, he increased his correspondence with Fromme as well as the vestiges of his once robust "family." Having witnessed firsthand the declining interest in all things Manson, Fromme understood that he desperately needed a forum to spread his message in a new way. Mystical prognostications and veiled threats were not successful, and so a dramatically altered strategy was necessary. Around this time, she learned that President Ford was scheduled to visit Sacramento. An idea formed, one shared by many presidential assailants. Shooting a president provided the largest forum imaginable for a discontented soul.[255]

Fromme did not hate Gerald Ford. She regarded him as a replica of the hated Richard Nixon, but otherwise was indifferent to the man and his politics. As has happened many times in American history, it was the visibility of his public position and not any specific policy position that drove a would-be assassin to act. Had he not fortuitously appeared in her own backyard at precisely the moment when she was searching for a new means of publicizing Charlie Manson's vitriol, she probably would never have crossed paths with Ford.[256]

But cross paths they did. In September 1975, President Ford was thinking about his reelection campaign. He had announced his candidacy two months prior. As an incumbent president, especially an antidote to the embattled Richard Nixon, who had resigned in disgrace thirteen months earlier,

8.1 In September 1975, two different women attempted to assassinate President Gerald R. Ford, pictured here. Courtesy of the Library of Congress.

Ford enjoyed all the advantages that office-holders possess: widespread name recognition, a reasonably well-established fundraising machine, and an ability to bestow patronage on key constituencies. Yet he faced severe challenges as well. As an accidental president, Ford knew that some Americans questioned his legitimacy. Moreover, his critics lambasted Ford as inept. On his watch, the unemployment rate kept ticking higher—over nine percent that June—and one foreign policy crisis after another emerged. In April 1975, the Asian nation of Cambodia fell to the bloodthirsty Khmer Rouge. That same month, Saigon finally fell to the communists, thus emphasizing the complete failure of American policy in Southeast Asia stretching back to the 1950s. In May, Cambodia seized the US merchant ship *Mayaguez* in the Gulf of Siam, taking the crew hostage. Although Ford sent in the Marines and eventually secured their release after a brief round of fighting, he was enduring a tough period that highlighted his leadership failures. Ford was a nice man who may have been in a job that was too big for him. He couldn't even control his wife. In an appearance on the television news show *60 Minutes* in August, Betty Ford discussed a range of topics that shocked Americans, expressing forthright opinions on extramarital affairs, marijuana use, and the need to legalize abortion.[257]

He came to California that September to address the Host Breakfast, an annual gathering of affluent California businessmen. The event was scheduled for September 5 in the Sacramento Convention Center. The group claimed that California Governor Jerry Brown, a Democrat, had refused to commit to speak; therefore, President Ford, a Republican, was invited as Brown's replacement. The governor later claimed that it was a big misunderstanding. He admitted that he had provided a "dilatory response" to the speaking invitation, but he had intended to participate until the organizers jumped the gun and invited Ford. In any case, Ford was happy to accept. California was the country's most populous state, and he could use its electoral votes to secure his election in 1976.[258]

On the morning of September 5, 1975, President Ford appeared at the Host Breakfast and delivered his prepared remarks. The meeting went as expected. At 9:26 a.m., he returned to his suite in the Senator Hotel on L Street near the state capitol in Sacramento. He had intended to drive over to pay a courtesy call on Governor Brown, but it was a beautiful day. Ford decided to walk.[259]

The Secret Service was already on heightened alert about Ford's California visit. A former convict, Thomas D. Elbert, had called the Secret Service office in Sacramento on August 15 and said, "I'm going to kill your boss, Ford." He was arrested the following day. Elbert had already served five years in prison for having threatened to kill President Nixon. He received a new five-year term as a result of the Ford threat.[260]

Unperturbed, the president started off across the road and into Capitol Park on foot. He shook hands and spoke with people he encountered as he made his way toward the entrance to the state capitol. As he smiled and exchanged pleasantries, Ford noticed a childlike woman dressed in red. It was Squeaky Fromme adorned in her red outfit "for the animals and earth colors." In her pocket she carried a .45-caliber M1911 pistol she borrowed from a Manson family "sugar daddy," Harold E. "Zeke"/"Manny" Boro.

Fromme was standing about two feet from the president, behind a row of people, when she reached into her robe and drew the pistol. She was not able to raise the weapon high enough for a head shot—too many people surrounded her to allow for such precision—but she aimed the barrel at the area between Ford's knees and his waist. The president caught sight of the gun. He later recalled that "as I stopped, I saw a hand come through the crowd in the first row, and that was the first active gesture that I saw, but in the hand there was a gun."

It was the moment of decision. If Fromme's paramount objective was to wound or kill the president, she could have pulled the trigger and been done with it. Yet she did not fire. The pistol contained four bullets, but a round was not in the chamber. Instead, she spoke. Witnesses differed slightly on her wording, but it was something to the effect of, "The country is a mess. This man is not your president."[261]

The hesitation allowed time for Secret Service Agent Larry Buendorf to step in front of Ford. "Gun," he called out as he wrestled with Fromme. "She's screaming," Buendorf explained later. "I've got the gun and I've got her and I'm not letting go so I just pushed her away from the president." It was over in a matter of seconds.[262]

The diminutive young woman was easily restrained and handcuffed. "Easy, guys, don't batter me," she asked of the agents as they whisked her away. "The gun didn't go off." She was incredulous. "Can you believe it? It didn't go off."[263]

8.2 On September 5, 1975, Lynette "Squeaky" Fromme, a follower of the cult leader Charles Manson, attempted to assassinate President Ford in Sacramento, California. She is shown here being escorted by police and Secret Service officers following her capture. Photo by Dick Schmidt/*Sacramento Bee*/ZUMA Press. Courtesy of Alamy Stock Photos.

Held for trial on attempted murder charges, Fromme intended to represent herself. She wanted to use the publicity from the proceedings as the bully pulpit that Manson needed to spread his message. US District Court Judge Thomas J. McBride would condone none of the shenanigans that occurred during earlier trials involving Manson family members. He refused the defendant's request to represent herself, appointing attorneys to act on her behalf.[264]

When she repeatedly disrupted the proceedings, the judge removed her from the courtroom. Each morning, he would ask whether she wished to participate in the trial. When she demurred or mentioned that a fair trial was impossible as long as Manson was behind bars, Judge McBride would order her removed to an adjacent room where she could watch the proceedings on closed-circuit television.[265]

The defense contended that Fromme had never intended to shoot President Ford. The absence of a round in the pistol chamber was proof that she merely wanted to generate sensational headlines to support Manson's cause. Her statement that the gun did not go off was a plea to the arresting officers in hopes that they would not treat her harshly, not a lament over Ford's successful escape from a bullet.

The jury did not believe Fromme's defense. She aimed a loaded gun at the president of the United States in hopes of attracting attention. Shooting the president would have attracted even more attention than attempting to shoot him. Despite her strange, mystical ties to Charles Manson, she had acted on her own free will to kill the president. She was sane, not acting under duress, free of drugs and alcohol, and therefore responsible for her actions. Convicted of the crime, Lynette Fromme was sentenced to serve life in prison.[266]

When she heard the verdict, she screamed "you animals" and hurled herself to the floor. She also threw an apple at the US attorney who prosecuted the case, hitting him and knocking the eyeglasses from his face. All she was doing, she claimed, was arguing for "clean air, healthy water and respect for creatures and creation."[267]

After the trial, Fromme settled down to serve her time, but occasionally she erupted in violence. In 1979, she attacked a fellow inmate with the claw end of a hammer. In 1987, she escaped from a federal prison camp in Alderson, West Virginia, to try and rendezvous with Manson. She had heard that he was suffering from testicular cancer and wanted to see him before he died. Despite her best efforts, Fromme was captured after two days on the lam.[268]

The passage of the years never softened her outlook. She remained as devoted to Manson as she had been when they first met. Paroled on August 14, 2009, she moved to Marcy, New York, and dropped out of sight.[269]

As for Gerald Ford, he recognized that he had escaped a close call. He had almost been another casualty in the political shootings that stretched back into the 1960s. Yet he refused to change his schedule. He was a politician seeking reelection, and he still needed to govern a nation riven by numerous partisan debates and political controversies. Little did he realize, however, that only seventeen days would pass before he again became a target for a female would-be assassin.[270]

Her name was Sara Jane Moore. She was a forty-five-year-old self-styled political radical from a middle class neighborhood in West Virginia. Born Sara Jane Kahn (and called "Sally") in 1930, nothing in her childhood suggested that she would one day shoot a gun at a president of the United States. One of five children, she grew up in a strict, religious family—and consequently was often at odds with her father—but she did not exhibit abnormal behavior.[271]

As a young woman, she ran through a series of would-be professions—nursing student, Women's Army Corps recruit, and accountant among them—and suffered through five marriages, bearing four children. She tried being a housewife and mother, but those roles were deeply unsatisfying. In her view, the American dream of settling down and raising a family in a comfortable middle class home was vacuous and unfulfilling. She seemed to be searching for something to fill a void in her otherwise empty life when she finally decided to throw herself into politics, particularly the radical politics of a specific segment of young people in California during the 1970s. Abandoning three of her children to be raised by her parents, she became an underground radical.[272]

The transition from frumpy, middle-aged housewife to chic activist was not as seamless as she had hoped. She accepted a position working for the People in Need Program (PIN) established by the wealthy Randolph Hearst, son of the legendary newspaperman William Randolph Hearst. Randolph Hearst's daughter, Patty, had been kidnapped by a radical group calling itself the Symbionese Liberation Army (SLA). Patty Hearst's kidnapping initially was aimed at securing leverage to force the release of two radicals from prison. When that plan failed, the SLA instructed Hearst to feed all the hungry people in the San Francisco Bay Area, a demand that would have cost the Hearst family $400 million. Randolph was not the principal heir to his father's fortune and therefore could not afford to meet such an unreasonable demand. Instead, he created the PIN program to feed needy people through a food distribution program. The program never worked well, and the SLA refused to release Patty Hearst.[273]

As for Sara Jane Moore, she labored on with radical young people, but never felt completely at ease. When an agent of the Federal Bureau of Investigation (FBI) attempted to recruit her, she agreed to provide information. She now led an exciting life of danger and intrigue as a federal informant living and working among radicals that might represent a genuine threat to the American polity. After only three months, however, she felt guilty and confessed to her radical friends that she was an FBI informant. Ostracized from her circle of radical colleagues, Moore felt more alienated and freakish than ever before. She vacillated back and forth between providing information to the FBI and embracing her radical clique.[274]

The year 1975 proved to be a propitious. Moore's friend Wilbert "Popeye" Jackson, along with his girlfriend, was shot and killed. Three months later, on September 5, Lynette Fromme tried to shoot President Ford. On September 18, the FBI arrested Patty Hearst, the kidnapped heiress who now appeared to be in cahoots with her captors, robbing banks and engaging in lawlessness. All around her, radicals were living and dying for the cause, and Sara Jane Moore remained paralyzed by indecision. Something had to change.[275]

Through her association with both radicals and the FBI, Moore was known to be a quirky, perhaps unstable individual. The Secret Service had evaluated her earlier in the year, but agents did not believe she posed a risk to the president. She appeared to be a matronly radical wannabe who did not possess the wherewithal to assassinate a public figure. Even when she was picked up for carrying an illegal .44-caliber handgun the day before President Ford visited San Francisco, authorities were not overly concerned about Moore.

Having read about the president's visit, Moore resolved to act. She would prove to her friends within the radical community that she was a true believer. If attempting to assassinate Ford had garnered Fromme enormous headlines for the Manson family, it could do the same for Moore.[276]

On September 22, 1975, the day of Ford's visit, Moore contacted a local gun dealer, Mark Fernwood, and purchased a .38-caliber Smith and

Wesson revolver. She initially told him it was for a friend, to which Fernwood expressed misgivings. When Moore showed up at his home that morning, Fernwood sold her the gun, anyway. As with so many people, Moore's plain, non-threatening appearance deceived him. "Here's a middle-aged woman, a divorcee with a child," Fernwood explained after the shooting. "She is dressed conservatively. There's no way of knowing that she would do an insane thing like that."[277]

Moore later claimed that she did not really want to shoot the president. As she left the gun dealer's house, she deliberately exceeded the speed limit in hopes that the police would stop her. They did not. Instead, she drove to the Union Square parking garage in downtown San Francisco.[278]

Ford was a guest at the famous St. Francis Hotel near a popular city park. Moore milled about in a crowd outside of the hotel, waiting for three hours for her target to appear. She was not alone. A crowd estimated at 3,000 strong surrounded the hotel and spilled into Union Square. A chorus of protesters loudly remonstrated against US policies. Security personnel circulated throughout the crowd. Sara Jane Moore, the plain-looking housewife-type kept her revolver concealed. Because she was not a wild-eyed, mustachioed, strongly-built man, her appearance did not invite scrutiny.[279]

Carol Pogash, a reporter working with the *San Francisco Examiner*, recognized Moore and spoke to her. They had met previously when Pogash was researching a story on the PIN program and Moore was working there. "What are you doing here?" Pogash innocently asked.

Moore responded with what initially seemed to be a non sequitur. "The Secret Service visited my house yesterday," she said. It was an odd comment unless a context can be inferred: *The Secret Service visited my house yesterday, but since they did not detain me today, I am here to shoot the president.* Pogash, of course, had no reason to know of the subtext, and so she wandered away.[280]

Finally, around 3:38 p.m., President Ford appeared in the doorway of the hotel. He acknowledged the crowd and he stepped outside, heading for a nearby limousine. Ford genuinely enjoyed mingling with crowds, and he debated crossing the street to talk with people. Moore could not believe how exposed he was. "The security was so stupid," she subsequently commented. "It was like an invitation."[281]

With her opportunity at hand, Sara Jane Moore, standing forty feet away from the president of the United States with a clear, open line of fire, raised the revolver, aimed, and fired. She could not know as she squeezed the trigger that the sight was slightly off with her revolver. Had the weapon worked as designed, she probably would have struck her target. Instead, she missed. Although the president's forehead was perfectly lined up in her sight, the bullet ricocheted off the hotel wall next to Ford, sending a shower of concrete chips to the ground and slightly wounding a taxi driver, John Ludwig.[282]

While the excited crowd reacted to the sound of gunfire, Moore aimed again, intending to squeeze off a second shot. As luck would have it, an ex-Marine named Oliver Sipple was standing nearby. When he realized what had happened, he acted with dispatch, knocking the woman's hand downward and spoiling her aim. She did not get off a second shot.[283]

Now more familiar with gunshots than he had desired, Ford reacted quickly. He ducked down as Secret Service agents Ron Pontius and Jack Merchant intervened, pushing him to the sidewalk. Moments later, an agent opened the limousine door. President Ford, agents Pontius and Merchant, and Donald Rumsfeld, Ford's chief of staff, piled inside the car. The car sped away with Ford shaken but essentially unscathed.[284]

Across the street, San Francisco police officer Timothy Hettrich witnessed the shooting. "I was five or seven feet away from the suspect," he told the press. "I looked to my left and saw her raise her arm holding the gun, and I saw her fire a round. Then I saw Sipple's hand reach out and push her hand down. I grabbed the cylinder of the gun, took it away."[285]

Despite Hettrich's heft—he was six feet tall and weighed 200 pounds—he found Moore a surprisingly strong adversary. As he desperately tried to wrench the gun from her hand, Moore would not release the revolver. Worried that the assailant would fire blindly and wound bystanders, Hettrich grabbed Moore's thumb and twisted it, which "got her to release the weapon real fast." Within seconds, Secret Service agents converged on the scene, handcuffing the shooter and hustling her inside the St. Francis Hotel. With the onlookers now recovering from the initial shock of hearing gunfire, authorities wanted to ensure that angry citizens did not turn their wrath on the suspect before she could be interrogated.[286]

Questioned inside the Borgia Room of the hotel, Moore refused to reply to police inquiries until someone picked up her son, Frederic, from school. "In another minute, if the president had not come, I would have had to leave to pick up my boy," she said. It was an incongruous statement to be uttered by

8.3 Sara Jane Moore attempted to assassinate President Ford on September 22, 1975, just seventeen days after Lynette "Squeaky" Fromme's assault. Courtesy of Alamy Stock Photos.

a would-be presidential assassin, but much of Sara Jane Moore's chaotic life was incongruous. The Secret Service dispatched an unmarked automobile to retrieve the child. He eventually entered the foster-care system before finding a permanent home with Charles and Gail Roberts, a middle-aged couple that Moore claimed she had known for a decade.[287]

Moore did not express regret for attempting to shoot the president. Her initial reaction was to lament her failure as an assassin. "If I had had my .44 with me, I would have caught him," she casually observed. She may have been correct. When asked if she had planned the crime with others, she assured investigators that "I acted alone."[288]

Moore never adequately explained her motive for shooting at Ford that day. Apart from her amorphous desire to break out of a rut and demonstrate her commitment to radical politics, she could not articulate a reason for her actions. Her ambivalence and disinterest in most political topics suggested that she was motivated by some inner desire to distinguish herself from the pack, to fulfill her own neurotic needs at the expense of everything else.

Deemed mentally competent to stand trial, Moore ultimately entered a guilty plea. Her court-appointed attorney urged her to stand trial with a defense of diminished capacity, but she was adamant. She would accept responsibility for her actions. At her sentencing hearing on January 16, 1976, Moore issued a prepared statement. "Would I counsel anyone to attempt such an assassination? No. Do I think assassination is a valid political tool? Yes. Used selectively and with the purpose clearly and publicly stated, it can be, and has been, very effective." As for her own circumstances, Moore reflected on her ambivalence in shooting at the president:

> Am I sorry I tried? Yes and no. Yes, because it accomplished very little except to throw away the rest of my life, although I realize there are those who think that's the one good thing resulting from this. And no, I'm not sorry I tried, because at the time it seemed a correct expression of my anger and, if successful, the assassination combined with public disclosures of this government's own activities in this area just might have triggered the kind of chaos that could have started the upheaval of change.[289]

Federal District Court Judge Samuel Conti commented that "The only reason the President was not killed was not through any fault of your own; it was the malfunctioning of that gun. Your aim was straight. The gun shot to the right a little bit. If it were a correct gun, you would have killed the man." Accordingly, the judge assigned the maximum penalty. "So it is the judgment of the Court that you be confined to the custody of the Attorney General for the maximum term prescribed by law, and that term is life imprisonment."[290]

The following day, Sara Jane Moore began serving her life sentence. She was initially sent to the Federal Correctional Institutional in San Pedro, California, twenty miles south of Los Angeles. In 1979, while incarcerated at the Alderson Women's Reformatory in West Virginia, she and another inmate worked together to escape over a twelve-foot wall. Their freedom was short-lived. After a night on the lam, both women were rearrested. The escapade added two years and a $5,000 fine onto Moore's prison sentence.[291]

Throughout the years, Moore struggled with life behind bars. She sometimes tangled with other prisoners and guards, landing in solitary confinement. She went on a hunger strike to protest poor prison conditions. She wrote letters complaining of assaults on her dignity, but as the years wore on, she became less active and more accepting of her fate.[292]

Her situation changed early in the new century. Gerald Ford died at the age of 93 on December 26, 2006. A little more than a year later, on December 31, 2007, 77-year-old Sara Jane Moore, after serving thirty-two years of her life sentence, won her parole. She quietly disappeared from public view.[293]

Both Lynette Fromme and Sara Jane Moore were rarities in American history—female shooters. They also can be classified as Type 2 actors. Although both women claimed to act on the basis of politics—Fromme seeking to publicize Charles Manson's skewed world view and Moore to resolve her guilt about working as an FBI informant against the interests of her radical friends—in reality they acted on other motives. Neither person was political in the sense that she sought to remove an elected official because she disagreed with his doctrines or political programs. As with so many would-be killers, Fromme and Moore targeted Ford because he served as president and his appearance was relatively convenient. Had someone else occupied the office, regardless of his politics, and had the president not visited California on two separate occasions in September 1975, the shootings probably would not have occurred.

Type 2 actors seek acceptance, recognition, and attention. Fromme hoped her act would return Manson to the headlines and Moore apparently believed her actions would highlight her radical proclivities. They projected their own needs and desires onto a third party, assuming that their actions in shooting a public figure would alleviate their private sufferings. Type 2 actors set out to prove something to someone, often a significant other that has rejected them or pushed them toward action. Fromme needed to show Charles Manson that she was still a devoted follower and capable of serving him well. Moore needed to rehabilitate herself in the eyes of her radical set. Neither woman was crazy. Fromme and Moore knew what they were doing and they were steadfast in the desire to show the world what they could do. Both women paid a heavy price for their actions.[294]

Chapter 9

"AT LEAST GIVE ME THE CHANCE, WITH THIS HISTORICAL DEED, TO GAIN YOUR RESPECT AND LOVE": RONALD REAGAN (1981)

Sixty-nine days into his first term as president, Ronald Wilson Reagan became the target of an assassin. Struck in the chest by a bullet and badly wounded, the seventy-year-old president might not have survived. It was a close call. Political zealots familiar with Tecumseh's curse grimaced at the thought that another president elected in a year ending in zero stretching all the way back to 1840—William Henry Harrison (1840), Abraham Lincoln (1860), James A. Garfield (1880), William McKinley (1900), Warren G. Harding (1920), Franklin D. Roosevelt (1940), and John F. Kennedy (1960)—might yet die in office. It was not to be. Reagan survived his wound and lived through to the end of his second term in January 1989.[295]

Before he was shot that day in March 1981, Ronald Reagan had lived a charmed life. Born in Dixon, Illinois, in 1911, he was the son of an alcoholic salesman and might have been expected to remain a small-town boy, but he wanted more out of life. Young Reagan eventually landed a job reporting college football games on the radio before heading west to become a B-actor in Hollywood motion pictures. Originally a New Deal Democrat, Reagan changed his party affiliation as he came to view the excesses of liberal politics later in life.[296]

He emerged on the political scene in 1964 after delivering a rousing speech on behalf of conservative Republican presidential candidate Barry Goldwater. The party nominee lost to Democratic incumbent Lyndon B. Johnson in an epic landslide, thus setting back conservatism for years to come, but Reagan's political star was on the rise. Two years later, he was elected governor of California, and reelected in 1970. The affable Reagan challenged President Gerald Ford for the 1976 Republican nomination and came close to winning, but ultimately he could not overtake the incumbent. Yet numerous Republicans experienced buyers' remorse, lamenting that the party had failed to coalesce behind the right man.[297]

The 1976 defeat appeared to be the end of the road for Reagan's political ascendancy. Conventional wisdom suggested that he would be too old for another try in 1980. Yet he defied the odds. In many ways, the boy from Dixon had spent his life defying the odds. He could do it one more time. And so he did, winning his party's nomination and handily defeating the Democratic president, Jimmy Carter, in the general election.[298]

Reagan came into office at a difficult time. The 1970s had been a time of tremendous turmoil for many Americans. Aside from the instability of presidential politics, the economy suffered from stagflation—a stagnant economy that refused to grow at a time of enormous inflation. The Organization of the Petroleum Exporting Countries (OPEC) announced an oil embargo against the United States in 1973, leading to petroleum shortages and a spike in prices, not to mention long lines at the gas pumps. Violent anti-war demonstrations early in the decade gave rise to terrorist attacks on American soil and rising crime rates. The United States had withdrawn from Vietnam at the beginning of 1973, but the fall of Saigon to North Vietnamese communist forces in April 1975 reemphasized the resources that had been expended in the jungles of Southeast Asia for well over a decade. At home, racial tensions elevated. By 1979, post-Vietnam and post-Watergate America appeared enervated by all that had happened in the preceding decade. That same year, during a revolution in Iran, fifty-two American diplomats and citizens became hostages to a group of religious extremists who seized control of the US embassy in Tehran. President Carter commented in a famous speech that the country was suffering from a national malaise. (He never uttered the word "malaise," but the pejorative label became so commonly associated with the speech that he might as well have used it.)[299]

Ronald Reagan, the soon-to-be septuagenarian former movie star with a million-dollar smile, promised to restore the country's prestige to its rightful place. He would end the hostage crisis, rebuild the nation's military might and thereby oppose the Soviet Union, and curb the runway spending of the bloated, overly bureaucratic federal government. With his eternal optimism and his reaffirmation of the promise of America, Ronald Reagan seemed to be exactly what the country needed at exactly the right time, at least to the millions of voters disenchanted with the status quo of the Carter administration.[300]

Yet his term did not start off well. Yes, the hostages returned home on the day Reagan was inaugurated, but he was not personally responsible for the resolution. In those first two months, Democrats bitterly criticized the new president's plans to cut spending for social welfare programs. The nation's economic woes showed no signs of improving. He was sending military advisers to El Salvador, and detractors argued that such a move could be a precursor to another quagmire similar to Vietnam. By the middle of March 1981, Reagan's approval rating had fallen to 59 percent, historically low for a president in the opening months of his administration.[301]

The president doggedly persisted in promoting a conservative agenda. To that end, he frequently appeared before business conventions to promote his vision for America. On March 30, 1981, he appeared at one such event held in the Washington, DC, Hilton Hotel. He had been invited to address an afternoon session of the Building and Construction Trades Department of the American Federation of Labor and Congress of Industrial Organizations (AFL-CIO). It was supposed to be just another speech before just another group in a lifetime filled with these types of speeches. A man with a gun changed all that, making the day one of the most memorable in twentieth-century American history.[302]

During the four-minute limousine ride from the White House to the hotel on March 30, the president chatted with his labor secretary, Ray Donovan, who had addressed the crowd earlier in the day. Donovan warned the president of a potentially hostile audience. With characteristic equanimity, Reagan shrugged it off. "We're used to that, aren't we?"[303]

At 1:50 p.m., the car stopped at the curb. The president walked thirty feet from the limousine to an enclosed passageway leading into the hotel. A crowd of reporters and onlookers stood at a rope line near the entrance hoping to catch a glimpse of the president. One onlooker, John Warnock Hinckley, Jr., had not come to gawk. He had come to kill.[304]

Hinckley was a troubled twenty-five-year-old. The youngest of three, he had grown up as a child of privilege—his father had worked his way up in the oil business and become an affluent, self-made man. During his early years, John, Jr., enjoyed sports and music. He had his share of friends. As

9.1 Ronald Reagan became the target of an assassination attempt on March 30, 1981. Courtesy of the Library of Congress.

he entered adolescence, however, young Hinckley's personality changed. He became moody and withdrawn, spending much of his time hiding out in his room, watching television or listening to music. Although his parents were concerned, they believed he was experiencing typical teenage angst. It was a reasonable assumption, but their son was far too disturbed for that.[305]

He drifted in and out of college. Like so many young people, Hinckley eventually fled to Los Angeles. He resolved to try his hand at songwriting, but unable to make his mark in show business, Hinckley returned to his family's home in Colorado. He could not loaf around the house indefinitely, especially since his older siblings were living more accomplished lives than he. Hinckley's parents finally forced him out of the house when it became clear that he lacked ambition to do anything apart from lie around and write fanciful stories and poems or play his guitar.[306]

Always an avid movie fan, he became obsessed with a popular Martin Scorsese film, *Taxi Driver*. In that 1976 film, Robert De Niro played a character named Travis Bickle, a loner who plotted the assassination of a political candidate. Bickle also rescued a teenaged prostitute from her pimp. The story touched Hinckley, and he saw *Taxi Driver* at least fifteen times, drawing inspiration from De Niro's portrayal of Bickle, who was loosely based on Arthur Bremer, the would-be assassin who shot Alabama governor and presidential candidate George C. Wallace in 1972.[307]

Taxi Driver's protagonist was not the only character to catch Hinckley's attention. The actress who played the film's young prostitute, Jodie Foster, impressed him as an intelligent, down-to-earth, vivacious person—someone he would love to meet. As he obsessed over the young woman, Hinckley read a story in *People* magazine about her decision to leave Hollywood to earn a college degree at Yale University. He knew what he must do. He would make his way to New Haven, Connecticut, and establish contact. Telling his parents that he was enrolled in a writing workshop at Yale, he cashed in stock he owned in his father's company and set out on his quixotic quest to win the actress's heart.[308]

The reality could never match the fantasy. Hinckley had constructed an elaborate scenario where he would rescue Jodie from her drab life just as Travis Bickle had rescued her character in *Taxi Driver*. Increasingly erratic and fixated on impressing his true love, Hinckley became the classic stalker. On the few occasions when she spoke with him on the telephone, the actress sounded alarmed. She did not know this man or his intentions. She finally instructed him not to call again. Rebuffed, Hinckley sank into a deep depression.[309]

He knew that he and Jodie belonged together and eventually seized upon a strategy to impress the object of his affections. He would kill a well-known political figure, perhaps the president of the United States. Travis Bickle had become a political assassin, and he had rescued Jodie on screen. Now John W. Hinckley, Jr., would shoot a political figure and rescue Jodie in real life. It was a perfect plan, and he loved the symmetry of life imitating art.[310]

Alas, the course of true love never does run smooth. Hinckley was arrested on a firearms charge at the Nashville, Tennessee, airport as he tracked President Jimmy Carter's movements during the fall of 1980. Fortunately for Hinckley, the FBI never reported the arrest to the Secret Service, and therefore Hinckley escaped additional charges.[311]

Despite his narrow escape from serious law enforcement scrutiny—or perhaps because of it—Hinckley recognized that his life was spiraling out of control. He returned to his parent's home briefly and submitted to voluntary psychiatric treatment, but the sessions apparently had little effect. Following a brief interlude, Hinckley went back to stalking a political figure.[312]

Carter was no longer suitable. After the president lost the 1980 presidential election, the would-be killer realized that he needed a new target. He considered assassinating Edward M. Kennedy, the Massachusetts senator, but he eventually settled on the incoming president. If Hinckley wanted to call attention to his undying love for Jodie Foster, he needed to take down the biggest target he could find, and a president of the United States is the biggest target available. Anything less would hardly impress a girl of Jodie's refinement and sophistication.[313]

With a firm target in mind, Hinckley traveled to Washington, DC, to carry out his desperate act of love. He did not have to wait long before an opportunity arose. Modern presidents constantly are out and about, mingling with the public and bonding with the people. Reagan was no exception. He traveled widely and delivered numerous speeches throughout his long career. Reading that the president would speak to the AFL-CIO at the Washington Hilton Hotel, Hinckley at last had an action plan. He would show up at the hotel and wreak havoc in the name of love.[314]

In a rambling five-page letter he wrote (but never mailed) to Foster on March 30—the day of the shooting—the young man poured out his heart. "I feel very good about the fact that you at least know my name and know how I feel about you," he confessed. "Jodie, I would abandon the idea of getting Reagan in a second if I could only win your heart and live out the rest of my life with you, whether it be in total obscurity or whatever. I will admit to you that the reason I'm going ahead with this attempt now is because I just cannot wait any longer to impress you." He finished with a melodramatic flourish as only a deeply neurotic person can. "This letter is being written only an hour before I leave for the Hilton Hotel. Jodie, I'm asking you to please look into your heart and at least give me the chance, with this historical deed, to gain your respect and love. I love you forever, John Hinckley."[315]

With his course of action charted and his letter written, he was ready to carry out his plan. Hinckley stepped outside of the Park Central Hotel that afternoon carrying a concealed RG-14 revolver and hailed a taxicab to an area near the Hilton Hotel. He arrived a few minutes before the Reagan motorcade appeared. Hinckley's first order of business was to step inside a nearby Holiday Inn to use the restroom. Afterward, he ambled over to the Hilton Hotel and joined a group of spectators and reporters standing at a rope line outside the VIP entrance. He was just another anonymous warm body sandwiched among other warm bodies congregating near the hotel entrance.[316]

Minutes later, Hinckley experienced an electric bolt of excitement. The presidential motorcade roared up to the hotel and stopped. The car door flew open and there he was, the great man himself. Hinckley felt as though Reagan made eye contact with him when the president stepped from his limousine. Raising his hand to wave, he realized that Reagan had already turned away and was almost inside the hotel. If Hinckley wanted to shoot the man, he would have to wait until the president finished his speech and returned to the limousine. He would have to be patient.[317]

During the interim, Hinckley wandered around the hotel lobby with the gun nestled in his pocket. No one challenged his presence. He eventually returned to the rope line to stand guard. At no time did a security guard or Secret Service man approach anyone in the crowd to ask questions or search their clothing.

When Reagan finally emerged after his speech, everyone gazed at the president. Smiling, Reagan lifted his right arm and waved at the crowd as he

9.2 President Reagan waved to the crowd moments before would-be assassin John W. Hinckley, Jr., began shooting. Courtesy of the National Archives & Records Administration.

walked toward the limousine for his short ride back to the White House. Press Secretary James Brady and Deputy Chief of Staff Michael Deaver accompanied their boss. Secret Service Agent Jerry Parr, garbed in a gray trench coat, followed at the president's elbow.[318]

Realizing that he would never find a better opportunity, Hinckley pulled the revolver from his pocket, crouched, grasped the gun in both hands, and fired. He stood approximately fifteen feet from the president. It was 2:27 p.m.[319]

Eyewitnesses recalled the sounds. *Pop! Pop!* After a brief pause, the sounds continued. *Pop! Pop! Pop! Pop!* In 1.7 seconds, the gunman sent six bullets whizzing toward the crowd of people surrounding the president. His gun emptied, but the man kept pulling the trigger.[320]

Reagan's press secretary, Jim Brady, went down hard. A bullet slammed into his head and sent him to the pavement near Hinckley. The next man hit, police officer Thomas Delahanty, fell with a bullet in his back. "I am hit," he exclaimed.[321]

The third shot flew over the president's head. The fourth hit Secret Service Agent Tim McCarthy in the chest, knocking him to the ground. The fifth bullet struck the bulletproof window of the limousine. The sixth round whisked across the driveway, struck the limousine, and ricocheted.[322]

Within seconds, Secret Service agents and police officers responded, piling onto the gunman in a chaotic effort to wrench the revolver from his grip. Agent Dennis McCarthy later said he heard a "pop, no louder than a firecracker," and he instantly knew what was happening. After the third shot erupted, he saw the gun and headed toward the shooter. After the gunman had dropped his weapon, McCarthy understood that his duty had changed. With the assailant effectively immobilized, the task was to ensure the man's safety. The Secret Service did not want another Lee Harvey Oswald. No one knew whether this incident was part of a conspiracy; it was imperative that the gunman be kept alive for questioning.[323]

In the first minutes after the shooting, accurate information was lacking. Initially, Reagan did not think he had been struck. Secret Service agent Jerry Parr had shoved the president inside the limousine when the shooting started. As the two men rode away from the scene, the agent asked if Reagan was hit.

"I don't think so," Reagan replied. Still, he felt tremendous pain. "I think you hurt my chest when you landed on top of me."

Parr thought the president might have broken a rib and should be taken back to the White House for treatment. If the shooting was part of a conspiracy—and no one knew for sure what was happening, or why—the president would be safe in a secure location. The White House medical staff could handle a minor wound.[324]

Parr's decision changed as soon as he saw blood on Reagan's lips. The agent instructed the limousine driver to divert the car to George Washington University Hospital. Time was of the essence.[325]

To his credit, Reagan understood that the shooting of an American president was a traumatic event—not only for him, but for everyone across the globe. He was a product of Hollywood, and he understood the optics of the situation. As word spread of the assassination attempt, citizens would recall John F. Kennedy's murder and turn to their television sets for information. If they saw film of Reagan splayed out on a gurney as he was wheeled into the hospital, they might panic. The repercussions for American citizens, government agencies, allies, enemies, and even the stock market would be enormous, and potentially calamitous. To forestall such damage, he decided to walk into the hospital without assistance.[326]

It was a gutsy, cinematic move. Agent Parr thought, "I guess he wants to be a cowboy," and no doubt Reagan, always enamored of American westerns, sought to play the role of the brave hero. It was a purely unscripted, inspired moment in a highly-scripted presidency.[327]

It played out exactly as the president had foreseen. Reagan somehow stumbled into the hospital entrance on wobbly legs. The hospital door closed behind him, allowing him to abandon the public façade. Within seconds, he collapsed. Hospital staff guided him onto a gurney and headed into a trauma room for examination. Doctors soon realized that a bullet had ricocheted off the limousine and struck the president in the side of his chest. The slug rested an inch from his heart.[328]

The American public did not learn until much later how close Reagan came to dying that day. He lost half the volume of blood in his body. Only Agent Parr's quick thinking and the skills of the trauma team saved the president's life.[329]

Reagan played the part of a wounded lion to perfection, joking with doctors, nurses, and his staff despite his dire condition. Echoing a line from a movie, Reagan told his frantic wife, Nancy, who had raced over from the

White House when she learned of the incident, "Honey, I forgot to duck." Shepherded into the hospital room, Reagan said to surgeon Joseph Giordano and his staff, "I hope you are all Republicans!" The doctor assured Reagan that everyone was a Republican that day.[330]

In the meantime, Jim Brady, Reagan's press secretary, suffered a grievous head wound. He underwent surgery and barely survived. He lived until August 4, 2014, but he suffered permanent neurological and motor damage. He and his wife, Sarah, became proponents of gun control, and the 1993 law that limited certain types of assault weapons and required background checks for gun purchases bore his name. The two other men wounded that day, Officer Delahanty and Secret Service Agent McCarthy, recovered completely.[331]

The initial questions centered on what happened, and why. After interrogating Hinckley and sifting through the items he left in his hotel room, including his diary, investigators realized that an assassination conspiracy did not exist. Hinckley was the classic lone wolf, an alienated man who acted for reasons of his own. He did not hate Reagan or the president's politics. He sought to impress an actress by undertaking a grand, sweeping act of such audacity that she would know he was a devotee. Judging by his earlier interest in President Carter and his brief infatuation with Senator Edward M. Kennedy, Hinckley did not much care about the identity of his target. His goal was to call attention to his neurotic fixation on Jodie Foster.[332]

Based on his behavior, John Hinckley, Jr., appears to have been a Type 2 shooter. He acted for neurotic reasons, not political purposes. His need for acceptance, recognition, and status—at least from Jodie Foster—was fierce. As James W. Clarke observed in his book *American Assassins*, a Type 2 actor always has at least one significant other in his life, and the rejection or indifference of the significant other drives the shooter to act. Clarke wrote that a Type 2 actor is "an anxious, emotional, and ultimately depressed person who is primarily concerned with his or her personal problems and frustrations and only secondarily with causes or ideals."[333]

Complicating an analysis of Hinckley's motives is the thorny question of his state of mind. Typically, a Type 2 actor, for all of his depression and neurotic tendencies, is sane in the sense that he recognizes the nature of reality. He does not hear imaginary voices urging him to act. He does not believe he can fly. In short, he does not suffer from severe cognitive distortion.

9.3 John W. Hinckley, Jr., was booked for attempting to assassinate President Reagan on March 30, 1981. Courtesy of the United States Federal Bureau of Investigation.

By this definition, Hinckley was sane when he shot at President Reagan. He knew what he was doing and he understood that there would be repercussions. Nonetheless, he chose to act, as he explained in his letter to Jodie Foster, "because I just cannot wait any longer to impress you." The act, he believed, was his last opportunity to win the woman of his dreams. [334]

Prosecutors charged John Hinckley with thirteen criminal counts and put him on trial. In June 1982, a jury found him not guilty by reason of insanity on all charges. Psychologists and psychiatrists for the defense determined that he suffered from an unspecified psychotic disease as well as narcissistic personality disorder. His attorney contended that he suffered from schizophrenia as well. Hinckley was confined to St. Elizabeth's Hospital to be treated for mental illness. [335]

It was never clear to many Americans that John Hinckley suffered from a mental defect. In fact, public outrage at the verdict forever changed the way that federal courts and law enforcement agencies determine the legal standard for mental illness. In the Insanity Defense Reform Act of 1984, passed in response to the Hinckley verdict, Congress shifted the burden of proof from the prosecution to the defense, requiring the defendant to demonstrate through clear and convincing evidence that he was insane and was "unable to appreciate the nature and quality or wrongfulness" of his act.[336]

Despite this change in the law, John Hinckley was prosecuted under the older legal rules on insanity. He was sentenced to remain in a psychiatric hospital as long as he remained a threat to himself or to others. During his decades of confinement, he settled into a routine of playing his guitar and composing songs. He showed little emotion about his crime or its aftermath.[337]

In 1987, he petitioned the court to allow home visits, but the court denied the petition when investigators found photographs and letters in his hospital room indicating his continued fixation on Jodie Foster. Hinckley also had exchanged letters with serial killer Ted Bundy. Evidence suggested that he had requested the address of cult leader Charles Manson.[338]

By 1999, Hinckley was allowed to leave the hospital for brief, supervised visits with his family. The following year, he was allowed to enjoy unsupervised visits. Hospital staff revoked the privileges after they discovered evidence of his ongoing obsession with Jodie Foster, but the home visits resumed again in 2004 and 2005. The duration of the visits grew progressively longer until Hinckley won his release from the hospital in September 2016.[339]

As for Ronald Reagan, the shooting made him a wildly popular political figure. He emerged from the hospital twelve days after the episode and returned to the White House. On April 25, he held a cabinet meeting. On April 28, he addressed a joint session of Congress and was met with a standing ovation even from Democratic members. He had been struggling to find his way before Hinckley arrived at the Hilton Hotel that day. Afterward, Reagan's popularity skyrocketed. He became almost a mythic figure to many Americans, for he had faced the possibility of death with grace and wit. He was to endure many highs and lows during his tenure in office, but Reagan engendered tremendous good will as a result of his reaction to the shooting. Even events such as the Iran-Contra affair during his second term, which might have decimated another presidency, only marginally diminished his good standing with the public.[340]

Ronald Reagan retired from the presidency in January 1989, a month before his seventy-eighth birthday. During the 1990s, he was diagnosed with Alzheimer's disease, a degenerative condition that robs the afflicted of their memories and, to some extent, their identity. In his final public act, he issued a farewell letter to the American people in November 1994. "I now begin the journey that will lead me into the sunset of my life," he president wrote. "I know that for America there will always be a bright dawn ahead." Reagan died on June 5, 2004.[341]

PART III

TYPE 3 ACTORS

Chapter 10

"I HAVE THE GUN IN MY HAND. I KILL KINGS AND PRESIDENTS FIRST AND NEXT ALL CAPITALISTS": ANTON CERMAK (1933)

On February 15, 1933, Giuseppe Zangara, an Italian immigrant, fired gunshots at President-elect Franklin Delano Roosevelt, who rode in an open car near Bayfront Park in Miami, Florida. Roosevelt was not hit, but five other people were, including Chicago mayor Anton Cermak. Of those struck, two people died, including Cermak, who lingered for nineteen days before his death. Zangara was executed for the crime.[342]

Little is known of Zangara's early life. He was born in Ferruzzano, Italy, on September 7, 1900. He lived there until he and an uncle, Vincent Cafaro, sailed to the United States on the ship *Martha Washington* in August 1923. His childhood apparently left him alienated and bitter. His mother died when he was two years old and his father remarried shortly thereafter. Zangara's stepmother had six daughters, and the family was impoverished. He grew to adulthood feeling as though he was a stranger in his own family, little noticed or appreciated.

The most traumatic event occurred when the boy was six years old. Citing the need for money to support the large family, Zangara's father removed Giuseppe from school and put him to work. After he was arrested, he described his anger at his father for denying him an education and a chance for a better life. "I was two months in school," he said in his rudimentary English. "My father came and take me out like this [gesturing] and say, 'You don't need no school. You need to work.' He take me out of school. Lawyers ought to punish him—that's the trouble—he send me to school and I don't have this trouble. Government!" In Zangara's opinion, the need to scratch out a living, which was brought on by the brutal demands of a government based on capitalist principles, was directly responsible for his plight.

Apart from his lack of formal education, Zangara suffered from poor health, developing stomach problems as a child. They plagued him all of his life. He blamed the hard physical labor he endured as the cause of his malady, which meant that a corrupt capitalist government, because it caused his father to deny him a quality education and decent health care, ultimately destroyed his health. The tenuous connection between Zangara's problems and the specific policies and practices of the government apparently never occurred to him.[343]

A diminutive young man—he stood barely five feet tall and weighed about 105 pounds—Zangara was easy to ignore. He became moody and withdrawn, an invisible person. At the age of sixteen or seventeen, he enlisted in the Italian army, probably to escape from his father's discipline. He served during World War I in the Tyrolean Alps, but little is known of his military record or his experiences. He returned home to work various menial jobs. He later explained that he had mulled over the possibility of assassinating Italian King Victor Emmanuel III, but nothing came of the scheme.[344]

Italy during the post–World War I years was filled with strife and turmoil. The economy was devastated by the war, resulting in massive layoffs in the industrial sector and political unrest. By 1922, when Benito Mussolini and his Fascists seized power, working people had reached the end of their tether. Il Duce promised to restore Italy's pride and improve the condition of the working classes, but the violence that accompanied his rise did little to assuage the fears of persons who were not ardent Fascists.

So Zangara and his uncle left the country, bound for America and the promise of a better life. They arrived in Philadelphia on September 2, 1923. With the death of President Warren G. Harding a month earlier and the accession of Calvin Coolidge into the White House, the Roaring Twenties were off and running. It was a time when many men and women, both native-born and immigrants, enjoyed increased employment opportunities and the accompanying material successes provided by a booming economy.[345]

With his lack of education, inability to speak the English language, and his poor social skills, Giuseppe Zangara did not improve his lot in the land of milk and honey. He remained mired in poverty, still suffering from his stomach ailment. Nonetheless, he struggled to make the best of a terrible situation.

He worked as a bricklayer in Paterson, New Jersey, sharing a room with his uncle. He typically earned $14 a day, a decent wage for a laborer at the time. Living frugally and saving his money, Zangara was not living the American dream, but he had hopes for a brighter future.[346]

His hopes came crashing down when his uncle married, and the new bride, not caring for her nephew-in-law, insisted that Zangara vacate the premises. Having severed his last human connection, the young man was lost in the world. By all accounts, he had no friends, romantic relationships, or familial ties. Whatever hopes and desires he entertained, he entertained them alone. With nothing or no one to give his life meaning, Zangara seldom strayed from his room when he was not working. Instead, he brooded over his health, eventually having his appendix removed in 1926. He thought the operation would ease his pain and improve his life, but it did not. In hopes that a warmer climate would prove to be an effective tonic to his ailments, he moved to New Orleans the following year. When that plan failed, he returned to New Jersey and resumed his life as a laborer.[347]

During the late 1920s and early 1930s, as much of the nation reeled in the aftermath of the great stock market crash, Zangara appeared unperturbed. He traveled to California, Panama, and Florida. Because he did not correspond or associate with anyone, he left no record of what he did on those trips.

Zangara returned several times to Miami, presumably to enjoy the warm weather. He also found numerous betting opportunities in Florida. By February 1933, Zangara was living in Miami full-time, and was virtually destitute. With no prospects on the horizon, he grew increasingly bitter about his life. He resolved to lash out at the cause of his sorrows. Although he was not a political man and knew little or nothing of national affairs, Zangara picked up bits and pieces from his acquaintances. He heard that President Herbert Hoover had triggered the Great Depression, which caused untold suffering to working men and women. If anyone was to blame for Giuseppe Zangara's desperate predicament, it was Herbert Hoover. He must be made to pay.[348]

On Monday, February 13, Zangara strolled into Davis's Pawn Shop on Miami Avenue and bought a .32-caliber handgun for $8. He planned to buy a bus ticket for Washington, DC, and search for an opportunity to get close enough to President Hoover to use his newly acquired purchase to good effect. Having a purpose in life and acting on his plan allowed him a measure of control over his fate that had been missing for years.[349]

Before he bought the bus ticket, Zangara read a newspaper story about a visit from President-elect Franklin D. Roosevelt. FDR was coming to Miami the next day and promised to appear in Bayfront Park to address an expected crowd of people. Zangara recognized a prime opportunity to effect his plan with minimal inconvenience. Why spend the time and money to travel to Washington, DC, to assassinate the sitting president when the man who was slated to take office in less than a month would be in the neighborhood? Zangara was not personally upset at Herbert Hoover. He was simply trying to eliminate a symbol of the government. Roosevelt would do just as well as Hoover. As Zangara later told his interlocutors, "Hoover and Roosevelt—everybody the same."[350]

FDR was scheduled to swear the oath of office as the thirty-second president of the United States in seventeen days. He was enjoying an eleven-day Caribbean cruise on his friend Vincent Astor's 263-foot yacht, christened the *Nourmahal*, before assuming the burdens of the presidency, his one last, brief respite before he was no longer a private citizen. The plan was for the ship to dock in Miami on February 15. From there, the president-elect would be whisked over to Bayfront Park to deliver brief remarks before an expected crowd of between 10,000 and 20,000 people attending the annual American Legion encampment. To disguise his leg braces, Roosevelt would sit on the top of the back seat of an open-air automobile. All Zangara would need to do would be to position himself either at the dock when the boat arrived or in the park close enough to elbow himself up to the car and fire off as many shots as possible before police and security personnel could tackle him.[351]

The plot did not go as Zangara had expected. He could not find a spot close to the dock, and so he missed the president-elect when the *Nourmahal* arrived. Trailing the crowd into the park, he grew frustrated by the mass of people crammed into a tight space. Because he was barely five feet tall, Zangara could muscle his way through the throngs only with great difficulty. To make matters worse, Roosevelt's speech lasted only two minutes. It was a welcoming oration more than a genuine political speech. The would-be assassin had been convinced that politicians would yammer on at great length. The abrupt end meant that Zangara had missed his prime opportunity to shoot the president-elect.[352]

Dignitaries gathered around the car to speak with Roosevelt at the conclusion of his remarks. It would be only a matter of minutes before the greetings ended and the automobile lurched out of the park. If Zangara intended to carry out his scheme, he had to act fast.

Unable to see above the people ahead of him, he found a chair. Stepping up to peer over the other onlookers at a distance of forty feet from Roosevelt, Zangara whipped out his .32 and squeezed off five shots. A woman standing nearby, Lillian Cross, saw a man with a gun and reached out to hit his arm with her handbag. Perhaps as a result, the shots missed hitting FDR, although others were hit. Mrs. Joseph (Mabel) Gill, wife of the president of Florida Power & Light, was seriously wounded. William Sinnott, a detective traveling with Roosevelt, felt a bullet crease his head. A Miami resident in the crowd suffered a nicked scalp. A New Jersey native was struck in the hand. Chicago Mayor Anton Cermak, fifty-nine years old, had been standing on the car's running board and speaking to Roosevelt when the shooting commenced. Struck in the chest, he staggered and fell.[353]

Cermak had served as Chicago's mayor since 1931. Although he and the president-elect publicly claimed to enjoy a warm relationship, their association had suffered after the mayor assisted Al Smith, the 1928 Democratic Party nominee, in trying to wrench the nomination from FDR in 1932. Now that Roosevelt was poised to assume high office, Cermak had traveled to Miami to play nice and assure the new president of his fidelity.[354]

While others screamed and frantically sought cover when the shooting began, Franklin Roosevelt kept calm. At no time did he panic or outwardly exhibit concern for his safety. Raymond Moley, a Columbia University political scientist who spent time advising FDR on prison reform, was on hand to witness Roosevelt's reaction immediately following the assassination attempt. He found the man unflappable. "FDR had talked to me once or twice during the campaign about the possibility that someone would try to assassinate him," Moley wrote. "To that extent, I knew, he was prepared for Zangara's attempt." Still, public figures sometimes talk about death in a cavalier fashion, but they succumb to paralyzing fear when the bullets fly. As Moley noted, "it is one thing to talk philosophically about assassination, and another to face it. And I confess that I have never in my life seen anything more magnificent than Roosevelt's calm that night."[355]

FDR did not dwell on the possibility of death by a determined gunman, but he knew it was a risk he must take to serve as the nation's chief magistrate. His version of events was low-key and devoid of histrionics. "I heard what I thought was a firecracker; then several more," he wrote of the incident. "The chauffer started the car." Prepared to race away from the danger, the driver halted when FDR instructed him to stop. "I looked around and saw Mayor Cermak doubled up," the president-elect recalled. He ordered that the mayor be loaded into the car and taken to a nearby hospital. Roosevelt's men complied at once.[356]

Cermak reputedly looked up at the president-elect either during the car ride or shortly after entering the hospital and uttered a classic line: "I am glad it was me instead of you." A reporter printed the comment in the newspaper, where it was picked up and widely circulated, entering the annals of American folklore. The phrase was even carved onto Cermak's tombstone, although most scholars doubt whether the mayor actually uttered the remark.[357]

As he rode the train back to New York days later, Roosevelt wired his gratitude to Lillian Cross for deflecting the shots. "How much greater and sadder a tragedy was averted by your unselfish courage and quick thinking of course no one can estimate. It now appears that by Divine Providence the lives of the victims of the assassin's disturbed aim will be spared."[358]

Alas, Roosevelt was too quick to praise divine providence. The mayor lingered in Miami's Jackson Memorial Hospital for nineteen days after the shooting, but he never recovered. He died on March 6. His personal physician later attributed Cermak's death to ulcerative colitis. The mayor probably would have recovered from the bullet wound itself, but the combination of the shooting and the disease was too much. Mabel Gill died of her wounds as well.[359]

As for the shooter, Zangara did not try to escape. Police officers immediately arrested him and transported him to the nineteenth floor of Miami's city hall building. The Dade County sheriff, prosecutors, and FBI agents arrived and interrogated the prisoner. As with any shooting aimed at a high-profile target, the interrogators wanted to know whether the gunman was part of a wider conspiracy. When questioned on whether he had enlisted accomplices in his plot, Zangara assured investigators that he was a loner, which did not take long to confirm. In fact, he was a nihilist in the sense that he was so disgusted with the world and his life that nothing mattered to him anymore. Suffering from chronic pain, with $43 in his pocket, and with no clear future ahead, he had nothing to lose by shooting at Roosevelt.[360]

When pressed to reveal his motives, Zangara spoke matter-of-factly about his designs on the president-elect. "Because the President—rich

10.1 Anton Cermak served as mayor of Chicago from 1931 until his death. He was shot on February 15, 1933, and died nineteen days later. Courtesy of the Library of Congress.

people—capitalists—spoil me when I'm six years old," he said. He confessed that he bore Roosevelt no ill will: "As a man I like him all right." His motive for firing a gun into a crowd, he said, was because the he wanted to hit Roosevelt. The individual mattered not to the gunman. In his view, one leader was the same as another: "President—always the same bunch." He said he did not know Mayor Cermak and had never visited Chicago. He did not intend to harm him. "I just went there to kill the president."[361]

Despite no clear evidence of a conspiracy, a rumor circulated that Zangara, as an Italian immigrant, was an anarchist or associated with the Black Hand, an infamous terrorist group best known as the instigator of the assassination of Archduke Franz Ferdinand, the event that triggered the First World War in 1914. Some stories suggested that Cermak had been the intended target because, as mayor of Chicago, he was trying to clean up the rampant corruption that had produced gangsters such as Al Capone. As the FBI pursued the leads, they encountered persons who claimed to have seen or heard Zangara associate with nefarious confederates who voiced anti-Roosevelt sentiments or wished to eliminate the Chicago mayor. All the supposed leads failed to yield a scintilla of credible information. Investigators concluded that Zangara was exactly what he appeared to be—a loner acting on his anger against the world of unnamed government officials and capitalists who had wrecked his life.[362]

The shooter made no effort to rationalize his actions or hide his guilt. In one astonishing exchange with his interrogators, Zangara bluntly offered that "I have the gun in my hand. I kill kings and presidents first and next all capitalists." He was unapologetic.

Five days after the event, he was hustled into a Dade County courtroom to face charges on four counts of attempted murder. He entered a "guilty" plea on all counts. His court-appointed defense attorneys wanted to explore an insanity plea, but their client would not hear of it. "My client has insisted on his guilt," the head attorney exclaimed. "He scoffs at the idea that he may be insane."[363]

To no one's surprise, Judge E. C. Collins sentenced Zangara to four twenty-year terms for the shootings. Far from expressing remorse for his actions, the defendant defiantly challenged the judge to increase the penalty. "Don't be stingy," he shouted. "Give me more—give me one hundred years."[364]

At the time of the original sentencing, Cermak and Gill, the two most grievously wounded victims, had not yet died. The judge told Zangara that he could face the death penalty if either or both perished. The defendant shrugged. "I no care. I sick all the time. I just think maybe cops kill me if I kill President. Somebody hit my arm when I try it."[365]

Following Mayor Cermak's death on March 6, prosecutors filed a first-degree murder charge on the theory of transferred intent. Zangara intended to kill someone—Franklin Roosevelt—but he accidentally killed someone else. The *mens rea* (guilty mind) existed and was sufficient to allow the judge to impose capital punishment. Circuit Judge Ely O. Thompson accepted Zangara's guilty plea on the new charge and told the defendant that he would die in Florida's electric chair.

The death sentence brought an angry response from the guilty man. "You give me electric chair," he snapped at the judge. "I'm no afraid that chair. You're one of capitalists. You is crook man, too. Put me in electric chair. I no care."[366]

True to his word, Giuseppe Zangara went to his death in Old Sparky, the electric chair located in the Florida state prison in Raiford, on March 20, 1933, unrepentant and apparently unafraid. In an astonishingly short

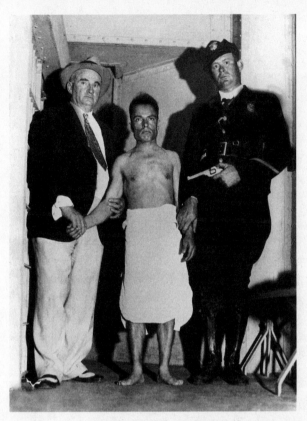

10.2 Giuseppe Zangara, an Italian immigrant, shot Chicago Mayor Anton Cermak, although President-elect Franklin D. Roosevelt probably was the intended target. Zangara (center) is shown here flanked by law enforcement officers shortly after his arrest. Courtesy of the Library of Congress.

time—thirty-three days after he shot at Franklin Roosevelt in Bayfront Park—he entered the legal system, offered his guilty pleas, received his sentence, and surrendered his life.

Strapped into the electric chair, Zangara bitterly denounced the "lousy capitalists" who would kill him as punishment for his crimes. The executioner slipped the shroud over his head, but Zangara was not quite finished. "Go ahead," he exclaimed, "push the button." He died without a single friend, family member, or loved one to offer him comfort or bear witness to his passing.[367]

As for the man he sought to kill, Franklin Roosevelt arrived for his inauguration in Washington, DC, on Saturday, March 4, 1933. It was a dreary,

10.3 Franklin D. Roosevelt (right) is shown on inauguration day, March 4, 1933, with the outgoing president, Herbert Hoover, just seventeen days after Giuseppe Zangara shot Chicago Mayor Anton Cermak. Cermak died two days after FDR's inauguration. Courtesy of the Library of Congress.

overcast day and the outgoing president, Herbert Hoover, barely spoke to him. Their ride in an automobile from the White House to the US Capitol was brief and uneventful. Roosevelt stepped into office at one of the most critical junctures in American history. The Great Depression had decimated the global economy, and fascism was on the rise in Europe. The nation's future looked bleak as the incoming executive set about offering a New Deal to the American people. FDR would enjoy a storied presidency for a dozen years, the longest in American history, until his death from a cerebral hemorrhage on April 12, 1945. If Giuseppe Zangara had succeeded in his quest to kill the president-elect, the Roosevelt administration would never have been born.[368]

Zangara's actions suggest that he was a Type 3 actor, although an argument can be made that he properly belonged in the Type 2 category or possibly in Type 1. A Type 1 actor, however, feels compelled to assassinate a public figure because he vehemently disapproves of the figure's ideology or public policy. By his own admission, Zangara did not hold a grudge against Franklin Roosevelt or the man's politics. He probably would have been hard pressed to summarize Roosevelt's political philosophy or even name any of his policy promises. In Zangara's view, one president was exactly the same as another. He was striking out against a symbol of the corrupt political and economic systems that had caused his health and educational problems. Yet Zangara did not understand how those systems worked. As far as he knew, capitalism (an economic system) and a republic (a political system) were one and the same. He did not object to specific policies because he understood nothing about public policy.

As for a neurotic Type 2 actor who seeks to compensate for a personality flaw by showing the world—and especially a real or imagined loved one—that his life has value, Zangara did not direct his act toward someone else. Lee Harvey Oswald, President John F. Kennedy's assassin, was proving to his wife, Marina, that he, Lee, could take action in the world and influence the course of world events. When he shot President Ronald Reagan, John W. Hinckley, Jr., was demonstrating to Jodie Foster that his life was valuable and that his love for her was real. Zangara, by contrast, had no one to impress, no one to show what he could do. He lashed out at a public figure because he had reached the end of the road and had nothing left to lose.

The Type 3 actor is a nobody without any hope of ever becoming a somebody. Earlier in his life, he might have struggled to find meaning, but by the time he takes up arms against his sea of troubles, he has lost hope. The world is meaningless, and the Type 3 actor has wallowed in its meaninglessness long enough. Because he is miserable with no end of the misery in sight, he will share the misery by assaulting a public figure. Killing a famous person probably will not alleviate his suffering, but at least it will resolve his existential crisis, albeit temporarily. In a strange way, assailing a public figure tells a Type 3 actor that he is still alive and, perversely, he functions as a rational actor in an irrational universe.[369]

Chapter 11

"LOOKING BACK ON MY LIFE, I WOULD HAVE LIKED IT IF SOCIETY HAD PROTECTED ME FROM MYSELF": GEORGE C. WALLACE (1972)

On Monday afternoon, May 15, 1972, Alabama Governor George Corley Wallace appeared at a shopping center in Laurel, Maryland, to address a crowd of supporters congregating to hear the presidential candidate speak. It was the kind of appearance that Wallace had made many times throughout his political career. Known as a conservative firebrand who dished out vitriolic rhetoric condemning an out-of-control federal government, a lax criminal justice system, and the fear of ascendant ethnic and racial minorities, Wallace was a master at playing on people's fears of a changing America. This was supposed to be another stop in a long list of stops for the energetic demagogue. He briefly considered cancelling the event—he had been heckled at a previous appearance and he was tired—but he persevered. As Wallace would soon learn, this campaign stop was anything but ordinary.

He had been worried about threats to his life. Ever since his emergence on the national scene as a proponent of state rights and white supremacy during the early 1960s, Wallace had attracted attention among fringe figures on both the left and right of the political spectrum. Now, as he campaigned to secure the 1972 Democratic presidential nomination, he was more prominent than ever. With strong primary showings, Wallace recognized that he might win his party's nomination and advance to the general election to challenge the perennially unpopular incumbent, President Richard M. Nixon. The vocal southern populist from the Southland could not be ignored.[370]

With his growing notoriety came growing worries. No one familiar with American politics during the preceding decade could forget the assassinations of JFK in 1963 or RFK in 1968, as well as the murders of Malcolm X in 1965 and Dr. Martin Luther King, Jr., in 1968. Fearful that a crazed assassin might assault him, Governor Wallace typically spoke in front of a bullet-proof shield attached to the speaker's podium while wearing a bullet-proof vest. As fate would have it, on May 15, 1972, he left the vest behind because the heat and humidity were oppressive.

The open-air rally that Monday afternoon followed the usual pattern. A country-western band played music to keep onlookers entertained while the faithful assembled to hear the candidate dish out red meat. Security personnel, including Secret Service agents, circulated through the crowd to keep an eye out for dangerous-looking characters that might wish the candidate harm. Anything out of the ordinary would be viewed with suspicion. Familiar faces and innocent-looking, fresh-faced attendees received less scrutiny than foreigners and oddly-dressed hippie-types.

A smiling man in his early twenties with a short blonde haircut wearing red, white, and blue clothing along with several Wallace campaign buttons was a familiar figure that day. He arrived at the rally in a red 1967 Rambler automobile, parked in the shopping center lot, and joined the crowd. Nothing seemed amiss. The young man had attended several Wallace rallies lately and appeared to be one of the governor's most loyal fans. Given his ongoing presence and his apparent innocuousness, no one thought the odd little fellow hiding behind sunglasses and a grinning visage presented a clear and present danger.[371]

His name was Arthur Herman Bremer and, unbeknownst to Wallace and the security personnel, he was not a Wallace groupie. The twenty-one-year-old Milwaukee, Wisconsin, native was later described as an "intelligent, rational, sometimes humorous, even thoughtful" man who knew "exactly what he was doing and why—and it had little to do with politics." Bremer was a nihilistic personality whose life was so meaningless and isolated that he believed he could create meaning only by assassinating a prominent person. After initially focusing on President Nixon as a suitable target, he settled on George Wallace because a presidential contender was not as insulated as an incumbent president. Far from a benign presence, the clean-cut young man nursed a secret, singular goal—to assassinate George Corley Wallace. He had attempted to carry out the deed previously, but his plans had been thwarted. Today would be the day.[372]

Oblivious to the plot unfolding on May 15, the candidate took to the stage and launched into his standard tirade. He was in his element that day.

11.1 Alabama Governor George C. Wallace ran for president in 1972, making him an attractive assassination target. Courtesy of the Library of Congress.

Wallace was a gifted public speaker, always ready with an insightful barb or a sharp retort. When he hurled vile epithets against elites in power, the governor reveled in the response of the faithful. Crowds never failed to take the bait, bellowing back their agreement with his odious attacks on unforeseen forces conspiring to rob the common man of his rightful heritage.

At the end of his talk, he emerged from behind the bulletproof glass to wade into the crowd standing before him. Wallace enjoyed mingling; he was a southern populist—a man of the people—and he drew energy from his raucous crowds. They fed his enormous ego and a seemingly insatiable need for adulation. One newspaper reporter described the typical Wallace rally. "It had become a ritual of the pugnacious little man's angry pursuit of the Presidency: His speech would end to deafening applause, his eyes would sparkle at the sight of the hundreds or thousands cheering him—and off would come his coat and into the crowd he would go, grasping for those eager, straining hands reaching towards him."[373]

Bremer had watched enough Wallace rallies to recognize the ritual. Away from his bulletproof podium and far enough removed from his security detail, the candidate would be easy prey for anyone willing to aim a pistol and discharge it. As long as he did not lose his nerve, Bremer could prove himself that very day. He could shoot the would-be president and become a famous sensation in the time it took to point, aim, and unload his fury on the world.

It unfolded precisely as the blonde, smiling man with the closely cropped hair and .38-caliber handgun envisioned. As the excited throng called out, "over here, over here," to the governor, Wallace happily reached out to his adoring fans. Bremer saw his chance, aimed his weapon, and pulled the trigger, sending five bullets hurdling toward the governor. Struck in his mid-section, right arm, shoulder, and chest, Wallace fell backward onto the pavement. A Secret Service agent, an Alabama state trooper, and a Maryland campaign worker were also struck. Everyone survived, but George Wallace would never walk again.[374]

Members of the crowd and police officers pounced on the gunman, pummeling him mercilessly, but it was too late. The damage was done. Wallace lay writhing in agony on the ground while his wife, Cornelia, crouched beside him. His blood quickly soaked her yellow suit.[375]

No one understood his motives at the time, but Bremer had been mulling over a high-profile assassination since earlier in the year. Yet the roots of his nihilism went much deeper, perhaps all the way back to a troubled childhood. The third of four boys, he was born on August 21, 1950, in Milwaukee. Bremer's mother, Sylvia, had lived a hardscrabble life, which left her a bitter, cold woman seething with resentment at the fundamental unfairness of existence. By all accounts, she was prone to erratic, angry outbursts against members of her family, especially her husband, William, who appeared to be an invisible ne'er-do-well. In a household riven by an unpredictable matriarch and an almost non-existent patriarch, most of the Bremer children fled the home as soon as they were old enough to emancipate themselves and seek solace from the harsh vicissitudes of a house filled with nearly constant acrimony.

Young Arthur was the exception that proved the rule. He was the object of Sylvia's special attention. Although she was never warm or loving toward the boy, she kept a fierce eye on his activities from the time he was a small child. She noted his bowel movements, his exterior comings and goings, and his level of cleanliness. No one knew precisely what would set her off. Perhaps in response, Arthur learned to hide his interior life. According to family members, he never cried as a child and waited to speak until he was four years old. Whether he would have grown up to be an odd character without his mother's peculiar brand of quasi-affection is a matter of no small conjecture.[376]

It is tempting to psychoanalyze how much of the son's behavior was attributable to the example set by his embittered mother and how much could be laid at the doorstep of DNA—the timeless nurture vs. nature debate. Most observers would have labeled young Arthur his father's son, a quiet, reserved oddball who appeared indifferent to the exterior sound and fury erupting all around him. With hindsight, an astute commentator might surmise that beneath the surface of the boy's placidity lurked a boiling cauldron of white hot anger reflecting his mother's fiery temperament.

In any case, it was clear that Arthur Bremer was not altogether well-adjusted. In school, he seldom made friends. After he failed the fifth grade, he considered suicide, but could not go through with it. Drifting through his teenage years, he was the odd, quiet fellow sitting in the back of the room with his head down. He did not date. Except for a year he spent as a second-string member of the South Division High School football team, he took no part in organized activities. By the time he graduated with a high-school diploma in 1968, Arthur Bremer was practically invisible. Few former class-mates could recall his presence in the school.[377]

He spent most of his time alone inside his house. This isolated condition existed for years, but his parents did not intervene. They noticed a marked change in the young man's behavior during his senior year in high school. To adults who did not care to look beyond appearances, he had always been neat, quiet, and mostly passive, perhaps unconsciously emulating his father's behavior, the textbook definition of the perfect child who is seen and not heard. Now he became aggressive and insulting, criticizing his mother, dressing flamboyantly, and leaving pornographic materials littered about his room. Something happened to Arthur Bremer that year, but no one could say what it was.[378]

Bremer had never been ambitious. After high school he fell into a series of menial jobs. He worked as a busboy at the Milwaukee Athletic Club as well as in the Pieces of Eight, a swanky local restaurant. For a time, he served as a janitor in Milwaukee's Story Elementary School. In the fall of 1970, he enrolled as a student in Milwaukee Technical College, but he left after a year. Continuing the pattern set early in life, he made no impact. Peers could not recall much about the shy, quiet young man who floated along the fringes of their lives.

Matters reached a breaking point in October 1971. During a heated argument, Arthur struck his father and haughtily told his family that he would no longer live there. For someone who had always appeared indifferent about his life and surroundings, the change was stunning. Bremer found a $138.50-a-month apartment on West Michigan Avenue in Milwaukee and made good on his promise to leave his childhood home.[379]

Freed from the constraints of his dysfunctional family, the young man enjoyed his newfound independence. Around this same time, he met a sophomore at West Division High School, Joan Pembrick. The twenty-one-year-old janitor was smitten with the fifteen-year-old high-school student. She initially agreed to go on a date because she was flattered by the attention she received from an older man. Arthur Bremer was elated. He had never before enjoyed the company of a young woman, and he was eager to impress her with his cosmopolitan ways.

For once, he made an impression, but not in the way he intended. It quickly became clear that Bremer was anything but sophisticated. He uttered crude comments about the young lady and her friends. Having never mastered basic social relationships, Bremer believed that he could impress Joan with vulgar language and allusions to fornication. All he knew of women was the misogyny he had viewed in pornography, and it showed.

During one memorable outing, as Bremer and his date listened to a concert featuring the rock band Blood, Sweat, and Tears shortly before Christmas 1971, the exuberant young man jumped from his seat and danced in wild gyrations. Joan was mortified. Bremer did not understand how embarrassing his behavior had become, but she realized that the relationship was doomed. On January 13, 1972, the girl's mother informed Bremer on the telephone that Joan did not wish to see him again.[380]

The one and only love affair of his life was over. He was devastated. Bremer had never before experienced romantic love, and he did not know how to take rejection. The same day he learned that the relationship was over, he purchased a .38-caliber pistol from Casanova Guns in Milwaukee. It was the weapon he would use against Governor Wallace four months later. His initial reason for purchasing the gun was never clear, but the young man felt good about his acquisition.[381]

His always-odd behavior became even odder. Two days after he bought the gun, Bremer shaved his head, leaving only his sideburns. Perhaps he thought his altered appearance would favorably impress Joan. Whatever his motive, he must now present himself to the object of his affections. He knew he could not call Joan and risk another conversation with her mother. Instead, he confronted her in person while he wore a knit cap. When she saw him, Bremer broke into a grin and yanked off the cap, revealing his bald head. Horrified, the girl rushed past him.[382]

Arthur Bremer's world imploded. He finally understood that the romance had ended, never to return. Having lost his only love interest and estranged from his family, he became more isolated than ever. He sat in his desolate apartment eating cereal and peanut butter or whatever remnants he could scrounge from the Milwaukee Athletic Club. In February, despondent, he quit his job. Now he had nothing and no one.[383]

Everything he had tried to accomplish in his short, pathetic life had ended in dismal failure. During the months that followed, Bremer considered suicide. He inked the word "KILLER" on his forehead one evening, hiding the message under his knit cap as he entered a diner for his last meal. He intended to throw a rope around his neck and tie it over the railing of a nearby bridge so he could jump to his death. In the last act of a desperate life, Arthur Bremer would allow Milwaukee motorists to react to his body dangling from a noose above a commuter bridge during rush-hour traffic. He was certain that people would notice him this time.

He might have gone through with the plan but for a waitress in the diner who showed him a little kindness during his meal. Thankful for her pleasant demeanor, he left her a large tip. When he fortuitously saw her again after her shift ended, he changed his mind. Suicide was not the answer.[384]

He hatched a plan in coming months. Somewhere in his musings, as he sought to instill meaning in his life, he realized that killing himself was a poor substitute for what he really wanted to do. He wanted to prove to the world that he was someone, a person to be reckoned with and respected. Although he had never shown an interest in politics, he also mused over the possibility of killing a well-known political figure. The incumbent president, Richard Nixon, was an obvious choice. Bremer was not interested in politics and bore no grudge against Richard Nixon, but he understood that assassinating a sitting president would transform him into a celebrity as no other act would.[385]

In a diary that he began writing on April 4, 1972, Bremer described his plans to stalk the president and shoot him. He also expressed disdain for anti-Nixon activists who marched around with signs and criticized the president without taking concrete action. Bremer's nihilistic perspective, with occasionally humorous outbursts, revealed a man contemptuous of almost everyone, even himself. In the end, he appeared indifferent about whether he or anyone else lived or died. Nothing mattered anymore.

As he reconnoitered the field, Bremer realized that the problem with killing Nixon was that the man was so well-protected. In the wake of other high-profile assassinations, presidents had received heightened security. He understood that he probably would not succeed in such a quixotic quest. Early in May 1972, therefore, he turned his attention to Governor Wallace, who was almost as high profile a target as Nixon was, but was far more accessible.[386]

And so on the hot, humid afternoon of May 15, George C. Wallace lay bleeding in the parking lot of a Maryland shopping center, the victim of a lone oddball anxious to make a name for himself. Arthur Bremer, a man who had failed at virtually every goal he had ever set, finally had succeeded in a self-appointed task. True, he had not killed Wallace, but to a man who cares not whether anyone lives or dies, killing his prey had never been the objective. He had wanted only to act, to move beyond the tired rut of his sad, sordid life. His mission had been accomplished.[387]

Within seconds of the shooting, bystanders grabbed the gunman and restrained him until he could be taken into custody. Bremer never attempted to escape. He craved attention and respect, which he would never receive if he fled the scene before people could know who he was, what he had done, and why he had done it. It did not take long for investigators to search his apartment and find his stash of pornography, Black Panther literature, and the diary outlining his bizarre desire to slay a public figure.[388]

As with all would-be assassins, the initial question was whether Arthur Bremer was sane. Determining a shooter's state of mind is almost as much an art as a science. Absent physical abnormalities such as a recent head injury or a brain tumor, causes and effects are not altogether clear. Psychologists and psychiatrists sifted through the detritus of the man's life searching for clues. They drew myriad, sometimes conflicting conclusions, but all agreed on the symptoms of a troubled life. As for the court system, a jury believed that

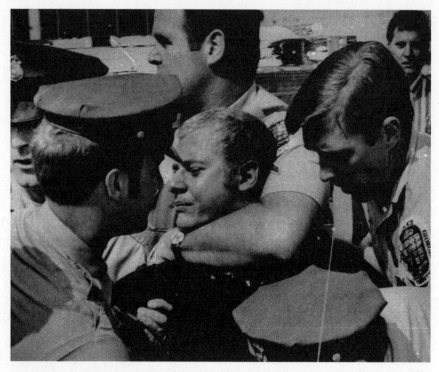

11.2 Arthur Bremer is shown here being restrained after he shot presidential candidate George Wallace in a shopping center in Laurel, Maryland, on May 15, 1972. Courtesy of the Associated Press.

Bremer could distinguish right from wrong and therefore was competent to stand trial for his crime.[389]

Five weeks after he shot Governor Wallace, Arthur Bremer was tried in a court of law. His trial focused on the writings in his diary, which revealed an emotionally disturbed but essentially sane defendant. Jurors delivered a guilty verdict in ninety-five minutes. The presiding judge sentenced Bremer to sixty-three years in the Maryland State Penitentiary, although the sentence later was reduced to fifty-three years.

Before sentencing, Bremer spoke to the court. Referring to the prosecutor, he said, "Well, Mr. Marshall mentioned that he would like society to be protected from someone like me. Looking back on my life, I would have liked it if society had protected me from myself." Society was protected from Bremer for thirty-five years, before he was released on parole on November 9, 2007.[390]

Perhaps to the gunman's delight, he became an indelible part of American popular culture. The fictional Travis Bickle character in Martin Scorsese's 1976 film *Taxi Driver* loosely resembles Bremer. Rock musician Peter Gabriel based his 1980 song "Family Snapshot" on Bremer's diary. In a curious art-imitates-life-imitates-art evolution, John W. Hinckley, Jr., President Ronald Reagan's would-be assassin, drew inspiration from *Taxi Driver* when he shot the president in 1981. In 1990, Stephen Sondheim's musical *Assassins* featured Bremer's offstage voice speaking to characters on stage. The 1994 film *Forrest Gump* briefly showed a clip of the Wallace shooting, although Bremer was not mentioned by name. Stephen King referenced Wallace's shooter in the acclaimed novel *11.22.63*.[391]

As for the man who took four bullets on May 15, 1972, George Wallace underwent multiple surgeries. Somehow he survived the ordeal. Although doctors saved his life, the governor's spine was severely damaged. He never walked again. Much of the rest of his life was filled with pain. He lived until 1998 and served as governor for many more years, but he was never the same man he once had been. The feisty segregationist eventually renounced his racist past and sought redemption late in life. Whether his change of heart was sincere or expedient, Wallace lived out his days a remnant of his former self.[392]

Even with the benefit of hindsight, categorizing Arthur Bremer is a difficult enterprise. Clearly he was not a Type 1 assailant. He expressed no interest in achieving a political goal. By his own admission, his interest in shooting Richard Nixon was not related to disagreements over the president's policy positions. When he realized that he would never get close enough to Nixon to shoot the man, he seamlessly changed course and stalked George Wallace. If Wallace had proved to be inaccessible, no doubt Bremer would have selected another target. His interest in shooting a political figure was related to the prominence of the target, not the target's politics.

Bremer also was not a Type 4 actor. He did not suffer from severe cognitive distortion. He never spoke of hallucinations or strange visions directing his actions. By all accounts, he was lucid and able to distinguish between reality and flights of fancy.[393]

The difficulty in categorization therefore lies in determining whether Arthur Bremer was a Type 2 or Type 3 shooter. The suggestion here is that he belongs in the Type 3 category. A Type 2 actor seeks recognition and hopes that assassinating a famous public figure will provide the fame he desperately craves. This description seems to apply to Bremer. He was not a political ideologue infuriated with George Wallace's racial views or the candidate's rigid stance on law and order. Bremer was a non-entity seeking to become an entity.

Yet seeking attention was not the central feature of Arthur Bremer's distorted personality. As his diary revealed, he had lost his way, viewing life as purposeless. His absurd attempts to provide meaning in his life ended in abject failure; thus, he believed that existence was a matter of no great consequence. Shooting George Wallace was his method of imposing the meaninglessness of his life onto another person.

In some ways, the distinction between Type 2 and Type 3 actors is a matter of degree. Type 2 actors possess low self-esteem and use violence as a means of invigorating their lives. They hope that somehow the fame that flows from the act will ease their pain. Type 3 actors have given up on easing their pain. They hope for nothing and seek to share their misery, projecting their nihilism into a public realm. As commentator James W. Clarke noted, Type 3 actors appear to "derive some satisfaction, perhaps pleasure, in their own debasement." A Type 3 assailant "is not someone who has lost his reason; rather he is someone who has lost everything *but* his reason."[394]

Chapter 12

"I'VE NEVER KILLED A PERSON WHO WAS UNDESERVING OF IT": JOHN H. WOOD, JR. (1979)

On Tuesday morning, May 29, 1979, John Howland Wood, Jr., a judge on the United States District Court for the Western District of Texas, walked outside of his townhouse in San Antonio and opened the door to his automobile. As he lifted his leg to step inside, a dumdum bullet fired from a high-velocity rifle slammed into his back, shattering into multiple fragments and knocking him to the ground. Judge Wood died instantly. He was sixty-three years old.[395]

The murder of a federal judge, the first such slaying of the twentieth century, generated massive news coverage. It was little wonder. Judges and justices at all levels of government spend much of their careers issuing judicial orders and opinions that affect the lives of ordinary citizens as well as large companies and institutions of government. As the final arbiter of legal matters in a nation built on the landmark principle of the rule of law, judicial officers must be able to act independently without fear of political reprisals or physical violence.[396]

Judge Wood's murder was deeply unsettling because he was well known for his handling of high-profile criminal cases. He had served on the bench for eight years. President Richard Nixon originally appointed Wood, a prominent Texas attorney, to the bench in 1970. The native Texan was exactly the sort of man that the Nixon administration, with its emphasis on law and order, was looking to appoint to the judiciary. As a judge, the former World War II naval officer established a reputation as tough on crime. "Maximum John" was especially harsh in sentencing drug traffickers.[397]

As soon as reports of the crime filtered in, agents from the FBI sprang into action. One agent characterized the shooting as the "crime of the century." Under pressure to solve the murder as quickly as possible, the Bureau dispatched agents into the field as part of "the most extensive FBI investigation since the assassination of President John F. Kennedy." Given the judge's propensity to sentence defendants to the maximum prison term allowed by law, investigators suspected that his shooting was related to his docket of pending criminal cases. They were correct.[398]

The difficulty was that Judge Wood had made many enemies during his tenure on the bench. A day after the shooting, a law enforcement officer confessed to reporters that the task was daunting. In his view, investigators would have to "follow up a lot of leads—this thing is going in four or five different directions." One direction was to examine a motorcycle group known as the Banditos. Several group members had appeared before Judge Wood previously, and others were suspects in an attack on Assistant US Attorney James Kerr in November 1978.[399]

When agents failed to establish a link, the case expanded rapidly. As one investigative reporter colorfully put it, "From the oil-stained driveway in San Antonio where Federal District Judge John H. Wood, Jr. fell last week, mortally wounded, the trail leads in many directions—to the sunny back streets of El Paso and Juarez, Mexico; to the Florida Everglades and the jungles of northern Colombia; to Boston and even to the gambling palaces of this Nevada city [Las Vegas]. And at the hub of it all is narcotics."[400]

As it turned out, the narcotics linkage became the central factor in the case. The trail eventually led to a notorious Texas drug kingpin, Jamiel "Jimmy" Chagra. Chagra was worried that Judge Wood, who was scheduled to preside over Chagra's pending trial, would favor prosecutors and, after ensuring a conviction, mete out the maximum penalty allowed by law. To prevent Wood from handling the case, Chagra hired a career criminal, Charles Voyde Harrelson (the father of movie actor Woody Harrelson), to kill the judge.[401]

The route from Jimmy Chagra to Charles Harrelson was long and circuitous. Police officials caught up with the triggerman owing to an anonymous tip and a tape recording of Jimmy talking with his brother, Joe (who also served as his attorney), during a visit to the United States Penitentiary in Leavenworth, Kansas, where Jimmy was incarcerated. On April 2, 1979, Joe Chagra had asked Judge Wood to recuse himself from Jimmy's trial. When the judge denied the request and set the trial to begin on May 29, 1979, the brothers discussed the means for assassinating Wood. The FBI recorded the conversation on tape, as well as conversations with Elizabeth Nichols Chagra, Jimmy's wife, and Jo Ann Harrleson, Charles Harrelson's wife.

A search of Joe Chagra's house revealed a map that Joe had discussed with Jimmy in the prison recording. The map supposedly showed the location of the rifle used to kill Judge Wood. FBI agents searched for the rifle in Forney, Texas, the site indicated on the map. Although they could not find the weapon, the agents received assistance from local residents, who provided them with the rifle stock. Investigators traced the rifle back to Jo Ann Harrelson, who had acquired the rifle for her husband.[402]

Subpoenaed to testify before a grand jury, Jo Ann Harrelson invoked her Fifth Amendment privilege, refusing to speak because she might incriminate herself. Government prosecutors granted her use immunity in exchange for her testimony, which she reluctantly provided during the summer of 1981. In September, the government indicted her for "knowingly making false and fictitious statements" during her testimony. Investigators had uncovered evidence that Jo Ann had purchased the rifle under an assumed name, Faye L. King—a play on the word "faking"—and provided false information about her address, birthdate, and driver's license number. After she was convicted, Jo Ann Harrelson received a twenty-year prison sentence. She was released in 1997, after serving almost sixteen years.[403]

Prosecutors indicted the remaining defendants on April 15, 1982. Joe Chagra faced charges for conspiring to commit first-degree murder of a federal judge, first-degree murder, conspiring to obstruct justice, and conspiracy to possess marijuana. He agreed to a guilty plea on the first charge in exchange for a ten-year prison sentence. As part of his agreement, Joe testified against Jo Ann Harrelson, Elizabeth Chagra, and Jo Ann's daughter, Teresa Starr, who carried the $250,000 "blood money" from Elizabeth Chagra to Charles Harrelson to pay for the murder. After serving six years, Joe earned his parole in March 1988. He died in 1996 as the result of injuries he suffered in an automobile accident.[404]

Elizabeth Chagra was convicted of conspiring to commit first-degree murder of a federal judge and sentenced to thirty years in prison. After her original conviction was reversed, she was convicted for conspiracy to commit second degree murder. Once again, she received a thirty-year sentence. She died of ovarian cancer in prison in 1997.[405]

Jimmy Chagra faced the same charges as his brother, but unlike Joe, he was acquitted of conspiring to commit first-degree murder of a federal judge and first-degree murder. Convicted instead of conspiring to obstruct justice and conspiracy to possess marijuana, Jimmy received a fifteen-year sentence. When he subsequently admitted that he had plotted to kill an assistant US attorney, Jimmy received a life sentence. In 2003, he earned his parole before being transferred to an undisclosed location, reputedly as part of the federal witness protection program.[406]

As for the triggerman, the story of his involvement gradually became clear. By all accounts, Charles Harrelson was a charismatic small-time criminal who turned to murder for hire. One observer concluded that "Charlie was without question a charmer—handsome, self-confident, and surprisingly polished, though he had barely finished high school. Obsessively neat, he had a taste for expensive clothes and cars and the finest Scotch whiskey and wine." During his closing argument, the lead prosecutor, Assistant US Attorney Ray Jahn, said that "Charles Harrelson had three talents. He was a cheat, he was a con man and he was a murderer." On another occasion, members of Jahn's team described Harrelson as "highly intelligent and cunning" as well as "an amoral, cold-blooded killer."[407]

Harrelson's life of crime was long and sordid. He served a prison term in California for theft in 1960. In 1968, Harrelson was tried and acquitted for the murder of Alan Berg, a man last seen alive riding in Harrelson's red Cadillac. Earlier that year, Harrelson was tried for killing a South Texas grain dealer, Sam Degelia, Jr. After his first trial ended with a hung jury, Harrelson was convicted in a second trial and sentenced to serve fifteen years. He was released for good behavior in 1978 after serving five years.[408]

Charles Harrelson met Jimmy Chagra during the spring of 1979. Chagra was known as "the highest of the high rollers," flying on private jets and placing six-figure bets at Las Vegas gaming tables. The purpose of the initial meeting remains unclear. Harrelson later testified that he wanted to engage Chagra in a card game in hopes of scoring a big payday. In his version of events, Harrelson did not ask Chagra for money to kill Judge Wood. Someone set him up as the fall guy for another assassin. Other versions of the tale suggest that Jimmy Chagra complained about Judge Wood and Charles Harrelson took it upon himself to kill the offending judge as a favor to Chagra.[409]

Harrelson reportedly told Joe Chagra the details of Judge Wood's murder. As Joe remembered it, Harrelson confessed that he stalked the judge for several weeks. On May 29, 1979, the morning that Jimmy Chagra's trial was set to commence, Harrelson hid in the judge's carport. When he saw Wood enter his car, Harrelson aimed his .243-caliber hunting rifle, squeezed off a single round, and saw his target collapse. "I watched him quiver for a fraction of a second, then twist and drop in his tracks," Harrelson supposedly said. "I knew it had been a clean, perfect shot."[410]

Despite his claims of innocence in the Wood murder, Harrelson often bragged about how little human life mattered to him. He sometimes said that as far as he was concerned, a human head was nothing more than "a watermelon with hair on it." He also said that "I've never killed a person who was undeserving of it."[411]

When investigators learned of Harrelson's involvement in the shooting, the alleged gunman faced charges of conspiring to commit first-degree murder of a federal judge, first-degree murder, and obstruction of justice. By this time, he was on the run. Harrelson spent part of his time on the lam hiding out in a rented room in Atlanta, Georgia. Armed with growing evidence, investigators pursued the fugitive for months.

Harrelson eventually surrendered to authorities following a standoff with police in September 1980. Subsequently claiming he was high on cocaine at the time, Harrelson confessed to killing Judge Wood, although he eventually recanted. He also said that he had taken part in the plot to assassinate President Kennedy in 1963. "At the same time I said I had killed the judge, I said I had killed Kennedy, which might give you an idea to the state of my mind at the time," he explained in a later interview. Investigators came to see that nothing Charles Harrelson said could be taken at face value. As with most pathological liars, he mixed the truth with lies so confidently that it was virtually impossible to distinguish between fact and fiction.[412]

Placed on trial in 1982 for Judge Wood's murder, Harrelson's charms could not sway the jury. Nine men and three women returned a guilty verdict after eighteen hours of deliberation. Judge William S. Sessions meted out two life sentences for the defendant.

Transferred to a federal prison in Atlanta, Harrelson disappeared from public notice until he attempted an escape in 1995. He died of a heart attack on March 15, 2007, in the United States Penitentiary, Administrative Maximum Facility (ADX)—the infamous Supermax facility—near Florence, Colorado. He was sixty-eight years old.[413]

Although he was the first federal judge murdered in the United States during the twentieth century, John H. Wood, Jr., was not the last. Judge Richard J. Daronco was killed in 1988, Judge Robert Smith Vance was assassinated in 1989, and Judge John Roll was shot and killed during an assault on

12.1 Charles V. Harrelson, a career criminal, shot and killed Judge John H. Wood, Jr., in 1979. Harrelson is pictured here in 1982. Courtesy of the Associated Press.

Congresswoman Gabrielle Giffords in 2011 (although presumably Roll was not the intended target).[414]

The assassination of a federal judge by a hitman hired to prevent a drug kingpin from standing trial might appear apolitical. Unlike elected officials who are killed because gunmen disagree with their policies, a federal judge is appointed for life and does not make overtly political decisions. In the examples cited above (except for Judge Roll), the judges died because someone decided that he was dissatisfied with the judge's rulings from the bench. The motives were far more personal than political.

Yet judges serve as representatives of the American system of government. They are integral to the smooth functioning of the judicial branch in a system of shared powers and checks and balances. To strike out at a symbol of the judiciary is to threaten the political system with chaos. Individual assassins may not seek the destruction of the political system, but their actions potentially have that effect.

As for Charles Harrelson, he was a classic Type 3 killer. Type 3 personalities are remorseless actors, sociopaths driven by a lack of empathy to snuff

12.2 John H. Wood, Jr., is remembered as a conscientious federal judge who meted out harsh sentences for criminal offenses. Courtesy of the Administrative Office of the United States Courts.

out the lives of others. Charles Harrelson admitted that he regarded a human head as "a watermelon with hair on it." To someone who genuinely sees his fellow human beings this way, firing a rifle into a person's back is not an especially noteworthy act. Jimmy Chagra allegedly paid Harrelson $250,000 to commit the crime, but even this motive was not the primary force influencing the assassin's actions. Harrelson had killed people for a lot less money than $250,000. Perhaps he acted for inscrutable reasons: to prove he was tough, to exercise control over hairy watermelons, or to experience the thrill of flaunting societal conventions and eluding capture from bumbling law enforcement officers. Whatever his motive, Harrelson reveled in his notoriety.

Type 3 actors such as Harrelson believe they are entitled to act however they see fit. The rules of human interaction simply do not apply to them. Immanuel Kant argued that every morally autonomous person should act as though his actions were a universal moral precept. If they knew anything of Kantian moral philosophy, no doubt Type 3 actors would denounce such abstractions as hogwash unworthy of anyone's time or attention. For Type 3 actors, life is a game to play. Either a player wins or he loses, but he never places himself into another man's shoes to experience life from another perspective. These emotionally stunted individuals cannot see beyond their own selfish desires.[415]

PART IV

TYPE 4 ACTORS

Chapter 13

"LET ME GO, GENTLEMEN—I AM *NOT* AFRAID—THEY *CAN'T* KILL ME—I CAN PROTECT MYSELF": ANDREW JACKSON (1835)

Andrew Jackson, military hero of the Battle of New Orleans and seventh president of the United States, was forty-four days shy of his sixty-eighth birthday when a failed house painter named Richard Lawrence tried to assassinate him on Friday, January 30, 1835. The harsh winter that year had kept the ailing, aged hero confined to the executive mansion on all but the rarest of occasions. The gray, damp last Friday in January was one such exception. Jackson ventured forth to attend funeral services for Congressman Warren Ransom Davis of South Carolina, who had died the previous day. Davis originally had been elected to the House as a Jacksonian man, a public servant who championed the rights of the people above elites, as did Jackson. Yet Davis eventually fell under the spell of fellow South Carolinian John C. Calhoun, vice president of the United States under John Quincy Adams as well as most of Jackson's first term as chief executive. The commanding, charismatic Calhoun was a well-known proponent of state rights and an ardent apologist for slavery. Proclaiming himself a Nullifier—a short-lived offshoot of the Democratic Party that proved to be popular in South Carolina during the early to mid-1830s—Davis agreed with Calhoun that states could nullify odious federal laws with the assent of a concurrent majority, a constitutional interpretation at odds with Jackson's views.

The president retained enough good will with the congressman to allow for a frank discussion of their differences. According to one oft-repeated, possibly apocryphal story, Jackson summoned Davis to his office not long after the South Carolina convention nullified the Tariff of 1832. Explaining his unbridled opposition to nullification, Jackson instructed Davis "to go back home and tell the people of South Carolina to quit their foolishness" and "return their allegiance to the United States." When the congressman demurred, Jackson allegedly opened a desk drawer and pointed inside. "Warren," he reputedly exclaimed, "in that drawer I have offers of three hundred thousand volunteers to march to South Carolina." Even if the exchange never took place, it illustrated the nature of Jackson's relationship with Warren R. Davis. The old president could disagree vehemently with the young representative, but they still bridged the divide with a measure of civility. Not all of the president's adversaries were so accommodating.[416]

Now, alas, Davis, one of the more sensible legislators from the Palmetto State, was gone, struck down in his prime with a liver ailment. At the time of his death, the forty-one-year-old congressman, who had been elected to his fifth term in November 1834, had been looking forward to taking his seat in the 24th Congress, scheduled to convene on March 4. Despite his political differences with Davis and the Nullifiers, Jackson thought enough of the man to pay his respects to the fallen South Carolinian in the midst of a brutal winter that found the nation's chief magistrate physically indisposed.[417]

The president arrived at the Capitol at the appointed hour on January 30. The solemn ceremony unfolded in the chambers of the US House of Representatives before members of Congress as well as cabinet officers and the president himself. Although the orations seemed to drag on interminably, Jackson eventually emerged and headed through the Capitol rotunda toward the east portico where a horse and carriage waited nearby to whisk him back to the security and comfort of the White House. Appearing frail and unwell, he sported a cane in one hand and clutched onto the arm of Treasury Secretary Levi Woodbury with his other hand as he slowly shuffled along the route.[418]

Unbeknownst to anyone, Richard Lawrence, an unemployed laborer, waited along with hundreds of onlookers for the president to exit the building. Old Hickory was not seen in public very much anymore, and a crowd had gathered. Most gawkers had arrived to catch a glimpse of the legendary general-turned-politician, perhaps to regale friends and family with tales of their encounter with the great man. Lawrence was not among the well-wishers that day. He had come for one purpose: he was armed with two brass pistols to kill Jackson. Anxious to complete the deed, Lawrence had been milling about the Capitol for hours. He had planned his actions as methodically as his diseased mind would allow. After considering whether to force his way into the middle of the funeral services inside the House chamber, he resolved to wait outside to slay the foul creature who had wronged him. In an era before Americans thought it necessary to protect their presidents from the depredations of wicked or disturbed souls, Richard Lawrence prowled about on the fringes of the crowd unmolested by law enforcement officials.[419]

Lawrence knew with absolute certainty that his cause was righteous; Andrew Jackson must die. As subsequent legal proceedings revealed, Lawrence believed that in opposing the Second National Bank of the United States, Jackson had caused the bank to withhold funds from Lawrence, and the destitute painter needed money to travel to England. On another occasion, Lawrence lamented the treatment of Native Americans, whose land had been stolen by the British before the colonies declared their independence. Jackson was a symbol of the obdurate federal government that had mistreated Native Americans. Adding insult to injury, somehow the president and Lawrence's brother-in-law were in cahoots to hurt Lawrence and all that he held dear. By the time he marched to the Capitol building on that dreary Friday in January 1835, Richard Lawrence was in a delusional state.[420]

If Lawrence's mind was sick, his prey faced a similar physical deterioration. In Jackson's case, however, his body was wearing out after decades of hard frontier living. The renowned frontiersman had spent much of his life as a vigorous man of action, making his name during the War of 1812. Now, in the middle of his second term of office, his gray hair had turned white, and his body was on the verge of collapse.[421]

When Jackson ambled out of the Capitol building that day, Lawrence saw his opportunity to slay the villain and enter the pages of history. He seized the moment. In a swift, sure motion, he stepped away from the throng and rushed toward the president. Before anyone could react, Lawrence reached into his right pocket and produced a pistol, aiming it at his nemesis. Onlookers gasped in horror. Accounts vary as to the where the assailant stood. Some witnesses estimated the distance between Lawrence and Jackson at six feet while others believed it was eight, ten, or thirteen feet. Whatever the exact distance, everyone agreed that a shot from point-blank range almost certainly would be fatal.

Amazingly, as Lawrence pulled the trigger, the pistol misfired. In the colorful words of one historian, "the explosion of the percussion cap echoed

ANDREW JACKSON.

13.1 Andrew Jackson was in the middle of his second term as president when a would-be assassin struck in 1835. Courtesy of the Library of Congress.

through the colonnade." Senator Thomas Hart Benton recalled that "the explosion of the cap was so loud that many persons thought the pistol had fired. I heard it at the foot of the steps, far from the place, and a great crowd between." In the wake of the loud explosion, the spectators froze in place. After a few seconds, as they realized what had occurred, men and women scattered in a mad dash for safety. Several eyewitnesses remembered that Jackson, far from being cowed, reacted in a fury, lifting his cane to strike the would-be assassin. As several men moved to protect the president, he called out, "Let me go, gentlemen—I am *not* afraid—they *can't* kill me—I can protect myself."[422]

Lawrence was almost as dumbfounded as everyone else. Realizing that he had failed in his quest, he discarded the first pistol and reached into his left pocket to produce a second gun. By this time, men were in motion. A navy

13.2 Richard Lawrence fired two pistols at President Jackson on January 30, 1835. Courtesy of the Library of Congress.

officer, Lieutenant Gedney, and Secretary Woodbury, among others, lunged toward the attacker. As they reached for him, Lawrence pulled the trigger of the second gun, which also misfired. Perhaps the damp weather had caused the surprising results. Experts later estimated that the odds of two pistols misfiring under such circumstances were 125,000 to 1.[423]

Having failed to assassinate the president, Lawrence focused on his escape. Before he could flee, however, the crowd knocked him to the ground. All the while, an enraged President Jackson waved his cane about. He was heard to shout, "Let me alone! Let me alone! I know where this came from." Convinced that his Whig opponents were behind the assassination plot, Jackson would show his enemies his wrath. He would not be intimidated.[424]

Jackson was no stranger to violence. It was a violent era, and he had been in the thick of many confrontations throughout his long life. He killed a Nashville man, Charles Dickinson, in a duel in Kentucky in 1806. In 1813, he was shot in the upper left arm during a street brawl.[425]

Even as president, Jackson was not safe from violent episodes. On May 6, 1833, Robert B. Randolph, a disgruntled naval officer who had been discharged from the service for allegedly misappropriating money, bloodied Jackson's face before being restrained. The president was a passenger on a steamboat heading to Fredericksburg, Virginia, when the attack occurred. Sitting with a table between him and the assailant, Jackson had little chance to defend himself. Andrew Jackson Donelson, the president's nephew and private secretary, pulled the man away from the president with assistance from several onlookers. Randolph fled with Jackson's men in hot pursuit. The author Washington Irving, who happened to be on hand, was among the spectators who chased the fleeing suspect. Irving later wrote that "It is a brutal transaction, which I cannot think of without indignation, mingled with a feeling of almost despair, that our national character should receive such crippling wounds from the hands of our own citizens." Jackson, in keeping with his reputation as a combative frontiersman, later told his vice president, Martin Van Buren, that he did not fear Randolph, or any man. If Jackson had been standing instead of sitting at the time, the president bragged that Randolph "never would have moved with life from the tracks he stood in." It was unclear whether the disaffected officer meant to kill the president or wished only to administer a beating. With the Lawrence incident, by contrast, it was clear that murder was the intended result. Most historians thus mark the 1835 episode as the first documented instance of a presidential assassination attempt in American history.[426]

The initial question after Lawrence was disarmed was whether the gunman acted alone or was part of a murderous cabal. Jackson thought he knew what had happened. He was convinced that his Whig political enemies had conspired with Lawrence to effect a *coup d'état*. Pointing to Lawrence after the gunman had been wrestled to the ground, the president proclaimed that "this man has been hired by that damned rascal Poindexter to assassinate me." The damned rascal in question was Mississippi Senator George Poindexter, former president *pro tempore* of the Senate and a long-time political foe who was engaged in an ongoing, vitriolic public feud with Andrew Jackson.

As a prominent anti-Jackson man, Poindexter had opposed virtually all of the president's policies despite his professed support for Jackson early in the careers of both men. By the 1830s, the senator frequently denounced "King Andrew's" policies, especially the president's decision to veto the bill re-chartering the Second Bank of the United States. Poindexter also expressed sympathy for South Carolinians in the 1832 nullification crisis.[427]

When the Mississippi senator learned of the accusations that he had hired an assassin, he dashed off a letter to the president demanding that Jackson avow or disavow the charge. He received no response. Poindexter soon heard rumors that Jackson was seeking sworn statements from witnesses who could tie him to Lawrence. Outraged, the senator publicly requested an investigation. He dramatically claimed that an official inquiry was necessary so that "if found guilty, I may no longer disgrace the seat which I occupy in this body."

In due course, Poindexter appealed to Vice President Van Buren, as president of the Senate, to create a special investigative committee. The vice president was no fan of the senator, but he had little choice politically but to accede to the aggrieved man's wishes. Even amidst the overheated political rancor of the time, it seemed incredible to believe that a sitting United States senator would hire a gunman to shoot the president of the United States in front of a crowd of eyewitnesses. Senator John Tyler of Virginia, one of the five men selected to serve, found the entire matter distasteful. Writing to his son, Tyler observed that if the investigation determined that Poindexter hired an assassin, he "deserves to be hung," but if the charges proved to be false, "his accusers would disgrace the gallows."[428]

Much to Jackson's chagrin, the resultant investigation could find no credible evidence that Senator Poindexter had hired Richard Lawrence, or anyone else, to kill the president. Jackson had procured signed affidavits from two men who claimed to have seen Lawrence inside Poindexter's house, but their allegations did not withstand scrutiny. The first man, Mordecai Foy, performed blacksmith work for the White House from time to time. Foy swore that he had seen Lawrence enter Poindexter's house three days before the assassination attempt. On cross examination, Foy could not identify Poindexter's house. Skeptics questioned how a man could precisely recall the date and time of the interaction but could not accurately identify the place where the nefarious exchange had occurred. The other witness, David Stewart, admitted that Lawrence owed him money, although he vehemently denied that the debt influenced the facts as he recalled them in his affidavit. Stewart was an especially poor witness. Not only was he seen in a shop more than a mile away from Poindexter's house at the time that he allegedly witnessed Lawrence enter the premises, but Stewart could not accurately describe Lawrence's appearance. The investigative committee dismissed the testimony of these two men. Foy, they concluded, was not to be believed because of "his habits of inebriation," while Stewart was a man whose character was "devoid of truth." As for anyone who influenced these two men to lie under oath, the committee recommended that such scoundrels "be held up to public odium and scorn."[429]

The president had no choice but to accept the committee's findings. Despite his best efforts, Jackson could not show that a conspiracy existed, although his followers argued that the toxic atmosphere among anti-Jackson partisans ultimately drove the shooter to commit his deed.[430]

Lacking an overtly political reason, Lawrence's motives remained murky. A mental defect of some sort apparently compelled him to appear at the Capitol that day with two pistols in his pockets. He confessed that he had listened to the heated congressional debates of 1833 and 1834, but he insisted that the incendiary rhetoric did not figure into his decision-making.

During his trial, which commenced on Saturday, April 11, 1835, it became clear that Lawrence was deranged. His friends recounted the background of a man who once had been industrious and ambitious, a fellow who was not destined for great things, but was nonetheless a productive member of society. According to acquaintances, eighteen months before he attacked the president, Lawrence's behavior changed markedly. Two brothers-in-law testified that Lawrence announced in November 1832 that he intended to travel to England. He left Washington, DC, where he resided, presumably to complete his journey. A month later, he returned home. Without explaining where he had been, Lawrence told his family that he had changed his mind because the "weather was too cold." He observed that the Philadelphia newspapers contained multiple stories about him, and he could not enjoy the anonymity he sought in his travels.

Lawrence boarded with his sister and her husband for six months. The testimony revealed the extent of his increasingly erratic behavior. He tried to kill his sister and threatened to kill his landlady and her husband. Hailed before a judge, he was warned to change his ways, but Lawrence was never jailed or committed to a mental institution.

He claimed to be King Richard III of England on more than one occasion. Having been born in Great Britain, Lawrence boasted that he retained great estates there, although his family protested that the assertion was delusional. He also believed that the United States government owed him money, and his frequent appearances at congressional debates apparently were his way of keeping tabs on the progress of his claims. Lawrence came to believe that President Jackson somehow was the main culprit responsible for his woes. He was unable to explain how killing the president would improve his life, but he harbored little doubt that it would.[431]

Throughout the trial, Lawrence rose from the defense table to shout out opinions. He questioned whether a United States court of law could exercise jurisdiction over him since he was an English king. As the proceedings continued, he blurted out all manner of bizarre ravings about the jurors and the proceedings.[432]

Above the din, prosecutor Francis Scott Key set forth his case. He told the jury that the charges against the defendant were unusual "for this part of the world." Key remarked that the defense probably would raise an insanity defense, and he intimated that he would not oppose such a plea if Lawrence were insane when he shot the pistols at the president.

Key patiently explained that insanity is not a singular state of mind, but depends on numerous factors. A defendant can be totally insane, that is, unable to distinguish between reality and fantasy at any time. Alternatively, a person may be insane for brief intervals, but lucid at other times. Finally, a person may be insane about a specific topic, but essentially reasonable about other issues. The question, therefore, was Richard Lawrence's state of mind when he sought to kill the president. Perhaps he was totally insane all the time, or only insane when he pulled the triggers of the pistols, or insane specifically about Andrew Jackson. Any of these conditions would necessitate a verdict of not guilty by reason of insanity, for a man cannot be held legally responsible when he does not appreciate what he has done.[433]

By the end of the trial, few people doubted that Lawrence was insane. Aside from the eighteen-month history of his descent into madness, the proceedings revealed that the young man hailed from a family with a history of derangement. His father had died in England in 1822 while suffering from delusions. His aunt died in the United States under similar circumstances. The doctors who testified agreed that Lawrence was partially insane on essentially every issue and completely insane concerning money owed to him by the United States government, which he believed President Jackson had prevented him from receiving.[434]

The jury was convinced. After only five minutes of deliberation, the jurors returned a verdict of not guilty by reason of insanity. Whisked away into a mental institution, the disturbed former house painter spent the rest of his days confined to a series of asylums until he died on June 13, 1861, two months after the first shots of the Civil War were fired and sixteen years after Old Hickory died.[435]

As for Lawrence's target, Andrew Jackson remained in the White House until his term expired in March 1837. Despite his continual battles with his political enemies—the Senate censured him in March 1834 for removing deposits from the Second Bank of the United States, although a resolution expunged the censure three years later—he remained a popular incumbent. Jackson likely could have won a third term in office, but he chose to follow George Washington's example and voluntarily depart after serving eight years. Retiring to the Hermitage, his estate near Nashville, Tennessee, Old Hickory lived eight years and ninety-six days after he left the presidency. He died on June 8, 1845, at the age of seventy-eight.[436]

Richard Lawrence holds the dubious distinction of being the first man to attempt a presidential assassination. In the aftermath of his deed, legislators mulled over the possibility of enacting a new law to protect the president. With the political turmoil of the times, however, those plans fell by the wayside. The failure to realize the potential threat faced by presidents would have devastating consequences almost thirty years later when an aggrieved actor named John Wilkes Booth resolved to kill a president.[437]

Chapter 14

"I SHOT THE PRESIDENT AS I WOULD A REBEL, IF I SAW HIM PULLING DOWN THE AMERICAN FLAG. I LEAVE MY JUSTIFICATION TO GOD AND THE AMERICAN PEOPLE": JAMES A. GARFIELD (1881)

President James A. Garfield served the second shortest tenure as the nation's chief executive—a mere 199 days—before he died on September 19, 1881, as a result of an assassin's bullet. Today little is remembered of Garfield's time in political office, either as president or when he served as a prominent member of Congress. Moreover, his killer, Charles Julius Guiteau, is described as the proverbial "disgruntled office seeker"—one account characterized him as "a half-crazed, pettifogging lawyer, who has been an unsuccessful applicant for office under the Government"—but the gunman's life and descent into madness are seldom discussed. In each instance, the flesh-and-blood man is far more interesting than popular myth would suggest.[438]

Like Richard Lawrence, Andrew Jackson's would-be assassin, Charles Guiteau was one of the most deeply disturbed individuals to take up arms against an American political figure. He constructed a fantasy in his mind that President Garfield had promised him a high-ranking position within the new administration, despite Guiteau's lack of qualifications for a prominent government post. When an offer of employment failed to materialize, Guiteau took matters into his own hands and exacted vengeance, claiming that he alone could save the republic from the nefarious Garfield. He was disgruntled in the sense that he was delusional for believing that President Garfield owed him anything. Guiteau was the focus of his own life, and he assumed that he should be the focus of everyone else's life, including the chief magistrate of the United States.[439]

The second presidential assassin in American history was born in Freeport, Illinois, on September 8, 1841. His mother died when young Julius, as he was called until his adolescence, was seven years old. He and his siblings came of age under the heavy hand of their father, Luther Guiteau, an intensely religious man who disliked his son's rebelliousness. For the most part, Julius looked to his older sister, Frances, and her husband, George Scoville, for guidance as he grew to maturity. Scoville, a lawyer, later represented his brother-in-law when the young man was tried for shooting President Garfield.[440]

Julius Guiteau suffered from a speech impediment, but he was also a precocious boy. His father thought him lazy when it came to performing manual labor, but the child took to reading and writing immediately. Later, he attended the University of Michigan. At his father's insistence, he dropped out of Michigan and attended classes in a biblical institute in the Oneida Community of New York. A utopian religious commune founded in 1848, Oneida was dedicated to free love, communalism, and the notion that man could establish a kingdom of God on earth.

After living and studying at Oneida for a time, Charles, as he now called himself, decided that he was the anointed one. When Guiteau informed fellow communitarians that he required lengthy periods of solitude free from the manual labor expected of all community members, they suspected the worst. He was an indolent charlatan who was not devoted to the commune; he was devoted only to himself. Soon he became a pariah, earning the moniker Charles "Git-out."[441]

By April 1865, it was indeed time to get out. He had lived in Oneida for almost five years, and he had worn out his welcome. Guiteau departed before he was asked to leave. He explained his predicament in a letter to his father. "The cause of my leaving was because I could not conscientiously and heartily accept their views on the labor question," he wrote. "They wanted to make a hard-working businessman of me, but I could not consent to that, and therefore deemed it expedient to quietly withdraw, which I did last Monday." Instead of working on God's behalf inside a religious community, he would go his own way. The best method of serving the lord, he believed, was to publish his own religious newspaper, a "daily theocratic press."[442]

Always supremely confident that he could achieve anything he desired, Guiteau harbored no doubt that he could make his newspaper an ongoing concern, glorifying God while earning a handsome profit at the same time. He ventured into New York City to court investors, only to be rebuffed repeatedly. After three months of fruitlessly searching for financiers, advertisers, and subscribers, Guiteau returned to Oneida with little to show for his efforts. He rejoined the community for a short while, but eventually he left again.[443]

Upon his departure, Guiteau engaged in a war of words with Oneida members, including founder John Humphrey Noyles. Guiteau had asked for various sums (somewhere between $5,000 and $9,000) to reimburse him for the years he had spent as a member of the commune. When Noyles balked at the settlement, Guiteau threatened to publicize a story about financial and sexual improprieties at Oneida. Noyles and Guiteau exchanged angry letters, and Noyles involved Luther Guiteau as well. According to Noyles, Charles Guiteau had confessed to several sins such as stealing money, visiting brothels, and contracting a venereal disease. Embarrassed at his son's behavior, the elder Guiteau confirmed that he had lost faith in his wayward offspring, believing that Charles only lived at Oneida to enjoy "the free exercise of unbridled lust."[444]

Luther Guiteau believed that his son was a fit subject for a lunatic asylum, but Charles set out to prove the old man wrong. For a time, the younger man appeared to have turned a corner. Charles Guiteau settled into a more or less middle-class existence. He moved to Chicago and claimed to practice law, although he never made much of a living. In 1869, he married a timid young librarian whom he had met at the YMCA, Annie J. Bunn, but both his law practice and his marriage failed within a few years.[445]

Following his misadventures in Chicago, Guiteau returned to New York. He floated from one scheme to another, confidently predicting success before he failed miserably at each new, hopeless endeavor. When he tried to purchase a newspaper but could not secure financing, he turned to religion.[446]

The mid-1870s found him churning out pamphlets and advertisements about his prowess in addressing age-old theological questions. Despite all the great minds of the Western intellectual tradition that had poured over these existential riddles, only Charles Julius Guiteau had unraveled the mysteries of the universe. When he did not attract sufficient attention for his philosophical advances, he hoisted sandwich boards over his shoulders and marched through the streets. If he found a willing audience, he would launch into an improvised sermon about Hell, the second coming of Christ, and similar religious topics.

The would-be evangelist billed himself as "the Eloquent Chicago Lawyer." From beginning to end, however, his tirades were anything but eloquent. In fact, the harangues usually degenerated into an incoherent series of clichés and non sequiturs. Predictably, audience members either expressed anger at the waste of their time or they laughed uproariously at the odd little man who invariably lapsed into gibberish. Each diatribe became an exercise in cringe-worthy moments, sometimes excruciatingly long and boring.

To the extent that he developed a reputation, Guiteau subsisted as a freak on the fringes of society. He was arrested several times for leaving a trail of unpaid bills and broken promises, but he always went back to proselytizing as soon as secured his freedom. While religion remained a constant theme, he eventually turned his attention to politics.[447]

The 1880 election garnered attention because former President Ulysses S. Grant, who was considering another term after his retirement in 1877, was the choice of a Republican Party faction known as the Stalwarts. When Grant failed to gain enough support to secure the nomination, the Republicans chose a dark horse, James A. Garfield, to be their standard bearer. Guiteau watched the race with great interest. He initially supported Grant, but seemed unfazed when Garfield emerged victorious. Afterward, Guiteau took it upon himself to hang around campaign headquarters. He also wrote a speech favorably comparing Garfield to his Democratic rival, Winfield Scott Hancock. According to the speech, if Hancock captured the presidency, he and the Democrats, originally supporters of the traitorous South, would reignite the Civil War. Evidence suggests that Guiteau launched into his oration only once, but he stopped talking after uttering only a few sentences.[448]

Garfield won the presidency in November 1880, and Guiteau was convinced that his support, especially his aborted speech, had made the difference. In his customarily grandiose way, he believed that he was due a high-ranking post in the new administration. It was not uncommon for a large donor or an influential politico who assisted a candidate in winning political office to expect a reward. Patronage was considered a major perquisite for the winning party. To the victor belong the spoils, the old adage suggested, and Guiteau was anxious to share in those spoils.[449]

No sooner had Garfield settled into his office than Guiteau peppered the new president with notes asking about an appointment. Referring to the new secretary of state, James G. Blaine, Guiteau informed President Garfield that

"I think Mr. Blaine intends giving me the Paris consulship with your and Gen. Logan's approbation, and I am waiting for a break in the Senate. I have practiced law in New York and Chicago, and presume I am well qualified for it."[450]

Of course, Guiteau was not well qualified for a post in the Garfield administration, nor had Blaine promised him anything of the sort. Administration officials frequently fielded requests for government positions when a new president came into office. Yet even among the nags that pestered the secretaries for government largesse, Charles Guiteau stood in a class by himself as someone utterly devoid of ability or even common sense. The beleaguered secretary of state grew so exasperated with Guiteau's constant lobbying that he dreaded seeing the now-familiar figure approach him in the hallways of government buildings or on the street. On one occasion, Blaine saw Guiteau heading his way and roared, "Never speak to me again on the Paris consulship as long as you live!"[451]

Worried that Blaine might poison the well, Guiteau penned a private letter to Garfield complaining about the secretary of state. "Mr. Blaine is a wicked man," the office seeker informed the president, "and you ought to demand his *immediate* resignation." If Garfield failed to act with dispatch, "you and the Republican party will come to grief."[452]

In the aftermath of Garfield's assassination, this last comment might be perceived as a veiled threat. At the time, however, Garfield and Blaine could be forgiven for dismissing the aggravating Guiteau as just another hack seeking to enrich himself at government expense. Enduring this sort of persistent lobbying, although extreme in Guiteau's case, was part of the chore of being president of the United States late in the nineteenth century. Officer seekers, whether meritorious public servants or insufferable cranks, always came out of the woodwork at the start of a new presidential administration in search of a lucrative federal position.

In addition, the odd little man who pestered Secretary Blaine had never exhibited outward signs of being dangerous. No one thought he would be dangerous now. His extreme narcissism and short attention span often shielded him from crushing disappointment. By the time he failed at something, usually he was on to the next thing.[453]

It is difficult to understand why the failure to secure a position in the Garfield administration caused Guiteau to react violently. How often in American history does a mentally unbalanced loner immerse himself in the vitriolic public discourse of the day and accept the hyperbole of political

Charles J. Guiteau

14.1 Suffering from delusions, Charles J. Guiteau, pictured here, believed that President James A. Garfield threatened the American republic and must be killed. Courtesy of the Library of Congress.

opponents as license to lash out violently? The question is rhetorical, but clearly some men are mentally unstable, and they need only a gentle shove—often in the form of intemperate rhetoric—to permit them to act against a public figure they perceive to be injurious to the public good or to their private interests. In this instance, it appears that Guiteau believed Garfield had betrayed the public trust. Guiteau thought that his actions would save the republic, unite the Republican Party, and provide him with the status he had desperately craved all his life.

Guiteau later claimed that he thought up the assassination scheme while lying on the cot in his Washington, DC, boardinghouse sometime between 8:30 and 9:00 p.m. on Wednesday, May 18, 1881. It came to him in a flash. Perhaps it struck him as an epiphany at that moment, but the "irresistible pressure" had been building for many weeks as he read accounts of the insidious Garfield and his chief henchman, Blaine.[454]

Support for the notion that Guiteau found inspiration for his assassination scheme from news coverage of the president's political enemies came from a strange missive that Guiteau wrote in June 1881. Titled "Address to the American People," Guiteau wrote the piece in his typically bombastic style. "I conceived of the idea of removing the President *four weeks ago*. Not a soul knew of my purpose," he confessed. "I conceived the idea myself and kept it to myself. I read the newspapers carefully, for and against the Administration, and gradually the convictions settled on me that the President's removal was a political necessity, because he proved a traitor to the men that made him, and thereby imperiled the life of the Republic."

The indictment continued, relying on Guiteau's inimitable logic. "Ingratitude is the basest of crimes," he declared. "[T]he President, under the manipulation of his Secretary of State, has been guilty of the basest ingratitude to the Stalwarts admits of no denial . . . In the President's madness he has wrecked the one grand old Republican party; and for this he dies."

Because Garfield represented a threat to the American regime, someone had to act on behalf of the public good; that someone was Charles J. Guiteau. Admitting that "I had no ill-will to the President," the assassin nonetheless recognized his duty. "This is not murder. It is political necessity. It will make my friend Arthur President, and save the Republic. I have sacrificed only one, and here is the motive: I shot the President as I would a rebel, if I saw him pulling down the American flag. I leave my justification to God and the American people."[455]

Despite his propensity to hatch fanciful schemes and abandon them, Guiteau followed through with his plan in early June. After borrowing $15, he purchased a silver-mounted English .44-caliber revolver and shot at targets on the banks of the Potomac River. He also stalked Garfield, finding him easy prey in an era before security personnel shielded public figures from the masses. He bypassed several opportunities to kill the president, including one occasion when he saw Garfield with his wife, Lucretia, and decided not to act lest he upset the frail woman.[456]

The day of reckoning finally dawned on Saturday, July 2, 1881. Guiteau had rented a room at the Riggs House, a prominent Washington, DC, hotel. He rose early to prepare for his date with destiny. President Garfield was slated to board a train at the Baltimore and Potomac Railroad Station, and there his assassin would strike. After consuming a large breakfast, Guiteau got in a little target practice before arriving at the train station.

He arrived with time to spare. Wandering about, he used the restroom and had his shoes shined. He scribbled a note to General William T. Sherman as his last order of business. Worried that an angry mob might lynch him before the citizenry appreciated the public service he had performed in shooting the president, Guiteau wanted the General of the Army to dispatch troops as a precaution. "I have just shot the president," the note explained. "I shot him several times, as I wished him to go as easily as possible. His death was a political necessity. I am a lawyer, theologian and politician. I am a Stalwart of the Stalwarts. I was with General Grant and the rest of our men in New York during the canvass. I am going to jail. Please order your troops and take possession of the jail at once."[457]

As expected, President Garfield arrived at the train station around 9:20 a.m. Secretary of State Blaine as well as Garfield's sons, Jim and Harry, accompanied him. In keeping with the standards of the time, he did not employ presidential bodyguards or other security personnel. Guiteau stepped behind the president and raised his revolver, squeezing off a shot from a distance of three feet. The blast resulted in a comparatively minor wound in Garfield's arm, passing through his coat and lodging in a nearby workman's toolbox. The president turned to see what had happened, exclaiming, "My God! What is this?"[458]

Guiteau fired a second time. The bullet hurtled into the president's right posterior thorax, fracturing a rib and traveling to the first lumbar vertebra, barely missing the spine. As he was struck, Garfield crumpled to the ground, vomiting. He lay semi-conscious as a large red stain crept across his back.[459]

Onlookers described Guiteau as almost preternaturally calm when he pointed his revolver at Garfield's back. His demeanor soon changed. Having acted according to his plan, the shooter now considered his own fate and realized that his chance to escape would soon disappear. According to one eyewitness, Guiteau's face "blanched like that of a corpse." Shaking with fear, he darted toward a side door, but someone blocked his way. He lunged for a second exit, but Secretary of State Blaine, recovering his composure after the shock of seeing his friend and superior gunned down in front of him, called for the exits to be barred.[460]

Guiteau was trapped inside the train station. Before he could react, a ticket agent, Robert Parke, grabbed the assailant by the back of the neck. "This is the man," he said. A crowd of bystanders descended on Guiteau. Calls for the gunman to be lynched grew into a chorus. "I truly believe that if they hadn't been so many officers present, the man would have been strung up then and there," a porter recalled.[461]

14.2 This drawing imagines the scene when Guiteau shot President Garfield. Courtesy of the Library of Congress.

Patrick Kearney, a Metropolitan Police officer, took charge, much to the desperate man's relief. Recognizing that the mob might tear him to pieces, a frantic Guiteau implored the officer to remove him from the station. "I want to go to jail," he said.[462]

Hustled outside the station to be taken into custody, Guiteau repeatedly called out, "I have a letter that I want to see carried to General Sherman. I want Sherman to have this letter." Kearney said he would take care of the delivery. Satisfied that he would not become a victim of mob violence and that his correspondence would be handled, Guiteau grew calm again. In fact, he felt happy for the first time in memory. "Thank God it is all over," he reflected. He had performed his duty as he saw it, and soon the American people would realize the distinguished nature of his public service.[463]

Inside the station, Dr. Smith Townsend was the first physician to arrive on the scene. He would soon be joined by a multitude of doctors anxious to save the president's life. During those first minutes, the good doctor sought to keep the president conscious. He administered aromatic spirits of ammonia and encouraged Garfield to sip brandy after ensuring that the patient was situated prone on the floor of the train station. Ignorant of the need to prevent infection for open wounds, Dr. Townsend probed the bullet hole with his unsterilized finger. Someone brought a mattress made of hay and horsehair and lifted the president onto it. They carried him to a second-story room in the station.[464]

Passing in and out of consciousness, Garfield asked that he be taken back to the White House. He also worried about his wife, Lucretia, who was suffering from malaria and had traveled to the New Jersey shore to recuperate. In fact, Garfield had entered the train station that morning to join her. He feared that news of his shooting would worsen her condition. From the first few minutes after the shooting, the medical professional who attended to the president were never certain of his recovery. Nonetheless, they complied with his request to leave the station, loading him onto a horse-drawn ambulance for the short ride to the executive mansion.[465]

Had James A. Garfield suffered his wound in a later age, he probably would have recovered. Unfortunately, his doctors rejected the innovative ideas of the British surgeon Joseph Lister, who began arguing in favor of antiseptic medicine beginning in the 1860s. European medical doctors had embraced Lister's methods by the 1870s, but many American physicians scoffed at such silliness. Leaving cuts open, exposed to the air, and probing wounds to dislodge obstructions appeared far more to their liking, although such techniques more often than not led to serious difficulties, including the death of the patient.[466]

Initial medical bulletins indicated that the president's condition was grave, and the injury might prove fatal. False reports circulated that Garfield had already died. Traveling in New York City, Vice President Chester A. Arthur boarded a train to Washington, DC, arriving the day after the shooting. Although some critics charged that the vice president might have had a hand in the assault, Arthur was innocent. In fact, he feared that he might soon be called on to affirm the oath as president. Arthur was a political hack, and he knew it. Whatever else he was, Arthur was not a fellow who burned with presidential ambition.[467]

By the next day, Garfield's condition had improved marginally. In the days to come, however, his health spiked up and down. For the seventy-nine days of the president's incapacitation, the doctors issued regular updates, leaving the public with a confusing picture of Garfield's health. One bulletin indicated that he was on the mend, but a few days later the doctors would offer a grim assessment, suggesting that the president was not long for the world. During this time, Vice President Arthur refused to swear the oath of office, leaving the executive branch without a leader for more than two months. The Twenty-Fifth Amendment, ratified in 1967, later addressed the question of governance when the president is incapacitated, but no provisions existed at the time of Garfield's injury.[468]

As news of the shooting spread, an offer of assistance arrived from an unexpected source. Alexander Graham Bell, the thirty-four-year-old Scottish inventor of the telephone, had pioneered an "induction balance" machine that detected metal. He met with the attending physician, Dr. Doctor Willard Bliss (whose parents apparently named him "Doctor" to encourage him to pursue a career in medicine). Bell offered to bring his device to the White House in an effort to locate the bullet inside Garfield's body. Dr. Bliss eventually allowed the inventor to try out his machine. Alas, Bell was unable to find the bullet despite two attempts. During the second attempt, Dr. Bliss insisted that Bell search only on the right side of Garfield's body because Bliss had determined that the bullet must be lodged there. Believing that he heard a faint sound, Bell confirmed the doctor's belief that the bullet was to be found on the president's right side, although he harbored nagging doubts about possible interference. Bell subsequently decided that interference from metal in the bed created the sounds he heard, but Dr. Bliss had already announced that the test was successful.[469]

Doctors continued to probe the wound and to make incisions in the president's body. Despite nearly constant pain from this series of reckless experiments, Garfield retained his equanimity. Informed that his surgeons proposed to perform another painful procedure on his wound, he exhibited his "unfailing cheerfulness." "Very well," he said, "whatever you say is necessary must be done." Garfield's only source of comfort during that time was his family, especially Lucretia, who sat by his side for most of his convalesce.[470]

All the slicing and dicing left pockets of infection in the patient's body. An abscess on the patient's right parotid gland caused it to fill with pus, swelling his eye and check and paralyzing his face. Doctors evinced little apparent concern for Garfield's suffering. Whenever someone suggested an additional treatment, Dr. Bliss would authorize the new, typically invasive procedure. It was apparent to anyone who saw the president during this time that he was not likely to recover. He was malnourished and weak, seldom eating a mouthful of food and probably suffering from severe dehydration.[471]

On September 5, Garfield told his doctors that he wanted to escape the heat and humidity of the White House. The following day, he was hoisted onto a special train that transported him to the Franklyn Cottage, a wealthy New Yorker's twenty-two-room summer home in Elberon, New Jersey, a seaside town. When he finally caught sight of the ocean after his bed inside the cottage was positioned so he could look outside, Garfield, always grateful for life's simple pleasures, expressed his joy. "This is delightful," he said. "It is such a change."[472]

He lived another two weeks. At 10:35 p.m. on September 19, 1881, surrounded by his wife, loved ones, and attendants, James A. Garfield, two months shy of his fiftieth birthday, died. Dr. Bliss recalled a "faint, fluttering pulsation of the heart, gradually fading to indistinctness." When it was clear that the patient had passed, the doctor lifted his head from Garfield's chest and said, simply, "It is over."[473]

Today, Garfield's brief tenure is a mere footnote in American history, the man with the bushy beard who was assassinated by a crazy office seeker. As he lay dying in those final September days, Garfield thought about his legacy. Looking up at Captain Almon Rockwell, an old friend from the army,

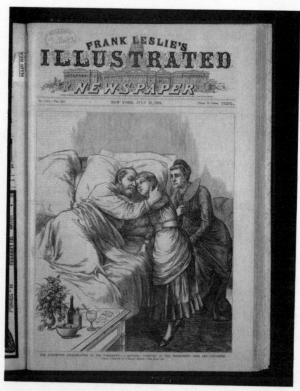

14.3 This drawing from the cover of *Frank Leslie's Illustrated Newspaper* shows Garfield being comforted by his family after the shooting. Courtesy of the Library of Congress.

the president asked, "Do you think my name will have a place in human history?" What could a treasured friend say to his mortally stricken comrade? "Yes," Rockwell replied, "a grand one, but a grander place in human hearts." It was a beautiful sentiment, but perhaps a false one.[474]

James Garfield died before he could fulfill his extraordinary promise. It is one of the genuine tragedies in the nation's history. The man who died that September day was far more than another nineteenth-century hack. Had he lived to complete a term or two in the presidential chair, he might have emerged as one of the immortals. He certainly exhibited the promise of a stellar leader. He was more or less honest, reasonably hard-working, and undeniably intelligent. Having served in the army and in Congress, he understood the demands of public service as well as the dictates of compromise and conciliation.

His biography only partially reveals the measure of the man. America's twentieth president, James Abram Garfield, was born on November 19, 1831, in a log cabin in Orange, Ohio, the fifth child in a family of five. His father died when the boy was not yet two years old. Raised poor and fatherless, Garfield experienced ridicule for his modest background, which caused him to retreat into reading as solace for the painful circumstances of his life. He was a scholarly child who grew up to become a brilliant teacher.[475]

During the Civil War, he served in uniform as a colonel and eventually a general before winning a seat in the US House of Representatives. He gravitated to the Radical Republicans in Congress, a group that found President Abraham Lincoln too plodding and vacillating for their tastes. When the party's standard bearer sought reelection, Garfield expressed his ambivalence. "He will probably be the man, though I think we could do better," he said when asked his opinion of the incumbent. In later years, after Lincoln's assassination, Garfield came to appreciate the man's singular virtues.[476]

As for his own career, he served in Congress for seventeen years. He was not a perennial presidential aspirant, preferring to spend his time legislating. His record in Congress met with success, but he experienced some failures as well. Garfield supported measures to allow blacks to vote, although he did not believe the races were equal in native ability. His reputation was tarnished by the Crédit Mobilier scandal, a corruption scheme involving construction of the Transcontinental Railroad, but he was never convicted of any crimes.[477]

Garfield served an important role in the disputed presidential election of 1876, when the Democrat, Samuel J. Tilden, appeared to have won the election while Republican nominee Rutherford B. Hayes claimed victory. With the election results confusing and perhaps fraudulent, Congress established a fifteen-member electoral commission to investigate disputed electoral votes from South Carolina, Louisiana, Florida, and Oregon. Garfield served on the commission, eventually voting with seven other Republicans to award all the delegates from the disputed states to Hayes. Recognizing that Democrats who controlled the House of Representatives were furious at the outcome, Garfield labored behind the scenes to engineer the Compromise of 1877, a deal which ended federal Reconstruction when US troops left the last southern statehouses. The supposedly corrupt bargain also ensured that one southern Democrat would serve in President Hayes's cabinet.[478]

During those turbulent times, Garfield navigated treacherous political waters by forging a career as a pragmatist. Whether he was a master legislator who understood the compromises necessary to enact bills into law or an unprincipled opportunist depended on one's point of view. As the House minority leader during the Hayes administration, Garfield sought to bridge the gap between two factions of the Republican Party. Garfield's ability to appease these warring factions led to his nomination as the party's presidential candidate when no other politician could win enough votes to emerge victorious during the 1880 convention. It was not a position that Garfield had sought, but once offered, he accepted.[479]

The general election on November 2, 1880, was a squeaker. Garfield defeated the Democrat, Winfield Scott Hancock, by 4,454,416 popular votes to 4,444,952—a mere 9,464 margin. In the Electoral College, the result was more decisive—Garfield received 57.99 percent (214 votes and nineteen states) to Hancock's 42.01 percent (155 votes and nineteen states).[480]

Garfield was sworn in as president on Friday, March 4, 1881. In his inaugural address, he pledged fidelity to the notion of good government prevalent at the time:

> Acting always within the authority and limitations of the Constitution, invading neither the rights of the States nor the reserved rights of the people, it will be the purpose of my Administration to maintain the authority of the nation in all places within its jurisdiction; to enforce obedience to all the laws of the Union in the interests of the people; to demand rigid economy in all the expenditures of

the Government, and to require the honest and faithful service of all executive officers, remembering that the offices were created, not for the benefit of incumbents or their supporters, but for the service of the Government.

He closed with an appeal to all Americans to assist him in making the country a better place. "And now, fellow-citizens, I am about to assume the great trust which you have committed to my hands. I appeal to you for that earnest and thoughtful support which makes this Government in fact, as it is in law, a government of the people."[481]

Garfield had been a promising public servant, and now, in September 1881, he was dead. His body returned by train from New Jersey to Washington, DC, where the murdered president lay in state in the Capitol rotunda for two days and nights. Mourners honored him with three funerals—one in Elberon, New Jersey, a second in Washington, DC, and a final service in Cleveland, Ohio, where the slain executive was buried.[482]

As for the man who killed him, Charles Guiteau languished behind bars in the District of Columbia jail. The public acclaim he had anticipated never came to pass. Even an optimistic egotist like Guiteau realized after a while that he was not the national hero he thought he should be. If he remained under any illusions to that effect, one of his guards, Sergeant William Mason, drove the point home. On September 11, 1881, eight days before Garfield's death, Mason fired a bullet through Guiteau's prison window, narrowly missing the assassin's head. When he was apprehended, Mason confessed that he was tired of protecting a wretch such as Guiteau. For his brash act, the sergeant received an eight-year prison term.[483]

Guiteau was not so fortunate. Many Americans wondered whether he would shield himself from punishment by employing an insanity defense, but it was not to be. Although Guiteau initially claimed insanity—"The Divine pressure on me to remove the president was so enormous that it destroyed my free agency, and therefore I am not legally responsible for my act," he said— the prosecution demonstrated that the gunman understood the consequences of his actions and knew what he did was wrong, which was enough to invalidate insanity as a defense.[484]

United States v. Charles J. Guiteau commenced on November 14, 1881, fifty-six days after Garfield's death. The assassin's brother-in-law, George

14.4 James A. Garfield died on September 19, 1881, owing to complications resulting from an assassin's bullet. Courtesy of the Library of Congress.

Scoville, served as his defense attorney. "If I didn't think the unfortunate man was insane, I would not defend him at all," Scoville explained.[485]

Guiteau's unstable personality was on display throughout the trial. He constantly sought to interject himself into the proceedings, complaining that he was not responsible for Garfield's death—the president's doctors were. He also berated his attorney, at one point telling Scoville, "You spoil everything by cross-examination." Calling out to witnesses, speaking to the judge, and even appealing for financial and legal assistance, he was the same ill-mannered, grating, obnoxious nuisance he had been throughout his adult life. When he learned that a fund had been established to care for Garfield's family, Guiteau exclaimed that it "was a splendid thing," but now, "I want them to give me some money."[486]

The central issue of the trial—the defendant's sanity, or lack thereof—seemed to many observers to be a waste of time. The man had shot the president, and the president eventually died. Everything else was irrelevant. The jury agreed. After suffering through two months of testimony, the jurors deliberated for less than an hour before returning a guilty verdict on January 13, 1882. As the courtroom burst into cheers and wild applause on learning of the verdict, Guiteau expressed his anger. "My blood be on the head of the jury, don't you forget it," he called out. "That is my answer. . . . God will avenge this outrage."[487]

Guiteau was one of the few Americans outraged at the verdict. Although Guiteau's siblings engaged in a concerted to effort forestall his execution, the public mood would allow for no leniency. This man Guiteau had committed a terrible crime, and he must pay the price. Just after noon on June 30, 1882, he did. He was forty years old when he died at the gallows.[488]

With the benefit of hindsight, and far removed from the passions of the day, Charles Guiteau can be seen for what he was—a delusional, mentally ill antagonist. His life-long pattern of hatching grandiose schemes based on an irrational belief in his own intellectual powers destroyed any chance that he had to live a normal, meaningful life. Everyone who came into contact with Guiteau as an adult recognized that there was something not quite right about this man. Until he shot President Garfield, however, no one thought him dangerous. He was odd, obnoxious, and difficult to take in large doses, but his eccentricities did not appear to have been harmful to others. Encountering him today, in an era when therapy and the use of medication to control mood swings and erratic behavior do not carry the same stigma as they did in bygone days, one would urge the gentleman to seek professional help.[489]

Guiteau seems to have been a Type 4 actor. He suffered from severe emotional and cognitive distortions. While he did not hear voices or believe that he could defy the laws of gravity, he was never able to perceive reality or his place within the world of other people. He believed that his actions were somehow supernatural in the sense that they were divinely inspired. God acted through him. The republic needed to be saved from a fiend, Garfield, and he, Guiteau, would be the instrument for carrying out the divine plan. Had the insanity defense not been so vilified in that era, he might have been declared insane and imprisoned in a psychiatric hospital for the balance of his life, as some later assassins and would-be assassins were. Charles J. Guiteau had the misfortune to be a delusional man who acted in a time and place where anyone, regardless of his motives, was required to pay the ultimate price for acting on a delusion.[490]

Chapter 15

"LOCK ME UP; I AM THE MAN WHO SHOT THE MAYOR": CARTER HARRISON, SR. (1893)

Mary Hanson, a domestic, told the tale eloquently: "Early last evening, there was a ring at the doorbell. I went to the door, and found a man I did not know. That was about seven o'clock. I asked the man what he wanted, and he said he wanted to see Mayor Harrison." Mayor Harrison was Carter Henry Harrison, Sr., then serving his fifth term as mayor of Chicago. The mention of a ringing doorbell referred to the mayor's residence located at 231 Ashland Boulevard. Last evening was Saturday, October 28, 1893.[491]

Earlier that day, Mayor Harrison had delivered a speech on American Cities Day before an estimated crowd of 5,000 people, most of whom were mayors and city councilmen attending the World's Columbian Exposition held in the Windy City from May 1 through October 31, 1893. The mayor was enjoying his twilight years. Although few political figures are universally loved, he was a generally revered figure in the city. He had amassed a tidy personal fortune during a lengthy business career, and his political future appeared bright. On a personal level, he was engaged to wed a much younger woman, Annie Howard, who was reputed to possess "a charming disposition" as well as a bank account estimated at three million dollars.[492]

Harrison's speech that day was an uplifting, albeit jingoistic, paean to the virtues of the Midwest's leading city. His enthusiasm was infectious. "I believe I shall see the day when Chicago will be the biggest city in America, and the third city on the face of the globe," he confidently told the crowd. The mayor was an optimistic soul. At sixty-eight years of age, he believed he had many years left to witness his beloved city's continued ascent. "I intend to live for more than half a century, and at the end of that half-century, London will be trembling lest Chicago shall surpass it."[493]

With his boosterism flaming white-hot, Harrison reveled in the warm glow of Chicago's successful world's fair. It had not proceeded flawlessly, but the event had gone well enough that the mayor could regale local officials with stories of mighty Chicago on the rise without risking ostracism or, worse, ridicule. In his view, the speech was a resounding success. He returned home from the day's festivities invigorated by all that he had seen, but he was also spent. One account described the crowded schedule as "having taxed his energies to the utmost."[494]

Harrison enjoyed dinner at his home with two of his children, Sophie and Preston, while struggling not to fall asleep at the table. With the meal ended, he wandered into the back parlor to nap on a couch. He was unaware that a visitor had appeared at the door a few minutes earlier.

Ms. Hanson was not disturbed by a stranger arriving to speak with the man of the house. As she well knew, Mayor Harrison prided himself on his accessibility to the citizens of Chicago. It was not uncommon for an unfamiliar figure to appear unannounced and request a meeting with his elected executive. Still, there were limits. "I told him Mr. Harrison was eating supper, and asked him to call again. About 7:45 he came back, and I went to the door and let him in."[495]

The fellow stood near the front door while Ms. Hanson ambled back to speak with the mayor. "Mr. Harrison was sitting in the second room to the front," she recalled. "I told him there was a man in the hall who wanted to see him, and I left the man in the hall and went to the kitchen." She had performed such duties numerous times, but this night was different. "Just as I got in the kitchen, I heard several shots fired and then I ran out from the kitchen to where I had left Mr. Harrison and the man. I saw the unknown man running out the door. Mr. Harrison staggered into the second room and out the door to the hall, where he fell."[496]

The mayor's son, Preston, was upstairs in his bedroom dressing for an engagement scheduled for later that evening. "It must have been about eight o'clock when I heard a noise," he said. "I was startled; it sounded like a picture falling." When Preston stepped into the upstairs hallway, he was surprised to see smoke wafting up from downstairs. Curious, he started for the staircase. As he descended, he heard two distinct pops. He realized that he had heard blasts from a revolver. To his horror, it reminded him of "a manhole explosion."[497]

Daughter Sophie was upstairs writing a letter after dinner when she heard an unusual sound. "I thought nothing of it," she later explained. She heard her father cry out, but she did not know he was in distress. She never entertained the notion that he had been hurt.[498]

In the meantime, as Preston Harrison entered the hall, he saw his father lying on his back on the floor. Servants surrounded the supine figure. "Father is not hurt, is he?"

Mayor Harrison, still conscious, answered. "Yes," he said. "I am shot. I will die."[499]

It was clear that someone—apparently the stranger who had appeared at the door at 7:00 p.m. and later returned—had shot the mayor with a revolver before escaping. "After he ran away," Mary Hanson said, "they went for doctors, who came right away." It was too late. The wounds were too extensive. The first bullet struck the mayor's hand and lodged in his abdomen. Another bullet struck him in the chest near the heart.[500]

Harrison's coachman, Paul Eliason Risberg, on hearing the sound of gunfire, retrieved his own revolver and got off two shots at the fleeing figure. The mayor's assailant returned fire. No one was injured in the exchange. By the time the coachman returned to the house, a crowd had gathered.[501]

One of the men in the crowd, a neighbor named William J. Chalmers, folded his coat and slid it beneath Harrison's head. The mayor remained prostrate on the floor. His friends lifted him from the floor and placed him on a couch, but to no avail. As Mary Hanson recalled, "Mr. Harrison died about twenty minutes after the shooting."[502]

As doctors and police officers descended on the house, stunned loved ones tried to make sense of what had happened. Harrison had amassed his share of political enemies, as any elected official does, but it was not readily obvious why anyone would murder him in such a brutal fashion. He had been elected to office five times, and was mostly beloved by his constituents.[503]

Unbeknownst to anyone inside the mayor's house, within half an hour of the shooting, a small, clean-shaven, poorly dressed man walked into the Desplaines Street police station. He carried a .38-caliber Smith and Wesson revolver, which he gingerly handed to the desk sergeant. Without fanfare or bombast, he uttered an astonishing announcement. "I did it," he said. When the sergeant asked what he meant, the fellow confessed. "Lock me up; I am the man who shot the mayor." The sergeant was incredulous until he examined the gun. It smelled of gunpowder and contained four spent cartridges.[504]

News of the assault had just begun circulating as this strange fellow entered the police station. When asked why he committed the crime, the man supplied a straightforward response. He killed the mayor, he said, because

15.1 Carter Harrison, Sr., was serving a fifth term as mayor of Chicago when an assailant murdered him in 1893. Courtesy of the Library of Congress.

"he betrayed my confidence. I supported him through his campaign and he promised to appoint me corporation counsel. He didn't live up to his word."[505]

When asked his name, he answered, "Prendergast, Patrick Eugene, or Eugene Prendergast. Makes no difference which. The last name is Patrick." When asked where he lived, Prendergast was not certain. "I don't know; I don't know where—around here somewhere, I guess. But, I do not live at the railroad tracks. I'll tell you that." Beyond the vague response, he could provide no details about his residence. It was difficult to tell whether his confusion was genuine or feigned.

One interlocutor asked if he had ever been a lawyer. Prendergast said he did not know, but he did not think he had ever been a lawyer.

"Then why did you expect to be made corporation counsel?"

Prendergast could not supply a satisfactory answer. "The mayor promised me—that's all," he said. Most of his responses following this admission were incomprehensible.[506]

Investigators later turned up information about the gunman. Patrick Eugene Joseph Prendergast was an Irish immigrant. Born in April 1868, he came to Chicago with his family in 1871. They arrived in time to experience the great fire that burned the city that October.[507]

According to his mother, with whom he lived all his life, Prendergast was "a shy and retiring kind of boy." He received a grade-school education— "nearly the equivalent to a high school degree"—which was common at the time. As he floated through school, he was quiet and unobtrusive, seldom participating in games with his peers. Prendergast's father died when the boy was thirteen, and his alienation was complete. The two apparently had been close, and the death deeply affected Eugene.[508]

As a young adult, he took an interest in law and politics, sometimes attending meetings of the Single-Tax Club, an organization that advocated for landowners to pay a tax on their real-estate holdings. The club subscribed to the tenets of an economic philosophy known as Georgism, named for the economist Henry George. A progressive, George believed that people should own the value they produce, but he argued that value found in land should belong to everyone equally. This popular doctrine appealed to poor workers who saw themselves as wage slaves, toiling away in grim factories for subsistence pay.[509]

Prendergast immersed himself in political treatises, obsessing over whatever issue he seized on. As with self-taught men who do not fully understand what they read, his political ideas did not always make sense. No matter; incoherence was not an impediment to free expression. Convinced that he possessed useful advice for political leaders, he frequently sent postcards to elected officials, addressing them as equals, offering ideas on legislation and policies that he deemed beneficial. The postcards numbered somewhere in the hundreds.[510]

He became fixated on one political leader in particular: Chicago Mayor Carter Henry Harrison, Sr. When Harrison ran for reelection in 1891, the young man, now a distributor that directed young boys to deliver newspapers throughout the city, threw himself into the campaign. His efforts went unappreciated. Harrison had no knowledge of Prendergast's contributions, for they mainly consisted of the man's trademark postcards mailed by the score, hastily scribbled appeals filled with non sequiturs and gibberish. Harrison lost that election, much to Prendergast's consternation, but two years later, the result was more positive. Harrison won reelection for a fifth term in April 1893.[511]

Confident that the mayor owed his election to Prendergast's postcard-writing, which he repeated in 1893, the young scribe naturally expected a reward. That was how politics worked. When your man won high office, he passed favors your way. To the victor belong the spoils.[512]

Why Prendergast decided that he would be rewarded with the job of corporation counsel is not clear. He later claimed that the mayor had promised him the position, but no record of such a promise exists. Prendergast had no legal training, nor had he ever made himself known in legal circles. Even at its most blatant, the spoils system did not reward people who lacked all qualification. Perhaps he imagined a meeting where a promise was made.[513]

Just as President Garfield's assassin, Charles Guiteau, with whom Prendergast has been compared, believed he was owed a high-ranking position in an incoming administration because of his campaign work, this young newspaper distributor had no doubt that he would soon receive a call from his patron. It was unrealistic, of course, but facts had ceased to matter for Prendergast. He was laboring under a powerful delusion, and nothing could disabuse him of the notion that he would ascend into high office.

Yet by October 1893, the fantasy had worn thin and Prendergast had lost patience. Harrison had won his new term six months earlier, and yet he had not contacted Prendergast to discuss the position. During the first week in October, the young hopeful appeared in City Hall and announced to a startled clerk that he, Prendergast, would soon become the new corporation counsel. The clerk laughed at the man's audacity as well as his delusions of grandeur.[514]

After Prendergast insisted on seeing the incumbent, the clerk scurried off to dredge up the current corporation counsel. The man, a Mr. Kraus, stepped into the waiting area. When Prendergast explained to the befuddled man that his successor had arrived, Kraus smiled. Something in the smile struck Prendergast as smug and condescending. No one understood that the mayor was about to make a change. In fact, they seemed downright contemptuous of the man who would soon occupy a lofty perch in the halls of power. He beat a hasty retreat.[515]

Brooding over the encounter, Prendergast at last recognized that he would not be appointed corporation counsel. Rather than attribute it to a delusion on his part, however, he decided that Mayor Harrison had promised the appointment would be forthcoming, and he had lied. To make matters worse, Prendergast's numerous entreaties were ignored. When he appeared at City Hall to claim the position that rightfully belonged to him, he was mocked and humiliated. The indignity was more than his fragile ego could take.[516]

Around two o'clock on American Cities Day—Saturday, October 28, 1893—Prendergast walked out of his mother's home, where he still lived, and visited a shoe dealer on Milwaukee Avenue. He paid $4 to purchase a revolver, which he loaded with five cartridges, leaving the chamber empty so the gun would not accidentally discharge. From there, he visited Illinois Governor John P. Altgeld's office in the Unity Building. Whether he intended to assassinate the governor is not known. Denied entry to the building because he "looked pale and strangely excited," he walked back out to the street. His whereabouts until 7:00 that evening are not known. Apart from shooting the mayor, the next time he attracted attention was when he walked into the Desplaines Street police station and confessed to shooting Harrison.[517]

The shocking murder cast a pall over the closing days of the Chicago World's Fair. The organizers canceled the planned closing ceremony. Instead, they held a memorial for Mayor Harrison complete with Chopin's "Funeral March" and a blessing and benediction. It was an anticlimactic ending to what had been an exciting and well-received international event.[518]

The mayor's funeral procession consisted of 600 carriages that stretched along the route for miles. Harrison's Kentucky mare trotted with stirrups crossed and an empty saddle. Flags flew at half-mast. By the time the procession reached Graceland Cemetery, darkness had descended, creating an eerie scene for participants at the graveside service.[519]

As for the man who shot the mayor, Prendergast remained behind bars. He confessed to the crime, but his state of mind became the crucial question. If he was mentally ill at the time of the murder, he would not be punished by the criminal justice system but would be sent to a hospital for the insane. During his trial in December 1893, his defense lawyers argued for insanity, but prosecutors countered by examining the man's actions on the day of the shooting.[520]

When he acquired the revolver, Prendergast had the presence of mind to ensure that a round was not loaded in the chamber. The type of weapon he purchased was well known for discharging prematurely when inadvertently jostled. If he had been genuinely insane, prosecutors argued, would he have known to exercise such care in handling the murder weapon? They did not think so, and neither did the jury.[521]

On December 29, 1893, after deliberating for one hour and three minutes, the jurors returned a guilty verdict. The punishment, they decided, was death. The defense attorneys had done their best to spare Prendergast. At a separate hearing to determine the defendant's sanity, or lack thereof, they even retained the services of Clarence Darrow, who was building a reputation as America's preeminent advocate—but it was not enough. Darrow convinced the court to allow the "poor demented imbecile," Prendergast, to submit to a sanity inquest, but the maneuver failed to save the defendant. Public demand for retribution was enormous. Grief-stricken Chicagoans insisted that Prendergast must pay the ultimate price, and their will was too strong to resist.[522]

Friday, July 13, 1894, was the appointed day. At ten o'clock that morning, the sheriff entered the condemned man's prison cell and read the death warrant. Prendergast did not reply, although he told a clergyman, "We may yet hear from the Governor." When the call did not come, at 11:35 a.m., the deputy sheriff climbed onto the scaffold and raised his hand, the signal for the procession to commence. A minute later, Prendergast and half a dozen law enforcement officers as well as the clergyman appeared. As he marched past 200 or so ticketholders watching from the so-called "Death Corridor," the prisoner stared straight ahead. His only reported reaction was to make the mark of the cross on his breast and forehead.

When the executioner fixed a white shroud over his head, Prendergast sighed. He seemed ready to launch into a long-winded diatribe, but the moment passed. Standing at the gallows with the noose adjusted around his neck, Prendergast knew his death was at hand and no last-minute reprieve would occur. He walked to the center of the platform and stood quietly. The hangman sprang the trap, the floor collapsed, and the assassin fell to his death. He was twenty-six years old. Two hundred and fifty-eight days had elapsed since he had shot and killed Mayor Harrison.[523]

In many ways, Patrick Eugene Joseph Prendergast resembles Charles J. Guiteau, who killed James A. Garfield. Both assassins invariably earned the description "a disgruntled officer seeker." In both instances, the men were delusional, possessing neither the ability nor the political connections to secure a place in the administration they believed had aggrieved them. Guiteau rationalized his act as bigger than his own disappointment, a grand gesture necessary to save the republic, deflecting attention from what was probably his true motive, namely his personal displeasure at failing to receive an appointment. Prendergast made no such grandiose claims. He shot Mayor Harrison because he believed that the mayor had lied about installing Prendergast as corporation counsel.[524]

Prendergast, like Guiteau, was a Type 4 actor. His life was filled with delusions that bore little relation to reality. He was not a lawyer, and therefore

ASSASSIN PATRICK EUGENE JOSEPH PRENDERGAST, TO BE HANGED TODAY.

15.2 This drawing of the assassin Prendergast appeared on page one of the *Chicago Daily Tribune* on the day he was executed, Friday, July 13, 1894. Reprinted from the *Chicago Daily Tribune*, July 13, 1894, page 1.

he was unqualified to serve as a lawyer in Harrison's administration. His efforts to secure the mayor's election in 1893 were marginal, at best. Firing off incomprehensible postcards to strangers was not an effective campaign tactic, and only a man suffering from some form of neurosis or psychosis would equate such actions with a promise of political reward.

In a later era, when mental illness was better understood, Prendergast probably would have escaped the gallows. In the late nineteenth century, however, insanity claims were regarded as a dodge, a careful trick manufactured by lawyers to allow criminal defendants to avoid punishment when they were adjudged guilty. Citizens screamed for vengeance, and so the harshest penalty possible was meted out. It also hurt Prendergast's cause that he was such an unsympathetic character. Strange, taciturn, and with a vaguely menacing look, he was the sort of expendable person that no one mourned apart from his family members. Sometimes the mentally ill cannot avoid paying a price for their violent actions.[525]

Chapter 16

"I DON'T KNOW WHETHER YOU FULLY UNDERSTAND THAT I HAVE JUST BEEN SHOT; BUT IT TAKES MORE THAN THAT TO KILL A BULL MOOSE": THEODORE ROOSEVELT (1912)

Theodore Roosevelt, twenty-sixth president of the United States, left office in March 1909. He had pledged to retire at the end of his second term, fulfilling a tradition that every president had observed since George Washington voluntarily departed in 1797. The wildly popular, energetic Roosevelt, nicknamed the Bull Moose for his seemingly unstoppable vitality, had enjoyed his time in office as few men ever had, but he was confident that his hand-picked successor, William Howard Taft, would continue his policies and secure TR's legacy. Roosevelt came to regret his decision to retire.[526]

By 1912, the former president believed that Taft was not sufficiently committed to progressive causes. Roosevelt had opposed powerful corporate forces because he believed they harmed the interests of working people. Much of his administration had been devoted to "trust-busting," or breaking up monopolies that took advantage of average men and women. In the years since TR had left the executive mansion, the conservative Republicans under Taft had turned a blind eye to corporate malfeasance, at least in Roosevelt's opinion. Bitterly disappointed in his friend's administration, Roosevelt publicly broke ranks with Taft. Unable to wrest the 1912 Republican presidential nomination away from the incumbent, Roosevelt led the Progressive wing of the Grand Old Party away to form a new organization, the Bull Moose Progressive Party. He was anointed the new party's candidate to challenge Taft and Democratic nominee Woodrow Wilson in the fall presidential election.[527]

Bull Moose supporters faced an uphill climb. After the two party system solidified in mid-nineteenth-century America, it became increasingly difficult for third parties to compete in presidential contests. Lacking the network of political operatives, grassroots mobilization resources, and financing of a major party, third-party candidates knew they must overcome formidable odds. Despite the challenges, TR believed that he could surmount any obstacles in his path. His widespread fame, exuberant personality, and tremendous self-confidence ensured that he would make a good showing. If any third-party candidate could win the White House, Roosevelt believed he could do it.

The colonel, as he liked to be called in his post-presidential years, set out on an exhausting, whirlwind campaign tour across the country. Everywhere he went, large crowds of excited well-wishers and curiosity seekers turned out to greet the famous man who sought a third term in office.[528]

Despite the raucous crowds and enthusiasm of the masses, Roosevelt's ambition was not met with universal approbation. One man, thirty-six-year-old bartender John Flammang Schrank of New York, became convinced that

16.1 Former President Theodore Roosevelt, pictured here, sought a third term as president in 1912. Courtesy of the Library of Congress.

no one should ever become president of the United States for a third term. Schrank had a dream, or perhaps it was a vision, in the wee morning hours of September 15, 1901, where the spirit of the assassinated President William McKinley instructed the German immigrant to avenge his death. Appearing only hours after McKinley had shuffled off his mortal coil, the apparition intimated that TR, who was serving as vice president at the time Leon Czolgosz shot and killed McKinley, was the mastermind behind the murder.[529]

Years passed and Schrank failed to act on his vision, but he never forgot what he had seen. On August 7, 1912, the same night that Roosevelt accepted the Bull Moose Party presidential nomination, Schrank experienced a new dream. This time, he awoke with a startling conviction: Theodore Roosevelt must not recapture the presidency. If the colonel recaptured the White House, he would become a new Napoleon. Even as Schrank wrestled with how he should interpret the dream, he awoke in the night five weeks later and encountered McKinley's ghost again. This time, Schrank realized that he could not shirk his duty. McKinley was instructing him to kill the Bull Moose, and he could no longer refuse.[530]

He bought a Colt .38 pistol for $14 and headed out on the road to follow Roosevelt as the old warhorse campaigned for the third term. Schrank headed to New Orleans before moving on to Atlanta, Georgia; Charleston, South Carolina; and Chattanooga, Tennessee. He came close to shooting the third termer in Chattanooga, but he lost his nerve and failed to act. Castigating himself for his timidity, he headed up the Midwest, trailing TR through Indiana and into Chicago. He probably could have done the deed in the Windy City, but he changed his plan at the last minute because he liked the city of Chicago and did not wish to tarnish its image.[531]

The moment of reckoning came in Milwaukee on October 14, 1912. The colonel was leaving the Hotel Gilpatrick on his way to a speaking engagement in the municipal auditorium before a crowd of some 9,000 supporters. As usual when Roosevelt was in town, a throng of citizens had appeared to cheer him on. Acknowledging the onlookers with a wave of his hand, the colonel stepped into an open car for the short ride to his venue.

Suddenly, a muzzle flash erupted from the crowd. Roosevelt's knees buckled and he staggered backward, collapsing into the seat. Elbert Martin, a stenographer traveling with the Roosevelt entourage, leapt from the car onto a man clutching a gun and tossed the fellow to the ground. Planting his knee on the man's back, Martin wrested the gun from his hand. Several police officers sprang into action as well. Witnessing the horrifying scene, members of the crowd gasped. Several onlookers screamed.[532]

Inside the car, Henry Cochems, TR's aide, asked if his boss was hit. The colonel confirmed that he was. "He pinked me, Harry," the wounded man said.

Despite his injury, Roosevelt had the presence of mind to ask about the gunman. "Don't hurt him," he called as the crowd chanted, "kill him! Kill him! Kill him!" TR was curious about the assailant. "Bring him to me!"

With Schrank now unarmed and restrained, the officers dragged the man over so that Roosevelt could look into his face. The assailant did not appear to be the stereotypical mustachioed, bomb-throwing, gun-wielding anarchist. In fact, he was a clean-shaved and ordinary looking. For a moment, the two men gazed at each other. "Officers, take charge of him and see that no harm is done to him," the colonel finally instructed.[533]

Although he was alert and ambulatory, TR had been shot and undoubtedly required medical attention. His aides insisted that his car be redirected to the closest hospital, but Roosevelt would have none of it. "You get me to that speech," he urged his driver. "It may be the last one I shall ever deliver, but I am going to deliver that one."[534]

His entourage was stunned. The Bull Moose's stamina was legendary, but this sort of bravado was taking things too far. Henry Cochems, in particular, continued to urge the candidate to cancel the speech. Ignoring his assistant, TR called out to the crowd, "We are going to the hall. We are going to the hall." Addressing his driver, the colonel instructed him to "start the machine. Go ahead, go on."

As the car moved slowly through the crowd, Roosevelt opened his heavy winter coat to reveal a large red bloodstain. John McGrath, another stenographer traveling with the campaign, exclaimed, "Why, colonel, you have a hole in your overcoat. He has shot you."

"I know it," TR replied.

It was an astonishing moment. The thought of moving on to the auditorium was almost inconceivable, yet TR would not yield. Reassuring his aides that he was up to the task, the colonel minimized the extent of his wound. "I know I am good now," he said. "I don't know how long I may be. This may be my last talk in this cause to our people, and while I am good I am going to

16.2 This John Falter painting depicts the moment when John Schrank shot former president Theodore Roosevelt in 1912. Courtesy of the Shapell Manuscript Collection.

drive to the hall and deliver my speech." Although no one was satisfied with the reassurances, the colonel's men did as they were told.

Arriving to a rousing welcome from a crowd amassed outside the auditorium, Roosevelt shuffled into a dressing room to wait for his dramatic entrance. While he was there, he allowed a doctor to examine his wound. Dr. Scurry Terrell, a throat specialist who was traveling with the party to keep TR's voice fit for the multitude of speeches the candidate would deliver, helped to unbutton Roosevelt's coat. The shirt and woolen undershirt were soaked in blood. Lifting the garments, Roosevelt exposed a half-inch bullet wound below his right breast. He took it as a good sign that he was not coughing up blood, which would indicate internal bleeding. "It's all right, doctor," Roosevelt said. "It didn't go through."[535]

Dr. Terrell joined the chorus of aides urging the colonel to head for a hospital in lieu of taking the stage. Despite continued protests, TR remained firm. He understood the political advantages of carrying on with a bullet lodged in his chest.

The man of the hour strode into the auditorium to thunderous applause. After he took his seat and listened to the invocation, Roosevelt leaned over to Henry Cochems, who had agreed to introduce the featured speaker, and directed, "You tell them, Harry." His aide nodded as he rose from his seat.

"We have with us a guest who embodies the Democratic qualities of Jefferson and the Republican qualities of Lincoln," Cochems told the crowd, "the one who towers above all others in service of his country—the good citizen, the good father, the good civilian, but above all, the good soldier. Ladies and gentlemen, I have something to tell you, and I hope you will receive it with calmness. As he left his hotel, a dastardly hand aimed a revolver at the Colonel, and he will speak to you, though there is a bullet somewhere in his breast."

It was almost too dramatic a tale to believe. Someone called out, "fake! Fake!"

TR stood and lifted his hand to quiet the crowd. Stepping downstage to begin his speech, he smiled. "No," he said in a voice that was surprisingly steady and loud, "it's no fake." He opened his coat to display the blood stains on his shirt. Many audience members gasped aloud. A few women could be heard screaming.[536]

Always a master thespian, the colonel knew how to milk the scene for maximum effect. "Friends, I shall ask you to be as quiet as possible. I don't know whether you fully understand that I have just been shot; but it takes more than that to kill a Bull Moose. But fortunately I had my manuscript, so you see I was going to make a long speech, and there is a bullet—there is where the bullet went through—and it probably saved me from it going into my heart." He lifted the pages for the crowd to see where the shot had passed through the paper. "The bullet is in me now, so that I cannot make a very long speech, but I will try my best."

The audience hushed, each man and woman no doubt astounded at the unfolding drama. TR delivered his lengthy address with his usual aplomb. Several times, as he paused, voices from the audience urged him to end the talk or at least sit down. Waving away concerns for his health, the Bull Moose persevered.

After eighty minutes, he finally wrapped it up. "I ask you to look at our declaration and hear and read our platform about social and industrial justice and then, friends, vote for the Progressive ticket without regard to me, without regard to my personality, for only by voting for that platform can you be true to the cause of progress throughout this Union." A plea for adherence to the party platform was a curious conclusion to a speech that commenced with a dramatic personal announcement. For all of his protests to the contrary, Teddy Roosevelt knew that the Bull Moose Progressive Party was embodied in one man, and he was that man.

With his speech concluded, he crept from the stage. He was a strong, energetic, barrel-chested man with an indefatigable will, but even Roosevelt had his limits. He was spent. Turning to Dr. Terrell, he finally surrendered. "Now, I am ready to go with you and do what you want."[537]

The good doctor, joined by TR's other aides, guided the injured man outside the auditorium and through the swarming crowds of people into a waiting car. Minutes later, they arrived at Johnson Emergency Hospital near Milwaukee's Union Station. TR was still on his feet as the hospital staff escorted him inside. Before he was treated, he insisted on dictating a telegram to his wife, Edith. "The wound is a trivial one," he explained.

It was not quite as trivial as he said. Examining x-rays later in the evening, the doctors could not determine whether the bullet had penetrated the lung. One fact was clear, however. The wound would have been far more severe if the bullet had not struck TR's folded speech as well as the eyeglasses case inside his jacket pocket. The Bull Moose had led a charmed life, and Lady Luck once again had favored him.

To ensure that he would recover, the doctors admitted the colonel into the hospital for observation. For once, the old warhorse acquiesced. He was pleased to learn that his wife was on her way. "I am the only person who can manage him," Edith Roosevelt remarked, "and therefore I am going to his bedside."[538]

In the meantime, Milwaukee police officers transported the would-be assassin to the downtown headquarters building for booking. Afterward, they escorted him into a sergeant's office. Chief of Police John T. Janssen was the first man to interrogate the gunman.[539]

Schrank initially refused to divulge his identity or any personal information, but as the interview progressed, he stated his name and revealed much about his thinking. Echoing comments uttered by other assailants of public figures, Schrank defended his act as "my duty as a citizen." He did not

16.3 John Schrank (left), pictured here under arrest, shot Theodore Roosevelt in 1912 because Schrank believed that no man should serve three terms as president. Courtesy of the Library of Congress.

believe that he had acted irrationally or that he was insane. During this first discussion, Schrank appeared to be a normal, well-functioning person. He had never been in legal trouble, nor had he been institutionalized for mental health reasons.

The gunman's troubled life and muddled thinking became evident as the police spent more time getting to know him. Born in Bavaria in 1876, John Schrank came to the United States to live with his aunt and uncle in New York City when he was twelve years old. His relatives operated a bar where Schrank worked for much of his young life. He was devastated when his aunt died in 1910, followed by his uncle a year later, but he was fortunate that they left him a business worth $25,000, a princely sum in 1911. He sold the business and lived off the proceeds before he resolved to stalk Theodore Roosevelt.

Not long after his initial vision, Schrank supposedly enjoyed a brief romance with a local woman named Elsie Ziegler. He later explained that he loved this young woman desperately. They were to be wed, he claimed, although Elsie's brother, Edward, said that his sister had only a "nodding acquaintance" with Schrank. Whatever the case, John Schrank was disconsolate after Elsie Ziegler died in a 1904 ferryboat accident in New York harbor. Her tragic death may have been the event that triggered his mental deterioration.[540]

Following Elsie's death, Schrank moved through his life strangely disconnected from other human beings. He might have lived out his days as a shy, awkward fellow who kept to himself, but it was not to be. He encountered the incorporeal McKinley yet again. Eleven years to the day after his first vision, Schrank was sitting at his desk writing a poem when the dead president reappeared. Schrank dashed off a note chronicling the encounter:

> Sept. 15th, 1912.
>> To the people of the United States
>> September 15 1901- 1:20 AM. in a dream I saw president McKinley sit up in his coffin. painting at (of) a man in a monk's attire in whom I recognized Theo. Roosevelt. The dead president said This is my murderer avenge my death.
>> To prevent is better than to defend.
>> Never let a third term party emblem appear on an official ballot
>> I am willing to die for my country, god has called me to be his instrument
>> So help me god.
>> Eine fester burg ist unser got [the opening line of "A Mighty Fortress is our God," the hymn that was playing as Elsie departed on her ill-fated ferryboat ride]
>> Innocent Guilty.[541]

The 1901 vision had left him perplexed, but with the 1912 vision, Schrank finally understood what he must do. President McKinley had instructed him to shoot the dangerous usurper, Theodore Roosevelt. The third-termer's audacity was breathtaking. He had not been satisfied with deposing McKinley eleven years earlier. Now TR sought a return to power, which surely portended only calamity for the American people. No man, least of all the power-hungry tyrant Theodore Roosevelt, should serve a third term in executive office.

With his duty clear, on September 14, 1912, John Schrank set out to avenge McKinley's murder. Armed with his .38-caliber pistol, he tracked the Bull Moose along a circuitous route that meandered from Charleston, South Carolina, all the way to Milwaukee, Wisconsin, and the fateful encounter outside the Hotel Gilpatrick on October 14.

Given this tale of visions and delusions of grandeur, it was hardly surprising that the alienists who were directed by the court to examine Schrank pronounced him insane. A man who acts at the direction of visions and dream-like apparitions is not someone who is mentally healthy. The presiding judge, August C. Backus, read the psychiatric evaluation and accepted the conclusions. "The court now finds that the defendant John Schrank is insane, and therefore incapacitated to act for himself," Judge Backus announced. "It is therefore ordered and adjudged that the defendant John Schrank be committed to the Northern Hospital for the Insane, near Oshkosh, in the County of Winnebago, state of Wisconsin, until such time when he shall have recovered from such insanity, when he shall be returned to this court for further proceedings according to law."[542]

16.4 A weary-looking Theodore Roosevelt returned to his home in Oyster Bay, New York, on October 22, 1912, eight days after John Schrank shot him in Milwaukee, Wisconsin. Courtesy of the Library of Congress.

Schrank cheerfully accepted the verdict. He told the doctors that he disagreed with their conclusions, but he thanked them for their efforts. Later, he bid farewell to the sheriff who had held him in custody. "I hope I haven't caused you much trouble," he said.

The sheriff assured him that all was well. "You've been the best prisoner we have had here since I have been in office."

"I am glad to hear that, for I do not like to cause people trouble," the amiable would-be assassin explained. "I am not crazy, but as the doctors have said I am, I must go to the asylum. There is nothing else for me to do."[543]

Having dispensed with the pleasantries, Schrank's jailers transferred him to the Northern Hospital for the Insane on the shores of Lake Winnebago near Oshkosh, Wisconsin. There he lived out his days, occasionally complaining about his treatment and always following the latest news. During more than three decades in confinement, Schrank never received a personal letter or a visitor. He must have been especially perturbed when TR's distant cousin, Franklin D. Roosevelt, dared to seek and win a third term as president in 1940. A few years later, on Wednesday, September 15, 1943, John Flammang Schrank, died of pneumonia. He was sixty-seven years old.[544]

As for the Bull Moose, he recovered from his injuries in due course. The same could not be said for his third-party presidential candidacy. Roosevelt stayed in the hospital briefly before returning to his home to recuperate. Within a few weeks, he was back on the campaign trail. He remained a popular, charismatic, larger-than-life character celebrated by Americans from all walks of life. Yet his personal popularity was not enough to overcome the structural difficulties inherent in any third-party challenge for elective office. The Progressives did not control the patronage, political operations, and ground-game resources that the major parties possessed. In pulling the progressive wing of the Republican Party away from Taft and the conservatives, Roosevelt weakened the entire party. The division allowed the Democratic candidate, Woodrow Wilson, to capture the office. When the votes were tabulated, Wilson won 6,293,454 popular votes and 435 electoral votes, carrying forty states. TR and the Progressives won 4,119,538 popular votes and eighty-eight electoral votes, taking six states. The incumbent, William Howard Taft, earned 3,484,980 popular votes, but only eight electoral votes and two states. The Socialist candidate, Eugene Victor Debs, earned 900,672 popular votes, but no electoral votes. Had Roosevelt and Taft joined forces, they probably could have defeated Wilson, but it was not to be. As Roosevelt later grumbled, "the country was sick and tired of reform."[545]

The story of John Flammang Schrank stalking and shooting Theodore Roosevelt has become the stuff of legend. The colonel's refusal to enter the hospital until he could deliver his speech has added to the lore of the tenacious, unstoppable, bear-of-a-man that became a force of nature. Schrank, in the meantime, became the prototype of the Type 4 assailant, suffering from severe cognitive deficiencies. Although he was not quite as impaired as, say, Richard Lawrence, the delusional housepainter who shot at President Andrew Jackson in 1835, Schrank was guided by voices and visions that existed only in his imagination. He was a classic would-be assassin who acted for reasons beyond perceived self-interest or political expediency.[546]

Chapter 17

"HE'S BEEN CONTROLLING MY MIND FOR YEARS. NOW I'VE PUT AN END TO IT": ALLARD K. LOWENSTEIN (1980)

A llard K. Lowenstein was one of a vanishing breed in American politics—
a progressive public figure who strove to promote social justice without
vilifying his opponents, a man who could reach across the aisle and embrace
persons diametrically opposed to his perspective. He counted among his
friends the liberal lion Edward M. "Ted" Kennedy, as well as the conservative
commentator William F. Buckley, Jr. He was a tireless campus activist during
the 1960s and 1970s, assuming prominent positions in both the civil-rights
and the anti-Vietnam movements. His 1980 murder by Dennis Sweeney, a
former protégé, sent shock waves through the community of social activists
and arguably served as a death knell for progressive ideals of the 1960s.[547]

Lowenstein was born in Newark, New Jersey, on January 16, 1929—
coincidentally, the day after Martin Luther King, Jr., was born in Atlanta,
Georgia. The middle child in a family of three, Allard seems to have adored
his father, a doctor who later became a restaurateur, but he felt that his mother
was distant and reserved. He grew up in a comfortable upper-middle-class
home, although he remembered those years as awkward. "As a kid," he once
remarked, "I was always being beaten up and I was funny looking and ended
up feeling left out. I find I can always identify with the people who are left
out."[548]

Educated at the prestigious Horace Mann School in the Bronx,
Lowenstein was enormously ambitious and relentlessly intellectual, but
unwilling to follow established rules or fall into the career pattern set by his
parents. He demonstrated his independent streak by forgoing an Ivy League
college education. Instead, he enrolled in the University of North Carolina in
Chapel Hill. He was enamored of the school's liberal president, Frank Porter

Graham, and he approved of UNC's highly regarded intercollegiate wrestling team, a sport that interested him greatly.

Graham became Lowenstein's idol. Later, Lowenstein served as Graham's special assistant when the college president briefly served as a US senator. Reflecting on Graham's heroic qualities, Lowenstein wrote that, "If iron could be gentle, it would be Frank Graham, a man who could lose his seat in the United States Senate . . . rather than filibuster in violation of his conscience or cheat a Negro boy of his due."[549]

Lowenstein excelled at UNC, serving as president of the National Student Association in 1950. After he graduated from college, he enrolled in Yale Law School. During his law school years, his lifelong habits became evident. One newspaper account later commented on the "ebullient—some would say, frenetic—style of advocacy for the underdog" that emerged as the young man studied law. "While he was earning a law degree at Yale University," the article continued, "he telephoned so many people in search of support for various causes that New Haven telephone operators knew his telephone number from memory."[550]

Following graduation from Yale, Lowenstein served for two years in the army. With his military service behind him, he embarked on a storied career as an educator, activist, and intellectual, eventually teaching at Stanford University, North Carolina State University, and the City College of New York. He also became a crusader extraordinaire, especially among college students. He earned the tongue-in-cheek title "the world's oldest student activist."[551]

Having served with one of his idols as a young man, he enjoyed the privilege of serving with another as he grew to maturity. Lowenstein described Eleanor Roosevelt as "the greatest of human beings, if greatness can be measured by numbers of people helped and quantities of energy guided to useful purpose." To his delight, he worked with her at the American Association for the United Nations in 1957. She later wrote the foreword to his one and only book, *Brutal Mandate: A Journey to South West Africa*, published in 1962. The book recounted the young man's trip to the nation now known as Namibia, a United Nations trust territory at the time, where he surreptitiously collected information about apartheid practices in South Africa.[552]

As he launched his academic career, Lowenstein came to Stanford University in 1961 to serve as assistant dean of men and director of Stern Hall, a men's dormitory complex. He also taught courses in the political science department. From his first day, he connected with young people. In an era where adolescents were becoming more politically conscious and the so-called generation gap was emerging, Lowenstein appeared to have his feet planted in both worlds. He was thirty-two years old and a college administrator, but he dressed informally, refused to talk to students in a condescending manner, and appeared genuinely interested in young people. It was a tribute that Stanford administrators hired such an iconoclast because Lowenstein, in the words of one commentator, "had few of the traditional qualities expected of assistant deans. He dominated conversations, invariably believing he knew best, and, never really comfortable working for anyone but himself, he was not much of a company man." He was, however, empathetic, energetic, and charismatic.[553]

During this time, Lowenstein encountered a young man who would play a pivotal role in his life and death. Dennis Sweeney was a freshman history major at Stanford in the fall of 1961. He was born in Oregon in 1943, but his parents separated when he was an infant. His father later died in an accident while serving in the army. The boy's stepfather, Gabriel Sweeney, adopted the young man when Dennis was fourteen. He took the name "Sweeney" at that time.[554]

As he did with many students, Lowenstein took Sweeney under his wing, providing him with positive reinforcement and introducing him to the world of political activism. It was an era brimming with youthful exuberance as adolescents learned that they could exercise substantial power. Causes abounded, and Al Lowenstein never found a liberal cause he could not support.

He seemed to be everywhere during the late 1950s and early 1960s. He worked on behalf of liberal figures such as Illinois Governor Adlai E. Stevenson and Minnesota Senator Hubert H. Humphrey. He was an early supporter of the Freedom Summer in Mississippi. After Lowenstein was arrested in December 1963 for leading a voter-registration effort in Mississippi, he worked with other civil rights activists to bring college students into the state to register black voters. It was dangerous work, but idealistic young men and women signed on to help. Dennis Sweeney was among the Stanford students who answered the call.[555]

When he committed to a cause, Sweeney did not believe in half measures. Like his mentor, he engaged in frenetic activity. In Sweeney's case, he spent time in McComb, Mississippi, one of the most dangerous places in a dangerous state. He survived two bombing attacks on offices where he worked. He was repeatedly arrested. By the time Freedom Summer concluded in 1964, Sweeney was seen as one of the most battle-hardened white civil rights activists involved with the Student Nonviolent Coordinating Committee (SNCC).[556]

Even as Dennis Sweeney became radicalized by his experiences, Allard Lowenstein backed away from extreme responses to southern provocations. Their different responses to the civil rights activism of the 1960s eventually led to a painful split between the two men. Lowenstein initiated a revolution among his followers, but he did not follow them to their conclusion. As a board member of Martin Luther King, Jr.'s Southern Christian Leadership Conference (SCLC), Lowenstein shared Dr. King's judgment that extremism and violence only beget extremism and violence. Sweeney was moving away from a moderate position, believing that the electoral process, with its incremental approach to change, only prolonged the misery and degradation of poor people of color.[557]

The dispute over whether to seat the Mississippi Freedom Democratic Party (MFDP) delegates, who represented black voters, instead of allowing the white-dominated Mississippi Democratic Party to become credentialed at the 1964 party convention further alienated Sweeney from Lowenstein. Sweeney believed the MFDP was the true party of the people, and therefore the delegates were legitimate. Lowenstein, by contrast, worried that a fissure within the Democratic Party would accomplish little other than to empower and embolden the Republicans in the pending fall 1964 election cycle. Thus, Lowenstein believed that the regular party delegates would have to be seated. It was a classic split between the activist who seeks progress by working through established political channels (Lowenstein) and the young upstart who seeks to step outside the mainstream and work for immediate change through alternative means (Sweeney).[558]

Worse was yet to come. With the rise of the black power movement and the ascendancy of a more radical element within SNCC, Dr. King and his associates appeared quaint and out of touch. Sweeney shared the sentiment that his former mentor was obsolete and weak-willed. New revelations appeared to support his opinion. A few years later, when Americans learned that the CIA had financed Lowenstein's beloved National Student Association, Sweeney and members of the New Left denounced their old professor as, at best, a CIA stooge and, as worst, an active CIA agent.[559]

Sweeney and Lowenstein parted company on bitter terms. Years later, the teacher remembered the break with his former student, calling it "one of the most bitter experiences I had in Mississippi, in personal terms." Lowenstein understood how and why Sweeney became radicalized, especially in light of the dangers the young man faced in McComb. The problem, however, was that Sweeney believed that Lowenstein and his moderate colleagues "were the enemy much more than the white power structure." This kind of personal repudiation was difficult to accept. "We were good friends," Lowenstein said, but "we met under very ugly kinds of circumstances where he would attack me from a very personal feeling."[560]

Another source of personal animosity may have been Lowenstein's confused sexuality. While he married a woman and fathered three children, he was an older man who spent much of his time surrounded by much younger men, many of whom were impressionable and hero-worshipped Lowenstein. Several men later claimed that Lowenstein hugged them inappropriately, although it was never clear whether the physical contact extended beyond undesired touching. Evaluating such claims is difficult because no one filed formal charges or launched an investigation at the time. The allegations did not surface until years after the fact. Dismissing the claims out of hand risks traumatizing victims of sexual assault, but accepting them at face value arguably besmirches the reputation of a well-regarded political figure. In any case, if Sweeney was not a recipient of such clumsy attempts at affection, he probably heard the rumors and concluded that his slightly tarnished hero was more than slightly tarnished.[561]

Whatever the truth behind the claims of an inappropriate relationship with his male protégés, Allard Lowenstein continued his prominent activism throughout the years. In 1962, he left Stanford to teach at North Carolina State College in Raleigh, North Carolina, where he became a vocal champion of desegregation. He also attended the Democratic National Convention in 1960, 1964, and 1968. In 1966, he worked with Senator Robert F. Kennedy to write an influential speech, the Day of Affirmation Address that Kennedy delivered in Cape Town, South Africa, calling for an end to apartheid.[562]

The apogee of Lowenstein's power and influence occurred in 1968 when he became the leader of the "Dump Johnson" movement. As the 1968 presidential election approached, Lowenstein and several other politically liberal activists worried that the incumbent, Lyndon B. Johnson, was too mired down in the Vietnam War to ever recapture his bona fides as a progressive politician. Moreover, even if Johnson somehow could be persuaded to abandon Vietnam, which seemed unlikely, the Democratic Party probably would go down in defeat to the Republicans during the general election unless an alternate candidate could be found.[563]

Lowenstein initially approached his good friend Robert Kennedy to run against Johnson—there was no love lost between LBJ and RFK—but the senator was not yet ready to commit. After South Dakota Senator George McGovern also resisted the opportunity to challenge LBJ in the primaries, Lownstein helped to recruit Minnesota Senator Eugene McCarthy to run. Although McCarthy eventually lost the nomination to Hubert H. Humphrey—and Humphrey lost the general election to Republican Richard M. Nixon—Lowenstein believed that his decision to find someone to challenge Johnson in the primaries pushed the incumbent to withdraw from the race.[564]

Also in 1968, Lowenstein announced his candidacy for a seat in the US House of Representatives for the fifth congressional district of New York, which included Nassau County, Long Island. It was a fairly liberal area, which allowed Lowenstein to win his election. He served but a single term. When the Republican-controlled state legislature gerrymandered the district, he lost his reelection bid. Lowenstein tried several times to win another seat in Congress, but he was unsuccessful. Instead, he channeled his enormous energies into a new position—chairman of the Americans for Democratic Action, an organization that promotes social justice and progressive candidates. He served as chairman from 1971 until 1973.[565]

For all his successes in 1968, Lowenstein was devastated when his friend Robert F. Kennedy died from an assassin's bullet on June 6. In later years, Lowenstein lobbied to have investigators open the case and reexamine the evidence. He was worried that accused gunman Sirhan Sirhan did not act alone that night in the kitchen of the Ambassador Hotel. Although most experts who have examined the evidence still believe that Sirhan acted alone, conflicting accounts and missing evidence suggest to others that a conspiracy existed.[566]

Lowenstein continued his interest in international affairs and social justice during the 1970s. He accepted an appointment as head of the US delegation to the 33rd annual session of the United Nations Commission on

17.1 Allard K. Lowenstein was a well-known progressive figure in twentieth-century American politics. Courtesy of the Special Collections Research Center at North Carolina State University.

Human Rights. During part of the Carter administration, from August 1977 to June 1978, he acted as the alternate US Representative for Special Political Affairs to the United Nations, with ambassadorial rank.[567]

Allard Lowenstein and Dennis Sweeney lost contact with each other after their falling out. During the late 1960s and early 1970s, as the old mentor moved from one high profile position to another, Sweeney dropped out of political movements and gradually succumbed to mental illness. One commentator characterized Sweeney as a "paranoid schizophrenic of the chronic type." The disease of schizophrenia typically appears when the patient is somewhere between his late teens and early thirties. He will hear voices and believe that conspiracies exist to harm or kill him. He can become a danger to himself or to others if left untreated.[568]

Sweeney's symptoms appeared when he was in his late twenties. His parents were so concerned about their son that they sought treatment for him in 1973 after he became convinced that the voices echoing in his head emanated from a transmitter that somehow had been planted in his teeth, perhaps by a dentist who inserted a bridge in his mouth when Dennis was five years old. Anxious to disrupt the transmissions, Sweeney used a pair of pliers to rip out the bridge, leaving a bloody mess in his mouth. Only his front teeth remained. His disfigured jaw gave him a sinister, crazed look.[569]

Distraught, his mother and stepfather had Sweeney committed for a ten-day observation at the Oregon State Mental Hospital. After the doctors concluded that they could not hold him any longer unless he consented, Sweeney strolled out of the hospital. He later bragged that he had learned how to fool the naïve, pathetic doctors. Whenever they asked whether the transmissions had stopped, he said yes. It was a lie, of course. The trick was simple: "Just don't talk about your transmissions."[570]

With the rise of his illness, Sweeney's academic achievements and political activism declined precipitously. He was no longer a brilliant Stanford student with a promising future or a cutting-edge civil rights activist. He was an oddball who floated from one menial job to another. Following a well-worn pattern among schizophrenics, Sweeney spent years figuring out ways to minimize the effect of the voices in his head. The odd jobs he held were far below the standards of the work he had performed in his salad days, but they suited his condition because they required little public interaction or intellectual fatigue. In the meantime, he cut off close ties with his old friends. When he did see his past associates at brief intervals, they winced when they saw his mouth and heard him speak about the voices in his head.

Sweeney's life fell into a routine. He spent most of his time alone, out of sight, fearful that unseen enemies were closing in, sending him damaging transmissions through his mouth. His best bet was to stay off the radar. Despite this strange behavior, outwardly he was no different than anyone else. To an outsider who met him for the first time, he did not appear "crazy" in the conventional sense of the word. His conversations sounded rational and focused. He could speak about the normal fixtures of life, and his words made sense. To the average person who spoke with him in passing, he seemed slightly moody or withdrawn, but nothing suggested that he was dangerous. If they saw his mangled bridgework, they would inquire about the circumstances, but otherwise he was just another quiet man living an unremarkable life.[571]

A decade passed before protégé and mentor briefly reconnected. Lowenstein was mounting another bid for Congress in 1974 when Sweeney suddenly appeared, seemingly out of nowhere. He said he wanted to help with the campaign. As a thirty-one-year-old volunteer, he stood out among the teens and twenty-somethings who worked in the trenches stuffing envelopes, cold-calling voters, and canvassing shopping center parking lots. Sweeney could not fit in, try as he might. After he showed his fellow volunteers his teeth and told them wild stories about tearing out a transmitter, they laughed or rolled their eyes. He was the creepy older man with horrible teeth and a weird way of talking. They made fun of him behind his back, but no one thought him a dangerous figure.

Alerted to Sweeney's presence, Lowenstein stopped in to say hello. He soon realized that his ex-student had endured a terrible ordeal. All this talk of transmissions and strange voices was worrisome. He offered to help Sweeney find a therapist, but the younger man, apparently unsettled at seeing his ex-teacher again, insisted that he was fine. Sweeney recently had worked in a mattress factory in Lynn, Massachusetts. After his short conversation with Lowenstein, he had had enough. He left the campaign and returned to Lynn.[572]

Once again, he dropped out of sight. A year later, Sweeney was living with a United Church of Christ minister and working as a freelance carpenter in Philadelphia. He called Lowenstein on the telephone, angry that the former mentor's CIA operatives were tormenting him. According to Lowenstein's version, Sweeney said, "Call your dogs off."[573]

Lowenstein recognized that Sweeney was delusional. "Dennis, let me help you," he said. "I know people who can help you. I would be happy to get you that help. I'd like to do it." The conversation ended with Sweeney angrily insisting that he was not delusional. He knew that Lowenstein had ordered the CIA to transmit messages into his head.[574]

A friend named Ed Pincus recollected a similar encounter with Sweeney sometime early in 1976. They had spoken on the telephone previously, so Pincus knew that Sweeney was suffering from mental illness. He did not realize how bad it was, however, until Sweeney showed up in Pincus's office. The goofy oddball of earlier times was replaced by an angry, desperate character that said he could no longer endure the transmissions. Something had to change. Pincus feared for his life as the raving man in his office insisted that he was a victim of a conspiracy involving Pincus, radical political activist Angela Davis, and Allard Lowenstein. Pincus ushered Sweeney out of his office as soon as possible, but the disturbed fellow kept turning up in the weeks and months that followed. Pincus worried that his stalker eventually would turn violent.[575]

Sweeney wandered in and out of people's lives in the ensuing years. One constant refrain was his growing hatred for Allard Lowenstein. He became fixated on the man, believing that his former teacher was causing the non-stop transmissions that were driving him to distraction. Sweeney rambled on about somehow making the transmissions end.

The impetus for finally taking action occurred when Sweeney's step-father, Gabriel, died of a heart attack on February 24, 1980. The grieving stepson flew back to Portland, Oregon, for the funeral convinced that the voices inside his head had caused his stepfather's death. He also believed that Lowenstein was directly responsible because he had sued Gabriel Sweeney in court, harassing the poor man and pushing him into an early grave. Investigators never found evidence that such a lawsuit ever existed.[576]

On March 3, not long after he returned from Portland, Sweeney walked into Raub's Sporting Goods store in New London, Connecticut, and purchased a Llama .380-caliber automatic pistol. On his firearms application, he answered "no" to the question, "Have you ever been adjudicated mentally defective or have you ever been committed to a mental institution?" The form went to the New London police department, which found no evidence that Dennis Sweeney was a risk to anyone. He was allowed to purchase the gun eight days after he submitted his application.[577]

By this time, Allard Lowenstein was working in a private law practice in New York City. Sweeney made an appointment to see his old teacher on Friday, March 14, 1980. He arrived on time for his 4:00 p.m. meeting, but Lowenstein was running late, so Sweeney was invited to sit and wait in an outer office. People who saw him that day described him as "expressionless" and "calm." He smoked a Winston cigarette while he waited.

Lowenstein eventually floated out and warmly greeted Sweeney, inviting him inside his private office. The door closed and the two men spoke for several minutes. Witnesses reported that the meeting lasted between ten and twenty minutes. No one knows exactly what they said, but they were seated on opposite sides of the desk. They had not seen each other more than three or four times during the previous fifteen years.

The two men stood to say their goodbyes. Sweeney reported that he told Lowenstein, "We've got to put an end to this, Al." A moment later, he whipped the pistol from his pocket. Realizing that Sweeney meant to shoot him, Lowenstein raised his arm and shouted, "No." Sweeney fired seven times, hitting Lowenstein with five bullets. Three shots came while Lowenstein was lying on the floor.[578]

The gunman made no attempt to flee. He calmly left Lowenstein's private office, laid his pistol on the receptionist's work tray, sat down in a chair, and lit another Winston. Frantic office workers called the police and scrambled over to check on Lowenstein. Robert Layton, a lawyer in the firm, approached Sweeney. "I asked him if he had a gun. He said very calmly, 'I'm not armed anymore.'"[579]

Officers quickly arrived and arrested Sweeney where he sat. They took him to Bellevue Hospital for one night before transferring him to the mental health wing at the Riker's Island Reformatory for Men. "He's been controlling my mind for years," he told his interrogators. "Now I've put an end to it."[580]

Lowenstein's wounds were extensive. His left arm was broken and one lung was irreparably damaged. He took two bullets in the chest. Transferred to St. Clare's Hospital in New York City, he was unconscious but alive. Doctors operated for five and a half hours in a desperate attempt to save the patient's life, but he had lost too much blood and the shock to his system was too massive. He died just after 11:00 p.m. He was fifty-one years old. "His heart just failed to continue to pump," Dr. William F. Mitty, Jr., chairman of the hospital's surgery department, told reporters gathered for an update.[581]

Stunned reactions poured in from across the nation and the world. Senator Ted Kennedy, challenging President Carter for the Democratic nomination, spoke from Chicago. Lowenstein had completed a campaign trip for Kennedy just days before the murder. The senator described his long-time friend and supporter as "a man of enormous concern about this country and about the cause of peace and the cause of social justice." No stranger to assassinations among his friends and family members, Kennedy lamented that,

"Once again, we've seen violence in our society. As one whose family has been touched by violence, I deplore this senseless act."[582]

Congressman Andrew Jacobs, Jr., who knew Lowenstein from their time together in the US House of Representatives, called Lowenstein a "gentle tornado" who "lost a lot of elections but he won a lot of hearts." New York Mayor Ed Koch said, "I met Al Lowenstein in the late 1950s. He was an extraordinary man—very gentle, educated. Everything he did was decent." New York Governor Hugh Carey described Lowenstein as "a tireless fighter for the poor and victimized and the causes he believed in." President Carter issued a statement saying that "the senseless and violent death has cut short a life devoted to reason and justice. From the sit-ins to the campuses to the halls of Congress, Al Lowenstein was a passionate fighter for a more humane, more democratic world. In the civil rights and anti-war movements, his eloquent dedication to nonviolent change inspired many thousands of Americans."[583]

Lowenstein's family held a private funeral service on March 16. A day later, a crowd estimated at 2,500—500 more than capacity—attended a public memorial service held in the Central Synagogue on 55th Street in Manhattan. The service drew people from all walks of life—Republicans, Democrats, elected officials, writers, reporters, lawyers, artists, students, and housewives—who had known Allard Lowenstein for much of his life. The folk trio Peter, Paul, and Mary performed "Amazing Grace," appearing along with popular singer Harry Chapin, who had volunteered for Lowenstein's campaigns. Coretta Scott King and Jacqueline Kennedy Onassis, two of the nation's best known widows, attended the memorial service, as did Andrew Young, a well-known civil rights activist and former United Nations ambassador, and conservative columnist William F. Buckley, Jr.[584]

Allard K. Lowenstein was laid to rest in Arlington National Cemetery, not far from the graves of the Kennedy brothers. The inscription on Lowenstein's headstone came from a note that his friend Robert F. Kennedy once gave him, quoting Emerson: "If a single man plant himself on his convictions and there abide, the huge world will come around to him." In death, he became an untouchable liberal hero, revered as a champion of human rights and a symbol of social and political justice. Yale University students created the Allard K. Lowenstein International Human Rights Project in 1981 in his honor, and the project led to the Allard K. Lowenstein International Human Rights

Clinic. In 2007, Hofstra University endowed the Allard K. Lowenstein Civil Rights Scholarship.[585]

For all of the fond eulogies and tributes following his death, Lowenstein's legacy was mixed. To admirers, he was a hero of the liberal perspective, a man who demonstrated what government could accomplish in the lives of ordinary citizens, while detractors dismissed him as an opportunist and charlatan who stirred up trouble with his activism but failed to effect substantive change. He virtually invented the left-wing student movement of the 1960s, and yet the more radical members of the movement came to despise him as a summer soldier and a sunshine patriot. He alienated as many civil rights activists as he inspired. He served but a single term in the House of Representatives, despite waging multiple campaigns to win another seat in Congress. In his personal life, he stumbled through a painful divorce. His homosexual impulses, which he did not publicly acknowledge, may have led him to abuse young men under his tutelage, although this observation has never been verified and is especially murky and controversial. One writer summed it up well when he wrote that "Lowenstein never quite fit. He was one of those people who helped define an era without ever quite being part of it."[586]

As for the man who pulled the trigger, Dennis Sweeney pleaded not guilty by reason of insanity for shooting Allard Lowenstein. Prosecutors did not dispute his insanity. Accordingly, he was committed to the custody of the New York state mental health system. For eight years, he lived in the Mid-Hudson Psychiatric Center in Hampton, New York, the state's maximum security psychiatric hospital. Doctors eventually transferred him to the Middletown Psychiatric Center, where he worked in the community and earned furloughs to live outside the facility from time to time. By 1992, he was working as a carpenter and cabinetmaker in a woodworking store. In 1995, he was moved to the most lenient psychiatric confinement possible, reporting to the hospital for only one night every two weeks. In 2000, he was released from all state custody.[587]

Dennis Sweeney undoubtedly fit the mold of a Type 4 political assassin. Owing to his schizophrenia, he was suffering from severe cognitive impairment when he shot Allard Lowenstein. A case can be made that he nursed a vendetta against his former mentor for genuine differences arising out of their time working together, but the old grievances served as but a starting point for Sweeney's simmering anger. His paranoid delusions about Lowenstein's

17.2 Dennis Sweeney pleaded not guilty by reason of insanity for shooting his former mentor and friend Allard Lowenstein. This drawing shows Sweeney during a 1980 courtroom appearance. Courtesy of the Courtroom Sketches of Ida Libby Dengrove, University of Virginia Law Library.

supposed involvement in a CIA-hatched scheme to send electric transmissions through Sweeney's teeth pushed the gunman to act. After the sudden death of his stepfather, which he also attributed to the transmitted voices, Sweeney felt that he had little choice but to eliminate the source of his problems. "We've got to put an end to this, Al," he said, and so he did.[588]

Chapter 18

"I BELIEVE THAT FOR ALL OUR IMPERFECTIONS, WE ARE FULL OF DECENCY AND GOODNESS, AND THAT THE FORCES THAT DIVIDE US ARE NOT AS STRONG AS THOSE THAT UNITE US": GABRIELLE GIFFORDS (2011)

Gabrielle Dee "Gabby" Giffords had just entered her third term in the United States House of Representatives from Arizona on January 8, 2011, when she held a "Congress on Your Corner" event to meet constituents outside a Safeway store in Casa Adobes, a suburb of Tucson, Arizona. She had no reason to believe that the event would be dangerous, although she was not a stranger to politically charged controversy and even threats of violence. Arizona was a deeply conservative western state, and Congresswoman Giffords was generally more moderate than her colleagues in the state's congressional delegation. Some constituents also found her politics far too left of center to suit their tastes.

The political culture had grown increasingly divisive and bitter in recent years, especially after voters elected Barack Obama as the first black American president and the Tea Party brand of conservatives became prominent critics of big government and anyone who smacked of statist tendencies. In this new era of 24/7-electronic vitriol, an elected official had to expect that disgruntled individuals would demonstrate their displeasure in sometimes not-so-appropriate ways. It first happened to Giffords in 2009 when a protestor arrived at a town hall meeting packing a gun. After the police arrived, the congresswoman shrugged off the episode. "When you represent a district that includes the home of the O.K. Corral and Tombstone, 'The Town Too Tough to Die,' nothing's a surprise out in Cochise County," she joked. During an interview on the television station MSNBC the next day, the congresswoman lamented that "our office corner has become a place where the Tea Party movement congregates and the rhetoric is incredibly heated, not just the calls but the emails, the slurs."[589]

The slurs continued, and the language escalated into overt action. In March 2010, not long after the congresswoman supported President Barack Obama's Affordable Care Act, someone shot or kicked her Tucson office door hard enough to shatter the glass. Later in the year, her political opponents labeled her a menace to the American way of life in a series of campaign advertisements. In the wake of these political attacks, people telephoned her office and asked to speak to the "communist bitch." Around that same time, someone smashed the lights surrounding a campaign sign outside of a volunteer's home and used a marker to scrawl the word "slut" on Giffords's name.[590]

It was a virulent campaign in a brutal election cycle that coincided with the mental decline of a twenty-two-year-old Pima County resident named Jared Lee Loughner, a young man who would cross paths with Gabby Giffords in 2011. By the fall of 2010, Loughner's life was spiraling out of control as he showed signs of developing mental illness. It hadn't always been that way. In high school, he was withdrawn and moody, but not out of line with many adolescents. He played the saxophone and enjoyed music. He had friends. Sometime during his senior year, he changed, imperceptibly at first, but inexorably. By the time that Loughner dropped out of Mountain View High School, his personality had changed dramatically. An acquaintance, Kylie Smith, later commented that she had known Loughner since preschool, but they lost touch. When she saw him again after a two-year lapse, the change in his appearance and attitude startled her. "He seemed out of it, like he was somewhere else," she subsequently said in an interview. "I could tell he wasn't just drunk and he wasn't just high." Although drugs and alcohol were not solely responsible for his personality changes, he frequently abused substances as his life unraveled. The abuse may have exacerbated Loughner's paranoia and delusional thinking.[591]

From time to time during the years 2006 to 2010, he rallied, briefly getting his life on track before sliding back into the old patterns. Loughner eventually earned his high school diploma from an alternative school and enrolled in courses at Pima Community College. He tried to join the army in

18.1 Gabrielle Giffords, pictured here in 2010, served as a moderate congresswoman in a predominantly conservative district. Courtesy of the Office of the Clerk, United States House of Representatives.

2008. After traveling to a military processing station in Phoenix, Loughner flubbed his interview when he confessed that he smoked marijuana regularly. The admission disqualified him from military service even though he passed an army-mandated drug test that same day.[592]

During his four-year stint at Pima, Loughner mostly floated through his classes without attracting much attention. Beginning in 2010, however, students and teachers began to notice his increasingly erratic behavior. In one memorable classroom outburst, he spoke of using bombs to blow up babies. On another occasion, Loughner made so much noise in the library that a librarian alerted campus police and the officers instructed Loughner that he must comply with college rules or vacate the premises. He promised to behave. A month later, the young man became so hostile toward an instructor that she requested that a campus police officer physically watch over her class.[593]

On still another occasion, Loughner disrupted a math class. Benjamin McGahee, Loughner's math professor, recalled that he "had this hysterical kind of laugh, laughing to himself." Loughner rambled on about "denying math" and similar nonsensical concepts. "One lady in the back of the classroom said she was scared for her life, literally," McGahee remembered. The instructor felt the same way. "When I turned my back to write on the board, I would always turn back quickly—to see if he had a gun." On a math exam, Loughner wrote, "Eat + Sleep + Brush Teeth = Math."[594]

Pima students who encountered the strange young man recognized that he was a problem in the classroom. One student dashed off an email to a classmate, "He scares me a bit. The teacher tried to throw him out and he refused to go." Two weeks later, the same student admitted that "He scares the living crap out of me."[595]

On September 23, 2010, six days before Loughner was suspended from the university, a police officer confronted the student about another outburst. In his report, the officer described Loughner's "incomprehensible" speech, his "jittery" eyes, and his "awkwardly tilted" head. "He very slowly began telling me in a low and mumbled voice that under the Constitution, which had been written on the wall for all to see, he had the right to his 'freedom of thought' and whatever he thought in his head he could also put on paper." The officer concluded that it "was clear he was unable to fully understand his actions." Altogether, college police responded to five separate incidents involving Loughner on two campuses.[596]

When they informed him of the suspension, school administrators also told Loughner and his parents that he could not return to classes until he submitted to a mental health examination demonstrating that he was not a danger to himself or to others. He never submitted such a report. College administrators later received scathing criticism for not taking additional steps to ensure that Loughner received the psychiatric care he needed. A spokesman explained that the college had few options. Loughner's "behavior, while clearly disturbing, was not a crime, and we dealt with it in a way that protected our students and our employees." Insisting that a disruptive student present the results of a mental health exam before returning to classes was the extent of what a college could compel a person to do.[597]

Loughner was bitter about his run-ins with campus administrators and police. In a YouTube video that he posted after his suspension, he complained about the unfair treatment. As far as he was concerned, he had been ill-served by the educational system. "Every Pima Community College class is always a scam!"[598]

While he was descending into mental illness, Loughner held a series of low-paying, low status jobs, mostly in fast food restaurants. His inability to follow directions and his strange behavior led him to quit or be fired from each position. By November 2010, he was at a low point in his life. On November 30, he visited a Sportsman's Warehouse in Tucson and purchased a 9-millimeter Glock pistol. He passed the required National Instant Check System (NICS) background check.[599]

It was unclear how much, if at all, the divisive political culture influenced Loughner's state of mind. Perhaps he focused on Congresswoman Giffords because he had read or heard the vitriol that her political enemies spread across the media. Alternatively, in light of his resistance to authority, he might have sought vengeance against anyone who occupied her position in public life.

His only known contact with the congresswoman before January 2011 occurred in 2007 when he approached her during a public forum and asked "what is government if words have no meaning?" Giffords apparently skirted over the incomprehensible question, and Loughner was incensed. He walked away from the encounter holding a grudge. He began to see her as a phony. Some reports suggested that he believed women should not hold positions of power. In a missive found among his possessions, he wrote "Die bitch!" in reference to the congresswoman. It was one thing to disapprove of an elected official, but somewhere along the line, he decided to act on his thoughts and feelings.[600]

His opportunity arose a little more than a month after he purchased his Glock. Giffords scheduled her "Congress on Your Corner" session, a familiar event in Tucson. The only difference this time was that Jared Lee Loughner took notice and resolved to shoot the phony congresswoman for her supposed transgressions.[601]

Loughner's movements on January 8 were not difficult to trace because he made no effort to disguise his activities. At 2:05 that morning, he called a friend's phone and left a voice message. "Hey man, it's Jared," he said. "Me and you had good times. Peace out. Later." A little over two hours after the call, he posted a rambling comment on the social media site MySpace. "Goodbye friends. Please don't be mad at me. The literacy rate is below 5%. I haven't talked to one person who is literate. I want to make it out alive. The longest war in the history of the United States. Goodbye. I'm saddened with the current currency and job employment. I had a bully at school. Thank you. P.S.—Plead the Fifth!"[602]

Loughner traveled to a Walmart store just after 7:00 a.m. to purchase ammunition for his Glock, but left before he completed the purchase. He entered another Walmart a few minutes later and found what he needed. At 7:34 a.m., Arizona Game and Fish Department officer Alen Edward Forney stopped Loughner's car after it ran a red light. Because Loughner had no outstanding warrants for his arrest, the officer allowed him to leave with only a warning. "The contact was very cordial," a police department spokesman later explained.

Another report cast the incident in a slightly different light. Forney described Loughner as "calm but nervous" as they discussed the traffic violation. When the officer told Loughner that he would not receive a ticket, the young man burst into tears. Forney noted that eventually "Loughner composed himself and said he was headed to his home and that he did not live far away." It was an unusual exchange, to be sure, but nothing about the incident indicated to the patrolman that Loughner was minutes away from murdering half a dozen people.[603]

Following the encounter, Loughner drove to the home he shared with his parents, Randy and Amy. At approximately 8:00 a.m., Randy Loughner saw his son remove a black bag—apparently a backpack—from the trunk of the car. The elder Loughner was not oblivious to his son's deteriorating state of mind, although he was not sure how to respond. He and his wife had discussed ways to curb their son's odd behavior. Sometimes at night they disabled his car to prevent him from leaving. They also confiscated a shotgun that Jared owned and locked it away for safekeeping.

As Jared entered the house on the morning of January 8, his father confronted him with questions about where he had been and what he had been doing. The young man mumbled something unintelligible and abruptly rushed outside. "He came in and I wanted to talk to him. And he took off," Mr. Loughner later told reporters. Sometimes Randy Loughner could sit and talk with his son in a calm, reasonable manner. On this morning, however, the young man would not be dissuaded from his task. Randy jumped in his car to follow his son, but Jared was already gone.[604]

Records indicate that Loughner walked to a nearby Circle K convenience store and called a taxicab at 9:18 a.m. Twenty-three minutes later, the taxi arrived to pick him up. Loughner provided the address of the Safeway store where Congresswoman Giffords was scheduled to speak with her constituents. At 9:59 a.m., the taxicab arrived at the shopping center where the store was located. Loughner and the taxi driver entered the Safeway so that Loughner could obtain change to pay his fare. Twelve minutes after his arrival, Loughner removed his Glock from the backpack and set out to kill the legislator.[605]

Unaware of the lurking danger, Congresswoman Giffords sent a tweet from her iPad that "My 1st Congress on Your Corner starts now. Please stop by to let me know what is on your mind." She was a Democrat in a Republican district; consequently, she knew that some constituents would let her know how much they disapproved of her policies. Yet Gabby Giffords believed that frank discussions among elected officials and the people they represented were a necessary part of a well-functioning republic.[606]

No sooner had the event opened than Loughner emptied his clip— thirty bullets discharged in fifteen seconds—striking nineteen people, killing six of them. Congresswoman Giffords collapsed after a bullet passed through her brain. Only the quick thinking of her intern, Daniel Hernandez, Jr., who immediately administered first aid, saved the congresswoman's life. In the meantime, bystanders wrestled Loughner to the ground and detained him until police arrived. Giffords was the intended target, but six people died because they were in the wrong place at the wrong time—so-called collateral damage.[607]

Grievously wounded, Giffords was transported to the University Medical Center of Tucson for treatment. The bullet had traveled through her head without crossing the midline of the brain, which meant she had hopes for surviving the attack. Several media stories immediately following the attack concluded that she had died, but the reports of her death were greatly exaggerated.[608]

Public reaction was swift. Although virtually everyone denounced the shooting and held Loughner responsible for the carnage, opinions differed on the underlying causes. Pima County Sheriff Clarence W. Dupnik, a friend of both Congresswoman Giffords and another victim, Judge John Roll, held a press conference not long after the attack. The sheriff was understandably emotional. He blamed the "vitriol that has permeated the political scene and left elected officials facing constant threats." In Dupnik's view, "I think it's time as a country that we do a little soul-searching. Because I think it's the vitriolic rhetoric that we hear day in and day out, from people in the radio business, and some people in the TV business . . . that this has not become the nice United States of America that most of us grew up in [*sic*]." The poisoned political climate "may be free speech, but it may not be without consequences."609

A chorus of supporters agreed with Sheriff Dupnik that the incivility of the partisan political rhetoric set the conditions for a deranged gunman to fire a gun at a public official standing in a crowd of people. The response was typified by Jeffrey Swanson, a professor of psychiatry at Duke University School of Medicine. "Take something you or I might find mildly threatening," he explained. "For a person with impaired perception of reality, that can get exaggerated to the point of being incredibly threatening." Alex Spillius, a correspondent for the British publication the *Daily Telegraph*, observed that "The gunman will, before long, have his day in court, but for now the tenor of political rhetoric is in the dock." Critics pointed to a map created by the interest group sarahpac.com and distributed by former vice presidential candidate Sarah Palin in 2009 showing vulnerable congressional districts that might switch from the Democrats to the Republicans in the 2010 elections. An illustration superimposed on top of the map featured Democratic congressional candidates, including Gabby Giffords, in the crosshairs of a gun sight. The implication was plain: Palin and her Tea Party colleagues did not pull the trigger on Gabby Giffords, but they all but urged someone with a diseased mind to do so.610

Politically conservative commentators expressed outrage that leftists would blame the Tea Party or right-wing political discourse when, in fact, Loughner was solely responsible. Writing in *The New American*, Alex Newman succinctly set forth the conservative party line. "The facts are still not yet all in," he wrote, "but from what is known so far, neither guns nor the Tea Party and its rhetoric were responsible for this tragedy—a sick individual was."611 Selwyn Duke, another commentator writing in *The New American*, concluded that "[w]hatever Jared Lee Loughner once was or could have been, he is now thoroughly twisted and totally immersed in a world inaccessible to those beyond the only thing he believes exists: his own mind."612 In an editorial appearing in *Commentary*, editor John Podhoretz, a prominent conservative polemicist, wrote that the "political attacks on the right that instantly followed the assassination attempt on Democratic Rep. Gabrielle Giffords represented a brazen effort on the part of liberals and the left to discredit, delegitimize, and silence their conservative opposition."613

As the political fallout resonated throughout the media, President Obama was invited to speak during a "Together We Thrive: Tucson and America" memorial held in honor of the shooting victims on January 12, 2011, in the McKale Memorial Center on the University of Arizona campus in Tucson. Sidestepping the political debate and the culture wars brewing in the background, Obama assumed the role of "healer in chief." "There is nothing I can say that will fill the sudden hole torn in your hearts," he remarked at the beginning of his talk. "But know this: The hopes of a nation are here tonight. We mourn with you for the fallen. We join you in your grief. And we add our faith to yours that Representative Gabrielle Giffords and the other living victims of this tragedy will pull through."[614]

The most poignant part of the address focused on each of the six people who died. "Judge John Roll served our legal system for nearly 40 years," the president said of the federal judge who was shot dead that day. "His colleagues described him as the hardest-working judge within the Ninth Circuit."[615]

He next acknowledged a septuagenarian couple gunned down on January 8. "George and Dorothy Morris—'Dot' to her friends—were high school sweethearts who got married and had two daughters. They did everything together—traveling the open road in their RV, enjoying what their friends called a fifty-year honeymoon. Saturday morning, they went by the Safeway to hear what their congresswoman had to say. When gunfire rang out, George, a former Marine, instinctively tried to shield his wife. Both were shot. Dot passed away."[616]

The third person shot dead was a seventy-nine-year-old woman. "A New Jersey native, Phyllis Schneck retired to Tucson to beat the snow. But in the summer, she would return East, where her world revolved around her three children, her seven grandchildren and two-year-old great-granddaughter. . . A Republican, she took a liking to Gabby, and wanted to get to know her better."[617]

One of the most dramatic stories from that day involved a man who threw his body over his wife to shield her from bullets. "Dorwan and Mavy Stoddard grew up in Tucson together—about seventy years ago," the president observed. "They moved apart and started their own respective families. But after both were widowed they found their way back here, to, as one of Mavy's daughters put it, 'be boyfriend and girlfriend again.'" Thanks to her husband's quick thinking, Mavy Stoddard survived, but he did not.[618]

Obama moved on to describe Giffords's thirty-year-old community outreach director from the congresswoman's district office. "Everything—everything—Gabe Zimmerman did, he did with passion. But his true passion was helping people. As Gabby's outreach director, he made the cares of thousands of her constituents his own, seeing to it that seniors got the Medicare benefits that they had earned, that veterans got the medals and the care that they deserved, that government was working for ordinary folks," the president mournfully recounted. "He died doing what he loved—talking with people and seeing how he could help."[619]

He saved the most gut-wrenching description for last. "And then there is nine-year-old Christina Taylor Green. Christina was an A student; she was a dancer; she was a gymnast; she was a swimmer. She decided that she wanted to be the first woman to play in the Major Leagues, and as the only girl on her Little League team, no one put it past her." Christina was interested in government, and so she had accompanied a neighbor to the Safeway that morning to meet her congresswoman. "She showed an appreciation for life uncommon for a girl her age. She'd remind her mother, 'We are so blessed. We have the best life.' And she'd pay those blessings back by participating in a charity that helped children who were less fortunate."[620]

President Obama struggled to make sense of a seemingly senseless act, briefly touching on the roiling debate about the gunman's motives, but quickly skirting past the sensitive topic. Recognizing that "our discourse has become so sharply polarized," he urged his audience to "pause for a moment and make sure that we're talking with each other in a way that heals, not in a way that wounds." Near the conclusion of the speech, the president grew wistful. "I believe that for all our imperfections, we are full of decency and goodness, and that the forces that divide us are not as strong as those that unite us," he said.[621]

In the final passage, he returned to the life and death of little Christina Taylor Green:

> Imagine—imagine for a moment, here was a young girl who was just becoming aware of our democracy; just beginning to understand the obligations of citizenship; just starting to glimpse the fact that some day she, too, might play a part in shaping her nation's future. She had been elected to her student council. She saw public service as something exciting and hopeful. She was off to meet her congresswoman,

someone she was sure was good and important and might be a role model. She saw all this through the eyes of a child, undimmed by the cynicism or vitriol that we adults all too often just take for granted. I want to live up to her expectations. I want our democracy to be as good as Christina imagined it. I want America to be as good as she imagined it. All of us—we should do everything we can to make sure this country lives up to our children's expectations."[622]

Reminding the nation that Christina was born on September 11, 2001—the day of the worst terrorist attack on American soil—the president concluded by promising that "we place our hands over our hearts, and we commit ourselves as Americans to forging a country that is forever worthy of her gentle, happy spirit."[623]

Obama's eloquent words did much to help Americans understand what had happened, but words can only do so much. In the wake of the shooting, Congresswoman Giffords faced a long road toward recovery, and Jared Lee Loughner entered the criminal justice system. Their respective experiences served as dual codas to the saga of the deranged gunman firing on the unsuspecting congresswoman.

After surviving the initial trauma and undergoing surgery, Giffords entered a long rehabilitation phase. She eventually transferred to the Institute for Rehabilitation and Research at the Memorial Hermann-Texas Medical Center in Houston. There she learned new techniques for communicating, a necessary component of her therapy owing to the damage her brain suffered from the shooting. On May 16, 2011, she was present as her husband, astronaut Mark Kelly, lifted off in the space shuttle *Endeavor* for its final flight.[624]

In August 2011, she appeared in the House of Representatives for the first time since the shooting to cast a ballot in favor of raising the debt ceiling. Later that same year, she and her husband released a book, *Gabby: A Story of Courage and Hope*, reviewing the Congresswoman's life story and political philosophy. Toward the end of the book, Giffords acknowledged the terrible toll the shooting had taken. She also discussed her new life and the challenges ahead. In a passage deliberately written to reflect her new style of speaking, she wrote, "Lot of people died. Six wonderful people. So many people hurt. Always connected to them. Long ways to go. Grateful to survive." She concluded on a hopeful note: "I will get stronger. I will return."[625]

18.2 Jared Lee Loughner, pictured here in his mug shot following his arrest, assaulted Congresswoman Gabrielle Giffords, among others, in 2011. Courtesy of the United States Marshals Service.

It became clear, however, that no matter how miraculous her recovery was, she could no longer function as a working member of Congress. On January 22, 2012, Giffords posted a video on YouTube telling her constituents that she intended to resign from her seat in the House of Representatives. "I don't remember much from that horrible day," she told her audience, "but I will never forget the trust you've placed in me." Two days later, she appeared in the audience for Obama's State of the Union address. The president's warm embrace of the courageous congresswoman received a hearty round of applause from her colleagues. The following day, January 25, 2012, Giffords delivered a letter to Speaker of the House John Boehner officially resigning from Congress to focus on improving her health.[626]

As for her assailant, Jared Lee Loughner was charged with one count of attempted assassination of a member of Congress, two counts of murder of a federal employee (Giffords's aide, Gabe Zimmerman, and Judge John Roll), and two counts of attempting to murder a federal employee, based on his injury of two of Giffords's aides. On January 19, a grand jury indicted him on three counts, not including the murder of Judge Roll or the murder of Gabe Zimmerman. On March 3, 2011, the grand jury indicted Loughner on additional charges of murder and attempted murder of the other shooting victims in the Safeway parking lot, for a total of forty-nine counts. He entered "not guilty" pleas on all charges.[627]

Following the arrest, authorities held Loughner in the Federal Correctional Institution in Phoenix until he was transferred to the United States penitentiary in Tucson on February 24, 2011. The United States District Court in Phoenix assigned Judy Clarke, we well known federal public defender, to represent Loughner in court. Clarke had made a name for herself defending high-profile, mostly unsympathetic criminal defendants, including Unabomber Theodore Kaczynski, Atlanta Olympic Park bomber Eric Rudolph, and 9/11 co-conspirator Zacarias Moussaoui. The Ninth Circuit Court of Appeals assigned the case to Larry A. Burns, a US District Court judge for the Southern District of California, to avoid a conflict of interest. All the federal judges in Arizona knew Judge Roll and therefore recused themselves from participating in the case.[628]

Judge Burns initially determined that Loughner was mentally incompetent to stand trial owing to the results of two medical examinations. The proceedings were suspended so that Loughner could be treated for paranoid schizophrenia. Loughner objected to the treatment, but the judge insisted that he could be forcibly treated against his will so that he would be competent to stand trial. The Ninth Circuit Court of Appeals rejected this rationale, but Judge Burns later ordered the continuation of the forcible treatment on the grounds that Loughner needed medication so that he would not harm himself or others. When the defense objected, the Ninth Circuit refused to intercede.[629]

After numerous medical and legal hearings, Judge Burns found that Loughner was competent to stand trial. To avoid the death penalty, the defendant agreed to plead guilty to nineteen felony counts. In November 2012, Judge Burns sentenced Loughner to seven consecutive life terms plus 140 years in prison without the possibility of parole. He was sent to the United States Medical Center for Federal Prisoners in Springfield, Missouri, a prison that provides medical and psychological services for inmates, before being transferred to the Federal Medical Center in Rochester, Minnesota.[630]

Jared Lee Loughner joined the ranks of many other American assassins and would-be assassins. He was a mentally disturbed Type 4 loner who had difficulty making friends or holding a job for a long period of time. He somehow transferred his own feelings of inadequacy and his disaffection for the world onto a public figure. If he showed no remorse for his violent deeds, it was because he was incapable of looking beyond himself and empathizing with another person. Like so many assassins, Loughner believed that it was right and necessary to visit his pain on others. Terrorists and conspirators frequently plan their crimes ahead of time and leave a distinct trail of clues if investigators know how and where to look. Mentally disturbed loners, by contrast, act for their own confused reasons, usually without leaving a clear trail. If they do leave clues behind, their ravings can be confusing and perhaps incomprehensible.

Many persons entertain feelings of despair, and utter threats against public figures for slights, real or imagined. Few act on their impulses. Ferreting out genuine threats from the multitudes who threaten violence but represent no significant danger to others remains a challenge. As this book attempts to demonstrate, the challenge has affected the course of American history since the 1830s.

PART V

UNKNOWN OR MIXED MOTIVES

Chapter 19

"OH LORD, MY GOD, IS THERE NO HELP FOR A WIDOW'S SON?": JOSEPH SMITH, JR. (1844)

Joseph Smith, Jr., founding father of the Church of Jesus Christ of Latter Day Saints (LDS), also known as the Mormons, never held political office or directly affected the operation of governmental institutions, yet he became an important political figure in nineteenth-century America. Prominent religious leaders attracted enormous attention in newspapers of the day, and Smith proved to be an especially charismatic figure that made for fascinating copy. Brigham Young, Smith's successor in the church, recalled that when he first heard Joseph preach, the effect was mesmerizing. In Young's view, Smith "took Heaven, figuratively speaking, and brought it down to earth." As the head of the LDS Church, Smith's outrageous public pronouncements and seemingly hostile activities alarmed residents who feared the Mormons as a strange, potentially dangerous sect. LDS members employed militant rhetoric, subscribed to odd customs and beliefs, and sometimes defended plural marriage. When an angry mob murdered Joseph Smith and his brother, Hyrum, in 1844, Americans were divided about whether the Mormon Church represented a distinct threat to the polity or existed simply as a misunderstood offshoot of the Christian faith.[631]

Smith was an imposing physical presence, six feet tall with a solid build, magnetic blue eyes, a long nose, and a receding hairline. A chipped front tooth and a slight limp suggested that he had lived a hard life. Indeed, he had. In less than four decades on earth, Joseph Smith was tarred and feathered, tried by legal authorities for crimes he and the Mormons allegedly committed, exiled, jailed, and eventually murdered. He believed that trailblazing religious prophets often were victims of persecution, and his life was proof of that assumption.[632]

Nothing in Smith's early life suggested that he would become a polarizing public figure. Born in Vermont shortly before Christmas 1805, his origins were humble. Perhaps the most propitious development in his young life occurred when his parents moved to western New York. It was an area colloquially known as the "burned-over district," Minister Charles Grandison Finney's colorful phrase describing an area that had been so heavily evangelized that no fuel (unconverted individuals) could be found.[633]

During the eighteenth century, upstate New York was one of many places in colonial America that experienced a religious revival known as the First Great Awakening. Its message resonated among the unwashed masses: people must accept the faith and embrace Christ or face eternal damnation. A religious war was underway, and it was a war for a person's immortal soul. Revivalists tapped into a deep undercurrent of fear and resentment, especially among lower-class colonists who yearned for the promise of something better—if not in this life, perhaps in the next.

The First Great Awakening changed many Americans' concept of religion. The self-taught preachers—sometimes called "new lights" to distinguish them from the "old lights," those stodgy ministers who intellectualized religion—who roamed the countryside beginning in the 1740s disagreed with their more learned brethren. Intellectual mastery of obscure texts was unnecessary. Religion was not about the head; it was about the heart. A conversion experience was available to anyone, no matter how poorly educated, rural, or ignorant of the ways of an organized church. The only way to know God was through emotion, and nothing stirred emotion quite like the fire-and-brimstone rhetoric of a new-light sermon.[634]

The evangelism of the First Great Awakening never died, but it lay dormant in some areas as the colonists separated from England and formed a new nation toward the end of the eighteenth century. Eight decades after the original movement, the Second Great Awakening infused the spirit of the Lord into a new generation of rural Americans. To be a messenger of God, a self-styled minister needed only to feel the calling. As with the First Great Awakening, mastering Latin, Greek, or Hebrew was unnecessary. Esoteric arguments on theology or schools of religious thought contaminated the religious experience.[635]

Charles Grandison Finney was perhaps the most popular evangelist of the Second Great Awakening, and he was a role model for anyone who sought a career in the ministry. The young Joseph Smith surely knew of the great Finney and his exploits. Beginning his career as an attorney in upstate New York, Finney converted at the age of twenty-nine when a bright light inexplicably filled his law office one fine day. Interpreting this extraordinary occurrence as the light of revelation from Jesus Christ, Finney changed his life from that day forward. Setting aside the trappings of his former life, he set out to preach a message far different from the Calvinism and Unitarianism of his neighbors. In a career that spanned five decades, Finney made a name for himself holding numerous tent revivals to convert non-believers to the Holy Band through the New Measures. To his everlasting credit, Finney was a vocal critic of slavery and a leading, if somewhat shrill, voice in the abolitionist movement of the antebellum period. At the end of his life, the great man served as the head of Oberlin College in Ohio and authored an influential "how-to" manual on conducting revivalist rituals.[636]

Coming of age in a religious area ensured that Joseph Smith was exposed to the ideas and concepts that Finney popularized. He was a willing recipient. By his early teens, Smith already knew that he would become a spiritual leader. Around the same time, he claimed that he possessed magical powers that would help him find buried treasure. While still in his teens, Smith developed a reputation as a "glass looker," a seer who used folk medicine to interpret signs leading to long-lost riches.[637]

Psychologists might trace young Joseph's beliefs to his unconventional parents. His father, Joseph, Sr., claimed to be a deist while his mother, Lucy, clung to Christian Primitivism. They were subsistence farmers, but they could never quite eke out a living. The boy knew hunger, both physically and spiritually.[638]

The turning point came when the adolescent Joseph met a traveling diviner who stopped in the community on his way to collect buried treasure. The man told all who would listen that he possessed magic stones directing his search. Skeptics dismissed such claims as gibberish, but Joseph Smith did not share their faithlessness. Enraptured, the young man spent time with the diviner seeking answers to the mysteries of the magic stones. Not long thereafter, Joseph acquired his own magic stones. Neighbors paid him money to discover buried gold, but he was never able to unearth anything of monetary value. Nonetheless, Joseph Smith's early forays into mysticism laid the groundwork for his later work pioneering a new religion.[639]

At the age of fourteen, he said that he had been visited by two "personages," God the Father and Jesus Christ. Whether the visit was mystical, divine inspiration or a lie—or perhaps the imaginings of a mentally disturbed, malnourished adolescent boy—depends on one's opinion of Joseph Smith. LDS supporters contend that religious pioneers invariably are denounced as

delusional lunatics or pathological liars. Later, after a religion has been institutionalized and accepted in mainstream society, the original founder is recognized as an insightful, wise prophet.[640]

Three years after the first experience, the elements of Smith's life—his
spirituality as well as his desire to find buried gold—came together in the
form of a celestial vision. The young man, a few months shy of his eighteenth
birthday, claimed that an angel, Moroni, appeared to him one evening and
revealed that the North American continent was the site of God's interaction
with an ancient race. Moroni told Smith of a book "written upon gold plates"
and buried in Cumorah, a hill conveniently located near the Smith home.
The message was clear: Joseph Smith, Jr., was the chosen one. He was called
to reveal the word of God as described on the golden plates.

For four long years, he attempted to retrieve the plates. Apparently not
yet ready to receive the word of God, Smith's early efforts were frustrated.
When he finally discovered the mysterious plates in 1827, he recognized that
only he could see the plates or the "reformed hieroglyphics" imprinted on the
holy relics. As he transcribed the words into paper, he relied on his new young
wife, Emma, to serve as his scribe, or secretary. Smith refrained from claiming that he translated the text, insisting that God spoke to Joseph and that He
alone produced the "gold bible" that became known as the Book of Mormon.
The 600-page work appeared in print in March 1830, a month before Smith
established his first church.[641]

The story held within the Book of Mormon's pages appealed to some
Americans anxious to know what happened to Jesus after he rose from the
dead. By asserting that North America was the holy land, in addition to the
Middle East, Joseph Smith's adherents could take comfort in the knowledge
that they, too, were special people in the eyes of the Lord. In some ways, the
Book of Mormon served as a sequel to the Bible, a proposition that attracted
some believers even as it repelled others.[642]

On April 6, 1830, Joseph Smith boldly proclaimed himself a "Seer, a
Translator, a Prophet, an Apostle of Jesus Christ, and Elder of the Church to
the Will of God the Father, and the grace of your Lord Jesus Christ." His
new Church of Christ quickly grew to forty members even as Smith haltingly
developed a theology of Mormonism. Building on Charles Grandison Finney's
example, Smith attracted new members to his flock through his personal charisma and frequent reliance on oratorical flourishes in melodramatic sermons.[643]

Joseph and Emma Smith had been living with Emma's father, Isaac Hale, who harbored deep suspicions about his son-in-law. Hale once described Smith as "saucy and insolent," a belief that never softened with the passing of years. Concerned about his daughter's welfare, Hale feared that Mormonism was little more than a scam perpetuated by a self-aggrandizing charlatan. In addition to his father-in-law's hostility, Smith found himself among unsympathetic neighbors who denounced the book of Mormon as blasphemous. Smith had worn out his welcome; thus, he resolved to escape to a more hospitable locale. While the church was still in its infancy, Smith relocated to Kirtland, Ohio. It was an inspired choice. Sidney Rigdon, a local preacher, had converted his entire congregation to Mormonism. Moving his flock to a ready-made church sustained Smith during a low period in his career.[644]

Smith soon rebounded from his early troubles. During the 1830s, the LDS Church expanded dramatically. By 1844, approximately 25,000 men and women in North America and Europe claimed membership in Joseph Smith's church. The new minister's personal charisma was largely responsible for this phenomenal growth, but his message of Christ in the New World also inspired the faithful. The 1830s and 1840s were a time of many new religions and churches, but few captured the imagination of large numbers of congregants. It was a testament to Joseph Smith's iron will and steady leadership that the Mormons bested their competitors.[645]

By most accounts, Smith possessed a prickly, unpredictable personality, easy to anger but quick to forgive. He was self-absorbed and confrontational, frequently seeking out conflicts that might have been avoided had he been less gruff and hostile to dissenters. He also caused rifts among even his most ardent followers. Sometimes the breach could be repaired, other times not. As the church expanded, Smith's supposed advances toward an adolescent girl and his defense of polygamy created large fissures that could not be repaired.[646]

Polygamy was not an original church tenet, but Smith embraced the concept early in the 1830s. Recognizing that the practice would be controversial, he seldom spoke of it in public. Privately, he defended polygamy by citing a concept he called the "New and Everlasting Covenant." According to Smith, the covenant transcended earthly law. Marriages recognized by governments were legal contracts, and nothing more. The New and Everlasting Covenant, however, promised a man and a woman exaltation, or godhood after death. To enter the covenant, a series of anointments must be sealed. Fortunately for

19.1 Joseph Smith founded the Mormon Church in 1830. Courtesy of the Library of Congress.

Smith, only he could seal the covenant. Despite Smith's efforts to keep this practice secret, news of the church's stance on polygamy invariably leaked out, incensing an already suspicious populace.[647]

Aside from polygamy, the Mormons encountered resistance from outsiders fearful of the church's willingness to employ violence. Smith insisted that he was a pacifist, but as his membership rolls expanded, church members faced hostile populations. Refusing to turn the other cheek indefinitely, he instructed his flock to train on military tactics and maneuvers. As the 1830s continued, the Mormons assembled a paramilitary force.[648]

Church members were destined to generate excitement, hostility, and fear wherever they settled. Perhaps Joseph Smith intended this result. Nothing ensures spiritual connectedness and bonding among the faithful as much as persecution from outsiders. Whenever non-believers assailed the church, Smith cemented the loyalty of his congregants by promising protection in this life and heavenly rewards in the next.

Always a restless soul, he resolved to move on in search of the true Zion almost as soon as he landed in Kirtland. After he was tarred and feathered in 1832, he knew the time was right. He sent a delegation to Missouri to scout for suitable locations, but the expedition proved to be a mistake when several leaders challenged Smith's authority. Mormons living in Ohio and Missouri soon struggled for control of the church.[649]

A pattern emerged. Smith would move into a community, build his church and populate it with his flock, announce that he was a community leader, and alienate indigenous residents. Sooner or later, angry, frightened neighbors banded together to drive the interlopers away. The cycle originated when Smith fled from Ohio to avoid creditors. Mormons also were driven out of Missouri. By the late 1830s, Smith and his loyal church members had landed in Nauvoo, Illinois. He soon declared that he was the mayor of the town as well as commander of his own private militia, the Nauvoo Legion. The year was 1843, and Joseph Smith had reached the pinnacle of his power and influence.[650]

A year later, Smith's empire crumbled when a newspaper, the *Nauvoo Expositor*, appeared. In its one and only edition, the *Expositor* revealed secrets about the Mormons and Smith's almost dictatorial power over the church. Published by apostates who had confronted Smith and insisted that he repudiate polygamy, the accounts were difficult to refute. Predictably, the detailed stories about polygamy ignited a firestorm of controversy, inflaming an already hostile anti-Mormon audience throughout Illinois. Smith might have salvaged his reputation, if not his life, had he responded to the accusations calmly and rationally. He did no such thing. Instead, he ordered soldiers of the Nauvoo Legion to destroy the press that had printed the offending newspaper. Acting as though he were a political authority, Smith also declared martial law. These reckless acts, coupled with the allegations recounted in the newspaper, all but sealed his fate.[651]

Confident that he could raise more troops through the Nauvoo Legion than Illinois Governor Thomas Ford could field with the state militia, Smith issued his imperious orders. Not surprisingly, Illinoisans reacted with alarm, calling for the government to suppress the Mormons through force of arms. For his part, Governor Ford feared that civil war would break out on the frontier. He appealed to Smith to surrender and submit to arrest or trigger a level of mob violence that no one could control. The prophet reluctantly agreed. He and seventeen high-ranking co-defendants from the LDS church, including his brother Hyrum, agreed to travel to Carthage, Illinois, and submit to a trial for inciting a riot.[652]

The governor had guaranteed Smith's safety, but the swiftly accumulating mob in Carthage had other plans. If Ford had been less cavalier in exercising security precautions, the situation might have ended differently.

Yet either astonishing naiveté or callous indifference led the man to assume that he could enforce law and order even as circumstances deteriorated and large groups of angry farmers roamed the streets of Carthage. "Your friends shall be protected, and have a fair trial by the law," the governor had assured the prophet. Joseph Smith did not place much faith in the pledge; he finally understood how unpopular he was. As he left his wife and family, he bid them farewell as though he would never see them again. "I go as a lamb to the slaughter," he said.[653]

Sitting in a jail cell awaiting trial or, more likely, mob justice, Smith thought that members of the Nauvoo Legion might break in and secure his release. A day earlier, friends had smuggled in two guns and two hickory canes in case they were needed for self-defense. It was not impossible to think that more help was on the way.[654]

Sometime between 4:00 and 5:00 on the afternoon of June 27, 1844, Joseph and Hyrum Smith sat in their cell on the second floor of the Carthage jail along with LDS disciples John Taylor and Willard Richards. They heard a commotion downstairs. Initially exultant, believing that their liberation was at hand, they recoiled in horror when gunfire erupted. The prisoners realized that an angry mob had broken into the jail and was coming for them. Hyrum Smith and Willard Richards threw their bodies against the wooden door of the cell to prevent the throng from entering the room, but bullets soon slammed against the barrier, tearing chunks from the wood and leaving holes. One shot smashed into Hyrum Smith's face on the left side of his nose. A second bullet tore into his back. "I am a dead man," he exclaimed as he collapsed and died.[655]

Joseph Smith and John Taylor hurled themselves against the door in a doomed effort to forestall the mob. Overwhelmed by the force pushing him back into the room, Joseph aimed his pistol through the opening between the door and the frame. He got off three shots, wounding two or three would-be assassins as they rushed up the staircase. The enraged citizens would not be thwarted. Rifle barrels and bayonets pushed through the doorway. John Taylor tried to bat them away with a cane, but he was outnumbered. Taylor later recalled that the situation was desperate; it "looked like certain death." Joseph Smith agreed with the dismal assessment. "While I was engaged in parrying the guns, Brother Joseph said, 'That's right, Brother Taylor, parry them off as well as you can.' Those were the last words I ever heard him speak on earth."[656]

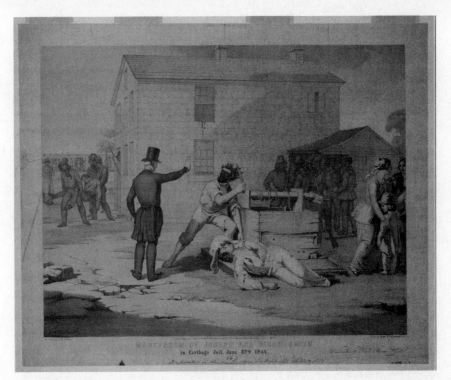

19.2 An 1851 lithograph, *Martyrdom of Joseph and Hiram Smith in Carthage Jail, June 27th, 1844,* shows the mutilation of Joseph Smith's body immediately following his murder. Courtesy of the Library of Congress.

Taylor took a bullet in the thigh as well as another in the midriff. Falling to the ground, he rolled under the bed to avoid further abuse. The gang of assassins shot at the prostrate man twice, but he was not the intended target. Legend has it that a bullet ripped through his stopwatch, freezing the moment forever at 5:16 p.m., although some historians argue that no bullets struck the watch.[657]

Joseph Smith moved toward the window. As he hoisted himself up to jump, a bullet from inside the room struck his back. Several bullets fired from the crowd outside the window hit him in the back and chest. Tumbling from the window, Smith reputedly cried out, "Oh Lord, my God, is there no help for a widow's son?" or words to the effect. Eyewitnesses disagreed on the exact phraseology. Smith, a Mason, may have been uttering a masonic plea for assistance.

What happened next has been told and retold many times, although accounts vary. The prophet was pushed against a well where he was either shot by a makeshift firing squad or mutilated by one or more members of the crowd. Joseph Smith was already dead as members of the mob continually fired bullets into his lifeless body. An 1851 lithograph, *Martyrdom of Joseph and Hiram Smith in Carthage Jail, June 27th, 1844*, painted by the artist G. W. Fasel, shows a black-faced figure—undoubtedly a member of the lynch mob—mutilating Smith's body.[658]

During the melee, Willard Richards escaped serious injury by hiding behind the door until the mob had dispersed. With only a minor scratch to his earlobe, he waited until he was certain that the crowd had departed before emerging from his hiding place. John Taylor, still cowering under the bed and bleeding profusely, begged Richards, a medical doctor, to help him. Both Richards and Taylor survived. The former recalled staring out the window and seeing at least one hundred people gathered around Joseph Smith's body. The following day, Samuel Smith and his brethren retrieved his brothers' bodies and placed them in temporary coffins to be returned to Nauvoo.[659]

Reactions to the murder varied, as had so many opinions about the Mormons. "Smith was killed, as he should have been," a Reverend William Brownlow gushed in a southern Illinois newspaper. "THREE CHEERS to the brave company who shot him to pieces!" An Illinois newspaperman named Thomas Sharp, a frequent LDS critic, defended the lynching as necessary. "True, the act of an armed body going to the jail and killing prisoners does appear at first sight dastardly, but we look at it as though these men were the executioners of justice." James Gordon Bennett, the idiosyncratic editor of the *New York Daily Tribune*, expressed horror at the "cold-blooded, barbarous, brutal outrage," while fellow editor Horace Greeley of the *New York Herald* suggested that the "blood of Joseph Smith, spilled by murderous hands" either would inspire Mormons to achieve great things or end the religion if a suitable successor could not be found. Governor Ford condemned "the recent disgraceful affair at Carthage," but found no fault with anyone, including himself, for failing to protect the Smith brothers from a vengeful mob. Nine defendants eventually tried for the murder, predictably, secured acquittals.[660]

Killers working as part of a mob are difficult to fit into a typology of political assassins because the motives of the individual members are not known, or else they are difficult to separate from the mob mentality. The motives of individual participants can be as numerous, various, or amorphous as the hopes, desires, and fears of the individuals themselves. Persons acting as part of a mob will commit atrocities they might never have attempted alone. Working in tandem with other persons creates an illusion of anonymity and passionate camaraderie that defies reasoned discourse. Mob members may be actuated by an intense dislike for the target of their violence or they may be along for the ride, motivated by little more than a desire to take part in an action that is bigger and seemingly more important than they are. Human nature lends itself to mob activity.

Joseph Smith did not deserve to be killed—no one "deserves" to be murdered at the hands of an extralegal band—but he had tempted the fates on the nineteenth-century American frontier. The Mormons espoused an alien set of beliefs that upset their neighbors. Rather than smooth over differences by reaching out to the community and promoting tolerance and understanding, Smith courted controversy through intemperate rhetoric and divisive claims. Even when he sought to keep his affairs secret, as with his private preference for plural marriage, his actions leaked out into the community and caused no small measure of consternation among non-believers. If Joseph Smith's example provides any lessons, it is that a stranger living among persons of different beliefs would be wise to emphasize inclusiveness and transparency in lieu of exclusivity and secretiveness. An iconoclast who ignores this insight does so at his peril.

Chapter 20

"I ASK NO QUARTER AND I FEAR NO FOE": WILLIAM GOEBEL (1900)

William J. Goebel, the recently inaugurated governor of the common-wealth of Kentucky, lay dead, the victim of an unknown assassin's bullet. Early on the morning of Tuesday, February 6, 1900, a slow-moving train carried his body to his hometown of Covington, Kentucky, to lie in state. When the great hall was opened so the throngs could view the cas-ket, onlookers estimated that 100,000 people filed past to pay their respects. The following day, the body was transported back to Frankfort for interment. Goebel's remains followed a circuitous route on the Queen and Crescent line, avoiding the more direct Louisville and Nashville rail line in memory of the governor's long-running feud with L & N officers. As the train chugged past numerous Kentucky hamlets, citizens lined the tracks to pay silent homage to their slain leader. They grieved for a man who had become in death what he never had been in life—a popular figure mourned as a fallen hero of the commonwealth. As of this writing, he remains the only US governor killed in office by an assassin.[661]

He was born Wilhelm Justus Goebel in Sullivan County, Pennsylvania, on January 4, 1856, but opponents claimed he was born in Europe. Although his name eventually was anglicized to William, he was proud of his strong Germanic roots. In fact, he spoke no English until he was six years old. His father fought for the Union during the Civil War. Upon returning home, the elder Goebel moved his family to Covington, Kentucky, for reasons unknown today. The oldest of four children, William worked hard during his youth as his father flitted from one job to another. After graduating from the law school at Cincinnati College, Goebel read law with a prominent Covington lawyer, John White Stevenson, a former congressman and Kentucky gover-nor. The association proved to be fruitful, an invaluable aid in Goebel's rise from poverty and obscurity to the pinnacle of Kentucky politics.

It helped that Goebel had a knack for his chosen profession. Stevenson was impressed with the young man's legal acumen. Consequently, he introduced his protégé to leaders in Kentucky business and politics, and promoted the junior lawyer to become a partner in his law firm. The association became so close that Goebel served as the executor of Stevenson's estate when the old man died in 1886.

A former governor's patronage was instrumental in ensuring Goebel's political ascendancy, but he was not the only important benefactor to show an interest in the young lawyer. Goebel met another influential Covington attorney who would prove to be a strong ally. John G. Carlisle was an up-and-coming Kentucky politician who also started his career in law and politics under Stevenson's tutelage. Carlisle later became speaker of the US House of Representatives, a US senator, and treasury secretary during Grover Cleveland's second term. Carlisle and Goebel served as law partners for a time, further improving Goebel's legal pedigree.

By all accounts, Goebel was an excellent lawyer and deserving of the early accolades he received. He was always well-prepared and well-spoken. He was not an orator of the first rank, but what he lacked in oratorical flourishes he compensated for in the clarity of his argument. The logic and precision of his public addresses could not be denied. In addition, he was an indefatigable worker who poured his energies into preparation. According to virtually everyone who knew him, Goebel was a workaholic's workaholic, never marrying or raising a family. His work was his life. Consumed by the public issues of the day, it was a natural and relatively seamless transition from law to politics.

Goebel entered the Kentucky senate at the end of 1887, shortly before his thirty-second birthday. He was a Democrat in a commonwealth where his party's power was declining. Kentucky had always been a rough-and-tumble place where the political agenda was muddled. During the Civil War, it had been a Border State where pro-Union forces battled with secessionists for control. After the war ended, Kentucky was among the states that experienced an internecine struggle between unreconstructed ex-Confederate veterans who sought to control political power and pro-Union Republicans.[662]

Goebel was a progressive Democrat who championed causes near and dear to the rural inhabitants he represented—reducing charges on toll roads, regulating railroads, improving schools and prisons, allowing women to vote for school board positions, and providing increased opportunities for blacks. Unlike many southern politicians, Goebel showed no interest in race-baiting as a means of garnering white votes. He continually won reelection to the state senate even though he frequently ran afoul of entrenched Kentucky politicians who were less-than-enamored of Goebel's supposed populism.

He could be warm and witty among friends, but in public Goebel appeared aloof and unapproachable. Despite his populist tendencies, he was hardly a hail-fellow-well-met personality, often refusing to shake hands and unwilling to smile. He could come off as gruff and abrasive, especially among strangers. He was tall, thin, and seemingly humorous; his pale skin and sharp nose made him appear sickly and repulsive. One reporter who followed Goebel's political career later recalled, "I never saw a man who, physically, so closely suggested the reptilian as this man did."[663]

But it was his politics that gave him his first significant political enemy. When Goebel sponsored a bill reducing the tolls charged by a corporation that had built a road on behalf of the commonwealth, John L. Sanford, a wealthy Covington banker and ex-Confederate soldier suspicious of Goebel's Union leanings, was incensed. Later, after Goebel worked to rewrite the state constitution to provide for a railroad commission to regulate Kentucky railroads and the rates they could charge, Sanford was heard to mutter that he would kill the young upstart. In the Kentucky politics of the time, such threats had to be taken seriously.

Their war of words escalated after someone posted a series of anonymous attacks on Goebel's reputation. Angered by these assaults on his character, Goebel responded with charges of his own. In one article published on April 6, 1895, Goebel alleged that Sanford, whom he did not know personally, suffered from gonorrhea. Goebel believed, with good reason, that Sanford had blocked Goebel's attempts to become an appellate judge. He also suspected that Sanford was involved in the anonymous attacks on Goebel's good name. These two proud, violent men in a proud, violent state were bound to erupt into violence before their confrontation was concluded.

Five days after Goebel's gonorrhea charge appeared, the two men met on the street. Goebel and the state attorney general, William J. "Jack" Hendrick, accompanied by Frank P. Helm, president of the First National Bank, were walking down the street toward Helm's bank in Covington. As they approached their destination, they came upon Sanford.

"Hey," Helm reputedly said. "There's Sanford."

Goebel replied curtly. "Yes, there's the son of a bitch."

Sanford acknowledged Hendrick and Helm, shaking hands with his left hand while his right hand remained hidden in his pocket. He turned his attention to Goebel, who also had his right hand in his pocket. "I understand that you assume the authorship of the article," he said, referring to Goebel's allegation that Sanford suffered from gonorrhea.

"I do," his nemesis replied.

In the next instant, violence erupted. As soon as Goebel admitted that he had written the salacious remark, Sanford pulled his right hand from his pocket to reveal a pistol. Goebel produced a pistol of his own. Two shots occurred in rapid succession. Messrs. Hendrick and Helm could not state definitively who fired first. By one account, Sanford pointed his gun at Goebel's abdomen and pulled the trigger. Remarkably, the shot passed through Goebel's coat and trousers, but did not injure him. Unfortunately for Sanford, Goebel's bullet struck the man in the brain. Sanford fell to the ground, mortally stricken. He died an hour later.

Goebel appeared unfazed by the episode. He calmly slipped his pistol back into his pocket and walked over to police headquarters. He telephoned his brother, Justus, and informed police officials that he had come to surrender. "Well, I suppose you have heard of it," he said. After posting the required bond, Goebel left the police station. He had spent only a few hours in custody.

During a preliminary hearing in the case, the judge dismissed the charges owing to "reasonable doubt" about who fired the first shot. If Sanford acted on his threat to kill Goebel, the latter's decision to shoot Sanford in the head was justifiable self-defense. A $100,000 civil suit filed by Sanford's widow three years also resulted in a judgment favorable to Goebel. Thus, he emerged from the sordid affair legally unscathed, but with a black mark against his name. That the son of an ex-Union man would shoot an ex-Confederate soldier to death did not sit well with many pro-southern Kentuckians. US Senator J. C. S. Blackburn, Sanford's close friend and political ally, typified the anti-Goebel feeling that arose from the incident. "I shall make it my life's mission to avenge him by burying his slayer in the depths of merited public execration," Blackburn vowed.[664]

Goebel patiently bided his time before seeking higher political office. While he waited for passions involving the Sanford episode to subside, he built a strong political base among laborers, denouncing big business and special interests in a populist appeal that rapidly gained traction. By 1897, his control over the local Democratic Party was so complete that he was known as the "Kenton King," a reference to the county where he exercised power.[665]

By 1898, the king was ready to make his move. He began organizing to run for governor the following year. First, he had to capture his party's nomination at the Democratic Convention. The nine-day convention held at the old Music Hall on Market Street in Louisville in June 1899 was a raucous affair. A correspondent for the *New York Times* described the assemblage as "the most uproarious and disorderly body of men ever gathered together for the transaction of political or other business."[666]

Goebel knew he would have his hands full securing the gubernatorial nomination. His opponents included old Parker Watkins Hardin (known affectionately to his supporters as P. Wat or Polly Wolly), a tall, handsome ex-Confederate who perennially campaigned for governor. He had lost the nomination in 1891. Hardin won his party's blessing four years later, but lost in the general election. Now he was seeking the post one final time. Backed by officers of the powerful L & N Railroad, who bitterly resented Goebel's attempted to regulate their business, ol' Polly Wolly was a formidable candidate. Goebel admitted as much in a letter to his brother. "There is going to be a hot fight between me and Hardin for the nomination," he wrote with considerable understatement.[667]

The other opponent, William J. Stone, a one-legged Confederate veteran, was a darling of the populists. Recognizing that he and Stone shared a similar political outlook but could not overcome Hardin's advantages alone, Goebel cut a deal with his rival. Stone and Goebel promoted Circuit Judge David B. Redwine, an intimate of both men, as the temporary convention chairman over Hardin's man. By ramming through their confidant, Goebel and Stone ensured that Redwine would seat more of their delegates than Hardin's delegates. The tactic worked like a charm. Goebel successfully maneuvered to control the convention and the platform on terms favorable to his candidacy.

During the convention, the delegates debated the merits of the three candidates in round after round of balloting that stretched across four days and nights. Facing a tired group of delegates, Goebel proposed that after the next ballot, the candidate with the lowest vote tally of the three should drop out. To ensure the result, he surreptitiously threw enough votes to Hardin to make Stone the odd man out. It was a cunning, if seemingly treacherous treatment of an ally. Goebel gambled that Stone's populist supporters, faced with a choice between the elitist Hardin and the more plebeian Goebel, would not hesitate to choose the latter. The gamble worked. With Stone out of the race, his votes gravitated to Goebel, and the Kenton King handily secured his party's nomination. Despite bitter charges of chicanery, Goebel insisted that he had simply practiced good, sharp convention politics.

It was a triumphant moment for the masterful political operative. "I never got anything in my life that was worth having without a hard fight," he admitted in a short speech before the delegates. "I believe the governorship is worth fighting for." The rest of the party, no matter how disappointed the individual delegates felt, soon fell in line behind the nominee. The state's largest newspaper, the *Courier-Journal*, marveled at Goebel's political canniness, proclaiming his efforts "the most masterly management ever witnessed in a Kentucky convention" and characterizing the new Democratic gubernatorial nominee as "a genius of political strategy."[668]

The genius still had to win the general election. Fortunately for the Democrats, the Republicans nominated a man, William Sylvester Taylor, who lacked even Goebel's nominal social graces. Taylor was reputed to be an adequate speaker, but not a first-class intellect. Known for his ill-fitting clothes, long, shaggy hair, and bony physique, "Tom-Tit" Taylor was not an impressive candidate. "Hogjaw" was even ridiculed by one newspaper as possibly industrious, but "a slouch in his gait, a boor in his manner, and the butt of the entire bar of Kentucky."[669]

Goebel and his base understood that Taylor was a proxy for his old enemy, the L & N Railroad. During his campaign stops, Goebel wasted no time in attacking the company as oppressive and exploitative of the common man. He was defiant and unrepentant in his appeal to the lowly citizen. "I ask no quarter and I fear no foe," he remarked on one occasion. As part of his manly promises to oppose entrenched power and the elites in the railroad companies, Goebel developed tried-and-true stump-pleasing tactics. His favorite rhetorical scheme was to ask the crowd if the railroad should be "the master or the servant of the people." Invariably, the response was "servant!"[670]

Wallowing in his populism, Goebel assured the voters that he was a man of the people. "I have not had a powerful family connection nor wealth to aid me," he cried. To shore up his populist bona fides, he even campaigned briefly with the well-known populist William Jennings Bryan, the Democratic Party's unsuccessful 1896 presidential nominee, a righteous man who approved of Goebel's message but frowned on the candidate's willingness to use profanity.[671]

Goebel believed he had captured the momentum going into Election Day on November 7, 1899. Yet when the votes were tallied, he lost by slightly more than 2,000 votes. Anxious to ratify the results, Republicans moved quickly to have Taylor sworn into office on December 12, 1899. The matter appeared to have ended after the disappointed Goebel graciously accepted the verdict.

Goebel's backers would not be placated. They located thousands of ballots they believed were fraudulent and asked the candidate to demand a recount. According to the state constitution, when a gubernatorial election was contested, an eleven-member contest committee was created by randomly drawing names of state legislators from a box. The committee would prepare a recommendation for the state legislature. Much to Goebel's delight, when the clerk drew the names for Goebel's challenge, nine Democrats, one Republican, and one Populist who usually sided with the Democrats, all ended up on the committee. Taylor was the temporary governor, but the election results might yet be reversed.[672]

On Tuesday morning, January 30, 1900, Goebel confidently strode across the capitol grounds in Frankfort accompanied by Eph Lillard, warden of the local penitentiary, and Jack P. "Dirk Knife" Chinn. They were anxious to meet with supporters and plot strategy before the contest committee convened. The capitol complex normally was the scene of much activity, but on this morning no one was bustling about. Mobs of men from both sides of the aisles had converged on the capital in recent days, and everyone feared that violence would erupt at the slightest provocation. Rumors had circulated that Goebel might be in danger and so he had taken precautions. Lillard and Chinn had been recruited to serve as bodyguards.

Unfortunately, Goebel had refused to alter his routine, which meant that anyone who wished him harm would know when and where he would be vulnerable. Perhaps he appeared at the capitol to demonstrate his bravery in the face of danger, or perhaps he believed that little harm would come to him from the faceless, nameless men who hid behind the mob. Whatever the reason, Goebel's final gamble proved to be foolish. When he was a few feet from the steps leading to the capitol entrance, the sound of a rifle shot echoed across the courtyard.

No one could be sure where the shot originated, but the result was devastating. A bullet struck William Goebel in the chest on the right side of his body. He crumpled to the ground. When Goebel tried to stand, Chinn called out, "Lie down or they will shoot you again." It was sage advice.[673]

After a few moments, satisfied that no additional shots would be fired, bystanders frantically rushed to Goebel's aid. Bleeding profusely, the wounded man remained conscious but in obvious distress. Several men gathered him up and carried him to the nearby Capitol Hotel, where a medical doctor, E. E. Hume, maintained an office. As luck would have it, Hume was in his office that morning. The doctor examined Goebel, who appeared "white as a sheet" from shock and loss of blood. A small rifle bullet had torn through his chest above the nipple, shattering a rib and penetrating his lung. It exited his back near the vertebrae. Dr. Hume understood that the wound was fatal, although Goebel insisted that he would recover.

Carried to the second floor of the hotel, the patient fought for his life as news of the incident circulated throughout the town. Republicans, fearful of swift retaliation from vengeful Democrats, hastily organized into small armed bands. They were wise to be worried. A headline appearing in the *Courier-Journal* before the shooting announced that "Armed Mob of Mountaineers Invade Frankfort to Bully the Legislature." The mountaineers appeared presumably at the behest of the anti-Goebel forces headed by the L & N Railroad. Governor Taylor feared that he might be seen as the leader of the mountaineer forces and thus become a target of armed marauders seeking retribution for the Goebel shooting. Accordingly, he declared a state of emergency and mobilized the state militia to ensure that law and order reigned in Frankfort.[674]

In light of the violence that had already occurred as well as the violence that might yet occur, legislators debated whether the contest committee should postpone its meeting. Republicans preferred this arrangement for several reasons, although Democrats recognized the risk inherent in allowing a delay. At the Democrats' direction, the contest committee met that afternoon and recommended that Goebel be installed as the rightful governor. Committee members announced their decision at 8:00 p.m.

The state legislature still had to adopt the committee's recommendation before the election results could be obviated. An hour after the public announcement, Governor Taylor issued a proclamation disbanding the legislature until it could reconvene a week later in London, Kentucky. He claimed that he based his action on a state constitutional provision stating that the legislature must meet in Frankfort "except in case of war, insurrection and pestilence." Arguing that the many groups of armed thugs roaming the streets of Frankfort constituted an insurrection, Taylor presented his proclamation as necessary to preserve order in the state. A majority of state legislators questioned the legality of the governor's proclamation. Instead of obeying the order, a quorum of state lawmakers met in the Capitol Hotel on January 31 and signed off on the contest committee report indicating that William Goebel must be sworn into office as governor.

At 9:00 p.m. on January 31, James H. Hazelrigg, chief justice of the Kentucky Supreme Court, administered the oath of office. Stories quickly spread that Goebel was already dead, but eyewitnesses reported that the new governor was alive. As his first act, Goebel signed a proclamation countermanding Taylor's proclamation. He also ordered the militia removed from the state capital and directed the state legislature to reassemble as soon as possible.[675]

With Taylor and Goebel both claiming the governor's chair, a potential crisis loomed. To ensure that their actions were viewed as constitutionally legitimate, Democrats met a second time and reenacted the procedure. They readopted the committee report and Goebel swore the governor's oath again, this time before Circuit Judge James E. Cantrill.[676]

Even as he assumed the mantle of power, Goebel knew that his condition was deteriorating. His death was imminent. Although he had remained conscious during most of his convalescence, he experienced considerable pain and grew weaker with each passing hour. Goebel gradually succumbed to uremic poisoning, his lungs filling with blood and his breathing growing labored. Several doctors attended to him, injecting pain medication, as necessary. On February 2, three days after the shooting, his fever spiked. A newspaper report informed the citizenry that the governor lived through the night only with help from "artificial stimulants."

At 10:00 in the morning on February 3, Goebel's condition took a turn for the worse. Despite frequent morphine injections and the administration of other drugs, he could not rally. His fever worsened. Yet somehow, he limped on. He spoke to a minister and assured the man, "I do not hold myself in open violation of the word of God."[677]

20.1 William Goebel served as governor of Kentucky for four days after he was mortally wounded by an unknown assailant. Courtesy of the Library of Congress.

Told late in the afternoon that he probably would die soon, Goebel stoically accepted the news. He asked for a drink of water at 5:45 p.m., lapsing into unconsciousness shortly thereafter. He died in his sleep at 6:44 p.m. He was forty-four years old, having survived just over one hundred hours after he was shot. His last words supposedly contained advice for his supporters: "Tell my friends to be brave, fearless and loyal to the great common people."[678]

The political hack that had been so reviled during his life suddenly became a martyred folk hero in death. Even his legion of political enemies found much to praise. Senator J. C. S. Blackburn, the man who had sworn to make it his life's mission to oppose Goebel, delivered the funeral oration, waxing eloquent about his fallen foe. He wistfully discovered virtues where once he had only seen vices. Blackburn told mourners that Goebel "lived an honest life and gave his life for your deliverance. Of him, no eulogy, but truth may say, 'Earth never pillowed upon her bosom a truer son, nor heaven opened wide her portals to receive a manlier spirit.'"[679]

The search for Goebel's assassin lasted for years. In the partisan atmosphere of the time, Democrats discovered a number of Republican-leaning would-be assassins who bragged about their participation in the crime. Caleb Powers, secretary of state under a Republican governor; Henry Youtsey, a young lawyer working with the state auditor's office; and James Howard, an outlaw with one murder charge pending, all came under fire. Indictments, trials, and convictions followed, as did appellate court reversals. The men supposedly were part of a conspiracy to kill Goebel, but the contradictory testimony, conflicting accounts from various witnesses, and dearth of physical evidence made the record unclear. The trial transcripts and other contemporaneous records were simply too unreliable and the passions were too intense to produce useful leads. To this day, the identity of the killer or killers remains unknown.[680]

The assassin's motives probably were political. If so, the act of killing the offending politician was rational and the killer probably was a classic Type 1 assassin. Without knowing more about the triggerman or the existence of any conspiracies, however, any assessment of motives or the state of mind of the killer is nothing more than conjecture. It is an unsatisfying end to an unsatisfying episode.

Reflecting on his brother's life in December 1900, ten months after the murder, Arthur Goebel wrote that "It is almost a year since William died, and he lives in the minds of the people as much as ever." The reason he was remembered, and would be remembered for years to come, seemed obvious to a grieving brother. "Why is it? He is Goebel; that is all."[681]

Chapter 21

"EVERY MAN A KING, BUT NO ONE WEARS A CROWN": HUEY P. LONG (1935)

Huey P. Long was one of those colorful populist characters that southern history occasionally produces. A poor-boy-made-good, he rose from humble beginnings to capture the governorship of Louisiana, a US Senate seat, and the imagination of a nation reeling from the devastation of the Great Depression. Public opinion was divided: supporters viewed him as a savior of the masses while detractors feared the populist-run-amok was a genuinely dangerous demagogue who would wreak havoc on the American political system. With his talk of sharing the wealth and ensuring that the common man grabbed a large slice of the economic pie, Long was jockeying for a presidential bid, perhaps in 1936 or 1940. It was not to be. He died from an assassin's bullet in September 1935.[682]

His biography reads like a clichéd Horatio Alger story. He was born Huey Pierce Long, Jr., in Winn Parish, a backwater hamlet in north central Louisiana, on August 30, 1893. The seventh of nine surviving children, Huey proved to be a bright, albeit rebellious boy. After protesting the twelfth-grade graduation requirement, he was expelled and never officially graduated from high school. Despite this technical deficiency, Long earned a scholarship to attend Louisiana State University. Unable to afford textbooks, he launched himself into business, traveling around the state as an auctioneer and salesman. He told audiences that he earned his education in the school of hard knocks, and to some extent it was true. He was the epitome of the self-made man.

Throughout his life, Long prided himself on his identity as a man of the people. The connection came from his years growing up poor and later traipsing along innumerable backroads hawking his wares as a salesman. Louisiana was a terribly poor state in a terribly poor region of the country. Class tensions festered as poor whites worried that the country was oblivious to their desperate plight. Long knew these people—he was one of these people—and he never forgot his humble origins. He understood what it was to be poor and fearful of the future. He would use this hard-got knowledge to good effect throughout his storied political career.

Eventually tiring of the itinerant life, the ambitious young man pondered his employment prospects. He longed to be a professional man, well respected, revered as an opinion leader. After attending a few classes at a seminary, he realized that preaching was not for him. Long intuitively recognized that a theatrical presence and a bombastic oratorical style could be used to great advantage. Perhaps his personality was suited for a career in law or politics. With these vague ambitions in mind, he drifted into law classes at the University of Oklahoma and Tulane University. He never graduated. In an era when a law degree from an accredited institution was not required to practice law, Huey Long sat for and passed the state's bar exam without holding a degree.

He was on his way. As a young lawyer, he handled cases for individuals, sometimes against large corporations such as Standard Oil Company, the behemoth that Long came to hate with a passion. He practiced law in the small town of Winnfield before moving on to Shreveport. Reflecting on that time in his life and career, he boasted that he never accepted a case against a poor man.[683]

When Long earned a seat on the Louisiana Railroad Commission (renamed the Louisiana Public Service Commission in 1921) at the age of twenty-five, he found a platform for his populist ideals. It was clear at the outset that he would not follow well-established rules whereby a young lawyer gradually ascended through the ranks, paying his dues by becoming a good, reliable party man. Long was determined to create his own path, and he found a winning formula. With his eyes firmly set on the prize, he saturated the political landscape with posters and leaflets outlining his ideas. He also pursued an exhaustive travel schedule, shaking hands and introducing himself to potential voters. Never a genteel soul, Long enthusiastically attacked his political opponents at every opportunity. No rhetoric was too hyperbolic or vitriolic for Huey P. Long. By 1922, his combative style had earned him the position of chairman of the Louisiana Public Service Commission.[684]

He was a young man in a hurry. Aiming for the governor's mansion, Long threw his hat in the ring in 1924. He had originally supported the outgoing incumbent, John M. Parker, Sr., but Long soon changed his mind. He believed that Governor Parker had kowtowed to the special interests, especially powerful corporations. The only effective method of opposing rich corporate leaders was to mount an insurgent campaign. Always the fiery populist, Long did exactly that. He took to the radio airwaves, blasting his message far and wide. He also used sound trucks patrolling through neighborhoods and backwoods bayous to promote his candidacy. Wearing his soon-to-be iconic white linen suits, the candidate never met a forum he didn't like. He appeared at numerous speaking engagements calling for a new administration that would pay special attention to the poor of Louisiana.

Although the message was effective and well-received, Long lost the gubernatorial election of 1924, placing third behind Lieutenant Governor (and former state house speaker) Hewitt Leonidas Bouanchaud and the winner, Henry L. Fuqua, warden of the Louisiana State Penitentiary. But no matter; he would live to fight another day. He had tasted defeat in 1924, but he would try again, and this time he would pull out the stops.[685]

By 1928, Long was ready. He had spent the intervening years building political support, especially among rural Catholics who might make a difference in a close election. He threw himself into the race with his customary abandon, traveling everywhere, visiting even the tiny towns and villages ignored by the New Orleans elites who promoted statewide candidates. His slogan—"Every man a king, but no one wears a crown"—appealed to impoverished citizens who felt marginalized by their elected leaders. Huey Long would be the king who made them kings, too.

He knew that while a majority of the state population lived in rural areas, it would be difficult to entice these folks to vote. Louisiana featured a poll tax that prevented the poor from voting. Black citizens had been disenfranchised by the state constitution of 1898. The voters who could be expected to support a populist candidate generally watched unfolding political events from the sidelines.

Despite the forces arrayed against him, Long captured the governorship in 1928. His passionate appeals to the poor overcame the skewed electoral system in the state. Although he failed to win a majority of the vote in the Democratic primary, his opponents bowed out of the race rather than face a runoff contest. In the general election, Long trounced Republican businessman Etienne J. Caire, hardly a surprise in the heavily Democratic state.[686]

Huey Long's election ushered in a sea change in Louisiana politics. When he campaigned against the established political order, he meant what he said. As soon as he had sworn the oath of office, he cleaned house inside the state bureaucracy, replacing members of the old guard with his own supporters. He had promised to attack the unacceptably high illiteracy rate in the state, and he was as good as his word. His administration offered free textbooks to school children, organized adult literacy programs, and launched large-scale public works programs to put unemployed workers on the government payroll and improve the state's dilapidated infrastructure.[687]

As much as the state's rural citizens appreciated their iconoclastic governor, corporate lobbyists and Long's partisan opponents came to loathe the man ensconced in the governor's mansion. When Long proposed an occupational license tax on refined oil produced in Louisiana, they reacted with predicable outrage. Two freshmen lawmakers pushed to impeach the governor owing to his abuses of power. A ferocious battle ensued. In the end, Long's enemies failed to secure the necessary two-thirds vote in the state senate to remove him from office.[688]

A triumphant Governor Long felt emboldened to act on his numerous predilections. Virtually everything he did was aimed at consolidating his political power. In recognition of the power of the press, in March 1930 he established his own newspaper, *Louisiana Progress*, to provide a forum for denouncing his enemies and promoting his agenda. The governor made it clear that a private company bidding on state contracts must purchase advertisements in Long's newspaper if the company hoped to succeed.[689]

He also exacted vengeance for real or perceived indignities. Anyone who was with him could count on patronage positions inside government institutions. Anyone who supported impeachment or moved to block his legislative initiatives would feel the fury of the man known as the Kingfish. He simply would not or could not tolerate dissent. The idea of a loyal opposition was alien to his nature. "I used to try to get things done by saying 'please,'" the governor remarked on one occasion. Confronted with opponents to his plans following the impeachment imbroglio, he articulated a simple strategy for success. "That didn't work and now I'm a dynamiter. I dynamite 'em out of my path."[690]

The governor received a growing number of death threats around the time he won the impeachment battle. Although he downplayed the risks publicly, he was not willing to take chances. He surrounded himself with a cadre of bodyguards. Adorned in a white suit and flanked by armed guards, the governor became a familiar site marching around the state capitol in Baton Rouge.[691]

Frustrated at efforts to block his plans in the state legislature, Long made a surprising announcement in 1930. He would run for a seat in the United States Senate representing Louisiana. Confident of success, he vowed to resign as governor and retire from politics if he lost the election. If he won, he would consider his Senate victory a popular referendum on his policies. As he expected, Long defeated the incumbent, Joseph E. Ransdell, by a resounding margin. Yet he surprised people once again in victory. He refused to resign his seat as governor, which ended in 1932, to head off to Washington, DC. Consequently, the US Senate seat remained vacant. Long rejected any criticism of this power play, telling reporters that "with Ransdell as Senator, the seat was vacant, anyway."[692]

During his remaining time as governor, he championed massive public works projects, notably the construction of a new state capitol building. He also earmarked funds for educational institutions, especially Louisiana State University. A laundry list of infrastructure improvement projects led to a flurry of road construction across the state, which improved his popularity, reduced unemployment, and modernized the state's still-antiquated road system.[693]

As prominent as Governor Long was inside Louisiana, he was not well-known elsewhere. That situation soon changed. He captured the national spotlight when he took his seat in the Senate. A fierce critic of President Herbert Hoover, Long spoke of his "share our wealth" ideas, which sounded suspiciously like socialism to some conservative Americans. Undaunted, the Louisiana senator became renowned for his fiery speeches in defense of wealth redistribution, which he unapologetically bellowed from the well of the Senate.[694]

If ever there was a kindred spirit with Franklin Delano Roosevelt, the former New York governor who defeated Hoover in the 1932 presidential election, Huey P. Long appeared to be it. The two men recognized, as few other political leaders did, that the American people longed for leadership that would act on their behalf. Long threw his support behind FDR, although he believed that the candidate did not go far enough. "I don't like your son of a bitch," he told a Roosevelt confederate. "But I'll be for him."[695]

Despite their similar goals, President Roosevelt and Senator Long found themselves at odds. The patrician Roosevelt mistrusted the demagogic, unrefined Long. The senator had performed his duty during the campaign, but after Roosevelt's inauguration, the Kingfish became a vocal critic, one of the few detractors from the left of the political spectrum.

The feeling was mutual. In Roosevelt's view, Long was more interested in self-aggrandizement and building a political empire than in ameliorating the ill effects of poverty and hopelessness during the Depression. A White House meeting in June 1933 only reinforced their shared animosity toward each other when Long initially refused to remove his straw hat and referred to the president by his first name, discourtesies that outraged FDR's assistants. The old man took the boorishness in stride. The Louisianan's hillbilly persona did not bother Roosevelt, but the talk about sharing the wealth and mobilizing the populace did.[696]

During 1933, as he basked in the glow of his newfound national fame, Long's antics grew in frequency and intensity. His zany behavior was already becoming the stuff of legend.

21.1 Huey P. Long of Louisiana was a legendary southern populist whose zany antics became well known during his time in office. Courtesy of the Library of Congress.

As governor, he had occasionally conducted state business wearing pajamas in his hotel room. He had been known to trade body blows with political opponents. As a senator, he showed no signs of changing his ways. In fact, he seemed proud of his outlandish escapades.[697]

A well-publicized incident during a charity revue at the exclusive Sands Point Bath Club in Long Island, New York, in August 1933 made the rounds amidst much guffawing and eye rolling among the Washington elite. The facts were never altogether clear, but apparently the inebriated senator demonstrated his clownish manners during a formal dinner by openly flirting with women and muttering offensive comments to his fellow diners. While adolescent behavior was good for a laugh or two, Washington movers and shakers did not understand how Huey Long could be taken seriously amidst such silliness. In all likelihood, he was playing the part of the southern hillbilly to capture headlines, and perhaps to disarm his political enemies. It was easy to underestimate a crazy fool—even if the fool proved to be crazy like a fox.[698]

Some politicos dismissed the Louisiana senator as a country bumpkin, but FDR never underestimated a populist politician with a knack for attracting attention. For all the infantile hijinks, the man was amassing a substantial following as Share Our Wealth clubs sprang up across the country. Long also delivered a series of nation-wide radio addresses arguing for a radical redistribution of wealth. He bitterly criticized the Federal Reserve as well as Wall Street financiers. In an era when citizens were desperate for food, shelter, and a measure of economic security, Long set forth a platform that struck a resonant chord with millions: a free college education as well as vocational training for young people; federal assistance for workers in the agricultural sector; increased federal regulation of the economy; a guaranteed income for workers; a substantial uptick on federal public works projects; and a permanent old age pension for the elderly.[699]

Many of Long's proposals were unworkable and unlikely to pass muster with conservative members of Congress, to say nothing of a cautious, reactionary Supreme Court majority that appeared all too willing to strike down New Deal programs as unconstitutional when they were challenged in court. Nonetheless, the radical concepts propelled Huey P. Long to the center of American politics. Watching from his perch inside the White House, Roosevelt feared that the sensationalistic senator might mount a credible challenge in the 1936 presidential election. The fellow was becoming too powerful to ignore. Anxious to curb Long's growing influence, the president blocked the senator's patronage requests, which infuriated the Kingfish. A US senator, especially if he belonged to the same party as the president, could expect to award a certain number of federal positions to friends and supporters as a matter of senatorial courtesy. FDR's unusual interference with these prerogatives looked too much like a declaration of war for the Louisiana senator to stand by idly. If FDR wanted a war, he would have it.

Their political battles degenerated into internecine warfare within the Democratic Party. Genuinely fearful that Long was employing fascist tactics and thereby exercising dictatorial control over Louisiana politics, President Roosevelt believed he had an obligation to do everything within his power to stymie the senator's ascent. To that end, FDR directed the Internal Revenue Service to investigate Long's tax returns. He also promoted political opposition to the Kingfish within Louisiana.

For his part, Long joined the loud chorus of FDR critics assailing the New Deal at every opportunity. The senator contended that Roosevelt was not a friend to the working-man. He was protecting the capitalist class at the expense of the little guy. If the president seemed to be an advocate for federal assistance to the poor, it was a façade. A genuine revolution whereby institutions of government were profoundly altered to control the private sector was needed, but the administration's programs were too limited to trigger the kind of change necessary to end the Great Depression.[700]

Even as he battled the president over federal patronage, Long was determined to keep tight control over jobs and money inside Louisiana. As always, he attacked his opponents with a ruthlessness and zeal that bordered on fanatical. In early September 1935, the senator focused his attention on one man in particular, Judge Benjamin Henry Pavy. Long directed his minions to introduce state legislation to gerrymander the district so that Pavy would lose his judgeship in 1936. The Kingfish's critics viewed this effort as yet another unprincipled attempt by an unprincipled authoritarian to smite his opponents and consolidate his power. They were exactly correct, and Long made no attempt to disguise his motives.[701]

Watching as the Pavy saga unfolded, a Baton Rouge physician, Dr. Carl Austin Weiss, became a major player in the Huey P. Long story. The quiet young surgeon entered the state capitol on the evening of Sunday, September 8, carrying a .32-caliber pistol. Dr. Weiss, Judge Pavy's son-in-law, apparently was upset by Long's style of politics in general and his attack on Pavy in particular. What happened that evening remains a matter of intense dispute. The generally accepted story is that Weiss arrived in the capitol building hell-bent on shooting the loudmouth senator who had attacked a noble public servant for no good reason.[702]

Several observers spotted Dr. Weiss happily chatting with bystanders in the capitol hallway that evening. He appeared relaxed and convivial. After that, eyewitnesses lost sight of him. Apparently, he loitered in an alcove outside the governor's office waiting for Long to arrive.

A few minutes later, at 9:20 p.m., his target appeared, briskly charging along the corridor, surrounded by his bodyguards, his jacket coat flapping, his big belly bouncing up and down. It was a familiar scene. Weiss stepped forward and aimed his pistol at Long from a distance of four feet. Without speaking a word, he squeezed off a shot, striking the governor in the abdomen.[703]

Screaming, Long grabbed his stomach and staggered out of the hallway. His bodyguards were slow to respond, but after a moment they sprang into action. They first attempted to wrench the gun from the assailant's hand. As he fell to the floor, the gunman may have fired another shot, but accounts differ. The young fellow tried to get back on his feet even as the bodyguards overreacted with a vengeance. Drawing their guns, the senator's henchmen pumped at least sixty-one bullets into the assailant's body, knocking Weiss to the floor. They fired long past the time the shooter had died.[704]

As the bullets flew behind him, Governor Long managed to stay on his feet long enough to climb down a stairwell. He experienced excruciating pain. Finding his boss in agony and about to collapse, an aide flagged down a car to transport the wounded man to Our Lady of the Lake Hospital. The patient arrived within ten minutes of the shooting.[705]

Dr. Arthur Vidrine, Long's friend as well as superintendent of Charity Hospital–New Orleans, happened to be in Baton Rouge on business when he learned of the shooting. He took charge of admitting the patient into the hospital. Vidrine was not an experienced surgeon, but he examined the senator and realized that surgery was necessary to stem interior hemorrhaging. The doctor had the good sense to send for experts. Unfortunately, they would not arrive for several hours, and Long's condition was rapidly deteriorating. Something had to be done or he would not survive. An informal committee

21.2 This drawing, "The Shooting of Huey Long" by Louisiana artist John McCrady, appeared in the June 26, 1939, issue of *Life* Magazine. Courtesy of the Manuscript Collection, Mss. 2525, Louisiana and Lower Mississippi Valley Collections, LSU Libraries, Baton Rouge, LA.

of medical personnel convened and agreed that they must operate immediately. Despite his lack of relevant experience, Vidrine agreed to act as lead surgeon.[706]

One commentator later characterized the surgery as "one of the most bizarre and unreal operating room settings that one could possibly imagine.

Spectators, bodyguards, and medical professionals elbowed each other for space in the operating room." The public spectacle made for a chaotic procedure. It lasted about an hour, ending shortly before experienced surgeons arrived at the hospital.[707]

Recriminations commenced when the experienced surgeons learned that no x-rays were taken preoperatively and the patient had not undergone urinary catheterization until after the operation. In their haste, Dr. Vidrine and his team failed to diagnose a hemorrhaging kidney, and they never rectified the error. By the time a second set of doctors realized the likely cause of the patient's massive internal injuries, it was too late to save the governor. Huey P. Long lingered until 4:10 a.m. on Tuesday, September 10, 1935, some thirty hours and thirty minutes after the shooting, when he died. He was forty-two years old. Details about the exact cause of death were difficult to pinpoint because an autopsy was supposed to be performed, but Mrs. Long asked that the body be left intact. Consequently, no physicians performed a postmortem examination.[708]

For all the unanswered questions about the doctors' actions at Our Lady of the Lake Hospital, they pale in comparison to the controversy over the shooter's motives. Carl Weiss was not the typical assassin discussed in this book. Virtually every other assailant characterized in these pages evinced emotional or psychological troubles. At some time in the person's life, one or more eyewitnesses described the person as odd, obsessed, dangerous, or crazy.

Carl Weiss was none of these things. The eldest of three children, he was born into an upper-middle-class Catholic family in Baton Rouge on December 18, 1905. His father was a physician. As a child, Carl was quiet and highly intelligent. Always a precocious boy, he loved mechanics, electricity, and music, learning to play the piano, clarinet, and saxophone. Although he was interested in target-shooting guns, he did not enjoy hunting live targets. Everyone who knew him well believed him to be the gentlest of souls.

Judging by virtually every objective measure, Carl Weiss was a prodigy. He graduated from St. Vincent's Academy, an all-male Catholic high school in Baton Rouge, in 1921. He was fifteen years old. Afterward, he enrolled in Louisiana State University, eventually pursuing a pre-medical program. These were successful years for young Weiss. He was an introverted young man, but he still engaged in social activities such as joining a college fraternity. He graduated with a Bachelor of Science degree in 1925.

Two years later, he earned his MD from Tulane University at the age of twenty-one. As a newly minted physician, he accepted a prestigious internship to study in Paris. He later studied in Vienna and toured other parts of Europe. After completing another internship at Bellevue Hospital in New York, where he specialized in eye, ear, nose, and throat medicine, as his father had done, Weiss returned to join his father's practice in 1932.[709]

In 1933, Weiss married Yvonne Louise Pavy from the little town of Opelousas. With this marriage, Dr. Weiss was thrust into the middle of a long-simmering feud between two rival factions in Louisiana politics. Yvonne's father, Judge Benjamin Pavy, was a prominent and vocal critic of Governor Huey P. Long. The governor was incensed that he could not control the judge. Rumors circulated that Long had dredged up an ugly rumor indicating that the Pavy family possessed black blood, a smear that held genuine legal ramifications. In the highly segregated South of the 1930s, a family sporting Negro ancestry would face a host of legal and cultural impediments. Long was not the typical racist white politician of his time, but he was not above using whatever means were necessary to win a political fight. Judge Pavy, no stranger to rough-and-tumble politics, ignored the rumor.

The standard narrative suggests that when Governor Long introduced a bill to redistrict Judge Pavy out of office as political retribution for the judge's opposition, something snapped inside of Carl Austin Weiss. It was the last straw after Long's previous affronts. (In addition to the rumors of racial impurity in the Pavy family, Yvonne's uncle, Paul Pavy, and her sister, Marie, employed in the state's public schools, lost their jobs because they were not certified by the state board of education, controlled by Governor Long.) When he learned of the anti-Pavy legislation, the brilliant, good-natured Weiss simply had reached the end of his tether. He carried a gun with him, as many doctors did in that time and place, for personal protection. Realizing that Huey Long was out to destroy his family, he decided to use that gun for another purpose. The normally gentle family man became a determined political assassin who refused to be thwarted from his duty. In short, he sought revenge for past slights or to prevent future depredations.[710]

Other theories abound. Perhaps Weiss did not kill Governor Long as a premeditated act. Instead, it might have been a spur-of-the-moment decision. Looking back on his actions earlier in the day, his behavior was not the behavior of a man about to commit an infamous crime. Weiss spent time with his family and nothing seemed amiss. From everything that he said and did, he was looking to the future. He scheduled time to perform surgery the following day. He loved his family passionately, and he planned on seeing his beloved son grow to maturity. Because Governor Long was known to travel with bodyguards, Weiss must have realized that he would be shot down if he tried to kill the governor. Nothing in his behavior indicated that he was a calculating killer. In fact, throughout his life he appeared to be an emotionally healthy, happy, well-grounded, intelligent human being without a penchant for violence.[711]

One version of events suggests that Carl Weiss was part of a conspiracy to kill Huey Long. Many people wanted the governor dead. Weiss may have been an idealistic young man induced to eliminate a problem not only for his family, but also for the good of Louisiana—and perhaps the nation, if one believed that the popular demagogue planned to mount a presidential bid in 1936 or 1940.

Alternatively, Weiss might have been a Manchurian candidate–style assassin who was programmed to kill the governor without realizing that he was doing so. According to this narrative, Weiss was a malleable personality who became the unwitting tool of the powers-that-be, namely the corporate interests (or FDR operatives) that feared the rise of a powerful populist. Alas, as with many conspiracy theories, the idea of shadowy, nefarious forces acting behind the scenes is tantalizing, but not a shred of credible evidence indicates that anyone else was involved.[712]

A more plausible scenario is that Weiss did not plan to kill Governor Long. Perhaps he wanted to speak to the man, to share his outrage at the governor's ill treatment of the Pavy family. According to this theory, Weiss lunged at Governor Long to give the fat political boss a piece of his mind. The exchange went horribly wrong. Long's bodyguards, caught off-guard and overreacting, whipped out their guns and started shooting. In the crowded hallway, they not only hit the unknown assailant, but they inadvertently shot their boss. Rather than confess their misdeeds, they planted the gun on the dead Dr. Weiss and concocted the tale of a crazy physician who shot the governor. Because Long could not provide insights into what occurred and the doctors never performed an autopsy to establish a definitive cause of death, determining what happened is almost impossible after the passage of many decades.

21.3 Dr. Carl Austin Weiss, pictured here, has been identified as Huey P. Long's assassin, although many questions about his motives and actions remain unanswered. Courtesy of the State Library of Louisiana.

Whatever happened that late summer evening in September 1935, assessing Carl Austin Weiss's motives—assuming he committed the crime in the first place—is impossible. Nothing in his background suggested that he would become a political assassin. He appeared to be a well-adjusted, productive citizen. Because he was cut down in a hail of bullets before he could be interrogated, his secrets died with him.[713]

Chapter 22

"I LIVE LIKE A MAN WHO'S ALREADY DEAD": MALCOLM X (1965)

Malcolm X arrived in Manhattan's Audubon Ballroom early on the afternoon of Sunday, February 21, 1965. He was scheduled to speak at an Organization of Afro-American Unity (OAAU) rally. The controversial thirty-nine-year-old civil rights activist was in the midst of a difficult, divisive time in his life. His home had been firebombed a week earlier, and his escalating fears for his own safety and the safety of his family had left him shaken and out of sorts. On the morning of the 21st, he had been awakened in his room at the Hilton Hotel by a telephone call from an unknown man. "Wake up, brother," a strange voice said ominously.[714]

Anxious to protect his pregnant wife and four daughters from harm, he had transported them to a friend's house after the bombing. He decided to stay elsewhere in case he was the target of assassins. On February 20, he checked into a room in the New York Hilton Hotel. Malcolm knew that his enemies, especially former colleagues within the Nation of Islam (NOI), wanted to see him dead. He told friends and news reporters that he probably was not long for the world. "I live like a man who's already dead," he said in an interview he granted shortly before he died. "I'm a marked man. It doesn't frighten me for myself as long as I felt they would not hurt my family."[715]

Coming from someone else, such remarks might have sounded unnecessarily melodramatic and absurd, but Malcolm X was not a man to traffic in hyperbole. His life had been dramatic enough without resorting to theatrics. The question was not why he was the target of men who wished to do him harm, but how had he stayed alive as long as he had?

He was born in Omaha, Nebraska, on May 19, 1925, as Malcolm Little, the fourth of seven children of a self-styled Baptist orator, Earl Little, who served as a local leader in the Universal Negro Improvement Association, a black nationalist fraternal organization. When Malcolm was six years old, his

278 • POLITICAL ASSASSINATIONS AND ATTEMPTS IN US HISTORY

father died under mysterious circumstances. Officially, his death was attributed to an unfortunate streetcar accident, but family members believed that a local white supremacist group, the Black Legion, murdered Earl for his "uppity ways." Earl was convinced that the Black Legion had burned down the family's home in Lansing, Michigan, and he shared his opinion freely.[716]

The Little family never fully rebounded from the patriarch's death. Following the birth of her eighth child, Malcolm's mother, Louise, suffered a nervous breakdown. Early in 1939, she entered the Kalamazoo State Hospital while her children were shipped off to foster homes. Malcolm was thirteen years old. (Later, he moved in with Ella, his older half-sister, who lived near Boston.)[717]

His early life fell into a predictable pattern. Malcolm was a bright child, but he could see no path toward fulfilling his ambitions. Had he been white, he probably would have enjoyed a prosperous future. Under a racist regime, however, a Negro child, no matter how gifted, was seldom valued for his professional promise. Even living in a progressive northern state, a Negro child felt the daunting burden of discrimination. Discouraged by a white teacher from pursuing a career in the law owing to his race, young Malcolm more or less gave up. Channeled into a series of menial, dead-end jobs, he eventually turned to a life of crime. In 1946, the street tough known as "Detroit Red" was caught after committing multiple burglaries, and sentenced to an eight-to-ten-year sentence in the Charlestown State Prison in Boston.[718]

While he was incarcerated in Charlestown, he met a man, John Bembry, who impressed young Malcolm as a genuine intellectual, well read and informed on numerous issues. Their association awakened a long-dormant interest in reading that would characterize the remainder of Malcolm's life. A second major change occurred soon thereafter. Early in 1948, Malcolm's brother, Philbert, sent him a letter discussing the family's newfound interest in the Nation of Islam. At first, Malcolm dismissed his brother's entreaties—Philbert "was forever joining something," he said—but gradually other family members worked on him, and he became intrigued. After he was transferred to the Norfolk Prison Colony in March 1948, Malcolm agreed to refrain from eating pork or smoking cigarettes. By the end of the year, he was writing letters to Elijah Muhammad, head of the NOI.[719]

Muhammad, born Elijah Robert Poole in Georgia in 1897, was a former sharecropper, day laborer, and factory worker who joined the Great Migration out of the South, eventually ending up in Michigan. He gravitated toward

Marcus Garvey's philosophy of black nationalism and Pan-Africanism, but floundered after Garvey's decline during the late 1920s. After seeing a charismatic preacher, Wallace D. Fard, speak, Poole was hooked. Poole joined Fard's fledging group, the Nation of Islam, and rose through the ranks. When Fard disappeared in 1934, Poole, who had assumed the surname "Muhammad," stepped up as the NOI's leader. Ruthless infighting characterized his early years as the Nation's leader, but by the 1940s—after serving four years in prison for failing to register for the draft—he was firmly in control of the organization. He moved around repeatedly before finally setting up shop in Chicago.[720]

Under Muhammad's leadership, the Nation's goal was to lift blacks up from their debased condition. To that end, Muhammad instructed his followers to refrain from using tobacco or drinking alcohol. Moreover, they must become self-reliant, building up black businesses and working hard. Coupled with a plea for members to embrace Muslim culture and traditions, the NOI appealed to many black Americans who felt beaten down by the Jim Crow regime as well as lingering effects of the Great Depression. While many blacks wholeheartedly embraced the Christian Faith, Muhammad's adherents believed that Christianity, with its emphasis on turning the other cheek and its promises of the meek inheriting the earth, had become a tool of social control for whites to keep blacks oppressed with false promises of a delayed reward in the hereafter.[721]

Despite his initial skepticism, Malcolm Little found much to appreciate in the Nation's teachings. The more he learned, the more he moved toward conversion. By 1950, he was signing his surname as "X" rather than "Little" because the latter was his slave name. He initiated an ongoing correspondence with Elijah Muhammad that would change both men's lives forever.[722]

After he earned his release from prison in 1952, Malcolm pledged his fidelity to the NOI. To bolster his bona fides, he delivered a series of well-regarded speeches about how Elijah Muhammad had changed his life. The NOI leader recognized that Malcolm was a powerful speaker and a potent recruitment tool. Standing six-foot, three-inches tall, Malcolm was always impeccably groomed and well spoken. His charisma attracted men and women in equal measure. Muhammad agreed to promote his young disciple into a position of leadership as a NOI minister.[723]

In 1954, Malcolm moved to Harlem and led Temple Number 7 there for almost a decade. Although officially he was only one among many NOI ministers, it quickly became evident that Malcolm X was something special.

22.1 Elijah Muhammad led the Nation of Islam and recruited Malcolm X to join the group in the early 1950s. Courtesy of the Library of Congress.

He traveled constantly, promoting the Nation and pushing for new members. His fiery rhetorical style and growing fame catapulted him to prominence as the civil rights movement gained momentum in the late 1950s. When he joined the Nation, the group boasted of somewhere between 400 and 1,200 members. Within a decade, the rolls contained between 50,000 and 75,000 members. Although Malcolm was not solely responsible for the exponential growth, he was the most visible and active of the Nation's ministers. His powerful oratory was sure to attract an audience wherever he preached. He brought in members from all parts of the social strata, including black professionals and even the boxing legend Cassius Clay, soon to be known as Muhammad Ali.[724]

In contrast to Martin Luther King, Jr., and proponents of non-violent protest, Malcolm let it be known that he would not turn the other cheek. Malcolm X did not believe the races could live together side by side. Whites by their nature would always seek to oppress blacks. It was an immutable fact of life. The goal for Malcolm and his compatriots was to separate from whites and build a black society that was not dependent on white largesse. If blacks passively assumed that whites would come around to see the immorality of segregation and racial inequities, it would be a long, lonely wait. Rather than supplicate themselves before a handful of benevolent whites, black nationalists preferred to take matters into their own hands. "We want freedom *by any means necessary*. We want justice *by any means necessary*. We want equality *by any means necessary*," he said in one of his most famous speeches, delivered in June 1964, toward the end of his life.[725]

In 1957, Malcolm became nationally known when he confronted New York Police Department (NYPD) officers after an NOI member was severely beaten and was not allowed to seek treatment in a hospital. A throng of thousands surrounded the police station until Malcolm was satisfied that his brother would be treated. At his signal, the crowd dispersed. Worried about the influence of this possibly dangerous radical in their midst, state and federal law enforcement officials took note. They had placed Malcolm under surveillance as far back as 1953, but now they ratcheted up their interest in him lest he unleash violent forces on white society. He had arrived on the scene, and no one could forget it. For the rest of his life, he would remain a target of law enforcement surveillance.[726]

As Malcolm's national recognition grew, so did his power. In retrospect, it is clear that Malcolm X and Elijah Muhammad were on a collision course from the moment the younger man became a media star. They were two powerful personalities that, as it turned out, pursued different agendas. Muhammad saw the NOI as his personal fiefdom with his ministers as components in a larger organizational structure. As Malcolm X continually took center stage, Elijah Muhammad became increasingly jealous of the media attention showered on the charismatic minister, believing that the talented subordinate might present a leadership threat. For his part, Malcolm saw himself as a good soldier who did as he was told. He wholeheartedly believed the Nation's teachings about developing strong black men who refrained from the sins of smoking cigarettes, drinking alcohol, abusing drugs, and deserting their families. When Malcolm learned of Muhammad's sexual escapades with comely young NOI secretaries, he was appalled at what he viewed as personal hypocrisy. He thought that such dalliances revealed an unacceptable level of sin in a religious leader.[727]

Aside from their personal differences, Muhammad and Malcolm drifted apart when it came to organizational goals. Muhammad was careful to refrain from adopting a political stance, believing that the Nation would avoid undue government scrutiny if it did not engage in the civil rights brouhahas that engulfed other black organizations. Elijah Muhammad, the former field hand made good, enjoyed a lavish lifestyle with considerable prestige and financial rewards. He wanted to do nothing that upset the apple cart. Having already tangled with the US government to his detriment during the 1940s, he knew that needlessly aggravating federal officials would accomplish nothing.

Malcolm, by contrast, was not content to sit on the sidelines and watch white America continually berate the black man. He genuinely believed his own rhetoric about the actions of white devils and their corrosive effect on non-white races. In his view, the Nation of Islam could serve as a powerful vehicle for promoting social, political, and religious changes in the country. All that was required was effective leadership. After the Los Angeles Police Department raided an NOI temple and viciously beat several members in 1962—even shooting one man to death—Malcolm longed to rage against police brutality aimed at members who were derided in the press as "Black Muslims" and treated as though they were the perpetrators of crimes when in reality they were the victims of an unchecked white power structure. Yet when Malcolm requested permission to speak out, Muhammad refused to countenance any sort of public protest. Malcolm was dismayed at what he saw as an unconscionable abdication of leadership in a time of racial turmoil.[728]

Even with their different agendas, a public split between Muhammad and Malcolm was not a foregone conclusion. Malcolm had been associated with the NOI most of his adult life. Elijah Muhammad had reached out to him during those dark days when Malcolm was languishing in prison and uncertain about what he should do with his life. The NOI gave his life purpose and meaning. The thought of leaving his only place of employment—indeed, his main claim to a professional identity—bothered him immensely. It was not a decision to be made lightly.[729]

He might have reached a rapprochement with Muhammad but for a high-profile incident that occurred at the end of 1963. On December 1 of that year, Malcolm delivered a speech in New York City. During the question-and-answer session afterward, a reporter asked him to comment on John F. Kennedy's recent assassination. A stunned nation was still mourning its martyred chief executive. Recognizing that reporters hungered for provocative statements from what they believed were radical groups seeking to undermine the safety and integrity of the republic, Elijah Muhammad had made it clear that he did not want NOI members to denigrate the popular president in public.

Malcolm let his rhetoric get the better of him that day. He responded to the reporter's query with an instantly quotable remark that reinforced the stereotype of the Nation of Islam as a black extremist group with Malcolm at the helm as demagogue-in-chief. It was, he said, a case of "the chickens coming home to roost." Had the remark been uttered in another time and in the context of the historical violence in American society, it might have been less sensational. At the time, however, Americans were still reeling from the shock of the president's sudden murder. Even Republicans and conservative Democrats who had bitterly opposed Kennedy's agenda were singing his praises in December 1963. He had entered the pantheon of immortal American leaders, fairly or unfairly. To denigrate his memory or even to speak of him in less-than-glowing terms was to invite anger and hostility on a grand scale. To hear anyone—much less a prominent black radical known for his attacks on white America—implicitly criticize the dead president or the society that produced him was too much. Not surprisingly, the next day's headlines resoundingly condemned the incendiary comments.[730]

The following day, Elijah Muhammad suspended Minister Malcolm X for ninety days. It was an astonishing public rebuke for the Nation's most valuable player. Muhammad's critics saw the action as a convenient pretext for the leader to call Malcolm to task, something he had wanted to do for quite a while.

Initially bewildered by the decision, Malcolm believed that he had made a valid point. He had long preached that white society was violent and oppressive. He was simply pointing out that any nation whose citizens engage in violent acts should expect that violence will be used against its own leaders. No matter; a punishment had been decreed, and the NOI would allow no appeal.

Most NOI members thought that the suspension would stay in place, and after ninety days life would go on as before. Circumstances changed quickly. Muhammad initially said that the suspension would be in place temporarily, but sometime during the following month, he changed his mind. Malcolm had grown too powerful and needed to be silenced permanently. It was obvious that the talented minister was unhappy with the NOI; he had voiced his concern over the Nation's anti-political stance on more than one occasion. Malcolm was not a man who could be controlled for long. Although he claimed to be contrite in accepting his punishment, Malcolm appeared to be anything but humbled by his silencing. If Malcolm continued his association with the Nation, it was only a matter of time before he challenged Elijah Muhammad's leadership.[731]

As late as February 1964, Malcolm was lobbying to be reinstated in the Nation of Islam. He seemed oblivious to the level of animosity that the rank-and-file members felt toward him. While some of the Nation's adherents remained personally loyal to Malcolm, a majority stayed loyal to Muhammad, expressing their anger at the apostate who had grown too big for his britches. He had finally received his comeuppance, they believed. Malcolm's friends inside the group finally convinced him that the level of hostility aimed at him was too intense to ever allow a return to the fold. "They're talking about killing you," a friend and colleague bluntly told him.[732]

Malcolm X finally understood that he no longer had a home within the Nation. Never a man to employ half measures, he publicly announced his split on March 8, 1964. Speaking to M. S. Handler of the *New York Times*, Malcolm explained that "I remain a Muslim," but it was time to move on. He said he would start a new movement by creating a "black nationalist party." The "main emphasis of the new movement will be black nationalism as a political concept and form of social action against the oppressors." He had eschewed direct political involvement in the past, but the future would be different, he said. "I have reached the conclusion that I can best spread Mr. Muhammad's message by staying out of the Nation of Islam and continuing to work on my own among America's twenty-two million non-Muslim Negroes."[733]

He put a brave face on a lonely, desperate situation, but in announcing his break, he also conveyed conflicting messages. Malcolm remained committed to spreading "Mr. Muhammad's message," he said, but the split threatened to undermine the legitimacy of the NOI. In pursuing his own political agenda, he risked confusing the public, which viewed all "Black Muslims" as indistinguishable from each other. The Nation of Islam had seen factions break away in the past, but none were headed by a leader like Malcolm X. He had become bigger than the NOI.[734]

Within the Nation of Islam, a debate ensued about what to do concerning Minister Malcolm. Muhammad might let him go his own way in peace, but would there ever be genuine peace as long as this man preached his own brand of Islam coupled with a potent message of Negro empowerment and social justice? From the NOI perspective, Malcolm compounded the problem by creating two competing organizations: Muslim Mosque, Inc., primarily a religious group for black Muslims, and the OAAU, a Pan-African group modeled on the Organization of African Unity (OAU), which Malcolm greatly admired. Although both nascent organizations were so small that they hardly posed a current threat to the NOI, they were poised to cipher off members from the Nation in time. In light of Malcolm's electrifying oratorical style and his ability to galvanize the media, Muhammad saw him as a festering problem that eventually must be addressed. He might have to be silenced—not for ninety days, but permanently.[735]

Confronted with the enormity of his bold actions, Malcolm understood that his break with the NOI held potentially violent consequences. The price of heresy might be death. He had come to understand that, in his words, "those folks down at 116th Street and that man in Chicago" would profit from his timely demise. They probably would orchestrate an assassination if they could. Yet he felt that he had no choice but to forge ahead.[736]

Malcolm spent the last year of his life in deep reflection as he traveled throughout Africa and Europe, during which time he became a Sunni Muslim. In April 1964, he completed the Hajj, an annual pilgrimage to Mecca, the holy city revered by Muslims around the world. As he was exposed to new ideas, Malcolm modified his beliefs. He still thought that powerful whites in American society caused untold suffering for people of color, but the answers were no longer as clear cut as he had originally believed. In his book *The Autobiography of Malcolm X*, published after his death by his ghost-writer, Alex Haley, Malcolm explained that he had experienced an epiphany. "I have never before seen *sincere* and *true* brotherhood practiced by all colors together, irrespective of their color." Islam was an all-encompassing religion, and it could erase distinctions such as creed or color. "You may be shocked by these words coming from me," he concluded. "But on this pilgrimage, what I have seen, and experienced, has forced me to *re-arrange* much of my thought-patterns previously held, and to *toss aside* some of my previous conclusions. This was not too difficult for me. Despite my firm convictions, I have been always a man who tries to face facts, and to accept the reality of life as new experience and new knowledge unfolds it. I have always kept an open mind, which is necessary to the flexibility that must go hand in hand with every form of intelligent search for truth."[737]

Malcolm's extensive international travel schedule kept him away from the NOI soldiers, who had decided that he must be assassinated. His return to the United States in February 1965 again put him at risk. He had been home for less than a day when they struck. Around 2:45 a.m. on February 14, one or more persons hurled Molotov cocktails at his house, setting a fire and awakening his family. Betty, his wife, was pregnant with twins. With Malcolm's assistance, she and her four girls rushed away from the flames. Everyone got out unscathed, but it was clear that Malcolm's enemies were closing in on him.

Most scholars have concluded that NOI operatives probably firebombed the home that night, but others question why the Nation would have done so. The NOI owned the property, and Malcolm was about to be evicted. FBI agents who had been watching Malcolm and NOI members for years might have thrown the bombs, although this course of action appears unlikely. The agents had been instructed to monitor his actions surreptitiously. Tossing Molotov cocktails at his house would have violated their instructions. Some cynics suggested that Malcolm himself burned the house as a means of exacting vengeance against the Nation. Most researchers who have examined the case have concluded that the Nation of Islam probably was responsible. NOI members were so angry with Malcolm and anxious to kill him that they acted even if it destroyed the organization's property. Several NOI members later claimed to know which persons had participated in the raid.[738]

22.2 Malcolm X, a controversial member of the Nation of Islam, split from the group in 1964. The photograph was taken after his April 1964 pilgrimage to Mecca. Courtesy of the Library of Congress.

Regardless of who participated, the bombing unnerved Malcolm. Yet he refused to alter his hectic speaking schedule during February 1965. Consequently, his lieutenants resolved to search anyone admitted to the auditoriums and ballrooms where he customarily spoke. As Malcolm well understood, however, a public figure is never completely safe when a determined assassin or group of assassins plots to take his life. He might have taken stronger precautions, but he would not yield. Perhaps Malcolm's sense of fatalism prevented him from turning away from his fate.

In light of recent events, when Malcolm entered the Audubon Ballroom early on the afternoon of Sunday, February 21, he knew that he might become a target of assassins at any moment. Curiously, he had invited his wife and daughters to attend the meeting. Perhaps he missed them and wanted them by his side. Perhaps he thought that no one would dare harm him in the presence of his family. Perhaps he simply was heedless of the risk. In any event, they became spectators to his grisly fate.[739]

The lax security arrangements struck many people as strange. NYPD officers normally appeared wherever Malcolm spoke, but they were noticeably absent outside the ballroom that day. Malcolm's aides apparently had asked them to stand in a less conspicuous place. In a bizarre development, especially given the lack of a police presence, the Muslim Mosque security detail, on orders from Malcolm, did not frisk audience members for weapons. It was a simple matter for gunmen to enter the ballroom without fear of detection. In the aftermath of the episode, Malcolm's supporters wondered whether he had harbored a secret death wish.[740]

He was not his usual equable self that day. By his own admission, Malcolm had reached his "wit's end." To the people who saw him immediately before he took the stage, he appeared angry and distracted, a man suffering from unrelenting stress. Usually unflappable, his demeanor worried his entourage. Still, he would press on, stubbornly keeping to his schedule.[741]

Shortly before 3:00 p.m., Malcolm stepped onto the plywood stage. Benjamin 2X Goodman, unnerved by Malcolm's bitter mood, was still sputtering through his introduction when he saw the minister arrive. He hastily wrapped up his remarks.[742]

The enthusiastic audience of 400 souls applauded for almost a full minute. "As-salāmu 'alaykum," Malcolm said as the noise subsided. It was the traditional Muslim greeting, Arabic for "peace be upon you." The crowd answered with the usual response, "wa'alaykumu s-salām," Arabic for "and upon you, peace."

At that instant, a disturbance erupted about six or eight rows from the stage. Several men appeared to be involved. According to one account, someone involved in the confrontation called out, "Get your hands out of my pocket," or words to that effect. Seeing the struggle, Malcolm called out, although eyewitnesses differed on precisely what he said. One version recounted his words as, "Be cool now, and don't get excited." Another eyewitness heard him repeatedly calling out, "Hold it! Hold it! Hold it! Hold it!"[743]

As Malcolm's bodyguards moved toward the commotion, a smoke bomb ignited in the rear of the auditorium. The scene quickly degenerated into pandemonium, exactly as planned. While everyone was distracted and Malcolm stood on the stage undefended, a burly figure, Willie X Bradley, stepped forward, aimed a sawed-off shotgun and fired, striking his target in the left side of his chest. Two other men advanced, Talmadge Hayer (who sometimes used the alias Thomas Hagan) and Leon X Davis, firing handguns at Malcolm, who had remained on his feet following the shotgun blast. In the face of the furious fusillade, Malcolm X toppled backward, his head smacking the stage with a thud. He had suffered twenty-one gunshot wounds, but the initial shotgun blast killed him.[744]

The three shooters fled the scene. Bradley ducked into a women's bathroom sixty feet from the stage, threw his shotgun away, and headed down a seldom-used flight of stairs to safety. Hayer and Davis ran through a gauntlet of bystanders and chairs. In the confusion, Davis disappeared into the throngs of clamoring people. Hayer did not. Malcolm's security chief, Reuben X Francis, shot Hagan in the thigh. The crowd descended on the wounded assassin and might have killed him but for the arrival of police officers, who took the suspect into custody.[745]

Malcolm's wife, Betty, screamed, "They're killing my husband!" She had fallen to her knees instinctively when the shooting commenced, but as she struggled to stand, her friends interceded. They escorted her and the children outside so they would not see the after-effects of the gunfire.[746]

Gene Roberts, an undercover policeman who had been attached to the Muslim Mosque guard detail, rushed to the stage. He could tell that Malcolm probably was dead, but he attempted mouth-to-mouth resuscitation, anyway. Bystanders ripped open the wounded man's shirt, but they could not revive him.[747]

In the minutes after the assault, an ambulance failed to appear on the scene. Someone retrieved a gurney from the nearby Columbia Presbyterian Hospital, and Malcolm's followers lifted his body onto it. As they pushed him outside the ballroom and moved toward the hospital, NYPD officers arrived and provided an escort.[748]

Emergency room doctors immediately took charge when Malcolm appeared at the hospital. They cut a tracheotomy in his throat to allow him to breathe, but it made no difference. For fifteen minutes, they labored over his unresponsive form before declaring him dead at 3:30 p.m.[749]

The news rapidly spread that Malcom had been assassinated. Martin Luther King, Jr., lamented that "our society is still sick enough to express dissent through murder." Roy Wilkins of the National Association for the Advancement of Colored People (NAACP) remarked that the episode was a "shocking and ghastly demonstration of the futility of resorting to violence as a means of settling differences."[750]

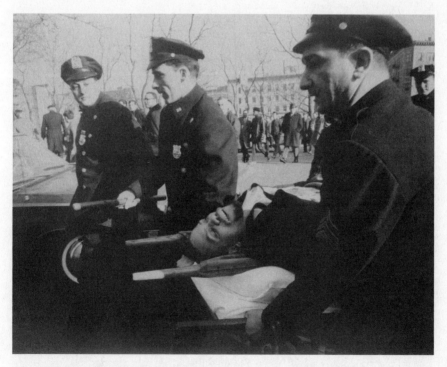

22.3 In this photograph, New York City policemen escort Malcolm X's body to Columbia Presbyterian Hospital following his shooting on February 21, 1965. Courtesy of Alamy Stock Photos.

When he was told of the incident, Elijah Muhammad gasped, "oh, My God!" He paused before murmuring, "Um, um, um." Although he probably did not directly order his former protégé's murder, Muhammad had to know that his faithful minions were plotting revenge. Retaliation against Muhammad was possible, for Malcolm still had his trusted lieutenants within the NOI ranks. Also recognizing that he might become the chief suspect in the murder, Muhammad wisely retreated behind closed doors at his well-fortified Chicago estate and kept a low profile.[751]

The reaction to Malcolm's murder ranged the gamut from those who believed he had it coming to those who mourned the loss of a great civil rights leader. An exchange that played out in the pages of the *New York Times* illustrated the opposing perspectives. The *Times* editors reflected the views of many whites when they opined that "the life and death of Malcolm X provides a discordant but typical theme for the times in which we live. He was a case history, as well as an extraordinary and twisted man, turning many true gifts to evil purpose."

Just as Malcolm had remarked that John F. Kennedy's assassination was a case of the chickens coming home to roost, his detractors believed that he who lives by the sword, dies by the sword. "Malcolm X's life was strangely and pitifully wasted," the *Times* concluded. "But this was because he did not seek to fit into society or into the life of his own people. He could not even come to terms with his fellow black extremists. The world he saw through those horn-rimmed glasses of his was distorted and dark. But he made it darker still with his exaltation of fanaticism." His murder was the logical extension of the forces he unleashed: "Yesterday someone came out of that darkness that he spawned, and killed him."[752]

A rebuttal appeared as a letter to the editor five days later. James Loomis of Brooklyn wrote that "Malcolm X did not 'spawn the darkness' of the Negro's fanaticism [Editorial Feb. 22]. He came out of it, and with clarity and precision focused the light of his own honesty on it to show us the danger in which we all walk, white and black alike." According to Loomis, "He was assassinated not because he was a violent man but because he longed for peace and believed that it could only come when were honest with each other. He knew that murder is spawned in the darkness of men's minds."[753]

While people reacted to news of the murder, investigators descended on the Audubon Ballroom to search for clues. In the opinion of some observers, the police appeared nonchalant in their efforts. Perhaps the observers were correct. Quite a few officers thought that Malcolm X was little more than a thug. His break with the Nation of Islam merely represented internecine warfare between rival gangs. The inevitable result of this kind of public feud was death and destruction. Accordingly, why spend considerable time and energy investigating shootings among warring factions?[754]

Although police officers arguably performed only a perfunctory examination, they nonetheless interviewed witnesses, snapped photographs, and attempted to figure out what happened. Incredibly, they also surrendered the crime scene to the Audubon Ballroom staff so that a scheduled dance could be held that evening at 7:00 p.m.—less than four hours after the murder. Without completing a full forensic examination, police officials allowed Malcolm's blood to be mopped up and chairs to be rearranged. They departed with bullet holes still plainly visible in the walls behind the speaker's lectern.[755]

Within days, three suspects emerged. Aside from Hayer, wounded and captured at the scene, the NYPD focused on two NOI soldiers: Norman 3X Butler and Thomas 15X Johnson. Numerous eyewitnesses placed the men in the ballroom that afternoon. Police promptly arrested the men and charged them with Malcolm's murder. Conspiracy theorists suggested that others had been involved, too, including undercover FBI agents who had planned to kill Malcolm X many times in the past.[756]

Hayer eventually confessed his role in the shooting. He said that he had been aided by accomplices, but he would not provide their names. He insisted, however, that Butler and Johnson did not participate. His remarks did not prevent a jury from convicting all three defendants of first-degree murder. Sentenced to serve life in prison, all three survived captivity. Butler was paroled in 1985, Johnson in 1987, and Hayer in 2010. Willie X Bradley and Leon X Davis were never hauled into court to account for their crimes.[757]

As for Malcolm X, he was laid to rest on Saturday, February 27, 1965, after a service held in the Faith Temple Church of God in Christ on Amsterdam Avenue in Harlem, a mile or so from the Audubon Ballroom. A thousand people packed the auditorium to remember his life and death. Although a number of civil rights activists appeared—Bayard Rustin, James Farmer, Dick Gregory, John Lewis, and James Forman among them—many others did not. Muhammad Ali, once Malcolm's close friend, had stayed loyal to Elijah Muhammad and the Nation of Islam. Adam Clayton Powell, Jr.,

22.4 Malcolm X was shot and killed on February 21, 1965, as he appeared in Manhattan's Audubon Ballroom. This photograph shows the immediate aftermath of the shooting. The circles on the backdrop indicate bullet holes. Courtesy of the Library of Congress.

the controversial Harlem congressman, had known Malcolm, but he did not attend the service, nor did many other prominent black leaders.[758]

Ossie Davis and Ruby Dee, a prominent black couple known for their work as actors on the stage and screen, presided over the service. Davis captured the headlines when he eloquently summarized Malcolm X's legacy. "Here—at this final hour, in this quiet place—Harlem has come to bid farewell to one of its brightest hopes—extinguished now, and gone from us forever," he stated. "Malcolm was our manhood, our living, black manhood! This was his meaning to his people. And, in honoring him, we honor the best in ourselves." Malcolm X was a civil rights leader whose faith and philosophy were constantly evolving up until the day he was cut down by assassins' bullets. "Consigning these mortal remains to earth, the common mother of all, secure in the knowledge that what we place in the ground is no more now a man—but a seed—which, after the winter of our discontent, will come forth again to meet us. And we will know him then for what he was and is—a Prince—our own black shining Prince!—who didn't hesitate to die, because he loved us so."[759]

When Malcolm X died, many Americans, black and white, did not share Ossie Davis's assessment of the former NOI minister as a black shining prince. Instead, the popular perception held that he was a racist demagogue who was killed because he broke ranks with his former gang.[760]

Time has changed the popular perspective of Malcolm, although not completely. With the publication of *The Autobiography of Malcolm X*—a book that has sold upwards of six million copies since it first appeared in print late in 1965—and the success of the civil rights movement of the last half of the twentieth century, Malcolm X has been transformed into a cultural icon. The subject of articles, books, and films, he has become larger than life, an icon revered by generations of people, in the United States and abroad, of all races who see him as a symbol of determined resistance to entrenched power. When information surfaced about the FBI's COINTELPRO (short for COunter INTELligence PROgram) operations in 1971, critics realized that civil rights activists such as Malcolm X had been targeted by federal law enforcement officials in a smear campaign designed to undermine their legitimacy. In the wake of such revelations, Malcolm's seemingly outrageous claims about the evils of the white power structure suddenly sounded less outrageous.[761]

In a final analysis, it is difficult to grapple with the twin perspectives on Malcolm X. His legacy is complicated. To critics he will always be a demagogue who answered white supremacy and bigotry with black supremacy and bigotry of his own. His admirers believe he was an important civil rights leader who stepped beyond Dr. King and the forces of moderation to offer a different, yet equally valid method for improving the lives of American blacks. He refused to be pinned down to a single position. His life was an evolving story, a work forever in progress. The nuances of his views in life transformed him into a *tabula rasa* after his death. The onlooker sees in Malcolm what he wants to see.

His assassins do not fit into a neat category, either. The Nation of Islam gunmen shot Malcolm X because he separated from the NOI and dared to criticize Elijah Muhammad. They saw in Malcolm a man who refused to be cowed, who would not temper his views even when he might have profited by toning down his rhetoric. They probably were Type 1 assassins, seeking to accomplish what amounted to a political objective by dispatching a political enemy. The zeal and commitment of these NOI soldiers were based on rational, supposedly principled motives. They possessed an objective—to rid the NOI of an intractable problem—and they took steps to achieve that objective.

Yet there are elements of Type 2 and Type 3 motives as well. As members of a religious group based largely on a cult of personality—namely, Elijah Muhammad's personality and his enigmatic brand of Islam—the assassins had to demonstrate to their leader that they were loyal subjects. Because Malcolm X had become a pariah, they decided that the most effective means of demonstrating their fidelity to the leader was to eliminate the problem through violence. Their personalities were subsumed by Elijah Muhammad's personality, making the gunmen appear to be Type 2 actors—needy, possessing low self-esteem, neurotic. They would show their significant other—Muhammad—that they were worthy disciples.

Yet the cavalier manner in which they shot Malcolm X suggests that one or more of the gunmen may have been psychopathic personalities. They did not hesitate to fire multiple shots inside a crowded ballroom, assassinating a public figure in front of his family as well as 400 potential eyewitnesses. Type 3 actors are so contemptuous of ordinary social mores that they feel no compunction about lashing out violently against a target. They are indifferent to the feelings of others, indifferent to death, and nihilistic in their outlook.

Add the concept of a group dynamic to the possibly mixed motives of the assassins and the analysis becomes even murkier. Most of the assailants profiled in this book acted alone. Even if they were part of a larger conspiracy, the would-be assassins perpetrated the deed alone. In the murder of Malcolm X, three gunmen, acting in concert, shot him down in cold blood. Whenever a group acts violently, it becomes difficult to assess individual motives. It is likely that the men were fortified by the knowledge that they were part of a larger organization. The NOI sustained them and steeled their nerves. They shared responsibility for the brutal deed and, therefore, if they were capable of feeling remorse for their crime, they could take comfort in their joint culpability. A mob mentality has allowed many a man to act when he might have abandoned the quest were he acting alone.

As for Malcolm X, he knew that he was marked for death. He spoke of it many times during his last year. His trusted aide Benjamin 2X Goodman perhaps put it best when he remarked, "Death ends a thing on time. Whatever may be the instruments to bring it about, when it comes, it comes on time."[762]

Chapter 23

"I MAY NOT GET THERE WITH YOU. BUT I WANT YOU TO KNOW TONIGHT, THAT WE, AS A PEOPLE, WILL GET TO THE PROMISED LAND": DR. MARTIN LUTHER KING, JR. (1968)

Dr. Martin Luther King, Jr., was thirty-nine years old on April 3, 1968, but he was almost as weary as a man twice his age. The constant, exhaustive travel, the stress of protests and marches, and the struggle to unite the disparate elements inside the increasingly discordant civil rights movement were almost more than a single man could bear. Coupled with the weight of so many expectations from black Americans caught in the clutches of the sputtering Jim Crow regime—a regime that King had helped to undermine—he was tired and ill. The burdens of living a life and constructing a legend had left him spent and frequently depressed.

He had hoped for a night off, a respite from his hectic schedule. It was not to be. As he stepped to the microphone on the Mason Temple stage in Memphis, Tennessee, that stormy Wednesday evening to discuss his efforts to mediate the city-wide sanitation strike, King nursed a cold. He had not planned to speak until his friend and colleague, Ralph David Abernathy, had called King's hotel room from the church and asked him to address an expectant crowd of almost 3,000 hopeful souls, many of whom were sanitation workers and their families. They had braved the elements to see the great man, and they must not be denied.

It was the usual plea. Whenever King waved away a speaking engagement or a commitment, someone pleaded with him to make an exception. He was the indispensable man. He must make an appearance. The faithful expected to see him and hear what he had to say. They expected him to be "on," ready to pass along pearls of wisdom in eloquent speeches that uplifted the audience to a higher plane. They expected the legend to appear. The flesh-and-blood man no longer mattered.

As he almost always did, King relented. He traveled over from the Lorraine Motel like the dutiful preacher he had always tried to be. It was to be a short appearance. Yet he was a gifted, natural speaker who often came alive when he stepped into the spotlight. And so now, on the last night of his life, Martin Luther King, Jr., came alive once again.[763]

"Something is happening in Memphis," he said, and "something is happening in our world." The world was sick, he said, sick with prejudice and fear and hatred. Nonetheless, he would not want to live in any other era, because "somehow . . . only when it is dark enough, can you see the stars." For all of the troubles in the world, the human condition was improving. It was a long, laborious, tension-filled process filled with innumerable missteps and reversals, but progress had been made. As King had said on several occasions, paraphrasing a quote by the nineteenth-century minister and abolitionist Theodore Parker, "The arc of the moral universe is long, but it bends towards justice." He had no doubt that justice would occur, but not necessarily on his timetable.[764]

Without becoming too maudlin, he reflected on his own mortality. "You know, several years ago, I was in New York City autographing the first book that I had written. And while sitting there autographing books, a demented black woman came up. The only question I heard from her was, 'Are you Martin Luther King?' And I was looking down writing, and I said yes. And the next minute I felt something beating on my chest. Before I knew it I had been stabbed by this demented woman." The black woman, Izola Curry, stabbed King in 1958 and was later judged to be insane. As for her target, he survived the attack, but it was a close call. Doctors told him that if he had sneezed, the blade might have punctured his aorta. "I'm so happy that I didn't sneeze," he said. If he had sneezed, he would have missed the wonders of the civil rights movement.

He did not know how much longer he would live given the threats he faced. "I left Atlanta this morning, and as we got started on the plane, there were six of us, the pilot said over the public address system, 'We are sorry for the delay, but we have Dr. Martin Luther King on the plane. And to be sure that all of the bags were checked, and to be sure that nothing would be wrong with the plane, we had to check out everything carefully. And we've had the plane protected and guarded all night." It was a chilling reminder of the dangers he faced each day.

"And then I got to Memphis," he continued. "And some began to say the threats, or talk about the threats that were out. What would happen to me from some of our sick white brothers?" He shrugged off such fatalism. It was not for a human being to know the answers.

What he did know was that much was left to be done. "Well, I don't know what will happen now," he confessed. "We've got some difficult days ahead. But it doesn't matter with me now. Because I've been to the mountaintop. And I don't mind." A burst of staccato applause fueled him forward. "Like anybody, I would like to live a long life. Longevity has its place. But I'm not concerned about that now. I just want to do God's will. And He's allowed me to go up to the mountain. And I've looked over. And I've seen the Promised Land . . . I may not get there with you. But I want you to know tonight, that we, as a people, will get to the Promised Land. So I'm happy tonight. I'm not worried about anything. I'm not fearing any man. Mine eyes have seen the glory of the coming of the Lord."[765]

With his last remark, delivered in a deep, rich, powerful voice, Dr. King moved away from the podium. The impromptu speech, so masterfully delivered, struck many listeners as prophetic, a great man's farewell to his followers, his soulful lamentation of things to come. He had been the leader of the civil rights movement, but his time was almost at an end.[766]

Perhaps he was prescient. Less than twenty-four hours later, he was dead.

After his murder, Dr. King became a larger-than-life icon. His name and legacy are revered today, but during his time he was seen by many Americans, especially whites, as a dangerous rabble-rouser dedicated to upending long-standing strictures of American society. He didn't start out that way. In the beginning, he was a Baptist preacher who hoped to establish a church and do what he could to minister to his congregation. Somewhere along the way, his life took an unexpected turn.

The turn started in Montgomery, Alabama. He was twenty-six years old at the time, a pastor at the Dexter Avenue Baptist Church. On December 1, 1955, Rosa Parks was arrested for refusing to get up from her seat when a white person wanted the seat on a Montgomery city bus. Predictably, she was charged with violating the city's segregation law. Using her arrest as a springboard for action, the Montgomery Improvement Association (MIA), a grassroots organization formed to lead a boycott against the city buses, lobbied to change the segregation laws. The boycott lasted 382 days, and pushed the city to comply with the

23.1 Dr. Martin Luther King, Jr., a black minister from Georgia, became a leading spokesman for the civil rights movement of the 1950s and 1960s. Courtesy of the Library of Congress.

activists' demands. King had been selected to serve as the public face for the MIA-led boycott, and the episode transformed him into a national figure.[767]

Martin Luther King, Jr., had impressed people all his life. Unlike some civil rights leaders who rose to prominence by overcoming seemingly insurmountable obstacles imposed on them by Jim Crow laws, he was reared in a middle-class family of ministers. In some ways, he was groomed to become a leader, although he never imagined the contours of his ministry.

Born on January 15, 1929, in Atlanta, Georgia, Michael King, Jr., was the middle child of Michael King, Sr., and Alberta Williams King. His maternal grandfather, A. D. Williams, originally a rural minister, moved to Atlanta at the end of the nineteenth century and stepped into the pulpit of the struggling Ebenezer Baptist Church, building a thirteen-member congregation into a successful, well-respected mainstay of the black community. Michael, Sr., took his over his father-in-law's duties after the older man died.

After visiting Germany in 1934, Michael, Sr., changed his name to honor the German theologian Martin Luther. His changed his son's name as well. The family sheltered Martin, Jr., from segregation as much as possible, although a young man could not help but understand the realities of Negro life in the mid-twentieth century when he was forced to attend segregated schools in Georgia.

Young Martin proved to be an eager pupil. Entering school at age five, he quickly mastered his subjects, and in high school, he skipped the ninth and twelfth grades. At the age of fifteen, he was ready for college. He enrolled in Morehouse College, a renowned historically black school in Atlanta, in 1944. He earned a BA in sociology from Morehouse in 1948, a divinity degree from Crozer Theological Seminary in Pennsylvania in 1951, and a PhD from Boston University in 1955. While he was studying in Boston, he married Coretta Scott, and the couple eventually had four children. Shortly before he completed his doctoral studies, he accepted a position at the Dexter Avenue Baptist Church.[768]

In 1957, King was one of sixty ministers who formed the Southern Christian Leadership Conference (SCLC) to help organize black churches in a bid to improve Negro civil rights. He headed the organization until his death eleven years later. King participated in landmark civil rights marches and protests under the SCLC auspices. With a talent for oratory and a willingness to wade into dangerous situations, he became in many ways the leading spokesman for the civil rights movement of the 1950s and 1960s. King's commitment to Mahatma Gandhi's philosophy of non-violent protest established the moral authority of the mainstream civil rights movement of his era. Owing in no small measure to King's leadership, Congress enacted and President Lyndon B. Johnson signed two major laws—the Civil Rights Act of 1964 and the Voting Rights Act of 1965—that eventually destroyed legal segregation in the United States. King won the Nobel Peace Prize for his efforts in 1964.[769]

By the time he stepped onto the balcony outside Room 306 of the Lorraine Motel on April 4, 1968, King was struggling to retain his authority in the civil rights community. His greatest triumphs were behind him, and he knew it. A group of young Turks from more militant organizations challenged the old man's non-violent approach. They were frustrated by conservative black leaders who turned the other cheek. If white Americans insisted on employing violence, the new civil rights leaders were prepared to answer with a similar, proportional response.[770]

King had visited Memphis to mediate a sanitation strike as part of his Poor People's Campaign to promote economic justice. Unfortunately, events had spiraled out of control as militant young blacks calling themselves the Black Organizing Project (BOP), or the "Invaders," refused to protest peacefully. King had been deeply unnerved by violence that erupted during a march in the city, fearing that such acts undermined the moral authority of his protests. To his dismay, the civil rights movement, already fractious and undisciplined, appeared to be splintering before his eyes.[771]

All these matters weighed heavily on King as he leaned on the balcony railing that evening. He had been moody and out of sorts lately, fatigued from overwork. Tonight, he resolved, he would lay aside his burdens and allow himself a brief respite.[772]

Now, as dusk approached, King and friends prepared for a relaxing dinner. Feeling playful, King leaned on the railing and looked down from the balcony, trading quips with Jesse Jackson, who stood in the courtyard below. The banter was light and easy.

"Our leader," the young civil rights activist called out in an exaggerated tone. He was teasing, obliquely referring to King's exalted status among the factious civil rights groups. As always with Jesse, the remark was meant as good-natured banter with a hint of impudence lurking just beneath the surface.

"Jesse!" King replied. In recent days, King had been aggravated with the headstrong civil rights activists who surrounded him. He especially felt peevish when it came to Jesse Jackson. King had recently exploded in frustration at his people, reserving special rage for young Jesse. Now it was time for a rapprochement. "I want you to come to dinner with me tonight," he told the young upstart. The group was heading over to the home of a local minister, Billy Kyles, for soul food. It would be a small, informal gathering. Asking Jackson to accompany him was a thoughtful gesture toward improving relations.

Overhearing the remark, Kyles called out, "Doc, Jesse took care of that before you did. He got himself invited!"

King laughed at Jackson's audacity.

Perhaps anxious to change the subject, Jackson introduced Ben Branch, a saxophonist scheduled to play that night at the Mason Temple, where King and his entourage planned to appear after dinner.

"Oh, yes," the reverend called down to the musician. "He's my man. How are ya, Ben?"

"Glad to see you, Doc," the saxophonist responded.

Still leaning on the railing, King called down a request. Referring to Branch's signature tune, he said, "Ben, I want you to sing for me tonight at the meeting. I want you to do that song, 'Take My Hand, Precious Lord.'" The melancholy song from the Great Depression had long been one of his favorites. "I want you to sing it like you've never sung it before. Sing it real pretty."

"I sure will, Doc."

Solomon Jones, the evening's chauffeur, called up to King. "It's getting chilly. I think you'll need a topcoat."

"Okay, Jonesy," he said. "You really know how to take good care of me." Fishing a cigarette from his pocket, he turned as if to retreat back into his hotel room to search for his coat.[773]

At that moment, a rifle shot echoed across the courtyard and a bullet smacked into the right side of King's face, destroying his jaw and traveling down into his neck. It tore the necktie from his shirt and violently hurled him backward. Gasping, he clutched at his throat with his right hand while he clawed at the railing with his left. Unable to remain on his feet, he collapsed, his legs becoming entangled in the railing as he fell.[774]

From inside Room 306, Ralph Abernathy was preparing for a long evening. He heard a sound, he later said, that reminded him of a car backfiring. With the door open, he had been listening to King's banter with the staff. After he heard the strange sound and realized that Martin had stopped talking, Abernathy rushed to the doorway to see what had caused the commotion. To his amazement, he saw his good friend splayed out on the concrete, his arms spread wide like a figure nailed to a cross.

"Oh my God," he exclaimed, "Martin's been shot!"

Everyone in the courtyard below called out for Abernathy to duck. An unseen gunman might still be lurking around. No one knew precisely where he was. Leaning down so that he would not become a convenient target, Abernathy stepped over the prone figure. King seemed to be looking up, fear in his eyes. The hole in his jaw was massive. Blood gushed out of the man's neck, pooling on the concrete.

Abernathy realized the injury was grievous, possibly fatal, but he wanted to comfort his friend in his desperate hour. "Martin, it's all right. Don't worry. This is Ralph. This is Ralph."[775]

But it was not all right. The life was draining out of Martin Luther King, Jr., as blood cascaded about his head. One eyewitness later described the thick puddle of liquid as "crimson molasses." Within minutes, King's eyes glazed over and his skin turned ashen. He slipped into shock.[776]

Satisfied that the gunman did not intend to fire a second shot, King's supporters raced up to the balcony. Marrel McCullough, an undercover policeman, grabbed a motel towel and slid it under King's jaw, wrapping it around the dying man's head. Andrew Young, a long-time trusted aide and friend, huddled over King, as did other members of the entourage.[777]

Young saw the size of the gaping hole and recognized that King's lethargy was an ominous sign. He felt for a pulse. It was there, but faint. Young was the first person on the scene to accept the inevitable outcome. "Ralph," he said in a soft, sad voice. "It's over."

Abernathy was no fool. He knew the odds of survival were arrayed against his friend. Nonetheless, he could not give up yet. "Don't say that," he urged Young. "Don't say that."[778]

Billy Kyles stood in Room 306, frantically dialing the telephone to summon an ambulance. Encountering a busy signal, he could not get through. Slamming his hand against the wall in frustration, he repeatedly shouted, "Answer the phone! Answer the phone!"

A subdued Ralph Abernathy turned to him. "Let's not lose our heads," he said.[779]

Everyone was stunned by how rapidly a pleasant evening of fun and frivolity had turned so horribly wrong. Throughout the motel, people milled about, desperate to help, but unsure of what to do. Solomon Jones, the man who was supposed to chauffer Dr. King to the evening's festivities, gunned the Cadillac around the parking lot in a fit of rage. When Loree Bailey, co-owner of the Lorraine Motel, learned of the shooting, she was disconsolate. Wandering in a circle, she muttered, "Why? Why? Why?" Within minutes, she suffered a cerebral hemorrhage. She died on April 9, the day Dr. King was laid to rest in Atlanta, Georgia.[780]

South African journalist Joseph Louw was staying in Room 309. After he heard the ruckus, he emerged from the room with his 35-millimeter camera in hand. He instantly recognized that history was unfolding before his eyes. Frustrated and feeling impotent, he aimed the camera at the balcony where Dr. King lay sprawled before the group of supporters and friends, depressing the button to capture a series of photographs documenting the scenes of unfolding horror. Louw was still snapping photographs when police officers wearing helmets arrived and asked where the rifle shot had originated. Seconds later, Louw snapped a dramatic photograph of the figures gathered around a bleeding Martin Luther King, Jr.—frantic aides pointing in the direction of the gunshot.[781]

The scene was surreal. King's lieutenants were accustomed to white police officers being part of the problem, not the solution, so they greeted the arrival of multiple uniformed law enforcement personnel with skepticism and concern. Fortunately, emergency medical technicians provided relief. As soon as they pulled up in an ambulance, the EMTs passed a stretcher upstairs so the wounded man could be loaded and driven off to the hospital. Six men, including Andrew Young, carried King down the stairs to a waiting ambulance. He was still alive, but barely.

With its famous passenger tucked inside, at 6:09 p.m.—eight minutes after the gunfire—the ambulance raced to nearby St. Joseph's Hospital. When it arrived six minutes later, the vehicle jerked to a stop. Abernathy, grim-faced and weary, jumped from the ambulance and accompanied King, now unconscious, as doctors wheeled the wounded man on a gurney down the hospital hallway to prepare for emergency surgery.

Surgeons took charge in a crowded operating room. Because King was struggling to breathe, a doctor performed a tracheotomy. Connected to a respirator, King appeared to recover slightly, his breathing settling into a rhythm. Doctors opened his chest cavity to repair the extensive damage. All the while Ralph Abernathy, now joined by Reverend Bernard Lee, stood off to the side, watching.[782]

Outside the hospital, a crowd gathered. Wild rumors circulated through the ranks: Abernathy had been hit and was mortally wounded. Dr. King was not seriously injured and would emerge at any moment to reassure the world that all was well. The assassin had been captured and killed by an enraged mob. President Lyndon Johnson had hopped aboard Air Force One and was on his way to Memphis.

Even as the unsubstantiated speculation spread, inside the hospital, the end was near. The trauma had been too great, and King had lost too much blood. The surgeons massaged his heart, but to no avail. Dr. Jerome Barrasso pronounced Martin Luther King, Jr., dead at 7:05 p.m., slightly more than an hour after the bullet had slammed into MLK's jaw.[783]

As the news hit the airwaves, prominent figures reacted with dispatch. Inside the White House, President Johnson had been preparing to depart for a Democratic Party fundraiser followed by meeting with General William Westmoreland and his military commanders in Hawaii to discuss strategy for fighting the Vietnam War. He cancelled the trip when his press secretary

23.2 In this iconic Joseph Louw photograph, Andrew Young and members of Dr. Martin Luther King, Jr.'s entourage point in the direction of a gunshot that mortally wounded the civil rights leader as he stood on the balcony of the Lorraine Motel in Memphis, Tennessee. Dr. King lies at their feet. Courtesy of the Everett Collection Historical/ Alamy Stock Photos.

told him the news at 8:20 p.m. "A jumble of anxious thoughts ran through my mind," he said later. "What does it mean? Was it the act of one man or a group? Was the assassin black or white? Would the shooting bring violence, more catastrophe, and more extremism?"[784]

Although Dr. King was a private citizen and his murder investigation technically should have been handled by the Memphis police, the president understood that this was an unusual case. He decided to assign the investigation to his attorney general, Ramsey Clark. Unbeknownst to Johnson, Clark had already heard the news and had spoken with Assistant FBI Director Cartha "Deke" DeLoach, directing the Bureau to take charge. DeLoach reported the details of his assignment to J. Edgar Hoover, the aging FBI director who loathed Dr. King. Hoover believed that King was a subversive black radical with ties to communist organizations seeking to overthrow the United States government. The director also detested Attorney General Clark—the two men were barely on speaking terms—but Hoover understood politics.

He had not retained his position as the FBI chief for forty-four years without learning a few things about political survival. Recognizing a fait accompli, Hoover reluctantly assigned FBI agents to the manhunt for King's assassin. The agency that had once tracked Dr. King's movements would now hunt down his assassin and, if possible, bring him to justice.[785]

President Johnson knew that he must calm the nation's fears. He had little doubt that many young people, especially blacks, would feel hurt and angry. The possibility of riots and additional violence was worrisome. He intended to order flags hung at half-staff—the first time such an honor had been bestowed on a private citizen. To stave off undue criticism among King's fellow activists, he would invite civil rights leaders to Washington for a presidential meeting. He also would declare Sunday, which happened to be Palm Sunday, a day of national mourning. Releasing a public telegram of condolence to King's widow would underscore White House concern.[786]

In the meantime, the president personally called Dr. King's widow in Atlanta to express his sorrow. When she first heard that her husband had been shot, Coretta Scott King had raced to the airport to board a flight to Memphis. As she arrived at the airport, Atlanta mayor Ivan Allen, Jr., who had accompanied her, answered a page over the public intercom system. Returning to her side, the ashen-faced mayor informed her that Martin was dead. Grief-stricken, she had returned home to comfort her children. President Johnson found her there and spoke with her privately for a few minutes.[787]

At 9:00 p.m. the president appeared on television. "America is shocked and saddened by the brutal slaying tonight of Dr. Martin Luther King," he said in a somber tone. "I ask every citizen to reject the blind violence that has struck Dr. King, who lived by nonviolence. I pray that his family can find comfort in the memory of all he tried to do for the land he loved so well."[788]

Black leaders were divided in their reactions. The old guard that Dr. King represented—the small band still committed to nonviolence—urged calm. "Dr. King would be greatly distressed to find that his blood had triggered off bloodshed and disorder," James Farmer, Jr., an organizer of the 1961 Freedom Rides, said. He urged everyone to be in a "prayerful mood, which would be in keeping with his life." The response to his death should honor the sacrifices he made during his life.[789]

Stokely Carmichael, a veteran of the Freedom Rides, offered a far more militant response. "White America killed Dr. King last night. She made it a whole lot easier for a whole lot of black people today. There no longer needs to be intellectual discussions; black people know that they have to get guns." Floyd McKissick of the Congress of Racial Equality (CORE) reflected the bitterness that many young blacks felt. "King was the last prince of nonviolence," he said. "Nonviolence is now a dead philosophy."[790]

Senator Robert F. Kennedy, campaigning for president in Indianapolis, offered perhaps the most eloquent remarks. Appearing wounded and grief-stricken and speaking without a prepared text as he stood in the back of a flatbed truck, he addressed a crowd of supporters, many of whom were black. Without glancing at the notes he clutched in his hand, he spoke from the heart. "I have some very sad news for all of you, and, I think, sad news for all of our fellow citizens, and people who love peace all over the world; and that is that Martin Luther King was shot and was killed tonight in Memphis, Tennessee."

Audience members gasped in horror. They had not heard the awful news.

RFK plowed on. "Martin Luther King dedicated his life to love and to justice between fellow human beings. He died in the cause of that effort. In this difficult day, in this difficult time for the United States, it's perhaps well to ask what kind of a nation we are and what direction we want to move in. For those of you who are black—considering the evidence evidently is that there were white people who were responsible—you can be filled with bitterness, and with hatred, and a desire for revenge."

The crowd watched, rapt and mostly silent, as a man obviously in pain, a man struggling to make sense of a seemingly senseless world, consoled them as best he could. "We can move in that direction as a country, in greater polarization—black people amongst blacks, and white amongst whites, filled with hatred toward one another. Or we can make an effort, as Martin Luther King did, to understand, and to comprehend, and replace that violence, that stain of bloodshed that has spread across our land, with an effort to understand, compassion and love."

To the astonishment of his aides, who had never heard Bobby Kennedy speak of his brother's assassination in public, he alluded to the horrific time when he had suffered a loss inflicted by an assassin's bullet. "For those of you who are black and are tempted to be filled with hatred and mistrust of the injustice of such an act, against all white people, I would only say that I can also feel in my own heart the same kind of feeling. I had a member of my family killed, but he was killed by a white man. But we have to make an effort in the United States, we have to make an effort to understand, to get beyond, or go beyond these rather difficult times."

Wrapping up, Kennedy urged his listeners to forge a better world, a world that Martin Luther King, Jr., would appreciate. "What we need in the United States is not division; what we need in the United States is not hatred; what we need in the United States is not violence and lawlessness, but is love and wisdom, and compassion toward one another, and a feeling of justice toward those who still suffer within our country, whether they be white or whether they be black." He concluded with a simple plea: "Let us dedicate ourselves to what the Greeks wrote so many years ago: to tame the savageness of man and make gentle the life of this world. Let us dedicate ourselves to that, and say a prayer for our country and for our people."[791]

It was a stunning performance, an extemporaneous speech that did much to soothe the people of Indianapolis. Unlike other cities across the country, the Indiana capital city did not erupt into flames. RFK, who would die by the hand of an assassin in two months' time, had exhibited a rare brand of leadership and courage in one of the nation's darkest hours.[792]

Despite his call for unity and compassion, not everyone was so forgiving. Riots broke out in more than one hundred cities. Washington, DC, Baltimore, and Chicago, with large black populations, saw the worst of the outbreaks, with hundreds of fires deliberately set. When all was said and done, dozens of people had died and property damage numbered in the millions of dollars. National Guard units mobilized in at least eighteen states and thirty-six cities. Some 14,800 National Guardsmen were federalized in two states as well as Washington, DC. Some commentators believe that the aftermath of the assassination changed Americans' perceptions of urban crime and decay as well as their fear of violent crime. The concept of "white flight" was already well known, but the riots of 1968 accelerated the phenomenon. The police overreaction to the riots at the Democratic National Convention in Chicago later that summer no doubt occurred, at least in part, because Mayor Richard J. Daley and his police officers feared the eruption of violent disturbances similar to the April riots.[793]

Even as word of the shooting spread and the world reacted, police officers and FBI agents in Memphis fanned out to search for the assailant. At 6:10 p.m., after interviewing witnesses who saw a man apparently fleeing the area, officers issued a bulletin to be on the lookout for a "young white male, well dressed, believed in late-model white Mustang, going north on Main from scene of shooting." Twenty minutes later, investigators discovered a bundle of items discarded adjacent to the Canipe Amusement Company located next to Bessie Brewer's Rooming House. They decided to check out the rooming house. A man named John Willard had rented Room 8 in the rooming house earlier that day, although he later changed to Room 5B. Upon entering Room 5B, police realized that it overlooked the Lorraine Motel courtyard. A nearby communal bathroom offered an unobstructed view of the balcony outside of Room 306. They concluded that the rifle shot probably had come from the bathroom.[794]

Perhaps the now-missing John Willard shot Dr. King and immediately fled, dropping the bundle in his haste to escape. When investigators unwrapped the strange bundle, they found a Remington 760 Gamemaster .30-06 rifle, binoculars, clothing, a Memphis *Commercial Appeal* newspaper story about Dr. King checking into the Lorraine Motel, two beer cans, and a radio. It was a treasure trove of clues. Fingerprints found on the items would help break the case.[795]

Several names emerged during the early stages of the investigation. Police discovered laundry tags on the clothing and traced them to the Home Service Laundry in Los Angeles, California. When investigators contacted laundry workers, they learned that the clothing belonged to a man named Eric S. Galt. A pair of pliers inside the bundle came from Rompage Hardware, two blocks from Home Service Laundry. With the rifle in hand, FBI agents traced the gun to the Aeromarine Supply Company in Birmingham, Alabama. A man named Harvey Lowmeyer had signed a receipt for the gun. Based on these leads, within hours of the shooting, police believed that a conspiracy existed among three men: John Willard, Eric S. Galt, and Harvey Lowmeyer. It would be some time before they understood that all three names were the aliases used by a single individual.[796]

In the meantime, the circumstantial evidence continued to mount. After a citizen phoned in a tip to the Atlanta police, investigators discovered a white Mustang parked in a housing project in Atlanta. On closer inspection, they realized it was Eric S. Galt's car. A sticker on the car revealed that it had been serviced at a dealership in Hollywood, California. The dealership provided an address for an apartment that Galt had rented. The forwarding address was for general mail delivery in Atlanta, Georgia. The FBI soon learned that aside from Los Angeles and Atlanta, Galt had lived in Birmingham.

It was only a matter of time before agents made sense of the clues. They found a photograph of Galt. Soon they found his rooming house in Atlanta.

Inside was a map with pencil scribblings showing that Galt had stalked Dr. King at Ebenezer Baptist Church as well as his office at SCLC headquarters, his home, and the Capitol Homes public housing project. As a bonus, the map contained a clear thumbprint.[797]

The forensics team sprang into action. After painstakingly sifting through hundreds of fingerprints, FBI agents stumbled upon a match. The fingerprint belonged to a small-time career criminal named James Earl Ray. Sentenced to serve a twenty-year sentence for robbery at the Missouri State Penitentiary in Jefferson City, Ray had escaped in 1967 and disappeared from sight. Now, he had turned up again.[798]

James Earl Ray was born in Alton, Illinois, on March 10, 1928, the first of nine children. His parents, George and Lucille, were poor farmers who struggled to earn a living even before the Great Depression hit. Ray's childhood was filled with misery. Recognizing that he could never support his large brood, George Ray spiraled downward, eventually turning to a life of petty crime. In 1935, his family abruptly fled from Illinois for safer environs in Ewing, Missouri, after police came looking for the family patriarch, who was facing a forgery charge. Two years later, Ray's sister Marjorie died after she was playing with matches and accidentally set herself on fire.

These terrible incidents left an emotional scar on Jimmy Ray. Desperate to escape his sordid circumstances, he left school in the eighth grade to live with his grandmother. At the age of sixteen, Ray entered the adult world, leaving behind his sad, abbreviated childhood.

He worked in a tannery in Hartford, Illinois, for two years before enlisting in the US Army in 1946, around his eighteenth birthday. Shipped off to serve in occupied Germany in the aftermath of World War II, he chafed at the rigid army discipline. As a young man with no obligations and lacking a moral compass, Ray was anxious to sow his wild oats. He constantly indulged in the vice available to a soldier in that time and place—drinking, fighting, visiting prostitutes, and trafficking in black market cigarettes. The army discharged him in 1948.

By 1949, he had moved to Los Angeles and embarked on a life of crime. For the next decade, Ray was in and out of prison for burglary and theft. In March 1960, he received a twenty-year sentence. Housed in the Missouri State Penitentiary, he escaped by hiding inside a bakery truck as it left the prison facility.

Ray lived an itinerant life after he escaped from prison, traveling to St. Louis, Chicago, Toronto, Montreal, and Birmingham. While he was in

Alabama, he bought the 1966 Mustang that he used to drive to and from Memphis. He also visited Mexico, staying in Acapulco and Puerta Vallarta. While in the latter city, Ray adopted the pseudonym Eric Starvo Galt and entertained vague notions of becoming a pornographic film director.[799]

Not long after he returned to the United States in November 1967, Ray showed his first interest in politics. He became enamored of George C. Wallace's presidential campaign and volunteered to work for the cause. The former Alabama governor had rocketed to national attention in 1963 when he emerged as a strong proponent of segregation. His 1968 presidential campaign was predicated on the innate inferiority of blacks and white fears over Negro ascendancy. In offering his time and energy to the Wallace campaign, Ray demonstrated his bias against people of color. He even entertained notions of moving to Rhodesia (present-day Zimbabwe), a notorious white supremacist regime in Africa. Later, after Dr. King was dead and Ray was fleeing justice, he sought asylum in Rhodesia.[800]

It is unclear when or why Ray resolved to murder Martin Luther King, Jr., but by early 1968 he was behaving like a man on a mission. On March 5, he visited a doctor, Russell Hadley, who performed facial reconstruction surgery, a form of rhinoplasty, to alter his appearance. He drove from Los Angeles, checked into an Atlanta rooming house, and apparently began stalking Dr. King. On March 30, he purchased a Remington 760 Gamemaster .30-06 rifle in Birmingham. He eventually returned to Atlanta and read an article about King's plans to fly to Memphis in early April. On April 2, Ray hopped into his Mustang and headed to a rendezvous with infamy.[801]

Two days later, Ray, using his "John Willard" alias, wasted no time in fleeing from Bessie Brewer's Rooming House after Dr. King collapsed with a bullet lodged in his neck. From there, he drove to Toronto, Canada, and stayed out of sight for a month as the FBI launched one of the most extensive manhunts in American history. While he was in Canada, he acquired a Canadian passport under the name Ramon George Sneyd. Afterward, the fugitive contemplated his next move. He had hoped to buy a plane ticket to Rhodesia, but the expensive fare convinced him to opt for London, England. Once he was overseas, he embarked on a brief trip to Lisbon, Portugal, before returning to London.[802]

On June 8, 1968, authorities arrested Ray at Heathrow Airport as he sought to leave England on a false Canadian passport. The name "Sneyd" appeared on a Royal Canadian Mounted Police watch list. Extradited back to the Tennessee to stand trial, Ray realized that he faced the death penalty if a jury convicted

23.3 James Earl Ray, shown here in a 1955 mug shot, assassinated Martin Luther King, Jr., in Memphis, Tennessee, on April 4, 1968. Courtesy of the Federal Bureau of Prisons.

him. The evidence against him was overwhelming. For starters, FBI agents had established a trail showing where and when he purchased the rifle. They also tied him to other items inside the discarded bundle. Fingerprints linked him to the rifle and the map found in the Atlanta rooming house. On and on it went. To avoid what appeared to be an almost certain conviction, Ray entered a guilty plea to the murder charge and, in exchange, avoided execution. The court sentenced him to serve ninety-nine years in prison.[803]

Three days after he agreed to plead guilty, James Earl Ray recanted. He said that he had confessed on the advice of his attorney, the prominent criminal defense lawyer Percy Foreman, but that he had changed his mind. Ray claimed he was innocent, but such a statement was hardly surprising; defendants charged with a capital offense frequently insist on their lack of culpability. In his defense, Ray explained that in 1967, he had met with a shadowy figure known as Raoul (sometimes spelled "Raul") who plotted Dr. King's murder.

True or false, it was a fantastic narrative, casting Raoul as the evil puppet-master and Ray as the unwitting puppet. Raoul directed Ray to buy the .30-06 Remington rifle used in the crime. Raoul also met Ray the night before the assassination, took possession of the rifle, and ordered Ray to rent a room in Bessie Brewer's Rooming House. Ray did as he had been instructed, but otherwise took no part in the shooting. Raoul or one of his associates murdered King with Ray's rifle, and left an innocent man behind as a convenient patsy.

On one level, Ray's story was laughably absurd. This Raoul character came out of nowhere, orchestrated the assassination of a major public figure, and disappeared without a trace. He also picked James Earl Ray, a lifelong ne'er-do-well with a long history of committing petty crimes, to serve as his primary confidant when he might have employed any number of more reputable criminals to execute the plot. For his part, Ray went along with the scheme more or less passively because he either needed a payoff from Raoul or detested blacks in general (or Martin Luther King, Jr., in particular) so much that he was willing to risk life and limb to kill the nation's most prominent civil rights activist.[804]

On another level, however, one does not need to be a dyed-in-the-wool aficionado of conspiracy theories to recognize that Dr. King was a much-reviled figure among large groups of Americans. Under J. Edgar Hoover's leadership, many FBI agents abhorred King. The Bureau had engaged in all manner of dirty tricks and illegal wiretapping schemes under the COINTELPRO umbrella, including a plot aimed at monitoring King's movements and activities. It does not require a tremendous leap of faith to assume that if the FBI was willing to violate numerous state and federal laws to prosecute a personal vendetta against King and other civil rights activists, the agency would conspire to kill him. Similarly, other organizations—the Ku Klux Klan, the CIA, or the Memphis Police Department—might have been involved in the murder. Of all the political figures portrayed in this book, Martin Luther King, Jr., had the largest number of active plotters who sought to discredit him personally or otherwise limit his effectiveness.[805]

Confined to prison until his death in 1998, James Earl Ray spent his time hiring and firing a series of fringe lawyers to promote his alibi and present fantastic tales of shadowy figures engaged in nefarious plots. Reminiscent of the brouhaha surrounding President John F. Kennedy's 1963 assassination, the public remained fascinated about what really happened in Memphis, Tennessee, on April 4, 1968. The "truth about the MLK murder" became a popular topic in a seemingly endless parade of books, articles, news stories, documentaries, and films.[806]

Despite the cottage industry centered on the King assassination, James Earl Ray's name disappeared from the headlines. He sometimes reemerged, as when he and six inmates escaped from the Brushy Mountain State Penitentiary in Petros, Tennessee, on June 11, 1977. After the fugitives were apprehended two days later, Ray received an extra year on his sentence.[807]

In the late 1990s, Martin Luther King, Jr.'s family called for a new trial to clear up the mystery about whether Ray participated in the crime. Dexter King, the civil rights icon's second son, met face-to-face with Ray on March 27, 1997. As they stood looking at each other, Dexter stammered, "I just want to ask you, for the record, did you kill my father?" The convicted killer replied, "No, no, I didn't, no. But like I say, sometimes these questions are difficult to answer, and you have to make a personal evaluation."[808]

The King family pushed for a new trial, but their efforts were too late. Suffering from complications associated with Hepatitis C, James Earl Ray died on April 23, 1998, at the Columbia Nashville Memorial Hospital. He was seventy years old.[809]

As for the man killed that long-ago day in Memphis, Dr. King immediately was hailed as an enormously influential, albeit controversial public figure. On April 9, the family held funeral services at Ebenezer Baptist Church for 1,300 people. Afterward, tens of thousands marched in a funeral procession covering three-and-a-half miles from Ebenezer Baptist Church to Morehouse College. The crowd was estimated at somewhere between 50,000 and 100,000 people, including dignitaries such as Robert F. Kennedy and his brother, Ted, Vice President Hubert H. Humphrey, former Vice President Richard Nixon, Senator Eugene McCarthy, and numerous civil rights leaders.[810]

In the years that followed, Martin Luther King, Jr.'s reputation grew and his image evolved. He had been a controversial man in his time, but with the passing decades he became a larger-than-life legend and his name entered the pantheon of great American political figures.[811]

It seemed that virtually every American city of any size scrambled to name a street or school after him. In 1983, President Ronald Reagan signed a bill into law creating a federal holiday in Dr. King's honor. Reagan had initially opposed the measure, explaining that it would cost too much money to create a new federal holiday. Some conservative Republicans objected to honoring a private citizen with a national holiday, especially because they believed that King was a closet communist. Recognizing the popularity of the bill—the House of Representatives passed it with a veto-proof majority of 338 to 90—Reagan acquiesced. The federal government first observed the holiday on January 20, 1986, although some states were slower in observing the occasion. In 1991, New Hampshire created Civil Rights Day and in 2000, Utah changed "Human Rights Day" to "Martin Luther King, Jr., Day."[812]

On August 22, 2011, the National Park Service unveiled a memorial to King near the National Mall in Washington, DC. A formal dedication ceremony was scheduled for August 28, 2011, commemorating the forty-eighth anniversary of King's most famous speech, his "I Have a Dream" address that he delivered on the steps of the Lincoln Memorial in 1963. The threat posed by Hurricane Irene forced the organizers to postpone the event, however, until October 16, the 16th anniversary of the 1995 Million Man March on the National Mall. President Barack Obama delivered remarks on the auspicious occasion, which the president called "a day that would not be denied."[813]

Even as time has passed and Martin Luther King, Jr., has become a distant, revered icon, questions linger about his assassin. Did James Earl Ray act alone or was he part of a larger cabal? Was he even involved?

The circumstantial evidence against Ray was overwhelming. He left a large trail of eyewitnesses and documents implicating him in the crime. Conspiracy buffs contend that the trail was too large and the clues too obvious to be anything other than a classic hatchet job. Ray was framed, they believe, by the elusive Raoul character. Perhaps such a man existed—books and articles published over the years claimed to have discovered the man's true identity—but no credible evidence has ever demonstrated his participation.

In addition, during most of Ray's life, he was the quintessential lone wolf. He was somewhat close to his siblings—and they may have helped him evade capture in 1968, as well as possibly aided in his prison escape in 1977—but they were never charged with a crime in connection with his actions in Memphis, Tennessee, in April 1968. The weight of the evidence suggests that James Earl Ray assassinated Martin Luther, Jr., and that he acted alone.

The difficulty arises in understanding his motives. Ray shared the racial biases of poor whites of his generation and he also demonstrated his allegiance to the renowned segregationist George C. Wallace when he volunteered to work on Wallace's 1968 presidential campaign. Yet for all his animosity toward people of color, Ray's actions throughout his life before he stalked Martin Luther King, Jr., do not suggest that he was a virulent,

23.4 The National Park Service added a memorial to Dr. Martin Luther King, Jr., near the National Mall in Washington, DC, in 2011. Courtesy of the Library of Congress.

obsessive racist. Plenty of figures in American history have been compelled to act owing to their hatred of the "other," but those bigots were obsessed with the mongrelization of the white race through miscegenation. Ray's animus appeared to be casual. He hated blacks because that is what poor white trash did in the South during the early to mid-twentieth century. For anyone who knew him well, the idea that he would upend his life to stalk a prominent black leader because he hated the man's skin color or ideology seemed far-fetched. His brother, Jerry Ray, candidly said that in his view, if Ray committed the crime, he would have "done it for the money."[814]

Therein lies the rub. James Earl Ray may have been paid to snuff out Dr. King's life. As a life-long hustler, Ray spent much of his adult life searching for the perfect score. His schemes and dreams typically imploded and left him bitter and hostile, a bumbling failure with little to show for it despite his planning. As with his claim that Raoul was the mastermind behind the assassination, Ray never supplied verifiable details about others involved in the plot. When he described his actions leading up to the murder, crucial information about the story changed over time. The truth is that James Earl Ray was a congenital liar, and it was difficult to believe anything he said.[815]

Classifying Ray according to his motives is difficult because his motives were anything but clear. If he is placed in the Type 1 category, it implies that Ray focused on eliminating King because he disagreed with the civil rights leader's political goals. Except for his brief foray into electoral politics working as a volunteer on the George C. Wallace presidential campaign, however, Ray never demonstrated much interest in, or awareness of, politics before he set his sights on killing Martin Luther King, Jr.

If he is considered a Type 2 killer, Ray must have been desperate to become famous by killing a prominent person. Yet his frenzied attempt to evade capture, his decision to recant his confession, and his insistence for three decades that he was a patsy suggested that he did not crave attention for his actions. Type 2 killers seek out media exposure. It is entirely possible that Ray reveled in his infamy, but it is not clear that he did so. He was such a perverse personality that understanding his motives poses an enormous challenge.

If he pulled the trigger to secure a monetary payoff, Ray might have been a Type 3 sociopath who acted with little regard for the immorality of his actions. A classic nihilist, the Type 3 actor acts because his life is empty and devoid of meaning. This category appears to be an appealing place to place Ray. Yet the evidence that he was a sociopath seeking a payday is non-existent. Shadowy figures, hidden conspiracies, and lurking clues are interesting to contemplate, but they do not amount to much in the final analysis.

From all accounts, Ray was not a delusional Type 4 actor. He never claimed to hear voices or suffer from severe cognitive distortion. What he did—assuming he did it—he probably did for rational reasons even if the reasons were not clear to anyone else. Then again, perhaps James Earl Ray was as confused about his motives as everyone else. Perhaps he went to his grave with the same questions as everyone who has reviewed his case: Did he do it and, if so, why?[816]

Chapter 24

"IF YOU SEE ME AS YOUR SAVIOR, I'LL BE YOUR SAVIOR. IF YOU SEE ME AS YOUR GOD, I'LL BE YOUR GOD": LEO RYAN (1978)

Leo Joseph Ryan, Jr., handily won reelection to the United States House of Representatives representing California's 11th congressional district six days before he departed on a fact-finding trip to Guyana, South America. He had heard disturbing rumors of inhumane treatment at the Peoples Temple in Jonestown, Guyana, the site of a religious compound founded by a charismatic minister from the United States, the Reverend Jim Jones. Ryan might have declined to intervene. Guyana, after all, was outside the direct jurisdiction of the United States. Yet Ryan was not a quiet, unobtrusive personality. He often stuck his nose into things that bothered him, and Jonestown bothered him. The congressman was friends with the father of former Temple member Bob Houston. Bob was found dead not long after he spoke with his ex-wife about leaving the Temple. As he read about the group and met with concerned relatives of Temple members, Ryan resolved to investigate a laundry list of allegations lodged against Reverend Jones and his heavy-handed henchmen.[817]

Ryan knew that the trip might be dangerous. Reports suggested that Jones was something of a Kurtz figure, the corrupt Ivory dealer in Joseph Conrad's 1899 novella *Heart of Darkness* who travels deep into the African hinterlands and succumbs to illness (and madness), dying with infamous words on his lips: "The horror! The horror!" Whether Jones would prove to be as demented as a fictional character certainly remained to be seen, but the congressman had reason to be worried. If the information he had received was accurate, Jim Jones was a cult leader with a messianic complex. The strange man and his adherents were burrowed deep within the bowels of a mostly primitive, developing nation situated far from American soil.[818]

Despite the risks and challenges, Leo Ryan was never one to shy away from difficult issues. His political career was filled with instances in which he put himself in harm's way to uncover an inconvenient truth about a festering problem. During the 1960s, he wanted to understand why the Watts section of Los Angeles had erupted into violence in August 1965. Ryan was a California state legislator at the time. Using an assumed name, he moved into the home of a black family, took a job as a substitute teacher, and set out to understand a complex social problem from the inside.

He repeated his role as a cultural anthropologist a few years later when he sought to understand prison life. Once again slipping into a separate identity, Ryan allowed himself to be transported to Folsom State Prison in leg irons and handcuffs. He lived for a week as an inmate, talking with his fellow prisoners in an effort to appreciate their concerns. Reflecting on Ryan's up-close-and-personal investigative style, G. W. (Joe) Holsinger, the congressman's administrative assistant in Washington, DC, remarked in 1978 that "He felt it was his job to inspect things personally."[819]

This dedication to a personal touch led the congressman into the jungles of South America. On November 1, 1978, Ryan announced that he would travel to Guyana to launch an investigation owing to his role as chairman of a congressional subcommittee exercising jurisdiction over American citizens living in foreign countries. He would get to the bottom of what was going on inside the Peoples Temple.[820]

He had his task cut out for him, for the Peoples Temple of the Disciples of Christ was a religious cult founded in 1955. The brainchild of James Warren Jones, the Peoples Temple was supposed to be a new-age religious movement based on Christianity mixed with socialism and principles of racial equality. Jones believed that he could achieve politically liberal social goals by creating a Pentecostal church that attracted a wide group of misfits who might otherwise never belong to a formal organization. In later years, he confessed that he was using religion as a cover for spreading Marxist ideology throughout the United States.[821]

Jones was always an odd personality. Born in rural Crete, Indiana, on May 13, 1931, he knew poverty intimately as a child. In 1934, his family, struggling to survive in the depths of the Great Depression, moved to Lynn, Indiana, where young Jim grew up in a house without indoor plumbing. Aside from living in poverty, he had a difficult time making friends. He was

24.1 Leo Ryan, pictured here, was a three-term United States congressman when he investigated disturbing tales about the Peoples Temple. Courtesy of the Office of the Clerk, United States House of Representatives.

a bookish child, always reading about historical figures and philosophers, including Mahatma Gandhi, Karl Marx, and Adolf Hitler. His peers recalled him as a "really weird kid" obsessed with religion and death. He reputedly killed household pets so he could stage elaborate funerals.

He may have been an odd character, but Jones proved to be a bright student, graduating from Richmond High School in Richmond, Indiana, in December 1948, on the eve of his seventeenth birthday. The following year, he married a nurse named Marceline Baldwin, and the couple moved to Bloomington, Indiana. Two years later, they moved to Indianapolis. Jones attended night school and eventually earned a degree in secondary education.[822]

He joined the Communist Party of the United States (CPUSA) in 1951, but he grew impatient when it became clear that he was destined to play a bit part in the communist movement. Ironically, given the hysteria among Americans about the extreme ideas of the CPUSA during the early 1950s, Jones's politics became far more radical than the communists' beliefs. Many idealistic young liberals who joined the CPUSA during the 1930s and 1940s left the organization when it became clear that totalitarians such as Joseph

Stalin and Mao Zedong were using the ideology as a convenient pretext for their authoritarian regimes to murder millions of people. Jones was not bothered by tales of slaughter and abuses of power. An admirer of the repressive North Korean regime, which he believed to be the purest expression of socialist ideals, Jones adopted three children of Korean ancestry as a demonstration of his allegiance to North Korea.[823]

Always a keen student of human behavior, he realized that he could advance his goals by adopting the persona of a minister. As the head of what he originally called the Peoples Temple Christian Church Full Gospel, Jones cynically set out on a mission of faith healing. He practiced the old-time method of placing his hands on people in the audience and "curing" the afflicted wretches during his public performances. Of course, he had planted the lucky invalid beforehand. It was the hokiest form of fraud and yet, amazingly, it worked more often than not.[824]

The sleight-of-hand chicanery may have played well among the hoi polloi, but Jones also had to win over the state's elite opinion leaders. They would not be swayed by religious mumbo jumbo. Yet as all great con men know, the way to overcome objections is to play to a mark's sentimental beliefs. Jones realized that most politicians appreciate works that ostensibly benefit the community. Accordingly, the reverend became adept at philanthropic endeavors—donating money to worthy causes and caring for the homeless and needy—thereby ingratiating himself with the mayor of Indianapolis as well as local reporters, who found the energetic preacher man good copy for the daily news.[825]

By the early 1960s, Jones felt that he had outgrown the provincialism of Indiana. Obsessed with the likelihood of an imminent nuclear war, he and Marceline relocated to Brazil because he had read that the country was a suitable place to ride out the apocalypse. They lived there for three years, ministering to the powerless and downtrodden. After the day of reckoning was inexplicably delayed, he and his wife returned to the United States. They stopped on the way home in a small, out-of-the-way country, Guyana, a remote outpost that would play a pivotal role in their later lives.[826]

Back in Indiana after his lengthy absence, Jones realized that his church had grown as much as possible in the Midwest. He resolved to pick up and move on to California. In the 1960s and 1970s, the Golden State was an ideal spot for someone pedaling a new brand of mysticism or a social utopia. Disaffected young people from across the country—indeed, from everywhere on the globe—gravitated to the West Coast of the United States in search of a dream. Setting up shop in Ukiah, in the Redwood Valley, Jones's move paid rich dividends. The Peoples Temple attracted a following far beyond what Reverend Jones could have imagined when he eked out a living in Indiana. He eventually opened churches in Sacramento, Santa Rosa, Fresno, Bakersfield, and Los Angeles.[827] Impressionable young people felt an immediate connection with the hip preacher who admitted all races and ethnicities into his church. Jones called his multi-racial flock his "Rainbow Family." Faux religious themes scattered in with Marxist doctrines and promises of love and understanding appealed to people who felt they were outcasts from the white, conservative, materialistic, middle class world of their parents. As one follower recalled of Jones, "I was convinced that this man truly and unconditionally loved me." Someone else commented that "He is trying to teach us that socialism is God."[828]

As his congregation grew throughout the 1970s—some estimates suggested that as many as 20,000 people claimed membership at the height of the Temple's popularity, although sober assessments placed the number at closer to 3,000—Jones became a force to be reckoned with in Northern California politics. San Francisco Mayor George Moscone appointed Jones to serve on the San Francisco Housing Authority. California Lieutenant Governor Mervyn Dymally became a fan. Jones met with California Governor Jerry Brown, vice presidential candidate Walter F. Mondale, First Lady-to-be Rosalynn Carter, and numerous local officials. To outward appearances, he was a politically astute, morally straight religious leader—a bit goofy, perhaps, but a man committed to good works on behalf of his fellow man.[829]

Appearances were deceiving. In private, Jim Jones was a markedly different man than he was in public. He urged his followers, even married couples, to abstain from sexual intercourse, but behind the scenes Jones demonstrated a voracious sexual appetite for men and women, regardless of their marital status. In public he appeared to be a Christian minister, but among his adherents he did not try to hide his atheism, denouncing the "fly-away" religion of an unseen, unknown "Sky God." Jones came to see himself as a secular savior. "What you need to believe in is what you can see," he said, explaining his unorthodox, self-serving perspective. "If you see me as your friend, I'll be your friend. If you see me as your father, I'll be your father.... If you see me as your savior, I'll be your savior. If you see me as your God, I'll be your God."[830]

As the self-proclaimed messiah's behavior became increasingly erratic, less-committed members of his flock strayed. Even worse, they talked. By 1977, wild stories circulated about Jones's sexual escapades, drug abuse, atheism, and other-worldly views about his own divinity.

In January 1977, Jones learned that Marshall Kilduff, a reporter with the *San Francisco Chronicle*, was planning to write a story on the goings-on within the Peoples Temple. Until 1976, the media coverage of Jones and his movement had been mostly positive, but it began to change as ex-Temple members blabbed to investigative journalists. Fearful that Kilduff might perform a hatchet job on the church, Jones considered a move away from the United States. His instincts were correct. Kilduff eventually shopped his story to an independent outlet, *New West* magazine, which published the exposé in August. Other negative stories followed closely behind. Political figures who had counted Jones as a friend and confidant suddenly no longer returned his phone calls. The tide was turning.[831]

Jones had been ruminating about establishing an isolated compound in the jungles of Guyana, South America, for years. If he exercised total authority over church members—including the ability to control media access and contact with outside parties—he could become the absolute leader he had always longed to be. The problem with operating a socialist church inside the United States was that too many eyes were on him. Members contacted their loved ones; newspaper and television outlets were ubiquitous; ex-members ran to the press and offered salacious details about church business. It was almost too much for an autocrat to bear. Once and for all, Reverend Jones needed to consolidate his power.[832]

Immigration and Naturalization officials in San Francisco noticed a curious phenomenon throughout much of 1977. Small bands of people requested passports to leave the United States and emigrate to a primitive South American country that few people had ever heard of: Guyana. The nation had only won its independence from Great Britain in 1966. Headed by a self-professed Socialist, the strongman Forbes Burnham, Guyana was known to be friendly with the Soviet Union, North Korea, and Cuba. In 1970, Burnham announced that his new nation was a "Cooperative Republic" dedicated to the ideals of communist regimes everywhere.

Here was a man after Jim Jones's own heart. He found much to admire in this isolated nation-state ruled over by a totalitarian thug. Although many

Americans recoiled at the retrograde politics of such a backward country, the reverend saw opportunity. If he could find refuge in a faraway land, he could build the utopian conclave he had dreamed of for much of his adult life. No matter that Georgetown, the country's capital, was infested with armed gangs that preyed on the populace by night or that Burnham's regressive policies had impoverished his people and bankrupted the country. Jim Jones had found a home at last.[833]

The reverend had been laying the groundwork for the mass exodus for years. He had dispatched attractive female Temple members to mingle with the Burnham regime and smooth the way. The plan worked. Government operatives granted permission for the strange white minister from the United States to clear off vegetation and establish a commune known, appropriately enough, as Jonestown.[834]

Propaganda painted a portrait of Jonestown as a utopian collectivity where everyone would live and work together in brotherly love. Presumably a community based on shared sacrifices and common core beliefs would eradicate all petty jealousies, fears, and animosity. As with most such collective towns constructed on lofty ideals, however, the utopian promises quickly degenerated into a dystopian nightmare.[835]

Guyana held little promise for a burgeoning community of idealistic misfits. Blessed with neither the pristine, idyllic beaches of neighboring countries nor the oil deposits that allowed ruthless South American dictators to finance their depredations against an unwitting citizenry at will, Guyana was simply an undeveloped, untamed, and perhaps untamable jungle. The advance guard sent by Jones literally and figuratively to clear the way soon found the going rough. Cutting back the brush to plant crops, Jonestown workers discovered how quickly the jungle reclaimed its own. Even when they managed to deposit seeds, the nutrient-starved soil made short work of the workers' efforts. Animals died rapidly, the heat was oppressive, flying insects struck incessantly, and the work was slow. By most accounts, it was a wretched hellhole destined for a bad end even before the compound was constructed.[836]

None of that mattered, for Jim Jones would not be dissuaded from carrying out his plans. Throughout the spring and summer of 1977, he and his followers engaged in a flurry of activity, moving supplies and equipment to Guyana. Groups of disciples soon departed from the United States in search of paradise.[837]

In the wake of the exodus, a spirited debate raged about the virtues and vices of the Peoples Temple. Some politically liberal officials continued to defend the movement and its controversial leader. California State Assemblyman (and later San Francisco mayor) Willie Brown remained a staunch champion until the end. Harvey Milk, a prominent gay activist in San Francisco, knew a thing or two about persecution, and he evinced sympathy when Jones complained of his poor treatment. In a letter to President Jimmy Carter dated February 19, 1978, Milk wrote, "Rev. Jones is widely known in the minority communities here and elsewhere as a man of the highest character, who has undertaken constructive remedies for social problems which have been amazing in their scope and effectiveness. He is also highly regarded amongst church, labor, and civic leaders of a wide range of political persuasions." Despite misgivings, San Francisco Mayor George Moscone had appointed Jones to the San Francisco Housing Authority. He continued to voice public support for the enigmatic reverend, although later Moscone offered apologies for allowing himself to be duped by a master charlatan.[838]

Other observers told a vastly different tale about the strange, atheistic reverend. Leon Broussard, a Temple member who managed to escape from Jonestown, reported on brutal conditions inside the compound. Jones forced rank-and-file members to labor under armed guard. Fearful that outsiders would attack Jonestown, the reverend staged mock assaults using live ammunition. He also appeared at night-time rallies urging his followers to embrace his own brand of extreme socialism and denounce the United States for its ill treatment of the Peoples Temple. Perhaps most disturbing of all, Jones spoke repeatedly of "revolutionary suicide." The "really weird kid" obsessed with religion and death was now a grown man who remained fixated on the twin themes of his bizarre life.[839]

Back in the United States, as stories circulated and other defectors came forth, a "Concerned Relatives" group formed. They traveled to Washington, DC, to lobby federal elected officials to investigate the strange goings-on within the Peoples Temple. Congressman Leo Ryan learned of their actions and met with the group during the summer of 1978. He promised to fly down to Guyana after the November election and personally investigate. As a member of the International Operations Subcommittee of the House Foreign Affairs Committee, the congressman could legitimately claim as his mission the protection of US citizens' lives and property while they lived abroad. The relatives had found a tenacious, sympathetic champion.[840]

Still, months passed and nothing appeared to happen. A child custody battle finally brought matters to a head. John Victor Stoen was six years old in 1978. His parents, Grace and Tim Stoen, were Peoples Temple members when the child was born on January 25, 1972. On February 6, 1972, Tim signed an affidavit acknowledging that he was not the boy's father. Reverend Jones, he claimed, was John's biological father. He had allowed Jones to father a child with his wife because he, Tim, was unable to do so and because Jones was "the most compassionate, honest and courageous human being the world contains." Jones's wife, Marceline, witnessed the affidavit signing.[841]

Grace Stoen left the Temple in July 1976 and instituted divorce proceedings against Tim. In the meantime, Jones instructed Tim to take the boy to Guyana in February 1977, presumably to frustrate Grace's efforts to gain custody in a US court of law. Tim Stoen did as he was instructed, but he soon entertained second thoughts. In June 1977, Tim defected from the Peoples Temple, but John remained in Jonestown with Reverend Jones. When Grace sought custody of her son, Jones produced the affidavit and argued that she was mentally unstable. The back-and-forth custody battle lent an air of urgency to the appeals by the Concerned Relatives group. On November 18, 1977, a California judge awarded custody to Grace and ordered US officials to take steps to enforce the court order.[842]

Jones's paranoia and oft-expressed feelings of persecution intensified after the custody dispute. Throughout 1978, he spoke of mass suicide and the need for his followers to stick together. Although he retained his grip on his most zealous supporters, others became disillusioned. While he was inside the United States, Jones maintained his mystique by limiting Temple members' access to his private life. Few people knew of his insatiable sexual appetite or his almost debilitating drug addiction. The façade, when viewed at short intervals, could fool most of the people most of the time. In addition, his grandiose claims of the jungle paradise that awaited them in a far-off land enchanted Temple members.

After the move, Jones could no longer keep members at arm's length. The more skeptical among his followers saw him as a drug-addled megalomaniac determined to rule over the compound with an iron fist. He was dangerous, and quite possibly crazy. Moreover, it was obvious to anyone but the most deluded soul that Jonestown was anything but an idyllic socialist community. Food was running out, sanitation was abysmal, pests were everywhere, and the muddy, isolated outpost was no one's idea of paradise.[843]

Congressman Ryan had promised to visit Guyana and check on conditions at the Peoples Temple compound after the election, and he remained true to his word. Accompanied by reporters as well as 17 concerned relatives, he departed from the United States on November 14, 1978. When they arrived in Georgetown on November 15, their reception was not cordial. Ryan stayed overnight with US Ambassador John Burke, but other members of his party found that the hotel staff had inexplicably botched their reservations. As a result, several travelers were forced to sleep in the hotel lobby.[844]

Officials of the Guyanese government initially blocked the group's travel plans. In the meantime, representatives of the Peoples Temple negotiated with Ryan about the conditions of his visit. The congressman grew increasingly frustrated with what he believed were obstructionist tactics. In a fit of pique, he insisted that he be allowed to visit Jonestown to assess the situation on the ground. Ryan eventually arranged for a small plane to fly his group to an airfield adjacent to Port Kaituma near Jonestown on November 17—regardless of any objections from Guyanese government representatives or Peoples Temple members.[845]

State Department officials had visited the compound previously, but their time on the premises had been limited and their questions more or less perfunctory. During a short visit, Jones could orchestrate an elaborate ruse to convince his visitors that Temple members were healthy, happy, and free to come and go at their leisure. Congressman Ryan's lengthy visit, which might include private interviews and discussions with Temple members, challenged the reverend's ability to stage a well-rehearsed pageant.

Nonetheless, Jones did his best to deceive the Ryan party. He hosted a reception, complete with a musical performance by Jonestown singers, for the congressman and his entourage at the compound's central pavilion during their first evening. Congressman Ryan even addressed brief remarks to the assemblage, receiving a standing ovation when he said that "for some of you, for a lot of you that I talked to, Jonestown is the best thing that ever happened to you in your lives."[846]

Despite the outward attempts at civility by all parties, the tension was palpable. Ryan had not come to participate in a pageant. He was determined to find answers. In an interview with the reverend, the congressman asked questions about life inside Jonestown. Jones complained to his distinguished visitor about exaggerated reports of abuses that were part of a conspiracy against the Peoples Temple. He produced a child that he said was John Victor Stoen, and asked if the child wished to leave. The boy said no.

Ryan bluntly asked about the talk of a mass suicide. Jones assured him that the comments should not be taken literally. "I only said it is better that we commit suicide than kill. Why hurt social progress?" Jones grumbled about the smear campaign launched against him in the media. "It would have been easier if someone had shot me as they did Malcolm X and Martin Luther King."[847]

Ryan had not seen a "smoking gun" suggesting that Jonestown was an armed concentration camp, yet he had an uneasy feeling. He and his traveling companions agreed to complete their investigation the next day. The group had hoped to spend the night inside the compound, but Jones argued that he did not have suitable accommodations for everyone. Only Congressman Ryan and a handful of his party stayed onsite. The other visitors bedded down in nearby Port Kaituma.[848]

The next morning, Ryan and his entourage continued interviewing members of the commune. The congressman announced that anyone who wished to leave could join him and his group when they departed. Although no one came forth at first, a reporter accompanying the tour received a note saying, "Vernon Gosney, Monica Bagby. Help us get out of Jonestown." When the reporter showed the note to Jones, the reverend was visibly angry. Ryan and his assistant, Jackie Speier, resolved to gather as many defectors as they could and leave as soon as possible.[849]

The visit was drawing to an end. As the congressman addressed Reverend Jones and said that he would soon depart, Temple member Don Sly approached. "Congressman Ryan, you motherfucker," he cried as he attacked the interloper with a knife. Several bystanders wrestled the knife away from Sly. Ryan was not hurt in the exchange, but Sly was cut. His blood decorated the congressman's shirt. Jones watched the attack impassively.[850]

Angry and shaken, Ryan urged his group to hasten away from Jonestown. The congressman had considered staying another night, but embassy personnel had persuaded him to leave. The delegation piled into a Peoples Temple truck accompanied by 16 departing members and headed for the airfield.

Reverend Jones had appeared ill and out of sorts all morning, but he did not attempt to stop them. The congressman and the reporters did not know whether they should be relieved or worried by the reverend's passivity as they drove away from the compound.[851]

Bouncing along the road in the direction of the airfield, Ryan realized that he had a problem. The group of defectors was larger than he had anticipated. His staff already had placed a call to the embassy in Georgetown for an additional airplane, but no one knew when it would arrive. As it turned out, the group arrived at the airstrip at Port Kaituma between 4:30 pm and 4:45 p.m., but the airplanes did not appear until approximately 5:10 p.m.[852]

The group anxiously milled around the waiting for the planes to arrive. Everyone glanced back at the jungle, wondering if they would encounter resistance from Jones or his zealots. Finally, after what seemed an interminable time, a six-seater Cessna appeared, followed by a larger Guyana Airways Otter. The airplanes landed on the small runway and taxied over to where the passengers stood in line.

The relieved travelers seemed to be on their way unscathed. Perhaps they had overreacted, succumbing to irrational fears about Jones's mental instability. Nevertheless, it was wise to take no chances. To ensure that an impostor had not infiltrated the defectors' ranks, the staff searched everyone boarding the planes. Finally, passengers crowded onto the Cessna and it taxied to the end of the runway to prepare for takeoff.[853]

As passengers stepped onto the Otter, a Temple dump truck and a red tractor trailer appeared out of the jungle and idled 150 to 200 yards away from the waiting throng. A dozen or so stone-faced men stood silently near the vehicles. Their presence made the pilgrims feel nervous, and with good reason.[854]

The episode erupted quickly. Without warning, the men standing near the vehicles produced guns and fired toward the crowd. The fusillade of bullets lasted four or five minutes. When it ended, the gunmen melted back into the jungle. NBC cameraman Bob Brown, correspondent Don Harris, *San Francisco Chronicle* photographer Greg Robinson, defector Patricia Parks, and Congressman Ryan died during the ambush. Eleven other people suffered bullet wounds. Mindful that the gunmen might return, the survivors hid in the jungle until a rescue plane landed the following day.[855]

At the same moment the gunfire commenced, Larry Layton, a mole planted among the passengers, whipped out a pistol on board the Cessna and fired, wounding two people. Dale Parks, a twenty-eight-year-old defector, wrestled the gun out of Layton's hand. The two men fell from the small airplane as they fought. As soon as Layton and Parks were on the ground, the Cessna pilot gunned the engine and took off, fleeing the carnage on the runway. Layton was later arrested and extradited to the United States after a jury in Guyana concluded that he was not guilty of murder. He was tried twice on four charges, including a count of conspiring to kill a United States congressman. His first trial ended in a hung jury. A jury convicted him at a second trial, and Layton served eighteen years in prison (including time in a Guyanese jail) before securing his parole in 2002.[856]

After presumably ordering his men to assault Ryan's party, Jones knew that judgment day had arrived. With the cold-blooded murder of the investigators, including a United States congressman, it was only a matter of time before authorities descended on Jonestown seeking retribution. Let them come. The reverend would deny them the satisfaction of dismantling Jonestown and exposing the secrets of the Peoples Temple. Addressing his most loyal lieutenants, he told them to prepare for the revolutionary suicide they had rehearsed. A tape recording captured his words. "My opinion is that we be kind to children and be kind to seniors and take the potion like they used to take in ancient Greece, and step over quietly because we are not committing suicide. It's a revolutionary act. We can't go back."[857]

Loyal followers distributed Flavor-Aid drink laced with Valium and cyanide. The Valium was supposed to render members unconscious while the cyanide killed them. Jones's helpers squirted the liquid into children's mouths with a syringe while adults swallowed the concoction from disposable drinking cups. The tape recording picked up a woman's voice urging the members not to panic. "There's nothing to worry about, so everybody keep calm and try and keep your children calm. And the oldest children can help love the little children and reassure them. They're not crying from pain. It's just a little bitter tasting but, they're not crying out of any pain." Despite such assurances, the cyanide worked faster than the Valium. In their final moments on earth, parents witnessed their children writhing in agony.[858]

"Don't be afraid to die," Jones told his flock. "If these people land out here, they'll torture some of our children here. They'll torture our people, they'll torture our seniors. We cannot have this." Even at the hour of his death, Jim Jones lied to one and all.[859]

24.2 A Guyanese government representative examines dead bodies inside the Jonestown compound shortly after the mass suicide in November 1978. Courtesy of Bettmann/ Getty Images.

The death toll that day reached 918—five at the Port Kaituma airstrip, four members in Georgetown when a zealous mother slit the throats of her three children before killing herself, and 909 people (including 278 children) in Jonestown. It was the largest mass slaughter of Americans until the terrorist attacks of September 11, 2001. Reverend Jim Jones was among the dead. He was found with a gunshot wound to the head. His body contained the barbiturate Pentobarbital.[860]

Assessing the motives of the killers who shot Congressman Ryan is difficult for many reasons. First, it is not altogether clear who these individuals were, so determining their intentions is an uncertain enterprise. It is safe to assume, however, that the men (and perhaps women) who pulled the triggers that day in the jungles of Guyana were the most zealous of the zealous. They were cult members who had surrendered some portion of their individualism to the Reverend Jim Jones and the Peoples Temple.

Research indicates that men and women of all ages, education and income levels, race, religious beliefs, and ideology can become cult members.

The one commonality among cult members appears to be a desperate desire for friendship, identity, respect, and security. The cult offers them something that no other institution or group has provided.[861]

Not surprisingly, members of the Peoples Temple tended to be young people who felt alienated from conventional society—racial and ethnic minorities, runaways, drug-users, prostitutes, mentally ill misfits, hippies, and outcasts of all sorts. The Peoples Temple offered them a home where supposedly they would be loved, respected, and valued. The reality differed markedly from the promise, but by the time the members understood the horrors of life inside the People Temple, they were caught in the trap.[862]

As for the man who built the cult around his strange personality, Jim Jones has been characterized as a drug-addicted, militantly homosexual, delusional psychopath. He was a paranoid authoritarian maniac who brooked no dissent and insisted on absolute loyalty. Presumably, he ordered his disciples to murder Leo Ryan as well as the staff members, reporters, and defectors who accompanied the congressman to the Port Kaituma airstrip on November 18, 1978.[863]

Of the types of political assailants discussed in this book, it seems unlikely that Jones was a Type 1 actor. He did not instruct his followers to kill a United States congressman because he passionately held a set of political views diametrically opposed to the congressman's policies. Type 1 actors seek out political figures to kill. In the Jim Jones case, a political figure sought him out while Jones would have preferred to be left alone. The isolated figure living in the jungle compound was, if anything, apolitical. Jones befriended political figures during his time in Indiana and California—and he flattered Forbes Burnham to grease the skids for the relocation to Guyana—but those associations were a means to an end. He professed to be a socialist who performed good works on behalf of the poor and disaffected, but those actions, too, smacked of rank opportunism. Jones did what was necessary to attract adherents, charm politicians, and repel perceived enemies. Political issues did not drive his actions.

Similarly, Jones probably was not a Type 2 actor seeking to kill a famous political figure to enhance his own status. Inside his own carefully crafted community, he already enjoyed the highest status possible. He claimed to be superhuman, and the Peoples Temple cult was essentially a cult of personality centered on Jim Jones. A classic Type 2 actor feels marginalized and ignored.

24.3 The Reverend Jim Jones, pictured here in 1977, was the charismatic leader of the Peoples Temple. Courtesy of Nancy Wong.

Jones was hardly ignored. In fact, he wanted Congressman Ryan and the press to ignore him, but they would not.

Was Jim Jones a Type 3 assassin—so nihilistic and divorced from society that he no longer believed life was worth living? Perhaps he was a Type 4 assassin, descending into madness in the jungles of South America surrounded by his brainwashed automatons. It is difficult to say. His cavalier manner in discussing mass suicide suggested that he was a Type 3 actor who did not distinguish between living and dying. His willingness to send more than 900 men, women, and children to their deaths with little or no compunction makes a persuasive case for a genuinely alienated human being.

It is tempting to see Jim Jones as insane—the quintessential Type 4 actor—an unhinged madman peddling his dangerous, quasi-socialist doctrines to an audience comprised of brainwashed zealots and unwilling slaves trapped in a hellish prison. Without a diagnosis from a competent psychiatrist or psychologist, determining whether Jones suffered from a mental defect is impossible to state with high confidence. Some of his actions suggested he was not in his right mind.

Yet to some extent, his actions were rational. Congressman Ryan interfered with church business and threatened to destroy the Peoples Temple; therefore, he needed to be removed. If the cause of a problem could be eliminated, the solution would advance the assassin's interests. Yet murdering a United States congressman only exacerbated Jones's predicament, hastening the apocalypse. If he was worried about the level of outside scrutiny, ordering the assassination of a congressman ensured a far greater level of scrutiny.

One school of thought hints at the possibility that Jones purposely acted to eliminate other options. The only way he could guarantee that he and his followers would commit revolutionary suicide was to force their hand. Killing Ryan and members of his entourage was a rational means of moving the Peoples Temple toward the next step of the journey. "We can't go back," Jones said, and he was correct.

Jim Jones and his henchmen fall into the Type 5 category because no one will ever know precisely what depths of despair or delusion drove them to commit their crimes. Intentionality is always a difficult concept to pin down. When cult members are involved, understanding their motivations becomes almost impossible owing to the large number of people involved and their varying motives and differing states of mind. Whatever demons drove them to act, the demons died with them in the South American jungle in November 1978.[864]

Chapter 25

"WE'VE SAID ALL ALONG THERE WERE THREE VICTIMS IN THIS. TODAY DAN WHITE BECAME THE THIRD VICTIM": GEORGE MOSCONE AND HARVEY MILK (1978)

The mayor's bodyguard called in a frantic plea for police assistance at 10:56 a.m. on Monday, November 27, 1978. The first officer on the scene confirmed the urgency with a simple five-word declarative sentence uttered into his walkie-talkie: "We've got a homicide here." The "here" was San Francisco City Hall.

As police and rescue personnel converged on the second floor offices of the Board of Supervisors, they found a horrific scene. George Moscone, the free-wheeling mayor who had celebrated his forty-ninth birthday three days earlier, lay sprawled on the floor, his famously silver hair discolored by blood. He had been shot once in the chest and shoulder and twice in the head. He still held a burning cigarette in has hand when the first paramedics arrived. Down the hall they found his colleague, Supervisor Harvey Milk, lying face down on the floor, dead. He had been shot five times, including twice in the head.[865]

Some observers initially wondered whether Mayor Moscone and Supervisor Milk had been victims of a hit squad dispatched by a religious cult known as the Peoples Temple. (For more on the Peoples Temple, see Chapter 24 of this book.) During the time that the Peoples Temple operated in San Francisco, Moscone had come to know the group's charismatic leader, Reverend Jim Jones. The mayor even appointed Jones to the San Francisco Housing Authority. After Jones and his followers departed for a new com-pound located in Guyana, South America, Moscone announced that his office would not launch an investigation into the Temple's supposedly nefarious activities. Critics charged that Moscone was beholden to Jones for helping him win the mayoral election. Jones was said to have bussed in supporters to vote, in some cases illegally, thereby electing Moscone. Other critics charged that Moscone had accepted sexual favors from attractive Peoples Temple members in exchange for casting a blind eye toward the cult's illegal conduct.

With Jones's departure and lingering questions about the cult's authoritarian proclivities, Moscone quietly backed away from his former affiliation. According to rumor, Jones took offense at his former ally's betrayal. The reverend left behind a list of people who should be killed after the Peoples Temple members committed suicide, and George Moscone's name was on the list.

For his part, Harvey Milk had met many times with Reverend Jones and expressed his admiration for the Temple's good deeds in ministering to the poor. Milk was on record singing the group's praises and publicly writing letters extolling Jones's virtues as an exemplary public servant. It seemed impossible that Harvey Milk, champion of the strange cult, would be its target. As with so much in Moscone's and Milk's lives, however, it was difficult to separate fact from fiction. Despite the insanity in thinking they had been murdered by cult members exacting vengeance for real or perceived transgressions, crazy things happened in San Francisco during the 1970s.[866]

The confusion did not last long. Within minutes, investigators realized that a Peoples Temple hit squad was not involved. Police officers had a reasonably good idea of the shooter's identity, and he likely acted alone. A male dispatcher spoke into the police radio within minutes. "Attention all units: Suspect on the 187 at City Hall, suspect named Dan White. White adult male. Thirty-two years. Six feet. One hundred eighty-five pounds. Wearing a three-piece suit. Considered armed and dangerous." The usual dispatcher, Patty, had stepped away from the microphone. Dan White was her brother.[867]

Investigators were still organizing the manhunt when, at 11:37 a.m., the temporary dispatcher reported that the suspect had voluntarily turned himself in at the Northern Police Station near city hall. He had once served as a police officer there. Examining the circumstances, investigators believed that his motive was straightforward. It was revenge, pure and simple.[868]

A Vietnam veteran and former police officer, Dan White served on the San Francisco Board of Supervisors from January through November 1978. Elected in 1977, White initially worked well with his colleagues. As the year progressed, however, he clashed with his fellow supervisors.

By all accounts, White was a straight-laced, politically conservative representative on a city council that was mostly liberal and free-spirited. In some cases, he was the deciding vote on issues important to the buttoned-down, middle-class Republican crowd. He defined his role as a "defender of the home, the family and religious life against homosexuals, pot smokers and cynics." His was an increasingly isolated voice amidst of cacophony of diverse chatter about which types of activities constituted appropriate behavior. San Francisco city government was renowned (or notorious, depending on one's perspective) for its tolerance of alternative lifestyles and titillating peccadilloes. Mayor Moscone was reputed to cavort with loose women—the scuttlebutt was that once upon a time a couple of beat cops had discovered him *in flagrante delicto* with a black prostitute—but who knew if the rumors were credible? Supervisor Harvey Milk was, if anything, even more outlandish than Moscone. Milk openly—even proudly—cavorted with gay men! In fact, he was a gay man. Harvey Milk was the first openly homosexual elected official in California, and an influential voice for a growing gay constituency. The prudish White disapproved of their lifestyle choices, but his animosity toward Moscone and Milk was not limited to distaste for their sexual histories and scandalous hanky-panky.[869]

The events leading up to the murders originated, as such things often do, over money. Aside from White's political confrontations with fellow municipal officials, he was experiencing financial difficulties. The $9,600 annual salary of a Supervisor was not enough money for a man with a wife and a baby to live on in the style to which White had grown accustomed. He had worked out a plan, however, that potentially would alleviate his monetary woes. White had obtained a lease for a fast food franchise, the Hot Potato, on one of the most desirable sites in the city—on Pier 39 at the edge of a Fisherman's Wharf, a popular tourist destination. He had opened his small franchise—not a genuine sit-down restaurant, but a serving cart—in October. He had not yet turned a profit, but he hoped to turn things around.[870]

On November 10, 1978, White appeared in the mayor's office and handed him a letter of resignation. "I have been proud to represent the people of San Francisco as their elected Supervisor from District Eight for the past ten months, but due to my personal responsibilities which I feel must take precedent *(sic)* over my legislative duties, I am resigning my position effective today," it read. Whether he did so because he wanted to devote himself full-time to the Hot Potato, as he claimed, or he acted impulsively because he was tired of the confrontational style of local politics was not altogether clear. Perhaps White did not know his own mind, either. Moscone asked, "are you sure, absolutely certain, that you've explored every avenue, every financial alternative?"

White said he was sure. "This is what I've got to do," he said. Whatever his motives, his letter of resignation appeared to end his brief political career. Moscone wished him well. "I admire that," he said, "putting your family first. You do what you have to do." The men shook hands and White left the office.[871]

When they learned of his seemingly impulsive decision, White's supporters and family members urged him to reconsider. They would help out with money—working at the Hot Potato for no wages, arranging interest free loans, or whatever it took to keep him afloat. He resisted at first, but over the weekend he came to regret his haste. White admitted to at least one friend that money was not the reason he had resigned. He was frustrated with the "bullshit" spouted out by the "fools and idiots" on the Board of Supervisors. These "goddamn people" had driven him to resign. Because he realized how much it meant to his supporters that he continue to serve, however, he changed his mind. Swallowing his pride, White called Moscone on the telephone to ask if he could rescind his resignation. Alternatively, the mayor could appoint him to his old position. Moscone told White to come down to city hall to discuss the matter.[872]

The mayor had never heard of someone rescinding a resignation, but he did not know the law. He asked the city attorney to investigate. During his meeting with White, Moscone said that he was researching whether a letter of resignation could be rescinded. If it could not, the mayor would reappoint White to the board.[873]

Much to his chagrin, Moscone learned that the letter could not be rescinded. The decision about whether to reappoint White was his problem, dropped into his lap by the city attorney. Unfortunately for the mayor, it was shaping up to be a major hassle. During the week after White submitted his letter, the young conservative's political foes relentlessly pressured the mayor to appoint someone in his stead. Harvey Milk, a supervisor with whom White occasionally argued, proved to be especially vehement. Milk and White had started out on good terms early in the year—they voted together on several measures, and White invited Milk to attend his child's baptism—but they eventually had a falling out. White was convinced that Milk was lobbying the mayor not to reappoint him, and he was correct. Milk repeatedly reached out to Moscone, reminding him that reappointing White, a notorious homophobe, would upset the gay community. Moscone would be a one-term mayor if he lost his gay constituency.[874]

Dan White thought that he had reached an ironclad agreement with the mayor to receive the reappointment. He was flabbergasted when Moscone wrote him a letter, soon released to the press, indicating that opposition to the reappointment was building and that the mayor needed an additional week to mull it over. In the meantime, White's supporters discussed the possibility of filing a lawsuit arguing that the resignation letter should never have been submitted so quickly to the Board of Supervisors. Thus, White technically might not have resigned as a matter of law.[875]

The back-and-forth maneuvering left Dan White with a whirlwind of emotions. He felt upbeat one moment, believing that he would soon win back his old job, and despondent the next, recognizing the depths of his own self-inflicted wound. The entire fiasco was enervating. He wished he could climb into a deep hole and never come out.[876]

It is difficult to know exactly when he decided to assault Moscone and Milk, but possibly he reached the tipping point when a reporter, Barbara Taylor of ABC News, telephoned on Sunday evening, November 26. "I can tell you from a very good source in the Mayor's office that you won't be reappointed," she said bluntly. "Can you comment on that?"

Taken aback, White put her off. "I don't want to talk about it," he replied. "I don't know anything about that." He hung up before she could pepper him with more questions. With his future plans in doubt, he retreated to his couch. He did not wish to disturb his wife, so he spent the night in the living room brooding about Moscone's duplicity.[877]

In the light of day, Dan White knew what he must do. He would charge into San Francisco City Hall and confront Moscone. If the mayor would not fulfill his promise to reappoint White, well, there would be hell to pay. Three other enemies—Carol Ruth Silver, Harvey Milk, and California Assembly Speaker and future San Francisco Mayor Willie Brown—would feel his wrath as well.[878]

When a former aide, Denise Apcar, picked White up the next morning at 10:15, he emerged from his garage instead of his house, where he usually greeted her. Pacing around the garage, he had been sifting through old news clippings, most of which showed his political defeats. He had spent God-knows-how-long anguishing over the compendium of slights and humiliations. Although Apcar did not know it at the time, White also had been rooting around in the garage for his .38-caliber service revolver, a remnant of his days as a policeman. He retrieved ten cartridges and slid them into his pocket wrapped in a handkerchief so they would not make noise rattling in his pocket. He wasn't sure whether he would find the nerve to use the weapon, but it never hurt to be prepared.

When they arrived at city hall, Apcar dropped White off at the Polk Street entrance sometime before 11:00 a.m. He did not recognize the security guard working the metal detector, so he broke away from the crowd shuffling through the entrance and circled around the building. Finding a large unlocked basement window, he stepped inside with his gun still concealed under his coat.[879]

A few minutes later, White appeared at the reception area outside Moscone's office and asked the receptionist if he could see the mayor. She knew it might be an unpleasant encounter, so she retreated into the inner office and told Moscone that Dan White wanted to see him. Moscone reluctantly agreed, and she went back to her desk outside. After a minute or two to reflect on what he would say, the mayor buzzed the receptionist to send White into the office.[880]

Moscone was scheduled to hold a press conference at 11:30 a.m. to announce the appointment of Donald T. Horanzy, a real estate broker, to replace White on the Board of Supervisors. Pressed for time, he decided not to beat around the bush. The mayor sat in the chair behind his desk and looked the younger man squarely in the eye. When White asked for the reappointment, Moscone told him no. White demanded to know why.

Moscone lit a cigarette. "Well," he said as he took a puff, "you know how it is, Dan. I've had a lot of people in from your district saying they didn't want you."

White's temper slipped. "That's a lie," he said. "Didn't you see the petitions?" He was referring to a list of signatures on his behalf submitted by his backers. "A thousand signatures in one day. I mean, those are the same people who brought false charges against me, you know that, you're in politics, you know what it's like. Those people, they're the same ones that are doggin' me ever since I've been elected. I've been a good supervisor, you know that. I'm honest. I work hard. Those people, they're snakes. They tried to hurt me and hurt my family with their lies."

On and on it went. He expressed the hurt, anger, and humiliation he felt from his treatment at the hands of the mayor and the Board of Supervisors. Moscone had decided on another appointment, but he recognized that Dan White was in pain. He believed it was important to allow the young man to vent, so he remained seated and quiet.

"Weren't you ever going to tell me? Why? Why aren't you going to reappoint me?"

Moscone was sympathetic to White's outrage, but he was tired of the conversation and ready for the meeting to end. "It's just a political decision, Dan, like we talked about, and that's that. There's nothing more I can say."

Moscone stood, walked around the desk and put his arm around White. "C'mon, let's go sit down in back and we'll talk it over. I'll pour us a drink." He pointed toward a different part of the office, gesturing for White to go on ahead. Sticking his head outside to view the reception area, Moscone saw his receptionist as well as his assistant, Rudy Nothenberg. Winking, he told the receptionist to hold his calls.

The two men entered the back room in the mayor's office. Moscone fixed two drinks from a liquor cabinet and handed one to White. White was not a drinker, so he placed the glass on the table next to a ceremonial couch. Moscone slid into a nearby chair. White paced back and forth, his rage building as Moscone tried to soothe his hurt feelings.

"What're you gonna do now—have you thought about it?" Moscone oozed sincerity, but White was convinced it was a phony act, a final attempt to appease the man he had just screwed over. Moscone suggested that he might be able to help out with White's financial problems.[881]

It was too late for that. White whipped out his .38 and pointed it at the mayor. Moscone tried to stand, but the first hollow-point bullet tore into his chest. As he fell toward the floor, White got off another shot. It hit Moscone in the shoulder. The mayor lay on the floor as the gunman stepped forward, his rage at full peak. He leaned down close and placed the gun barrel next to the injured man's ear. Squeezing off two more rounds, Dan White knew that he had accomplished his objective. The phony, conniving, slimy liar was dead.[882]

With the dirty deed done, he scurried out through the office door, past the receptionist and the mayor's assistant, down the hall. He had a few more appointments to keep before he surrendered his firearm. He must act quickly.

Dianne Feinstein, another Supervisor who had served with White, saw him hurry by. She knew there might be an ugly confrontation at the afternoon board meeting and hoped to forestall the unpleasantness. "Dan," she called out as he flew past her.

He stopped and looked at her. "It'll have to wait, Dianne," he said before continuing on his way.

A few doors down, he came upon his second appointment of the day. He had hoped to visit Carol Ruth Silver and Willie Brown to afford them the same treatment he had extended to Mayor Moscone, but they were absent from city hall. Still, he was satisfied when he came upon Harvey Milk, who stood in his office talking with someone. "Harvey," White asked, trying to keep his voice neutral, his emotions even-keeled, "can I see you for a minute?"

Milk must have sensed that White was unhappy. Still, he had no idea of the depths of the man's rage. "Sure," he said as he followed the former supervisor into White's old office, which had been cleared of personal effects. White shut the door and turned. Harvey Milk leaned against the edge of the empty desk.

White shouted at the object of his anger. "What the hell are you doing to me? Why do you want to hurt my name, my family? You cheated me."

Milk never spoke, but White thought he saw a smirk on the man's face. He would wipe the smirk right off. Pulling the pistol from beneath his coat, he fired the first of five shots. It tore into Milk's stomach. A second shot hit the man as he collapsed, striking his arms and passing in and out of his chest. White was not finished. He fired a shot into Milk's back, followed by a shot at the base of his skull. One final shot, delivered point blank into his head, ensured that the traitor would not recover.[883]

His work done, White opened the door and stepped into the hallway. Clerks and office workers looked on, some apparently befuddled, others horrified. Jogging down the hallway, White greeted a woman he had known for years. "Hi, Anne," he said as he dashed for the stairwell.

Dianne Feinstein was the first person to reach Harvey Milk's body lying on the floor of Dan White's former office. She could tell immediately that he was dead. No one could sustain that much damage—blood was everywhere and Milk was unresponsive—and live to tell the tale. She instructed

25.1 Harvey Milk became the first openly gay person in California to hold political office when he was elected to the San Francisco Board of Supervisors. He is pictured here (left) with San Francisco Mayor George Moscone in April 1977. Former Supervisor Dan White murdered both men on November 27, 1978. Courtesy of the Associated Press.

a bystander to call for help, but the man was distraught. Feinstein took the telephone from his hand. "Here, let me." Her calm composure in a crisis served her well that day. Feinstein would go on to serve as mayor of the city and eventually a United States senator representing California.[884]

As for Dan White, he found Denise Apcar and asked to borrow her car. She was unaware of the havoc he had wreaked in the Board of Supervisors offices moments earlier, so she surrendered her keys without protest. White had borrowed her car previously; it was nothing out of the ordinary. Fleeing the premises, he used a nearby pay phone to call his wife, who was working at the Hot Potato. He begged her to meet him at St. Mary's Cathedral. He did not tell her why, but she knew he was distraught. Jumping into a taxicab, she arrived as soon as she could.

Her husband confessed the unimaginable. "I shot the mayor and Harvey," he said. She had known of his moodiness and irritability lately, his mixed emotions as he debated whether he should return to the Board of Supervisors, and then his agony as he waited for George Moscone to decide his fate. Like everyone else who heard the news, she was stunned by his actions.

"I love you Danny," she told him. "I'll stick by you no matter what, but please, please don't, please." She could not bear to finish the sentence. What she meant was *please don't turn the gun on yourself.* Satisfied that he would not take his own life, she told him that he had to turn himself into the police. "Let's walk down to Northern Station now," she said, and he complied with her request.[885]

After he was booked and taken into custody, White granted an interview to an old friend on the police force, Frank Falzon, and he confessed to the crimes. His statement was recorded. With numerous eyewitnesses to place him at the scene and his tape-recorded confession, guilt was never in doubt. What was in doubt was his state of mind at the time he pulled the trigger. White's wife hired a defense attorney, Douglas Schmidt, to argue that the former supervisor was depressed and suffering from diminished capacity when he confronted George Moscone and Harvey Milk in city hall on November 27, 1978.[886]

The Dan White homicide trial commenced on May 1, 1979. Assistant District Attorney Tom Norman presented the state's case against the defendant, guiding the jury through the events leading up to the shootings. He noted the significance of Dan White's preparations on November 27 as well as his need to reload the .38 between the time he shot Moscone and when he shot Milk. If White had been engulfed in the heat of passion, he would not have acted so methodically in executing the two victims. It was a clear case of premeditated, first degree "malice" murder.[887]

Schmidt had anticipated the prosecution's case. The evidence against White was overwhelming, so there was no point in challenging the facts about what happened. Instead, he told the jurors that he intended to "show not so much *what* happened on November twenty-seventh, but rather *why* those tragedies occurred." According to the defense attorney, "I think that when all the facts are out the charge of first-degree murder simply will not be supported here." Schmidt's opening statement revealed his central theory of the case: "Good people, fine people, with fine backgrounds, simply don't kill people in cold blood." Dan White shot these two men because he was suffering from depression.[888]

Prosecutors believed the tape-recorded confession would convince the jury that White had acted with premeditation and did not deserve sympathy or compassion. Yet, strangely enough, the recordings had the opposite effect. Several jurors wept when they heard White describe his state of mind. "Well, it's just that I've been under an awful lot of pressure lately, financial pressure, because of my job situation, family pressure because of, ah... not being able to have time with my family." What was supposed to be a conventional murder case buttressed by a taped confession became a referendum on the defendant's state of mind.[889]

Reporters seized on one aspect of the defense that came to be known derisively as the "Twinkie Defense." Schmidt argued that White was suffering from a series of mental problems in the days and weeks leading up to the shootings. Testimony indicated that White had consumed prodigious quantities of sugary snack foods, allowing Schmidt to argue that the defendant's abnormally high blood sugar level contributed to his depressive state. The reliance on a poor diet was only a small part of the defense strategy, but reporters breathlessly penned stories and articles on the gullibility of the jurors in accepting such a patently absurd argument.[890]

Schmidt's strategy was far more subtle and sophisticated than the Twinkie Defense suggested. He carefully constructed a narrative that portrayed Dan White as a courageous, hard-working, honest, straight-shooting supervisor surrounded by lying politicians who broke their promises; opportunistic, backbiting homosexuals; and self-absorbed city hall cronies who cared more about their own career advancement than they did about the public interest. It was a brilliant tale, masterfully crafted. Dan White, the perennially unpopular and moody outcast who chafed at the political system, was transformed into a white knight, a devoted public servant and dedicated family man—a pillar of the community, really—who desired nothing so much as an opportunity to fight for truth, justice, and the American way. He had snapped in a moment of weakness caused by his deep depression, but he was hardly a cold-blooded killer.[891]

Prosecutors knew their case was imploding, but they were at a loss to regain control of the narrative. Even the prosecution witnesses failed to support their argument. Dianne Feinstein, the supervisor who became mayor after Moscone's death, had been the first person to arrive at Harvey Milk's side in the seconds after the shooting. Feinstein was horrified by the crime and appeared as a key prosecution witness. Yet she admitted on cross examination that Dan White did not seem to be the type of person who would shoot two people. The admission supported the defense theory that White was not in his right mind when he pulled the trigger that day.[892]

On May 21, 1979, after thirty-six hours of deliberations stretching across six days, the jury of seven women and five men announced its verdict: Dan White was guilty of two counts of voluntary manslaughter. Based on the verdict, Judge Walter Calcagno sentenced the defendant to the maximum term allowed under California law: seven years and eight months in prison. If White behaved while he was confined, he would be eligible for parole in five years.[893]

District Attorney Joseph Freitas, Jr., addressed the press immediately. "I'm very, very disappointed," he said. "It was a wrong decision. The jury was overwhelmed by emotions and did not sufficiently analyze the evidence that this was deliberate, calculated murder."[894]

Predictably, the defense attorney viewed the result differently. "It's the verdict that was supported by the evidence," Doug Schmidt said. "It was voluntary manslaughter. It was an awful thing, and I don't want to make light of it." His client was out of the public eye, but Schmidt assured the press that White was "filled with remorse and I think he's in very bad condition."[895]

Many San Franciscans did not care about Dan White's bad condition. They were outraged at what they viewed as undeniably unjust verdicts. The gay community found the Milk murder especially egregious. As the first openly gay person elected to public office in California, he was a prominent activist and beloved by many. Already convinced that Dan White was homophobic, gay activists saw the jury verdicts as additional evidence that homosexuals were discriminated against in the criminal justice system. If Harvey Milk had been a straight, conservative businessman, his murderer would have been held accountable.[896]

On the evening of May 21, 1979—hours after the verdict was announced—between 3,000 and 5,000 demonstrators took to the streets to protest the travesty of justice. Coincidentally, it was the evening before Harvey Milk's forty-ninth birthday. During the so-called "White Night Riots," protestors broke windows, set fire to police cars, and railed against the crooked legal system. Carol Ruth Silver, one of the supervisors targeted by White who escaped injury or death because she was absent from city hall, tried to address the crowd and was struck in the head by a flying object.[897]

Harry Britt, the gay man selected to replace Milk on the Board of Supervisors after the shooting, held a press conference to express the mood of the crowd. "Harvey Milk's people do not have anything to apologize for. Now the society is going to have to deal with us not as nice little fairies who have hairdressing salons, but as people capable of violence. We're not going to put up with Dan Whites anymore." Gay activist Cleve Jones bitterly commented that "Today, Dan White was essentially patted on the back. He was convicted of manslaughter—what you get for hit and run. We all know this violence has touched all of us. It was not manslaughter. I was there that day at City Hall. I saw what the violence did. It was not manslaughter, it was murder."[898]

Dan White lay in his jail cell during the melee, apparently oblivious to the level of pain and outrage his sentencing had caused in the community. Following the eruptions in May 1979, he headed off to prison and gradually faded from public view. Corrections officials segregated him from the general population, fearful that another inmate might attack the former police officer to exact vengeance. Although his name surfaced in occasional "where are they now?" segments on television or in the newspaper, he hunkered down and quietly served his time, becoming, in the words of the old cliché, a model prisoner.[899]

White's notoriety resurfaced when he was granted parole. He had served five years, one month, and nine days of a seven-year sentence by the time he was released from the Soledad Correctional Facility on January 6, 1984. He had asked to return to San Francisco, but authorities sent him to Los Angeles instead, fearing that his presence in his hometown would trigger a community backlash and perhaps endanger White's safety. When he learned of the decision, Los Angeles Mayor Tom Bradley sent a letter to the Department of Corrections objecting to the release, but to no avail. White left prison, as planned. He rented an apartment and kept a low profile, growing a beard, dying his hair, and living under a Scottish pseudonym. Although many close family members and friends welcomed his return to society, White was a pariah among the professional men and women he had known before the shootings. His parole ended after a year, and he returned to his San Francisco home. He later visited Ireland for four months, a trip he had frequently talked about while he was in prison.[900]

On October 21, 1985, White called his brother, Tom, on the telephone and asked him to come to the house that afternoon. When Tom arrived around 2:00 pm, he discovered Dan White's body lying inside a white Buick sedan. Dan had deliberately left the automobile engine running inside the garage. A garden hose ran from the exhaust pipe to the partially opened car window. The thirty-nine-year-old ex-con died of carbon monoxide poisoning. Before he died, White left three suicide notes taped to the car—one to his wife, one to Tom, and one to his mother.[901]

25.2 Dan White, pictured here on January 9, 1978, shortly after he joined the San Francisco Board of Supervisors, shot and killed Supervisor Harvey Milk and Mayor George Moscone on November 27, 1978. Courtesy of Alamy Stock Photos.

Doug Schmidt, White's former lawyer and architect of the Twinkie Defense, was saddened by news of the suicide. "We've said all along there were three victims in this," he said. "Today Dan White became the third victim." He added, "This was a sick man."[902]

San Francisco Mayor Dianne Feinstein spoke of White without anger despite her aversion to his politics and his crimes. "I am very sorry to hear that Dan White has taken his life," she remarked. "My sympathy goes to his widow, Mary Ann, and his children who have suffered very much. This latest tragedy should close a very sad chapter in this city's history."[903]

In the gay community, they noted White's passing without glee, but certainly with a sense of relief. "I'm glad his conscience caught up with him," one observer commented. Supervisor Harry Britt said that "It comes as no surprise that Dan White was a very disturbed man. The assassination of Harvey Milk and George Moscone are proof of that fact. Dan White is in death as he was in life."[904]

With Dan White's death, the sad saga of three San Francisco municipal officials locked in a web of destruction faded from memory. San Franciscans and gays undoubtedly remembered, but for almost every else, it was one of those crazy things that happened in a crazy city during a crazy era.[905]

Hollywood resurrected interest in Harvey Milk's story over the years, most notably in Gus Van Sant's critically acclaimed 2008 film *Milk*, starring Sean Penn as Harvey Milk and Josh Brolin as Dan White. Penn earned a Best Actor Academy Award for his portrayal. The screenwriter, gay activist Dustin Lance Black, intimated in the film that White might have been a closeted gay man who shot his victims as an act of self-loathing, although most sources familiar with the real-life events believe that revenge for Moscone's decision not to reappoint White was the primary motive.[906]

The difficulty with pinpointing Dan White's motives is that he was an odd person who may have suffered from mental illness. A case can be made, however, that he understood exactly what he was doing. Perhaps he was a Type 1 killer. He accepted the consequences of his action, lashing out to accomplish a political purpose. George Moscone and Harvey Milk stood in White's way of becoming a Supervisor again and earning the respect and admiration of his family and friends. As he contemplated the humiliation of not being reappointed, he reached the end of his tether.

Perhaps he was a Type 4 assassin. As he descended into deep depression, White became convinced that he had no recourse but to murder the men who had occasioned his misery. He was incapable of appreciating the consequences of his actions. Had he been in his right mind, Dan White would have understood that shooting two men to death would not restore his exalted status in the community or in the eyes of his loved ones. As his attorney, Doug Schmidt, argued, White was suffering from diminished capacity when he pulled the trigger that awful day. The old Dan White that everyone knew before November 27, 1978, would never had behaved in such a violent, irresponsible manner. He was a difficult man to deal with, but he was not a murderer.

Perhaps his neuroses compelled him to act as a Type 2 killer or his nihilism pushed him to become a Type 3 killer. Although these categorizations are possible, they seem less compelling than a Type 1 or Type 4 classification. In any event, it is difficult to pin down why Dan White acted as he did. Observers and loved ones did not fully understand his motives in 1978, and no one fully understands them now.[907]

PART VI

CONCLUSION

AFTERWORD

Categorizing assassins and would-be assassins according to their suspected motives is a potentially perilous exercise. Understanding the intricacies of the human heart is never easy. The criminal law attempts to assign penalties to offenders based on whether they possess the requisite *mens rea* (guilty mind) at the time an action occurs as well as whether their conduct (*actus reus*) fits the elements of a crime, but this business of evaluating intentions is always an uncertain endeavor. Educated guesses must be made, often based on incomplete, missing, or conflicting data. It is an art, not a science, and judgments are open to interpretation and dispute.

Even if the motives of assailants can be understood and categorized, the next question remains problematic. Does studying the behavior of past actors allow researchers to predict the behavior of future actors? The answer invariably is "no." The varieties of human experience do not lend themselves to definitive prognostication. So-called "warning signs" of mental illness or aggressive egocentric neediness do not indicate an assassin in the making. For every disturbed individual who acts violently against a public figure, untold thousands suffer silently, act out against friends and family members, or seek and receive professional treatment. Philip K. Dick imagined a world where persons could be arrested for their future crimes, but the criminal justice system had not advanced (or devolved, as they case may be) to that extent quite yet.[908]

Having said these things, figuring out why historical persons did what they did can yield insight into patterns of behavior. The purpose of exploring the crimes of past attackers, as with any trek through history, is to understand, to the extent possible, what happened and why. All history is an effort to make sense of events and the people who participated in them. If subsequent writers take issue with the conclusions, they can and should make the case for accepting alternative explanations. History therefore becomes a conversation among defenders of differing schools of thought.

This book argues for a school of thought based on human psychology. An actor who strikes out against a political figure does so for reasons that

Table 1: Categorization of Assailants According to Type.

TYPE 1	TYPE 2	TYPE 3	TYPE 4	TYPE 5
Booth (Lincoln)	Oswald (JFK)	Zangara (FDR/ Cermak)	Lawrence (Jackson)	Mob (Smith)
Czolgosz (McKinley)	Byck (Nixon)	Bremer (Wallace)	Guiteau (Garfield)	Unknown (Goebel)
Orchard, *et al.* (Steunenberg)	Fromme and Moore (Ford)	Harrelson (Wood)	Prendergast (Harrison)	Weiss (Long)
Collazo and Torresola (Truman)	Hinckley (Reagan)		Schrank (TR)	Nation of Islam soldiers (Malcolm X)
Sirhan (RFK)			Sweeney (Lowenstein)	Ray (MLK)
			Loughner (Giffords)	Jones (Ryan, *et al.*)
				White (Moscone and Milk)

can be classified in one of five categories. See Table 1. As discussed in the Introduction, Type 1 actors are rational persons who assail a public figure for relatively straightforward reasons—namely, they wish to institute political changes. Type 2 actors are needy individuals who seek to prove something to a significant other. They may possess political motives, but such considerations are secondary. The main goal of a Type 2 personality is to fill an emotional need through violence. To use the colloquial expression, Type 3 actors are psychopaths who believe that nothing matters and existence is a curse. These nihilists seek to visit their misery on others. Type 4 actors are cognitively impaired—"crazy," in modern parlance. Not surprisingly, wide variations exist in the nature and extent of the impairment, but all Type 4 actors suffer from some form of mental illness. The Type 5 category is reserved for assailants whose motives are unknown, mixed, or simply not properly classified elsewhere.

No doubt a discerning reader can take issue with some or all of these characterizations. Is Lee Harvey Oswald, John F. Kennedy's assassin, so distinct from Sirhan Sirhan, Robert F. Kennedy's assassin, that the two men belong in separate categories? A case can be made that both assailants were driven by their egocentric needs to shoot a member of the Kennedy family, therefore placing both in the Type 2 category. Alternatively, a critic might argue that they belong in the Type 1 or Type 3 category. On and on the debate continues.

The purpose of placing the actors in the categories listed herein is to make a plausible case for understanding why these marginalized figures believed that it was necessary to employ violence. The majority of people are socialized to obey the law, acquire an education, take part in social activities, seek employment, support their families, and seek out whatever measure of happiness they can find in their lives. If meaning is to be found, it is found in living a life in accordance with societal customs and mores. Yet the men and women in these pages were not content to fall in line with societal dictates. Whether they suffered from mental illness, social ostracism, or nihilistic tendencies, they thought that violence somehow would improve their lot.

Aside from focusing on the individual actors, a broader line of inquiry concerns why so many American political figures have been the targets of violence. Commentators have examined the historical record and argued that individuals take up arms for a variety of reasons aside from mental illness. First, they live in a society that glorifies violence. Television programs, films, podcasts, social media postings, newspapers, articles, and books report on killers with glee, transforming violence into an acceptable form of human interaction. Serial killers and infamous assassins become celebrities in a culture that worships celebrity. In the news business, if it bleeds, it leads.

The coarse nature of American political discourse encourages marginalized people to act out their grievances, or so the argument goes. A polarized electorate that refuses to consider the merits of opposing parties and ideals, a rapacious media driven to cover "gotcha" moments emphasizing the peccadillos of public figures, and a public with an ever-dwindling attention span hungry for titillating stories ensure that narratives grounded in the least common denominator receive maximum attention. For a person already predisposed to act on their violent predilections, incendiary rhetoric exerts a powerful influence, providing a tacit permission slip for someone of a less-than-healthy psychological state to take up arms.

Some critics contend that the ease with which anyone in the United States can acquire firearms or bomb-making materials facilitates violence. Such an observation quickly degenerates into the old adage that "guns don't kill people; people kill people." Perhaps the cliché holds a measure of wisdom, but it is equally true that people with guns kill people with more precision. Yet recognizing a problem and fixing it are separate endeavors. It is doubtful that strict gun-control measures would have prevented the assassinations and attempts described in this book. Most of the people discussed in these pages were committed actors who planned their crimes and pursued their prey with single-minded purposefulness. Their inability to acquire a weapon on one occasion probably would not have frustrated their scheme indefinitely. They likely would have found another means of acting.

Scholars and medical professionals sometimes contend that a more robust mental health system in the United States would ameliorate the underlying causes of some political assassinations. Although the stigma of seeking out and obtaining help for mental illness has lessened in the twenty-first century compared with times past, no one would argue that everyone who needs treatment receives it. Failure to recognize the need, concerns about costs, and the lack of access to mental health resources are among the many impediments to effective treatment.

Mental diseases are not like physical diseases. A broken arm is relatively easy to diagnose and treat. Cause and effect are more or less linear. Mental illnesses, by contrast, wear many faces; some are hidden from view. Too often a person who needs treatment does not receive it. Even when he does, the variables of the human personality cannot be isolated with precision. A patient can relapse, suffer from a different problem, or escape detection. Even when a person receives treatment, the process is not always straightforward, and a "cure" is not guaranteed.

To understand the how and why of political assassinations and attempts is to look through a glass darkly. Patterns emerge even if they are not always clear and distinct. The purpose of this book has been to offer one means of recognizing those patterns. It remains to be seen whether such recognition can lead to improved outcomes in future cases.

NOTES

1 The Second Amendment reads: "A well regulated Militia, being necessary to the security of a free State, the right of the people to keep and bear Arms, shall not be infringed."

2 James W. Clarke, *American Assassins: The Darker Side of Politics* (Princeton, NJ: Princeton University Press, 1982).

3 "The Assassination of Mr. Lincoln: Interesting Particulars of the Tragedy," *New York Times*, April 18, 1865, 4; James F. Kirkham, Sheldon Levy, and William J. Crotty, *Assassination and Political Violence: A Report to the National Commission on the Causes and Prevention of Violence*, Vol. 8 (Washington, DC: U.S. Government Printing Office, October 1969), 50-52; Philip B. Kunhardt, Jr., Philip B. Kunhardt, III, and Peter W. Kunhardt, *Lincoln: An Illustrated Biography* (New York: Knopf, 1992), 352-59; Jay Winik, *April 1865: The Month That Saved America* (New York: HarperCollins, 2001), 223, 259-62.

4 Lincoln's comment about the annals of the poor is quoted in David Herbert Donald, *Lincoln* (New York: Simon & Schuster, 1995), 19. See also Douglas R. Egerton, *Year of Meteors: Stephen Douglas, Abraham Lincoln, and the Election that Brought on the Civil War* (New York: Bloomsbury Press, 2010), 111-48; Lewis L. Gould, *Grand Old Party: A History of the Republicans* (New York: Random House, 2003), 24-28.

5 Doris Kearns Goodwin, *Team of Rivals: The Political Genius of Abraham Lincoln* (New York: Simon & Schuster, 2005), 28-59; Harold Holzer, *Lincoln President-Elect: Abraham Lincoln and the Great Secession Winter 1860-1861* (New York: Simon & Schuster, 2008), 11-14; James M. McPherson, *Battle Cry of Freedom: The Civil War Era* (New York: Ballantine Books, 1988), 216-21; Ronald C. White, Jr., *A. Lincoln: A Biography* (New York: Random House, 2009), 325-29.

6 Eric H. Walther, *The Shattering of the Union: America in the 1850s* (Wilmington, DE: Scholarly Resources, 2004), 57-60; Jules Witcover, *Party of the People: A History of the Democrats* (New York: Random House, 2003), 141-46.

7 Quoted in Kunhardt, Kunhardt, and Kunhardt, *Lincoln: An Illustrated Biography*, 28.

8 Michael Burlingame, *Abraham Lincoln: A Life*, Vol. II (Baltimore, MD: The Johns Hopkins University Press, 2008), 131-38; David Detzer, *Allegiance: Fort Sumter, Charleston, and the Beginning of the Civil War* (New York: Harcourt, 2001), 210-31; Kunhardt, Kunhardt, and Kunhardt, *Lincoln: An Illustrated Biography*, 148, 149

9 William C. Harris, *Lincoln's Rise to the Presidency* (Lawrence: University Press of Kansas, 2007), 5-6, 13-16, 329-30; William Nester, *The Age of Lincoln and the Art of American Power, 1848-1876* (Lincoln, NE: Potomac Books, 2013), 289-312.

10 See, for example, Eric Foner, *Forever Free: The Story of Emancipation and Reconstruction* (Illustrations Edited with a Commentary by Joshua Brown. New York: Knopf, 2005), 62-63; Eric Foner, *Reconstruction: America's Unfinished Revolution: 1863-1877* (New York: Francis Parkman Prize Edition, History Book Club, 2005 [1988]), 66-68; Charles Bracelen Flood, *1864: Lincoln at the Gates of History* (New York: Simon & Schuster, 2009), 362-70; Harold Holzer, *Lincoln: How Abraham Lincoln Ended Slavery in America* (New York: Newmarket Press, an Imprint of HarperCollins, 2012), 155-74; McPherson, *Battle Cry of Freedom*, 712-13, 838-40; James Oakes, *Freedom National: The Destruction of Slavery in the United States, 1861-1865* (New York and London: W. W. Norton, 2013), 430-88; Michael Vorenberg, *Final Freedom: The Civil War, the Abolition of Slavery, and the Thirteenth Amendment* (Cambridge and New York: Cambridge University Press,

2001), 53-60; John C. Waugh, *Re-Electing Lincoln: The Battle for the 1864 Presidency* (New York: Crown Books, 1997), 271-72.

11 Michael W. Kauffman, *American Brutus: John Wilkes Booth and the Lincoln Conspiracies* (New York: Random House, 2004), 6; Kunhardt, Kunhardt, and Kunhardt, *Lincoln: An Illustrated Biography*, 321, 343; Winik, *April 1865*, 203-206.

12 James W. Clarke, *American Assassins: The Darker Side of Politics* (Princeton, NJ: Princeton University Press, 1982), 20-25; Kauffman, *American Brutus*, 81-92.

13 Clarke, *American Assassins*, 22-25; Kauffman, *American Brutus*, 98-99, 125. See also "Booth's End; The Shooting of the Assassin of the President; His Flight and Desperate Resistance," *The New York Herald*, April 28, 1865, 1.

14 Clarke, *American Assassins*, 25-28; Kauffman, *American Brutus*, 124-25; James L. Swanson, *Manhunt: The 12-Day Chase for Lincoln's Killer* (New York: William Morrow, 2006), 4-5.

15 Clarke, *American Assassins*, 33; Kirkham, Levy, and Crotty, *Assassination and Political Violence*, 51-52; Swanson, *Manhunt*, 23-26.

16 Clarke, *American Assassins*, 33-34; Kirkham, Levy, and Crotty, *Assassination and Political Violence*, 51-52; Winik, *April 1865*, 345.

17 Kauffman, *American Brutus*, 173-80; Winik, *April 1865*, 345-46.

18 Quoted in Donald, *Lincoln*, 584-85. See also Richard Carwardine, *Lincoln: A Life of Purpose and Power* (New York: Knopf, 2003), 308-309; William Harris, *With Charity for All: Lincoln and the Restoration of the Union* (Lexington: University Press of Kentucky, 1999), 2; Hans Trefousse, *The Radical Republicans: Lincoln's Vanguard for Racial Justice* (New York: Knopf, 1969), 300-304.

19 Quoted in Swanson, *Manhunt*, 6. See also: Donald, *Lincoln*, 585-88; Kauffman, *American Brutus*, 209-10; White, *A. Lincoln: A Biography*, 672.

20 Clarke, *American Assassins*, 34-35; Swanson, *Manhunt*, 28-29.

21 Quoted in Clarke, *American Assassins*, 34.

22 Kauffman, *American Brutus*, 225; Swanson, *Manhunt*, 38-39.

23 Kauffman, *American Brutus*, 219, 225; Kunhardt, Kunhardt, and Kunhardt, *Lincoln: An Illustrated Biography*, 352; Swanson, *Manhunt*, 28, 32.

24 "The Assassination of Mr. Lincoln: Interesting Particulars of the Tragedy," 4; Kauffman, *American Brutus*, 226; Swanson, *Manhunt*, 38-46.

25 Swanson, *Manhunt*, 46-48; Kunhardt, Kunhardt, and Kunhardt, *Lincoln: An Illustrated Biography*, 353; Winik, *April 1865*, 223-24.

26 Kauffman, *American Brutus*, 3-19, 79; Elizabeth D. Leonard, *Lincoln's Avengers: Justice, Revenge, and Reunion After the Civil War* (New York: Norton, 2004), 4-5; Swanson, *Manhunt*, 38-49; White, *A. Lincoln*, 672-75.

27 Kauffman, *American Brutus*, 9-14; Kunhardt, Kunhardt, and Kunhardt, *Lincoln: An Illustrated Biography*, 356; Swanson, *Manhunt*, 83-86.

28 Kauffman, *American Brutus*, 26-27; Kunhardt, Kunhardt, and Kunhardt, *Lincoln: An Illustrated Biography*, 356-57; Swanson, *Manhunt*, 93-94.

29 Kunhardt, Kunhardt, and Kunhardt, *Lincoln: An Illustrated Biography*, 356-59; Swanson, *Manhunt*, 110-22.

30 Quoted in Donald, *Lincoln*, 599. See also Goodwin, *Team of Rivals*, 744; Naveh, "'Now He Belongs to the Ages,'" 49-56; Peterson, *Lincoln in American Memory*, 3-4. For a discussion of what Stanton actually said—he may have said, "Now he belongs to the angels"—see Adam Gopnik, *Angels and Ages: A Short Book about Darwin, Lincoln, and Modern Life* (New York: Random House, 2009), 24-26.

31 "Important. Assassination of President Lincoln," *The New York Herald*, April 15, 1865, 1; Kauffman, *American Brutus*, 134-38; Leonard, *Lincoln's Avengers*, 33-65, 67-130; "Trial of the Assassins; The Suppressed Testimony Now Made Public; Highly Important Revelations; Implication of Jeff. Davis in the Assassination," *The Boston Herald*, June 5, 1865, 2.

32 Clarke, *American Assassins*, 25-28; Kunhardt, Kunhardt, and Kunhardt, *Lincoln: An Illustrated Biography*, 400-401; Naveh, "'Now He Belongs to the Ages,'" 49-56; Peterson, *Lincoln in American Memory*, 3-4.

33 Quoted in Carwardine, *Lincoln: A Life of Purpose and Power*, 319. See also Eval Naveh, "'He Belongs to the Ages': Lincoln's Image and the American Historical Consciousness," *Journal of American Culture* 16, no. 4 (Winter 1993): 49-50, 53-56; Merrill Peterson, *Lincoln in American Memory* (New York and Oxford: Oxford University Press, 1995), 21; White, *A. Lincoln*, 675-76.

34 Kauffman, *American Brutus*, 240-41, 278-80; Leonard, *Lincoln's Avengers*, 33; Peterson, *Lincoln in American Memory*, 14; Winik, *April 1865*, 355-59.

35 Kauffman, *American Brutus*, 14-15; "The President's Assassin," *The Boston Herald*, April 17, 1865, 4; Swanson, *Manhunt*, 112-21.

36 Kauffman, *American Brutus*, 227-30; Swanson, *Manhunt*, 66-68, 80-83.

37 Kauffman, *American Brutus*, 230-31, 243-45; Leonard, *Lincoln's Avengers*, 59-63; Swanson, *Manhunt*, 129-32.

38 "Booth's End; The Shooting of the Assassin of the President; His Flight and Desperate Resistance," 1; Kauffman, *American Brutus*, 309-13; Swanson, *Manhunt*, 278-80, 287-92.

39 Kauffman, *American Brutus*, 312-16; Swanson, *Manhunt*, 308-23.

40 Kauffman, *American Brutus*, 317-18; Leonard, *Lincoln's Avengers*, 38; Swanson, *Manhunt*, 323-31.

41 "Booth's End; The Shooting of the Assassin of the President; His Flight and Desperate Resistance," 1; Kauffman, *American Brutus*, 318-20; Swanson, *Manhunt*, 331-43.

42 *The Assassination of President Lincoln and the Trial of the Conspirators* (New York: Moore, Wilstach & Baldwin, 1865), 97-112, 248-49; Leonard, *Lincoln's Avengers*, 54-56, 289, 293-94

43 *The Assassination of President Lincoln and the Trial of the Conspirators*, 168-242, 248-49; Kauffman, *American Brutus*, 386-87; Leonard, *Lincoln's Avengers*, 49-50, 129-30, 137-38, 140-41, 276.

44 Kauffman, *American Brutus*, 387-90; Leonard, *Lincoln's Avengers*, 187-90, 237-38, 256, 282, 287, 294-96.

45 *Ex Parte Milligan*, 71 U.S. 2 (1866). See also *The Assassination of President Lincoln and the Trial of the Conspirators*, 17; Kauffman, *American Brutus*, 386-87; Leonard, *Lincoln's Avengers*, 72-73, 148-49; Howard Means, *The Avenger Takes His Place: Andrew Johnson and the 45 Days That Changed a Nation* (New York: Harcourt, 2006), 147-49.

46 "The Assassination Conspiracy," *The Boston Herald*, July 10, 1865, 2; *The Assassination of President Lincoln and the Trial of the Conspirators*, 85-143, 248; Kauffman, *American Brutus*, 375-76; Leonard, *Lincoln's Avengers*, 42-45, 130, 133-34, 266, 270-73.

47 *The Assassination of President Lincoln and the Trial of the Conspirators*, 17-23; Kauffman, *American Brutus*, 354-63.

48 *The Assassination of President Lincoln and the Trial of the Conspirators*, 249-50; Leonard, *Lincoln's Avengers*, 128-33; "The Sentences of the Assassination Conspirators," *The Boston Herald*, July 7, 1865, 2; Swanson, *Manhunt*, 362-64.

49 Kauffman, *American Brutus*, 373; Leonard, *Lincoln's Avengers*, 133; Swanson, *Manhunt*, 364.

50 Powell is quoted in Kauffman, *American Brutus*, 373. The other quotes are from Swanson, *Manhunt*, 364-65.

51 Atzerodt is quoted in Kauffman, *American Brutus*, 374. See also Leonard, *Lincoln's Avengers*, 133; Swanson, *Manhunt*, 364-65.

52 Kauffman, *American Brutus*, 374; Kunhardt, Kunhardt, and Kunhardt, *Lincoln: An Illustrated Biography*, 392; Leonard, *Lincoln's Avengers*, 133-34; Swanson, *Manhunt*, 364-65.

53 Kauffman, *American Brutus*, 375-98; Kunhardt, Kunhardt, and Kunhardt, *Lincoln: An Illustrated Biography*, 392; Leonard, *Lincoln's Avengers*, 133-34.

54 Clarke, *American Assassins*, 38-39; Allen C. Guelzo, "The Redemption of Abraham Lincoln," *The Civil War Monitor* 6, no. 2 (Summer 2016): 30-38, 74-75; Peterson, *Lincoln in American Memory*, 3-4.

55 Ronald L. Feinman, *Assassinations, Threats, and the American Presidency: From Andrew Jackson to Barack Obama* (Lanham, MD: Rowman & Littlefield, 2015), 37; Scott Miller, *The President and the Assassin: McKinley, Terror, and Empire at the Dawn of the American Century* (New York: Random House, 2011), 6-7.

56 Quoted in Miller, *The President and the Assassin*, 48.

57 Feinman, *Assassinations, Threats, and the American Presidency*, 37-39; Wyatt Kingseed, "The Assassination of William McKinley," *American History* 36, no. 4 (October 2001): 24; Miller, *The President and the Assassin*, 27-30.

58 Quoted in Miller, *The President and the Assassin*, 18. See also Feinman, *Assassinations, Threats, and the American Presidency*, 37-38; "President McKinley's Illustrious Career; Entered Army When a Mere Boy and Made a Brilliant Record; His Successes in Congress," *New York Times*, September 7, 1901, 5.

59 Feinman, *Assassinations, Threats, and the American Presidency*, 38; Miller, *The President and the Assassin*, 21-23; "President McKinley's Illustrious Career," 5.

60 James W. Clarke, *American Assassins: The Darker Side of Politics* (Princeton, NJ: Princeton University Press, 1982), 56; "President McKinley's Illustrious Career," 5.

61 Quoted in Richard Hofstadter, *The American Political Tradition and the Men Who Made It* (New York: Vintage Books, 1989 [1948]), 245. See also Lawrence Goodwyn, *The Populist Movement: A Short History of the Agrarian Revolt in America* (New York and Oxford: Oxford University Press, 1978), 216-17; Robert C. McMath, Jr., *American Populism: A Social History, 1877–1898* (New York: Hill and Wang, 1993), 200-1.

62 The speech is reprinted in many sources. See, for example, William Safire, editor, *Lend Me Your Ears: Great Speeches in History* (New York and London: W. W. Norton, 2004), 923-26, and William Jennings Bryan, *The Cross of Gold: Speech Delivered Before the National Democratic Convention at Chicago, July 9, 1896* (Lincoln: University of Nebraska Press, 1996). See also Hofstadter, *The American Political Tradition and the Men Who Made It*, 241-43; Michael Kazin, *A Godly Hero: The Life of William Jennings Bryan* (New York: Knopf, 2006), 59-61.

63 Goodwyn, *The Populist Movement*, 282-86; Joseph Nathan Kane, *Facts About the Presidents* (New York: Ace Books, 1976), 262; Kazin, *A Godly Hero*, 76-79, 84; R. Hal Williams, *Realigning America: McKinley, Bryan, and the Remarkable Election of 1896* (Lawrence: The University Press of Kansas, 2001), 149-50.

64 Miller, *The President and the Assassin*, 50-51; "President McKinley's Illustrious Career," 5.

65 Feinman, *Assassinations, Threats, and the American Presidency*, 38-39; Kingseed, "The Assassination of William McKinley," 24; James F. Kirkham, Sheldon Levy, and William J. Crotty, *Assassination and Political Violence: A Report to the National Commission on the Causes and Prevention of Violence*, Vol. 8 (Washington, DC: U.S. Government Printing Office, October 1969), 54; Miller, *The President and the Assassin*, 129-35, 157-58, 178, 210-11.

66 Gerard Helferich, *Theodore Roosevelt and the Assassin: Madness, Vengeance, and the Campaign of 1912* (Guilford, CT: Lyons Press, 2013), x; Feinman, *Assassinations, Threats, and the American Presidency*, 39; Miller, *The President and the Assassin*, 50, 265, 270-71.

67 Feinman, *Assassinations, Threats, and the American Presidency*, 39; Helferich, *Theodore Roosevelt and the Assassin*, 18-20; Miller, *The President and the Assassin*, 200-201, 270, 271.

68 See, for example, Norman P. Barry, *On Classical Liberalism and Libertarianism* (New York: Macmillan, 1986), 161-91; Miller, *The President and the Assassin*, 60-62.

69 Joseph T. McCann, *Terrorism on American Soil: A Concise History of Plots and Perpetrators from the Famous to the Forgotten* (Boulder, CO: Sentient Publications, 2006), 64; Miller, *The President and the Assassin*, 109-110.

70 J. Michael Martinez, *Terrorist Attacks on American Soil: From the Civil War Era to the Present* (Lanham, MD: Rowman & Littlefield, 2012), 133-34; McCann, *Terrorism on American Soil*, 64; Miller, *The President and the Assassin*, 345.

71 John Chalberg, *Emma Goldman: American Individualist*, 2d. ed. (New York: Longman, 2008), 11-26; Kenneth M. Dolbeare, *American Political Thought* (Chatham, NJ: Chatham House, 1984), 392.

72 Andrew Cook, "Lone Assassins," *History Today* 53, no. 11 (November 2003): 26; Kingseed, "The Assassination of William McKinley," 25; Don Sneed, "Newspapers Call for Swift Justice: A Study of the McKinley Assassination," *Journalism Quarterly* 65, no. 2 (Summer 1988): 361-62.

73 Cary Federman, "The Life of an Unknown Assassin: Leon Czolgosz and the Death of William McKinley," *Crime, History & Societies* 14, no. 2 (2010): 92.

74 Kingseed, "The Assassination of William McKinley," 25; Andrew Milner, "C'mon and Shoot a President: The Historical People Behind the Characters in Assassins," *The Sondheim Review* 22, no. 1 (Winter 2015): 12.

75 Cook, "Lone Assassins," 26; Milner, "C'mon and Shoot a President," 12-13.

76 Clarke, *American Assassins*, 55-56; Miller, *The President and the Assassin*, 6.

77 Clarke, *American Assassins*, 56-57; Feinman, *Assassinations, Threats, and the American Presidency*, 39-40; Helferich, *Theodore Roosevelt and the Assassin*, xii-xiii; Miller, *The President and the Assassin*, 300-1.

78 Colegrove is quoted in Clarke, *American Assassins*, 57. See also Miller, *The President and the Assassin*, 9.

79 Parker is quoted in Miller, *The President and the Assassin*, 10. See also Clarke, *American Assassins*, 57; Miller, *The President and the Assassin*, 9.

80 Czolgosz is quoted in Helferich, *Theodore Roosevelt and the Assassin*, xiii. See also Clarke, *American Assassins*, 58; Feinman, *Assassinations, Threats, and the American Presidency*, 40; Miller, *The President and the Assassin*, 301.

81 McKinley is quoted in Miller, *The President and the Assassin*, 302. See also Kingseed, "The Assassination of William McKinley," 25; Milner, "C'mon and Shoot a President," 13.

82 Czolgosz is quoted in Miller, *The President and the Assassin*, 304. See also Clarke, *American Assassins*, 58; Feinman, *Assassinations, Threats, and the American Presidency*, 40; Miller, *The President and the Assassin*, 301.

83 Goldman is quoted in Miller, *The President and the Assassin*, 307. See also Clarke, *American Assassins*, 59-60; Kirkham, Levy, and Crotty, *Assassination and Political Violence*, 55.

84 McKinley is quoted in Miller, *The President and the Assassin*, 313.

85 Helferich, *Theodore Roosevelt and the Assassin*, xiii-xiv; Miller, *The President and the Assassin*, 313-14.

86 Kingseed, "The Assassination of William McKinley," 26; Miller, *The President and the Assassin*, 315-20.

87 "Nation Grieves at Loss of President; Funeral Service Arranged for Thursday; Mr. Roosevelt Sworn In; He Promises to Follow the Policy [of] Mr. McKinley," *New York Times*, September 15, 1901, 1.

88 Cook, "Lone Assassins," 26; Miller, *The President and the Assassin*, 321-25.

89 Czolgosz is quoted in Walter Channing, *The Mental Status of Czolgosz, the Assassin of President McKinley* (Charleston, SC: Nabu Press, 1913 [1902]), 22. See also Miller, *The President and the Assassin*, 324-25.

90 Czolgosz is quoted in "Assassin Czolgosz is Executed at Auburn; He Declared that He Felt No Regret for His Crime," *New York Times*, October 30, 1901, 5. See also Cook, "Lone Assassins," 26; Federman, "The Life of an Unknown Assassin," 87; Kingseed, "The Assassination of William McKinley," 30; Kirkham, Levy, and Crotty, *Assassination and Political Violence*, 55-56; Miller, *The President and the Assassin*, 323-25.

91 Quoted in Clarke, *American Assassins*, 59. See also "Czolgosz's Body to Be Destroyed at Auburn; Brother of Assassin Empowers Warden to Dispose of It," *New York Times*, October 29, 1901, 1.

92 Miller, *The President and the Assassin*, 348; "Nation Grieves at Loss of President," 1.

93 "Ex-Governor Killed by Dynamite Bomb; Frank Steunenberg of Idaho Victim of an Assassin; Governor from 1897 to 1901; The Bomb Had Been Placed at His Gate at Caldwell, and Exploded as He Entered," *New York Times*, December 31, 1905, 1. See also Allan Brinkley, "Who Killed Frank

Steunenberg?" *The New Republic* 217, no. 17 (October 27, 1997): 35; Stephen G. Christianson, "William 'Big Bill' Haywood Trial: 1907," in *Great American Trials: From Salem Witchcraft to Rodney King*, ed. Edward W. Knappman (Detroit, MI: Visible Ink Press, 2003), 245; Andrew E. Kersten, *Clarence Darrow: American Iconoclast* (New York: Hill and Wang, 2011), 125-26; J. Anthony Lukas, *Big Trouble: A Murder in a Small Western Town Sets Off a Struggle for the Soul of America* (New York: Simon & Schuster, 1997), 50-53.

94   Frank Steunenberg is quoted in Lukas, *Big Trouble*, 51. Belle is quoted in Lukas, *Big Trouble*, 53.

95   Brinkley, "Who Killed Frank Steunenberg?," 35; Christianson, "William 'Big Bill' Haywood Trial," 244-45; Lukas, *Big Trouble*, 108-18, 140-54.

96   Lukas, *Big Trouble*, 66-72. The quotes appear on page 68. See also Peter Carlson, *Roughneck: The Life and Times of Big Bill Haywood* (New York: W. W. Norton & Company, 1983), 86-88.

97   Harry Orchard, *The Confessions and Autobiography of Harry Orchard: Assassin and Terrorist for the Western Federation of Miners* (Calumet, MI: Calumet History and Hobby, 2013), 194-96. See also Lukas, *Big Trouble*, 69-70.

98   Lukas, *Big Trouble*, 70-71; Orchard, *The Confessions and Autobiography of Harry Orchard*, 197.

99   Carlson, *Roughneck*, 89; Lukas, *Big Trouble*, 158-69, 238-39.

100   Lukas, *Big Trouble*, 74-77.

101   Michael Burlingame, *Abraham Lincoln: A Life*, Vol. II (Baltimore, MD: The Johns Hopkins University Press, 2008), 32-39; Lukas, *Big Trouble*, 77-87.

102   Carlson, *Roughneck*, 89; Lukas, *Big Trouble*, 155-200.

103   Carlson, *Roughneck*, 89-90; Philip Dray, *There Is Power in a Union: The Epic Story of Labor in America* (New York: Anchor Books, 2011), 292; Lukas, *Big Trouble*, 172-95; Orchard, *The Confessions and Autobiography of Harry Orchard*, 205, 207.

104   Dray, *There Is Power in a Union*, 295; Lukas, *Big Trouble*, 447, 555-57.

105   Christianson, "William 'Big Bill' Haywood Trial," 244-45; Kersten, *Clarence Darrow*, 125; Lukas, *Big Trouble*, 197-200, 243-47.

106   Carlson, *Roughneck*, 93-94; Lukas, *Big Trouble*, 274-87, 299-300.

107   *Pettibone v. Nichols*, 203 US 192, 215-16 (1906). See also Carlson, *Roughneck*, 101-2.

108   Dray, *There Is Power in a Union*, 294; Lukas, *Big Trouble*, 329, 516-17, 565.

109   Carlson, *Roughneck*, 88; Lukas, *Big Trouble*, 288-93.

110   Carlson, *Roughneck*, 88, 102-3; Kersten, *Clarence Darrow*, 129; Lukas, *Big Trouble*, 333-35.

111   Christianson, "William 'Big Bill' Haywood Trial," 244, 247.

112   Kersten, *Clarence Darrow*, 129-30; Lukas, *Big Trouble*, 433-58, 460-64.

113   Carlson, *Roughneck*, 115-22; Kersten, *Clarence Darrow*, 131-32; Lukas, *Big Trouble*, 551-63.

114   Quoted in Lukas, *Big Trouble*, 708. See also Carlson, *Roughneck*, 124-26, 129-31; Dray, *There Is Power in a Union*, 295-96; Kersten, *Clarence Darrow*, 132-33.

115   Quoted in S. Paul O'Hara, *Inventing the Pinkertons; or Spies, Sleuths, Mercenaries, and Thugs: Being a Story of the Nation's Most Famous (and Infamous) Detective Agency* (Baltimore, MD: Johns Hopkins University Press, 2016), 132.

116   Quoted in John A. Farrell, *Clarence Darrow: Attorney for the Damned* (New York: Vintage, 2012), 179. See also Dray, *There Is Power in a Union*, 296.

117   Quoted in Farrell, *Clarence Darrow*, 180. See also Christianson, "William 'Big Bill' Haywood Trial," 246.

118   Quoted in Lukas, *Big Trouble*, 719. See also Kersten, *Clarence Darrow*, 130-31.

119   Quoted in Lukas, *Big Trouble*, 719. See also Christianson, "William 'Big Bill' Haywood Trial," 246.

120   Quoted in Lukas, *Big Trouble*, 719.

121   Quoted in Lukas, *Big Trouble*, 720. See also Carlson, *Roughneck*, 128-29, 131-33; Kersten, *Clarence Darrow*, 135.

122   Carlson, *Roughneck*, 134; Dray, *There Is Power in a Union*, 296; Kersten, *Clarence Darrow*, 135-36; Lukas, *Big Trouble*, 748.

123 Dray, *There Is Power in a Union*, 296; Lukas, *Big Trouble*, 750-54.

124 Lukas, *Big Trouble*, 705-12.

125 Joseph Nathan Kane, *Facts About the Presidents* (New York: Ace Books, 1976), 366-79; David McCullough, *Truman* (New York: Simon & Schuster, 1992), 808; Walter Russell Mead, *Special Providence: American Foreign Policy and How It Changed the World* (Oxford and New York: Routledge, 2002), 257.

126 John Lewis Gaddis, *Strategies of Containment: A Critical Appraisal of American National Security Policy During the Cold War*, 2d. ed. (Oxford and New York: Oxford University Press, 2005), 24-52; McCullough, *Truman*, 607-608.

127 Paul Kennedy, "Truman Death Aim Denied by Collazo," *New York Times*, March 2, 1951, A32; Joseph T. McCann, *Terrorism on American Soil: A Concise History of Plots and Perpetrators from the Famous to the Forgotten* (Boulder, CO: Sentient Publications, 2006), 86-87.

128 Quoted in James W. Clarke, *American Assassins: The Darker Side of Politics* (Princeton, NJ: Princeton University Press, 1982), 69. See also McCann, *Terrorism on American Soil*, 87-88; Elbert B. Smith, "Shoot-out on Pennsylvania Avenue," *American History* 32, no. 3 (July/August 1997): 16-17.

129 Clarke, *American Assassins*, 71; McCann, *Terrorism on American Soil*, 88-89; McCullough, *Truman*, 810; Smith, "Shoot-out on Pennsylvania Avenue," 17-19.

130 Clarke, *American Assassins*, 71-72; Kennedy, "Truman Death Aim Denied by Collazo," A32; Smith, "Shoot-out on Pennsylvania Avenue," 18-20.

131 Collazo is quoted in Mel Ayton, *Hunting the President: Threats, Plots, and Assassination Attempts— From FDR to Obama* (Washington, DC: Regnery History, 2014), 31. See also McCann, *Terrorism on American Soil*, 89-90; McCullough, *Truman*, 809-10; Smith, "Shoot-out on Pennsylvania Avenue," 16.

132 Clarke, *American Assassins*, 72-73; McCann, *Terrorism on American Soil*, 90; Smith, "Shoot-out on Pennsylvania Avenue," 18-20.

133 Quoted in McCullough, *Truman*, 810. See also Smith, "Shoot-out on Pennsylvania Avenue," 18-20.

134 Ayton, *Hunting the President*, 31-32; Clarke, *American Assassins*, 73; Stephen Hunter and Joseph Bainbridge, Jr., *American Gunfight: The Plot to Kill Harry Truman—And the Shootout That Stopped It* (New York: Simon & Schuster, 2005), 106-108; McCullough, *Truman*, 809-10; Smith, "Shoot-out on Pennsylvania Avenue," 18-20.

135 Clarke, *American Assassins*, 73; McCullough, *Truman*, 810; Smith, "Shoot-out on Pennsylvania Avenue," 19-21.

136 McCann, *Terrorism on American Soil*, 90-91; McCullough, *Truman*, 810-11.

137 McCann, *Terrorism on American Soil*, 90-91; Smith, "Shoot-out on Pennsylvania Avenue," 19.

138 Hunter and Bainbridge, *American Gunfight*, 159-60; McCullough, *Truman*, 808-13; Smith, "Shoot-out on Pennsylvania Avenue," 19-21.

139 McCann, *Terrorism on American Soil*, 91; McCullough, *Truman*, 810; "Oscar Collazo, 80, Truman Attacker in '50," *New York Times*, February 23, 1994, A16; Smith, "Shoot-out on Pennsylvania Avenue," 19-21.

140 McCann, *Terrorism on American Soil*, 91; McCullough, *Truman*, 811; Smith, "Shoot-out on Pennsylvania Avenue," 20-21.

141 Quoted in McCullough, *Truman*, 811. See also McCann, *Terrorism on American Soil*, 91.

142 McCullough, *Truman*, 811-12.

143 Quoted in McCann, *Terrorism on American Soil*, 91.

144 McCullough, *Truman*, 811-13.

145 Ayton, *Hunting the President*, 33; Clarke, *American Assassins*, 73-74.

146 Ayton, *Hunting the President*, 33-34; McCann, *Terrorism on American Soil*, 91; "Oscar Collazo, 80, Truman Attacker in '50," A16.

147 "Oscar Collazo, 80, Truman Attacker in '50," A16.

148 Clarke, *American Assassins*, 13-16.

149 Much has been written about the lives and times of the Kennedy family. Two especially good sources of information about Robert F. Kennedy are Arthur M. Schlesinger, Jr., *Robert Kennedy and His Times* (New York: Ballantine Books, 1978), and Evan M. Thomas, *Robert Kennedy: His Life* (New York: Simon & Schuster, 2000). See also Anne Mork, "The Once and Future King: Robert F. Kennedy as a Liberal Icon," *American Studies in Scandinavia* 44, no. 2 (2012): 29-50.

150 Schlesinger, *Robert Kennedy and His Times*, 671-74, 822-25, 884-86; Alden Whitman, "Robert Francis Kennedy: Attorney General, Senator and Heir of the New Frontier," *New York Times*, June 7, 1968, 18.

151 James W. Clarke, *American Assassins: The Darker Side of Politics* (Princeton, NJ: Princeton University Press, 1982), 82-83; Mork, "The Once and Future King," 34; Schlesinger, *Robert Kennedy and His Times*, 137, 522-37.

152 Schlesinger, *Robert Kennedy and His Times*, 400, 863; Whitman, "Robert Francis Kennedy," 18.

153 Schlesinger, *Robert Kennedy and His Times*, 717-18.

154 Clarke, *American Assassins*, 83; Mork, "The Once and Future King," 35; Schlesinger, *Robert Kennedy and His Times*, 932-33.

155 Quoted in Mel Ayton, *The Forgotten Terrorist: Sirhan Sirhan and the Assassination of Robert F. Kennedy* (Omaha, NE: The Notable Trials Library, 2012), 16.

156 Ayton, *The Forgotten Terrorist*, 16-17; Mark Kurlansky, *1968: The Year That Rocked the World* (New York: Ballantine Books, 2004), 261-62; Evan M. Thomas, "RFK's Last Campaign," *Newsweek* 131, no. 23, June 8, 1998, 46-53.

157 Ayton, *The Forgotten Terrorist*, 45-47; Clarke, *American Assassins*, 87.

158 Sirhan is quoted in Ayton, *The Forgotten Terrorist*, 53.

159 Ayton, *The Forgotten Terrorist*, 50-65; Clarke, *American Assassins*, 79-85; Peter Kihss, "Suspect, Arab Immigrant, Arraigned; Notes on Kennedy in Suspect's Home," *New York Times*, June 6, 1968, 1, 21; Terence Smith, "Father of Suspect 'Sickened' by News," *New York Times,* June 6, 1968, 1, 21.

160 Ayton, *The Forgotten Terrorist*, 67-70; Clarke, *American Assassins*, 85; Kihss, "Suspect, Arab Immigrant, Arraigned," 21.

161 Ayton, *The Forgotten Terrorist*, 70-71; Clarke, *American Assassins*, 87-88.

162 Ayton, *The Forgotten Terrorist*, 73-76; Clarke, *American Assassins*, 92-95; Kihss, "Suspect, Arab Immigrant, Arraigned," 1.

163 Ayton, *The Forgotten Terrorist*, 75-76; Clarke, *American Assassins*, 94.

164 Ayton, *The Forgotten Terrorist*, 78-80; Clarke, *American Assassins*, 78, 95.

165 Ayton, *The Forgotten Terrorist*, 81.

166 Ayton, *The Forgotten Terrorist*, 82-83; "2 Newsmen and Union Leader Among 5 Felled by Gunfire," *The Atlanta Constitution*, June 6, 1968, 2.

167 Ayton, *The Forgotten Terrorist*, 83; Wallace Turner, "The Shooting: A Victory Celebration That Ended with Shots, Screams and Curses," *New York Times,* June 6, 1968, 21.

168 Warren Rogers, *When I Think of Bobby: A Personal Memoir of the Kennedy Years* (New York: HarperCollins, 1993), 157, 158.

169 Romero and Kennedy are quoted in Ayton, *The Forgotten Terrorist*, 25.

170 Quoted in Thomas, *Robert Kennedy: His Life*, 391. See also Rogers, *When I Think of Bobby*, 159.

171 Rogers, *When I Think of Bobby*, 160.

172 Plimpton and Sirhan are quoted in Ayton, *The Forgotten Terrorist*, 83. See also Clarke, *American Assassins*, 78.

173 Ethel Kennedy is quoted in Rogers, *When I Think of Bobby*, 162. See also Ayton, *The Forgotten Terrorist*, 85.

174 Ayton, *The Forgotten Terrorist*, 26-27; Gladwin Hill, "Kennedy is Dead, Victim of Assassin," *New York Times*, June 6, 1968, 1, 20.

175 Mankiewicz is quoted in "Transcripts of Medical Statements," *New York Times*, June 6, 1968, 22. See also Gladwin Hill, "Kennedy is Dead, Victim of Assassin," 1; Thomas, *Robert Kennedy: His Life*, 392.

176 Unruh is quoted on page 86 and the officer is quoted on page 87 of Ayton, *The Forgotten Terrorist*. See also Clarke, *American Assassins*, 78; Turner, "The Shooting," 21.

177 Ayton, *The Forgotten Terrorist*, 88.

178 Sirhan is quoted in Ayton, *The Forgotten Terrorist*, 102.

179 Sirhan is quoted in Michael Newton, *Famous Assassinations in World History: An Encyclopedia*, Vol. I: A-P (Santa Barbara, CA: ABC-CLIO, 2014), 265. See also Ayton, *The Forgotten Terrorist*, 95-99.

180 Ayton, *The Forgotten Terrorist*, 103; Clarke, *American Assassins*, 100; Douglas Robinson, "Sirhan Convicted in First Degree; Jury to Fix Fate," *New York Times*, April 18, 1969, 1, 24.

181 The Kennedy family letter is quoted in Ayton, *The Forgotten Terrorist*, 105-106. See also Clarke, *American Assassins*, 101; Douglas Robinson, "Sirhan Sentenced to Gas Chamber on 5th Jury Vote," *New York Times*, April 24, 1969, 1.

182 493 P.2d 880, 6 Cal. 3d 628 (Cal. 1972).

183 Ayton, *The Forgotten Terrorist*, 107-202.

184 Ayton, *The Forgotten Terrorist*. See also Clarke, *American Assassins*, 101-4.

185 Quoted in Daniel Patrick Moynihan, *Daniel Patrick Moynihan: A Portrait in Letters of an American Visionary* (New York: Public Affairs, 2010), 70. See also James L. Swanson, *End of Days: The Assassination of John F. Kennedy* (New York: William Morrow, 2013), 204; Tom Wicker, "Gov. Connally Shot; Mrs. Kennedy Safe; President Is Struck Down by a Rifle Shot from Building on Motorcade—Johnson, Riding Behind, is Unhurt," *New York Times*, November 23, 1963, 1.

186 William Manchester, *The Death of a President: November 20–November 25, 1963*, 25th Anniversary Edition (New York: Perennial Library, 1988), 562.

187 Ronald L. Feinman, *Assassinations, Threats, and the American Presidency: From Andrew Jackson to Barack Obama* (Lanham, MD: Rowman & Littlefield, 2015), 84-87.

188 Nellie Connally is quoted in Swanson, *End of Days*, 112. See also: Swanson, *End of Days*, 60-63. Her comment is quoted in slightly different words in Vincent Bugliosi, *Reclaiming History: The Assassination of President John F. Kennedy* (New York: W. W. Norton & Company, 2007), 37. For more information on Kennedy's reasons for visiting Texas, see Feinman, *Assassinations, Threats, and the American Presidency*, 89-90, 91.

189 Feinman, *Assassinations, Threats, and the American Presidency*, 29-41, 63-71, 73-81; Swanson, *End of Days*, xv-xvi.

190 Feinman, *Assassinations, Threats, and the American Presidency*, 83-84.

191 Mel Ayton, *Hunting the President: Threats, Plots, and Assassination Attempts—From FDR to Obama* (Washington, DC: Regnery History, 2014), 69-70; Bugliosi, *Reclaiming History*, 419, 973, 1000, 1347.

192 Ayton, *Hunting the President*, 60-63; Feinman, *Assassinations, Threats, and the American Presidency*, 88; Larry J. Sabato, *The Kennedy Half Century: The Presidency, Assassination, and Lasting Legacy of John F. Kennedy* (New York: Bloomsbury USA, 2013), 235-36; Swanson, *End of Days*, 86.

193 Ayton, *Hunting the President*, 65-66; Feinman, *Assassinations, Threats, and the American Presidency*, 88-89.

194 Feinman, *Assassinations, Threats, and the American Presidency*, 90; Swanson, *End of Days*, 84-85.

195 Bugliosi, *Reclaiming History*, xii-xiii; Swanson, *End of Days*, 85-86.

196 Bugliosi, *Reclaiming History*, 13, 14, 28, 31; Feinman, *Assassinations, Threats, and the American Presidency*, 90; Swanson, *End of Days*, 93-103.

197 Feinman, *Assassinations, Threats, and the American Presidency*, 91; Swanson, *End of Days*, 106-17.

198 Bugliosi, *Reclaiming History*, 363, 548, 559, 562, 573-93; James W. Clarke, *American Assassins: The Darker Side of Politics* (Princeton, NJ: Princeton University Press, 1982), 109-11; Swanson, *End of Days*, 37-39; James F. Kirkham, Sheldon Levy, and William J. Crotty, *Assassination and*

Political Violence: A Report to the National Commission on the Causes and Prevention of Violence, Vol. 8 (Washington, DC: U.S. Government Printing Office, October 1969), 61.

199   Clarke, *American Assassins*, 113-14; Feinman, *Assassinations, Threats, and the American Presidency*, 92-94.

200   Clarke, *American Assassins*, 113-15; Feinman, *Assassinations, Threats, and the American Presidency*, 94-95; Swanson, *End of Days*, 39-44.

201   Bugliosi, *Reclaiming History*, 942, 967; Clarke, *American Assassins*, 114-16; Feinman, *Assassinations, Threats, and the American Presidency*, 95; Swanson, *End of Days*, 15-16.

202   Bugliosi, *Reclaiming History*, 707, 947; Clarke, *American Assassins*, 118; Kirkham, Levy, and Crotty, *Assassination and Political Violence*, 61; Swanson, *End of Days*, 57.

203   Bugliosi, *Reclaiming History*, 112; Clarke, *American Assassins*, 119-20; Feinman, *Assassinations, Threats, and the American Presidency*, 96; Kirkham, Levy, and Crotty, *Assassination and Political Violence*, 61; Swanson, *End of Days*, 58, 59.

204   Bugliosi, *Reclaiming History*, 6; Clarke, *American Assassins*, 120-21; Feinman, *Assassinations, Threats, and the American Presidency*, 96; Swanson, *End of Days*, 59.

205   Clarke, *American Assassins*, 120-24; Feinman, *Assassinations, Threats, and the American Presidency*, 96.

206   Clarke, *American Assassins*, 124; Swanson, *End of Days*, 72-75.

207   Bugliosi, *Reclaiming History*, 3-5; Clarke, *American Assassins*, 124-25; Feinman, *Assassinations, Threats, and the American Presidency*, 96; Swanson, *End of Days*, 75-79, 81-82, 83.

208   Bugliosi, *Reclaiming History*, 6-10; Clarke, *American Assassins*, 125; Swanson, *End of Days*, 86-90.

209   Bugliosi, *Reclaiming History*, 30-31; Swanson, *End of Days*, 105-6.

210   Bugliosi, *Reclaiming History*, 39-44; Manchester, *The Death of a President*, 153-58; Swanson, *End of Days*, 122-40.

211   Bugliosi, *Reclaiming History*, 45-47; Clarke, *American Assassins*, 125; Feinman, *Assassinations, Threats, and the American Presidency*, 96; Sabato, *The Kennedy Half Century*, 11; Swanson, *End of Days*, 144-45, 157-58.

212   Bugliosi, *Reclaiming History*, 70-71; Clarke, *American Assassins*,125; Sabato, *The Kennedy Half Century*, 12; Swanson, *End of Days*, 145, 156-57.

213   Bugliosi, *Reclaiming History*, 74, 78-80; Clarke, *American Assassins*, 125; Feinman, *Assassinations, Threats, and the American Presidency*, 96-97; Kirkham, Levy, and Crotty, *Assassination and Political Violence*, 61; Manchester, *The Death of a President*, 262, 282; Sabato, *The Kennedy Half Century*, 18; Swanson, *End of Days*, 171-74.

214   The quotes are found in Swanson, *End of Days*, 181. See also Bugliosi, *Reclaiming History*, 104-7; Feinman, *Assassinations, Threats, and the American Presidency*, 97; Sabato, *The Kennedy Half Century*, 18-19.

215   Bugliosi, *Reclaiming History*, 109, 114-15, 123-26, 129-31, 134; Feinman, *Assassinations, Threats, and the American Presidency*, 97; Gladwin Hill, "Evidence Against Oswald Described as Conclusive," *New York Times*, November 24, 1963, 1, 2; Swanson, *End of Days*, 182-86.

216   Bugliosi, *Reclaiming History*, 117-18; Swanson, *End of Days*, 178-80; Wicker, "Gov. Connally Shot," 1, 2.

217   Bugliosi, *Reclaiming History*, 205-6, 336; Swanson, *End of Days*, 217, 290, 295-98.

218   Bugliosi, *Reclaiming History*, 200-4, 270-78, 419; Feinman, *Assassinations, Threats, and the American Presidency*, 97-98; Anthony Lewis, "Johnson Spurs Oswald Inquiry; President Orders FBI to Check Death—Handling of Case Worries Capital," *New York Times*, November 25, 1963, 1, 11; Sabato, *The Kennedy Half Century*, 29; Swanson, *End of Days*, 232-42.

219   Bugliosi, *Reclaiming History*, xliv-xlvi; Feinman, *Assassinations, Threats, and the American Presidency*, 98-99; Swanson, *End of Days*, 295-98.

220   Bugliosi, *Reclaiming History*, xix, 324-46; Sabato, *The Kennedy Half Century*, 133-34; Swanson, *End of Days*, 264, 283, 295-97.

221   Ayton, *Hunting the President*, 70; Bugliosi, *Reclaiming History*, xix-xxii; 369; Feinman, *Assassinations, Threats, and the American Presidency*, 100-5; Swanson, *End of Days*, 295-97. See also *Report of*

the Warren Commission on the Assassination of President Kennedy (New York: McGraw-Hill Book Company, 1964); *Report to the President by the Commission on CIA Activities within the United States* (New York: Manor Books, 1975); *Report of the Select Committee on Assassinations of the US House of Representatives* (Washington, DC: United States Government Printing Office, 1979).

222   The lack of credible evidence has not stopped the conspiracy theorists from searching—in fact, it has encouraged them to do so. See, for example, Bugliosi, *Reclaiming History*, xv, xxvi, xxxvi, xliv; Jean Davison, *Oswald's Game* (New York: W. W. Norton, 1983); Mark Lane, *Rush to Judgment: A Critique of the Warren Commission's Inquiry into the Murders of President John F. Kennedy, Officer J. D. Tippit and Lee Harvey Oswald* (New York: Holt, Rinehart & Winston, 1966); Swanson, *End of Days*, 297-98; Robert A. Wagner, *The Assassination of JFK: Perspectives Half a Century Later* (Indianapolis, IN: Dog Ear Publishing, 2016), 59-76, 318-37.

223   Bugliosi, *Reclaiming History*, 4.

224   Clarke, *American Assassins*, 17, 126-28; Swanson, *End of Days*, 297.

225   Oswald is quoted in Bugliosi, *Reclaiming History*, 891.

226   Bugliosi, *Reclaiming History*, 313-14; Feinman, *Assassinations, Threats, and the American Presidency*, 99-100; Manchester, *The Death of a President*, 575-603; Swanson, *End of Days*, 201-2, 242-52; Tom Wicker, "A Hero's Burial; Million in Capital See Cortege Roll on to Church and Grave," *New York Times*, November 26, 1963, 1, 2.

227   Feinman, *Assassinations, Threats, and the American Presidency*, 83-84, 104-5.

228   James W. Clarke, *American Assassins: The Darker Side of Politics* (Princeton, NJ: Princeton University Press, 1982), 128; "Hijacker Kills 2 and Then Himself," *New York Times*, February 23, 1974, 65.

229   Byck's quote, "The next one will be in the head," is found in Clarke, *American Assassins*, 128. See also Sam MacDonald, "Hijacker Targeted President in 1974," *Insight on the News* 18, no. 23 (June 24, 2002): 24.

230   Loftin is quoted in Clarke, *American Assassins*, 128-29. See also Ronald L. Feinman, *Assassinations, Threats, and the American Presidency: From Andrew Jackson to Barack Obama* (Lanham, MD: Rowman & Littlefield, 2015), 140.

231   Clarke, *American Assassins*, 128-29; Feinman, *Assassinations, Threats, and the American Presidency*, 140; "Hijacker Kills 2 and Then Himself," 61, 65.

232   Clarke, *American Assassins*, 129; Feinman, *Assassinations, Threats, and the American Presidency*, 138.

233   Clarke, *American Assassins*, 129-30; "Hijacker Had Picketed White House," *New York Times*, February 24, 1974, 34.

234   Clarke, *American Assassins*, 130-31; Andrew Milner, "C'mon and Shoot a President: The Historical People Behind the Characters in Assassins," *The Sondheim Review* 22, no. 1 (Winter 2015): 13.

235   Richard Perlstein, *Nixonland: The Rise of a President and the Fracturing of America* (New York: Scribner, 2008), 23, 28-29, 340-43, 381-82, 516, 545, 547.

236   Clarke, *American Assassins*, 131; Feinman, *Assassinations, Threats, and the American Presidency*, 138; Milner, "C'mon and Shoot a President," 13.

237   The quotes appear in Clarke, *American Assassins*, 131. See also Feinman, *Assassinations, Threats, and the American Presidency*, 138.

238   Byck is quoted in Clarke, *American Assassins*, 131.

239   Clarke, *American Assassins*, 132; "Hijacker Had Picketed White House," 34.

240   Clarke, *American Assassins*, 132; Feinman, *Assassinations, Threats, and the American Presidency*, 138; "Hijacker Had Picketed White House," 34.

241   Clarke, *American Assassins*, 133; Milner, "C'mon and Shoot a President," 14.

242   Byck is quoted in "Hijacker Had Picketed White House," 34. See also Clarke, *American Assassins*, 133; Feinman, *Assassinations, Threats, and the American Presidency*, 138; Milner, "C'mon and Shoot a President," 14.

243   Byck is quoted in *American Assassins*, 134. See also Feinman, *Assassinations, Threats, and the American Presidency*, 139, 140; Milner, "C'mon and Shoot a President," 14.

244 Byck is quoted in *American Assassins*, 141. See also Feinman, *Assassinations, Threats, and the American Presidency*, 139.

245 Clarke, *American Assassins*, 141-42.

246 Clarke, *American Assassins*, 141-42; Feinman, *Assassinations, Threats, and the American Presidency*, 138-40; "Hijacker Had Picketed White House," 34; Milner, "C'mon and Shoot a President," 13-14.

247 Mel Ayton, *Hunting the President: Threats, Plots, and Assassination Attempts—From FDR to Obama* (Washington, DC: Regnery History, 2014), 109; Douglas Brinkley, *Gerald R. Ford* (New York: Times Books, 2007), 51-52, 62-63; "Gerald Ford Dies; Nixon's Successor in '74 Crisis was 93," *New York Times*, December 27, 2006, A1; James Naughton and Adam Clymer, "President Gerald R. Ford, Who Led US Out of Watergate Era, Dies at 93," *New York Times*, December 28, 2006, A31, A32.

248 Ayton, *Hunting the President*, 109-10; Brinkley, *Gerald R. Ford*, 60-61; 67-69; John Herbers, "No Conditions Set; Action Taken to Spare Nation and Ex-Chief, President Asserts," *New York Times*, September 9, 1974, 1; Tom Wicker, "A New Kind of Cover-up," *New York Times*, September 10, 1974, 41.

249 Brinkley, *Gerald R. Ford*, 120, 179; Mike Mayo, *American Murder: Criminals, Crimes and the Media* (Canton, MI: Visible Ink Press, 2008), 120.

250 Ayton, *Hunting the President*, 115-16; Brinkley, *Gerald R. Ford*, 120, 179; Vincent Bugliosi with Curt Gentry, *Helter Skelter: The True Story of the Manson Murders* (New York: Bantam Books, 1975), 135, 177-80; James W. Clarke, *American Assassins: The Darker Side of Politics* (Princeton, NJ: Princeton University Press, 1982), 144-45, 147; Ronald L. Feinman, *Assassinations, Threats, and the American Presidency: From Andrew Jackson to Barack Obama* (Lanham, MD: Rowman & Littlefield, 2015), 145-46; Mayo, *American Murder*, 120.

251 Ayton, *Hunting the President*, 116; Feinman, *Assassinations, Threats, and the American Presidency*, 146; Robert D. McFadden, "Suspect was Defender of the Manson 'Family,'" *New York Times*, September 6, 1975, 1, 26; James M. Naughton, "Ford Safe as Guard Seizes a Gun Woman Pointed at Him on Coast; Follower of Manson Is Charged; Two Feet Away; A Wan President Later Urges Fight on Crime in Sacramento Talk," *New York Times*, September 6, 1975, 26.

252 Clarke, *American Assassins*, 147-48; McFadden, "Suspect Was Defender of the Manson 'Family,'" 26; Naughton, "Ford Safe as Guard Seizes a Gun Woman Pointed at Him on Coast," 26.

253 Clarke, *American Assassins*, 149-50.

254 Fromme is quoted in James W. Clarke, *Defining Danger: American Assassins and the New Domestic Terrorists* (New Brunswick, NJ: Transaction Publishers, 2012), 152. Clarke, *American Assassins*, 150-51; Feinman, *Assassinations, Threats, and the American Presidency*, 146; McFadden, "Suspect Was Defender of the Manson 'Family,'" 26.

255 Clarke, *American Assassins*, 152; Clarke, *Defining Danger*, 155.

256 Ayton, *Hunting the President*, 116; Clarke, *American Assassins*, 153; Clarke, *Defining Danger*, 155.

257 Feinman, *Assassinations, Threats, and the American Presidency*, 143-45; "Gerald Ford Dies," A1; "Gerald R. Ford," *New York Times*, December 28, 2006, A34; David Kirkpatrick, "Moderate? Conservative? With Gerald Ford, Take Your Pick," *New York Times*, December 31, 2006, C1, C4; Naughton and Clymer, "President Gerald R. Ford, Who Led US Out of Watergate Era, Dies at 93," A31, A32.

258 Feinman, *Assassinations, Threats, and the American Presidency*, 145.

259 Ayton, *Hunting the President*, 116; Clarke, *American Assassins*, 152-53; Clarke, *Defining Danger*, 154-55.

260 Ayton, *Hunting the President*, 112; "Felon Admits Guilt in Threat on Ford," *New York Times*, September 13, 1975, 28.

261 Ford is quoted in "Ford Testimony Tape in Fromme Trial Freed," *Sacramento Bee*, April 7, 1987, B1. Fromme is quoted in Ayton, *Hunting the President*, 117. See also Clarke, *American Assassins*, 152-53; Clarke, *Defining Danger*, 155; Feinman, *Assassinations, Threats, and the American Presidency*, 146-47; Naughton, "Ford Safe as Guard Seizes a Gun Woman Pointed at Him on Coast," 1, 26.

262   Buendorf is quoted in Ayton, *Hunting the President*, 117. See also John Boertlein, *Presidential Confidential: Sex, Scandal, Murder, and Mayhem in the Oval Office!* (Cincinnati, OH: Clerisy Press, 2010), 73; Feinman, *Assassinations, Threats, and the American Presidency*, 147; Naughton, "Ford Safe as Guard Seizes a Gun Woman Pointed at Him on Coast," 1, 26.

263   Fromme is quoted in Ayton, *Hunting the President*, 118.

264   Clarke, *American Assassins*, 153-54; Clarke, *Defining Danger*, 156-57; Wallace Turner, "'The Gun Is Pointed,' Miss Fromme Says; Judge Ejects Her," *New York Times*, September 12, 1975, 23, 69.

265   Clarke, *American Assassins*, 154; Clarke, *Defining Danger*, 156-57; Turner, "'The Gun Is Pointed,' Miss Fromme Says," 23.

266   Clarke, *American Assassins*, 154; Clarke, *Defining Danger*, 156.

267   Fromme is quoted in Boertlein, *Presidential Confidential*, 73. See also Feinman, *Assassinations, Threats, and the American Presidency*, 147.

268   Feinman, *Assassinations, Threats, and the American Presidency*, 147.

269   Boertlein, *Presidential Confidential*, 73; Feinman, *Assassinations, Threats, and the American Presidency*, 147.

270   Clarke, *American Assassins*, 156; Feinman, *Assassinations, Threats, and the American Presidency*, 147.

271   Ayton, *Hunting the President*, 118-19; Clarke, *American Assassins*, 156; Feinman, *Assassinations, Threats, and the American Presidency*, 148; Geri Spieler, *Taking Aim at the President: The Remarkable Story of the Woman Who Shot at Gerald Ford* (New York: Palgrave Macmillan, 2009), 19-28.

272   Ayton, *Hunting the President*, 119; Clarke, *American Assassins*, 157-60; Spieler, *Taking Aim at the President*, 28-81.

273   Andrew H. Malcolm, "Accused Ford Assailant Has Led a Tangled Life," *New York Times*, September 24, 1975, 26; Jeffrey Toobin, *American Heiress: The Wild Saga of the Kidnapping, Crimes and Trial of Patty Hearst* (New York: Doubleday, 2016), 78, 86; Spieler, *Taking Aim at the President*, 81-91; Henry Weinstein, "Suspect Asserted She Helped FBI; Also Volunteered for Civil Rights and Leftist Groups and Worked for Hearst," *New York Times*, September 23, 1975; 77, 26.

274   Clarke, *American Assassins*, 160-61; Malcolm, "Accused Ford Assailant Has Led a Tangled Life," 26; Spieler, *Taking Aim at the President*, 93-128; Weinstein, "Suspect Asserted She Helped FBI," 77.

275   Clarke, *American Assassins*, 161-63; Spieler, *Taking Aim at the President*, 109-11, 116-19, 137; Toobin, *American Heiress*, 256-57.

276   Clarke, *American Assassins*, 164; Feinman, *Assassinations, Threats, and the American Presidency*, 148; Spieler, *Taking Aim at the President*, 147-49; Weinstein, "Suspect Asserted She Helped FBI," 77.

277   Fernwood is quoted in Spieler, *Taking Aim at the President*, 154. See also Clarke, *American Assassins*, 164.

278   Spieler, *Taking Aim at the President*, 154-55.

279   Ayton, *Hunting the President*, 119; Spieler, *Taking Aim at the President*, 154-55.

280   The exchange between Pogash and Moore, including the quotes, can be found in Spieler, *Taking Aim at the President*, 155.

281   Moore is quoted in Spieler, *Taking Aim at the President*, 155.

282   Ayton, *Hunting the President*, 119; Boertlein, *Presidential Confidential*, 74; Feinman, *Assassinations, Threats, and the American Presidency*, 148; Spieler, *Taking Aim at the President*, 156-57.

283   A difference of opinion exists as to whether Moore fired the first shot and then Sipple struck her hand before she could squeeze off a second shot or whether Sipple deflected the first shot and prevented even the possibility of a second shot. For information on Sipple acting after the first shot was fired, see, for example, Feinman, *Assassinations, Threats, and the American Presidency*, 148, and Spieler, *Taking Aim at the President*, 156. For the notion that Sipple deflected the first shot, see, for example, Ayton, *Hunting the President*, 119, and Philip Shabecoff, "2d Coast Episode: The Suspect Had Been Queried but Freed by Secret Service," *New York Times*, September 23, 1975, 1. All sources agree that Moore fired only one shot.

284 Spieler, *Taking Aim at the President*, 156.

285 Hettrich is quoted in Shabecoff, "2d Coast Episode," 1.

286 Hettrich is quoted in Spieler, *Taking Aim at the President*, 157.

287 Spieler, *Taking Aim at the President*, 161-62.

288 Moore is quoted in Spieler, *Taking Aim at the President*, 159, 160.

289 The statement is quoted in Spieler, *Taking Aim at the President*, 177-78. See also Ayton, *Hunting the President*, 119; Feinman, *Assassinations, Threats, and the American Presidency*, 149.

290 Judge Conti is quoted in Spieler, *Taking Aim at the President*, 183, 184.

291 Randal C. Archibold, "One of Ford's Would-Be Assassins Is Paroled," *New York Times*, January 1, 2008, A15; Spieler, *Taking Aim at the President*, 185-203.

292 Spieler, *Taking Aim at the President*, 205-15.

293 Archibold, "One of Ford's Would-Be Assassins is Paroled," A15; Ayton, *Hunting the President*, 119-20; Feinman, *Assassinations, Threats, and the American Presidency*, 149; "Gerald Ford Dies," A1; Naughton and Clymer, "President Gerald R. Ford, Who Led US Out of Watergate Era, Dies at 93," A31, A32; Spieler, *Taking Aim at the President*, 214-15.

294 Clarke, *American Assassins*, 165; 17, Mayo, *American Murder*, 120.

295 Mel Ayton, *Hunting the President: Threats, Plots, and Assassination Attempts—From FDR to Obama* (Washington, DC: Regnery History, 2014), 143-45; William S. Connery, "The Zero Year Curse," *World & I* 16, no. 6 (June 2001): 180-89; Ronald L. Feinman, *Assassinations, Threats, and the American Presidency: From Andrew Jackson to Barack Obama* (Lanham, MD: Rowman & Littlefield, 2015), 151-53.

296 H. W. Brands, *Reagan: The Life* (New York: Anchor Books, 2016), 10-12, 56-57; Del Quentin Wilber, *Rawhide Down: The Near Assassination of Ronald Reagan* (New York: Henry Holt, 2011), 9; Sean Wilentz, *The Age of Reagan: A History, 1974-2008* (New York: Harper, 2008), 130-31.

297 Brands, *Reagan*, 1-5, 192-206; Feinman, *Assassinations, Threats, and the American Presidency*, 152; Wilber, *Rawhide Down*, 9-10; Wilentz, *The Age of Reagan*, 65-69, 132-34.

298 Brands, *Reagan*, 237-38; Lou Cannon, *President Reagan: The Role of a Lifetime* (New York: Public Affairs Books, 2000); Feinman, *Assassinations, Threats, and the American Presidency*, 152; Wilber, *Rawhide Down*, 10.

299 Cannon, *President Reagan*, 85; Philip Jenkins, *Decade of Nightmares: The End of the Sixties and the Making of Eighties America* (Oxford and New York: Oxford University Press, 2006), 1-23, 153-62, 175, 217-18, 230-31; Wilentz, *The Age of Reagan*, 53-55, 85-92, 115-19, 123-24.

300 Jenkins, *Decade of Nightmares*, 171-88; Wilentz, *The Age of Reagan*, 127-29.

301 Cannon, *President Reagan*, 197; Jenkins, *Decade of Nightmares*, 179-83.

302 Brands, *Reagan*, 284-85; Richard Reeves, *President Reagan: The Triumph of Imagination* (New York: Simon & Schuster, 2005), 33; Wilber, *Rawhide Down*, 58-60.

303 The exchange is discussed and Reagan is quoted in Wilber, *Rawhide Down*, 65-66.

304 Feinman, *Assassinations, Threats, and the American Presidency*, 155; Wilber, *Rawhide Down*, 70-72.

305 "Agents Tracing Hinckley's Path Find a Shift to Violent Emotion," *New York Times*, April 5, 1981, A1, A30; Donald Capps, "John W. Hinckley, Jr.: A Case of Narcissistic Personality Disorder," *Pastoral Psychology* 62, no. 3 (June 2013): 252-53; Philip Taubman, "Suspect Was Arrested Last Year in Nashville on Weapons Charge," *New York Times*, March 31, 1981, A1, A2; Wilber, *Rawhide Down*, 21.

306 "Agents Tracing Hinckley's Path Find a Shift to Violent Emotion," A30; Feinman, *Assassinations, Threats, and the American Presidency*, 153; Wilber, *Rawhide Down*, 21-22.

307 "Agents Tracing Hinckley's Path Find a Shift to Violent Emotion," A30; Ayton, *Hunting the President*, 148; Capps, "John W. Hinckley, Jr.," 256; Feinman, *Assassinations, Threats, and the American Presidency*, 154; Jenkins, *Decade of Nightmares*, 239; Reeves, *President Reagan*, 45; Wilber, *Rawhide Down*, 37-38.

308 "Agents Tracing Hinckley's Path Find a Shift to Violent Emotion," A30; Capps, "John W. Hinckley, Jr.," 254; Feinman, *Assassinations, Threats, and the American Presidency*, 154; Jenkins, *Decade of Nightmares*, 239; Matthew L. Wald, "Teen-Age Actress Says Notes Sent by Suspect Did Not Hint Violence," *New York Times*, April 2, 1981, A1, A24; Wilber, *Rawhide Down*, 38, 54-55; Wilentz, *The Age of Reagan*, 142.

309 "Agents Tracing Hinckley's Path Find a Shift to Violent Emotion," A30; Wald, "Teen-Age Actress Says Notes Sent by Suspect Did Not Hint Violence," A24; Wilber, *Rawhide Down*, 55-57.

310 "Agents Tracing Hinckley's Path Find a Shift to Violent Emotion," A30; Wilber, *Rawhide Down*, 57-58.

311 "Agents Tracing Hinckley's Path Find a Shift to Violent Emotion," A30; Feinman, *Assassinations, Threats, and the American Presidency*, 154; Howell Raines, "Left Lung is Pierced; Coloradoan, 25, Arrested—Brady, Press Chief, Is Critically Injured," *New York Times*, March 31, 1981, A1; Taubman, "Suspect was Arrested Last Year in Nashville on Weapons Charge," A1, A2; Wilber, *Rawhide Down*, 70-71.

312 Wilber, *Rawhide Down*, 71.

313 Ayton, *Hunting the President*, 145-46.

314 Ayton, *Hunting the President*, 146; Wilber, *Rawhide Down*, 71-72.

315 Hinckley's letter is quoted in Wilber, *Rawhide Down*, 57-58. See also "Agents Tracing Hinckley's Path Find a Shift to Violent Emotion," A30; Ayton, *Hunting the President*, 146; Feinman, *Assassinations, Threats, and the American Presidency*, 155; Reeves, *President Reagan*, 45.

316 Ayton, *Hunting the President*, 146; Capps, "John W. Hinckley, Jr.," 255; Wilber, *Rawhide Down*, 69-70, 72.

317 Wilber, *Rawhide Down*, 72.

318 Feinman, *Assassinations, Threats, and the American Presidency*, 155; Raines, "Left Lung Is Pierced," A3; Wilber, *Rawhide Down*, 79-80.

319 Brands, *Reagan*, 286; Feinman, *Assassinations, Threats, and the American Presidency*, 156; Wilber, *Rawhide Down*, 77, 81-82.

320 Brands, *Reagan*, 286; Reeves, *President Reagan*, 34; Wilber, *Rawhide Down*, 80-81.

321 Delahanty is quoted and the incident is described in Wilber, *Rawhide Down*, 82. See also Ayton, *Hunting the President*, 146-47; Capps, "John W. Hinckley, Jr.," 255; Feinman, *Assassinations, Threats, and the American Presidency*, 156.

322 Ayton, *Hunting the President*, 147; Feinman, *Assassinations, Threats, and the American Presidency*, 156; Wilber, *Rawhide Down*, 82; Wilentz, *The Age of Reagan*, 142.

323 Wilber, *Rawhide Down*, 83-85.

324 The quotes and the incident appear in Wilber, *Rawhide Down*, 88-89. See also Brands, *Reagan*, 286; Feinman, *Assassinations, Threats, and the American Presidency*, 156; Raines, "Left Lung Is Pierced," A1, A3; Reeves, *President Reagan*, 34.

325 Raines, "Left Lung Is Pierced," A3; Reeves, *President Reagan*, 34-35; Wilber, *Rawhide Down*, 90-91.

326 Brands, *Reagan*, 286; Feinman, *Assassinations, Threats, and the American Presidency*, 157; Reeves, *President Reagan*, 35; Wilber, *Rawhide Down*, 94, 97, 98.

327 Parr is quoted in Wilber, *Rawhide Down*, 94. See also Reeves, *President Reagan*, 35.

328 Wilber, *Rawhide Down*, 97-100, 109-11.

329 Wilber, *Rawhide Down*, 111; Wilentz, *The Age of Reagan*, 142.

330 The exchange and quotes appear in Wilber, *Rawhide Down*, 138, 147. See also Brands, *Reagan*, 287; Cannon, *President Reagan*, 114; Feinman, *Assassinations, Threats, and the American Presidency*, 157; Raines, "Left Lung Is Pierced," A3; Reeves, *President Reagan*, 36, 38; Lynn Rosellini, "'Honey, I Forgot to Duck,' Injured Reagan Tells Wife," *New York Times*, March 31, 1981, A3; Wilentz, *The Age of Reagan*, 142.

331 Brands, *Reagan*, 286; Cannon, *President Reagan*, 90-91. On Brady's 2014 death, see, for example, Laurence Arnold, "James Brady: 1940-2014: Reagan Aide Became Gun Control Symbol; U of

I Graduate Wounded in 1981 Assassination Try," *Chicago Tribune*, August 5, 2014, 6; Feinman, *Assassinations, Threats, and the American Presidency*, 156; Jon Thurber, "Witty Reagan Aide and Gun Control Advocate," *The Washington Post*, August 5, 2014, A1.

332 Wilber, *Rawhide Down*, 228.

333 Clarke, *American Assassins*, 15.

334 Quoted in Wilber, *Rawhide Down*, 57-58.

335 Ayton, *Hunting the President*, 149; Capps, "John W. Hinckley, Jr.," 247-69; Feinman, *Assassinations, Threats, and the American Presidency*, 158; Jenkins, *Decade of Nightmares*, 239-40; Wilber, *Rawhide Down*, 228.

336 See, for example, Norman J. Finkel, PhD, "The Insanity Defense Reform Act of 1984: Much Ado About Nothing," *Behavioral Sciences & The Law* 7, no. 3 (Summer 1989): 403-19; Joe Palazzolo, "John Hinckley Case Led to Vast Narrowing of Insanity Defense," *Wall Street Journal Eastern Edition*, July 28, 2016, A3.

337 Capps, "John W. Hinckley, Jr.," 247-69.

338 "Doctor, Backing Hinckley, Tells of Letter to Murderer," *New York Times*, April 14, 1987, A18; Leslie Maitland Werner, "Request for Hinckley Leave Withdrawn: 'There Was No Attempt to Keep the Letters Secret,' Hospital Says," *New York Times*, April 16, 1987, A16.

339 Ayton, *Hunting the President*, 149-50; Jessica Gresko, "Reagan Shooter Leaves Mental Hospital," *Chicago Tribune*, September 11, 2016, 6. See also Capps, "John W. Hinckley, Jr.," 264-66.

340 Cannon, *President Reagan*, 197; Capps, "John W. Hinckley, Jr.," 159-60; Wilentz, *The Age of Reagan*, 209-44.

341 Brands, *Reagan*, 730-31; Cannon, *President Reagan*, xv; Capps, "John W. Hinckley, Jr.," 160; Wilber, *Rawhide Down*, 228-29.

342 James W. Clarke, *American Assassins: The Darker Side of Politics* (Princeton, NJ: Princeton University Press, 1982), 171-72; Harold Ivan Smith, "FDR's Near Assassination in Miami's Bay Front Park," *Illness, Crisis and Loss* 20, no. 2 (April 2012): 160; "Zangara Will Die in the Chair Today; Assassin Is to Pay Penalty in Florida State Prison at 9 AM for Cermak Slaying; Has Shown No Remorse; Eats Hearty Chicken Dinner Despite Previous Complaints—Clinics Seek His Body," *New York Times*, March 30, 1933, 11.

343 For more information on Zangara's early life and poor health, see, for example, Clarke, *American Assassins*, 167-69; "Zangara Planned Attack All Alone; Assassination Attempt Is Laid to Moroseness, Due to Chronic Ailment; Uncle Mystified by Act; Nephew, During Life in Paterson, Had No Friends and Sought Only Freedom from Pain," *New York Times*, February 17, 1933, 4.

344 H. W. Brands, *Traitor to His Class: The Privileged Life and Radical Presidency of Franklin Delano Roosevelt* (New York: Doubleday, 2008), 208; Clarke, *American Assassins*, 169; Ronald L. Feinman, *Assassinations, Threats, and the American Presidency: From Andrew Jackson to Barack Obama* (Lanham, MD: Rowman & Littlefield, 2015), 56; Smith, "FDR's Near Assassination in Miami's Bay Front Park," 169; Adrian Zita-Bennet, "Champion of the 'Forgotten Man?' FDR and the 1932 Election," *NeoAmericanist* 6, no. 2 (Spring/Summer 2013): 12.

345 Clarke, *American Assassins*, 169-70; Feinman, *Assassinations, Threats, and the American Presidency*, 56; "Zangara Planned Attack All Alone," 4.

346 Brands, *Traitor to His Class*, 208; Clarke, *American Assassins*, 169-70; Feinman, *Assassinations, Threats, and the American Presidency*, 56.

347 "Zangara Planned Attack All Alone," 4.

348 Brands, *Traitor to His Class*, 208; Clarke, *American Assassins*, 170-71.; Feinman, *Assassinations, Threats, and the American Presidency*, 57; "First Intended to Kill Hoover," *New York Times*, March 20, 1933, 11; Smith, "FDR's Near Assassination in Miami's Bay Front Park," 169; Zita-Bennet, "Champion of the 'Forgotten Man?'" 12. For more information on Zangara's travels, see especially "Zangara Planned Attack All Alone," 4.

349   Brands, *Traitor to His Class*, 208; Clarke, *American Assassins*, 171.

350   Zangara is quoted in Clarke, *American Assassins*, 171. See also Brands, *Traitor to His Class*, 208.

351   Mel Ayton, *Hunting the President: Threats, Plots, and Assassination Attempts—From FDR to Obama* (Washington, DC: Regnery History, 2014), 7-8; Clarke, *American Assassins*, 171-72.

352   Brands, *Traitor to His Class*, 208; Smith, "FDR's Near Assassination in Miami's Bay Front Park," 163.

353   Brands, *Traitor to His Class*, 209; Edward M. Burke, "Lunatics and Anarchists: Political Homicide in Chicago," *The Journal of Criminal Law & Criminology* 92, nos. 3-4 (Spring/Summer 2002): 796; Clarke, *American Assassins*, 172; Feinman, *Assassinations, Threats, and the American Presidency*, 56; Raymond Moley, "Bank Crisis, Bullet Crisis—Same Smile; Five Years of Roosevelt—and After," *The Saturday Evening Post* 212, no. 5 (July 29, 1939): 12; Smith, "FDR's Near Assassination in Miami's Bay Front Park," 163; Jean Edward Smith, *FDR* (New York: Random House Trade Paperbacks, 2008), 297.

354   Smith, "FDR's Near Assassination in Miami's Bay Front Park," 169; Smith, *FDR*, 297; "Zangara Will Die in the Chair Today," 11.

355   Moley is quoted in Brands, *Traitor to His Class*, 210. See also Moley, "Bank Crisis, Bullet Crisis," 12; Smith, *FDR*, 298.

356   Roosevelt is quoted in Brands, *Traitor to His Class*, 209. See also Feinman, *Assassinations, Threats, and the American Presidency*, 57; Moley, "Bank Crisis, Bullet Crisis," 12; Smith, *FDR*, 297.

357   The remark, probably apocryphal, is reported in several sources. See, for example, Feinman, *Assassinations, Threats, and the American Presidency*, 56.

358   Roosevelt's note is quoted in Smith, "FDR's Near Assassination in Miami's Bay Front Park," 162.

359   Brands, *Traitor to His Class*, 211; "Cermak Has Turn for the Worse; Doctors Late at Night Indicate That Crisis in Case Is at Hand; Opiate Is Administered; Zangara Blocks Move for Appeal and Lawyers Abandon the Idea," *New York Times*, February 22, 1933, 42; Feinman, *Assassinations, Threats, and the American Presidency*, 56; "First Intended to Kill Hoover," 11; Smith, *FDR*, 297-98; "Zangara Will Die in the Chair Today," 11.

360   Brands, *Traitor to His Class*, 209-11.

361   Zangara is quoted in Brands, *Traitor to His Class*, 209. See also Zita-Bennet, "Champion of the 'Forgotten Man?'" 12.

362   Brands, *Traitor to His Class*, 209, 210-11; Burke, "Lunatics and Anarchists," 797-98; Feinman, *Assassinations, Threats, and the American Presidency*, 56-57.

363   The attorney is quoted in Brands, *Traitor to His Class*, 210.

364   Zangara is quoted in Brands, *Traitor to His Class*, 210. See also Burke, "Lunatics and Anarchists," 797; "Cermak Has Turn for the Worse," 42; Clarke, *American Assassins*, 172; Feinman, *Assassinations, Threats, and the American Presidency*, 57-58; "First Intended to Kill Hoover," 11.

365   Zangara is quoted in Clarke, *American Assassins*, 172.

366   Zangara is quoted in Clarke, *American Assassins*, 172. See also Burke, "Lunatics and Anarchists," 797; Feinman, *Assassinations, Threats, and the American Presidency*, 58; "First Intended to Kill Hoover," 11.

367   Brands, *Traitor to His Class*, 211; Burke, "Lunatics and Anarchists," 797; Feinman, *Assassinations, Threats, and the American Presidency*, 58.

368   Brands, *Traitor to His Class*, 211-13; Joseph Nathan Kane, *Facts About the Presidents* (New York: Ace Books, 1976), 338-65.

369   Clarke, *American Assassins*, 173-74.

370   Dan T. Carter, *The Politics of Rage: George Wallace, the Origins of the New Conservatism, and the Transformation of American Politics*, 2d ed. (Baton Rouge: LSU Press, 2000), 418, 422; Ronald L. Feinman, *Assassinations, Threats, and the American Presidency: From Andrew Jackson to Barack Obama* (Lanham, MD: Rowman & Littlefield, 2015), 119-25; Jules Witcover, *Party of the People: A History of the Democrats* (New York: Random House, 2003), 509, 580-81.

371 Feinman, *Assassinations, Threats, and the American Presidency*, 125; James T. Wooten, "Again a Gun Alters the Politics of the Republic," *New York Times*, May 21, 1972, E1.

372 The quote appears in James W. Clarke, "Emotional Deprivation and Political Deviance: Some Observations on Governor Wallace's Would-Be Assassin, Arthur H. Bremer," *Political Psychology* 3, no. 1/2 (Spring 1981-Summer 1982): 85. See also James W. Clarke, *American Assassins: The Darker Side of Politics* (Princeton, NJ: Princeton University Press, 1982), 175-76.

373 Wooten, "Again a Gun Alters the Politics of the Republic," E1. See also Carter, *The Politics of Rage*, 418-19.

374 Carter, *The Politics of Rage*, 419-33; Feinman, *Assassinations, Threats, and the American Presidency*, 129-30.

375 Clarke, *American Assassins*, 176; Feinman, *Assassinations, Threats, and the American Presidency*, 127; Stephan Lesher, *George Wallace: American Populist* (Boston, MA: Da Capo Press, 1994), 481; Wooten, "Again a Gun Alters the Politics of the Republic," E1.

376 Carter, *The Politics of Rage*, 419.

377 Clarke, *American Assassins*, 178-79; Douglas E. Kneeland, "Now, Arthur Bremer Is Known," *New York Times*, May 22, 1972, 1, 28.

378 Clarke, *American Assassins*, 179; Clarke, "Emotional Deprivation and Political Deviance," 95; Kneeland, "Now, Arthur Bremer is Known," 28.

379 Carter, *The Politics of Rage*, 419; Kneeland, "Now, Arthur Bremer is Known," 28.

380 Clarke, *American Assassins*, 179-81; Clarke, "Emotional Deprivation and Political Deviance," 96-98; Feinman, *Assassinations, Threats, and the American Presidency*, 126-27; Kneeland, "Now, Arthur Bremer Is Known," 28.

381 Clarke, *American Assassins*, 181; Clarke, "Emotional Deprivation and Political Deviance," 98; Feinman, *Assassinations, Threats, and the American Presidency*, 126.

382 Clarke, *American Assassins*, 181; Clarke, "Emotional Deprivation and Political Deviance," 98; Kneeland, "Now, Arthur Bremer Is Known," 28.

383 Clarke, *American Assassins*, 181; Kneeland, "Now, Arthur Bremer Is Known," 28.

384 Clarke, *American Assassins*, 181-82; Clarke, "Emotional Deprivation and Political Deviance," 98-99; Kneeland, "Now, Arthur Bremer Is Known," 28.

385 Clarke, *American Assassins*, 181-83; Clarke, "Emotional Deprivation and Political Deviance," 98-100; Douglas E. Kneeland, "Police Suspect Governor Was Stalked," *New York Times*, May 17, 1972, 1, 29; Terence Smith, "Reports Hint Bremer Stalked Others: Reports That Bremer Also Stalked Nixon and Humphrey," *New York Times*, May 26, 1972, 1, 12; Martin Waldron, "Bremer, in Red, White and Blue, Was Conspicuous at Many Rallies," *New York Times*, May 29, 1972, 14; Jay Walz, "Ottawa Police Say Bremer Was Seen '10 or 12 Feet' from Nixon Motorcade," *New York Times*, June 2, 1972, 9.

386 Carter, *The Politics of Rage*, 433; Clarke, *American Assassins*, 182-86; Clarke, "Emotional Deprivation and Political Deviance," 99-103; Walz, "Ottawa Police Say Bremer Was Seen '10 or 12 Feet' from Nixon Motorcade," 9.

387 Clarke, *American Assassins*, 187-88; Clarke, "Emotional Deprivation and Political Deviance," 105-106; Kneeland, "Now, Arthur Bremer Is Known," 28; Smith, "Reports Hint Bremer Stalked Others: Reports That Bremer Also Stalked Nixon and Humphrey," 12.

388 Clarke, *American Assassins*, 183-91; Clarke, "Emotional Deprivation and Political Deviance," 105-110; Feinman, *Assassinations, Threats, and the American Presidency*, 127-28; Kneeland, "Now, Arthur Bremer Is Known," 28.

389 Clarke, *American Assassins*, 190-91; Feinman, *Assassinations, Threats, and the American Presidency*, 128; Terence Smith, "Bremer, in a Heavily Guarded Courtroom, Pleads Not Guilty to US Charges in Shooting of Wallace," *New York Times*, May 25, 1972, 30.

390 Bremer is quoted in Clarke, *American Assassins*, 191. See also Feinman, *Assassinations, Threats, and the American Presidency*, 128.

391   Scorsese's perspective is discussed in Thomas Schatz, *Hollywood: Crit Concepts V2* (New York: Routledge, 2004), 109. See also Feinman, *Assassinations, Threats, and the American Presidency*, 129.

392   Feinman, *Assassinations, Threats, and the American Presidency*, 129-30; Lesher, *George Wallace*, 482-83; James T. Wooten, "Wallace is Visited in Hospital by Nixon," *New York Times*, May 20, 1972, 1, 15.

393   Clarke, *American Assassins*, 191-93; Clarke, "Emotional Deprivation and Political Deviance," 110-12.

394   Clarke, *American Assassins*, 193.

395   M. Jackson Jones, "In the Line of Fire: A Tribute and Discussion About the Assassinations of Judge John H. Wood Jr., Richard J. Daronco, and Robert S. Vance," *Creighton Law Review* 49, no. 1 (December 2015): 3.

396   Bureau of Justice Assistance, *Protecting Judicial Officials: Implementing an Effective Threat Management Process* (Washington, DC: US Government Printing Office, June 2006), 1-2; Jones, "In the Line of Fire," 1.

397   John M. Crewdson, "El Paso is Called a Major New Hub of Drug Traffic," *New York Times*, June 17, 1979, 30; Jones, "In the Line of Fire," 2-3.

398   The quotes come from Jones, "In the Line of Fire," 3.

399   The quote "this thing is going in four or five different directions" comes from "Around the Nation: Hunt for U.S. Judge's Killer Includes Motorcycle Group," *New York Times*, May 31, 1979, 16. See also Wayne King, "New Criminal Class Is Flourishing in Sun Belt," *New York Times*, December 18, 1982, 1.

400   Quoted in Crewdson, "El Paso Is Called a Major New Hub of Drug Traffic," 1.

401   Crewdson, "El Paso Is Called a Major New Hub of Drug Traffic," 30; Jones, "In the Line of Fire," 3-4.

402   Gary Cartwright, "The Sins of the Father," *Texas Monthly* 22, no. 11 (November 1994): 100-104; Jones, "In the Line of Fire," 3-4.

403   Jones, "In the Line of Fire," 6; Wayne King, "Three Are Found Guilty in Assassination of Federal Judge," *New York Times*, December 15, 1982, A16.

404   Jones, "In the Line of Fire," 6.

405   Jones, "In the Line of Fire," 6; King, "New Criminal Class Is Flourishing in Sun Belt," 1.

406   Cartwright, "The Sins of the Father," 100-104; Jones, "In the Line of Fire," 6-7.

407   The quote "Charlie was without question a charmer" is from Cartwright, "The Sins of the Father," 101. Jahn's quote is found in King, "Three Are Found Guilty in Assassination of Federal Judge," A16. The quote that Harrelson was "highly intelligent and cunning" was found in "Convicted Killer Tells of Fear Youths Will Emulate Slaying," *New York Times*, December 16, 1982, D27.

408   Cartwright, "The Sins of the Father," 100-104.

409   Cartwright, "The Sins of the Father," 100-104; Crewdson, "El Paso Is Called a Major New Hub of Drug Traffic," 1, 30.

410   Harrelson is quoted in Cartwright, "The Sins of the Father," 103.

411   Harrelson is quoted in Cartwright, "The Sins of the Father," 103. See also "Obituaries: Florence, Colo.: Charles Harrelson, Actor's Dad and a Murderer, Dies in Prison," *The Atlanta Journal-Constitution*, March 23, 2007, D8.

412   Harrelson's quote about killing Kennedy is found in Jim Marrs, *Crossfire: The Plot that Killed Kennedy*, Revised and Expanded Edition (New York: Basic Books, 2013), 325.

413   "Obituaries: Florence, Colo.," D8; King, "Three Are Found Guilty in Assassination of Federal Judge," A16.

414   Jones, "In the Line of Fire," 1-22.

415   James W. Clarke, *American Assassins: The Darker Side of Politics* (Princeton, NJ: Princeton University Press, 1982), 15-16.

416   Jackson is quoted in Jon Meacham, *American Lion: Andrew Jackson in the White House* (New York: Random House, 2008), 221. See also Carlton Jackson, "—Another Time, Another Place—The Attempted Assassination of President Andrew Jackson," *Tennessee Historical Quarterly* 26, no. 2 (Summer

1967): 184; Meacham, *American Lion*, 298; Richard C. Rohrs, "Partisan Politics and the Attempted Assassination of Andrew Jackson," *Journal of the Early Republic* 1, no. 2 (Summer 1981): 149.

417 Tucker, "The Attempted Assassination of President Jackson: A Letter by Richard Henry Wilde," *The Georgia Historical Quarterly* 58, Supplement (1974): 194-95, 196.

418 Jackson, "—Another Time, Another Place—," 184; Meacham, *American Lion*, 298; Edward L. Tucker, "The Attempted Assassination of President Jackson,"194-95, 196.

419 Jackson, "—Another Time, Another Place—," 184; Tucker, "The Attempted Assassination of President Jackson," 194-95.

420 James W. Clarke, *American Assassins: The Darker Side of Politics* (Princeton, NJ: Princeton University Press, 1982), 196; Jackson, "—Another Time, Another Place—," 187-89; James F. Kirkham, Sheldon Levy, and William J. Crotty, *Assassination and Political Violence: A Report to the National Commission on the Causes and Prevention of Violence*, Vol. 8 (Washington, DC: U.S. Government Printing Office, October 1969), 50; Meacham, *American Lion*, 301.

421 Jackson, "—Another Time, Another Place—," 184; Tucker, "The Attempted Assassination of President Jackson," 194.

422 The historian is Tucker, "The Attempted Assassination of President Jackson," 197. Benton is quoted in H. W. Brands, *Andrew Jackson: His Life and Times* (New York: Doubleday, 2005), 503. Jackson is quoted in Tucker, "The Attempted Assassination of President Jackson," 197. See also Clarke, *American Assassins*, 195; Jackson, "—Another Time, Another Place—," 184-85; Robert V. Remini, *Andrew Jackson* (New York: Harper Perennial, 1999 [1966]), 201-202.

423 Meacham, *American Lion*, 298-99; Remini, *Andrew Jackson*, 201; Tucker, "The Attempted Assassination of President Jackson," 197-98.

424 Jackson is quoted in Jackson, "—Another Time, Another Place—," 184. See also Rohrs, "Partisan Politics and the Attempted Assassination of Andrew Jackson," 153; Tucker, "The Attempted Assassination of President Jackson," 197.

425 Brands, *Andrew Jackson*, 131-38, 188-91; Joseph Nathan Kane, *Facts About the Presidents* (New York: Ace Books, 1976), 96; Kirkham, Levy, and Crotty, *Assassination and Political Violence*, 50; Meacham, *American Lion*, 26, 29-30.

426 Irving is quoted in Meacham, *American Lion*, 254. Jackson is quoted in Meacham, *American Lion*, 255. See also Kane, *Facts About the Presidents*, 99; Kirkham, Levy, and Crotty, *Assassination and Political Violence*, 50; Meacham, *American Lion*, 254-55.

427 Jackson is quoted in Edwin A. Miles, "Andrew Jackson and Senator George Poindexter," *The Journal of Southern History* 24, no. 1 (February 1958): 62. See also Jackson, "—Another Time, Another Place—," 184; Meacham, *American Lion*, 300; Miles, "Andrew Jackson and Senator George Poindexter," 54-62; Rohrs, "Partisan Politics and the Attempted Assassination of Andrew Jackson," 154-55.

428 Poindexter is quoted in Miles, "Andrew Jackson and Senator George Poindexter," 63. Tyler is quoted in Rohrs, "Partisan Politics and the Attempted Assassination of Andrew Jackson," 155-56.

429 The Senate investigation is covered in Rohrs, "Partisan Politics and the Attempted Assassination of Andrew Jackson," 155-58. The quoted descriptions of Foy and Stewart are found on 158. See also Meacham, *American Lion*, 300-301.

430 Meacham, *American Lion*, 301; Miles, "Andrew Jackson and Senator George Poindexter," 63; in Rohrs, "Partisan Politics and the Attempted Assassination of Andrew Jackson," 158-59.

431 Brands, *Andrew Jackson*, 504-505; Clarke, *American Assassins*, 98; Jackson, "—Another Time, Another Place—," 185-90; Meacham, *American Lion*, 301.

432 Clarke, *American Assassins*, 197; Jackson, "—Another Time, Another Place—," 185-86; Tucker, "The Attempted Assassination of President Jackson," 198.

433 Key is quoted in Jackson, "—Another Time, Another Place—," 186. The discussion of insanity is found on 185-86. See also Kirkham, Levy, and Crotty, *Assassination and Political Violence*, 50; Meacham, *American Lion*, 301; Tucker, "The Attempted Assassination of President Jackson," 198.

434 Clarke, *American Assassins*, 195-98; Jackson, "—Another Time, Another Place—," 189-90; Meacham, *American Lion*, 301; Rohrs, "Partisan Politics and the Attempted Assassination of Andrew Jackson," 160; Tucker, "The Attempted Assassination of President Jackson," 198.

435 Brands, *Andrew Jackson*, 504-505; Clarke, *American Assassins*, 198; Jackson, "—Another Time, Another Place—," 190; Meacham, *American Lion*, 301; Remini, *Andrew Jackson*, 201-202; Rohrs, "Partisan Politics and the Attempted Assassination of Andrew Jackson," 160; Tucker, "The Attempted Assassination of President Jackson," 198.

436 Brands, *Andrew Jackson*, 557-58; Kane, *Facts About the Presidents*, 87; Meacham, *American Lion*, 343-45; Remini, *Andrew Jackson*, 224.

437 Kane, *Facts About the Presidents*, 99; Kirkham, Levy, and Crotty, *Assassination and Political Violence*, 49-50; Tucker, "The Attempted Assassination of President Jackson," 199.

438 The "half-crazed, pettifogging lawyer" description can be found in "A Great Nation in Grief; President Garfield Shot by an Assassin; Though Seriously Wounded He Still Survives; The Would-Be Murderer Lodged in Prison," *New York Times*, July 3, 1881, 1. See also James W. Clarke, *American Assassins: The Darker Side of Politics* (Princeton, NJ: Princeton University Press, 1982), 198-99; Ronald L. Feinman, *Assassinations, Threats, and the American Presidency: From Andrew Jackson to Barack Obama* (Lanham, MD: Rowman & Littlefield, 2015), 29; Lewis L. Gould, *Grand Old Party: A History of the Republicans* (New York: Random House, 2003), 99; James F. Kirkham, Sheldon Levy, and William J. Crotty, *Assassination and Political Violence: A Report to the National Commission on the Causes and Prevention of Violence*, Vol. 8 (Washington, DC: U.S. Government Printing Office, October 1969), 52; Richard Menke, "Media in America, 1881: Garfield, Guiteau, Bell, Whitman," *Critical Inquiry* 31, no. 3 (Spring 2005): 638.

439 Clarke, *American Assassins*, 198-99, 214; Feinman, *Assassinations, Threats, and the American Presidency*, 31-33.

440 "The Assassin's Career," *New York Times*, July 1, 1882, 1; Clarke, *American Assassins*, 199; Kirkham, Levy, and Crotty, *Assassination and Political Violence*, 52; Allan Peskin, "Charles Guiteau of Illinois: President Garfield's Assassin," *Journal of the Illinois State Historical Society (1908-1984)* 70, no. 2 (May 1977): 130.

441 "The Assassin's Career," 1; Clarke, *American Assassins*, 199-200; Feinman, *Assassinations, Threats, and the American Presidency*, 32; Kirkham, Levy, and Crotty, *Assassination and Political Violence*, 52-53; Candice Millard, *Destiny of the Republic: A Tale of Madness, Medicine and the Murder of a President* (New York: Doubleday, 2011), 48-51; Peskin, "Charles Guiteau of Illinois," 131-32.

442 Guiteau's letter is quoted in Clarke, *American Assassins*, 200. See also "The Assassin's Career," 1; Millard, *Destiny of the Republic*, 51; Peskin, "Charles Guiteau of Illinois," 132.

443 "The Assassin's Career," 1; Clarke, *American Assassins*, 201-2; Kirkham, Levy, and Crotty, *Assassination and Political Violence*, 53.

444 Luther Guiteau is quoted in Clarke, *American Assassins*, 202. See also Millard, *Destiny of the Republic*, 55; Peskin, "Charles Guiteau of Illinois," 132.

445 "The Assassin's Career," 1; Clarke, *American Assassins*, 202; Kirkham, Levy, and Crotty, *Assassination and Political Violence*, 53; Millard, *Destiny of the Republic*, 55-56, 105-6; Peskin, "Charles Guiteau of Illinois," 132-33.

446 "The Assassin's Career," 1; Peskin, "Charles Guiteau of Illinois," 133.

447 "The Assassin's Career," 1; Clarke, *American Assassins*, 202-4; Feinman, *Assassinations, Threats, and the American Presidency*, 32; Kirkham, Levy, and Crotty, *Assassination and Political Violence*, 53; Millard, *Destiny of the Republic*, 54-57; Peskin, "Charles Guiteau of Illinois," 133-34.

448 Clarke, *American Assassins*, 204; Kirkham, Levy, and Crotty, *Assassination and Political Violence*, 53; Menke, "Media in America, 1881," 643; Peskin, "Charles Guiteau of Illinois," 134; Russell Roberts, "Strangled for the Republic: The Assassination of President Garfield," *Timeline* 22, no. 3 (July–September 2005): 32.

449 Clarke, *American Assassins*, 204-5; Menke, "Media in America, 1881," 643; Millard, *Destiny of the Republic*, 95; Peskin, "Charles Guiteau of Illinois," 134; Roberts, "Strangled for the Republic," 32.

450 Guiteau's letter is quoted in Clarke, *American Assassins*, 205. See also Peskin, "Charles Guiteau of Illinois," 134-35; Roberts, "Strangled for the Republic," 33.

451 Blaine is quoted in Peskin, "Charles Guiteau of Illinois," 135. See also Clarke, *American Assassins*, 206; Kirkham, Levy, and Crotty, *Assassination and Political Violence*, 53; Menke, "Media in America, 1881," 643; Millard, *Destiny of the Republic*, 93-97, 106-8, Roberts, "Strangled for the Republic," 33.

452 Guiteau is quoted in Peskin, "Charles Guiteau of Illinois," 136. See also Clarke, *American Assassins*, 206.

453 Clarke, *American Assassins*, 206.

454 Menke, "Media in America, 1881," 643-44; Millard, *Destiny of the Republic*, 113-14; Peskin, "Charles Guiteau of Illinois," 130-36; Roberts, "Strangled for the Republic," 33; Bruce Watson, "The President and the Lunatic," *American Heritage* 61, no. 1 (Spring 2011): 38.

455 Menke, "Media in America, 1881," 643; Peskin, "Charles Guiteau of Illinois," 130.

456 Feinman, *Assassinations, Threats, and the American Presidency*, 33; Kirkham, Levy, and Crotty, *Assassination and Political Violence*, 53-54; Millard, *Destiny of the Republic*, 117, 120; Peskin, "Charles Guiteau of Illinois," 137; Roberts, "Strangled for the Republic," 34.

457 The note is quoted in "A Great Nation in Grief," 1. See also Clarke, *American Assassins*, 209; Watson, "The President and the Lunatic," 38-39.

458 Garfield is quoted in Peskin, "Charles Guiteau of Illinois," 138. See also "A Great Nation in Grief," 1; Millard, *Destiny of the Republic*, 131-32; Roberts, "Strangled for the Republic," 34; Watson, "The President and the Lunatic," 38-40.

459 Peter Carlson, "Alexander Graham Bell Scans James Garfield," *American History* 50, no. 6 (February 2016): 14; Feinman, *Assassinations, Threats, and the American Presidency*, 33; "A Great Nation in Grief," 1; Menke, "Media in America, 1881," 644; Roberts, "Strangled for the Republic," 34.

460 Millard, *Destiny of the Republic*, 131-32, 135-36.

461 The quotes come from Millard, *Destiny of the Republic*, 135-36. See also Peskin, "Charles Guiteau of Illinois," 139.

462 Guiteau is quoted in Millard, *Destiny of the Republic*, 136. See also "A Great Nation in Grief," 1; Roberts, "Strangled for the Republic," 34.

463 Guiteau is quoted in Millard, *Destiny of the Republic*, 136. See also Peskin, "Charles Guiteau of Illinois," 139.

464 Millard, *Destiny of the Republic*, 138-42; Roberts, "Strangled for the Republic," 35.

465 Millard, *Destiny of the Republic*, 139, 145-48.

466 Feinman, *Assassinations, Threats, and the American Presidency*, 33; Millard, *Destiny of the Republic*, 14-17, 156-59.

467 Millard, *Destiny of the Republic*, 207-9; "A Terrible Death Watch; Scenes in the President's Chamber Saturday Night; His Anxiety About Mrs. Garfield and His Joy on Her Arrival; Touching Incidents," *New York Times*, July 4, 1881, 1.

468 Millard, *Destiny of the Republic*, 209-10, 215-18, 224; "The President's Condition; Joyful News for the Patient Watchers in and About the White House Followed by Discouraging Tidings; His Tender Nurses; A Good Omen; No Visitors Allowed to See the Patient; Incidents of the Day," *New York Times*, July 4, 1881, 1.

469 Carlson, "Alexander Graham Bell Scans James Garfield," 14, 16; Feinman, *Assassinations, Threats, and the American Presidency*, 33-34; Menke, "Media in America, 1881," 646-47; Millard, *Destiny of the Republic*, 160-62, 173-75, 186-90, 198-204, 210-14.

470 Garfield is quoted in Millard, *Destiny of the Republic*, 216. See also Feinman, *Assassinations, Threats, and the American Presidency*, 33-34.

471 Feinman, *Assassinations, Threats, and the American Presidency*, 33-34.

472   Garfield is quoted in Millard, *Destiny of the Republic*, 227. See also Roberts, "Strangled for the Republic," 35, 36, 38.

473   Bliss is quoted in Millard, *Destiny of the Republic*, 229. See also "James A. Garfield," *New York Times*, September 20, 1881, 4. See also Carlson, "Alexander Graham Bell Scans James Garfield," 16; Clarke, *American Assassins*, 209; Feinman, *Assassinations, Threats, and the American Presidency*, 34; Menke, "Media in America, 1881," 653.

474   The exchange between Garfield and Rockwell is quoted in Millard, *Destiny of the Republic*, 228. See also Feinman, *Assassinations, Threats, and the American Presidency*, 29, 35.

475   Feinman, *Assassinations, Threats, and the American Presidency*, 29-30, 35; Millard, *Destiny of the Republic*, 19-23; "The President's Career; Heroic Work that Led Him to His Exalted Place; His Ancestors in the Revolution; Left Fatherless When a Child; Brave Efforts of His Mother to Educate Him; Services in the War and in Congress; Nominated for President; The Election and His Administration," *New York Times*, September 20, 1881, 8.

476   Feinman, *Assassinations, Threats, and the American Presidency*, 29, 30.

477   Feinman, *Assassinations, Threats, and the American Presidency*, 30; Millard, *Destiny of the Republic*, 27-28, 60.

478   Feinman, *Assassinations, Threats, and the American Presidency*, 30.

479   Feinman, *Assassinations, Threats, and the American Presidency*, 30; Kirkham, Levy, and Crotty, *Assassination and Political Violence*, 52; Millard, *Destiny of the Republic*, 42-47.

480   Feinman, *Assassinations, Threats, and the American Presidency*, 31; Gould, *Grand Old Party*, 84, 99; Joseph Nathan Kane, *Facts About the Presidents* (New York: Ace Books, 1976), 223-24.

481   James A. Garfield, "Inaugural Address," in *Inaugural Addresses of the Presidents of the United States*, Vol. I, *George Washington (1789) to James A. Garfield (1881)* (Bedford, MA: Applewood Books, 2000), 149.

482   Feinman, *Assassinations, Threats, and the American Presidency*, 34; Kane, *Facts About the Presidents*, 230; Millard, *Destiny of the Republic*, 234.

483   Millard, *Destiny of the Republic*, 234-35.

484   Guiteau is quoted in Millard, *Destiny of the Republic*, 237. See also Feinman, *Assassinations, Threats, and the American Presidency*, 35.

485   Scoville is quoted in Millard, *Destiny of the Republic*, 238. See also Stephen G. Christianson, "Charles Guiteau Trial: 1881," in *Great American Trials: From Salem Witchcraft to Rodney King*, ed. Edward W. Knappman (Detroit, MI: Visible Ink Press, 2003), 188; Clarke, *American Assassins*, 209-10; Watson, "The President and the Lunatic," 40-47.

486   Guiteau is quoted in Millard, *Destiny of the Republic*, 239. See also Carlson, "Alexander Graham Bell Scans James Garfield," 16; Christianson, "Charles Guiteau Trial," 188-89; Clarke, *American Assassins*, 209-11.

487   Guiteau is quoted in Millard, *Destiny of the Republic*, 242. See also Christianson, "Charles Guiteau Trial," 190; Clarke, *American Assassins*, 209-11; Feinman, *Assassinations, Threats, and the American Presidency*, 35; Watson, "The President and the Lunatic," 40-47.

488   "The Autopsy Begun; Guiteau's Brain Found in an Apparently Normal Condition," *New York Times*, July 1, 1882, 1; "Buried in the Jail Yard; The Last of the President's Murderer; Guiteau's Body Placed Where Body-snatchers Cannot Get at It; Carried to the Grave by Six Convicts and Interred Without Ceremony," *New York Times*, July 2, 1882, 1; Christianson, "Charles Guiteau Trial," 190; Clarke, *American Assassins*, 212-14; Feinman, *Assassinations, Threats, and the American Presidency*, 35; "The Gallows Prepared; Everything in Readiness for Guiteau's Death; No Chance of Executive Interference; The Murderer's Last Day; Visits from Relatives, Counsel, and Clergyman; The Demeanor of the Assassin," *New York Times*, June 30, 1882, 1; Millard, *Destiny of the Republic*, 244-46; Peskin, "Charles Guiteau of Illinois," 139; "A Great Tragedy Ended; The World Is Rid of a Wretched Assassin; Guiteau Expiates the Crime Upon the Scaffold; The Last Hours of a Murderer

of a President; The Scenes at the Gallows; Prayers to God and Curses for the Nation; Weeping and Sobbing, But Finally Meeting Firmly; Yells and Cheers Following the Fall of the Drop," *New York Times*, July 1, 1882, 1; Death"Guiteau's Crime," *New York Times*, July 1, 1882, 1; "Last Will of Guiteau; Disposing of His Body and His Book; a Letter to His Counsel," *New York Times*, June 30, 1882, 2; Watson, "The President and the Lunatic," 44-47.

489 Clarke, *American Assassins*, 194, 198, 214; Millard, *Destiny of the Republic*, 1, 184-86, 241.

490 Clarke, *American Assassins*, 17, 194.

491 Hanson is quoted in "The Coroner's Inquest: Story of the Assassination Told in Detail," *New York Times*, October 30, 1893, 1. See also A Member of the Chicago Press, with Author's Introductory, *Carter Harrison's Assassination: Giving a Full Account of His Tragic Death, with a Detailed Synopsis of His Eventful Life* (A. Theo. Patterson, Progressive Printer, 1893), 5-6; Richard Allen Morton, "A Victorian Tragedy: The Strange Deaths of Mayor Carter H. Harrison and Patrick Eugene Prendergast," *Journal of the Illinois State Historical Society (1998—)* 96, no. 1 (Spring 2003): 7-9, 17.

492 Edward M. Burke, "Lunatics and Anarchists: Political Homicide in Chicago," *The Journal of Criminal Law & Criminology* 92, nos. 3-4 (Spring/Summer 2002): 793; Erik Larson, *The Devil in the White City: Murder, Magic, and Madness at the Fair That Changed America* (New York: Crown Publishers, 2003), 308; A Member of the Chicago Press, *Carter Harrison's Assassination*, 5, 18-20, 27; Donald L. Miller, *The City of the Century: The Epic of Chicago and the Making of America* (New York: Simon & Schuster, 1997), 531; Morton, "A Victorian Tragedy," 6-7.

493 Harrison is quoted in Larson, *The Devil in the White City*, 328. See also Burke, "Lunatics and Anarchists," 799; "Harrison's Murder Avenged; Prendergast, the Assassin, Dies on the Scaffold," *New York Times*, July 14, 1894, 9; Miller, *The City of the Century*, 531-32; A Member of the Chicago Press, *Carter Harrison's Assassination*, 31-34; Morton, "A Victorian Tragedy," 7.

494 "Assassinated; Carter H. Harrison, Mayor of Chicago, Killed; Murderer in Custody; A Disappointed Office Seeker's Terrible Revenge; No Word of Warning; The Mayor Dies in Less Than an Hour," *New York Times*, October 29, 1893, 1. See also Morton, "A Victorian Tragedy," 7.

495 Hanson is quoted in "The Coroner's Inquest," 1. See also Larson, *The Devil in the White City*, 330; A Member of the Chicago Press, *Carter Harrison's Assassination*, 6; Morton, "A Victorian Tragedy," 7.

496 Hanson is quoted in "The Coroner's Inquest," 1. See also Burke, "Lunatics and Anarchists," 792-93; "Harrison's Murder Avenged," 9; A Member of the Chicago Press, *Carter Harrison's Assassination*, 6; Morton, "A Victorian Tragedy," 7-8.

497 Preston Harrison is quoted in Larson, *The Devil in the White City*, 330. See also "Assassinated; Carter H. Harrison, Mayor of Chicago, Killed," 1; "Harrison's Murder Avenged," 9.

498 Sophie Harrison is quoted in *The Devil in the White City*, 330. See also "Assassinated; Carter H. Harrison, Mayor of Chicago, Killed," 1.

499 The exchange between Preston Harrison and his father is quoted in Larson, *The Devil in the White City*, 330. See also "Assassinated; Carter H. Harrison, Mayor of Chicago, Killed," 1; "Shot by a Crank; Carter Harrison, Chicago's Mayor, Foully Murdered; No Word of Warning for Him; Prendergast, the Assassin, Gives Himself Up to the Police; The Mob Wanted to Lynch Him; So He was Quietly Taken to the City Hall and Put in a Dungeon; He is a Crazy Paper Carrier; Says the Mayor Promised to Appoint Him Corporation Counsel—Great Excitement and Deep Sorrow in the City," *The Atlanta Constitution*, October 29, 1893, 15; A Member of the Chicago Press, *Carter Harrison's Assassination*, 37, 39.

500 Hanson is quoted in "The Coroner's Inquest," 1. See also Larson, *The Devil in the White City*, 330-31; "Shot by a Crank," 15.

501 "Assassinated; Carter H. Harrison, Mayor of Chicago, Killed," 1; Morton, "A Victorian Tragedy," 8; "Prendergast Dies; Trembling, He Goes to His Infamous Death on the Gallows; Until the End He Hoped to Escape," *The Atlanta Constitution*, July 14, 1894, 1. One source claims that the coachman

chased the shooter to the police station and turned him into the authorities. See A Member of the Chicago Press, *Carter Harrison's Assassination*, 8-9.

502   Hanson is quoted in "The Coroner's Inquest," 1. See also "Harrison's Murder Avenged," 9; A Member of the Chicago Press, *Carter Harrison's Assassination*, 8, 37-39; Miller, *The City of the Century*, 436, 531-32.

503   "Carter H. Harrison's Career; His Stubborn Political Fights and Victories in Chicago," *New York Times*, October 29, 1893, 2; "A Great City in Mourning; Chicago Sorrows Over the Murder of Mayor Harrison; Her Citizens Grieved and Indignant; The Assassin Locked Up in the County Jail Safe from Violence; Doubts as to His Sanity," *New York Times*, October 30, 1893, 1; Morton, "A Victorian Tragedy," 9-10.

504   Prendergast is quoted in Larson, *The Devil in the White City*, 331. See also "Assassinated; Carter H. Harrison, Mayor of Chicago, Killed," 1; Burke, "Lunatics and Anarchists," 793; "Harrison's Murder Avenged," 9; Morton, "A Victorian Tragedy," 7; "Shot by a Crank," 15.

505   Prendergast is quoted in Larson, *The Devil in the White City*, 331. See also Burke, "Lunatics and Anarchists," 793; "Harrison's Murder; Inquest Over the Body of the Slain Mayor of Chicago; The Crank Prendergast in a Cell; He Coolly Reads Accounts of His Bloody Work; He Insists That He Did His Duty; The Question as to Who Will Succeed as Mayor; Testimony at the Coroner's Inquest," *The Atlanta Constitution*, October 30, 1893, 1; A Member of the Chicago Press, *Carter Harrison's Assassination*, 43-44.

506   The interrogation is quoted and summarized in "Shot by a Crank," 15. See also "Assassinated; Carter H. Harrison, Mayor of Chicago, Killed," 1; "Harrison's Murder," 1.

507   Larson, *The Devil in the White City*, 58-59.

508   Prendergast's mother is quoted in Larson, *The Devil in the White City*, 58. See also Morton, "A Victorian Tragedy," 13.

509   Larson, *The Devil in the White City*, 58; A Member of the Chicago Press, *Carter Harrison's Assassination*, 47-48; Morton, "A Victorian Tragedy," 14-15.

510   Burke, "Lunatics and Anarchists," 794; Larson, *The Devil in the White City*, 59, 183-84; A Member of the Chicago Press, *Carter Harrison's Assassination*, 56-58.

511   "Carter H. Harrison's Career," 2; Larson, *The Devil in the White City*, 214-16.

512   Larson, *The Devil in the White City*, 246, 317.

513   James F. Kirkham, Sheldon Levy, and William J. Crotty, *Assassination and Political Violence: A Report to the National Commission on the Causes and Prevention of Violence*, Vol. 8 (Washington, DC: U.S. Government Printing Office, October 1969), 31; Morton, "A Victorian Tragedy," 13.

514   Larson, *The Devil in the White City*, 317; Morton, "A Victorian Tragedy," 12.

515   Burke, "Lunatics and Anarchists," 794; Larson, *The Devil in the White City*, 317; A Member of the Chicago Press, *Carter Harrison's Assassination*, 48.

516   Larson, *The Devil in the White City*, 329.

517   Larson, *The Devil in the White City*, 331; Morton, "A Victorian Tragedy," 13.

518   Morton, "A Victorian Tragedy," 10-11.

519   "Harrison Lying in State; Viewed by Thousands in Chicago's City Hall," *New York Times*, November 1, 1893, 3; Larson, *The Devil in the White City*, 331-32; A Member of the Chicago Press, *Carter Harrison's Assassination*, 49-51; Morton, "A Victorian Tragedy," 10-11; "Victor F. Lawson's Estimate; The Editor of *The Chicago News* on Carter H. Harrison's Character," *New York Times*, October 30, 1893, 2.

520   Burke, "Lunatics and Anarchists," 794-95; Larson, *The Devil in the White City*, 382; Morton, "A Victorian Tragedy," 12-13, 16-17.

521   Larson, *The Devil in the White City*, 382-83; Morton, "A Victorian Tragedy," 17-20.

522   Darrow is quoted in Larson, *The Devil in the White City*, 382. See also Burke, "Lunatics and Anarchists," 794-95; Morton, "A Victorian Tragedy," 25-30.

523 Burke, "Lunatics and Anarchists," 795; "Harrison's Murder Avenged," 9; Morton, "A Victorian Tragedy," 30-32.

524 Morton, "A Victorian Tragedy," 32-33; 'Public Men and Cranks," *The Atlanta Constitution*, November 1, 1893, 4.

525 Morton, "A Victorian Tragedy," 32-33.

526 Gerard Helferich, *Theodore Roosevelt and the Assassin: Madness, Vengeance, and the Campaign of 1912* (Guilford, CT: Lyons Press, 2013), 23-31; Patricia O'Toole, *When Trumpets Call: Theodore Roosevelt After the White House* (New York: Simon & Schuster, 2005), 166-71.

527 Helferich, *Theodore Roosevelt and the Assassin*, 25-31; Lewis L. Gould, *Grand Old Party: A History of the Republicans* (New York: Random House, 2003), 181-91.

528 Gould, *Grand Old Party*, 189-91; Helferich, *Theodore Roosevelt and the Assassin*, 29-31.

529 James W. Clarke, *American Assassins: The Darker Side of Politics* (Princeton, NJ: Princeton University Press, 1982), 218-19; Ronald L. Feinman, *Assassinations, Threats, and the American Presidency: From Andrew Jackson to Barack Obama* (Lanham, MD: Rowman & Littlefield, 2015), 48; Helferich, *Theodore Roosevelt and the Assassin*, ix-xv; O'Toole, *When Trumpets Call*, 233.

530 Clarke, *American Assassins*, 218-19; Helferich, *Theodore Roosevelt and the Assassin*, 60-63; O'Toole, *When Trumpets Call*, 233.

531 Helferich, *Theodore Roosevelt and the Assassin*, 156-57; O'Toole, *When Trumpets Call*, 233-34.

532 Clarke, *American Assassins*, 214-15; Feinman, *Assassinations, Threats, and the American Presidency*, 48; James F. Kirkham, Sheldon Levy, and William J. Crotty, *Assassination and Political Violence: A Report to the National Commission on the Causes and Prevention of Violence*, Vol. 8 (Washington, DC: U.S. Government Printing Office, October 1969), 56; Rick Marschall, *Bully! The Life and Times of Theodore Roosevelt* (Washington, DC: Regnery History, 2011), 300; O'Toole, *When Trumpets Call*, 217-18.

533 Roosevelt is quoted in Helferich, *Theodore Roosevelt and the Assassin*, 174. The episode is also recounted in "His Good Nature Led Colonel into Danger," *New York Times*, October 16, 1912, 4.

534 Roosevelt is quoted in "His Good Nature Led Colonel into Danger," 4. See also Helferich, *Theodore Roosevelt and the Assassin*, 174; O'Toole, *When Trumpets Call*, 217-18.

535 The exchange and the quotes can be found in Helferich, *Theodore Roosevelt and the Assassin*, 174-76. See also Clarke, *American Assassins*, 215; O'Toole, *When Trumpets Call*, 217-18.

536 Roosevelt is quoted in Helferich, *Theodore Roosevelt and the Assassin*, 177-78. See also Feinman, *Assassinations, Threats, and the American Presidency*, 49; "His Good Nature Led Colonel into Danger," 4; O'Toole, *When Trumpets Call*, 218.

537 Roosevelt is quoted in Helferich, *Theodore Roosevelt and the Assassin*, 182. See also Feinman, *Assassinations, Threats, and the American Presidency*, 49; "His Good Nature Led Colonel into Danger," 4; Kirkham, Levy, and Crotty, *Assassination and Political Violence*, 56; O'Toole, *When Trumpets Call*, 218.

538 Edith Roosevelt is quoted in "Mrs. Roosevelt Goes to Join Her Husband," *New York Times*, October 16, 1912, 4. See also "The Attack upon Mr. Roosevelt," *New York Times*, October 16, 1912, 12; Helferich, *Theodore Roosevelt and the Assassin*, 193; "Roosevelt Gains, Bullet Located, Lodged in Rib," *New York Times*, October 17, 1912, 1.

539 Helferich, *Theodore Roosevelt and the Assassin*, 189-91.

540 Clarke, *American Assassins*, 218-19; Helferich, *Theodore Roosevelt and the Assassin*, 7-8, 9.

541 The text is quoted in Helferich, *Theodore Roosevelt and the Assassin*, 62-63. See also Clarke, *American Assassins*, 218.

542 Judge Backus is quoted in Helferich, *Theodore Roosevelt and the Assassin*, 226. See also Clarke, *American Assassins*, 220; "Schrank Owns Guilt, Callous, Then Sorry," *New York Times*, October 16, 1912, 2; "Traced on Roosevelt's Tour; Schrank Left Writings Assailing Colonel in Charleston—Movements Vague Elsewhere," *New York Times*, October 16, 1912, 5.

543 Schrank and the sheriff are quoted in Helferich, *Theodore Roosevelt and the Assassin*, 229.

544   Clarke, *American Assassins*, 220-21; Helferich, *Theodore Roosevelt and the Assassin*, 240-42; Kirkham, Levy, and Crotty, *Assassination and Political Violence*, 57.

545   Roosevelt is quoted in Helferich, *Theodore Roosevelt and the Assassin*, 237. See also Gould, *Grand Old Party*, 191-92; Joseph Nathan Kane, *Facts About the Presidents* (New York: Ace Books, 1976), 295; "World's Sympathy Shown; Crowned Heads of Send Messages to the Ex-President," *New York Times*, October 17, 1912, 2.

546   Clarke, *American Assassins*, 220-21; Kirkham, Levy, and Crotty, *Assassination and Political Violence*, 64, 65.

547   Carey Winfrey, "An Ebullient Advocate of Social Justice," *New York Times*, March 15, 1980, 23.

548   Quoted in Winfrey, "An Ebullient Advocate of Social Justice," 23. See also William H. Chafe, *Never Stop Running: Allard Lowenstein and the Struggle to Save American Liberalism* (New York: Basic Books, 1993), 1.

549   Quoted in See also David Harris, *Dreams Die Hard* (New York: St. Martin's/Marek, 1982), 10. See also Chafe, *Never Stop Running*, 88-89; Winfrey, "An Ebullient Advocate of Social Justice," 23.

550   Winfrey, "An Ebullient Advocate of Social Justice," 23.

551   Quoted in Harris, *Dreams Die Hard*, 8. See also page 11.

552   Chafe, *Never Stop Running*, 149-50; Winfrey, "An Ebullient Advocate of Social Justice," 23.

553   Harris, *Dreams Die Hard*, 17. See also Paul L. Montgomery, "Lowenstein Death Had Roots in Bitter 60's," *New York Times*, March 17, 1980, B1; Winfrey, "An Ebullient Advocate of Social Justice," 23.

554   "Ex-Rep. Lowenstein Killed by a Gunman; Antiwar Leader Shot at Law Office—Former Co-Worker is Held," *New York Times*, March 15, 1980, 1; Harris, *Dreams Die Hard*, 19-21; Montgomery, "Lowenstein Death Had Roots in Bitter 60's," B1; Paul L. Montgomery, "Lowenstein Hailed by Many Mourners; Suspect Is Arraigned as Kennedy, Carter and Carey Pay Tribute to Civil Rights Leader," *New York Times*, March 16, 1980, 43; Winfrey, "An Ebullient Advocate of Social Justice," 23.

555   "Ex-Rep. Lowenstein Killed by a Gunman," 1, 23; Montgomery, "Lowenstein Death Had Roots in Bitter 60's," B1, B9; Bruce Watson, *Freedom Summer: The Savage Season That Made Mississippi Burn and Made America a Democracy* (New York: Viking, 2010), 63.

556   Montgomery, "Lowenstein Hailed by Many Mourners," 43.

557   "Ex-Rep. Lowenstein Killed by a Gunman," 23; Montgomery, "Lowenstein Death Had Roots in Bitter 60's," B9.

558   Harris, *Dreams Die Hard*, 60-89; Montgomery, "Lowenstein Death Had Roots in Bitter 60's," B9.

559   Chafe, *Never Stop Running*, 104-5; Harris, *Dreams Die Hard*, 169-73; Montgomery, "Lowenstein Death Had Roots in Bitter 60's," B9.

560   Lowenstein quoted in Harris, *Dreams Die Hard*, 89.

561   Chafe, *Never Stop Running*, 83, 84, 122-30; Harris, *Dreams Die Hard*, 108-10; John B. Judis, "The Activist as Hero," *The New Republic* 209, no. 17 (October 25, 1993): 42.

562   Chafe, *Never Stop Running*, 270; Harris, *Dreams Die Hard*, 24-25, 125-39.

563   "Ex-Rep. Lowenstein Killed by a Gunman," 23; Harris, *Dreams Die Hard*, 187-88; Montgomery, "Lowenstein Hailed by Many Mourners," 43; Arthur M. Schlesinger, Jr., *Robert Kennedy and His Times* (New York: Ballantine Books, 1978), 886.

564   Chafe, *Never Stop Running*, 270-71; Harris, *Dreams Die Hard*, 193-94, 232-33; Schlesinger, *Robert Kennedy and His Times*, 886-87, 892, 903, 917; Winfrey, "An Ebullient Advocate of Social Justice," 23.

565   Harris, *Dreams Die Hard*, 238-41, 247-50, 262-67, 292-93; Judis, "The Activist as Hero," 45; "The Shadow of the Gunman," *New York Times*, March 18, 1980, A22; Winfrey, "An Ebullient Advocate of Social Justice," 23.

566   Chafe, *Never Stop Running*, 402-5.

567   Winfrey, "An Ebullient Advocate of Social Justice," 23.

568   The quote is found in Harris, *Dreams Die Hard*, 293-95. See also Montgomery, "Lowenstein Death Had Roots in Bitter 60's," B9.

569 Chafe, *Never Stop Running*, 453-54; Harris, *Dreams Die Hard*, 295-96; Montgomery, "Lowenstein Hailed by Many Mourners," 43.

570 Sweeney is quoted in Harris, *Dreams Die Hard*, 296.

571 Chafe, *Never Stop Running*, 453-56; Harris, *Dreams Die Hard*, 299.

572 Harris, *Dreams Die Hard*, 301.

573 Sweeney is quoted in Harris, *Dreams Die Hard*, 302. See also Chafe, *Never Stop Running*, 455-56; David Margolick, "Lowenstein Killer Moves Toward Freedom," *New York Times*, November 1, 1992, 49.

574 Lowenstein is quoted in Harris, *Dreams Die Hard*, 302. See also Chafe, *Never Stop Running*, 455-56.

575 Harris, *Dreams Die Hard*, 264-65, 299-300, 303-4.

576 "Ex-Rep. Lowenstein Killed by a Gunman," 1, 23; is quoted in Harris, *Dreams Die Hard*, 319-20; Montgomery, "Lowenstein Death Had Roots in Bitter 60's," B9; Montgomery, "Lowenstein Hailed by Many Mourners," 43.

577 The form is quoted in Harris, *Dreams Die Hard*, 320. See also "Ex-Rep. Lowenstein Killed by a Gunman," 23.

578 Sweeney is quoted in Harris, *Dreams Die Hard*, 324. See also Chafe, *Never Stop Running*, 458; "Ex-Rep. Lowenstein Killed by a Gunman," 23; Harris, *Dreams Die Hard*, 323-24; Watson, *Freedom Summer*, 290.

579 Layton is quoted in Montgomery, "Lowenstein Death Had Roots in Bitter 60's," B9. See also Chafe, *Never Stop Running*, 458; Harris, *Dreams Die Hard*, 324.

580 Sweeney is quoted in Harris, *Dreams Die Hard*, 324.

581 Mitty is quoted in "Ex-Rep. Lowenstein Killed by a Gunman," 23. See also Chafe, *Never Stop Running*, 458-59.

582 Kennedy is quoted in "Ex-Rep. Lowenstein Killed by a Gunman," 23. See also Harris, *Dreams Die Hard*, 325-26.

583 Jacobs is quoted in Laurie Johnston, "Services for Lowenstein Recall Activism of 1960's," *New York Times*, March 19, 1980, B6. Koch is quoted in "Ex-Rep. Lowenstein Killed by a Gunman," 23. Carey is quoted in Montgomery, "Lowenstein Hailed by Many Mourners," 43. Carter's statement is quoted in Montgomery, "Lowenstein Hailed by Many Mourners," 43.

584 "Funeral for Lowenstein to be Held Tomorrow," *New York Times*, March 17, 1980, B9; Johnston, "Services for Lowenstein Recall Activism of 1960's," B6.

585 The inscription is quoted in Chafe, *Never Stop Running*, 290. See also "Allard K. Lowenstein International Human Rights Clinic," Yale.edu, https://law.yale.edu/centers-workshops/orville-h-schell-jr-center-international-human-rights/lowenstein-clinic (accessed March 22, 2017); "Gift of Norman E. Kent '71, '75 Creates Allard K. Lowenstein Memorial Civil Rights Scholarship," Hofstra.edu, http://www.hofstra.edu/home/news/pressreleases/archive/101107_lowensteinkent.html (accessed March 22, 2017).

586 The quote is found in Judis, "The Activist as Hero," 45.

587 "The City: Insanity Plea Made in Lowenstein's Death," *New York Times*, March 21, 1980, B3; John Sullivan, "Plan to Release Notorious Killer Prompts Debate about Insanity," *New York Times*, July 14, 2000, B1; Watson, *Freedom Summer*, 290.

588 Sullivan, "Plan to Release Notorious Killer Prompts Debate about Insanity," B1.

589 The "O.K. Corral" quote is from Mark Z. Barabak, Lisa Mascaro, and Robin Abcarian, "The Nation; A Calm Voice in a Divided District; Giffords Had Brushes with Danger Before. Friends Say She Was Undaunted," *Los Angeles Times*, January 9, 2011, A12. The quote on the Tea Party movement is from Tom Zoellner, "Extreme Arizona," *High Country News* 44, no. 3 (February 20, 2012), 12.

590 Barabak, Mascaro, and Abcarian, "The Nation," A12; Sheryl Gay Stolberg and William Yardley, "For Giffords, Tucson Roots Shaped Views," *New York Times*, January 15, 2011, A15. Zoellner, "Extreme Arizona," 12.

591 Kylie Smith is quoted in John Cloud, "The Troubled Life of Jared Loughner," *Time* 177, no. 3 (January 24, 2011): n.p., Time.com. http://www.time.com/time/magazine/article/ 0,9171,2042358,00.html (accessed February 7, 2017). See also Selwyn Duke, "The Lost Man Behind the Leftist Myth," *The New American* 27, no. 3 (February 7, 2011): 15.

592 Cloud, "The Troubled Life of Jared Loughner," n.p.; Duke, "The Lost Man Behind the Leftist Myth," 15; "Reports Detail Loughner's Troubling Encounters with Pima Campus Police," *Community College Week* 23, no. 2 (January 24, 2011): 3.

593 Cloud, "The Troubled Life of Jared Loughner," n.p.; McCreary, "'Mentally Defective' Language in the Gun Control Act," 821; "Reports Detail Loughner's Troubling Encounters with Pima Campus Police," 15-16.

594 McGahee's comments about "this hysterical kind of laugh" and the "lady in the back of the classroom" are quoted in Cloud, "The Troubled Life of Jared Loughner," n.p. McGahee's comment that "I would always turn back quickly" is quoted in Duke, "The Lost Man Behind the Leftist Myth," 15. Loughner's math exam response "Eat + Sleep + Brush Teeth = Math" is quoted in Jana R. McCreary, "'Mentally Defective' Language in the Gun Control Act," *Connecticut Law Review* 45, no. 3 (February 2013): 821. See also David Von Drehle, *et al.*, "1 Madman and a Gun," *Time* 177, no. 3 (January 24, 2011): 26-31.

595 The unnamed student is quoted in McCreary, "'Mentally Defective' Language in the Gun Control Act," 821.

596 The officer is quoted in "Reports Detail Loughner's Troubling Encounters with Pima Campus Police," 3. See also Cloud, "The Troubled Life of Jared Loughner," n.p.; McCreary, "'Mentally Defective' Language in the Gun Control Act," 821.

597 The quote comes from "Reports Detail Loughner's Troubling Encounters with Pima Campus Police," 5. See also Cloud, "The Troubled Life of Jared Loughner," n.p.; Barry Gault, "Lay That Pistol Down: Mental-Health Laws Weren't the Problem in Tucson," *Commonweal* 138, no. 4 (February 25, 2011): 15; McCreary, "'Mentally Defective' Language in the Gun Control Act," 821-23.

598 Loughner is quoted in "Reports Detail Loughner's Troubling Encounters with Pima Campus Police," 5.

599 McCreary, "'Mentally Defective' Language in the Gun Control Act," 820; "Reports Detail Loughner's Troubling Encounters with Pima Campus Police," 3; Zoellner, "Extreme Arizona," 14.

600 Loughner is quoted in Zoellner, "Extreme Arizona," 14-15. See also Jonathan Alter and McKay Coppins, "American Assassins," *Newsweek* 157, no. 4 (January 24, 2011): 18-22; Duke, "The Lost Man Behind the Leftist Myth," 16; Von Drehle, *et al.*, "1 Madman and a Gun," 26-31.

601 Aimee Houser, *Tragedy in Tucson: The Arizona Shooting Rampage* (Minneapolis, MN: ABDO Publishing Company, 2012), 11; Francesca Marie Smith and Thomas A. Hollihan, "'Out of Chaos Breathes Creation': Human Agency, Mental Illness, and Conservative Arguments Locating Responsibility for the Tucson Massacre," *Rhetoric & Public Affairs* 17, no. 4 (Winter 2014): 586; Stolberg and Yardley, "For Giffords, Tucson Roots Shaped Views," A15.

602 Loughner's phone message and MySpace posting are quoted in Valrie Plaza, *American Mass Murderers* (Raleigh, NC: Lulu.com, 2015), 360. See also Houser, *Tragedy in Tucson*, 8.

603 The police department spokesman is quoted in Marc Lacey, Jo Becker, and Richard A. Oppel, Jr., "Suspect Ran Red Light and Was Stopped by Police Hours Before Attack," *New York Times*, January 13, 2011, A22. The quote about Loughner composing himself after breaking into tears is found in "Tucson Gunman Before Rampage: 'I'll See You on National TV,'" *CBS News* (online), April 11, 2014, http://www.cbsnews.com/news/jared-loughner-who-shot-gabrielle-giffords-in-tucson-ranted-online/ (accessed February 7, 2017). See also Houser, *Tragedy in Tucson*, 8-9; Lacey, Becker, and Oppel, "Suspect Ran Red Light and Was Stopped by Police Hours Before Attack," A22; Plaza, *American Mass Murderers*, 360.

604 Randy Loughner is quoted in in "Tucson Gunman Before Rampage" (online). See also Houser, *Tragedy in Tucson*, 8-9; Lacey, Becker, and Oppel, "Suspect Ran Red Light and Was Stopped by Police Hours Before Attack," A22.

605   Lacey, Becker, and Oppel, "Suspect Ran Red Light and Was Stopped by Police Hours Before Attack," A22.

606   Houser, *Tragedy in Tucson*, 10-11.

607   Smith and Hollihan, "'Out of Chaos Breathes Creation,'" 586; "Tucson Gunman Before Rampage" (online); Von Drehle, *et al.*, "1 Madman and a Gun," 26-31.

608   Smith and Hollihan, "'Out of Chaos Breathes Creation,'" 586;

609   Dupnik is quoted in Smith and Hollihan, "'Out of Chaos Breathes Creation,'" 590. See also G. Thomas Goodnight, "Gabrielle Giffords: A Study in Civil Courage," *Rhetoric & Public Affairs* 17, no. 4 (Winter 2014): 680; Zoellner, "Extreme Arizona," 15.

610   Swanson is quoted in Cloud, "The Troubled Life of Jared Loughner," n.p.. Spillius is quoted in Smith and Hollihan, "'Out of Chaos Breathes Creation,'" 591. See also Beth L. Boser and Randall A. Lake, "'Enduring' Incivility: Sarah Palin and the Tucson Tragedy," *Rhetoric & Public Affairs* 17, no. 4 (Winter 2014): 619-52; Smith and Hollihan, "'Out of Chaos Breathes Creation,'" 591-92; Von Drehle, *et al.*, "1 Madman and a Gun," 26-31.

611   Alex Newman, "Tragic Response to a Tragedy," *The New American* 27, no. 3 (February 7, 2011): 14.

612   Duke, "The Lost Man Behind the Leftist Myth," 16.

613   John Podhoretz, "Manipulating a Massacre," *Commentary* 131, no. 2 (February 2011): 1. See also Killings in Tucson," *Commonweal* 138, no. 2 (January 11, 2011): 5.

614   Barak Obama, "In Christina We See All of Our Children," *Vital Speeches of the Day* 77, no. 3 (March 2011): 86. See also Smith and Hollihan, "'Out of Chaos Breathes Creation,'" 604-605.

615   Ibid.

616   Ibid.

617   Ibid.

618   Ibid., 87.

619   Ibid. See also Katharine Q. Seelye, "Office Staff for Giffords is a 'Family,'" *New York Times*, January 10, 2011, A11.

620   Obama, "In Christina We See All of Our Children," 87.

621   Ibid., 87, 88.

622   Ibid., 88.

623   Ibid.

624   Goodnight, "Gabrielle Giffords," 689.

625   Gabrielle Giffords and Mark Kelly with Jeffrey Zaslow, *Gabby: A Story of Courage and Hope* (New York: Scribner, 2011), 299.

626   Goodnight, "Gabrielle Giffords," 690-92.

627   Marc Lacey, "In Tucson, Loughner Enters Plea: Not Guilty," *New York Times*, March 10, 2011, A17; "Not Guilty Plea Entered by Loughner on 49 Counts," *Inside Tucson Business* 20, no. 42 (March 11, 2011): 3.

628   Marisol Bello, "Loughner's Lawyer Is 'One-Woman Dream Team,'" *USA Today*, January 11, 2011, 7A. Jennifer Percy, "The Woman Who Saves the Worst People Among Us," *Esquire* 163, nos. 6/7 (June/July 2015): 106, 153; John Schwartz, "In Tucson Case, a Federal Judge Both 'General and Traffic Cop,'" *New York Times*, January 14, 2011, A18.

629   Andy Coghlan, "Gunman Might Stand Trial After Forcible Medication," *New Scientist* 211, no. 2820 (July 9, 2011): 11; Plaza, *American Mass Murderers*, 364; Gary Slapper, "Opinion: Changing Madness to Badness," *The Journal of Criminal Law* 75, no. 5 (October 2011): 337-40.

630   Jessie Kissinger, "I Cover My Face with My Hands," *Esquire* 158, no. 5 (December 2012): 130-32; Plaza, *American Mass Murderers*, 364; Fernanda Santos and Timothy Williams, "Gunman Gets 7 Life Terms in Tucson Shootings of Congresswoman and Others," *New York Times*, November 9, 2012, 16.

631   Brigham Young is quoted in Alex Beam, *America Crucifixion: The Murder of Joseph Smith and the Fate of the Mormon Church* (New York: Public Affairs, 2014), 7. See also Marvin S. Hill, "Carthage

Conspiracy Reconsidered: A Second Look at the Murder of Joseph and Hyrum Smith," *Journal of the Illinois State Historical Society (1998–)* 97, no. 2 (Summer 2004): 115; J. Kingston Pierce, "The Death of Joseph Smith," *American History* 36, no. 5 (December 2001): 54, 59-60.

632 Beam, *America Crucifixion*, 6-7.

633 Beam, *America Crucifixion*, 14-15; Pierce, "The Death of Joseph Smith," 56. See also Whitney R. Cross, *The Burned-Over District: The Social and Intellectual History of Enthusiastic Religion in Western New York, 1800-1850* (New York: Harper & Row, 1965).

634 See, for example, John Howard Smith, *The First Great Awakening: Redefining Religion in British America, 1725–1775* (Lanham, MD: Fairleigh Dickinson University Press and Rowman & Littlefield, 2015).

635 Daniel Walker Howe, *What Hath God Wrought: The Transformation of America, 1815–1848* (Oxford and New York: Oxford University Press, 2007), 312-13; Neil Meyer, "Falling for the Lord: Shame, Revivalism, and the Origins of the Second Great Awakening," *Early American Studies: An Interdisciplinary Journal* 9, no. 1 (Winter 2011): 142-66.

636 Charles E. Hambrick-Stowe, *Charles G. Finney and the Spirit of American Evangelicalism* (Grand Rapids, MI: William B. Eerdmans Publishing, 1996), 1-21; Rollin W. Quimby, "Charles Grandison Finney: Herald of Modern Revivalism," *Speech Monographs* 20, no. 4 (November 1953): 293-99.

637 Leonard J. Arrington and David Bitton, *The Mormon Experience: A History of the Latter Day Saints* (Champaign, IL: The University of Illinois Press, 1992), 5-7; Howe, *What Hath God Wrought*, 313; Jon Krakauer, *Under the Banner of Heaven: A Story of Violent Faith* (New York: Doubleday, 2003), 55-56.

638 Arrington and Bitton, *The Mormon Experience*, 9-14; Krakauer, *Under the Banner of Heaven*, 61-62; Ronald W. Walker, Richard E. Turley Jr., and Glen M. Leonard, *Massacre at Mountain Meadows* (New York and Oxford: Oxford University Press, 2008), 6-7.

639 Arrington and Bitton, *The Mormon Experience*, 5-7; Krakauer, *Under the Banner of Heaven*, 56.

640 Richard Lyman Bushman, *Joseph Smith: Rough Stone Rolling* (New York: Vintage, 2007), 41; Krakauer, *Under the Banner of Heaven*, 55-57.

641 Smith's description of Moroni is quoted in Beam, *America Crucifixion*, 16-17. See also Arrington and Bitton, *The Mormon Experience*, 8-12; Bushman, *Joseph Smith*, 44-45; Howe, *What Hath God Wrought*, 313-14; Krakauer, *Under the Banner of Heaven*, 57-58; Ann Tares, "History and the Claims of Revelation: Joseph Smith and the Materialization of the Golden Plates," *Numen: International Review for the History of Religions* 61, nos. 2/3 (2014): 182-207.

642 Arrington and Bitton, *The Mormon Experience*, 13-21; Bushman, *Joseph Smith*, xx, 35-36; Howe, *What Hath God Wrought*, 313-15.

643 Beam, *America Crucifixion*, 19-20; Pierce, "The Death of Joseph Smith," 58.

644 Isaac Hale is quoted in Beam, *America Crucifixion*, 16. See also Arrington and Bitton, *The Mormon Experience*, 21; Bushman, *Joseph Smith*, 89-90.

645 Beam, *America Crucifixion*, 21.

646 Beam, *America Crucifixion*, 23-24; Bushman, *Joseph Smith*, 178-79.

647 Bushman, *Joseph Smith*, 442-43; Krakauer, *Under the Banner of Heaven*, 5-6; Brian C. Hales, "Joseph Smith's Personal Polygamy," *Journal of Mormon History* 38, no. 2 (Spring 2012): 163-228.

648 Krakauer, *Under the Banner of Heaven*, 5-6; Walker, Turley, and Leonard, *Massacre at Mountain Meadows*, 6-8.

649 Bushman, *Joseph Smith*, 178-79; Walker, Turley, and Leonard, *Massacre at Mountain Meadows*, 8.

650 Arrington and Bitton, *The Mormon Experience*, 22; Bushman, *Joseph Smith*, 221; Howe, *What Hath God Wrought*, 318; Spencer W. McBride, "When Joseph Smith Met Martin Van Buren: Mormonism and the Politics of Religious Liberty in Nineteenth-Century America," *Church History* 85, no. 1 (March 2016): 150-51.

651 Beam, *America Crucifixion*, 109-25; George R. Gayler, "Governor Ford and the Death of Joseph and Hyrum Smith," *Journal of the Illinois State Historical Society (1908–1984)* 50, no. 4 (Winter

1957): 391-92; Joseph L. Lyon and David W. Lyon, "Physical Evidence at Carthage Jail and What It Reveals about the Assassination of Joseph and Hyrum Smith," *Brigham Young University Studies* 47, no. 4 (2008): 5; Pierce, "The Death of Joseph Smith," 59.

652   Bushman, *Joseph Smith*, 539-42; Howe, *What Hath God Wrought*, 725-26.

653   Governor Ford is quoted in Beam, *America Crucifixion*, 169. Joseph Smith's farewell statement to his family is found in Beam, *America Crucifixion*, 154. See also Gayler, "Governor Ford and the Death of Joseph and Hyrum Smith," 396-98.

654   Arrington and Bitton, *The Mormon Experience*, 22; Beam, *America Crucifixion*, 172-73; Bushman, *Joseph Smith*, 551-52; Howe, *What Hath God Wrought*, 725-26; Krakauer, *Under the Banner of Heaven*, 131-33, 191-92.

655   Beam, *America Crucifixion*, 178-79; Gayler, "Governor Ford and the Death of Joseph and Hyrum Smith," 406; Lyon and Lyon, "Physical Evidence at Carthage Jail and What It Reveals about the Assassination of Joseph and Hyrum Smith," 8-9, 11; Dallin H. Oaks and Marvin S. Hill, *Carthage Conspiracy: The Trial of the Accused Assassins of Joseph Smith* (Omaha, NE: The Notable Trials Library, 2013), 20-21.

656   John Taylor is quoted in Beam, *America Crucifixion*, 180. See also Lyon and Lyon, "Physical Evidence at Carthage Jail and What It Reveals about the Assassination of Joseph and Hyrum Smith," 4-50; Pierce, "The Death of Joseph Smith," 59.

657   Beam, *America Crucifixion*, 181-82; Gayler, "Governor Ford and the Death of Joseph and Hyrum Smith," 406-407.

658   Beam, *America Crucifixion*, 181-83; Barbara Hands Bernauer, "'Side by Side'—The Final Burial of Joseph and Hyrum Smith." *The John Whitmer Historical Association Journal* 11, no. 1 (1991): 17-18; Gayler, "Governor Ford and the Death of Joseph and Hyrum Smith," 407; Hill, "Carthage Conspiracy Reconsidered," 118; Oaks and Hill, *Carthage Conspiracy*, 21.

659   Beam, *America Crucifixion*, 189-91; Bernauer, "'Side by Side,'" 17-18.

660   Reverend William Brownlow is quoted in Pierce, "The Death of Joseph Smith," 59. Thomas Sharp and Governor Ford are quoted in Beam, *America Crucifixion*, 201. Bennett is quoted in Beam, *America Crucifixion*, 201, and Greely is quoted in Beam, *America Crucifixion*, 202. See also Beam, *America Crucifixion*, 207-27; Gayler, "Governor Ford and the Death of Joseph and Hyrum Smith," 408-11; Howe, *What Hath God Wrought*, 726-27; Krakauer, *Under the Banner of Heaven*, 192-96; Oaks and Hill, *Carthage Conspiracy*, 184-85.

661   James F. Kirkham, Sheldon Levy, and William J. Crotty, *Assassination and Political Violence: A Report to the National Commission on the Causes and Prevention of Violence*, Vol. 8 (Washington, DC: U.S. Government Printing Office, October 1969), 23; Marianne C. Walker, "The Late Governor William Goebel: He Fought, Killed, and Was Killed," *Humanities* 34, no. 4 (July/August 2013): 28.

662   The best source of information on Goebel's early life is James C. Klotter, *William Goebel: The Politics of Wrath* (Lexington: The University Press of Kentucky, 2009 [1977]), 5-21. See also Michael Newton, *Famous Assassinations in World History: An Encyclopedia*, Vol. I: A–P (Santa Barbara, CA: ABC-CLIO, 2014), 181.

663   The quote is found in Klotter, *William Goebel*, 2-3. See also Newton, *Famous Assassinations in World History*, 181.

664   For more on the Sanford episode, see Klotter, *William Goebel*, 33-36; Walker, "The Late Governor William Goebel," 31-32. Blackburn is quoted in Klotter, *William Goebel*, 35.

665   Walker, "The Late Governor William Goebel," 32.

666   The quote is found in Walker, "The Late Governor William Goebel," 32.

667   Goebel is quoted in Klotter, *William Goebel*, 52.

668   Goebel is quoted in Klotter, *William Goebel*, 63. The quote from the *Courier-Journal* is reproduced in Walker, "The Late Governor William Goebel," 33.

669   The quote is from Klotter, *William Goebel*, 66.

670   The quote "I ask no quarter and I fear no foe" is found in Klotter, *William Goebel*, 79. The master-servant call-and-response quote is found in Walker, "The Late Governor William Goebel," 48. See also Newton, *Famous Assassinations in World History*, 181.

671   Goebel is quoted in Walker, "The Late Governor William Goebel," 48. See also Kirkham, Levy, and Crotty, *Assassination and Political Violence*, 23, 25.

672   Klotter, *William Goebel*, 86-99; Walker, "The Late Governor William Goebel," 48.

673   Klotter, *William Goebel*, 100; Kirkham, Levy, and Crotty, *Assassination and Political Violence*, 23, 25; Newton, *Famous Assassinations in World History*, 182; Walker, "The Late Governor William Goebel," 48.

674   Klotter, *William Goebel*, 103.

675   Klotter, *William Goebel*, 103-104; Walker, "The Late Governor William Goebel," 49.

676   Klotter, *William Goebel*, 106-107; "Opinions in Washington: Effect of Goebel's Death on the Situation—Federal Troops to Leave Kentucky," *New York Times*, February 4, 1900, 2; Walker, "The Late Governor William Goebel," 49.

677   Goebel is quoted in Klotter, *William Goebel*, 107.

678   One popular anecdote has Goebel consuming his last meal and turning to his caretaker to quip, "Doc, that was a damned bad oyster." The story is probably apocryphal. Goebel's final words are quoted in Klotter, *William Goebel*, 108. See also "Death Comes to William Goebel; Hopeless Struggle for Life Continued All Day Yesterday," *New York Times*, February 4, 1900, 1.

679   Blackburn is quoted in Klotter, *William Goebel*, 2. See also "Goebel's Funeral Quiet; Great Crowd Attends the Ceremonies in the Downpour of Rain," *New York Times*, February 9, 1900, 2.

680   Kirkham, Levy, and Crotty, *Assassination and Political Violence*, 23, 25. See also "Opinions in Washington," 2.

681   Arthur Goebel is quoted in Klotter, *William Goebel*, 131.

682   Ernest G. Bormann, "Huey Long: Analysis of a Demagogue," *Today's Speech* 2, no. 3 (September 1954): 16-19; Peter J. King, "Huey Long: The Louisiana Kingfish," *History Today* 14, no. 3 (March 1964): 151; Richard D. White, Jr., *Kingfish: The Reign of Huey P. Long* (New York: Random House, 2006), ix-xii.

683   For more information on Long's early years, see, for example, Ernest G. Bormann, "A Rhetorical Analysis of the National Radio Broadcasts of Senator Huey Pierce Long," *Speech Monographs* 24, no. 4 (November 1957): 245-46; H. W. Brands, *Traitor to His Class: The Privileged Life and Radical Presidency of Franklin Delano Roosevelt* (New York: Doubleday, 2008), 296; J. Michael Hogan and Glen Williams, "The Rusticity and Religiosity of Huey P. Long," *Rhetoric & Public Affairs* 7, no. 2 (Summer 2004): 149; King, "Huey Long," 152-55; White, *Kingfish*, 5-13; T. Harry Williams, *Huey Long* (New York: Vintage, 1981 [1969]), 20-79.

684   Hogan and Williams, "The Rusticity and Religiosity of Huey P. Long," 149; King, "Huey Long," 155; White, *Kingfish*, 47-48; Williams, *Huey Long*, 90-93.

685   For information on the 1924 gubernatorial election, see, for example, Bormann, "A Rhetorical Analysis of the National Radio Broadcasts of Senator Huey Pierce Long," 244, 246; Brands, *Traitor to His Class*, 296; Hogan and Williams, "The Rusticity and Religiosity of Huey P. Long," 149; King, "Huey Long," 155; Rupert Peyton, "Reminiscences of Huey P. Long," *North Louisiana Historical Association Journal* 7, no. 4 (Summer 1976): 161; White, *Kingfish*, 18-19; Williams, *Huey Long*, 193-221, 241.

686   "Every man a king, but no one wears a crown" is quoted in Brands, *Traitor to His Class*, 296. See also Edward F. Haas, "Huey Long and the Dictators," *Louisiana History: The Journal of the Louisiana Historical Association* 47, no. 2 (Spring 2006): 136; Hogan and Williams, "The Rusticity and Religiosity of Huey P. Long," 149; Williams, *Huey Long*, 219-76.

687   Bormann, "Huey Long," 17; Peyton, "Reminiscences of Huey P. Long," 164; Jerry P. Sanson, "'What He Did and What He Promised to Do….' Huey Long and the Horizons of Louisiana Politics," *Louisiana History: The Journal of the Louisiana Historical Association* 47, no. 3 (Summer 2006): 266.

688   King, "Huey Long," 156; White, *Kingfish*, 62-87.

689   King, "Huey Long," 158.

690   Long is quoted in White, *Kingfish*, 90-91. See also Brands, *Traitor to His Class*, 296-97.

691   "Long Predicted He Would be Shot; He Told Senate Aug. 9 That Plot to Kill Him Had Been Overheard in New Orleans; Always Had a Bodyguard; Thomas Recalls Inquiry in Louisiana Revealed Hate and 'Almost Mob Desires,'" *New York Times*, September 9, 1935, 1, 3; Williams, *Huey Long*, 27, 385.

692   Long is quoted in Nicholas L. Henry, *Governing at the Grassroots: State and Local Politics* (Upper Saddle River, NJ: Prentice-Hall, 1987), 186. See also Bormann, "A Rhetorical Analysis of the National Radio Broadcasts of Senator Huey Pierce Long," 244; Hogan and Williams, "The Rusticity and Religiosity of Huey P. Long," 149; King, "Huey Long," 156; White, *Kingfish*, 105-14; Williams, *Huey Long*, 453-80.

693   John W. Scott, "Highway Building in Louisiana before Huey Long: An Overdue Re-appraisal," *Louisiana History: The Journal of the Louisiana Historical Association* 44, no. 1 (Winter 2003): 29-30, 36-38. See also Glen Jeansonne, "Huey P. Long: A Political Contradiction," *Louisiana History: The Journal of the Louisiana Historical Association* 31, no. 4 (Winter 1990): 380-81; King, "Huey Long," 156; Sanson, "'What He Did and What He Promised to Do…,'" 269.

694   Bormann, "Huey Long," 19; Bormann, "A Rhetorical Analysis of the National Radio Broadcasts of Senator Huey Pierce Long," 246, 248-49; Brands, *Traitor to His Class*, 299; Haas, "Huey Long and the Dictators," 147; Hogan and Williams, "The Rusticity and Religiosity of Huey P. Long," 150; Jeansonne, "Huey P. Long," 381; King, "Huey Long," 156-57; White, *Kingfish*, 195-200.

695   Long is quoted in Brands, *Traitor to His Class*, 297. See also Hogan and Williams, "The Rusticity and Religiosity of Huey P. Long," 149-50; Jeansonne, "Huey P. Long," 381.

696   Bormann, "A Rhetorical Analysis of the National Radio Broadcasts of Senator Huey Pierce Long," 251; Brands, *Traitor to His Class*, 195-96, 298; Hogan and Williams, "The Rusticity and Religiosity of Huey P. Long," 150; King, "Huey Long," 156-57; Sanson, "'What He Did and What He Promised to Do…,'" 264; White, *Kingfish*, 179-83.

697   Haas, "Huey Long and the Dictators," 149; Hogan and Williams, "The Rusticity and Religiosity of Huey P. Long," 157-59; Williams, *Huey Long*, 430-32.

698   "Long Predicted He Would be Shot," 3; White, *Kingfish*, 185-86; Williams, *Huey Long*, 649-52.

699   Bormann, "Huey Long," 18; Bormann, "A Rhetorical Analysis of the National Radio Broadcasts of Senator Huey Pierce Long," 255-56; Brands, *Traitor to His Class*, 323; Hogan and Williams, "The Rusticity and Religiosity of Huey P. Long," 154; King, "Huey Long," 157; Jean Edward Smith, *FDR* (New York: Random House Trade Paperbacks, 2008), 348; White, *Kingfish*, 145, 172.

700   Brands, *Traitor to His Class*, 298-99; Hogan and Williams, "The Rusticity and Religiosity of Huey P. Long," 161; Jeansonne, "Huey P. Long," 381, 383; White, *Kingfish*, 229-31.

701   White, *Kingfish*, 261-62; Williams, *Huey Long*, 861-66.

702   White, *Kingfish*, 264.

703   Brands, *Traitor to His Class*, 326; Jeansonne, "Huey P. Long," 384; "Long Predicted He Would Be Shot," 1, 3; White, *Kingfish*, 263; Williams, *Huey Long*, 864-65.

704   Alex Heard, "Exhumed Innocent," *The New Republic* 205, no. 6 (August 5, 1991): 14; White, *Kingfish*, 263-64; Williams, *Huey Long*, 865.

705   White, *Kingfish*, 263-64; Williams, *Huey Long*, 866.

706   Michael C. Trotter, "Huey P. Long's Last Operation: When Medicine and Politics Don't Mix," *The Ochsner Journal* 12, no. 1 (Spring 2012): 9, 10-12; White, *Kingfish*, 265-66; Williams, *Huey Long*, 873-75.

707   The commentator, Michael Trotter, is quoting author and amateur sleuth Ed Reed in Trotter, "Huey P. Long's Last Operation," 10.

708   Trotter, "Huey P. Long's Last Operation," 10-12. See also "Bury Senator Tomorrow; Tomb in Shadow of the Skyscraper Capitol Symbolizing Power; Baton Rouge Is Hushed; Flags Fly at Half

Staff and Silence Rules Over Boisterous State House Corridors; Legislature Works On; Coroner's Jury Returns Findings as Talk Is Heard That Killer Draws Lots in Plot," *New York Times*, September 11, 1935, 1, 17; Peyton, "Reminiscences of Huey P. Long," 164; White, *Kingfish*, 265-66, 267-68.

709   Williams, *Huey Long*, 867.

710   Bormann, "Huey Long," 17; Heard, "Exhumed Innocent," 14; White, *Kingfish*, 264; Williams, *Huey Long*, 867-69.

711   Heard, "Exhumed Innocent," 14; Williams, *Huey Long*, 870-71.

712   "Bury Senator Tomorrow," 1, 17; White, *Kingfish*, 267-68; Williams, *Huey Long*, 871-72.

713   Heard, "Exhumed Innocent," 14; Frances Frank Marcus, "Researchers Exhume Doctor's Grave to Resolve Part of Huey Long Legend," *New York Times*, October 21, 1991, A10.

714   Quoted in James W. Douglass, "The Murder and Martyrdom of Malcolm X," in *The Assassinations: Probe Magazine on JFK, MLK, RFK and Malcolm X*, eds. James DiEugenio and Lisa Peace (Port Townsend, WA: Feral House, 2003), 410. See also Peter Goldman, *The Death and Life of Malcolm X* (Omaha, NE: The Notable Trials Library, 2016 [1973]), 268; Manning Marable, *Malcolm X: A Life of Reinvention* (New York: Viking, 2011), 432-34.

715   Quoted in Theodore Jones, "Malcolm Knew He Was a 'Marked Man,'" *New York Times*, February 22, 1965, 1.

716   Philip Benjamin, "Malcolm X Lived in 2 Worlds, White and Black, Both Bitter," *New York Times*, February 22, 1965, 10; Malcolm X, *The Autobiography of Malcolm X: As Told to Alex Haley* (New York: Ballantine Books, 1992 [1965]), 1-10; Marable, *Malcolm X*, 16-32; Hans J. Massaquoi, "Mystery of Malcolm X," *Ebony* 48, no. 4 (February 1993): 40; Charles Whitaker, "Who Was Malcolm X?" *Ebony* 47, no. 4 (February 1992): 118.

717   Malcolm X, *The Autobiography of Malcolm X*, 21-23, 35-40; Massaquoi, "Mystery of Malcolm X," 40.

718   Benjamin, "Malcolm X Lived in 2 Worlds," 10; Peter Ling, "The Media Made Malcolm X," *History Today* 62, no. 1 (January 2012): 50; Malcolm X, *The Autobiography of Malcolm X*, 151-56; Marable, *Malcolm X*, 71; Massaquoi, "Mystery of Malcolm X," 42.

719   The quote about Philbert is found in Malcolm X, *The Autobiography of Malcolm X*, 158. See also Benjamin, "Malcolm X Lived in 2 Worlds," 10; Malcolm X, *The Autobiography of Malcolm X*, 156-58; Marable, *Malcolm X*, 73-74; Massaquoi, "Mystery of Malcolm X," 42, 44.

720   Will Lissner, "Malcolm Fought for Top Power in Muslim Movement, and Lost," *New York Times*, February 22, 1965, 11; Massaquoi, "Mystery of Malcolm X," 44.

721   Benjamin, "Malcolm X Lived in 2 Worlds," 10; Lissner, "Malcolm Fought for Top Power in Muslim Movement, and Lost," 11.

722   Marable, *Malcolm X*, 92-96; Massaquoi, "Mystery of Malcolm X," 44.

723   Lissner, "Malcolm Fought for Top Power in Muslim Movement, and Lost," 11; Marable, *Malcolm X*, 103-5; Massaquoi, "Mystery of Malcolm X," 44.

724   Benjamin, "Malcolm X Lived in 2 Worlds," 10; Massaquoi, "Mystery of Malcolm X," 44.

725   Quoted in Malcolm X, *By Any Means Necessary: Malcolm X—Speeches and Writings* (New York: Pathfinder Press, 1992), 61. Emphasis in the original. See also Ling, "The Media Made Malcolm X," 54; Marable, *Malcolm X*, 350-51.

726   Douglass, "The Murder and Martyrdom of Malcolm X," 380; Marable, *Malcolm X*, 127-34.

727   Douglass, "The Murder and Martyrdom of Malcolm X," 382-83.

728   Jones, "Malcolm Knew He Was a 'Marked Man,'" 1, 11; Peniel E. Joseph, *Waiting 'Til the Midnight Hour: A Narrative History of Black Power in America* (New York: Henry Holt, 2006), 76-77; Marable, *Malcolm X*, 208-10.

729   Marable, *Malcolm X*, 292-96.

730   Benjamin, "Malcolm X Lived in 2 Worlds," 10; Lissner, "Malcolm Fought for Top Power in Muslim Movement, and Lost," 11; "Malcolm X Scores US and Kennedy," *New York Times*, December 2, 1963, 21; Massaquoi, "Mystery of Malcolm X," 37.

731 R. W. Apple, Jr., "Malcolm X Silenced for Remarks on Assassination of Kennedy," *New York Times*, December 5, 1963, 22; Douglass, "The Murder and Martyrdom of Malcolm X," 383-84.

732 See also Lissner, "Malcolm Fought for Top Power in Muslim Movement, and Lost," 11.

733 M. S. Handler, "Malcolm X Splits with Muhammad; Suspended Black Leader Plans Black Nationalist Political Movement," *New York Times*, March 9, 1964, 1. See also Douglass, "The Murder and Martyrdom of Malcolm X," 378, 385; Ling, "The Media Made Malcolm X," 52; Lissner, "Malcolm Fought for Top Power in Muslim Movement, and Lost," 11.

734 Douglass, "The Murder and Martyrdom of Malcolm X," 385; Joseph, *Waiting 'Til the Midnight Hour*, 92-110.

735 Whitaker, "Who Was Malcolm X?" 122.

736 Quoted in Theodore Jones, "Malcolm Knew He Was a 'Marked Man,'" 1. See also Marable, *Malcolm X*, 418-27.

737 Malcolm X, *The Autobiography of Malcolm X*, 346-47. Emphasis in the original.

738 Joseph, *Waiting 'Til the Midnight Hour*, 114-15; Peter Kihss, "Malcolm X Shot to Death at Rally Here," *New York Times*, February 22, 1965, 10; "Malcolm Asked Gun Permit After Home Was Bombed," *New York Times*, February 22, 1965, 10; Whitaker, "Who Was Malcolm X?" 120.

739 Joseph, *Waiting 'Til the Midnight Hour*, 115; Marable, *Malcolm X*, 433.

740 Douglass, "The Murder and Martyrdom of Malcolm X," 408.

741 Goldman, *The Death and Life of Malcolm X*, 270; Marable, *Malcolm X*, 434.

742 Douglass, "The Murder and Martyrdom of Malcolm X," 412; Goldman, *The Death and Life of Malcolm X*, 271-73.

743 "Be cool now" is quoted in Kihss, "Malcolm X Shot to Death at Rally Here," 10. "Hold it!" is quoted in Douglass, "The Murder and Martyrdom of Malcolm X," 412. See also Goldman, *The Death and Life of Malcolm X*, 273.

744 Douglass, "The Murder and Martyrdom of Malcolm X," 412; Goldman, *The Death and Life of Malcolm X*, 273-74; Joseph, *Waiting 'Til the Midnight Hour*, 115; Kihss, "Malcolm X Shot to Death at Rally Here," 1.

745 Douglass, "The Murder and Martyrdom of Malcolm X,"412-13; Kihss, "Malcolm X Shot to Death at Rally Here," 1, 10; Gay Talese, "Police Save Suspect from the Crowd," *New York Times*, February 22, 1965, 10.

746 Betty is quoted in Kihss, "Malcolm X Shot to Death at Rally Here," 10.

747 Goldman, *The Death and Life of Malcolm X*, 276-77; Marable, *Malcolm X*, 439.

748 Goldman, *The Death and Life of Malcolm X*, 277; Kihss, "Malcolm X Shot to Death at Rally Here," 10; Marable, *Malcolm X*, 440.

749 Goldman, *The Death and Life of Malcolm X*, 277-78; Kihss, "Malcolm X Shot to Death at Rally Here," 10.

750 King and Wilkins are quoted in Marable, *Malcolm X*, 456.

751 Muhammad is quoted in Marable, *Malcolm X*, 446. See also Kihss, "Malcolm X Shot to Death at Rally Here," 10; Marable, *Malcolm X*, 446-47.

752 "Malcolm X," *New York Times*, February 22, 1965, 20.

753 James Loomis, "Letter to the Editor: Death of Malcolm X," *New York Times*, February 27, 1965, 24.

754 "Malcolm X," 20; Marable, *Malcolm X*, 443-46.

755 Marable, *Malcolm X*, 445.

756 Douglass, "The Murder and Martyrdom of Malcolm X," 413-14; Marable, *Malcolm X*, 451-52.

757 Douglass, "The Murder and Martyrdom of Malcolm X," 414-15.

758 Peter Kihss, "Hunt for Killers in Malcolm Case 'On Right Track,'" *New York Times*, February 25, 1965, 1, 18.

759 Ossie Davis, "Eulogy for Malcolm X: Faith Temple of God in Christ: New York City—February 27, 1965," in *Say It Loud: Great Speeches on Civil Rights and African American Identity*, eds. Catherine

Ellis and Stephen Drury Smith (New York and London: The New Press, 2010), 28-29. See also Marable, *Malcolm X*, 458-59.

760 Marable, *Malcolm X*, 454-56.

761 Nelson Blackstock, *COINTELPRO: The FBI's Secret War on Political Freedom* (New York: Pathfinder, 1988), 110-11; Taylor Branch, *Pillar of Fire: America in the King Years, 1963–65* (New York: Simon & Schuster, 1998), 243; Marable, *Malcolm X*, 293-96.

762 Quoted in Marable, *Malcolm X*, 441.

763 Taylor Branch, *At Canaan's Edge: America in the King Years, 1965–68* (New York: Simon & Schuster, 2006), 755-56; David J. Garrow, *Bearing the Cross: Martin Luther King, Jr., and the Southern Christian Leadership Conference* (New York: Quill, William Morrow, 1986), 620-21; Nick Kotz, *Judgment Days: Lyndon Baines Johnson, Martin Luther King Jr., and the Laws That Changed America* (Boston and New York: Houghton Mifflin, 2005), 412-13; Peter Ling, "Martin Luther King's Half-Forgotten Dream," *History Today* 48, no. 4 (April 1998): 18-19; Hampton Sides, *Hellhound on His Trail: The Stalking of Martin Luther King Jr. and the International Hunt for His Assassin* (New York: Doubleday, 2010), 138-40.

764 The *"arc of* the moral universe" quote can be found in many sources. See for example, Branch, *At Canaan's Edge*, 170, 771.

765 The text of the speech can be found in many sources. See, for example, Keith D. Miller, *Martin Luther King's Biblical Epic: His Final, Great Speech* (Jackson: University of Mississippi Press, 2012), Appendix A, 175-81.

766 Branch, *At Canaan's Edge*, 756-58; Garrow, *Bearing the Cross*, 621; Kotz, *Judgment Days*, 413; "Religion and Spirituality: Dr. Martin Luther King Jr.—'I've Seen the Promised land,'" *The New York Amsterdam News* 107, no. 14 (March 31-April 6, 2016): 33; Sides, *Hellhound on His Trail*, 141.

767 Garrow, *Bearing the Cross*, 11-24, 51-82; Ling, "Martin Luther King's Half-Forgotten Dream," 18; "Religion and Spirituality: Dr. Martin Luther King Jr.," 33; Alan F. Westin and Barry Mahoney, *The Trial of Martin Luther King* (New York: The Notable Trials Library, 1997), 25-31.

768 Garrow, *Bearing the Cross*, 36-51; Westin and Mahoney, *The Trial of Martin Luther King*, 23.

769 Garrow, *Bearing the Cross*, 111, 113-14, 354-55, 380-81, 387-88; Kotz, *Judgment Days*, xi-xviii.

770 Garrow, *Bearing the Cross*, 535, 609-19; Ling, "Martin Luther King's Half-Forgotten Dream," 18-19.

771 James W. Douglass, "The King Assassination: After Three Decades, Another Verdict," *Christian Century* 117, no. 9 (March 15, 2000): 309; Garrow, *Bearing the Cross*, 610-15; Kotz, *Judgment Days*, 402, 410-11, 420, 422.

772 Branch, *At Canaan's Edge*, 764; Kevin Chapell, "The Question That Won't Go Away: Who Killed King?," *Ebony* 52, no. 7 (May 1997): 37; Garrow, *Bearing the Cross*, 622-23; Sides, *Hellhound on His Trail*, 154.

773 The quotes from the exchange are found in Sides, *Hellhound on His Trail*, 163-64, 165-66. See also Branch, *At Canaan's Edge*, 766; Garrow, *Bearing the Cross*, 623; Chapell, "The Question That Won't Go Away," 37.

774 Branch, *At Canaan's Edge*, 767; Garrow, *Bearing the Cross*, 623; Kotz, *Judgment Days*, 414-15; Sides, *Hellhound on His Trail*, 166, 168-69.

775 Abernathy is quoted in Sides, *Hellhound on His Trail*, 170. Emphasis in the original.

776 Sides, *Hellhound on His Trail*, 171.

777 Ibid.

778 The exchange between Young and Abernathy is found in Ibid., 171.

779 Abernathy is quoted in Ibid., 171. See also Garrow, *Bearing the Cross*, 624.

780 Sides, *Hellhound on His Trail*, 172.

781 Chapell, "The Question That Won't Go Away," 37; Sides, *Hellhound on His Trail*, 173.

782 Sides, *Hellhound on His Trail*, 178-79, 184-86.

783   Chapell, "The Question That Won't Go Away," 37; Kotz, *Judgment Days*, 415; Sides, *Hellhound on His Trail*, 192-93.

784   Johnson is quoted in Sides, *Hellhound on His Trail*, 205. See also "Martin Luther King Is Slain in Memphis; A White Is Suspected; Johnson Urges Calm," *New York Times*, April 5, 1968, 1.

785   Sides, *Hellhound on His Trail*, 199-201.

786   Ibid., 205-6.

787   Ivan Allen, Jr., "The Night MLK Was Shot," *Atlanta* 43, no. 12 (April 2004): 49-50; Sides, *Hellhound on His Trail*, 198-99, 206.

788   Johnson is quoted in Christopher P. Lehman, *Power, Politics, and the Decline of the Civil Rights Movement: A Fragile Coalition, 1967-1973* (Santa Barbara, CA: Praeger, 2014), 42-43. See also "Martin Luther King Is Slain in Memphis," 1.

789   Farmer is quoted in "Martin Luther King Assassination," UPI.com Archives, http://www.upi.com/ Archives/Audio/Events-of-1968/Martin-Luther-King-Assassination/ (accessed March 25, 2017).

790   Carmichael is quoted in Shirley Sherrod with Catherine Whitney, *The Courage to Hope: How I Stood Up to the Politics of Fear* (New York: Atria Books, 2012), 81. McKissick is quoted in Sides, *Hellhound on His Trail*, 207. For other reactions, see, for example, Lawrence Van Gelder, "Dismay in Nation; Negroes Urge Others to Carry on Spirit of Nonviolence," *New York Times*, April 5, 1968, 1, 26.

791   The text of Kennedy's speech can be found in many sources. See, for example, Ray Boomhower, *Robert F. Kennedy and the 1968 Indiana Primary* (Bloomington: Indiana University Press, 2008), 135-36; "39 Years Ago: Robert F. Kennedy's Remarks on the Assassination of Martin Luther King Jr., April 4, 1968," *The Journal of Blacks in Higher Education* 55, no. 1 (Spring 2007): 5. For a discussion of the reaction to Kennedy's speech, see, for example, Zachary J. Martin, *The Mindless Menace of Violence: Robert F. Kennedy's Vision and the Fierce Urgency of Now* (Lanham, MD: Hamilton Books, 2009), 12-16; Jeffrey P. Mehltretter Drury and Cole A. Crouch, "Robert F. Kennedy, 'Statement on the Death of Reverend Martin Luther King, Rally in Indianapolis, Indiana' (4 April 1968) and Robert F. Kennedy, 'Remarks at the Cleveland City Club' (5 April 1968)," *Voices of Democracy* 11, no. 1 (2016): 1-24; Arthur M. Schlesinger, Jr., *Robert Kennedy and His Times* (New York: Ballantine Books, 1978), 938-43; Evan M. Thomas, *Robert Kennedy: His Life* (New York: Simon & Schuster, 2000), 366-67.

792   Drury and Crouch, "Robert F. Kennedy," 1-24; Thomas, *Robert Kennedy*, 366-68.

793   "55,000 Troops Readied for Riots," *The Atlanta Constitution*, April 9, 1968, 20; Martin Gansberg, "Damage Here Since Slaying of Dr. King is Near '64 Riot Level," *New York Times*, April 10, 1968, 35; C. Richard Hofstetter, "Political Disengagement and the Death of Martin Luther King," *Public Opinion Quarterly* 33, no. 2 (Summer 1969): 174-79; Kotz, *Judgment Days*, 415-16.

794   Chapell, "The Question That Won't Go Away," 36; Sides, *Hellhound on His Trail*, 175-77, 179-82.

795   Chapell, "The Question That Won't Go Away," 38; Sides, *Hellhound on His Trail*, 202-4; Lawrence Van Gelder, "James Earl Ray, 70, Killer of Dr. King, Dies in Nashville," *New York Times*, April 24, 1998, A25.

796   Sides, *Hellhound on His Trail*, 236-37.

797   Ibid., 249-50, 253-55, 270-71, 274-75, 282-84, 291-93, 294-305.

798   Ibid., 319-21.

799   James W. Clarke, *American Assassins: The Darker Side of Politics* (Princeton, NJ: Princeton University Press, 1982), 241-47; Richard Hammer, "Ray: Clues to a Man of Mystery," *New York Times*, June 16, 1968, E2; Van Gelder, "James Earl Ray, 70, Killer of Dr. King, Dies in Nashville," A25.

800   Clarke, *American Assassins*, 247-53.

801   Clarke, *American Assassins*, 248; Sides, *Hellhound on His Trail*, 129-30.

802   Clarke, *American Assassins*, 252-53; Hammer, "Ray," E2; Van Gelder, "James Earl Ray, 70, Killer of Dr. King, Dies in Nashville," A25.

803   Clarke, *American Assassins*, 253-54; Chapell, "The Question That Won't Go Away," 38; Fred P. Graham, "Suspect in Assassination of Dr. King is Seized in London; Ray Found Armed; Arrested at the Airport by Scotland Yard on Way from Lisbon," *New York Times*, June 9, 1968, 1; Hammer, "Ray," E2; Sides, *Hellhound on His Trail*, 390.

804   Clarke, *American Assassins*, 246-49; Chapell, "The Question That Won't Go Away," 38; Douglass, "The King Assassination," 311; "End of an Assassin," *New York Times*, April 24, 1998, A26; Sides, *Hellhound on His Trail*, 390-93.

805   Clarke, *American Assassins*, 249-57; Sides, *Hellhound on His Trail*, 390-93.

806   Chapell, "The Question That Won't Go Away," 38, 40; Sides, *Hellhound on His Trail*, 391-93; Van Gelder, "James Earl Ray, 70, Killer of Dr. King, Dies in Nashville," A25.

807   Sides, *Hellhound on His Trail*, 391-97; Van Gelder, "James Earl Ray, 70, Killer of Dr. King, Dies in Nashville," A25.

808   The exchange between Dexter King and James Earl Ray is recounted and quoted in Kevin Sack, "Dr. King's Son Says Family Believes Ray Is Innocent," *New York Times*, March 28, 1997, A22. See also Chapell, "The Question That Won't Go Away," 38, 40, 42; Douglass, "The King Assassination," 308.

809   In a wrongful death civil trial held after Ray's death, a jury determined that several conspirators, including Loyd Jowers, the white owner of a restaurant located near the Lorraine Motel, master-minded Dr. King's assassination. Despite this verdict, commentators remain divided over whether Ray acted alone—if he acted at all. See, for example, Ruben Castaneda, "A Conspiracy of Silence?," *American Journalism Review* 22, no. 2 (March 2000): 60-63; "King Family Rebukes Report That Says James Earl Ray Acted Alone in King's Death," *Jet* 98, no. 3 (June 26, 2000), 4, 6; Barbara Reynolds, "Assassins of Democracy: An American Nightmare," *Crisis* 105, no. 3 (July 1998): 10-12.

810   "Dr. Martin Luther King Buried in Atlanta; A Vast Cortege Follows Mule-Drawn Bier," *New York Times*, April 10, 1968, 1; Kotz, *Judgment Days*, 418-19.

811   Kevin Bruyneel, "The King's Body: The Martin Luther King Jr. Memorial and the Politics of Collective Memory," *History & Memory* 26, no. 4 (Spring/Summer 2014): 76-77.

812   Derek H. Alderman, "Martin Luther King Jr. Streets in the South: A New Landscape of Memory," *Southern Cultures* 14, no. 3 (Fall 2008): 88-105; Bruyneel, "The King's Body," 101-2; "President Ronald Reagan Signed Bill Establishing the Martin Luther King National Holiday," *Jet* 105, no. 26 (June 28, 2004): 56-58; "Rev. Martin Luther King Jr.'s Life and Legacy Celebrated on National Holiday," *Jet* 107, no. 5 (February 7, 2005): 5-12.

813   Barack Obama, "This is a Day That Would Not Be Denied: 'Let Us Keep Climbing Toward That Promised Land,'" *Vital Speeches of the Day* 77, no. 12 (December 2011): 421-23. See also Jeanine Barone, "In the Footsteps of a Dream: Relive the History of the Civil-rights Movement in Alabama and Georgia," *National Parks* 84, no. 4 (Fall 2010): 1; Bruyneel, "The King's Body," 75-108; Kelly Quinn, "Commemorating Martin Luther King, Jr.: The New Monument on the Mall," *Against the Current* 27, no. 1 (March/April 2012): 4-6.

814   Jerry Ray is quoted in Gerald Posner, *Killing the Dream: James Earl Ray and the Assassination of Martin Luther King, Jr.* (Boston: Mariner Books, 1999 [1998]), 54.

815   Douglas Brinkley and Anne Brinkley, "Lawyers and Lizard-Heads: The Prison Letters of James Earl Ray," *The Atlantic Monthly* 289, No. 5 (May 2002): 55-61; Castaneda, "A Conspiracy of Silence?," 60-63.

816   Clarke, *American Assassins*, 256-57; Sides, *Hellhound on His Trail*, 391-93.

817   *The Assassination of Representative Leo J. Ryan and the Jonestown, Guyana Tragedy: Report of the Staff Investigative Group to the Committee on Foreign Affairs* (Washington, DC: United States House of Representatives, May 15, 1979), 1; David Binder, "Coast Congressman Believed Slain Investigating Commune in Guyana," *New York Times*, November 19, 1978, 1, 22; Jon Nordheimer, "Leader of Sect Dies; Parents Reported to Give Children Poison Before Dying Beside Them," *New York Times*, November 21, 1978, A1; Tim Reiterman with John Jacobs, *Raven: The Untold Story of the*

Rev. Jim Jones and His People (New York: Jeremy P. Tarcher/Penguin, 2008 [1982]), 457-58, 459-60; Steven V. Roberts, "Wounded Aide to Ryan Worried and Wrote Her Will Before Trip," *New York Times*, November 21, 1978, A16; Charles Scaliger, "(South) American Killing Fields," *New American* 28, no. 6 (March 19, 2012): 38.

818   For more on the Kurtz connection, see, for example, "By Death Possessed: A Prophet, a Cult, and Mass Madness in Guyana Jungle," *New York Times*, November 26, 1978, E1. See also Scaliger, "(South) American Killing Fields," 38.

819   Holsinger is quoted in Joseph B. Treaster, "Ryan Was a Friend of Disadvantaged; Congressman's Investigations of Trouble Spots Were Marked by Personal Involvement," *New York Times*, November 20, 1978, A17. For more on Ryan's background, see, for example, Eric Pace, "He Enjoys Controversy," *New York Times*, November 19, 1978, 22.

820   *The Assassination of Representative Leo J. Ryan and the Jonestown, Guyana Tragedy*, 2. See also George Russell, "The Left's Great Crime: Jim Jones, Marxist Mass-murderer," *Commentary* 133, no. 1 (January 2012): 38; Treaster, "Ryan was a Friend of Disadvantaged," A17.

821   Scaliger, "(South) American Killing Fields," 33-34; Wallace Turner, "Dispute Over Baby Spurred Sect's Move to Guyana," *New York Times*, November 19, 1978, 22.

822   Reiterman with Jacobs, *Raven*, 24; Russell, "The Left's Great Crime," 39; Scaliger, "(South) American Killing Fields," 33-34; Julia Scheeres, *A Thousand Lives: The Untold Story of Hope, Deception, and Survival at Jonestown* (New York: Free Press, 2011), 5-6; Turner, "Dispute Over Baby Spurred Sect's Move to Guyana," 22.

823   Scaliger, "(South) American Killing Fields," 34.

824   Keith Harrary, "The Truth About Jonestown; 13 Years Later—Why We Should Still Be Afraid," *Psychology Today* 25, no. 2 (March/April 1992): 72; Reiterman with Jacobs, *Raven*, 44-46, 48-52, 53-54; Scaliger, "(South) American Killing Fields," 34; Scheeres, *A Thousand Lives*, 7-8.

825   "By Death Possessed," E1; Scaliger, "(South) American Killing Fields," 34.

826   Scaliger, "(South) American Killing Fields," 34.

827   *The Assassination of Representative Leo J. Ryan and the Jonestown, Guyana Tragedy*, 16; "By Death Possessed," E1; Russell, "The Left's Great Crime," 39; Scaliger, "(South) American Killing Fields," 34-35.

828   The quotes are found in Scaliger, "(South) American Killing Fields," 35. See also *The Assassination of Representative Leo J. Ryan and the Jonestown, Guyana Tragedy*, 16.

829   "By Death Possessed," E1; Reiterman with Jacobs, *Raven*, 268-69, 302-5, 306, 307, 573, 577; Russell, "The Left's Great Crime," 39-40; Turner, "Dispute Over Baby Spurred Sect's Move to Guyana," 22.

830   Jones is quoted in Scaliger, "(South) American Killing Fields," 34. See also Russell, "The Left's Great Crime," 39.

831   *The Assassination of Representative Leo J. Ryan and the Jonestown, Guyana Tragedy*, 16-17; Reiterman with Jacobs, *Raven*, 313-15, 324-27.

832   *The Assassination of Representative Leo J. Ryan and the Jonestown, Guyana Tragedy*, 16-17; Reiterman with Jacobs, *Raven*, 331-41; Scheeres, *A Thousand Lives*, 55-80.

833   Reiterman with Jacobs, *Raven*, 239, 272-73; Russell, "The Left's Great Crime," 40.

834   Reiterman with Jacobs, *Raven*, 246-48; Scaliger, "(South) American Killing Fields," 36.

835   Russell, "The Left's Great Crime," 40-41; Scaliger, "(South) American Killing Fields," 36-37.

836   Reiterman with Jacobs, *Raven*, 290-92; Russell, "The Left's Great Crime," 41; Scaliger, "(South) American Killing Fields," 36-37.

837   *The Assassination of Representative Leo J. Ryan and the Jonestown, Guyana Tragedy*, 16-17; Reiterman with Jacobs, *Raven*, 321-22, 333-34, 337; Scaliger, "(South) American Killing Fields," 36.

838   The text of Harvey Milk's letter can be found in "Letter of Harvey Milk to Pres. Jimmy Carter," February 19, 1978, "Alternative Considerations of Jonestown and Peoples Temple," San Diego State University

Department of Religious Studies, http://jonestown.sdsu.edu/?page_id=19042 (accessed March 27, 2017). See also Reiterman with Jacobs, *Raven*, 327, 331, 573; Russell, "The Left's Great Crime," 39-40; Scheeres, *A Thousand Lives*, 33; Turner, "Dispute Over Baby Spurred Sect's Move to Guyana," 22.

839 *The Assassination of Representative Leo J. Ryan and the Jonestown, Guyana Tragedy*, 17-19; Nordheimer, "Leader of Sect Dies," A1, A17; Russell, "The Left's Great Crime," 41.

840 *The Assassination of Representative Leo J. Ryan and the Jonestown, Guyana Tragedy*, 24-25; Scaliger, "(South) American Killing Fields," 38; Treaster, "Ryan was a Friend of Disadvantaged," A17.

841 Tim Stoen's affidavit is quoted in Reiterman with Jacobs, *Raven*, 131. See also Reiterman with Jacobs, *Raven*, 130-31; Russell, "The Left's Great Crime," 41; Turner, "Dispute Over Baby Spurred Sect's Move to Guyana," 22.

842 Nicholas M. Horrock, "FBI is Investigating Jones Plot, Using Statute on Assassinations," *New York Times*, November 22, 1978, A12; Russell, "The Left's Great Crime," 41; Turner, "Dispute Over Baby Spurred Sect's Move to Guyana," 22.

843 Russell, "The Left's Great Crime," 39, 40, 41; Scaliger, "(South) American Killing Fields," 37-38.

844 *The Assassination of Representative Leo J. Ryan and the Jonestown, Guyana Tragedy*, 3.

845 *The Assassination of Representative Leo J. Ryan and the Jonestown, Guyana Tragedy*, 3-4; "Binder, "Coast Congressman Believed Slain Investigating Commune in Guyana," 22; By Death Possessed," E1; Pranay Gupte, "Guyana Official Reports 300 Dead at Religious Sect's Jungle Temple; 6 Are Wounded Critically," *New York Times*, November 20, 1978, A16; Roberts, "Wounded Aide to Ryan Worried and Wrote Her Will Before Trip," A16; Scaliger, "(South) American Killing Fields," 38.

846 The episode is recounted and Ryan is quoted in *The Assassination of Representative Leo J. Ryan and the Jonestown, Guyana Tragedy*, 4.

847 Jones is quoted in Reiterman with Jacobs, *Raven*, 498. See also *The Assassination of Representative Leo J. Ryan and the Jonestown, Guyana Tragedy*, 4.

848 *The Assassination of Representative Leo J. Ryan and the Jonestown, Guyana Tragedy*, 5. Reiterman with Jacobs, *Raven*, 498; Scaliger, "(South) American Killing Fields," 38; "State Department Says It Told Ryan of Mission's Peril," *New York Times*, November 21, 1978, A16.

849 The note is quoted in Reiterman with Jacobs, *Raven*, 515. See also Gupte, "Guyana Official Reports 300 Dead at Religious Sect's Jungle Temple," A16; Reiterman with Jacobs, *Raven*, 473, 511, 518.

850 Sly is quoted in Reiterman with Jacobs, *Raven*, 520. See also *The Assassination of Representative Leo J. Ryan and the Jonestown, Guyana Tragedy*, 5; Gupte, "Guyana Official Reports 300 Dead at Religious Sect's Jungle Temple," A16; Scheeres, *A Thousand Lives*, 219.

851 *The Assassination of Representative Leo J. Ryan and the Jonestown, Guyana Tragedy*, 5-6; Reiterman with Jacobs, *Raven*, 520-21, 524; Scaliger, "(South) American Killing Fields," 38-39.

852 *The Assassination of Representative Leo J. Ryan and the Jonestown, Guyana Tragedy*, 5; Scheeres, *A Thousand Lives*, 219-21.

853 *The Assassination of Representative Leo J. Ryan and the Jonestown, Guyana Tragedy*, 5-6; Reiterman with Jacobs, *Raven*, 526-27.

854 *The Assassination of Representative Leo J. Ryan and the Jonestown, Guyana Tragedy*, 5-6; Gupte, "Guyana Official Reports 300 Dead at Religious Sect's Jungle Temple," A16; Reiterman with Jacobs, *Raven*, 525-26; Scaliger, "(South) American Killing Fields," 39.

855 "Binder, "Coast Congressman Believed Slain Investigating Commune in Guyana," 22; Gupte, "Guyana Official Reports 300 Dead at Religious Sect's Jungle Temple," A16; Nordheimer, "Leader of Sect Dies," A17; Jon Nordheimer, "Mystery Is Intensifying in Guyana Over Those Who Fled Suicide Rite," *New York Times*, November 23, 1978, A1, A16; Reiterman with Jacobs, *Raven*, 527-38; Russell, "The Left's Great Crime," 41; Scaliger, "(South) American Killing Fields," 39; Joseph B. Treaster, "Graves Team On Way; Identification of 400 Who Died in Mass Suicide is Due to Begin Today," *New York Times*, November 22, 1978, A1, A10; "Witness Tells How Cult Members Went to Deaths," *New York Times*, November 25, 1978, 8.

856   "Larry Layton Released from Federal Prison," "Alternative Considerations of Jonestown and Peoples Temple," San Diego State University Department of Religious Studies, http://jonestown.sdsu. edu/?page_id=19042 (accessed March 28, 2017). See also *The Assassination of Representative Leo J. Ryan and the Jonestown, Guyana Tragedy*, 5-6.

857   Jones is quoted on the "suicide tape" found in "Q042 Transcript, FBI Transcription," "Alternative Considerations of Jonestown and Peoples Temple," San Diego State University Department of Religious Studies, http://jonestown.sdsu.edu/?page_id=29081 (accessed March 28, 2017). See also *The Assassination of Representative Leo J. Ryan and the Jonestown, Guyana Tragedy*, 19-20; "By Death Possessed," E1; Harrary, "The Truth About Jonestown," 67; Nordheimer, "Leader of Sect Dies," A17; Jon Nordheimer, "Son Depicts Leader of Cult as a Fanatic and Paranoid," *New York Times*, November 22, 1978, A1, A10; "Witness Tells How Cult Members Went to Deaths," 8.

858   The woman is quoted on the "suicide tape" found in "Q042 Transcript, FBI Transcription." See also *The Assassination of Representative Leo J. Ryan and the Jonestown, Guyana Tragedy*, 19-20; "By Death Possessed," E1; Jon Nordheimer, "Guyana Toll Is Raised to At Least 900 by US, with 260 Children Among Victims at Colony; Total is Up by 120; A Survivor Says That Many Took Poison Willingly on Jones's Urging," *New York Times*, November 26, 1978, 1, 22; Nordheimer, "Leader of Sect Dies," A1, A17; Scaliger, "(South) American Killing Fields," 39; Scheeres, *A Thousand Lives*, 229-30.

859   Jones is quoted in Scheeres, *A Thousand Lives*, 228. See also the "suicide tape" found in "Q042 Transcript, FBI Transcription"; "Witness Tells How Cult Members Went to Deaths," 8.

860   Scaliger, "(South) American Killing Fields," 39; Scheeres, *A Thousand Lives*, 234.

861   The literature on the subject is voluminous. See, for example, *Cults and New Religious Movements: A Report of the American Psychiatric Association from the Commission on Psychiatry and Religion* (Arlington, VA: American Psychiatric Association Publishing, 1989). See also *The Assassination of Representative Leo J. Ryan and the Jonestown, Guyana Tragedy*, 26; Harrary, "The Truth About Jonestown," 88.

862   *The Assassination of Representative Leo J. Ryan and the Jonestown, Guyana Tragedy*, 19-20; Harrary, "The Truth About Jonestown," 72, 88; Scheeres, *A Thousand Lives*, 33.

863   Harrary, "The Truth About Jonestown," 64, 72; Scaliger, "(South) American Killing Fields," 39.

864   *The Assassination of Representative Leo J. Ryan and the Jonestown, Guyana Tragedy*, 19-20; "By Death Possessed," E1; Horrock, "FBI Is Investigating Jones Plot," A12; Scaliger, "(South) American Killing Fields," 39.

865   Randy Shilts, *The Mayor of Castro Street: The Life and Times of Harvey Milk* (New York: St. Martin's Press, 1982), xv; Mike Weiss, *Double Play: The San Francisco City Hall Killings* (Reading, MA: Addison-Wesley Publishing Company, 1984), 3; Wallace Turner, "Suspect Sought Job; Moscone Had Been Asked to Reappoint Him as a Board Member," *New York Times*, November 28, 1978, A1.

866   The concerns about Moscone's and Milk's links to the Peoples Temple and the possibility of a hit squad are discussed in Paul Krassner, "The Milk-Moscone Case Revisited," *The Nation* 238, no. 1 (January 14, 1984): 9-10; Turner, "Suspect Sought Job," B12; Weiss, *Double Play*, 4, 221.

867   The quote is found in Weiss, *Double Play*, 4. See also Cleve Jones, *When We Rise: My Life in the Movement* (New York: Hachette Books, 2016), 164; Turner, "Suspect Sought Job," A1, B12.

868   Shilts, *The Mayor of Castro Street*, xv-xvi; Weiss, *Double Play*, 4-9.

869   The quote "defender of the home, the family and religious life against homosexuals, pot smokers and cynics" is found in Turner, "Suspect Sought Job," B12. See also John M. Crewdson, "Harvey Milk, Led Coast Homosexual-Rights Fight," *New York Times*, November 28, 1978, B12; Krassner, "The Milk-Moscone Case Revisited," 9; Weiss, *Double Play*, 19-20, 31-38.

870   Krassner, "The Milk-Moscone Case Revisited," 9; Wallace Turner, "Ex-Official Guilty of Manslaughter in Slayings on Coast; 3,000 Protest," *New York Times*, May 22, 1979, D17; Turner, "Suspect Sought Job," B12. For more on the Hot Potato, see, for example, Kristan Lawson and Anneli Rufus, *California Babylon: A Guide to Sites of Scandal, Mayhem, and Celluloid in the Golden State* (New York: St. Martin's Press, 2000), 223.

871 The quotes and the exchange are found in Weiss, *Double Play*, 189-93. See also Jones, *When We Rise*, 159; Krassner, "The Milk-Moscone Case Revisited," 9.

872 Jones, *When We Rise*, 159; Turner, "Suspect Sought Job," B12; Weiss, *Double Play*, 203-4.

873 Weiss, *Double Play*, 203-4, 208-9.

874 Jones, *When We Rise*, 160; Krassner, "The Milk-Moscone Case Revisited," 9; Shilts, *The Mayor of Castro Street*, 250-51; Weiss, *Double Play*, 209-10.

875 Turner, "Suspect Sought Job," A1, B12; Weiss, *Double Play*, 218-19.

876 Weiss, *Double Play*, 219-26.

877 The exchange and quotes are found in Weiss, *Double Play*, 234-35. See also Jones, *When We Rise*, 160; Krassner, "The Milk-Moscone Case Revisited," 9.

878 Krassner, "The Milk-Moscone Case Revisited," 9; Weiss, *Double Play*, 239-42.

879 Colin Evans, "Daniel James White Trial: 1979," in *Great American Trials: From Salem Witchcraft to Rodney King*, ed. Edward W. Knappman (Detroit, MI: Visible Ink Press, 2003), 686; Krassner, "The Milk-Moscone Case Revisited," 9; Weiss, *Double Play*, 244-45, 248.

880 Krassner, "The Milk-Moscone Case Revisited," 9; Turner, "Suspect Sought Job," A1, B12; Weiss, *Double Play*, 248-50.

881 Moscone's quotes and the scene are found in Weiss, *Double Play*, 250-2.

882 Evans, "Daniel James White Trial," 686; Turner, "Ex-Official Guilty of Manslaughter in Slayings on Coast," D17; Weiss, *Double Play*, 252-53.

883 The quotes and scenes are found in Weiss, *Double Play*, 253-54. See also Evans, "Daniel James White Trial," 686; Krassner, "The Milk-Moscone Case Revisited," 9; Shilts, *The Mayor of Castro Street*, xvi; Turner, "Ex-Official Guilty of Manslaughter in Slayings on Coast," D17; Turner, "Suspect Sought Job," B12.

884 The quotes and scenes are found in Weiss, *Double Play*, 254. See also Krassner, "The Milk-Moscone Case Revisited," 9; Turner, "Suspect Sought Job," B12.

885 The quotes and scenes are found in Weiss, *Double Play*, 254-56. See also Evans, "Daniel James White Trial," 686; Shilts, *The Mayor of Castro Street*, xv-xvi.

886 Krassner, "The Milk-Moscone Case Revisited," 11; Weiss, *Double Play*, 7-9, 259-61, 262-71, 278-83.

887 Evans, "Daniel James White Trial," 687; Weiss, *Double Play*, 289-91.

888 Schmidt is quoted in Weiss, *Double Play*, 292, 293. Emphasis in the original. See also Evans, "Daniel James White Trial," 687.

889 The quote is found in Weiss, *Double Play*, 321. See also Evans, "Daniel James White Trial," 688; Krassner, "The Milk-Moscone Case Revisited," 11; Turner, "Ex-Official Guilty of Manslaughter in Slayings on Coast," D17.

890 Evans, "Daniel James White Trial," 688; Krassner, "The Milk-Moscone Case Revisited," 11; Weiss, *Double Play*, 342-43.

891 Evans, "Daniel James White Trial," 687; Weiss, *Double Play*, 393-97.

892 Evans, "Daniel James White Trial," 688; Turner, "Suspect Sought Job," B12; Weiss, *Double Play*, 308-12, 389-91.

893 Evans, "Daniel James White Trial," 688; Jones, *When We Rise*, 170-71; Shilts, *The Mayor of Castro Street*, 324-25; Paul Shinoff, "Jurors Found No Evidence White Slayings Premeditated," *The Atlanta Constitution*, May 23, 1979, 6A; Turner, "Ex-Official Guilty of Manslaughter in Slayings on Coast," A1; Weiss, *Double Play*, 398-404.

894 Freitas is quoted in Turner, "Ex-Official Guilty of Manslaughter in Slayings on Coast," D17. See also Weiss, *Double Play*, 403.

895 Schmidt is quoted in Turner, "Ex-Official Guilty of Manslaughter in Slayings on Coast," D17.

896 Evans, "Daniel James White Trial," 688-89; Robert Lindsey, "Slayer of Coast Mayor Released from Prison," *New York Times*, January 7, 1984, 9; Turner, "Ex-Official Guilty of Manslaughter in Slayings on Coast," A1, D17; Weiss, *Double Play*, 405-15.

897   Evans, "Daniel James White Trial," 688-89; Jones, *When We Rise*, 173-78; Shilts, *The Mayor of Castro Street*, 329-31; Turner, "Ex-Official Guilty of Manslaughter in Slayings on Coast," A1, D17; Weiss, *Double Play*, 412.

898   Britt is quoted in Shilts, *The Mayor of Castro Street*, 334-35. Jones is quoted in Shilts, *The Mayor of Castro Street*, 327. See also Jones, *When We Rise*, 171.

899   Nancy Skelton and Mark A. Stein, "SF Assassin Dan White Kills Himself," *Los Angeles Times*, October 22, 1985, 1; Weiss, *Double Play*, 415-16.

900   Evans, "Daniel James White Trial," 689; Robert Lindsey, "Dan White, Killer of San Francisco Mayor, a Suicide," *New York Times*, October 22, 1985, A18; Lindsey, "Slayer of Coast Mayor Released from Prison," 9.

901   Evans, "Daniel James White Trial," 689; Lindsey, "Dan White, Killer of San Francisco Mayor, a Suicide," A18; Skelton and Stein, "SF Assassin Dan White Kills Himself," 1.

902   Schmidt is quoted in Lindsey, "Dan White, Killer of San Francisco Mayor, a Suicide," A18.

903   Feinstein is quoted in Skelton and Stein, "SF Assassin Dan White Kills Himself," 1.

904   The quotes are found in Skelton and Stein, "SF Assassin Dan White Kills Himself," 1. See also Lindsey, "Dan White, Killer of San Francisco Mayor, a Suicide," A18.

905   Jones, *When We Rise*, 251; Shilts, *The Mayor of Castro Street*, 347-8; Skelton and Stein, "SF Assassin Dan White Kills Himself," 1.

906   See, for example, Michael Bronski, "Milk," *Cineaste* 34, no. 2 (Spring 2009): 71-73; Patrick McCreery, "Of Medals and Myths," *New Labor Forum* 19, no. 1 (Winter 2010): 113-16.

907   Evans, "Daniel James White Trial," 689; Shilts, *The Mayor of Castro Street*, 342.

908   Philip K. Dick, *Minority Report* (New York: Pantheon, 2002 [1956]).

REFERENCES

"Agents Tracing Hinckley's Path Find a Shift to Violent Emotion." *New York Times*, April 5, 1981.

Alderman, Derek H. "Martin Luther King Jr. Streets in the South: A New Landscape of Memory." *Southern Cultures* 14, no. 3 (Fall 2008): 88-105.

Allen, Ivan, Jr. "The Night MLK Was Shot." *Atlanta* 43, no. 12 (April 2004): 46-59.

Alter, Jonathan, and McKay Coppins. "American Assassins." *Newsweek* 157, no. 4 (January 24, 2011): 18-22.

Apple, R. W., Jr. "Malcolm X Silenced for Remarks on Assassination of Kennedy." *New York Times*, December 5, 1963.

Archibold, Randal C. "One of Ford's Would-Be Assassins Is Paroled." *New York Times*, January 1, 2008.

Arnold, Laurence. "James Brady: 1940–2014: Reagan Aide Became Gun Control Symbol; U of I Graduate Wounded in 1981 Assassination Try." *Chicago Tribune*, August 5, 2014.

"Around the Nation: Hunt for U.S. Judge's Killer Includes Motorcycle Group." *New York Times*, May 31, 1979.

Arrington, Leonard J., and David Bitton. *The Mormon Experience: A History of the Latter Day Saints*. Champaign, IL: The University of Illinois Press, 1992.

"Assassin Czolgosz is Executed at Auburn; He Declared That He Felt No Regret for His Crime." *New York Times*, October 30, 1901.

"Assassinated; Carter H. Harrison, Mayor of Chicago, Killed; Murderer in Custody; A Disappointed Office Seeker's Terrible Revenge; No Word of Warning; The Mayor Dies in Less Than an Hour." *New York Times*, October 29, 1893.

"The Assassination Conspiracy." *The Boston Herald*, July 10, 1865.

"The Assassination of Mr. Lincoln: Interesting Particulars of the Tragedy." *New York Times*, April 18, 1865.

The Assassination of President Lincoln and the Trial of the Conspirators. New York: Moore, Wilstach & Baldwin, 1865.

"The Assassin's Career." *New York Times*, July 1, 1882.

"The Attack upon Mr. Roosevelt." *New York Times*, October 16, 1912.

"The Autopsy Begun; Guiteau's Brain Found in an Apparently Normal Condition." *New York Times*, July 1, 1882.

Ayton, Mel. *The Forgotten Terrorist: Sirhan Sirhan and the Assassination of Robert F. Kennedy*. Omaha, NE: The Notable Trials Library, 2012.

———————. Mel. *Hunting the President: Threats, Plots, and Assassination Attempts—From FDR to Obama*. Washington, DC: Regnery History, 2014.

Barabak, Mark Z.; Lisa Mascaro; and Robin Abcarian. "The Nation; A Calm Voice in a Divided District; Giffords Had Brushes with Danger Before. Friends Say She Was Undaunted." *Los Angeles Times*, January 9, 2011.

Barone, Jeanine. "In the Footsteps of a Dream: Relive the History of the Civil-rights Movement in Alabama and Georgia." *National Parks* 84, no. 4 (Fall 2010): 1-5.

Barry, Norman P. *On Classical Liberalism and Libertarianism*. New York: Macmillan, 1986.

Beam, Alex. *America Crucifixion: The Murder of Joseph Smith and the Fate of the Mormon Church*. New York: Public Affairs, 2014.

Bello, Marisol. "Loughner's Lawyer Is 'One-Woman Dream Team.'" *USA Today*, January 11, 2011.

Benjamin, Philip. "Malcolm X Lived in 2 Worlds, White and Black, Both Bitter." *New York Times*, February 22, 1965.

Bernauer, Barbara Hands. "'Side by Side'—The Final Burial of Joseph and Hyrum Smith." *The John Whitmer Historical Association Journal* 11, no. 1 (1991): 17-33.

Binder, David. "Coast Congressman Believed Slain Investigating Commune in Guyana." *New York Times*, November 19, 1978.

Blackstock, Nelson. *COINTELPRO: The FBI's Secret War on Political Freedom.* New York: Pathfinder, 1988.

Boertlein, John. *Presidential Confidential: Sex, Scandal, Murder, and Mayhem in the Oval Office!* Cincinnati, OH: Clerisy Press, 2010.

Boomhower, Ray. *Robert F. Kennedy and the 1968 Indiana Primary.* Bloomington: Indiana University Press, 2008.

"Booth's End; The Shooting of the Assassin of the President; His Flight and Desperate Resistance." *The New York Herald*, April 28, 1865.

Bormann, Ernest G. "Huey Long: Analysis of a Demagogue." *Today's Speech* 2, no. 3 (September 1954): 16-19.

—————. "A Rhetorical Analysis of the National Radio Broadcasts of Senator Huey Pierce Long." *Speech Monographs* 24, no. 4 (November 1957): 244-57.

Boser, Beth L., and Randall A. Lake. "'Enduring' Incivility: Sarah Palin and the Tucson Tragedy." *Rhetoric & Public Affairs* 17, no. 4 (Winter 2014): 619-52.

Branch, Taylor. *At Canaan's Edge: America in the King Years, 1965–68.* New York: Simon & Schuster, 2006.

—————. *Pillar of Fire: America in the King Years, 1963–65.* New York: Simon & Schuster, 1998.

Brands, H. W. *Andrew Jackson: His Life and Times.* New York: Doubleday, 2005.

—————. *Reagan: The Life.* New York: Anchor Books, 2016.

—————. *Traitor to His Class: The Privileged Life and Radical Presidency of Franklin Delano Roosevelt.* New York: Doubleday, 2008.

Brinkley, Alan. "Who Killed Frank Steunenberg?" *The New Republic* 217, no. 17 (October 27, 1997): 35-37.

Brinkley, Douglas. *Gerald R. Ford.* New York: Times Books, 2007.

—————, and Anne Brinkley. "Lawyers and Lizard-Heads: The Prison Letters of James Earl Ray." *The Atlantic Monthly* 289, No. 5 (May 2002): 55-61.

Bronski, Michael. "Milk." *Cineaste* 34, no. 2 (Spring 2009): 71-73.

Bruyneel, Kevin. "The King's Body: The Martin Luther King Jr. Memorial and the Politics of Collective Memory." *History & Memory* 26, no. 4 (Spring/Summer 2014): 75-108.

Bryan, William Jennings. *The Cross of Gold: Speech Delivered Before the National Democratic Convention at Chicago, July 9, 1896.* Lincoln: University of Nebraska Press, 1996.

Bugliosi Vincent. *Reclaiming History: The Assassination of President John F. Kennedy.* New York: W. W. Norton & Company, 2007.

—————, with Curt Gentry. *Helter Skelter: The True Story of the Manson Murders.* New York: Bantam Books, 1975.

Bureau of Justice Assistance. *Protecting Judicial Officials: Implementing an Effective Threat Management Process.* Washington, DC: US Government Printing Office, June 2006.

"Buried in the Jail Yard; The Last of the President's Murderer; Guiteau's Body Placed Where Body-snatchers Cannot Get at It; Carried to the Grave by Six Convicts and Interred Without Ceremony." *New York Times*, July 2, 1882.

Burke, Edward M. "Lunatics and Anarchists: Political Homicide in Chicago." *The Journal of Criminal Law & Criminology* 92, nos. 3-4 (Spring/Summer 2002): 791-804.

Burlingame, Michael. *Abraham Lincoln: A Life.* Vol. II. Baltimore, MD: The Johns Hopkins University Press, 2008.

"Bury Senator Tomorrow; Tomb in Shadow of the Skyscraper Capitol Symbolizing Power; Baton Rouge Is Hushed; Flags Fly at Half Staff and Silence Rules Over Boisterous State House Corridors; Legislature Works On; Coroner's Jury Returns Findings as Talk Is Heard That Killer Draws Lots in Plot." *New York Times*, September 11, 1935.

Bushman, Richard Lyman. *Joseph Smith: Rough Stone Rolling*. New York: Vintage, 2007.

"By Death Possessed: A Prophet, a Cult, and Mass Madness in Guyana Jungle." *New York Times*, November 26, 1978.

Cannon, Lou. *President Reagan: The Role of a Lifetime*. New York: Public Affairs Books, 2000.

Capps, Donald. "John W. Hinckley, Jr.: A Case of Narcissistic Personality Disorder." *Pastoral Psychology* 62, no. 3 (June 2013): 247-69.

Carlson, Peter. "Alexander Graham Bell Scans James Garfield." *American History* 50, no. 6 (February 2016): 14, 16.

_____. *Roughneck: The Life and Times of Big Bill Haywood*. New York: W. W. Norton & Company, 1983.

Carter, Dan T. *The Politics of Rage: George Wallace, the Origins of the New Conservatism, and the Transformation of American Politics*, 2d ed. Baton Rouge: LSU Press, 2000.

"Carter H. Harrison's Career; His Stubborn Political Fights and Victories in Chicago." *New York Times*, October 29, 1893.

Cartwright, Gary. "The Sins of the Father." *Texas Monthly* 22, no. 11 (November 1994): 100-104.

Carwardine, Richard. *Lincoln: A Life of Purpose and Power*. New York: Knopf, 2003.

Castaneda, Ruben. "A Conspiracy of Silence?" *American Journalism Review* 22, no. 2 (March 2000): 60-63.

"Cermak Has Turn for the Worse; Doctors Late at Night Indicate That Crisis in Case Is at Hand; Opiate Is Administered; Zangara Blocks Move for Appeal and Lawyers Abandon the Idea." *New York Times*, February 22, 1933.

Chafe, William H. *Never Stop Running: Allard Lowenstein and the Struggle to Save American Liberalism*. New York: Basic Books, 1993.

Chalberg, John. *Emma Goldman: American Individualist*. 2d. ed. New York: Longman, 2008.

Channing, Walter. *The Mental Status of Czolgosz, the Assassin of President McKinley*. Charleston, SC: Nabu Press, 1913 [1902].

Chapell, Kevin. "The Question That Won't Go Away: Who Killed King?" *Ebony* 52, no. 7 (May 1997): 36-38, 40, 42.

Christianson, Stephen G. "William 'Big Bill' Haywood Trial: 1907." In *Great American Trials: From Salem Witchcraft to Rodney King*, edited by Edward W. Knappman, 244-47. Detroit, MI: Visible Ink Press, 2003.

_____. "Charles Guiteau Trial: 1881." In *Great American Trials: From Salem Witchcraft to Rodney King*, edited by Edward W. Knappman, 187-91. Detroit, MI: Visible Ink Press, 2003.

"The City: Insanity Plea Made in Lowenstein's Death." *New York Times*, March 21, 1980.

Clarke, James W. *American Assassins: The Darker Side of Politics*. Princeton, NJ: Princeton University Press, 1982.

_____. *Defining Danger: American Assassins and the New Domestic Terrorists*. New Brunswick, NJ: Transaction Publishers, 2012.

_____. "Emotional Deprivation and Political Deviance: Some Observations on Governor Wallace's Would-Be Assassin, Arthur H. Bremer." *Political Psychology* 3, no. 1/2 (Spring 1981–Summer 1982): 84-115.

Cloud, John. "The Troubled Life of Jared Loughner." *Time* 177, no. 3 (January 24, 2011): n.p. Time.com. http://www.time.com/time/magazine/article/0,9171,2042358,00.html (accessed February 7, 2017).

Coghlan, Andy. "Gunman Might Stand Trial After Forcible Medication." *New Scientist* 211, no. 2820 (July 9, 2011): 11.

Connery, William S. "The Zero Year Curse." *World & I* 16, no. 6 (June 2001): 180-89.

"Convicted Killer Tells of Fear Youths Will Emulate Slaying." *New York Times*, December 16, 1982.

Cook, Andrew. "Lone Assassins." *History Today* 53, no. 11 (November 2003): 25-31.

"The Coroner's Inquest: Story of the Assassination Told in Detail." *New York Times*, October 30, 1893.

Crewdson, John M. "El Paso Is Called a Major New Hub of Drug Traffic." *New York Times*, June 17, 1979.

_____. "Harvey Milk, Led Coast Homosexual-Rights Fight." *New York Times*, November 28, 1978.

Cross, Whitney R. *The Burned-Over District: The Social and Intellectual History of Enthusiastic Religion in Western New York, 1800–1850.* New York: Harper & Row, 1965.

Cults and New Religious Movements: A Report of the American Psychiatric Association from the Commission on Psychiatry and Religion. Arlington, VA: American Psychiatric Association Publishing, 1989.

"Czolgosz's Body to Be Destroyed at Auburn; Brother of Assassin Empowers Warden to Dispose of It." *New York Times*, October 29, 1901.

Davis, Ossie. "Eulogy for Malcolm X: Faith Temple of God in Christ: New York City—February 27, 1965." In *Say It Loud: Great Speeches on Civil Rights and African American Identity*, edited by Catherine Ellis and Stephen Drury Smith, 25-29. New York and London: The New Press, 2010.

Davison, Jean. *Oswald's Game.* New York: W. W. Norton, 1983.

"Death Comes to William Goebel; Hopeless Struggle for Life Continued All Day Yesterday." *New York Times*, February 4, 1900.

Detzer, David. *Allegiance: Fort Sumter, Charleston, and the Beginning of the Civil War.* New York: Harcourt, 2001.

Dick, Philip K. *Minority Report.* New York: Pantheon, 2002 [1956].

"Doctor, Backing Hinckley, Tells of Letter to Murderer." *New York Times*, April 14, 1987.

"Dr. Martin Luther King Buried in Atlanta; A Vast Cortege Follows Mule-Drawn Bier." *New York Times*, April 10, 1968.

Dolbeare, Kenneth M. *American Political Thought.* Chatham, NJ: Chatham House, 1984.

Donald, David Herbert. *Lincoln.* New York: Simon & Schuster, 1995.

Douglass, James W. "The King Assassination: After Three Decades, Another Verdict." *Christian Century* 117, no. 9 (March 15, 2000): 308-13.

———. "The Murder and Martyrdom of Malcolm X." In *The Assassinations: Probe Magazine on JFK, MLK, RFK and Malcolm X*, edited by James DiEugenio and Lisa Peace, 376-424. Port Townsend, WA: Feral House, 2003.

Dray, Philip. *There Is Power in a Union: The Epic Story of Labor in America.* New York: Anchor Books, 2011.

Drury, Jeffrey P. Mehltretter, and Cole A. Crouch. "Robert F. Kennedy, 'Statement on the Death of Reverend Martin Luther King, Rally in Indianapolis, Indiana' (4 April 1968) and Robert F. Kennedy, 'Remarks at the Cleveland City Club' (5 April 1968)." *Voices of Democracy* 11, no. 1 (2016): 1-24.

Duke, Selwyn. "The Lost Man Behind the Leftist Myth." *The New American* 27, no. 3 (February 7, 2011): 15-16.

Egerton, Douglas R. *Year of Meteors: Stephen Douglas, Abraham Lincoln, and the Election that Brought on the Civil War.* New York: Bloomsbury Press, 2010.

"End of an Assassin." *New York Times*, April 24, 1998.

Evans, Colin. "Daniel James White Trial: 1979." In *Great American Trials: From Salem Witchcraft to Rodney King*, edited by Edward W. Knappman, 686-89. Detroit, MI: Visible Ink Press, 2003.

"Ex-Governor Killed by Dynamite Bomb; Frank Steunenberg of Idaho Victim of an Assassin; Governor from 1897 to 1901; The Bomb Had Been Placed at His Gate at Caldwell, and Exploded as He Entered." *New York Times*, December 31, 1905.

Ex Parte Milligan, 71 U.S. 2 (1866).

"Ex-Rep. Lowenstein Killed by a Gunman; Antiwar Leader Shot at Law Office—Former Co-Worker Is Held." *New York Times*, March 15, 1980.

"55,000 Troops Readied for Riots." *The Atlanta Constitution*, April 9, 1968.

Farmer, James, Jr. "Martin Luther King Assassination." UPI.com Archives. http://www.upi.com/Archives/Audio/Events-of-1968/Martin-Luther-King-Assassination/ (accessed March 25, 2017).

Farrell, John A. *Clarence Darrow: Attorney for the Damned.* New York: Vintage, 2012.

Federman, Cary. "The Life of an Unknown Assassin: Leon Czolgosz and the Death of William McKinley." *Crime, History & Societies* 14, no. 2 (2010): 85-106.

Feinman, Ronald L. *Assassinations, Threats, and the American Presidency: From Andrew Jackson to Barack Obama*. Lanham, MD: Rowman & Littlefield, 2015.

"Felon Admits Guilt in Threat on Ford." *New York Times*, September 13, 1975.

Finkel, PhD, Norman J. "The Insanity Defense Reform Act of 1984: Much Ado About Nothing." *Behavioral Sciences & The Law* 7, no. 3 (Summer 1989): 403-19.

"First Intended to Kill Hoover." *New York Times*, March 20, 1933.

Flood, Charles Bracelen. *1864: Lincoln at the Gates of History*. New York: Simon & Schuster, 2009.

Foner, Eric. *Forever Free: The Story of Emancipation and Reconstruction*. Illustrations Edited with a Commentary by Joshua Brown. New York: Knopf, 2005.

_____. Eric. *Reconstruction: America's Unfinished Revolution: 1863–1877*. New York: Francis Parkman Prize Edition, History Book Club, 2005 [1988].

"Ford Testimony Tape in Fromme Trial Freed." *Sacramento Bee*, April 7, 1987.

"Funeral for Lowenstein to Be Held Tomorrow." *New York Times*, March 17, 1980.

Gaddis, John Lewis. *Strategies of Containment: A Critical Appraisal of American National Security Policy During the Cold War*. 2d. ed. Oxford and New York: Oxford University Press, 2005.

"The Gallows Prepared; Everything in Readiness for Guiteau's Death; No Chance of Executive Interference; The Murderer's Last Day; Visits from Relatives, Counsel, and Clergyman; The Demeanor of the Assassin." *New York Times*, June 30, 1882.

Gansberg, Martin. "Damage Here Since Slaying of Dr. King is Near '64 Riot Level." *New York Times*, April 10, 1968.

Garfield, James A. "Inaugural Address." In *Inaugural Addresses of the Presidents of the United States*, Vol. I, *George Washington (1789) to James A. Garfield (1881)*, 143-49. Bedford, MA: Applewood Books, 2000.

Garrow, David J. *Bearing the Cross: Martin Luther King, Jr., and the Southern Christian Leadership Conference*. New York: Quill, William Morrow, 1986.

Gault, Barry. "Lay That Pistol Down: Mental-Health Laws Weren't the Problem in Tucson." *Commonweal* 138, no. 4 (February 25, 2011): 15-16.

Gayler, George R. "Governor Ford and the Death of Joseph and Hyrum Smith." *Journal of the Illinois State Historical Society (1908–1984)* 50, no. 4 (Winter 1957): 391-411.

"Gerald Ford Dies; Nixon's Successor in '74 Crisis was 93." *New York Times*, December 27, 2006.

"Gerald R. Ford." *New York Times*, December 28, 2006.

Giffords, Gabrielle, and Mark Kelly with Jeffrey Zaslow. *Gabby: A Story of Courage and Hope*. New York: Scribner, 2011.

"Gift of Norman E. Kent '71, '75 Creates Allard K. Lowenstein Memorial Civil Rights Scholarship." Hofstra.edu. http://www.hofstra.edu/home/news/pressreleases/archive/101107_lowensteinkent.html (accessed March 22, 2016).

"Goebel's Funeral Quiet; Great Crowd Attends the Ceremonies in the Downpour of Rain." *New York Times*, February 9, 1900.

Goldman, Peter. *The Death and Life of Malcolm X*. Omaha, NE: The Notable Trials Library, 2016 [1973].

Goodnight, G. Thomas. "Gabrielle Giffords: A Study in Civil Courage." *Rhetoric & Public Affairs* 17, no. 4 (Winter 2014): 679-710.

Goodwin, Doris Kearns. *Team of Rivals: The Political Genius of Abraham Lincoln*. New York: Simon & Schuster, 2005.

Goodwyn, Lawrence. *The Populist Movement: A Short History of the Agrarian Revolt in America*. New York and Oxford: Oxford University Press, 1978.

Gopnik, Adam. *Angels and Ages: A Short Book About Darwin, Lincoln, and Modern Life*. New York: Random House, 2009.

Gould, Lewis L. *Grand Old Party: A History of the Republicans*. New York: Random House, 2003.

Graham, Fred P. "Suspect in Assassination of Dr. King Is Seized in London; Ray Found Armed; Arrested at the Airport by Scotland Yard on Way from Lisbon." *New York Times*, June 9, 1968.

"A Great City in Mourning; Chicago Sorrows Over the Murder of Mayor Harrison; Her Citizens Grieved and Indignant; The Assassin Locked Up in the County Jail Safe from Violence; Doubts as to His Sanity." *New York Times*, October 30, 1893.

"A Great Nation in Grief; President Garfield Shot by an Assassin; Though Seriously Wounded He Still Survives; The Would-Be Murderer Lodged in Prison." *New York Times*, July 3, 1881.

"A Great Tragedy Ended; The World Is Rid of a Wretched Assassin; Guiteau Expiates the Crime Upon the Scaffold; The Last Hours of a Murderer of a President; The Scenes at the Gallows; Prayers to God and Curses for the Nation; Weeping and Sobbing, But Finally Meeting Firmly; Yells and Cheers Following the Fall of the Drop." *New York Times*, July 1, 1882.

Gresko, Jessica. "Reagan Shooter Leaves Mental Hospital." *Chicago Tribune*, September 11, 2016.

Guelzo, Allen C. "The Redemption of Abraham Lincoln." *The Civil War Monitor* 6, no. 2 (Summer 2016): 30-38, 74-75.

"Guiteau's Crime." *New York Times*, July 1, 1882.

Gupte, Pranay. "Guyana Official Reports 300 Dead at Religious Sect's Jungle Temple; 6 Are Wounded Critically." *New York Times*, November 20, 1978.

Haas, Edward F. "Huey Long and the Dictators." *Louisiana History: The Journal of the Louisiana Historical Association* 47, no. 2 (Spring 2006): 133-51.

Hales, Brian C. "Joseph Smith's Personal Polygamy." *Journal of Mormon History* 38, no. 2 (Spring 2012): 163-228.

Hambrick-Stowe, Charles E. *Charles G. Finney and the Spirit of American Evangelicalism.* Grand Rapids, MI: William B. Eerdmans Publishing, 1996.

Hamilton, Alexander, James Madison, and John Jay. *The Federalist Papers.* Edited by Clinton Rossiter. New York: The New American Library, 1961.

Hammer, Richard. "Ray: Clues to a Man of Mystery." *New York Times*, June 16, 1968.

Handler, M. S. "Malcolm X Splits with Muhammad; Suspended Black Leader Plans Black Nationalist Political Movement." *New York Times*, March 9, 1964.

Harrary, Keith. "The Truth About Jonestown; 13 Years Later—Why We Should Still Be Afraid." *Psychology Today* 25, no. 2 (March/April 1992): 62-67, 72, 88.

Harris, David. *Dreams Die Hard.* New York: St. Martin's/Marek, 1982.

Harris, William C. *Lincoln's Rise to the Presidency.* Lawrence: University Press of Kansas, 2007.

——————. *With Charity For All: Lincoln and the Restoration of the Union.* Lexington: University Press of Kentucky, 1999.

"Harrison Lying in State; Viewed by Thousands in Chicago's City Hall." *New York Times*, November 1, 1893.

"Harrison's Murder Avenged; Prendergast, the Assassin, Dies on the Scaffold." *New York Times*, July 14, 1894.

"Harrison's Murder; Inquest Over the Body of the Slain Mayor of Chicago; The Crank Prendergast in a Cell; He Coolly Reads Accounts of His Bloody Work; He Insist That He Did His Duty; The Question As to Who Will Succeed as Mayor; Testimony at the Coroner's Inquest." *The Atlanta Constitution*, October 30, 1893.

Heard, Alex. "Exhumed Innocent." *The New Republic* 205, no. 6 (August 5, 1991): 12, 14.

Helferich, Gerard. *Theodore Roosevelt and the Assassin: Madness, Vengeance, and the Campaign of 1912.* Guilford, CT: Lyons Press, 2013.

Henry, Nicholas L. *Governing at the Grassroots: State and Local Politics.* Upper Saddle River, NJ: Prentice-Hall, 1987.

Herbers, John. "No Conditions Set; Action Taken to Spare Nation and Ex-Chief, President Asserts." *New York Times*, September 9, 1974.

"Hijacker Had Picketed White House." *New York Times*, February 24, 1974.

"Hijacker Kills 2 and Then Himself." *New York Times*, February 23, 1974.

Hill, Gladwin. "Evidence Against Oswald Described as Conclusive." *New York Times*, November 24, 1963.

_____. "Kennedy Is Dead, Victim of Assassin." *New York Times*, June 6, 1968.

Hill, Marvin S. "Carthage Conspiracy Reconsidered: A Second Look at the Murder of Joseph and Hyrum Smith." *Journal of the Illinois State Historical Society (1998–)* 97, no. 2 (Summer 2004): 107-34.

"His Good Nature Led Colonel into Danger." *New York Times*, October 16, 1912.

Hofstadter, Richard. *The American Political Tradition and the Men Who Made It*. New York: Vintage Books, 1989 [1948].

Hofstetter, C. Richard. "Political Disengagement and the Death of Martin Luther King." *Public Opinion Quarterly* 33, no. 2 (Summer 1969): 174-79.

Hogan, J. Michael, and Glen Williams. "The Rusticity and Religiosity of Huey P. Long." *Rhetoric & Public Affairs* 7, no. 2 (Summer 2004): 149-72.

Holzer, Harold. *Lincoln: How Abraham Lincoln Ended Slavery in America*. New York: Newmarket Press, an Imprint of HarperCollins, 2012.

_____. *Lincoln President-Elect: Abraham Lincoln and the Great Secession Winter 1860–1861*. New York: Simon & Schuster, 2008.

Horrock, Nicholas M. "FBI Is Investigating Jones Plot, Using Statute on Assassinations." *New York Times*, November 22, 1978.

Houser, Aimee. *Tragedy in Tucson: The Arizona Shooting Rampage*. Minneapolis, MN: ABDO Publishing Company, 2012.

Howe, Daniel Walker. *What Hath God Wrought: The Transformation of America, 1815–1848*. Oxford and New York: Oxford University Press, 2007.

Hunter, Stephen, and Joseph Bainbridge, Jr. *American Gunfight: The Plot to Kill Harry Truman—And the Shootout That Stopped It*. New York: Simon & Schuster, 2005.

"Important. Assassination of President Lincoln." *The New York Herald*, April 15, 1865.

Jackson, Carlton. "—Another Time, Another Place—The Attempted Assassination of President Andrew Jackson." *Tennessee Historical Quarterly* 26, no. 2 (Summer 1967): 184-90.

"James A. Garfield." *New York Times*, September 20, 1881.

Jeansonne, Glen. "Huey P. Long: A Political Contradiction." *Louisiana History: The Journal of the Louisiana Historical Association* 31, no. 4 (Winter 1990): 373-85.

Jenkins, Philip. *Decade of Nightmares: The End of the Sixties and the Making of Eighties America*. Oxford and New York: Oxford University Press, 2006.

Johnston, Laurie. "Services for Lowenstein Recall Activism of 1960's." *New York Times*, March 19, 1980.

Jones, Cleve. *When We Rise: My Life in the Movement*. New York: Hachette Books, 2016.

Jones, M. Jackson. "In the Line of Fire: A Tribute and Discussion About the Assassinations of Judge John H. Wood Jr., Richard J. Daronco, and Robert S. Vance." *Creighton Law Review* 49, no. 1 (December 2015): 1-22.

Jones, Theodore. "Malcolm Knew He was a 'Marked Man.'" *New York Times*, February 22, 1965.

Joseph, Peniel E. *Waiting 'Til the Midnight Hour: A Narrative History of Black Power in America*. New York: Henry Holt, 2006.

Judis, John B. "The Activist as Hero," *The New Republic* 209, no. 17 (October 25, 1993): 42-45.

Kane, Joseph Nathan. *Facts About the Presidents*. New York: Ace Books, 1976.

Kauffman, Michael W. *American Brutus: John Wilkes Booth and the Lincoln Conspiracies*. New York: Random House, 2004.

Kazin, Michael. *A Godly Hero: The Life of William Jennings Bryan*. New York: Knopf, 2006.

Kennedy, Paul. "Truman Death Aim Denied by Collazo." *New York Times*, March 2, 1951.

Kersten, Andrew E. *Clarence Darrow: American Iconoclast*. New York: Hill and Wang, 2011.

Kihss, Peter. "Hunt for Killers in Malcolm Case 'On Right Track.'" *New York Times*, February 25, 1965.

_____. "Malcolm X Shot to Death at Rally Here." *New York Times*, February 22, 1965.

_____. "'Sublime Heroism' Cited in Shooting." *New York Times*, March 3, 1954.

_____. "Suspect, Arab Immigrant, Arraigned; Notes on Kennedy in Suspect's Home." *New York Times*, June 6, 1968.

"Killings in Tucson." *Commonweal* 138, no. 2 (January 11, 2011): 5.

"King Family Rebukes Report That Says James Earl Ray Acted Alone in King's Death." *Jet* 98, no. 3 (June 26, 2000), 4, 6.

King, Peter J. "Huey Long: The Louisiana Kingfish." *History Today* 14, no. 3 (March 1964): 151-60.

King, Wayne. "New Criminal Class Is Flourishing in Sun Belt." *New York Times*, December 18, 1982.

——————. "Three Are Found Guilty in Assassination of Federal Judge." *New York Times*, December 15, 1982.

Kingseed, Wyatt. "The Assassination of William McKinley." *American History* 36, no. 4 (October 2001): 22-30.

Kirkham, James F.; Sheldon G. Levy; and William J. Crotty. *Assassination and Political Violence: A Report to the National Commission on the Causes and Prevention of Violence*. Vol. 8. Washington, DC: US Government Printing Office, October 1969.

Kirkpatrick, David. "Moderate? Conservative? With Gerald Ford, Take Your Pick." *New York Times*, December 31, 2006.

Kissinger, Jessie. "I Cover My Face with My Hands." *Esquire* 158, no. 5 (December 2012): 130-32.

Klotter, James C. *William Goebel: The Politics of Wrath*. Lexington: The University Press of Kentucky, 1977.

Kneeland, Douglas E. "Now, Arthur Bremer Is Known." *New York Times*, May 22, 1972.

——————. "Police Suspect Governor Was Stalked." *New York Times*, May 17, 1972.

Kotz, Nick. *Judgment Days: Lyndon Baines Johnson, Martin Luther King Jr., and the Laws That Changed America*. Boston and New York: Houghton Mifflin, 2005.

Krakauer, Jon. *Under the Banner of Heaven: A Story of Violent Faith*. New York: Doubleday, 2003.

Krassner, Paul. "The Milk-Moscone Case Revisited." *The Nation* 238, no. 1 (January 14, 1984): 9, 11-12.

Kunhardt, Philip B., Jr.; Philip B. Kunhardt, III; and Peter W. Kunhardt. *Lincoln: An Illustrated Biography*. New York: Knopf, 1992.

Kurlansky, Mark. *1968: The Year That Rocked the World*. New York: Ballantine Books, 2004.

Lacey, Marc. "In Tucson, Loughner Enters Plea: Not Guilty." *New York Times*, March 10, 2011.

——————; Jo Becker; and Richard A. Oppel, Jr. "Suspect Ran Red Light and Was Stopped by Police Hours Before Attack." *New York Times*, January 13, 2011.

Lane, Mark. *Rush to Judgment: A Critique of the Warren Commission's Inquiry into the Murders of President John F. Kennedy, Officer J. D. Tippit and Lee Harvey Oswald*. New York: Holt, Rinehart & Winston, 1966.

Langdon, Emma Florence. *The Cripple Creek Strike: A History of Industrial Wars in Colorado, 1903–4–5*. Denver, CO: The Great Western Publishing Company, 1904-5.

"Larry Layton Released from Federal Prison." "Alternative Considerations of Jonestown and Peoples Temple," San Diego State University Department of Religious Studies. http://jonestown.sdsu.edu/?page_id=19042 (accessed March 28, 2017).

Larson, Erik. *The Devil in the White City: Murder, Magic, and Madness at the Fair That Changed America*. New York: Crown Publishers, 2003.

"Last Will of Guiteau; Disposing of His Body and His Book; a Letter to His Counsel." *New York Times*, June 30, 1882.

Lawson, Kristan, and Anneli Rufus. *California Babylon: A Guide to Sites of Scandal, Mayhem, and Celluloid in the Golden State*. New York: St. Martin's Press, 2000.

Lehman, Christopher P. *Power, Politics, and the Decline of the Civil Rights Movement: A Fragile Coalition, 1967–1973*. Santa Barbara, CA: Praeger, 2014.

Leonard, Elizabeth D. *Lincoln's Avengers: Justice, Revenge, and Reunion After the Civil War*. New York: Norton, 2004.

Lesher, Stephan. *George Wallace: American Populist*. Boston, MA: Da Capo Press, 1994.

Lewis, Anthony. "Johnson Spurs Oswald Inquiry; President Orders FBI to Check Death—Handling of Case Worries Capital." *New York Times*, November 25, 1963.

Lindsey, Robert. "Dan White, Killer of San Francisco Mayor, a Suicide." *New York Times*, October 22, 1985.

_____. "Slayer of Coast Mayor Released from Prison." *New York Times*, January 7, 1984.

Ling, Peter. "Martin Luther King's Half-Forgotten Dream." *History Today* 48, no. 4 (April 1998): 17-22.

_____. "The Media Made Malcolm X." *History Today* 62, no. 1 (January 2012): 49-55.

Lissner, Will. "Malcolm Fought for Top Power in Muslim Movement, and Lost." *New York Times*, February 22, 1965.

"Long Predicted He Would Be Shot; He Told Senate Aug. 9 That Plot to Kill Him Had Been Overheard in New Orleans; Always Had a Bodyguard; Thomas Recalls Inquiry in Louisiana Revealed Hate and 'Almost Mob Desires.'" *New York Times*, September 9, 1935.

Loomis, James. "Letter to the Editor: Death of Malcolm X." *New York Times*, February 27, 1965.

Lukas, J. Anthony. *Big Trouble: A Murder in a Small Western Town Sets Off a Struggle for the Soul of America*. New York: Simon & Schuster, 1997.

Lyon, Joseph J., and David W. Lyon. "Physical Evidence at Carthage Jail and What It Reveals about the Assassination of Joseph and Hyrum Smith." *Brigham Young University Studies* 47, no. 4 (2008): 4-50.

MacDonald, Sam. "Hijacker Targeted President in 1974." *Insight on the News* 18, no. 23 (June 24, 2002): 24-25.

Malcolm, Andrew H. "Accused Ford Assailant Has Led a Tangled Life." *New York Times*, September 24, 1975.

"Malcolm Asked Gun Permit After Home Was Bombed." *New York Times*, February 22, 1965.

Malcolm X. *By Any Means Necessary: Malcolm X—Speeches and Writings*. New York: Pathfinder Press, 1992.

"Malcolm X." *New York Times*, February 22, 1965.

Malcolm X. *The Autobiography of Malcolm X: As Told to Alex Haley*. New York: Ballantine Books, 1992 [1965].

"Malcolm X Scores US and Kennedy." *New York Times*, December 2, 1963.

Manchester, William. *The Death of a President: November 20–November 25, 1963*. 25th Anniversary Edition. New York: Perennial Library, 1988.

Marable, Manning. *Malcolm X: A Life of Reinvention*. New York: Viking, 2011.

Marcus, Frances Frank. "Researchers Exhume Doctor's Grave to Resolve Part of Huey Long Legend." *New York Times*, October 21, 1991.

Margolick, David. "Lowenstein Killer Moves Toward Freedom." *New York Times*, November 1, 1992.

Marrs, Jim. *Crossfire: The Plot That Killed Kennedy*. Revised and Expanded Edition. New York: Basic Books, 2013.

Marschall, Rick. *Bully! The Life and Times of Theodore Roosevelt*. Washington, DC: Regnery History, 2011.

"Martin Luther King Is Slain in Memphis; A White is Suspected; Johnson Urges Calm." *New York Times*, April 5, 1968.

Martin, Zachary J. *The Mindless Menace of Violence: Robert F. Kennedy's Vision and the Fierce Urgency of Now*. Lanham, MD: Hamilton Books, 2009.

Martinez, J. Michael. *Terrorist Attacks on American Soil: From the Civil War Era to the Present*. Lanham, MD: Rowman & Littlefield, 2012.

Massaquoi, Hans J. "Mystery of Malcolm X." *Ebony* 48, no. 4 (February 1993): 36-40, 42, 44.

Mayo, Mike. *American Murder: Criminals, Crimes and the Media*. Canton, MI: Visible Ink Press, 2008.

McBride, Spencer W. "When Joseph Smith Met Martin Van Buren: Mormonism and the Politics of Religious Liberty in Nineteenth-Century America." *Church History* 85, no. 1 (March 2016): 150-58.

McCann, Joseph T. *Terrorism on American Soil: A Concise History of Plots and Perpetrators from the Famous to the Forgotten*. Boulder, CO: Sentient Publications, 2006.

McCreary, Jana R. "'Mentally Defective' Language in the Gun Control Act." *Connecticut Law Review* 45, no. 3 (February 2013): 813-64.

McCreery, Patrick. "Of Medals and Myths." *New Labor Forum* 19, no. 1 (Winter 2010): 113-16.

McCullough, David. *Truman*. New York: Simon & Schuster, 1992.

McFadden, Robert D. "Suspect was Defender of the Manson 'Family.'" *New York Times*, September 6, 1975.

McMath, Robert C., Jr. *American Populism: A Social History, 1877–1898*. New York: Hill and Wang, 1993.

McPherson, James M. *Battle Cry of Freedom: The Civil War Era*. New York: Ballantine Books, 1988.

Meacham, Jon. *American Lion: Andrew Jackson in the White House*. New York: Random House, 2008.

Mead, Walter Russell. *Special Providence: American Foreign Policy and How It Changed the World*. Oxford and New York: Routledge, 2002.

Means, Howard. *The Avenger Takes His Place: Andrew Johnson and the 45 Days That Changed a Nation*. New York: Harcourt, 2006.

A Member of the Chicago Press, with Author's Introductory. *Carter Harrison's Assassination: Giving a Full Account of His Tragic Death, with a Detailed Synopsis of His Eventful Life*. A. Theo. Patterson, Progressive Printer, 1893.

Menke, Richard. "Media in America, 1881: Garfield, Guiteau, Bell, Whitman." *Critical Inquiry* 31, no. 3 (Spring 2005): 638-64.

Meyer, Neil. "Falling for the Lord: Shame, Revivalism, and the Origins of the Second Great Awakening." *Early American Studies: An Interdisciplinary Journal* 9, no. 1 (Winter 2011): 142-66.

Miles, Edwin A. "Andrew Jackson and Senator George Poindexter." *The Journal of Southern History* 24, no. 1 (February 1958): 51-66.

Milk, Harvey. "Letter of Harvey Milk to Pres. Jimmy Carter," February 19, 1978. "Alternative Considerations of Jonestown and Peoples Temple," San Diego State University Department of Religious Studies. http://jonestown.sdsu.edu/?page_id=19042 (accessed March 27, 2017).

Millard, Candice. *Destiny of the Republic: A Tale of Madness, Medicine and the Murder of a President*. New York: Doubleday, 2011.

Miller, Donald L. *The City of the Century: The Epic of Chicago and the Making of America*. New York: Simon & Schuster, 1997.

Miller, Keith D. *Martin Luther King's Biblical Epic: His Final, Great Speech*. Jackson: University of Mississippi Press, 2012.

Miller, Scott. *The President and the Assassin: McKinley, Terror, and Empire at the Dawn of the American Century*. New York: Random House, 2011.

Milner, Andrew. "C'mon and Shoot a President: The Historical People Behind the Characters in Assassins." *The Sondheim Review* 22, no. 1 (Winter 2015): 12-15.

Moley, Raymond. "Bank Crisis, Bullet Crisis—Same Smile; Five Years of Roosevelt—and After." *The Saturday Evening Post* 212, no. 5 (July 29, 1939): 12-13, 52, 54-55, 57-58.

Montgomery, Paul L. "Lowenstein Death Had Roots in Bitter 60's." *New York Times*, March 17, 1980.

―――――――――. "Lowenstein Hailed by Many Mourners; Suspect Is Arraigned as Kennedy, Carter and Carey Pay Tribute to Civil Rights Leader." *New York Times*, March 16, 1980.

Mork, Anne. "The Once and Future King: Robert F. Kennedy as a Liberal Icon." *American Studies in Scandinavia* 44, no. 2 (2012): 29-50.

Morton, Richard Allen. "A Victorian Tragedy: The Strange Deaths of Mayor Carter H. Harrison and Patrick Eugene Prendergast." *Journal of the Illinois State Historical Society (1998–)* 96, no. 1 (Spring 2003): 6-36.

Moynihan, Daniel Patrick. *Daniel Patrick Moynihan: A Portrait in Letters of an American Visionary*. New York: Public Affairs, 2010.

"Mrs. Roosevelt Goes to Join Her Husband." *New York Times*, October 16, 1912.

"Nation Grieves at Loss of President; Funeral Service Arranged for Thursday; Mr. Roosevelt Sworn In; He Promises to Follow the Policy [of] Mr. McKinley." *New York Times*, September 15, 1901.

Naughton, James, and Adam Clymer. "President Gerald R. Ford, Who Led US Out of Watergate Era, Dies at 93." *New York Times*, December 28, 2006.

Naughton, James M. "Ford Safe as Guard Seizes a Gun Woman Pointed at Him on Coast; Follower of Manson is Charged; Two Feet Away; A Wan President Later Urges Fight on Crime in Sacramento Talk." *New York Times*, September 6, 1975.

Naveh, Eyal. "'He Belongs to the Ages': Lincoln's Image and the American Historical Consciousness." *Journal of American Culture* 16, no. 4 (Winter 1993): 49-57.

Nester, William. *The Age of Lincoln and the Art of American Power, 1848–1876.* Lincoln, NE: Potomac Books, 2013.

Newman, Alex. "Tragic Response to a Tragedy." *The New American* 27, no. 3 (February 7, 2011): 10-14.

Newton, Michael. *Famous Assassinations in World History: An Encyclopedia.* Vol. I: A-P. Santa Barbara, CA: ABC-CLIO, 2014.

Nordheimer, Jon. "Guyana Toll is Raised to At Least 900 by US, with 260 Children Among Victims at Colony; Total Is Up by 120; A Survivor Says That Many Took Poison Willingly on Jones's Urging." *New York Times*, November 26, 1978.

_____. "Leader of Sect Dies; Parents Reported to Give Children Poison Before Dying Beside Them." *New York Times*, November 21, 1978.

_____. "Mystery Is Intensifying in Guyana Over Those Who Fled Suicide Rite." *New York Times*, November 23, 1978.

_____. "Son Depicts Leader of Cult as a Fanatic and Paranoid." *New York Times*, November 22, 1978.

"Not Guilty Plea Entered by Loughner on 49 Counts." *Inside Tucson Business* 20, no. 42 (March 11, 2011): 3.

Oakes, James. *Freedom National: The Destruction of Slavery in the United States, 1861–1865.* New York and London: W. W. Norton, 2013.

Oaks, Dallin H., and Marvin S. Hill. *Carthage Conspiracy: The Trial of the Accused Assassins of Joseph Smith.* Omaha, NE: The Notable Trials Library, 2013.

Obama, Barak. "In Christina We See All of Our Children." *Vital Speeches of the Day* 77, no. 3 (March 2011): 86-88.

_____. "This Is a Day That Would Not Be Denied: 'Let Us Keep Climbing Toward That Promised Land.'" *Vital Speeches of the Day* 77, no. 12 (December 2011): 421-23.

"Obituaries: Florence, Colo.: Charles Harrelson, Actor's Dad and a Murderer, Dies in Prison." *The Atlanta Journal-Constitution*, March 23, 2007.

O'Hara, S. Paul. *Inventing the Pinkertons; or Spies, Sleuths, Mercenaries, and Thugs: Being a Story of the Nation's Most Famous (and Infamous) Detective Agency.* Baltimore, MD: Johns Hopkins University Press, 2016.

"Opinions in Washington: Effect of Goebel's Death on the Situation—Federal Troops to Leave Kentucky." *New York Times*, February 4, 1900.

Orchard, Harry. *The Confessions and Autobiography of Harry Orchard: Assassin and Terrorist for the Western Federation of Miners.* Calumet, MI: Calumet History and Hobby, 2013.

"Oscar Collazo, 80, Truman Attacker in '50." *New York Times*, February 23, 1994.

O'Toole, Patricia. *When Trumpets Call: Theodore Roosevelt After the White House.* New York: Simon & Schuster, 2005.

Pace, Eric. "He Enjoys Controversy." *New York Times*, November 19, 1978.

Palazzolo, Joe. "John Hinckley Case Led to Vast Narrowing of Insanity Defense." *Wall Street Journal Eastern Edition*, July 28, 2016.

The People of the State of California v. Robert Page Anderson, 493 P.2d 880, 6 Cal. 3d 628 (Cal. 1972).

Percy, Jennifer. "The Woman Who Saves the Worst People Among Us." *Esquire* 163, nos. 6/7 (June/July 2015): 106, 153.

Perlstein, Richard. *Nixonland: The Rise of a President and the Fracturing of America.* New York: Scribner, 2008.

Peskin, Allan. "Charles Guiteau of Illinois: President Garfield's Assassin." *Journal of the Illinois State Historical Society (1908–1984)* 70, no. 2 (May 1977): 130-39.

Peterson, Merrill D. *Lincoln in American Memory.* New York and Oxford: Oxford University Press, 1995.

Pettibone v. Nichols, 203 US 192 (1906).

Peyton, Rupert. "Reminiscences of Huey P. Long." *North Louisiana Historical Association Journal* 7, no. 4 (Summer 1976): 161-64.

Pierce, J. Kingston. "The Death of Joseph Smith." *American History* 36, no. 5 (December 2001): 54-60.

Plaza, Valrie. *American Mass Murderers.* Raleigh, NC: Lulu.com, 2015.

Podhoretz, John. "Manipulating a Massacre." *Commentary* 131, no. 2 (February 2011): 1-2.

Posner, Gerald. *Killing the Dream: James Earl Ray and the Assassination of Martin Luther King, Jr.* Boston: Mariner Books, 1999 [1998].

"Prendergast Dies; Trembling, He Goes to His Infamous Death on the Gallows; Until the End He Hoped to Escape." *The Atlanta Constitution,* July 14, 1894.

"President McKinley's Illustrious Career; Entered Army When a Mere Boy and Made a Brilliant Record; His Successes in Congress." *New York Times,* September 7, 1901.

"President Ronald Reagan Signed Bill Establishing the Martin Luther King National Holiday." *Jet* 105, no. 26 (June 28, 2004): 56-58.

"The President's Assassin." *The Boston Herald,* April 17, 1865.

"The President's Career; Heroic Work that Led Him to His Exalted Place; His Ancestors in the Revolution; Left Fatherless When a Child; Brave Efforts of His Mother to Educate Him; Services in the War and in Congress; Nominated for President; The Election and His Administration." *New York Times,* September 20, 1881.

"The President's Condition; Joyful News for the Patient Watchers in and About the White House Followed by Discouraging Tidings; His Tender Nurses; A Good Omen; No Visitors Allowed to See the Patient; Incidents of the Day." *New York Times,* July 4, 1881.

"Q042 Transcript, FBI Transcription." "Alternative Considerations of Jonestown and Peoples Temple," San Diego State University Department of Religious Studies. http://jonestown.sdsu.edu/?page_id=29081 (accessed March 28, 2017).

Quimby, Rollin W. "Charles Grandison Finney: Herald of Modern Revivalism." *Speech Monographs* 20, no. 4 (November 1953): 293-99.

Quinn, Kelly. "Commemorating Martin Luther King, Jr.: The New Monument on the Mall." *Against the Current* 27, no. 1 (March/April 2012): 4-6.

Raines, Howell. "Left Lung Is Pierced; Coloradoan, 25, Arrested—Brady, Press Chief, Is Critically Injured." *New York Times,* March 31, 1981.

Reeves, Richard. *President Reagan: The Triumph of Imagination.* New York: Simon & Schuster, 2005.

Reiterman, Tim, with John Jacobs. *Raven: The Untold Story of the Rev. Jim Jones and His People.* New York: Jeremy P. Tarcher/Penguin, 2008 [1982].

"Religion and Spirituality: Dr. Martin Luther King Jr.—'I've Seen the Promised land.'" *The New York Amsterdam News* 107, no. 14 (March 31-April 6, 2016): 33.

Remini, Robert V. *Andrew Jackson.* New York: Harper Perennial, 1999 [1966].

Report to the President by the Commission on CIA Activities within the United States. New York: Manor Books, 1975.

Report of the Select Committee on Assassinations of the US House of Representatives. Washington, DC: United States Government Printing Office, 1979.

Report of the Warren Commission on the Assassination of President Kennedy. New York: McGraw-Hill Book Company, 1964.

"Reports Detail Loughner's Troubling Encounters with Pima Campus Police." *Community College Week* 23, no. 2 (January 24, 2011): 3, 5.

"Rev. Martin Luther King Jr.'s Life and Legacy Celebrated on National Holiday." *Jet* 107, no. 5 (February 7, 2005): 5-12.

Reynolds, Barbara. "Assassins of Democracy: An American Nightmare." *Crisis* 105, no. 3 (July 1998): 10-12.

Roberts, Russell. "Strangled for the Republic: The Assassination of President Garfield." *Timeline* 22, no. 3 (July-September 2005): 30-43.

Roberts, Steven V. "Wounded Aide to Ryan Worried and Wrote Her Will Before Trip." *New York Times*, November 21, 1978.

Robinson, Douglas. "Sirhan Convicted in First Degree; Jury to Fix Fate." *New York Times*, April 18, 1969.

——————————. "Sirhan Sentenced to Gas Chamber on 5th Jury Vote." *New York Times*, April 24, 1969.

Rogers, Warren. *When I Think of Bobby: A Personal Memoir of the Kennedy Years*. New York: HarperCollins, 1993.

Rohrs, Richard C. "Partisan Politics and the Attempted Assassination of Andrew Jackson." *Journal of the Early Republic* 1, no. 2 (Summer 1981): 149-63.

Roosevelt, Eleanor. Foreword to *Brutal Mandate: A Journey to South West Africa*, by Allard K. Lowenstein. New York: The MacMillan Company, 1962.

"Roosevelt Gains, Bullet Located, Lodged in Rib." *New York Times*, October 17, 1912.

Rosellini, Lynn. "'Honey, I Forgot to Duck,' Injured Reagan Tells Wife." *New York Times*, March 31, 1981.

Russell, George. "The Left's Great Crime: Jim Jones, Marxist Mass-murderer." *Commentary* 133, no. 1 (January 2012): 38-41.

Sabato, Larry J. *The Kennedy Half Century: The Presidency, Assassination, and Lasting Legacy of John F. Kennedy*. New York: Bloomsbury USA, 2013.

Sack, Kevin. "Dr. King's Son Says Family Believes Ray is Innocent." *New York Times*, March 28, 1997.

Safire, William, Editor. *Lend Me Your Ears: Great Speeches in History*. New York and London: W. W. Norton, 2004.

Sanson, Jerry P. "'What He Did and What He Promised to Do....' Huey Long and the Horizons of Louisiana Politics." *Louisiana History: The Journal of the Louisiana Historical Association* 47, no. 3 (Summer 2006): 261-76.

Santos, Fernanda, and Timothy Williams. "Gunman Gets 7 Life Terms in Tucson Shootings of Congresswoman and Others." *New York Times*, November 9, 2012.

Scaliger, Charles. "(South) American Killing Fields." *New American* 28, no. 6 (March 19, 2012): 33-39.

Schatz, Thomas. *Hollywood: Crit Concepts V2*. New York: Routledge, 2004.

Scheeres, Julia. *A Thousand Lives: The Untold Story of Hope, Deception, and Survival at Jonestown*. New York: Free Press, 2011.

Schlesinger, Arthur M. Jr. *Robert Kennedy and His Times*. New York: Ballantine Books, 1978.

"Schrank Owns Guilt, Callous, Then Sorry." *New York Times*, October 16, 1912.

Schwartz, John. "In Tucson Case, a Federal Judge Both 'General and Traffic Cop.'" *New York Times*, January 14, 2011.

Scott, John W. "Highway Building in Louisiana before Huey Long: An Overdue Re-appraisal." *Louisiana History: The Journal of the Louisiana Historical Association* 44, no. 1 (Winter 2003): 5-38.

Seelye, Katharine Q. "Office Staff for Giffords is a 'Family.'" *New York Times*, January 10, 2011.

"The Sentences of the Assassination Conspirators." *The Boston Herald*, July 7, 1865.

Shabecoff, Philip. "2d Coast Episode: The Suspect Had Been Queried but Freed by Secret Service." *New York Times*, September 23, 1975.

"The Shadow of the Gunman." *New York Times*, March 18, 1980, A22.

Sherrod, Shirley, with Catherine Whitney. *The Courage to Hope: How I Stood Up to the Politics of Fear*. New York: Atria Books, 2012.

Shilts, Randy. *The Mayor of Castro Street: The Life and Times of Harvey Milk*. New York: St. Martin's Press, 1982.

Shinoff, Paul. "Jurors Found No Evidence White Slayings Premeditated." *The Atlanta Constitution*, May 23, 1979.

"Shot by a Crank; Carter Harrison, Chicago's Mayor, Foully Murdered; No Word of Warning for Him; Prendergast, the Assassin, Gives Himself Up to the Police; The Mob Wanted to Lynch Him; So He Was Quietly Taken to the City Hall and Put in a Dungeon; He Is a Crazy Paper Carrier; Says the Mayor Promised to Appoint Him Corporation Counsel—Great Excitement and Deep Sorrow in the City." *The Atlanta Constitution*, October 29, 1893.

Skelton, Nancy, and Mark A. Stein. "SF Assassin Dan White Kills Himself." *Los Angeles Times*, October 22, 1985.

Slapper, Gary. "Opinion: Changing Madness to Badness." *The Journal of Criminal Law* 75, no. 5 (October 2011): 337-40.

Smith, Elbert B. "Shoot-out on Pennsylvania Avenue." *American History* 32, no. 3 (July/August 1997): 16-24.

Smith, Francesca Marie, and Thomas A. Hollihan. "'Out of Chaos Breathes Creation': Human Agency, Mental Illness, and Conservative Arguments Locating Responsibility for the Tucson Massacre." *Rhetoric & Public Affairs* 17, no. 4 (Winter 2014): 585-618.

Smith, Harold Ivan. "FDR's Near Assassination in Miami's Bay Front Park." *Illness, Crisis and Loss* 20, no. 2 (April 2012): 59-181.

Smith, Jean Edward. *FDR*. New York: Random House Trade Paperbacks, 2008.

Smith, John Howard. *The First Great Awakening: Redefining Religion in British America, 1725–1775*. Lanham, MD: Fairleigh Dickinson University Press and Rowman & Littlefield, 2015.

Smith, Terence. "Bremer, in a Heavily Guarded Courtroom, Pleads Not Guilty to US Charges in Shooting of Wallace." *New York Times*, May 25, 1972.

_____. "Father of Suspect 'Sickened' by News." *New York Times,* June 6, 1968.

_____. "Reports Hint Bremer Stalked Others: Reports That Bremer Also Stalked Nixon and Humphrey." *New York Times*, May 26, 1972.

Sneed, Don. "Newspapers Call for Swift Justice: A Study of the McKinley Assassination." *Journalism Quarterly* 65, no. 2 (Summer 1988): 360-67, 398.

Spieler, Geri. *Taking Aim at the President: The Remarkable Story of the Woman Who Shot at Gerald Ford*. New York: Palgrave Macmillan, 2009.

"State Department Says It Told Ryan of Mission's Peril." *New York Times*, November 21, 1978.

Stolberg, Sheryl Gay, and William Yardley. "For Giffords, Tucson Roots Shaped Views." *New York Times*, January 15, 2011.

Sullivan, John. "Plan to Release Notorious Killer Prompts Debate about Insanity." *New York Times*, July 14, 2000.

Swanson, James L. *End of Days: The Assassination of John F. Kennedy*. New York: William Morrow, 2013.

_____. *Manhunt: The 12-Day Chase for Lincoln's Killer*. New York: William Morrow, 2006.

"2 Newsmen and Union Leader Among 5 Felled by Gunfire." *The Atlanta Constitution*, June 6, 1968.

"39 Years Ago: Robert F. Kennedy's Remarks on the Assassination of Martin Luther King Jr., April 4, 1968." *The Journal of Blacks in Higher Education* 55, no. 1 (Spring 2007): 5.

Talese, Gay. "Police Save Suspect from the Crowd." *New York Times*, February 22, 1965.

Tares, Ann. "History and the Claims of Revelation: Joseph Smith and the Materialization of the Golden Plates." *Numen: International Review for the History of Religions* 61, nos. 2/3 (2014): 182-207.

Taubman, Philip. "Suspect was Arrested Last Year in Nashville on Weapons Charge." *New York Times*, March 31, 1981.

"A Terrible Death Watch; Scenes in the President's Chamber Saturday Night; His Anxiety About Mrs. Garfield and His Joy on Her Arrival; Touching Incidents." *New York Times*, July 4, 1881.

Thomas, Evan M. "RFK's Last Campaign." *Newsweek* 131, no. 23, June 8, 1998, 46-53.

_____. *Robert Kennedy: His Life*. New York: Simon & Schuster, 2000.

Thurber, Jon. "Witty Reagan Aide and Gun Control Advocate." *The Washington Post*, August 5, 2014.

Toobin, Jeffrey. *American Heiress: The Wild Saga of the Kidnapping, Crimes and Trial of Patty Hearst*. New York: Doubleday, 2016.

"Traced on Roosevelt's Tour; Schrank Left Writings Assailing Colonel in Charleston—Movements Vague Elsewhere." *New York Times*, October 16, 1912.

"Transcripts of Medical Statements." *New York Times*, June 6, 1968.

Treaster, Joseph B. "Graves Team On Way; Identification of 400 Who Died in Mass Suicide Is Due to Begin Today." *New York Times*, November 22, 1978.

_____. "Ryan Was a Friend of Disadvantaged; Congressman's Investigations of Trouble Spots Were Marked by Personal Involvement." *New York Times*, November 20, 1978.

Trefousse, Hans L. *The Radical Republicans: Lincoln's Vanguard for Racial Justice*. New York: Knopf, 1969.

"Trial of the Assassins; The Suppressed Testimony Now Made Public; Highly Important Revelations; Implication of Jeff. Davis in the Assassination." *The Boston Herald*, June 5, 1865.

Trotter, Michael C. "Huey P. Long's Last Operation: When Medicine and Politics Don't Mix." *The Ochsner Journal* 12, no. 1 (Spring 2012): 9-16.

Tucker, Edward L. "The Attempted Assassination of President Jackson: A Letter by Richard Henry Wilde." *The Georgia Historical Quarterly* 58, Supplement (1974): 193-99.

"Tucson Gunman Before Rampage: 'I'll See You on National TV.'" *CBS News* (online), April 11, 2014. http://www.cbsnews.com/news/jared-loughner-who-shot-gabrielle-giffords-in-tucson-ranted-online/ (accessed February 7, 2017).

Turner, Wallace. "Dispute Over Baby Spurred Sect's Move to Guyana." *New York Times*, November 19, 1978.

_____. "Ex-Official Guilty of Manslaughter in Slayings on Coast; 3,000 Protest." *New York Times*, May 22, 1979.

_____. "'The Gun Is Pointed,' Miss Fromme Says; Judge Ejects Her." *New York Times*, September 12, 1975.

_____. "The Shooting: A Victory Celebration That Ended with Shots, Screams and Curses." *New York Times*, June 6, 1968.

_____. "Suspect Sought Job; Moscone Had Been Asked to Reappoint Him as a Board Member." *New York Times*, November 28, 1978.

Van Gelder, Lawrence. "Dismay in Nation; Negroes Urge Others to Carry on Spirit of Nonviolence." *New York Times*, April 5, 1968.

_____. "James Earl Ray, 70, Killer of Dr. King, Dies in Nashville." *New York Times*, April 24, 1998.

"Victor F. Lawson's Estimate; The Editor of *The Chicago News* on Carter H. Harrison's Character." *New York Times*, October 30, 1893.

Von Drehle, David; Alex Altman; Katy Steinmetz; Cleo Brock-Abraham; Massimo Calabresi; Steven Gray; and Mark Thompson. "1 Madman and a Gun." *Time* 177, no. 3 (January 24, 2011): 26-31.

Vorenberg, Michael. *Final Freedom: The Civil War, the Abolition of Slavery, and the Thirteenth Amendment*. Cambridge and New York: Cambridge University Press, 2001.

Wagner, Robert A. *The Assassination of JFK: Perspectives Half a Century Later*. Indianapolis, IN: Dog Ear Publishing, 2016.

Wald, Matthew L. "Teen-Age Actress Says Notes Sent by Suspect Did Not Hint Violence." *New York Times*, April 2, 1981.

Waldron, Martin. "Bremer, in Red, White and Blue, Was Conspicuous at Many Rallies." *New York Times*, May 29, 1972.

Walker, Marianne C. "The Late Governor William Goebel: He Fought, Killed, and Was Killed." *Humanities* 34, no. 4 (July/August 2013): 28-33, 48-49.

Walker, Ronald W., Richard E. Turley, Jr., and Glen M. Leonard. *Massacre at Mountain Meadows*. New York and Oxford: Oxford University Press, 2008.

Walther, Eric H. *The Shattering of the Union: America in the 1850s*. Wilmington, DE: Scholarly Resources, 2004.

Walz, Jay. "Ottawa Police Say Bremer Was Seen '10 or 12 Feet' from Nixon Motorcade." *New York Times*, June 2, 1972, 9.

Watson, Bruce. *Freedom Summer: The Savage Season That Made Mississippi Burn and Made America a Democracy*. New York: Viking, 2010.

_____. "The President and the Lunatic." *American Heritage* 61, no. 1 (Spring 2011): 38-47.

Waugh, John C. *Re-Electing Lincoln: The Battle for the 1864 Presidency*. New York: Crown Books, 1997.

Weinstein, Henry. "Suspect Asserted She Helped FBI; Also Volunteered for Civil Rights and Leftist Groups and Worked for Hearst." *New York Times*, September 23, 1975.

Weiss, Mike. *Double Play: The San Francisco City Hall Killings*. Reading, MA: Addison-Wesley Publishing Company, 1984.

Werner, Leslie Maitland. "Request for Hinckley Leave Withdrawn: 'There Was No Attempt to Keep the Letters Secret,' Hospital Says." *New York Times*, April 16, 1987.

Westin, Alan F., and Barry Mahoney. *The Trial of Martin Luther King*. New York: The Notable Trials Library, 1997.

Whitaker, Charles. "Who Was Malcolm X?" *Ebony* 47, no. 4 (February 1992): 118, 120, 122, 124.

White, Richard D., Jr. *Kingfish: The Reign of Huey P. Long*. New York: Random House, 2006.

White, Ronald C., Jr. *A. Lincoln: A Biography*. New York: Random House, 2009.

Whitman, Alden. "Robert Francis Kennedy: Attorney General, Senator and Heir of the New Frontier." *New York Times*, June 7, 1968.

Wicker, Tom. "Gov. Connally Shot; Mrs. Kennedy Safe; President Is Struck Down by a Rifle Shot from Building on Motorcade—Johnson, Riding Behind, Is Unhurt." *New York Times*, November 23, 1963.

_____. "A Hero's Burial; Million in Capital See Cortege Roll on to Church and Grave." *New York Times*, November 26, 1963.

_____. "A New Kind of Cover-up." *New York Times*, September 10, 1974.

Wilber, Del Quentin. *Rawhide Down: The Near Assassination of Ronald Reagan*. New York: Henry Holt, 2011.

Wilentz, Sean. *The Age of Reagan: A History, 1974–2008*. New York: Harper, 2008.

Williams, R. Hal. *Realigning America: McKinley, Bryan, and the Remarkable Election of 1896*. Lawrence: The University Press of Kansas, 2001.

Williams, T. Harry. *Huey Long*. New York: Vintage, 1981 [1969].

Winfrey, Carey. "An Ebullient Advocate of Social Justice." *New York Times*, March 15, 1980.

Winik, Jay. *April 1865: The Month That Saved America*. New York: HarperCollins, 2001.

Witcover, Jules. *Party of the People: A History of the Democrats*. New York: Random House, 2003.

"Witness Tells How Cult Members Went to Deaths." *New York Times*, November 25, 1978.

Wooten, James T. "Again a Gun Alters the Politics of the Republic." *New York Times*, May 21, 1972.

_____. "Wallace Is Visited in Hospital by Nixon." *New York Times*, May 20, 1972.

"World's Sympathy Shown; Crowned Heads of Send Messages to the Ex-President." *New York Times*, October 17, 1912.

"Zangara Planned Attack All Alone; Assassination Attempt Is Laid to Moroseness, Due to Chronic Ailment; Uncle Mystified by Act; Nephew, During Life in Paterson, Had No Friends and Sought Only Freedom from Pain." *New York Times*, February 17, 1933.

"Zangara Will Die in the Chair Today; Assassin Is to Pay Penalty in Florida State Prison at 9 AM for Cermak Slaying; Has Shown No Remorse; Eats Hearty Chicken Dinner Despite Previous Complaints—Clinics Seek His Body." *New York Times*, March 30, 1933.

Zita-Bennet, Adrian. "Champion of the 'Forgotten Man?' FDR and the 1932 Election." *NeoAmericanist* 6, no. 2 (Spring/Summer 2013): 1-18.

Zoellner, Tom. "Extreme Arizona." *High Country News* 44, no. 3 (February 20, 2012): 12-18.

INDEX

and Martin Luther King, Jr., assassination,
303-304, 305
and Robert F. Kennedy, 61-62, 216
Johnson, Rafer, 67
Johnson, Thomas 15X, 291
Jones, Cleve, 346
Jones, Fred, 93, 94
Jones, James Warren (Jim), 334-35, 352
and assassination of Congressman Ryan,
328, 329
and Congressman Ryan's visit, 326-28
and Jonestown compound, 317, 322-24,
325-26
and "revolutionary suicide," 324, 327,
329-30
and Stoen case, 325
background of, 318-21
bizarre private life of, 321-22
death of, 330
motives of, 330-33, 352
Jones, Marceline, 319, 325
Jones, Solomon, 301, 302
Jones, Thomas, 16
Jonestown, Guyana, 317, 322-24, 325-26, 327,
329, 330
Jowers, Loyd, 393n809
Juarez, Mexico, 154

Kaczynski, Theodore, 237
Kahn, Sara Jane. *See* Moore, Sara Jane
Kalamazoo State Hospital, 278
Kansas City, Missouri, 52
Kant, Immanuel, 159
Kautz, August V., 19
Kearney, Patrick, 181
Keene, Laura, 13
Kelly, Mark, 235
Kennedy administration, 62
Kennedy, Caroline, 78
Kennedy, Edward M. (Ted), 61, 71, 121, 125,
211, 221-22, 313
Kennedy, Ethel, 69, 70
Kennedy, Jacqueline (Jackie), 70, 78, 80, 86-87,
91, 222
Kennedy, John F., xv, 64, 141, 222, 352
and conspiracy theories, 77, 78, 81, 82, 87-88,
89, 91, 157, 312
and previous assassination attempts, 77-78
and Texas trip, 76, 78-79

assassination of, 63, 75, 76-77, 80, 84-86,
116, 124, 142, 153, 282, 283, 290,
306, 352, 353
as president, 61, 62, 75-76, 77
background of, 78
funeral of, 91
memorialization of, 75, 90, 92
Kennedy, Joseph P., 61
Kennedy, Joseph P., Jr., 61
Kennedy, Robert F. (Bobby), xv, 215, 222, 352
and Martin Luther King, Jr., assassination,
306-307, 313
assassination of, xi, xii, 66-69, 71, 72, 77, 142,
216, 352, 353
as presidential candidate, 63-67, 216, 306
background of, 61-63
death of, 69-70
Kennedy, Rose Fitzgerald, 61
Kentucky, 89, 167, 252, 253, 257
Kentucky gubernatorial convention. *See*
Democratic Convention (Kentucky)
Kentucky Supreme Court, 260
Kentucky senate, 253, 254
Kerr, James, 154
Key, Francis Scott, 171
Khmer Rouge, 105
Khrushchev, Nikita, 80-81, 88
Kilduff, Marshall, 322
King, Alberta Williams, 298
King, Coretta Scott, 222, 299, 305
King, Dexter, 313
King, Faye L. *See* Harrelson, Jo Ann
King, Martin Luther, Jr., xvi, 211, 214, 280, 289,
293, 352
aftermath of the assassination, 303-307
and April 3 "mountaintop" speech, 295-97
assassination of, 64, 66, 76-77, 143, 300-303,
304, 327
background of, 297-300
conspiracy theories and, 311-13, 314-16
death of, 297, 303
funeral of, 313
memorialization of, 313-14, 315
King, Martin Luther, Sr., 298
King, Stephen, 151
Kirtland, Ohio, 245, 246
Koch, Ed, 222
Korean War, 53
Kraus, Mr., 195

ABOUT THE AUTHOR

J. Michael Martinez works in Monroe, Georgia, as corporate counsel for a manufacturing company. He also teaches as a part-time faculty member at Kennesaw State University and the University of Georgia. Martinez is the author of a dozen books, including *Terrorist Attacks on American Soil: From the Civil War Era to the Present* (2012) and *The Greatest Criminal Cases: Changing the Course of American Law* (2014). Visit him on the Internet at www.jmichaelmartinez.com.